ATION

REFL   OCIETY?

ISSN 1538-6694

EDUCATION
REFLECTING OUR SOCIETY?

Gina Giuliano

INFORMATION PLUS® REFERENCE SERIES
Formerly published by Information Plus, Wylie, Texas

GALE GROUP

THOMSON LEARNING

Detroit • New York • San Diego • San Francisco
Boston • New Haven, Conn. • Waterville, Maine
London • Munich

EDUCATION: REFLECTING OUR SOCIETY?

Gina Giuliano, *Author*

The Gale Group Staff:
Coordinating Editors: Ellice Engdahl, *Series Editor*; Charles B. Montney, *Series Graphics Editor*
Managing Editor: Debra M. Kirby
Contributing Editors: Elizabeth Manar, Kathleen Meek
Contributing Associate Editors: Paula Cutcher-Jackson, Prindle LaBarge, Heather Price, Michael T. Reade
Imaging and Multimedia Content: Barbara J. Yarrow, *Manager, Imaging and Multimedia Content*; Dean Dauphinais, *Imaging and Multimedia Content Editor*; Kelly A. Quin, *Imaging and Multimedia Content Editor*; Robyn Young, *Imaging and Multimedia Content Editor*; Leitha Etheridge-Sims, *Image Cataloger*; Mary K. Grimes, *Image Cataloger*; David G. Oblender, *Image Cataloger*; Lezlie Light, *Imaging Coordinator*; Randy Bassett, *Imaging Supervisor*; Robert Duncan, *Imaging Specialist*; Dan Newell, *Imaging Specialist*; Luke Rademacher, *Imaging Specialist*; Christine O'Bryan, *Graphic Specialist*
Indexing: Susan Kelsch, *Indexing Supervisor*
Permissions: Margaret A. Chamberlain, *Permissions Specialist*; Maria Franklin, *Permissions Manager*
Product Design: Michelle DiMercurio, *Senior Art Director and Product Design Manager*; Michael Logusz, *Graphic Artist*
Production: Evi Seoud, *Assistant Manager, Composition Purchasing and Electronic Prepress*; Keith Helmling, *Buyer*; Dorothy Maki, *Manufacturing Manager*
Cover photo © PhotoDisc.

ISBN 0-7876-5103-6 (set)
ISBN 0-7876-6055-8 (this volume)
ISSN 1538-6694 (this volume)
Printed in the United States of America
10 9 8 7 6 5 4 3 2 1

TABLE OF CONTENTS

CHAPTER 1

The United States is one of the most highly educated nations in the world. This chapter presents and interprets data about America's educational level, focusing on years of school completed; enrollment (historical, current, and projected); racial, ethnic, and gender differences in attainment; and spending on public and private schools from elementary through post-secondary.

CHAPTER 2

Chapter 2 covers topics relating to preprimary, elementary, and secondary schools. These include enrollment trends like preprimary growth, geographic shifts, racial and ethnic diversity, and declining poverty rate. A major topic is school financing, subdivided into types and sources, equalization, revenues, expenditures, and international comparisons. Public and private schools are also compared in this chapter, which ends with data on attendance and high school graduation rates.

CHAPTER 3

How does the American education system serve students with special needs? This chapter describes programs for the physically and mentally disabled, the gifted and talented, the financially disadvantaged, and those seeking vocational training. Legislation aimed at helping such students is discussed, along with trends in each of the four categories.

CHAPTER 4

Chapter 4 treats measures of academic success. Results from the National Assessment of Educational Progress in the categories of reading, mathematics, science, and writing are given and explained in the first part. Additional sections deal with international comparisons, Carnegie units and exit exams as requirements for high school graduation, and scores on college entrance exams.

CHAPTER 5

Eight National Education Goals were created between 1989 and 1994, after an influential report warned about mediocrity in American schools. This chapter lists the goals and measures progress toward meeting them. A version known as the National Urban Education Goals is also considered.

CHAPTER 6

Among the barriers to academic success examined in this chapter are poverty, lack of English proficiency, difficult transitions to middle school and junior high, dropping out, and school violence. Health-risk behaviors that may hinder educational achievement (like smoking, substance abuse, and early sexual activity) are treated extensively.

CHAPTER 7

As the result of controversial efforts to improve American education, students can now attend charter, parochial, or for-profit institutions; schools outside their immediate neighborhoods; or even home schools. Other politically sensitive issues touched on in this chapter include the role of religion and technology, bilingual education, site-based school management, and aging physical infrastructure.

CHAPTER 8

This chapter covers issues relating to teachers, such as employment situation, salaries, turnover, and preparedness for the job. It also presents results from Phi Delta Kappa/Gallup polls of teacher attitudes on various topics, including school quality, curriculum focus, attracting and retaining good staff, use of computers or the Internet, relations with parents, obstacles to improvement, and school safety.

CHAPTER 9

College and university enrollment is analyzed in this chapter (by student age, race, ethnicity, nationality, academic preparedness, degree level, and employment status). Other topics addressed here include post-secondary institutions serving specifically women, blacks, Hispanics, or Native Americans; degree-granting trends; faculty; rising costs and financial assistance; distance education; and substance abuse on campus.

CHAPTER 10

Chapter 10 concerns public opinion on education, as reflected by Phi Delta Kappa/Gallup polls. Answers to questions about public school problems and quality, performance standards, voucher programs, drug and alcohol possession, morals instruction, and provisions of the *No Child Left Behind Act* are tabulated and analyzed.

PREFACE

Education: Reflecting Our Society? is one of the latest volumes in the Information Plus Reference Series. Previously published by the Information Plus company of Wylie, Texas, the Information Plus Reference Series (and its companion set, the Information Plus Compact Series) became a Gale Group product when Gale and Information Plus merged in early 2000. Those of you familiar with the series as published by Information Plus will notice a few changes from the 2000 edition. Gale has adopted a new layout and style that we hope you will find easy to use. Other improvements include greatly expanded indexes in each book, and more descriptive tables of contents.

While some changes have been made to the design, the purpose of the Information Plus Reference Series remains the same. Each volume of the series presents the latest facts on a topic of pressing concern in modern American life. These topics include today's most controversial and most studied social issues: abortion, capital punishment, care for the elderly, crime, health care, the environment, immigration, minorities, social welfare, women, youth, and many more. Although written especially for the high school and undergraduate student, this series is an excellent resource for anyone in need of factual information on current affairs.

By presenting the facts, it is Gale's intention to provide its readers with everything they need to reach an informed opinion on current issues. To that end, there is a particular emphasis in this series on the presentation of scientific studies, surveys, and statistics. These data are generally presented in the form of tables, charts, and other graphics placed within the text of each book. Every graphic is directly referred to and carefully explained in the text. The source of each graphic is presented within the graphic itself. The data used in these graphics are drawn from the most reputable and reliable sources, in particular the various branches of the U.S. government and major independent polling organizations. Every effort has been made to secure the most recent information available. The reader should bear in mind that many major studies take years to conduct, and that additional years often pass before the data from these studies is made available to the public. Therefore, in many cases the most recent information available in 2002 dated from 1999 or 2000. Older statistics are sometimes presented as well, if they are of particular interest and no more recent information exists.

Although statistics are a major focus of the Information Plus Reference Series, they are by no means its only content. Each book also presents the widely held positions and important ideas that shape how the book's subject is discussed in the United States. These positions are explained in detail and, where possible, in the words of their proponents. Some of the other material to be found in these books includes: historical background; descriptions of major events related to the subject; relevant laws and court cases; and examples of how these issues play out in American life. Some books also feature primary documents, or have pro and con debate sections giving the words and opinions of prominent Americans on both sides of a controversial topic. All material is presented in an even-handed and unbiased manner; the reader will never be encouraged to accept one view of an issue over another.

HOW TO USE THIS BOOK

From escalating violence in the classroom to producing high school graduates capable of competing in today's global marketplace, education is a hotly disputed topic in America. This book presents a snapshot of education in the United States. Areas covered include an overview of American education; a discussion of primary, elementary, and secondary schools; public versus private schooling; special education; education of gifted children; testing and achievement of students at the primary, secondary, and college levels; national education goals; and "at-risk" students, including trends in dropout rates, drug use, and violence in schools. Also discussed are colleges and universities; issues in education such as home schooling, school choice and vouchers; trends in teacher supply and demand; and public opinions about education.

Education: Reflecting Our Society? consists of ten chapters and three appendices. Each of the chapters is devoted to a particular aspect of education. For a summary of the information covered in each chapter, please see the synopses provided in the Table of Contents at the front of the book. Chapters generally begin with an overview of the basic facts and background information on the chapter's topic, then proceed to examine sub-topics of particular interest. For example, Chapter Three: Education for Special School Populations begins with the definition of a disability and then goes on to discuss the characteristics of special education students and trends in special education. Discussions of gifted and talented students, disadvantaged students, and vocational education are also included. Readers can find their way through a chapter by looking for the section and sub-section headings, which are clearly set off from the text. Or, they can refer to the book's extensive index if they already know what they are looking for.

Statistical Information

The tables and figures featured throughout *Education: Reflecting Our Society?* will be of particular use to the reader in learning about this issue. These tables and figures represent an extensive collection of the most recent and important statistics on education, as well as related issues—for example, graphics in the book cover the percent of the population (3-34 years old) enrolled in school; sources of revenue for public elementary and secondary schools; subjects included in state assessment systems; average ACT and SAT scores of incoming college students; the National Education Goals; the percent of youths who are neither enrolled in school nor working; trends in the use of various drugs by eighth, tenth, and twelfth graders; the top ten reasons for homeschooling; the number of elementary and secondary teachers; enrollment in degree-granting institutions; and grading of public schools. Gale believes that making this information available to the reader is the most important way in which we fulfill the goal of this book: to help readers understand the issues and controversies surrounding education in the United States and reach their own conclusions.

Each table or figure has a unique identifier appearing above it, for ease of identification and reference. Titles for the tables and figures explain their purpose. At the end of each table or figure, the original source of the data is provided.

In order to help readers understand these often complicated statistics, all tables and figures are explained in the text. References in the text direct the reader to the relevant statistics. Furthermore, the contents of all tables and figures are fully indexed. Please see the opening section of the index at the back of this volume for a description of how to find tables and figures within it.

In addition to the main body text and images, *Education: Reflecting Our Society?* has three appendices. The first is the Important Names and Addresses directory. Here the reader will find contact information for a number of government and private organizations that can provide information on education. The second appendix is the Resources section, which can also assist the reader in conducting his or her own research. In this section, the author and editors of *Education: Reflecting Our Society?* describe some of the sources that were most useful during the compilation of this book. The final appendix is the index. It has been greatly expanded from previous editions, and should make it even easier to find specific topics in this book.

COMMENTS AND SUGGESTIONS

The editors of the Information Plus Reference Series welcome your feedback on *Education: Reflecting Our Society?* Please direct all correspondence to:

Editors
Information Plus Reference Series
27500 Drake Rd.
Farmington Hills, MI 48331-3535

ACKNOWLEDGEMENTS

The editors wish to thank the copyright holders of material included in this volume and the permissions managers of many book and magazine publishing companies for assisting us in securing reproduction rights. We are also grateful to the staffs of the Detroit Public Library, the Library of Congress, the University of Detroit Mercy Library, Wayne State University Purdy/Kresge Library Complex, and the University of Michigan Libraries for making their resources available to us.

Following is a list of the copyright holders who have granted us permission to reproduce material in Information Plus: Education. *Every effort has been made to trace copyright, but if omissions have been made, please let us know.*

Acknowledgements are listed in the order the tables and figures appear in the text of Education. *For more detailed citations, please see the sources listed under each table and figure.*

Table 1.1. Snyder, Thomas D. and Charlene M. Hoffman. "Table 1.—Estimated number of participants in elementary and secondary education and in degree-granting institutions: Fall 2000," in *Digest of Education Statistics, 2000,* NCES 2001-034. U.S. Department of Education, National Center for Education Statistics, January 2001.

Table 1.2. Snyder, Thomas D. and Charlene M. Hoffman. "Table 8.—Years of school completed by persons age 25 and over and 25 to 29, by race/ethnicity and sex: 1910 to 1999," in *Digest of Education Statistics, 2000,* NCES 2001-034. U.S. Department of Education, National Center for Education Statistics, January 2001.

Figure 1.1. Snyder, Thomas and Charlene M. Hoffman. "Figure 3.—Years of school completed by persons 25 years old and over: 1940 to 1999," in *Digest of Education Statistics, 2000,* NCES 2001-034. U.S. Depart-

ment of Education, National Center for Education Statistics, January 2001.

Table 1.3. Snyder, Thomas D. and Charlene M. Hoffman. "Table 7.—Percent of the population 3 to 34 years old enrolled in school, by race/ethnicity, sex, and age: October 1975 to October 1999," in *Digest of Education Statistics, 2000,* NCES 2001-034. U.S. Department of Education, National Center for Education Statistics, January 2001.

Table 1.4. Snyder, Thomas D. and Charlene M. Hoffman. "Table 3.—Enrollment in educational institutions, by level and by control of institution: 1869-70 to fall 2010," in *Digest of Education Statistics, 2000,* NCES 2001-034. U.S. Department of Education, National Center for Education Statistics, January 2001.

Table 1.5. Snyder, Thomas D. and Charlene M. Hoffman. "Table 31.—Total expenditures of educational institutions related to the gross domestic product, by level of institution: 1929-30 to 1999-2000," in *Digest of Education Statistics, 2000,* NCES 2001-034. U.S. Department of Education, National Center for Education Statistics, January 2001.

Table 2.1. Gerald, Debra E. and William J. Hussar. "Table 1.—Enrollment in grades K-8 and 9-12 of elementary and secondary schools, by control of institution, with projections: Fall 1986 to fall 2011," in *Projections of Education Statistics to 2011,* NCES 2001-083. U.S. Department of Education, National Center for Education Statistics, October 2001.

Figure 2.1. Wirt, John, Susan Choy, Debra Gerald, Stephen Provasnik, Patrick Rooney, Satoshi Watanabe, Richard Tobin, and Mark Glander. "School Enrollment: Public elementary and secondary school enrollment in Grades K-12 (in thousands), by grade level, with projections: Fall 1965-2010," in *The Condition of Education, 2001,* NCES 2001-

072. U.S. Department of Education, National Center for Education Statistics, June 2001.

Table 2.2. Snyder, Thomas D. and Charlene M. Hoffman. "Table 45.—Enrollment of 3-, 4-, and 5-year-old children in preprimary programs, by level and control of program and by attendance status: October 1965 to October 1999," in *Digest of Education Statistics, 2000,* NCES 2001-034. U.S. Department of Education, National Center for Education Statistics, January 2001.

Figure 2.2. Snyder, Thomas D. and Charlene M. Hoffman. "Figure 9.—Percentage change in public elementary and secondary enrollment, by state: Fall 1994 to fall 1999," in *Digest of Education Statistics, 2000,* NCES 2001-034. U.S. Department of Education, National Center for Education Statistics, January 2001.

Table 2.3. Snyder, Thomas D. and Charlene M. Hoffman. "Table 44.—Enrollment in public elementary and secondary schools, by race/ethnicity and state: Fall 1986 and fall 1998," in *Digest of Education Statistics, 2000,* NCES 2001-034. U.S. Department of Education, National Center for Education Statistics, January 2001.

Table 2.4. Dalaker, Joseph. "Table A-4. People and Families in Poverty by Selected Characteristics: 1993 and 2000," in *Poverty in the United States: 2000,* P60-214. U.S. Department of Commerce, U.S. Census Bureau, Economics and Statistics Administration, September 2001.

Figure 2.3. Snyder, Thomas D. and Charlene M. Hoffman. "Figure 11.—Sources of revenue for public elementary and secondary schools: 1970-71 to 1997-98," in *Digest of Education Statistics, 2000,* NCES 2001-034. U.S. Department of Education, National Center for Education Statistics, January 2001.

Table 2.5. "Table 3.6: Strategies and Results of State Efforts to Reduce Funding Gaps in

School Years 1991-92 and 1995-96," in *School Finance: State Efforts to Equalize Funding Between Wealthy and Poor School Districts,* GAO/HEHS-98-92. U.S. General Accounting Office, Health, Education, and Human Services Division, June 1998.

Table 2.6. Snyder, Thomas D. and Charlene M. Hoffman. "Table 159.—Revenues for public elementary and secondary schools, by source and state: 1997-98," in *Digest of Education Statistics, 2000,* NCES 2001-034. U.S. Department of Education, National Center for Education Statistics, January 2001.

Table 2.7. Hoffman, Charlene M. "Table 34.—Current expenditures per pupil in fall enrollment: 1979-80 to 1999-2000," in *Mini-Digest of Education Statistics, 2000,* NCES 2001-046. U.S. Department of Education, National Center for Education Statistics, August 2001.

Table 2.8. Snyder, Thomas D. and Charlene M. Hoffman. "Table 412.—Total public direct expenditures on education as a percentage of gross domestic product: Selected countries, 1985 to 1997," in *Digest of Education Statistics, 2000,* NCES 2001-034. U.S. Department of Education, National Center for Education Statistics, January 2001.

Figure 2.4. Wirt, John, et al. "International Expenditures for Education: Educational expenditures per student in relation to GDP per capita, by level of education for selected OECD countries: 1997," in *The Condition of Education, 2001,* NCES 2001-072. U.S. Department of Education, National Center for Education Statistics, June 2001.

Table 2.9. Broughman, Stephen P. and Lenore A. Colaciello. "Table 1.—Number and percentage distribution of private schools, students and FTE teachers, by NCES typology and selected characteristics: United States, 1999-2000," in *Private School Universe Survey: 1999–2000,* NCES 2001-330. U.S. Department of Education, National Center for Education Statistics, August 2001.

Table 2.10. Snyder, Thomas D. and Charlene M. Hoffman. "Table 86.—Public elementary and secondary students, schools, pupil/teacher ratios, and finances, by type of locale: 1997 and 1998," in *Digest of Education Statistics, 2000,* NCES 2001-034. U.S. Department of Education, National Center for Education Statistics, January 2001.

Table 2.11. Snyder, Thomas D. and Charlene M. Hoffman. "Table 65.—Public and private elementary and secondary teachers and pupil/teacher ratios, by level: Fall 1955 to fall 1999," in *Digest of Education Statistics, 2000,* NCES 2001-034. U.S. Department of Education, National Center for Education Statistics, January 2001.

Table 2.12. Snyder, Thomas D. and Charlene M. Hoffman. "Table 94.—Public ele-

mentary and secondary schools, by type and size of school: 1998-99," in *Digest of Education Statistics, 2000,* NCES 2001-034. U.S. Department of Education, National Center for Education Statistics, January 2001.

Table 2.13. Johnson, Frank. "Table 5—Student membership and current expenditures per pupil in membership for public elementary and secondary schools, by function and state: School year 1998-99," in *Statistics in Brief: Revenues and Expenditures for Public Elementary and Secondary Education: School Year 1998-99,* NCES 2001-321. U.S. Department of Education, National Center for Education Statistics, March 2001.

Figure 2.5. "Exhibit 25 Extended-Time Instructional Programs During the School Year: Availability and Participation, 1997-98," in *High Standards for All Students: A Report from the National Assessment of Title I on Progress and Challenges Since the 1994 Reauthorization.* U.S. Department of Education, Planning and Evaluation Service, January 2001.

Table 2.14. Snyder, Thomas D. and Charlene M. Hoffman. "Table 101.—High school graduates compared with population 17 years of age, by sex and control of school: 1869-70 to 1999-2000," in *Digest of Education Statistics, 2000,* NCES 2001-034. U.S. Department of Education, National Center for Education Statistics, January 2001.

Table 2.15. Snyder, Thomas D. and Charlene M. Hoffman. "Table 104.—General Educational Development (GED) credentials issued, and number and age of test takers: United States and outlying areas, 1971 to 1996," in *Digest of Education Statistics, 2000,* NCES 2001-034. U.S. Department of Education, National Center for Education Statistics, January 2001.

Table 3.1. Snyder, Thomas D. and Charlene M. Hoffman. "Table 53.—Children 0 to 21 years old served in federally supported programs for the disabled, by type of disability: 1976-77 to 1998-99," in *Digest of Education Statistics, 2000,* NCES 2001-034. U.S. Department of Education, National Center for Education Statistics, January 2001.

Table 3.2. "Table II-2 Number of Students Ages 6-21 Served Under IDEA, in the 1989-90 and 1998-99 School Year," in *22nd Annual Report to Congress on the Implementation of the Individuals with Disabilities Act.* U.S. Department of Education, Office of Special Education and Rehabilitative Services, 2000.

Table 3.3. Snyder, Thomas D. and Charlene M. Hoffman. "Table 54.—Percentage distribution of disabled persons 3 to 21 years old receiving education services for the disabled, by age group and educational environment: 1997-98," in *Digest of Education Statistics, 2000,* NCES 2001-034. U.S. Department of

Education, National Center for Education Statistics, January 2001.

Figure 3.1. Thompson, Sandra L. and Martha L. Thurlow. "Figure 1. Positive Consequences of the Participation of Students with Disabilities in Standards, Assessments, and Accountability," in *2001 State Special Education Outcomes: A Report on State Activities at the Beginning of a New Decade* [Online] http://www.coled.umn.edu/NCEO/OnlinePubs/2001StateReport.html [accessed February 1, 2002]. University of Minnesota, National Center on Educational Outcomes. Reproduced by permission.

Figure 3.2. Thompson, Sandra L. and Martha L. Thurlow. "Figure 2. Negative Consequences of the Participation of Students with Disabilities in Standards, Assessments, and Accountability Systems," in *2001 State Special Education Outcomes: A Report on State Activities at the Beginning of a New Decade* [Online] http://www.coled.umn.edu/NCEO/OnlinePubs/2001StateReport.html [accessed February 1, 2002]. University of Minnesota, National Center on Educational Outcomes. Reproduced by permission.

Table 3.4. Snyder, Thomas D. and Charlene M. Hoffman. "Table 108.—Students with disabilities exiting the educational system, by age, type of disability, and basis of exit: The United States and outlying areas, 1996-97 and 1997-98," in *Digest of Education Statistics, 2000,* NCES 2001-034. U.S. Department of Education, National Center for Education Statistics, January 2001.

Table 3.5. Ross, Pat O'Connell. "1972 Marland Definition (Public Law 91-20, section 806)," in *National Excellence: A Case for Developing America's Talent.* U.S. Department of Education, Office of Educational Research and Improvement, October 1993.

Table 3.6. Snyder, Thomas D. and Charlene M. Hoffman. "Table 106.—Percent of high school dropouts (status dropouts) among persons 16 to 24 years old, by sex and race/ethnicity: April 1960 to October 1999," in *Digest of Education Statistics, 2000,* NCES 2001-034. U.S. Department of Education, National Center for Education Statistics, January 2001.

Figure 3.3. Kaufman, Philip, Martha Naomi Alt, and Christopher D. Chapman. "Figure 1.—Event dropout rates of 15- to 24-year-olds who dropped out of grades 10-12, by family income: October 1972 to October 2000," in *Dropout Rates in the United States: 2000,* NCES 2002-114, U.S. Department of Education, National Center for Education Statistics, November 2001.

Table 3.7. Snyder, Thomas D. and Charlene M. Hoffman. "Table 366.—Appropriations for Title I and Title VI, Elementary and Secondary Education Act (ESEA) of 1994, by state or other area: 1998-99 and 1999-2000," in *Digest of Education Statistics, 2000,* NCES 2001-034. U.S. Department of Education, National Center for Education Statistics, January 2001.

Figure 3.4. "Exhibit 1 Funding for Title I and Other Federal Elementary-Secondary Programs, FY 1994 to FY 2001," in *High Standards for All Students: A Report from the National Assessment of Title I on Progress and Challenges Since the 1994 Reauthorization.* U.S. Department of Education, Planning and Evaluation Service, January 2001.

Figure 3.5. Sinclair, Beth. "Figure 6: Title I Participation, by Grade Span, 1998-99," in *State ESEA Title I Participation Information for 1998-99: Final Summary Report.* Westat prepared for the U.S. Department of Education, Office of the Deputy Secretary, Planning and Evaluation Service, October 2001.

Figure 3.6. "Exhibit 27 Title I Part D Services Offered in Juvenile and Adult Institutions for Neglected and Delinquent Children," in *High Standards for All Students: A Report from the National Assessment of Title I on Progress and Challenges Since the 1994 Reauthorization.* U.S. Department of Education, Planning and Evaluation Service, January 2001.

Figure 3.7. "Traditional Streams of Migration," in *Migrant Children—Education and HHS Need to Improve the Exchange of Participant Information,* GAO/HEHS-00-4. U.S. General Accounting Office, October 1999.

Table 3.8. "Head Start Facts FY–2000 Data," in *Head Start Fact Sheet* [Online] http://www2.acf.dhhs/programs/hsb/about/fact2001.htm [accessed November 7, 2001]. U.S. Department of Health and Human Services, Administration for Children and Families.

Table 3.9. Snyder, Thomas D. and Charlene M. Hoffman. "Table 371. U.S. Department of Health and Human Services allocations for Head Start and enrollment in Head Start, by state or other area: Fiscal years 1996 to 1999," in *Digest of Education Statistics, 2000,* NCES 2001-034. U.S. Department of Education, National Center for Education Statistics, January 2001.

Figure 3.8. Hurst, David and Lisa Hudson. "Figure 1. Average number of Carnegie units accumulated by public high school graduates, by type of coursework: 1982 and 1998," in *Changes in High School Vocational Coursetaking in a Larger Perspective,* NCES 2001-026. U.S. Department of Education, National Center for Education Statistics, December 2000.

Figure 3.9. Phelps, Richard P., et al. "Figure 7. Percent of public secondary schools offering at least one listed occupational program that report using each of five procedures to

ensure they teach job skills in at least one program, by school type: 1999," in *Features of Occupational Programs at the Secondary and Postsecondary Levels,* NCES 2001-018. U.S. Department of Education, National Center for Education Statistics, June 2001.

Figure 3.10. Phelps, Richard P., et al. "Figure 11. Percent of public secondary schools offering at least one listed occupational program that report different levels of involvement by educators and industry in developing or adopting skill competency lists for at least one program, by school type: 1999," in *Features of Occupational Programs at the Secondary and Postsecondary Levels,* NCES 2001-018. U.S. Department of Education, National Center for Education Statistics, June 2001.

Figure 3.11. Phelps, Richard P., et al. "Figure 5. Percentage distribution of types of less-than-4-year postsecondary institutions that offer at least one listed occupational program, for all program areas, and in each broad program area: 1999," in *Features of Occupational Programs at the Secondary and Postsecondary Levels,* NCES 2001-018. U.S. Department of Education, National Center for Education Statistics, June 2001.

Figure 3.12. Phelps, Richard P., et al. "Figure 8. Percent of less-than-4-year postsecondary institutions offering at least one listed occupational program that report using each of five procedures to ensure they teach job skills, by type of institution: 1999," in *Features of Occupational Programs at the Secondary and Postsecondary Levels,* NCES 2001-018. U.S. Department of Education, National Center for Education Statistics, June 2001.

Figure 3.13. Phelps, Richard P., et al. "Figure 12. Percent of less-than-4-year postsecondary institutions offering at least one listed occupational program that report different levels of involvement by educators and industry in developing or adopting skill competency lists for at least one program, by type of institution: 1999," in *Features of Occupational Programs at the Secondary and Postsecondary Levels,* NCES 2001-018. U.S. Department of Education, National Center for Education Statistics, June 2001.

Figure 3.14. Phelps, Richard P., et al. "Figure 13. Percent of less-than-4-year postsecondary institutions offering at least one occupational program, that offer each type of credential for at least one program, by type of institution: 1999," in *Features of Occupational Programs at the Secondary and Postsecondary Levels,* NCES 2001-018. U.S. Department of Education, National Center for Education Statistics, June 2001.

Figure 4.1. "Exhibit 14. States with Content and Performance Standards in Mathematics and Reading/Language Arts," in *High Stan-*

dards for All Students: A Report from the National Assessment of Title I on Progress and Challenges Since the 1994 Reauthorization. U.S. Department of Education, January 2001.

Figure 4.2. Goertz, Margaret E., Mark C. Duffy, and Kerstin Carlson Le Floch. "Figure 1. Subjects Included in State Assessment Systems, 1999-2000," in *Assessment and Accountability Systems in the United States: 1999-2000.* University of Pennsylvania, Graduate School of Education, Consortium for Policy Research in Education, March 2001. Reproduced by permission.

Table 4.1. Rose, Lowell C. and Alec M. Gallup. "In your opinion, is there too much emphasis on achievement testing in the public schools in your community, not enough emphasis on testing, or about the right amount?," in "The 33rd Annual Phi Delta Kappa/Gallup Poll of the Public's Attitude Toward the Public Schools." *Phi Delta Kappan,* v. 83, n. 1, September 2001. Reproduced by permission.

Figure 4.3. Rose, Lowell C. and Alec M. Gallup. "Figure 12. Opinions Regarding Standardized Testing," in "The 33rd Annual Phi Delta Kappa/Gallup Poll of the Public's Attitude Toward the Public Schools." *Phi Delta Kappan,* v. 83, n. 1, September 2001. Reproduced by permission.

Figure 4.4. Donahue, Patricia L., et al. "Figure i.3. Achievement Levels," in *The Nation's Report Card: Fourth Grade Reading 2000,* NCES 2001-499. U.S. Department of Education, National Center for Education Statistics, April 2001.

Table 4.2. Snyder, Thomas D. and Charlene M. Hoffman. "Table 110.—Average student proficiency in reading, by age and selected characteristics of students: 1971 to 1999," in *Digest of Education Statistics, 2000,* NCES 2001-034. U.S. Department of Education, National Center for Education Statistics, January 2001.

Figure 4.5. Donahue, Patricia L., et al. "Figure 1.3. Reading Achievement Levels," in *The Nation's Report Card: Fourth Grade Reading 2000,* NCES 2001-499. U.S. Department of Education, National Center for Education Statistics, April 2001.

Figure 4.6. Donahue, Patricia L., et al. "Figure 1.1. Scale Score Results," in *The Nation's Report Card: Fourth Grade Reading 2000,* NCES 2001-499. U.S. Department of Education, National Center for Education Statistics, April 2001.

Figure 4.7. "Exhibit 10 Reading Performance on the Trend NAEP, by School Poverty Level, 1988 to 1999," in *High Standards for All Students: A Report from the National Assessment of Title I on Progress and Challenges Since the 1994 Reauthorization.* U.S.

Department of Education, Planning and Evaluation Service, January 2001.

Figure 4.8. Donahue, Patricia L., et al. "Figure 2.3. Scale Score Results by Race/Ethnicity," in *The Nation's Report Card: Fourth Grade Reading 2000*, NCES 2001-499. U.S. Department of Education, National Center for Education Statistics, April 2001.

Figure 4.9. Donahue, Patricia L., et al. "Figure 2.1. Scale Score Results by Gender," in *The Nation's Report Card: Fourth Grade Reading 2000*, NCES 2001-499. U.S. Department of Education, National Center for Education Statistics, April 2001.

Figure 4.10. Wirt, John, et al. "Preschool Reading Activities: Percentage of 3- to 5-year-old children not yet enrolled in kindergarten who participated in home literacy activities with a family member three or more times in the week before the survey, by number of risk factors: 1999," in *The Condition of Education, 2001*, NCES 2001-072. U.S. Department of Education, National Center for Education Statistics, June 2001.

Figure 4.11. Braswell, James S., et al. "Figure 1.4. NAEP mathematics achievement levels: Grade 4," in *The Nation's Report Card: Fourth Grade Mathematics 2000*, NCES 2001-517. U.S. Department of Education, National Center for Education Statistics, August 2001.

Figure 4.12. Braswell, James S., et al. "Figure 2.1. National Scale Score Results," in *The Nation's Report Card: Fourth Grade Mathematics 2000*, NCES 2001-517. U.S. Department of Education, National Center for Education Statistics, August 2001.

Table 4.3. Snyder, Thomas D. and Charlene M. Hoffman. "Table 123. Percent of students at or above selected mathematics proficiency levels, by sex, race/ethnicity, control of school, and age: 1978 to 1999," in *Digest of Education Statistics, 2000*. U.S. Department of Education, National Center for Education Statistics, January 2001.

Figure 4.13. "Exhibit 11 Mathematics Performance on the Trend NAEP, by School Poverty Level, 1986 to 1999: Average Scale Scores of 9-Year-Old Public School Students," in *High Standards for All Students: A Report from the National Assessment of Title I on Progress and Challenges Since the 1994 Reauthorization*. U.S. Department of Education, Planning and Evaluation Service, January 2001.

Table 4.4. "Achievement Levels," in *The Nation's Report Card: Science Highlights 2000*, NCES 2002-452. U.S. Department of Education, Office of Educational Research and Improvement, National Center for Education Statistics, November 2000.

Figure 4.14. "Percentile Scores, Grades 4, 8, and 12: 1996," in *The Nation's Report Card:*

Science Highlights 2000, NCES 2002-452. U.S. Department of Education, Office of Educational Research and Improvement, National Center for Education Statistics, November 2000.

Figure 4.15. "Average Science Scores by Race/Ethnicity, Grades 4, 8, and 12: 1996-2000," in *The Nation's Report Card: Science Highlights 2000*, NCES 2002-452. U.S. Department of Education, Office of Educational Research and Improvement, National Center for Education Statistics, November 2000.

Table 4.5. Wirt, John, et al. "Table 13—1. Average science scale scores, by race/ethnicity and age: 1970-1999," in *The Condition of Education, 2001*, NCES 2001-072. U.S. Department of Education, National Center for Education Statistics, June 2001.

Figure 4.16. "Average Science Scores by Gender, Grades 4, 8, and 12: 1996-2000," in *The Nation's Report Card: Science Highlights 2000*, NCES 2002-452. U.S. Department of Education, Office of Educational Research and Improvement, National Center for Education Statistics, November 2000.

Table 4.6. Wirt, John, et al. "Table 13—3. Average science scale scores, by sex and age: 1970-1999," in *The Condition of Education, 2001*, NCES 2001-072. U.S. Department of Education, National Center for Education Statistics, June 2001.

Table 4.7. Greenwald, Elissa, et al. "Table 1.2. Percentage of students at or above the writing achievement levels for the nation: 1998," in *NAEP 1998 Writing Report Card for the Nation and the States*, NCES 1999-462. U.S. Department of Education, National Center for Education Statistics, September 1999.

Table 4.8. Greenwald, Elissa, et al. "Table 2.2. Average writing scale scores by race/ethnicity: 1998," in *NAEP 1998 Writing Report Card for the Nation and the States*, NCES 1999-462. U.S. Department of Education, National Center for Education Statistics, September 1999.

Table 4.9. Greenwald, Elissa, et al. "Table 2.1. Average writing scale scores by gender: 1998," in *NAEP 1998 Writing Report Card for the Nation and the States*, NCES 1999-462. U.S. Department of Education, National Center for Education Statistics, September 1999.

Figure 4.17. Greenwald, Elissa, et al. "Figure 4.9. Students' reports on the presence of four types of reading materials in their home (a newspaper, an encyclopedia, magazines, and more than 25 books): 1998," in *NAEP 1998 Writing Report Card for the Nation and the States*, NCES 1999-462. U.S. Department of Education, National Center for Education Statistics, September 1999.

Table 4.10. "Table F.1. Trends in mean achievement scores in the 8th grade, by subject (1995 and 1999)," in *Education at a Glance: OECD Indicators*. Organisation for Economic Co-operation and Development, Paris, France, 2001, p. 310. Reproduced by permission.

Figure 4.18. "Chart A2.1. Educational attainment of the population (1999)," in *Education at a Glance: OECD Indicators*. Organisation for Economic Co-operation and Development, Paris, France, 2001, p. 36. Reproduced by permission.

Table 4.11. Snyder, Thomas D. and Charlene M. Hoffman. "Table 138.—Average number of Carnegie units earned by public high school graduates in various subject fields, by student characteristics: 1982 to 1998," in *Digest of Education Statistics, 2000*, NCES 2001-034. U.S. Department of Education, National Center for Education Statistics, January 2001.

Table 4.12. "Table 2: Average SAT Scores of Entering College Classes: 1967-2001," in "2001 College Bound Seniors are the Largest, Most Diverse Group in History" [Online] http://www.collegeboard.org/press/senior01/html/082801.html [accessed November 5, 2001]. The College Board. Reproduced by permission. All rights reserved. www.collegeboard.com.

Table 4.13. "Average ACT Scores by Level of Academic Preparation," in *2001 ACT National and State Scores* [Online] http://www.act.org/research/ [accessed November 5, 2001]. The American College Testing Program. Reproduced by permission.

Table 4.14. "Table 6: Average ACT Scores and Standard Deviations for Males and Females," in *2001 ACT National and State Scores* [Online] http://www.act.org/research/ [accessed November 5, 2001]. The American College Testing Program. Reproduced by permission.

Table 4.15. "Table 1: Average ACT Scores by Academic Preparation for Different Ethnic Groups," in *2001 ACT National and State Scores* [Online] http://www.act.org/research/ [accessed November 5, 2001]. The American College Testing Program. Reproduced by permission.

Figure 5.1. Price, Cynthia. "The National Education Goals," in *The National Educational Goals Report: Building a Nation of Learners, 1999*. National Education Goals Panel, 1999.

Table 5.1. Price, Cynthia. "Goal 1," in *The National Educational Goals Report: Building a Nation of Learners, 1999*. National Education Goals Panel, 1999.

Table 5.2. "Goal 1: Ready to Learn," in *Promising Practices: Progress Toward the*

Goals 2000. National Education Goals Panel, December 2000.

Table 5.3. Price, Cynthia. "Goal 2," in *The National Educational Goals Report: Building a Nation of Learners, 1999*. National Education Goals Panel, 1999.

Table 5.4. "Goal 2: School Completion," in *Promising Practices: Progress Toward the Goals 2000*. National Education Goals Panel, December, 2000.

Table 5.5. Price, Cynthia. "Goal 3," in *The National Educational Goals Report: Building a Nation of Learners*. National Education Goals Panel, 1999.

Table 5.6. Barton, Paul E. "Gap Closing," in *Raising Achievement and Reducing Gaps: Reporting Progress Toward Goals for Academic Achievement*. National Education Goals Panel, March 2001.

Table 5.7. "Goal 3: Student Achievement and Citizenship," in *Promising Practices: Progress Toward the Goals 2000*. National Education Goals Panel, December 2000.

Table 5.8. Price, Cynthia. "Goal 4," in *The National Educational Goals Report: Building a Nation of Learners*. National Education Goals Panel, 1999.

Table 5.9. "Goal 4: Teacher Education and Professional Development," in *Promising Practices: Progress Toward the Goals 2000*. National Education Goals Panel, December 2000.

Table 5.10. Price, Cynthia. "Goal 5," in *The National Educational Goals Report: Building a Nation of Learners*. National Education Goals Panel, 1999.

Table 5.11. Barton, Paul E. "4th Grade Math," in *Raising Achievement and Reducing Gaps: Reporting Progress Toward Goals for Academic Achievement*. National Education Goals Panel, March 2001.

Table 5.12. Barton, Paul E. "8th Grade Math," in *Raising Achievement and Reducing Gaps: Reporting Progress Toward Goals for Academic Achievement*. National Education Goals Panel, March 2001.

Table 5.13. Barton, Paul E. "4th Grade Reading," in *Raising Achievement and Reducing Gaps: Reporting Progress Toward Goals for Academic Achievement*. National Education Goals Panel, March 2001.

Table 5.14. "Goal 5: Mathematics and Science," in *Promising Practices: Progress Toward the Goals 2000*. National Education Goals Panel, December 2000.

Table 5.15. Price, Cynthia. "Goal 6," in *The National Educational Goals Report: Building a Nation of Learners*. National Education Goals Panel, 1999.

Table 5.16. "Goal 6: Adult Literacy and Lifelong Learning," in *Promising Practices: Progress Toward the Goals 2000*. National Education Goals Panel, December 2000.

Table 5.17. Price, Cynthia. "Goal 7," in *The National Educational Goals Report: Building a Nation of Learners*. National Education Goals Panel, 1999.

Table 5.18. "Goal 7: Safe, Disciplined and Alcohol- and Drug-Free Schools," in *Promising Practices: Progress Toward the Goals 2000*. National Education Goals Panel, December 2000.

Table 5.19. Price, Cynthia. "Goal 8," in *The National Educational Goals Report: Building a Nation of Learners*. National Education Goals Panel, 1999.

Table 5.20. "Goal 8: Parental Participation," in *Promising Practices: Progress Toward the Goals 2000*. National Education Goals Panel, December 2000.

Figure 6.1. Dalaker, Joseph. "Figure 3. Poverty Rates by Race and Hispanic Origin: 1959 to 2000," in *Poverty in the United States: 2000*, P60-214. U.S. Department of Commerce, U.S. Census Bureau, Economics and Statistics Administration, September 2001.

Table 6.1. "Table ED2. Early childhood care and education: Percentage of children ages 3 to 5 who are enrolled in center-based early childhood care and education programs by child and family characteristics, selected years 1991-99," in *America's Children: Key National Indicators of Well-Being, 2001*. Federal Interagency Forum on Child and Family Statistics, July 2001. Reproduced by permission.

Table 6.2. Snyder, Thomas D. and Charlene M. Hoffman. "Table 106.—Percent of high school dropouts (status dropouts) among persons 16 to 24 years old, by sex and race/ethnicity: April 1960 to October 1999," in *Digest of Education Statistics, 2000*, NCES 2001-034. U.S. Department of Education, National Center for Education Statistics, January 2001.

Table 6.3. Snyder, Thomas D. and Charlene M. Hoffman. "Table 378.—Unemployment rate of persons 16 years old and over, by age, sex, race/ethnicity, and highest degree attained: 1997, 1998, and 1999," in *Digest of Education Statistics, 2000*, NCES 2001-034. U.S. Department of Education, National Center for Education Statistics, January 2001.

Table 6.4. Wirt, John, et al. "Table 18—1 Median annual earnings (in constant 2000 dollars of all wage and salary workers ages 25-34, by sex and educational attainment level: March 1970-99," in *The Condition of Education, 2001*, NCES 2001-072. U.S. Department of Education, National Center for Education Statistics, June 2001.

Table 6.5. Tim, Jan and Charita Castro. "Table A—1. Average Monthly Program Participation Rates for Any Means-Tested Programs by Selected Characteristics: 1993-95," in *Dynamics of Economic Well-Being: Program Participation, 1993 to 1995, Who Gets Assistance?* U.S. Census Bureau, September 2001.

Figure 6.2. "Indicator ED6. Percentage of youth ages 16 to 19 who are neither enrolled in school nor working by gender, race, and Hispanic origin, 1984-2000," in *America's Children: Key National Indicators of Well-Being, 2001*. Federal Interagency Forum on Child and Family Statistics, July 2001.

Table 6.6. Johnson, Lloyd D., Patrick M. O'Malley, and Jerald G. Bachman. "Table 8—1 Trends in Harmfulness of Drugs as Perceived by Eighth and Tenth Graders, 1991-2000," in *Monitoring the Future: National Survey Results on Drug Use 1975-2000, Volume I: Secondary School Students*, NIH Publication No. 01-4924. National Institute on Drug Abuse, August 2001. Reproduced by permission.

Table 6.7. Johnson, Lloyd D., Patrick M. O'Malley and Jerald G. Bachman. "Table 5—5a Trends in Prevalence of Use of Various Drugs for Eighth, Tenth, and Twelfth Graders," in *Monitoring the Future: National Survey Results on Drug Use 1975-2000, Volume I: Secondary School Students*, NIH Publication No. 01-4924. National Institute on Drug Abuse, August 2001. Reproduced by permission.

Table 6.8. Kann, Laura, et al. "Table 20. Percentage of high school students who drank alcohol and used marijuana, by sex, race/ethnicity, and grade - United States, Youth Risk Behavior Survey, 1999," in *Youth Risk Behavior Surveillance - United States, 1999, Morbidity and Mortality Weekly Report/ CDC Surveillance Summaries*, v. 49, n. ss-5, June 9, 2000. Reproduced by permission.

Figure 6.3. Johnson, Lloyd D., Patrick M. O'Malley, and Jerald G. Bachman. "Figure 8-10a Trends in Perceived Harmfulness of Smoking One or More Packs of Cigarettes per Day for Eighth, Tenth, and Twelfth Graders," in *Monitoring the Future: National Survey Results on Drug Use 1975-2000, Volume I: Secondary School Students*, NIH Publication No. 01-4924. National Institute on Drug Abuse, August 2001.

Figure 6.4. Johnson, Lloyd D., Patrick M. O'Malley, and Jerald G. Bachman. "Figure 8-10b Trends in Disapproval of Smoking One or More Packs of Cigarettes per Day for Eighth, Tenth, and Twelfth Graders," in *Monitoring the Future: National Survey Results on Drug Use 1975-2000, Volume I: Secondary School Students*, NIH Publication No. 01-4924. National Institute on Drug Abuse, August 2001.

Table 6.9. "Table 4. Percentage of middle school and high school students who were current users of any tobacco product, cigarettes, cigars, smokeless tobacco, pipes, bidis, or kreteks, by sex and race/ethnicity," in *Youth Tobacco Surveillance: United States, 1998-99, Morbidity and Mortality Weekly Report*/CDC Surveillance Summaries, v. 49, n. ss-10, October 13, 2000.

Table 6.10. Kann, Laura, et al. "Table 14. Percentage of high school students who used tobacco by sex, race/ethnicity, and grade - United States, Youth Risk Behavior Survey, 1999," in *Youth Risk Behavior Surveillance - United States, 1999, Morbidity and Mortality Weekly Report*/CDC Surveillance Summaries, v. 49, n. ss-5, June 9, 2000. Reproduced by permission.

Table 6.11. Kann, Laura, et al. "Table 30. Percentage of high school students who engaged in sexual behaviors, by sex, race/ethnicity, and grade - United States, Youth Risk Behavior Survey, 1999," in *Youth Risk Behavior Surveillance - United States, 1999, Morbidity and Mortality Weekly Report*/CDC Surveillance Summaries, v. 49, n. ss-5, June 9, 2000. Reproduced by permission.

Table 6.12. Moore, Kristin Anderson, et al. "Teen Birth Rate (Births per 1,000 Females Ages 15-19, 15-17, and 18-19)," in *CTS Facts at a Glance.* Child Trends, August 2001. Reproduced by permission.

Figure 6.5. Moore, Kristin Anderson, et al. "U.S. Teen Birth Rate by Race/Ethnicity 1990-1999," in *CTS Facts at a Glance.* Child Trends, August 2001. Reproduced by permission.

Table 6.13. Moore, Kristin Anderson, et al. "Marital and Non-marital Birth Rate (Births per 1,000 Females)," in *CTS Facts at a Glance.* Child Trends, August 2001. Reproduced by permission.

Table 6.14. "Table 7. AIDS cases by sex, age at diagnosis, and race/ethnicity, reported through December 2000, United States," in *HIV/AIDS Surveillance Report.* Centers for Disease Control and Prevention, v. 12, n. 2, 2000.

Table 6.15. Kann, Laura, et al. "Table 10. Percentage of high school students who engaged in violence and in behaviors resulting from violence on school property, by sex, race/ethnicity, and grade - United States, Youth Risk Behavior Survey, 1999," in *Youth Risk Behavior Surveillance - United States, 1999, Morbidity and Mortality Weekly Report*/CDC Surveillance Summaries, v. 49, n. ss-5, June 9, 2000. Reproduced by permission.

Table 6.16. Rennison, Callie Marie. "Table 2. Rates of violent crime and personal theft, by gender, age, race, and Hispanic origin, 2000," in *Criminal Victimization 2000: Changes 1999-2000 with Trends 1993-2000.*

U.S. Department of Justice, Bureau of Justice Statistics, June 2001.

Table 7.1. Nelson, Beryl, et al. "Estimated Percentage of Charter Schools by Source of Primary Control for Various School Decisions and Operations," in *The State of Charter Schools 2000: Fourth-Year Report.* U.S. Department of Education, Office of Educational Research and Improvement, January 2001.

Figure 7.1. Nelson, Beryl, et al. "Estimated Percentage of Charter Schools that are Externally Monitored on Accountability Measures," in *The State of Charter Schools 2000: Fourth-Year Report.* U.S. Department of Education, Office of Educational Research and Improvement, January 2000.

Figure 7.2. Rose, Lowell C. and Alec M. Gallup. "Figure 4. Awareness of Charter Schools," in "The 33rd Annual Phi Delta Kappa/Gallup Poll of the Public's Attitude Toward the Public Schools." *Phi Delta Kappan,* v. 83, n. 1, September 2001. Reproduced by permission.

Table 7.2. Rose, Lowell C. and Alec M. Gallup. "As you may know, charter schools operate under a charter or contract that frees them from many of the state regulations imposed on public schools and permits them to operate independently. Do you favor or oppose the idea of charter schools?" in "The 33rd Annual Phi Delta Kappa/Gallup Poll of the Public's Attitude Toward the Public Schools." *Phi Delta Kappan,* v. 83, n. 1, September 2001. Reproduced by permission.

Table 7.3. Rose, Lowell C. and Alec M. Gallup. "Do you favor or oppose allowing students and parents to choose a private school to attend at public expense?" in "The 33rd Annual Phi Delta Kappa/Gallup Poll of the Public's Attitude Toward the Public Schools." *Phi Delta Kappan,* v. 83, n. 1, September 2001. Reproduced by permission.

Table 7.4. Langdon, Carol A. and Nick Vesper. "In the voucher system, parents are given a voucher which can be used to pay all the tuition for attendance at a private or church-related school. Parents can then choose any private school, church-related school, or public school for their child. If a parent chooses a public school, the voucher would not apply. Would you favor or oppose the use of the voucher system in your state?" in "The Sixth Phi Delta Kappa Poll of Teachers' Attitudes Toward the Public Schools." *Phi Delta Kappan,* v. 81, n. 8, April 2000. Reproduced by permission.

Figure 7.3. Bielick, Stacey, et al. "Figure 2. Ten reasons for homeschooling and the percentage of home schooled students whose parents gave each reason," in *Homeschooling in the United States: 1999,* NCES 2001-033. U.S. Department of Education,

National Center for Education Statistics, July 2001.

Table 7.5. Langdon, Carol A. and Nick Vesper. "Would you favor or oppose requiring children who are schooled at home to take all the state and national assessment tests that public school students are required to take?" in "The Sixth Phi Delta Kappa Poll of Teachers' Attitudes Toward the Public Schools." *Phi Delta Kappan,* v. 81, n. 8, April 2000. Reproduced by permission.

Table 7.6. Rose, Lowell C. and Alec M. Gallup. "In your opinion, should faith-based or religious organizations receive public tax money for providing after-school programs designed to improve students' academic performance?" in "The 33rd Annual Phi Delta Kappa/Gallup Poll of the Public's Attitude Toward the Public Schools." *Phi Delta Kappan,* v. 83, n. 1, September 2001. Reproduced by permission.

Figure 7.4. Smerdon, Becky, et al. "Figure 4.8. Percent of Public School Teachers Reporting Student Use of Various Technologies in Schools and Classrooms: 1999," in *Teachers' Tools for the 21st Century: A Report on Teachers' Use of Technology,* NCES 2000-102. U.S. Department of Education, National Center for Education Statistics, September 2000.

Figure 7.5. Smerdon, Becky, et al. "Figure 3.7. Percent of Elementary and Secondary Teachers and Adults in Other Occupations Who Report Having Computers at Home: 1994, 1997 and 1998," in *Teachers' Tools for the 21st Century: A Report on Teachers' Use of Technology,* NCES 2000-102. U.S. Department of Education, National Center for Education Statistics, September 2000.

Figure 7.6. Smerdon, Becky, et al. "Figure 3.4. Percent of Public Schools and Instructional Rooms with Internet Access: 1994 to 1999," in *Teachers' Tools for the 21st Century: A Report on Teachers' Use of Technology,* NCES 2000-102. U.S. Department of Education, National Center for Education Statistics, September, 2000.

Figure 7.7. Whiten, Karen and Suzanne Lofhjelm. "Figure 2: Concentration of Students With Limited English Proficiency in the United States, School Year 1997-98," in *Bilingual Education: Four Overlapping Programs Could Be Consolidated,* GAO-01-657. U.S. General Accounting Office, May 2001.

Table 7.7. Lewis, Laurie, et al. "Table 4. Percent of public schools rating the condition of building features as less than adequate, by school characteristics: 1999," in *Condition of America's Public School Facilities: 1999,* NCES 2000-032. U.S. Department of Education, National Center for Education Statistics, June 2000.

Table 7.8. Wirt, John, et al. "Table 45–1. Percentage of public schools with an inadequate or unsatisfactory building, building feature, or environmental feature, by categories of under-enrolled and overcrowded: 1999," in *The Condition of Education 2001,* NCES 2001-072. U.S. Department of Education, National Center for Education Statistics, June 2001.

Figure 7.8. Rose, Lowell C. and Alec M. Gallup. "Figure 11. Variance in Funding and Quality of Schools," in "The 33rd Annual Phi Delta Kappa/Gallup Poll of the Public's Attitude Toward the Public Schools." *Phi Delta Kappan,* v. 83, n. 1, September 2001. Reproduced by permission.

Figure 8.1. Gerald, Debra E. and William J. Hussar. "Figure 45.—Elementary and secondary teachers, with alternative projections: Fall 1986 to fall 2011," in *Projections of Education Statistics to 2011,* NCES 2001-083. U.S. Department of Education, National Center for Education Statistics, October 2001.

Table 8.1. Gerald, Debra E. and William J. Hussar. "Table 31.—Elementary and secondary teachers, by control of institution and organizational level, with alternative projections: Fall 1986 to fall 2011," in *Projections of Education Statistics to 2011,* NCES 2001-083. U.S. Department of Education, National Center for Education Statistics, October 2001.

Table 8.2. Gerald, Debra E. and William J. Hussar. "Table 32.—Pupil/teacher ratios in elementary and secondary schools, by control of institution, with alternative projections: Fall 1986 to fall 2001," in *Projections of Education Statistics to 2011,* NCES 2001-083. U.S. Department of Education, National Center for Education Statistics, October 2001.

Table 8.3. Snyder, Thomas D. and Charlene M. Hoffman. "Table 67.—Teachers, enrollment, and pupil/teacher ratios in public elementary and secondary schools, by state: Fall 1993 to fall 1998," in *Digest of Education Statistics, 2000,* NCES 2001-034. U.S. Department of Education, National Center for Education Statistics, January 2001.

Table 8.4. Hoffman, Charlene M. "Table 16.—Average annual salary for public elementary and secondary schools (sic) teachers: 1970-71 to 1998-99 (in constant 1998-99 dollars)," in *Mini-Digest of Education Statistics, 2000,* NCES 2001-046. U.S. Department of Education, National Center for Education Statistics, August 2001.

Table 8.5. Snyder, Thomas D. and Charlene M. Hoffman. "Table 76.—Estimated average annual salary of teachers in public elementary and secondary schools, by state: 1969-70 to 1998-99," in *Digest of Education Statistics, 2000,* NCES 2001-034. U.S. Department of Education, National Center for Education Statistics, January 2001. Data

© 2000, NEA, Washington, D.C. Reproduced by permission.

Table 8.6. Nelson, F. Howard, Rachel Drown, and Jewell C. Gould. "Table II—5 Trends in Teacher Salaries Compared to the Average Annual Salaries of Selected White-Collar Occupations," in *Survey and Analysis of Teacher Salary Trends 2000.* Research & Information Services, American Federation of Teachers, AFL-CIO, Washington, DC. Reproduced by permission.

Figure 8.2. Ingersoll, Richard M. "Figure 1. Percent of employee turnover and percent of teacher turnover, by selected school characteristics," in *A Different Approach to Solving the Teaching Shortage Problem.* Center for the Study of Teaching and Policy, Seattle, WA, January 2001. Reproduced by permission.

Figure 8.3. Smerdon, Becky, et al. "Table 5.1. Percent of public school teachers reporting feeling not at all, somewhat, or well/very well prepared to use computers and the internet for classroom instruction, by years of teaching experience: 1999," in *Teachers' Tools for the 21st Century: A Report on Teachers' Use of Technology,* NCES 2000-102. U.S. Department of Education, National Center for Education Statistics, September 2000.

Table 8.7. Langdon, Carol A. and Nick Vesper. "Students are often given the grades A, B, C, D, and FAIL to denote the quality of their work. Suppose the public schools themselves, in this community, were graded in the same way. What grade would you give the public schools here — A, B, C, D, or FAIL?" in "The Sixth Phi Delta Kappa Poll of Teachers' Attitudes Toward the Public Schools." *Phi Delta Kappan,* v. 81, n. 8, April 2000. Reproduced by permission.

Table 8.8. Langdon, Carol A. and Nick Vesper. "Here are some ways that have been suggested for attracting and retaining good public school teachers. As you read each suggestion, would you indicate whether you favor it or oppose it as a way to attract and retain good teachers?" in "The Sixth Phi Delta Kappa Poll of Teachers' Attitudes Toward the Public Schools." *Phi Delta Kappan,* v. 81, n. 8, April 2000. Reproduced by permission.

Table 8.9. Langdon, Carol A. and Nick Vesper. "Here are different factors that might be considered in choosing a public school for a child, assuming free choice of public and private schools were allowed in this community. As you read each of these factors, would you indicate whether you consider it very important, fairly important, not too important, or not at all important in choosing a local school?" in "The Sixth Phi Delta Kappa Poll of Teachers' Attitudes Toward the Public Schools." *Phi Delta Kappan,* v. 81, n. 8, April 2000. Reproduced by permission.

Figure 8.4. Smerdon, Becky, et al. "Figure 6.1. Percent of Public School Teachers Reporting Small, Moderate, or Great Barriers to Their Use of Computers and the Internet for Instruction: 1999," in *Teachers' Tools for the 21st Century: A Report on Teachers' Use of Technology,* NCES 2000-102. U.S. Department of Education, National Center for Education Statistics, September 2000.

Table 8.10. Langdon, Carol A. and Nick Vesper. "What do you think are the biggest problems with which the public schools must deal?" in "The Sixth Phi Delta Kappa Poll of Teachers' Attitudes Toward the Public Schools." *Phi Delta Kappan,* v. 81, n. 8, April 2000. Reproduced by permission.

Table 8.11. Langdon, Carol A. and Nick Vesper. "In your opinion who or what is the main obstacle to improving the public schools in your community?" in "The Sixth Phi Delta Kappa Poll of Teachers' Attitudes Toward the Public Schools." *Phi Delta Kappan,* v. 81, n. 8, April 2000. Reproduced by permission.

Table 8.12. Langdon, Carol A. and Nick Vesper. "Thinking about the public schools in your community, how would you describe the learning environment for students in those schools - very safe and orderly, somewhat safe and orderly, not very safe and orderly, or not at all safe and orderly?" in "The Sixth Phi Delta Kappa Poll of Teachers' Attitudes Toward the Public Schools." *Phi Delta Kappan,* v. 81, n. 8, April 2000. Reproduced by permission.

Figure 9.1. Snyder, Thomas D. and Charlene M. Hoffman. "Figure 15.—Enrollment in degree-granting institutions, by age: Fall 1970 to fall 2010," in *Digest of Education Statistics, 2000,* NCES 2001-034. U.S. Department of Education, National Center for Education Statistics, January 2001.

Table 9.1. Gerald, Debra E. and William J. Hussar. "Table 10.—Total enrollment in all degree-granting institutions, by sex, attendance status, and control of institution, with alternative projections: Fall 1986 to fall 2011," in *Projections of Education Statistics to 2011,* NCES 2001-083. U.S. Department of Education, National Center for Education Statistics, October 2001.

Figure 9.2. Gerald, Debra E. and William J. Hussar. "Figure 31.—Enrollment in degree-granting institutions, by age group, with middle alternative projections: Fall 1991, 2001, and 2011," in *Projections of Education Statistics to 2011,* NCES 2001-083. U.S. Department of Education, National Center for Education Statistics, October 2001.

Table 9.2. Snyder, Thomas D. and Charlene M. Hoffman. "Table 208.—Total enrollment in degree-granting institutions, by level of study, sex, and race/ethnicity of student: 1976 to 1997," in *Digest of Education*

Statistics, 2000, NCES 2001-034. U.S. Department of Education, National Center for Education Statistics, January 2001.

Table 9.3. "Figure 16: Graduation Rates of Students Taking Remedial Courses as a Percent of Students Taking No Remedial Courses," in *Access Denied: Restoring the Nation's Commitment to Equal Educational Opportunity*. Advisory Committee on Student Financial Assistance, February 2001.

Table 9.4. "Figure 13: College Preparatory Core Course Completion for College-Bound High School Seniors," in *Access Denied: Restoring the Nation's Commitment to Equal Educational Opportunity*. Advisory Committee on Student Financial Assistance, February 2001.

Table 9.5. Snyder, Thomas D. and Charlene M. Hoffman. "Table 245.—Degree-granting institutions, by control and type of institution: 1949-50 to 1998-99," in *Digest of Education Statistics, 2000*, NCES 2001-034. U.S. Department of Education, National Center for Education Statistics, January 2001.

Table 9.6. Snyder, Thomas D. and Charlene M. Hoffman. "Table 223.—Selected statistics on degree-granting historically black colleges and universities: 1980, 1990, 1997 and 1998," in *Digest of Education Statistics, 2000*, NCES 2001-034. U.S. Department of Education, National Center for Education Statistics, January 2001.

Table 9.7. Gerald, Debra E. and William J. Hussar. "Table 19.—Total undergraduate enrollment in all degree-granting institutions, by sex, attendance status, and control of institution, with alternative projections," in *Projections of Education Statistics to 2011*, NCES 2001-083. U.S. Department of Education, National Center for Education Statistics, October 2001.

Table 9.8. Gerald, Debra E. and William Hussar. "Table 20.—Total graduate enrollment in all degree-granting institutions, by sex, attendance status, and control of institution, with alternative projections: Fall 1986 to fall 2011," in *Projections of Education Statistics to 2011*, NCES 2001-083. U.S. Department of Education, National Center for Education Statistics, October 2001.

Table 9.9. Gerald, Debra E. and William Hussar. "Table 21.—Total first-professional enrollment in all degree-granting institutions, by sex, attendance status, and control of institution, with alternative projections: Fall 1986 to fall 2011," in *Projections of Education Statistics to 2011*, NCES 2001-083. U.S. Department of Education, National Center for Education Statistics, October 2001.

Table 9.10. Snyder, Thomas D. and Charlene M. Hoffman. "Table 248.—Earned degrees conferred by degree-granting institutions, by level of degree and sex of student:

1869-70 to 2009-10," in *Digest of Education Statistics, 2000*, NCES 2001-034. U.S. Department of Education, National Center for Education Statistics, January 2001.

Table 9.11. Snyder, Thomas D. and Charlene M. Hoffman. "Table 259.—Degrees conferred by degree-granting institutions, by control of institution, level of degree and discipline division: 1997-98," in *Digest of Education Statistics, 2000*, NCES 2001-034. U.S. Department of Education, National Center for Education Statistics, January 2001.

Table 9.12. Snyder, Thomas D. and Charlene M. Hoffman. "Table 261.—First-professional degrees conferred by degree-granting institutions in dentistry, medicine, and law, by sex, and number of institutions conferring degrees: 1949-50 to 1997-98," in *Digest of Education Statistics, 2000*, NCES 2001-034. U.S. Department of Education, National Center for Education Statistics, January 2001.

Table 9.13. Snyder, Thomas D. and Charlene M. Hoffman. "Table 230.—Full-time instructional faculty in degree-granting institutions, by race/ethnicity, academic rank, and sex: Fall 1997," in *Digest of Education Statistics, 2000*, NCES 2001-034. U.S. Department of Education, National Center for Education Statistics, January 2001.

Table 9.14. "Table 4. Average Student Expenses, by College Board Region, 2000-2001," in *Trends in College Pricing*. The College Board, 2000. Reproduced by permission. All rights reserved. www.collegeboard.com.

Figure 9.3. "Figure 1: Median Annual Household Income by Educational Attainment of Householder, 1997," in *Access Denied: Restoring the Nation's Commitment to Equal Educational Opportunity*. Advisory Committee on Student Financial Assistance, Washington, DC, February 2001.

Table 9.15. "Figure 7: Pell Grant Maximum Award as a Percentage of Institutional Cost of Attendance," in *Access Denied: Restoring the Nation's Commitment to Equal Educational Opportunity*. Advisory Committee on Student Financial Assistance, Washington, DC, February 2001.

Table 9.16. "Figure 10: Unmet Need by Institution Type and Family Income," in *Access Denied: Restoring the Nation's Commitment to Equal Educational Opportunity*. Advisory Committee on Student Financial Assistance, Washington, DC, February 2001.

Table 9.17. Eaton, Judith S. "'New Providers' of Higher Education...," in *Distance Learning: Academic and Political Challenges for Higher Education Accreditation*. Council for Higher Education Accreditation, CHEA Monograph Series 2001, 2001.

Figure 9.4. Thompson, Chris. "Figure 1: State Activities in E-Learning Service Delivery," in *The State of E-Learning in the States*. National Governors Association Center for Best Practices, 2000. Reproduced by permission.

Table 9.18. Kriger, Thomas J. "Table 1. A Sampling of Colleges and Universities that Offer Online/Distance Education Programs," in *A Virtual Revolution: Trends in the Expansion of Distance Education*. American Federation of Teachers, May 2001. Reproduced by permission.

Table 9.19. "Table 2. Corporate-University Joint Ventures: Course Management System Vendors," in *A Virtual Revolution: Trends in the Expansion of Distance Education*. American Federation of Teachers, May 2001. Reproduced by permission.

Table 9.20. Kriger, Thomas J. "Table 3. Corporate-University Joint Ventures: Hybrid Course or Content Providers," in *A Virtual Revolution: Trends in the Expansion of Distance Education*. American Federation of Teachers, May 2001. Reproduced by permission.

Table 9.21. Kriger, Thomas J. "Table 4. Virtual Universities," in *A Virtual Revolution: Trends in the Expansion of Distance Education*. American Federation of Teachers, May 2001. Reproduced by permission.

Table 9.22. Johnson, Lloyd D., Patrick M. O'Malley, and Jerald G. Bachman. "Table 2-2 Trends in Annual and 30-Day Prevalence of Use of Various Drugs for Eighth, Tenth, and Twelfth Graders, College Students, and Young Adults (Ages 19-28)," in *Monitoring the Future: National Survey Results on Drug Use 1975-2000, Volume II: College Students & Adults Ages 19-40*, NIH Publication No. 01-4925. National Institute on Drug Abuse, August 2001.

Table 9.23. Johnson, Lloyd D., Patrick M. O'Malley, and Jerald G. Bachman. "Table 2-3 Trends in Daily Use of Various Drugs for Eighth, Tenth, and Twelfth Graders, College Students, and Young Adults (Ages 19-28)," in *Monitoring the Future: National Survey Results on Drug Use 1975-2000, Volume II: College Students & Adults Ages 19-40*, NIH Publication No. 01-4925. National Institute on Drug Abuse, August 2001.

Table 10.1. Rose, Lowell C. and Alec M. Gallup. "What do you think are the biggest problems with which the public schools of your community must deal?" in "The 33rd Annual Phi Delta Kappa/Gallup Poll of the Public's Attitude Toward the Public Schools." *Phi Delta Kappan*, v. 83, n. 1, September 2001. Reproduced by permission.

Table 10.2. Rose, Lowell C. and Alec M. Gallup. "Students are often given the grades A, B, C, D, and FAIL to denote the quality of their work. Suppose the public schools themselves, in this community, were graded in the same way. What grade would you give the public schools here—A, B, C, D, or FAIL?" in "The 33rd Annual Phi Delta Kappa/Gallup Poll of the Public's Attitude Toward the Public Schools." *Phi Delta Kappan,* v. 83, n. 1, September 2001. Reproduced by permission.

Table 10.3. Rose, Lowell C. and Alec M. Gallup. "How about the public schools in the nation as a whole? What grade would you give the public schools nationally - A, B, C, D, or FAIL?" in "The 33rd Annual Phi Delta Kappa/Gallup Poll of the Public's Attitude Toward the Public Schools." *Phi Delta Kappan,* v. 83, n. 1, September 2001. Reproduced by permission.

Figure 10.1. Wirt, John, et al. "Attitudes Toward School: Percentage of children in grades 3-12 whose parents were very satisfied with various aspects of their schools, by family income: 1993 and 1999," in *The Condition of Education, 2001,* NCES 2001-072. U.S. Department of Education, National Center for Education Statistics, June 2001.

Figure 10.2. Rose, Lowell C. and Alec M. Gallup. "Figure 13. Consequences for Schools That Do Not Progress Toward State Standards," in "The 33rd Annual Phi Delta Kappa/Gallup Poll of the Public's Attitude Toward the Public Schools." *Phi Delta Kappan,* v. 83, n. 1, September 2001. Reproduced by permission.

Table 10.4. Rose, Lowell C., and Alec M. Gallup. "Which one of these two plans would you prefer - improving and strength-

ening the existing public schools or providing vouchers for parents to use in selecting and paying for private and/or church-related schools?" in "The 33rd Annual Phi Delta Kappa/Gallup Poll of the Public's Attitude Toward the Public Schools." *Phi Delta Kappan,* v. 83, n. 1, September 2001. Reproduced by permission.

Table 10.5. Langdon, Carol A. and Nick Vesper. "In your opinion, are student achievement standards in the public schools in your community too high, about right, or too low?" in "The Sixth Phi Delta Kappa Poll of Teachers' Attitudes Toward the Public Schools." *Phi Delta Kappan,* v. 81, n. 8, April 2000. Reproduced by permission.

Table 10.6. Langdon, Carol A. and Nick Vesper. "Social promotion means moving children from grade to grade in order to keep them with others in their own age group. Would you favor stricter standards for social promotion in school even if it meant that significantly more students would be held back?" in "The Sixth Phi Delta Kappa Poll of Teachers' Attitudes Toward the Public Schools." *Phi Delta Kappan,* v. 81, n. 8, April 2000. Reproduced by permission.

Table 10.7. Langdon, Carol A. and Nick Vesper. "As you know, many high school students are allowed to choose many of their academic courses. Would you favor or oppose requiring high school students to take a standardized core curriculum of certain courses?" in "The Sixth Phi Delta Kappa Poll of Teachers' Attitudes Toward the Public Schools." *Phi Delta Kappan,* v. 81, n. 8, April 2000. Reproduced by permission.

Table 10.8. Rose, Lowell C. and Alec M. Gallup. "In your opinion, do all students have the ability to reach a high level of learning, or do only some have the ability to reach a high level of learning?" in "The 33rd Annual Phi Delta Kappa/Gallup Poll of the Public's Attitude Toward the Public Schools." *Phi Delta Kappan,* v. 83, n. 1, September 2001. Reproduced by permission.

Table 10.9. Langdon, Carol A. and Nick Vesper. "Some public schools have a so-called zero tolerance drug and alcohol policy, which means that possession of any illegal drugs or alcohol by students will result in automatic suspension. Would you favor or oppose such a policy in the public schools in your community?" in "The Sixth Phi Delta Kappa Poll of Teachers' Attitudes Toward the Public Schools." *Phi Delta Kappan,* v. 81, n. 8, April 2000. Reproduced by permission.

Table 10.10. Langdon, Carol A. and Nick Vesper. "Here is a list of different values that might be taught in the public schools. For each one, please indicate whether you think it should be taught to all students in the public schools of your community," in "The Sixth Phi Delta Kappa Poll of Teachers' Attitudes Toward the Public Schools." *Phi Delta Kappan,* v. 81, n. 8, April 2000. Reproduced by permission.

Figure 10.3. Rose, Lowell C. and Alec M. Gallup. "Figure 10. Percent Who Favor/ Oppose the President's Initiatives," in "The 33rd Annual Phi Delta Kappa/Gallup Poll of the Public's Attitude Toward the Public Schools." *Phi Delta Kappan,* v. 83, n. 1, September 2001. Reproduced by permission.

CHAPTER 1
AN OVERVIEW OF AMERICAN EDUCATION

American education has always faced challenges. Debates about the purposes of schools, the benefits of education, the best approach to teaching and learning, and calls for reform of the system have been common in the history of education in the United States. During the 1980s the nation became increasingly aware of critical issues such as low academic performance, high dropout rates, and drug use and violence in the schools. Parents worry about the escalating cost of a college education. Political and community leaders question the ability of the nation's schools to produce high school graduates capable of competing in an increasingly technical and international environment. Voters and legislators debate whether parents who educate their children in private schools should receive federal or state subsidies.

Despite these problems the United States remains one of the most highly educated nations in the world. In fall 2000 approximately 76.4 million Americans were involved either directly or indirectly in providing or receiving formal education. About 68 million students were enrolled in schools and colleges, and 4 million instructors were teaching at the elementary, secondary, or college level. Another 4.4 million persons were professional, administrative, and support personnel at educational institutions. (See Table 1.1.)

EDUCATION LEVEL OF POPULATION HAS GROWN

The number of school years completed among Americans age 25 and older has been increasing. In 1940 about one in four Americans (24.5 percent) 25 years old and older had completed four or more years of high school, and almost one in seven (13.7 percent) had completed fewer than five years of elementary school. By 1999 in the

TABLE 1.1

Estimated number of participants in elementary and secondary education and in degree-granting institutions, fall 2000

[In millions]

Participants	All levels (elementary, secondary, and higher education)	Elementary and secondary schools			Degree-granting institutions		
		Total	Public	Private	Total	Public	Private
Total	76.4	59.1	52.5	6.6	17.3	13.1	4.2
Enrollment	68.0	53.0	47.0	6.0	15.0	11.6	3.5
Teachers and faculty	4.0	3.3	2.9	0.4	0.7	0.5	0.2
Other professional, administrative, and support staff	4.4	2.9	2.6	0.2	1.5	1.0	0.5

NOTE: Includes enrollments in local public school systems and in most private schools (religiously affiliated and nonsectarian). Elementary and secondary includes most kindergarten and some nursery school enrollment. Excludes preprimary enrollment in schools that do not offer first grade or above. Degree-granting institutions comprises full-time and part-time students enrolled in degree-credit and nondegree-credit programs in universities, other 4-year colleges, and 2-year colleges that participated in Title IV federal financial aid programs. Data for teachers and other staff in public and private elementary and secondary schools and colleges and universities are reported in terms of full-time equivalents. Detail may not sum to totals due to rounding.

SOURCE: Thomas D. Snyder and Charlene M. Hoffman, "Table 1.—Estimated number of participants in elementary and secondary education and in degree-granting institutions: Fall 2000," in *Digest of Education Statistics, 2000*, NCES 2001-034, U.S. Department of Education, National Center for Education Statistics, Washington DC, January 2001

TABLE 1.2

Years of school completed by persons age 25 and over and 25–29, by race/ethnicity and sex, 1910–99

| | Percent, by years of school completed | | | | | | | | | | | |
| | All races | | | White, non-Hispanic[1] | | | Black, non-Hispanic[1] | | | Hispanic | | |
Age and year	Less than 5 years of elementary school	High school completion or higher[2]	4 or more years of college[3]	Less than 5 years of elementary school	High school completion or higher[2]	4 or more years of college[3]	Less than 5 years of elementary school	High school completion or higher[2]	4 or more years of college[3]	Less than 5 years of elementary school	High school completion or higher[2]	4 or more years of college[3]
						Males and females						
25 and over												
1910 [4]	23.8	13.5	2.7	—	—	—	—	—	—	—	—	—
1920 [4]	22.0	16.4	3.3	—	—	—	—	—	—	—	—	—
1930 [4]	17.5	19.1	3.9	—	—	—	—	—	—	—	—	—
April 1940	13.7	24.5	4.6	10.9	26.1	4.9	41.8	7.7	1.3	—	—	—
April 1950	11.1	34.3	6.2	8.9	36.4	6.6	32.6	13.7	2.2	—	—	—
April 1960	8.3	41.1	7.7	6.7	43.2	8.1	23.5	21.7	3.5	—	—	—
March 1970	5.3	55.2	11.0	4.2	57.4	11.6	14.7	36.1	6.1	—	—	—
March 1980	3.4	68.6	17.0	1.9	71.9	18.4	9.1	51.4	7.9	15.8	44.5	7.6
March 1985	2.7	73.9	19.4	1.4	77.5	20.8	6.1	59.9	11.1	13.5	47.9	8.5
March 1987	2.4	75.6	19.9	1.3	79.0	20.5	4.9	63.6	10.8	11.9	50.9	8.6
March 1988	2.5	76.2	20.3	1.2	79.8	21.8	4.8	63.5	11.2	12.2	51.0	10.0
March 1989	2.5	76.9	21.1	1.2	80.7	22.8	5.2	64.7	11.7	12.2	50.9	9.9
March 1990	2.5	77.6	21.3	1.1	81.4	23.1	5.1	66.2	11.3	12.3	50.8	9.2
March 1991	2.4	78.4	21.4	1.1	82.4	23.3	4.7	66.8	11.5	12.5	51.3	9.7
March 1992	2.1	79.4	21.4	0.9	83.4	23.2	3.9	67.7	11.9	11.8	52.6	9.3
March 1993	2.1	80.2	21.9	0.8	84.1	23.8	3.7	70.5	12.2	11.8	53.1	9.0
March 1994	1.9	80.9	22.2	0.8	84.9	24.3	2.7	73.0	12.9	10.8	53.3	9.1
March 1995	1.9	81.7	23.0	0.7	85.9	23.4	2.5	73.8	13.3	10.6	53.4	9.3
March 1996	1.8	81.7	23.6	0.6	86.0	25.9	2.2	74.6	13.8	10.4	53.1	9.3
March 1997	1.7	82.1	23.9	0.6	86.3	26.2	2.0	75.3	13.3	9.4	54.7	10.3
March 1998	1.7	82.8	24.4	0.6	87.1	26.6	1.7	76.4	14.8	9.3	55.5	11.0
March 1999	1.6	83.4	25.2	0.6	87.7	27.7	1.8	77.4	15.5	9.0	56.1	10.9
25 to 29												
1920 [4]	—	—	—	12.9	22.0	4.5	44.6	6.3	1.2	—	—	—
April 1940	5.9	38.1	5.9	3.4	41.2	6.4	27.0	12.3	1.6	—	—	—
April 1950	4.6	52.8	7.7	3.3	56.3	8.2	16.1	23.6	2.8	—	—	—
April 1960	2.8	60.7	11.0	2.2	63.7	11.8	7.2	38.6	5.4	—	—	—
March 1970	1.1	75.4	16.4	0.9	77.8	17.3	2.2	58.4	10.0	—	—	—
March 1980	0.8	85.4	22.5	0.3	89.2	25.0	0.7	76.7	11.6	6.7	58.0	7.7
March 1985	0.7	86.1	22.2	0.2	89.5	24.4	0.4	80.5	11.6	6.0	60.9	11.1
March 1987	0.9	86.0	22.0	0.4	89.4	24.7	0.4	83.5	11.5	4.8	59.8	8.7
March 1988	1.0	85.9	22.7	0.3	89.7	25.1	0.3	80.9	12.0	6.0	62.3	11.3
March 1989	1.0	85.5	23.4	0.3	89.3	26.3	0.5	82.3	12.7	5.4	61.0	10.1
March 1990	1.2	85.7	23.2	0.3	90.1	26.4	1.0	81.7	13.4	7.3	58.2	8.2
March 1991	1.0	85.4	23.2	0.3	89.8	26.7	0.5	81.8	11.0	5.8	56.7	9.2
March 1992	0.9	86.3	23.6	0.3	90.7	27.2	0.8	80.9	11.1	5.2	60.9	9.5
March 1993	0.7	86.7	23.7	0.3	91.2	27.2	0.2	82.7	13.3	4.0	60.9	8.3
March 1994	0.8	86.1	23.3	0.3	91.1	27.1	0.6	84.1	13.6	3.6	60.3	8.0
March 1995	1.0	86.9	24.7	0.3	92.5	28.8	0.2	86.7	15.4	4.9	57.2	8.9
March 1996	0.8	87.3	27.1	0.2	92.6	31.6	0.4	86.0	14.6	4.3	61.1	10.0
March 1997	0.8	87.4	27.8	0.1	92.9	32.6	0.6	86.9	14.2	4.2	61.8	11.0
March 1998	0.7	88.1	27.3	0.1	93.6	32.3	0.4	88.3	15.8	3.7	62.8	10.4
March 1999	0.6	87.8	28.2	0.1	93.0	33.6	0.2	88.7	15.0	3.2	61.6	8.9
						Males						
25 and over												
April 1940	15.1	22.7	5.5	12.0	24.2	5.9	46.2	6.9	1.4	—	—	—
April 1950	12.2	32.6	7.3	9.8	34.6	7.9	36.9	12.6	2.1	—	—	—
April 1960	9.4	39.5	9.7	7.4	41.6	10.3	27.7	20.0	3.5	—	—	—
March 1970	5.9	55.0	14.1	4.5	57.2	15.0	17.9	35.4	6.8	—	—	—
March 1980	3.6	69.2	20.9	2.0	72.4	22.8	11.3	51.2	7.7	16.5	44.9	9.2
March 1990	2.7	77.7	24.4	1.3	81.6	26.7	6.4	65.8	11.9	12.9	50.3	9.8
March 1994	2.1	81.1	25.1	0.8	85.1	27.8	3.9	71.8	12.7	11.4	53.4	9.6
March 1995	2.0	81.7	26.0	0.8	86.0	28.9	3.4	73.5	13.7	10.8	52.9	10.1
March 1996	1.9	81.9	26.0	0.7	86.1	28.8	2.9	74.6	12.5	10.2	53.0	10.3
March 1997	1.8	82.0	26.2	0.6	86.3	29.0	2.9	73.8	12.5	9.2	54.9	10.6
March 1998	1.7	82.8	26.5	0.7	87.1	29.3	2.3	75.4	14.0	9.3	55.7	11.1
March 1999	1.6	83.5	27.5	0.6	87.7	30.6	2.1	77.2	14.3	9.0	56.0	10.7

same age group, 83.4 percent of Americans had completed high school, while only 1.6 percent had fewer than five years of formal education. In 1940 less than 5 percent of the population 25 years old and older had completed four or more years of college; by 1999 more than 25 percent had done so. (See Table 1.2 and Figure 1.1.)

Among people ages 25 to 29 years, 87.8 percent had completed four or more years of high school in 1999,

TABLE 1.2

Years of school completed by persons age 25 and over and 25–29, by race/ethnicity and sex, 1910–99 [CONTINUED]

	Percent, by years of school completed											
	All races			White, non-Hispanic[1]			Black, non-Hispanic[1]			Hispanic		
Age and year	Less than 5 years of elementary school	High school completion or higher[2]	4 or more years of college[3]	Less than 5 years of elementary school	High school completion or higher[2]	4 or more years of college[3]	Less than 5 years of elementary school	High school completion or higher[2]	4 or more years of college[3]	Less than 5 years of elementary school	High school completion or higher[2]	4 or more years of college[3]
	Females											
25 and over												
April 1940	12.4	26.3	3.8	9.8	28.1	4.0	37.5	8.4	1.2	—	—	—
April 1950	10.0	36.0	5.2	8.1	38.2	5.4	28.6	14.7	2.4	—	—	—
April 1960	7.4	42.5	5.8	6.0	44.7	6.0	19.7	23.1	3.6	—	—	—
March 1970	4.7	55.4	8.2	3.9	57.7	8.6	11.9	36.6	5.6	—	—	—
March 1980	3.2	68.1	13.6	1.8	71.5	14.4	7.4	51.5	8.1	15.3	44.2	6.2
March 1990	2.2	77.5	18.4	1.0	81.3	19.8	4.1	66.5	10.8	11.7	51.3	8.7
March 1994	1.7	80.8	19.6	0.7	84.7	21.1	1.8	73.9	13.1	10.3	53.2	8.6
March 1995	1.7	81.6	20.2	0.6	85.8	22.2	1.8	74.1	13.0	10.4	53.8	8.4
March 1996	1.7	81.6	21.4	0.5	85.9	23.2	1.6	74.6	14.8	10.6	53.3	8.3
March 1997	1.6	82.2	21.7	0.5	86.3	23.7	1.3	76.5	14.0	9.5	54.6	10.1
March 1998	1.6	82.9	22.4	0.6	87.1	24.1	1.2	77.1	15.5	9.2	55.3	10.9
March 1999	1.6	83.4	23.1	0.5	87.7	25.0	1.5	77.5	16.5	9.0	56.3	11.0

—Not available.

[1]Includes persons of Hispanic origin for years prior to 1980.
[2]Data for years prior to 1993 include all persons with at least 4 years of high school.
[3]Data for 1993 and later years are for persons with a bachelor's or higher degree.
[4]Estimates based on Bureau of the Census retrojection of 1940 Census data on education by age.
NOTE: Data for 1980 and subsequent years are for the noninstitutional population.

SOURCE: Thomas D. Snyder and Charlene M. Hoffman, "Table 8.—Years of school completed by persons age 25 and over and 25 to 29, by race/ethnicity and sex: 1910 to 1999," in *Digest of Education Statistics, 2000,* NCES 2001-034, U.S. Department of Education, National Center for Education Statistics, Washington DC, January 2001

while 28.2 percent had completed four or more years of college. White Americans were more likely than black or Hispanic Americans to have completed both high school and college. (See Table 1.2.)

SCHOOL ENROLLMENT

Virtually all children 5 to 17 years old are enrolled in school. In 1999 more than 95 percent of all young people from 5 to 17 years old attended school. The enrollment of 3- and 4-year-olds has increased substantially since 1975, from 31.5 percent in that year to 54.2 percent in 1999. (See Table 1.3.)

The proportion of people enrolled in school drops sharply after age 18. By this age young people either graduate from or leave high school and may not immediately go on to any form of higher education. However, the proportion of older teens attending school has increased since 1980. In 1999 the proportion of 18- and 19-year-olds enrolled in school reached 60.6 percent, up from 46.9 percent in 1975. (See Table 1.3.)

Enrollment Numbers Change

The number of students enrolled in elementary and secondary schools and in colleges is directly proportional to the birth rates of the previous two decades. After World War II and the Korean conflict, the nation experienced a

FIGURE 1.1

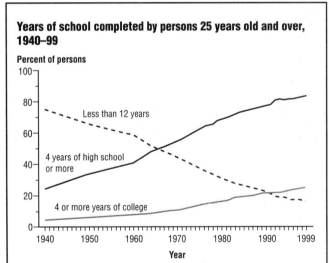

Years of school completed by persons 25 years old and over, 1940–99

SOURCE: Thomas D. Snyder and Charlene M. Hoffman, "Figure 3.—Years of school completed by persons 25 years old and over: 1940 to 1999," in *Digest of Education Statistics, 2000,* NCES 2001-034, U.S. Department of Education, National Center for Education Statistics, Washington DC, January 2001

"baby boom" (1946–1964) as returning soldiers settled down to start families. Consequently school enrollment grew rapidly during the 1950s and 1960s as these babies matured to school age. Total enrollment peaked at 61

TABLE 1.3

Percent of the population 3 to 34 years old enrolled in school, by race/ethnicity, sex, and age, October 1975–October 1999

Year and age	Total				Male				Female			
	All races	White, non-Hispanic	Black, non-Hispanic	Hispanic origin	All races	White, non-Hispanic	Black, non-Hispanic	Hispanic origin	All races	White, non-Hispanic	Black, non-Hispanic	Hispanic origin
1975												
Total, 3 to 34 years	53.7	53.0	57.7	54.8	56.1	55.2	60.4	58.1	51.5	50.8	55.3	51.7
3 and 4 years	31.5	31.0	34.4	27.3	30.9	31.1	31.4	26.7	32.1	30.9	37.5	27.9
5 and 6 years	94.7	95.1	94.4	92.1	94.4	94.8	94.8	89.7	95.1	95.4	94.0	94.4
7 to 9 years	99.3	99.4	99.3	99.6	99.2	99.2	99.4	99.6	99.5	99.6	99.2	99.5
10 to 13 years	99.3	99.3	99.1	99.2	98.9	99.0	98.9	98.8	99.6	99.6	99.3	99.7
14 and 15 years	98.2	98.5	97.4	95.6	98.4	98.6	97.6	97.4	98.0	98.4	97.2	93.8
16 and 17 years	89.0	89.5	86.8	86.2	90.7	91.2	88.1	88.3	87.2	87.8	85.5	84.0
18 and 19 years	46.9	46.8	46.9	44.0	49.9	49.4	49.6	51.9	44.2	44.2	44.6	37.1
20 and 21 years	31.2	32.1	26.7	27.5	35.3	36.7	28.4	31.3	27.4	27.8	25.3	24.3
22 to 24 years	16.2	16.4	13.9	14.1	20.0	20.8	14.5	15.9	12.6	12.2	13.4	12.5
25 to 29 years	10.1	10.1	9.4	8.3	13.1	13.2	11.6	11.9	7.2	7.2	7.6	5.3
30 to 34 years	6.6	6.6	7.1	5.5	7.7	7.5	8.7	7.2	5.6	5.8	5.9	4.1
1980												
Total, 3 to 34 years	49.7	48.8	54.0	49.8	50.9	50.0	56.2	49.9	48.5	47.7	52.1	49.8
3 and 4 years	36.7	37.4	38.2	28.5	37.8	39.2	36.4	30.1	35.5	35.5	40.0	26.6
5 and 6 years	95.7	95.9	95.5	94.5	95.0	95.4	94.1	94.0	96.4	96.5	97.0	94.9
7 to 9 years	99.1	99.1	99.4	98.4	99.0	99.0	99.5	97.7	99.2	99.2	99.3	99.0
10 to 13 years	99.4	99.4	99.4	99.7	99.4	99.4	99.4	99.4	99.4	99.3	99.3	99.9
14 and 15 years	98.2	98.7	97.9	94.3	98.7	98.9	98.4	96.7	97.7	98.5	97.3	92.1
16 and 17 years	89.0	89.2	90.7	81.8	89.1	89.4	90.7	81.5	88.8	89.0	90.6	82.2
18 and 19 years	46.4	47.0	45.8	37.8	47.0	48.5	42.9	36.9	45.8	45.7	48.3	38.8
20 and 21 years	31.0	33.0	23.3	19.5	32.6	34.8	22.8	21.4	29.5	31.3	23.7	17.6
22 to 24 years	16.3	16.8	13.6	11.7	17.8	18.7	13.4	10.7	14.9	15.0	13.7	12.6
25 to 29 years	9.3	9.4	8.8	6.9	9.8	9.8	10.6	6.8	8.8	9.1	7.5	6.9
30 to 34 years	6.4	6.4	6.9	5.1	5.9	5.6	7.2	6.2	7.0	7.2	6.6	4.1
1985												
Total, 3 to 34 years	48.3	47.8	50.8	47.7	49.2	48.7	52.6	47.5	47.4	46.9	49.2	47.9
3 and 4 years	38.9	40.3	42.8	27.0	36.7	39.1	34.6	26.4	41.2	41.6	50.3	27.7
5 and 6 years	96.1	96.6	95.7	94.5	95.3	95.6	94.5	95.3	97.0	97.6	97.1	93.7
7 to 9 years	99.1	99.4	98.6	98.4	99.0	99.3	98.4	98.9	99.2	99.4	98.9	98.0
10 to 13 years	99.3	99.3	99.5	99.4	99.2	99.2	99.1	99.1	99.4	99.3	99.9	99.7
14 and 15 years	98.1	98.3	98.1	96.1	98.3	98.4	98.5	96.2	97.9	98.1	97.6	96.0
16 and 17 years	91.7	92.5	91.8	84.5	92.4	92.9	92.0	88.9	90.9	92.2	91.6	80.0
18 and 19 years	51.6	53.7	43.5	41.8	52.2	53.4	49.4	38.6	51.0	54.0	37.8	44.7
20 and 21 years	35.3	37.2	27.7	24.0	36.5	38.8	29.9	20.3	34.1	35.7	25.8	27.4
22 to 24 years	16.9	17.5	13.8	11.6	18.8	19.8	13.5	12.6	15.1	15.4	14.0	10.4
25 to 29 years	9.2	9.6	7.4	6.6	9.4	9.7	5.8	8.2	9.1	9.4	8.7	4.9
30 to 34 years	6.1	6.2	5.2	5.7	5.4	5.6	3.9	4.0	6.8	6.9	6.2	7.5
1990												
Total, 3 to 34 years	50.2	49.8	52.2	47.2	50.9	50.4	54.3	46.8	49.5	49.2	50.3	47.7
3 and 4 years	44.4	47.2	41.8	30.7	43.9	47.9	38.1	28.0	44.9	46.6	45.5	33.6
5 and 6 years	96.5	96.7	96.5	94.9	96.5	96.8	96.2	95.8	96.4	96.7	96.9	93.9
7 to 9 years	99.7	99.7	99.8	99.5	99.7	99.7	99.9	99.5	99.6	99.7	99.8	99.4
10 to 13 years	99.6	99.7	99.9	99.1	99.6	99.6	99.9	99.0	99.7	99.7	99.8	99.1
14 and 15 years	99.0	99.0	99.4	99.0	99.1	99.2	99.7	99.1	98.9	98.9	99.1	98.8
16 and 17 years	92.5	93.5	91.7	85.4	92.6	93.4	93.0	85.5	92.4	93.7	90.5	85.3
18 and 19 years	57.2	59.1	55.0	44.0	58.2	59.7	60.4	40.7	56.3	58.5	49.8	47.2
20 and 21 years	39.7	43.1	28.3	27.2	40.3	44.2	31.0	21.7	39.2	42.0	25.8	33.1
22 to 24 years	21.0	21.9	19.7	9.9	22.3	23.7	19.3	11.2	19.9	20.3	20.0	8.4
25 to 29 years	9.7	10.4	6.1	6.3	9.2	10.0	4.7	4.6	10.2	10.7	7.3	8.1
30 to 34 years	5.8	6.2	4.5	3.6	4.8	5.0	2.3	4.0	6.9	7.4	6.3	3.1
1995												
Total, 3 to 34 years	53.7	53.8	56.3	49.7	54.3	54.2	58.6	49.1	53.2	53.4	54.1	50.3
3 and 4 years	48.7	52.2	47.8	36.9	49.4	51.1	52.4	40.8	48.1	53.5	43.4	32.7
5 and 6 years	96.0	96.6	95.4	93.9	95.3	95.9	94.6	93.6	96.8	97.4	96.3	94.3
7 to 9 years	98.7	98.9	97.7	98.5	98.9	99.0	98.1	98.8	98.5	98.9	97.2	98.2
10 to 13 years	99.1	99.0	99.2	99.2	99.1	99.0	99.5	98.8	99.0	98.9	98.9	99.5
14 and 15 years	98.9	98.8	99.0	98.9	99.0	98.9	99.6	98.4	98.8	98.7	98.3	99.4
16 and 17 years	93.6	94.4	93.0	88.2	94.5	95.0	95.6	88.4	92.6	93.8	90.3	88.0
18 and 19 years	59.4	61.8	57.5	46.1	59.5	61.9	59.2	47.4	59.2	61.8	56.1	44.8
20 and 21 years	44.9	49.7	37.8	27.1	44.7	50.0	36.7	24.8	45.1	49.3	38.7	29.2
22 to 24 years	23.2	24.4	20.0	15.6	22.8	24.1	20.6	14.8	23.6	24.8	19.5	16.6
25 to 29 years	11.6	12.3	10.0	7.1	11.0	12.2	6.3	5.6	12.2	12.3	13.0	8.7
30 to 34 years	5.9	5.7	7.7	4.7	5.4	5.0	6.9	4.5	6.5	6.3	8.3	4.9

TABLE 1.3

Percent of the population 3 to 34 years old enrolled in school, by race/ethnicity, sex, and age, October 1975–October 1999 [CONTINUED]

Year and age	Total				Male				Female			
	All races	White, non-Hispanic	Black, non-Hispanic	Hispanic origin	All races	White, non-Hispanic	Black, non-Hispanic	Hispanic origin	All races	White, non-Hispanic	Black, non-Hispanic	Hispanic origin
1999												
Total, 3 to 34 years	56.0	56.2	58.6	51.1	56.4	56.7	60.3	50.3	55.5	55.7	56.9	52.1
3 and 4 years	54.2	58.6	56.7	36.9	53.3	59.2	52.8	33.5	55.2	57.9	60.5	40.5
5 and 6 years	96.0	96.0	97.7	93.9	95.9	96.1	98.2	92.8	96.1	95.9	97.1	95.0
7 to 9 years	98.5	98.4	98.1	99.0	98.3	98.4	97.6	98.7	98.7	98.5	98.6	99.2
10 to 13 years	98.8	98.9	98.7	98.3	98.7	98.7	98.9	98.5	98.9	99.1	98.5	98.0
14 and 15 years	98.2	98.4	98.1	97.6	98.0	98.2	97.8	98.1	98.3	98.6	98.4	96.9
16 and 17 years	93.6	94.5	93.9	88.1	93.7	94.3	94.5	87.9	93.5	94.8	93.2	88.2
18 and 19 years	60.6	64.1	57.2	44.5	60.3	63.7	59.3	45.3	60.9	64.6	55.3	43.6
20 and 21 years	45.3	50.0	40.4	22.6	44.7	48.9	43.2	21.5	45.8	51.1	37.9	23.6
22 to 24 years	24.5	26.3	21.9	15.0	23.6	26.8	16.4	11.2	25.4	25.7	26.0	19.2
25 to 29 years	11.1	10.9	10.7	9.1	10.7	10.7	9.4	8.6	11.4	11.0	11.8	9.5
30 to 34 years	6.2	5.9	7.8	5.6	5.8	5.8	6.6	3.9	6.6	6.1	8.8	7.3

NOTE: Includes enrollment in any type of graded public, parochial, or other private schools. Includes nursery schools, kindergartens, elementary schools, high schools, colleges, universities, and professional schools. Attendance may be on either a full-time or part-time basis and during the day or night. Enrollments in "special" schools, such as trade schools, business colleges, or correspondence schools, are not included. Beginning in 1995, preprimary enrollment was collected using new procedures. May not be comparable to figures for earlier years. Data are based upon sample surveys of the civilian noninstitutional population.

SOURCE: Thomas D. Snyder and Charlene M. Hoffman, "Table 7.—Percent of the population 3 to 34 years old enrolled in school, by race/ethnicity, sex, and age: October 1975 to October 1999," in *Digest of Education Statistics, 2000,* NCES 2001-034, U.S. Department of Education, National Center for Education Statistics, Washington DC, January 2001

million in 1975, a number not attained again until 1991. Elementary enrollment (36.7 million) reached a record high in 1969, and high school enrollment (15.7 million) peaked in 1976. (See Table 1.4.)

Birth rates declined as the baby boom waned, and so did school enrollments in the 1970s. An "echo effect" occurred in the 1980s, when those born during the baby boom started their own families. This increase in birth rates triggered an increase in school enrollment in the early 1990s. In 1991 the enrollment of students at schools of all levels was 61.6 million. In the years following 1991 school enrollment has grown about 1 to 2 percent annually. (See Table 1.4.)

Since 1969 elementary enrollment in public and private schools gradually declined from a high of 36.7 million. After leveling off in the late 1980s at around 33 million, elementary enrollment rose through the 1990s and is expected to stay fairly stable to 2010. (See Table 1.4.)

High school enrollment, which began to decline in the late 1970s, started to increase again in the mid-1990s and is expected to continue to grow. College enrollments, unlike elementary and secondary enrollments, have risen consistently and are expected to reach 17.4 million by 2010. (See Table 1.4.)

EDUCATIONAL DIFFERENCES

Race and Ethnicity

The marked difference in educational attainment that once existed between whites and minorities has narrowed, although there are still significant gaps. About 88 percent of white adults age 25 years and older were high school graduates in 1999, while 77.4 percent of blacks and 56.1 percent of Hispanics were graduates. The most significant advances can be seen among young adults ages 25 to 29, where 93 percent of whites, 88.7 percent of blacks, and 61.6 percent of Hispanics were high school graduates in 1999, compared to 41.2 percent of whites and 12.3 percent of blacks and other races in 1940. (See Table 1.2.)

In 1940 white adults age 25 and older were far more likely than blacks and other minorities to have completed four years of college (4.9 percent versus 1.3 percent). In 1999, nearly 60 years later 27.7 percent of whites, 15.5 percent of blacks, and 10.9 percent of Hispanics had completed four or more years of college. About one-third of white young adults (33.6 percent) ages 25 to 29 were college graduates, compared to 15 percent of blacks and 8.9 percent of Hispanics in the same age group. (See Table 1.2.)

Gender

Traditionally women were slightly more likely than men to complete high school but less likely to go on to college. In recent years the differences in high school graduation have disappeared. In 1999 more than 83 percent of both women and men age 25 and older had completed four or more years of high school. The proportion of women age 25 and older graduating from college has increased steadily, from 3.8 percent in 1940 to 23.1 percent in 1999. Nevertheless the proportion of male students

TABLE 1.4

Enrollment in educational institutions, by level and by control of institution, 1869–70 to fall 2010

[In thousands]

Year	Total enrollment, all levels	Elementary and secondary, total	Public elementary and secondary schools			Private elementary and secondary schools[1]			Degree-granting institutions[2]		
			Total	Pre-kindergarten through grade 8	Grades 9 through 12	Total	Kindergarten through grade 8	Grades 9 through 12	Total	Public	Private
1869–70	—	—	6,872	6,792	80	—	—	—	52	—	—
1879–80	—	—	9,868	9,757	110	—	—	—	116	—	—
1889–90	14,491	14,334	12,723	12,520	203	1,611	1,516	95	157	—	—
1899–1900	17,092	16,855	15,503	14,984	519	1,352	1,241	111	238	—	—
1909–10	19,728	19,372	17,814	16,899	915	1,558	1,441	117	355	—	—
1919–20	23,876	23,278	21,578	19,378	2,200	1,699	1,486	214	598	—	—
1929–30	29,430	28,329	25,678	21,279	4,399	2,651	2,310	341	1,101	—	—
1939–40	29,539	28,045	25,434	18,832	6,601	2,611	2,153	458	1,494	797	698
1949–50	31,151	28,492	25,111	19,387	5,725	3,380	2,708	672	2,659	1,355	1,304
Fall 1959	44,497	40,857	35,182	26,911	8,271	5,675	4,640	1,035	3,640	2,181	1,459
Fall 1964	52,996	47,716	41,416	30,025	11,391	[3]6,300	[3]5,000	1,300	5,280	3,468	1,812
Fall 1965	54,394	48,473	42,173	30,563	11,610	6,300	4,900	1,400	5,921	3,970	1,951
Fall 1966	55,629	49,239	43,039	31,145	11,894	[3]6,200	[3]4,800	[3]1,400	6,390	4,349	2,041
Fall 1967	56,803	49,891	43,891	31,641	12,250	[3]6,000	[3]4,600	[3]1,400	6,912	4,816	2,096
Fall 1968	58,257	50,744	44,944	32,226	12,718	5,800	4,400	1,400	7,513	5,431	2,082
Fall 1969	59,055	51,050	45,550	32,513	13,037	[3]5,500	[3]4,200	1,300	8,005	5,897	2,108
Fall 1970	59,838	51,257	45,894	32,558	13,336	5,363	4,052	1,311	8,581	6,428	2,153
Fall 1971	60,220	51,271	46,071	32,318	13,753	[3]5,200	[3]3,900	[3]1,300	8,949	6,804	2,144
Fall 1972	59,941	50,726	45,726	31,879	13,848	[3]5,000	[3]3,700	[3]1,300	9,215	7,071	2,144
Fall 1973	60,047	50,445	45,445	31,401	14,044	[3]5,000	[3]3,700	[3]1,300	9,602	7,420	2,183
Fall 1974	60,297	50,073	45,073	30,971	14,103	[3]5,000	[3]3,700	[3]1,300	10,224	7,989	2,235
Fall 1975	61,004	49,819	44,819	30,515	14,304	[3]5,000	[3]3,700	[3]1,300	11,185	8,835	2,350
Fall 1976	60,490	49,478	44,311	29,997	14,314	5,167	3,825	1,342	11,012	8,653	2,359
Fall 1977	60,003	48,717	43,577	29,375	14,203	5,140	3,797	1,343	11,286	8,847	2,439
Fall 1978	58,897	47,637	42,551	28,463	14,088	5,086	3,732	1,353	11,260	8,786	2,474
Fall 1979	58,221	46,651	41,651	28,034	13,616	[3]5,000	[3]3,700	[3]1,300	11,570	9,037	2,533
Fall 1980	58,305	46,208	40,877	27,647	13,231	5,331	3,992	1,339	12,097	9,457	2,640
Fall 1981	57,916	45,544	40,044	27,280	12,764	[3]5,500	[3]4,100	[3]1,400	12,372	9,647	2,725
Fall 1982	57,591	45,166	39,566	27,161	12,405	[3]5,600	[3]4,200	[3]1,400	12,426	9,696	2,730
Fall 1983	57,432	44,967	39,252	26,981	12,271	5,715	4,315	1,400	12,465	9,683	2,782
Fall 1984	57,150	44,908	39,208	26,905	12,304	[3]5,700	[3]4,300	[3]1,400	12,242	9,477	2,765
Fall 1985	57,226	44,979	39,422	27,034	12,388	5,557	4,195	1,362	12,247	9,479	2,768
Fall 1986	57,709	45,205	39,753	27,420	12,333	[3]5,452	[3]4,116	[3]1,336	12,504	9,714	2,790
Fall 1987	58,254	45,488	40,008	27,933	12,076	5,479	4,232	1,247	12,767	9,973	2,793
Fall 1988	58,485	45,430	40,189	28,501	11,687	[3]5,241	[3]4,036	[3]1,206	13,055	10,161	2,894
Fall 1989	59,436	45,898	40,543	29,152	11,390	[3]5,355	[3]4,162	[3]1,193	13,539	10,578	2,961
Fall 1990	60,267	46,448	41,217	29,878	11,338	5,232	4,095	1,137	13,819	10,845	2,974
Fall 1991	61,605	47,246	42,047	30,506	11,541	[3]5,199	[3]4,074	[3]1,125	14,359	11,310	3,049
Fall 1992	62,686	48,198	42,823	31,088	11,735	[3]5,375	[3]4,212	[3]1,163	14,487	11,385	3,103
Fall 1993	63,241	48,936	43,465	31,504	11,961	[3]5,471	[3]4,280	[3]1,191	14,305	11,189	3,116
Fall 1994	63,986	49,707	44,111	31,898	12,213	[3]5,596	[3]4,360	[3]1,236	14,279	11,134	3,145
Fall 1995	64,764	50,502	44,840	32,341	12,500	5,662	4,465	1,197	14,262	11,092	3,169
Fall 1996	65,762	51,394	45,611	32,764	12,847	[3]5,783	[3]4,486	[3]1,297	14,368	11,120	3,247
Fall 1997	66,490	51,987	46,127	33,073	13,054	5,860	4,552	1,308	14,502	11,196	3,306
Fall 1998	67,008	52,459	46,535	33,344	13,191	5,924	4,597	1,327	14,549	11,176	3,373
Fall 1999[4]	67,611	52,750	46,812	33,437	13,375	5,938	4,599	1,339	14,861	11,579	3,282
Fall 2000[4]	68,124	52,989	47,026	33,521	13,505	5,963	4,611	1,352	15,135	11,795	3,340
Fall 2001[4]	68,516	53,155	47,176	33,557	13,619	5,979	4,616	1,363	15,361	11,972	3,389
Fall 2002[4]	68,787	53,287	47,296	33,543	13,753	5,991	4,614	1,377	15,500	12,080	3,420
Fall 2003[4]	69,050	53,367	47,373	33,442	13,931	5,995	4,600	1,395	15,683	12,221	3,462
Fall 2004[4]	69,303	53,429	47,436	33,237	14,199	5,993	4,572	1,422	15,874	12,370	3,505
Fall 2005[4]	69,538	53,465	47,475	33,051	14,423	5,990	4,546	1,444	16,073	12,523	3,550
Fall 2006[4]	69,771	53,435	47,452	32,915	14,537	5,983	4,527	1,455	16,336	12,726	3,610
Fall 2007[4]	69,979	53,336	47,365	32,835	14,530	5,971	4,517	1,455	16,643	12,962	3,682

(27.5 percent in 1999) who completed four or more years of college was still higher. (See Table 1.2.)

PROJECTIONS TO 2010

The National Center for Education Statistics (NCES) estimates that the total public and private elementary and secondary enrollment will increase from 52.8 million in 1999 to 53.5 million in 2005, and then begin to fall to about 53 million in 2010. Enrollment in kindergarten through eighth grade is projected to decrease slightly by 2010, while enrollment in grades nine through twelve is expected to rise. The number of persons attending degree-granting institutions of higher learning is projected to increase from 14.9 million in 1999 to 17.5 million by 2010. (See Table 1.4.)

TABLE 1.4

Enrollment in educational institutions, by level and by control of institution, 1869–70 to fall 2010 [CONTINUED]

[In thousands]

Year	Total enrollment, all levels	Elementary and secondary, total	Public elementary and secondary schools			Private elementary and secondary schools[1]			Degree-granting institutions[2]		
			Total	Pre-kindergarten through grade 8	Grades 9 through 12	Total	Kindergarten through grade 8	Grades 9 through 12	Total	Public	Private
Fall 2008[4]	70,149	53,174	47,218	32,825	14,393	5,956	4,515	1,441	16,975	13,216	3,759
Fall 2009[4]	70,317	53,056	47,109	32,877	14,232	5,947	4,522	1,425	17,261	13,434	3,827
Fall 2010[4]	70,506	53,016	47,068	32,999	14,069	5,948	4,539	1,409	17,490	13,607	3,882

—Not available.

[1] Beginning in fall 1980, data include estimates for an expanded universe of private schools. Therefore, these totals may differ from figures shown in other tables, and direct comparisons with earlier years should be avoided.

[2] Data for 1869–70 through 1949–50 include resident degree-credit students enrolled at any time during the academic year. Beginning in 1959, data include all resident and extension students enrolled at the beginning of the fall term. Enrollment for 1996, 1997, and 1998 are for degree-granting institutions. All other years, including the projections are for institutions of higher education.

[3] Estimated.

[4] Projected.

NOTE: Elementary and secondary enrollment includes pupils in local public school systems and in most private schools (religiously affiliated and nonsectarian). Excludes home-schooled children. Based on U.S. Department of Education estimates, the home-schooled children numbered approximately 800,000 to 1,000,000 in 1997–98. Public elementary enrollment includes most preprimary school pupils. Private elementary enrollment includes some preprimary students. Higher education enrollment includes students in colleges, universities, professional schools, and 2–year colleges. Degree-granting institutions are 2-year and 4-year institutions that were eligible to participate in Title IV federal financial aid programs. Higher education enrollment projections are based on the middle alternative projections published by the National Center for Education Statistics. Detail may not sum to totals due to rounding.

SOURCE: Thomas D. Snyder and Charlene M. Hoffman, "Table 3.—Enrollment in educational institutions, by level and by control of institution: 1869–70 to fall 2010," in *Digest of Education Statistics, 2000,* NCES 2001-034, U.S. Department of Education, National Center for Education Statistics, Washington DC, January 2001

EDUCATION SPENDING

Expenditures for public and private education from preprimary through graduate school rose to an estimated high of $646.8 billion for the 1999–2000 school year. Expenditures for elementary and secondary schools reached $389 billion (60 percent of total education spending), and outlays for colleges and universities were estimated at $257.8 billion (40 percent). In 1999–2000 the United States spent 7 percent of its gross domestic product (GDP—the total value of goods and services produced within the United States) on education. Fifty years before, in the 1949–50 school year, the United States spent $8.9 billion, or 3.3 percent of its GDP, on education. (See Table 1.5.)

TABLE 1.5

Total expenditures of educational institutions related to the gross domestic product, by level of institution, 1929–1930 to 1999–2000

Year	Gross domestic product (in billions)	School year	Total expenditures for education (amounts in millions of current dollars)						
			All educational institutions		All elementary and secondary schools		All colleges and universities	
			Amount	As a percent of gross domestic product	Amount	As a percent of gross domestic product	Amount	As a percent of gross domestic product
1929	$103.7	1929–30	—	—	—	—	$632	0.6
1939	92.0	1939–40	—	—	—	—	758	0.8
1949	267.7	1949–50	$8,911	3.3	$6,249	2.3	2,662	1.0
1959	507.4	1959–60	23,860	4.7	16,713	3.3	7,147	1.4
1961	545.7	1961–62	28,503	5.2	19,673	3.6	8,830	1.6
1963	618.7	1963–64	34,440	5.6	22,825	3.7	11,615	1.9
1965	720.1	1965–66	43,682	6.1	28,048	3.9	15,634	2.2
1967	834.1	1967–68	55,652	6.7	35,077	4.2	20,575	2.5
1969	985.3	1969–70	68,459	6.9	43,183	4.4	25,276	2.6
1970	1,039.7	1970–71	75,741	7.3	48,200	4.6	27,541	2.6
1971	1,128.6	1971–72	80,672	7.1	50,950	4.5	29,722	2.6
1972	1,240.4	1972–73	86,875	7.0	54,952	4.4	31,923	2.6
1973	1,385.5	1973–74	95,396	6.9	60,370	4.4	35,026	2.5
1974	1,501.0	1974–75	108,664	7.2	68,846	4.6	39,818	2.7
1975	1,635.2	1975–76	118,706	7.3	75,101	4.6	43,605	2.7
1976	1,823.9	1976–77	126,417	6.9	79,194	4.3	47,223	2.6
1977	2,031.4	1977–78	137,042	6.7	86,544	4.3	50,498	2.5
1978	2,295.9	1978–79	148,308	6.5	93,012	4.1	55,296	2.4
1979	2,566.4	1979–80	165,627	6.5	103,162	4.0	62,465	2.4
1980	2,795.6	1980–81	182,849	6.5	112,325	4.0	70,524	2.5
1981	3,131.3	1981–82	197,801	6.3	120,486	3.8	77,315	2.5
1982	3,259.2	1982–83	212,081	6.5	128,725	3.9	83,356	2.6
1983	3,534.9	1983–84	228,597	6.5	139,000	3.9	89,597	2.5
1984	3,932.7	1984–85	247,657	6.3	149,400	3.8	98,257	2.5
1985	4,213.0	1985–86	269,485	6.4	161,800	3.8	107,685	2.6
1986	4,452.9	1986–87	291,974	6.6	175,200	3.9	116,774	2.6
1987	4,742.5	1987–88	313,375	6.6	187,999	4.0	125,376	2.6
1988	5,108.3	1988–89	346,883	6.8	209,377	4.1	137,506	2.7
1989	5,489.1	1989–90	381,525	7.0	230,970	4.2	150,555	2.7
1990	5,803.2	1990–91	412,652	7.1	248,930	4.3	163,722	2.8
1991	5,986.2	1991–92	432,987	7.2	261,255	4.4	171,732	2.9
1992	6,318.9	1992–93	456,070	7.2	274,335	4.3	181,735	2.9
1993	6,642.3	1993–94	477,237	7.2	287,507	4.3	189,730	2.9
1994	7,054.3	1994–95	503,925	7.1	302,400	4.3	201,525	2.9
1995	7,400.5	1995–96	529,596	7.2	318,246	4.3	211,350	2.9
1996	7,813.2	1996–97	562,251	7.2	338,951	4.3	223,300	2.9
1997	8,318.4	[1]1997–98	596,222	7.2	361,422	4.3	234,800	2.8
1998	8,790.2	[1]1998–99	623,200	7.1	376,900	4.3	246,300	2.8
1999	9,299.2	[2]1999–2000	646,800	7.0	389,000	4.2	257,800	2.8

—Not available.

[1]Preliminary data for elementary and secondary schools and estimates for colleges and universities.

[2]Estimated.

NOTE: Total expenditures for public elementary and secondary schools include current expenditures, interest on school debt, and capital outlay. Data for private elementary and secondary schools are estimated. Total expenditures for colleges and universities include current-fund expenditures and additions to plant value. Excludes expenditures of noncollegiate postsecondary institutions. Data for 1995–96 and later years are for 4-year and 2-year degree-granting institutions that were eligible to participate in Title IV federal financial aid programs. Detail may not sum to totals due to rounding.

SOURCE: Thomas D. Snyder and Charlene M. Hoffman, "Table 31.—Total expenditures of educational institutions related to the gross domestic product, by level of institution: 1929–30 to 1999–2000," in *Digest of Education Statistics, 2000,* NCES 2001-034, U.S. Department of Education, National Center for Education Statistics, Washington DC, January 2001

PREPRIMARY, ELEMENTARY, AND SECONDARY SCHOOLS

SCHOOL ENROLLMENTS

Preprimary, elementary, and secondary school enrollments reflect the number of births over a specific period. Because of the baby boom (1946–1964), school enrollment grew rapidly during the 1950s and 1960s and then declined steadily during the 1970s and 1980s. In 1985 public elementary and secondary school enrollment increased for the first time since 1971. Enrollment has grown slowly but steadily since, reaching an estimated 46.9 million in public schools and 6 million in private schools in fall 1999. Slow but steady growth is projected to continue until 2005, when it will begin to decline slightly. (See Table 2.1 and Figure 2.1.)

Preprimary Growth

In contrast to the declining elementary and secondary school enrollment during the 1970s and early 1980s, preprimary enrollment showed substantial growth. Between 1970 and 1980 preprimary enrollment rose from 4.1 million to 4.9 million preschool-age children. While the population of three- to five-year-olds grew 28 percent from 1980 to 1999, enrollment in preprimary programs rose 61 percent, to 7.8 million. This increase reflects not only the growth in the number of children, but also the greater availability of and interest in preschool education. In 1965 only 27.1 percent of the 12.5 million children in this age group were enrolled in nursery school or kindergarten. By October 1999, 65.8 percent of the 11.9 million preschool-age children in this country were enrolled in preprimary programs. (See Table 2.2.)

As the proportion of working mothers has grown, the proportion of young children in full-day preprimary programs has also increased. In 1999 more than one-half (53 percent) of children in preprimary programs attended school all day, compared to 31.8 percent in 1980 and 17 percent in 1970. (See Table 2.2).

Geographic Shifts

There have been significant changes in regional school enrollment. Between 1970 and 1980, school enrollment in 41 states and the District of Columbia dropped, with most of the decline occurring at the elementary level. Between fall 1994 and fall 1999, 20 states increased enrollment by 5 percent or more, while 17 other states reported increases of less than 5 percent. Alabama, Arkansas, the District of Columbia, Iowa, Kentucky, Louisiana, Mississippi, Montana, New Mexico, North Dakota, South Carolina, South Dakota, West Virginia, and Wyoming reported decreases in school enrollment. (See Figure 2.2.)

Racial and Ethnic Diversity

Public school enrollment has become more racially and ethnically diverse, reflecting the nation's changing demographics. Between 1986 and 1998 the proportion of non-Hispanic white students declined from 70.4 percent to 62.9 percent, while the proportion of non-Hispanic black students increased slightly, from 16.1 percent to 17.1 percent. The proportion of Hispanic students rose from 9.9 percent to 15 percent; Asian or Pacific Islander students from 2.8 percent to 3.9 percent; and American Indian/Alaskan Native students from less than 1 percent to slightly over 1 percent. (See Table 2.3.)

THE SCHOOL-AGE POPULATION

The 2000 Census counted approximately 61.3 million elementary- and secondary-age children (ages 5 to 19). About 22 percent of the total U.S. population were school-age children.

Poor School-Age Children

Poverty rates have declined significantly. From 1993 to 2000 the proportion of Americans living in poverty

TABLE 2.1

Enrollment in grades K–8 and 9–12 of elementary and secondary schools, by control of institution, with projections, Fall 1986–fall 2011

(In thousands)

Year	Total			Public			Private		
	K–12[1]	K–8[1]	9–12	K–12[1]	K–8[1]	9–12	K–12[1]	K–8[1]	9–12
1986[2]	45,205	31,536	13,669	39,753	27,420	12,333	5,452	4,116	1,336
1987[2]	45,487	32,165	13,323	40,008	27,933	12,076	5,479	4,232	1,247
1988[2]	45,430	32,537	12,893	40,188	28,501	11,687	5,242	4,036	1,206
1989[3]	45,741	33,187	12,553	40,543	29,152	11,390	5,198	4,035	1,163
1990[4]	46,451	33,962	12,488	41,217	29,878	11,338	5,234	4,084	1,150
1991[3]	47,322	34,619	12,703	42,047	30,506	11,541	5,275	4,113	1,162
1992[4]	48,145	35,263	12,882	42,823	31,088	11,735	5,322	4,175	1,147
1993[3]	48,813	35,719	13,093	43,465	31,504	11,961	5,348	4,215	1,132
1994[4]	49,609	36,233	13,376	44,111	31,898	12,213	5,498	4,335	1,163
1995[3]	50,502	36,806	13,697	44,840	32,341	12,500	5,662	4,465	1,197
1996[4]	51,217	37,157	14,060	45,611	32,764	12,847	5,606	4,393	1,213
1997[3]	51,652	37,380	14,272	46,127	33,073	13,054	5,525	4,307	1,218
1998[4]	52,319	37,891	14,428	46,539	33,346	13,193	5,780	4,545	1,235
1999[3]	52,875	38,253	14,623	46,857	33,488	13,369	6,018	4,765	1,254

Projected

Year	Total			Public			Private		
	K–12[1]	K–8[1]	9–12	K–12[1]	K–8[1]	9–12	K–12[1]	K–8[1]	9–12
2000	52,902	38,130	14,772	47,051	33,545	13,506	5,851	4,585	1,266
2001	53,065	38,163	14,902	47,213	33,587	13,626	5,852	4,576	1,276
2002	53,218	38,142	15,076	47,358	33,574	13,784	5,860	4,568	1,292
2003	53,293	38,026	15,267	47,432	33,475	13,957	5,861	4,551	1,310
2004	53,356	37,803	15,552	47,494	33,276	14,218	5,862	4,527	1,334
2005	53,397	37,601	15,796	47,536	33,091	14,445	5,861	4,510	1,351
2006	53,372	37,446	15,927	47,515	32,947	14,569	5,857	4,499	1,358
2007	53,279	37,362	15,917	47,430	32,868	14,562	5,849	4,494	1,355
2008	53,125	37,358	15,767	47,286	32,860	14,426	5,839	4,498	1,341
2009	53,014	37,422	15,592	47,178	32,913	14,265	5,836	4,509	1,327
2010	52,973	37,563	15,409	47,131	33,034	14,096	5,842	4,529	1,313
2011	53,026	37,732	15,294	47,170	33,179	13,991	5,856	4,553	1,303

[1] Includes most kindergarten and some nursery school enrollment.
[2] Private school numbers are estimated on the basis of past data.
[3] Private school numbers are from the Private School Universe Survey.
[4] Private school numbers are interpolated.

NOTE: Some data have been revised from previously published figures. Detail may not sum to totals due to rounding.

SOURCE: Debra E. Gerald and William J. Hussar, "Table 1.—Enrollment in grades K-8 and 9-12 of elementary and secondary schools, by control of institution, with projections: Fall 1986 to fall 2011," in *Projections of Education Statistics to 2011*, NCES 2001-083, U.S. Department of Education, National Center for Education Statistics, Washington, DC, October 2001

decreased from 15.1 percent to 11.3 percent. Among children under age 18, the proportions living in poverty were 22.7 percent in 1993, and 16.2 percent in 2000. (See Table 2.4.) Poverty remains a persistent problem for the nation and its schools. Children who are poor are more likely to be undernourished, subject to frequent illnesses, and generally much less ready for learning.

Poverty rates vary widely by race and ethnicity, as well as by the type of household in which a child lives. In 2000 the proportion of whites living in poverty was 7.5 percent, compared to 22.1 percent of blacks and 21.2 percent of Hispanics. White (16.9 percent), black (34.6 percent) and Hispanic (34.2 percent) families living in households headed by a female with no spouse present were more likely to be poor than white (3.3 percent), black (6.1 percent) or Hispanic (14.1 percent) families that were headed by a married couple. (See Table 2.4.)

FINANCING THE SCHOOLS

Sources of Funding

Public schools obtain funds from three sources: local, state, and federal governments. Typically, local governments rely on property taxes to finance education, while state governments use revenues from sales taxes and, in some instances, income taxes. Local and state governments have traditionally been the primary sources of revenues for elementary and secondary schools, with the federal government contributing a relatively small proportion. (See Figure 2.3.)

During the late 1970s the federal government supplied almost 10 percent of the revenues for public schools, while state and local authorities divided the remainder. Since 1980 the federal proportion has dropped, reaching about 6 percent in 1990. It increased slightly to 6.8

percent in the 1997–98 school year (see Figure 2.3). The dependence on state and local revenues has significant meaning for school funding.

State revenues, which rely on sales and income taxes, are tied to business cycles. Local school funding is usually tied to property taxes. When a recession occurs or businesses close or move away so that property values decline, school funding is directly affected. Also, per capita income and property values are typically lower in rural areas, and local taxes may not be enough to fund the district's schools. In these cases, states must find ways to fill the gap.

To try to resolve these problems, many states now use complex formulas for distributing state education funds to equalize the per pupil expenditure statewide—that is, they give proportionally more state funds per student to poor districts than to wealthy districts.

In *School Finance: State Efforts to Equalize Funding Between Poor and Wealthy School Districts* (Virginia Vandelinde and Nancy Purvine, Washington, DC, June 1998), the General Accounting Office (GAO), an agency of Congress, analyzed state efforts to equalize funding. Between November 1996 and May 1998, the GAO researched four states—Oregon, Kansas, Rhode Island, and Louisiana—which utilized a wide variety of school finance strategies. Two key factors were found to have reduced the size of the funding gap between poor and wealthy districts: 1) a greater tax effort by poor districts and 2) the state's effort to compensate for differences in district funding with specific equalization policies. (See Table 2.5.)

Attempts at equalization in the four states showed mixed results. Oregon and Kansas reduced their funding gaps between poor and wealthy districts. Oregon's success was largely the result of a 75 percent increase in its share of education funding. Louisiana's equalization efforts increased its funding gap, and Rhode Island's gap stayed about the same. (See Table 2.5.)

The GAO found that equalization efforts are undermined in states without some kind of ceiling on wealthy districts' spending. Even when states fund poor districts at a higher rate than wealthy districts, wealthy districts are able to raise more funds locally. In some states, wealthy districts may have to contribute locally raised revenue to the state for redistribution to poor districts.

A newer issue than financial equity is the issue of the adequacy of the education the state offers children. Education experts are developing standards—what it takes in terms of teachers, curriculum, and expenditures—to define an adequate education. The next step will be to determine how much money each school needs to meet those standards.

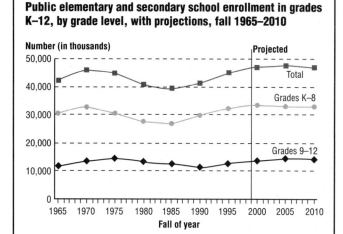

FIGURE 2.1

Public elementary and secondary school enrollment in grades K–12, by grade level, with projections, fall 1965–2010

NOTE: Includes most kindergarten and some nursery school enrollment.

SOURCE: John Wirt, et al., "School Enrollment: Public elementary and secondary school enrollment in Grades K-12 (in thousands), by grade level, with projections: Fall 1965–2010," in *The Condition of Education, 2001*, NCES 2001-072, U.S. Department of Education, National Center for Education Statistics, Washington, DC, June 2001

Revenues

In the 1997–98 school year revenues for public elementary and secondary schools totaled $326 billion. States (48.4 percent) and local authorities (42.3 percent) provided most of the revenues, with less than 7 percent coming from the federal government and less than 3 percent from private sources. The proportions of federal, state, and local funding varied by state. In Hawaii, the state provided 89 percent of revenue, while in New Hampshire, the state provided only 9.3 percent. The federal government supplied 16.5 percent of the school revenue for the District of Columbia and 3.6 percent for New Jersey. Local and intermediate sources accounted for 84.5 percent of school revenue in New Hampshire, and less than 1 percent in Hawaii. (See Table 2.6.)

Expenditures

According to the National Center for Education Statistics (NCES), in 1999 the nation spent $311.6 billion (in current expenditures) for public elementary and secondary education, which is a 98 percent increase since 1986. By 2004 the current expenditures are projected to reach $356.3 billion, and by 2011 the total is projected to be $418.3 billion (in constant 1999–2000 dollars, adjusted for inflation).

In 1999–2000 the average per pupil expenditure was estimated to be $6,584. Allowing for inflation (constant 1999–2000 dollars), the expenditure per student has risen significantly (45 percent) since 1979–80. (See Table 2.7.) The NCES projects that expenditures per student will reach $8,875 by 2011.

TABLE 2.2

Enrollment of 3-, 4-, and 5-year old children in preprimary programs, by level and control of program and by attendance status , October 1965–October 1999

[In thousands]

Year and age	Total population, 3 to 5 years old	Enrollment by level and control						Enrollment by attendance		
		Total	Percent enrolled	Nursery school Public	Private	Kindergarten Public	Private	Full-day	Part-day	Percent full-day
Total, 3 to 5 years old										
1965	12,549	3,407	27.1	127	393	2,291	596	—	—	—
1970	10,949	4,104	37.5	332	762	2,498	511	698	3,405	17.0
1975	10,185	4,955	48.7	570	1,174	2,682	528	1,295	3,659	26.1
1980	9,284	4,878	52.5	628	1,353	2,438	459	1,551	3,327	31.8
1985	10,733	5,865	54.6	846	1,631	2,847	541	2,144	3,722	36.6
1986	10,866	5,971	55.0	829	1,715	2,859	567	2,241	3,730	37.5
1987	10,872	5,931	54.6	819	1,736	2,842	534	2,090	3,841	35.2
1988	10,993	5,978	54.4	851	1,770	2,875	481	2,044	3,935	34.2
1989	11,039	6,026	54.6	930	1,894	2,704	497	2,238	3,789	37.1
1990	11,207	6,659	59.4	1,199	2,180	2,772	509	2,577	4,082	38.7
1991	11,370	6,334	55.7	996	1,828	2,967	543	2,408	3,926	38.0
1992	11,545	6,402	55.5	1,073	1,783	2,995	550	2,410	3,992	37.6
1993	11,954	6,581	55.1	1,205	1,779	3,020	577	2,642	3,939	40.1
1994[1]	12,328	7,514	61.0	1,848	2,314	2,819	534	3,468	4,046	46.2
1995[1]	12,518	7,739	61.8	1,950	2,381	2,800	608	3,689	4,051	47.7
1996[1]	12,378	7,580	61.2	1,830	2,317	2,853	580	3,562	4,019	47.0
1997[1]	12,121	7,860	64.9	2,207	2,231	2,847	575	3,922	3,939	49.9
1998[1]	12,078	7,788	64.5	2,213	2,299	2,674	602	3,959	3,829	50.8
1999[1]	11,920	7,844	65.8	2,209	2,298	2,777	560	4,154	3,690	53.0
3 years old										
1965	4,149	203	4.9	41	153	5	4	—	—	—
1970	3,516	454	12.9	110	322	12	10	142	312	31.3
1975	3,177	683	21.5	179	474	11	18	259	423	37.9
1980	3,143	857	27.3	221	604	16	17	321	536	37.5
1985	3,594	1,035	28.8	278	679	52	26	350	685	33.8
1986	3,607	1,041	28.9	257	737	26	21	399	642	38.3
1987	3,569	1,022	28.6	264	703	24	31	378	644	37.0
1988	3,719	1,027	27.6	298	678	24	26	369	658	35.9
1989	3,713	1,005	27.1	277	707	3	18	390	615	38.8
1990	3,692	1,205	32.6	347	840	11	7	447	758	37.1
1991	3,811	1,074	28.2	313	702	38	22	388	687	36.1
1992	3,905	1,081	27.7	336	685	26	34	371	711	34.3
1993	4,053	1,097	27.1	369	687	20	20	426	670	38.9
1994[1]	4,081	1,385	33.9	469	887	19	9	670	715	48.4
1995[1]	4,148	1,489	35.9	511	947	15	17	754	736	50.6
1996[1]	4,045	1,506	37.2	511	947	22	26	657	848	43.7
1997[1]	3,947	1,528	38.7	643	843	25	18	754	774	49.4
1998[1]	3,989	1,498	37.6	587	869	27	14	735	763	49.1
1999[1]	3,862	1,505	39.0	621	859	13	12	773	732	51.3
4 years old										
1965	4,238	683	16.1	68	213	284	118	—	—	—
1970	3,620	1,007	27.8	176	395	318	117	230	776	22.8
1975	3,499	1,418	40.5	332	644	313	129	411	1,008	29.0
1980	3,072	1,423	46.3	363	701	239	120	467	956	32.8
1985	3,598	1,766	49.1	496	859	276	135	643	1,123	36.4
1986	3,616	1,772	49.0	498	903	257	115	622	1,150	35.1
1987	3,597	1,717	47.7	431	881	280	125	548	1,169	31.9
1988	3,598	1,768	49.1	481	922	261	104	519	1,249	29.4
1989	3,692	1,882	51.0	524	1,055	202	100	592	1,290	31.4
1990	3,723	2,087	56.1	695	1,144	157	91	716	1,371	34.3
1991	3,763	1,994	53.0	584	982	287	140	667	1,326	33.5
1992	3,807	1,982	52.1	602	971	282	126	632	1,350	31.9
1993	4,044	2,178	53.9	719	957	349	154	765	1,413	35.1
1994[1]	4,202	2,532	60.3	1,020	1,232	198	82	1,095	1,438	43.2
1995[1]	4,145	2,553	61.6	1,054	1,208	207	84	1,104	1,449	43.3
1996[1]	4,148	2,454	59.2	1,029	1,168	180	77	1,034	1,420	42.1
1997[1]	4,033	2,665	66.1	1,197	1,169	207	92	1,161	1,505	43.5
1998[1]	4,002	2,666	66.6	1,183	1,219	210	53	1,179	1,487	44.2
1999[1]	4,021	2,769	68.9	1,212	1,227	207	122	1,355	1,414	48.9

International Comparisons of Expenditures Per Student

One method of measuring a country's commitment to education is to examine what portion of its GDP (gross domestic product, the total value of goods and services produced in the nation) goes to educating its people. In 1997 the United States government spent 5.2 percent of its GDP for education, 3.5 percent for primary and secondary

TABLE 2.2

Enrollment of 3-, 4-, and 5-year old children in preprimary programs, by level and control of program and by attendance status , October 1965–October 1999 [CONTINUED]

[In thousands]

Year and age	Total population, 3 to 5 years old	Enrollment by level and control						Enrollment by attendance		
		Total	Percent enrolled	Nursery school		Kindergarten		Full-day	Part-day	Percent full-day
				Public	Private	Public	Private			
5 years old [2]										
1965	4,162	2,521	60.6	18	27	2,002	474	—	—	—
1970	3,814	2,643	69.3	45	45	2,168	384	326	2,317	12.3
1975	3,509	2,854	81.3	59	57	2,358	381	625	2,228	21.9
1980	3,069	2,598	84.7	44	48	2,183	322	763	1,835	29.4
1985	3,542	3,065	86.5	73	94	2,519	379	1,151	1,914	37.6
1986	3,643	3,157	86.7	75	75	2,576	432	1,220	1,937	38.6
1987	3,706	3,192	86.1	124	152	2,538	378	1,163	2,028	36.4
1988	3,676	3,184	86.6	72	170	2,590	351	1,155	2,028	36.3
1989	3,633	3,139	86.4	129	132	2,499	378	1,255	1,883	40.0
1990	3,792	3,367	88.8	157	196	2,604	411	1,414	1,953	42.0
1991	3,796	3,267	86.0	100	143	2,642	382	1,354	1,913	41.4
1992	3,832	3,339	87.1	135	127	2,688	390	1,408	1,931	42.2
1993	3,857	3,306	85.7	116	136	2,651	403	1,451	1,856	43.9
1994[1]	4,044	3,597	88.9	359	194	2,601	442	1,704	1,893	47.4
1995[1]	4,224	3,697	87.5	385	226	2,578	507	1,830	1,867	49.5
1996[1]	4,185	3,621	86.5	290	202	2,652	477	1,870	1,750	51.7
1997[1]	4,141	3,667	88.5	368	219	2,616	465	2,007	1,660	54.7
1998[1]	4,087	3,624	88.7	442	211	2,437	535	2,044	1,579	56.4
1999[1]	4,037	3,571	88.4	376	212	2,557	426	2,027	1,544	56.8

— Not available.

[1] Data collected using new procedures. May not be comparable with figures prior to 1994.

[2] Enrollment data include only those students in preprimary programs.

NOTE: Data are based on sample surveys of the civilian noninstitutional population. Although cells with fewer than 75,000 children are subject to wide sampling variation, they are included in the table to permit various types of aggregations. Detail may not sum to totals due to rounding.

SOURCE: Thomas D. Snyder and Charlene M. Hoffman, "Table 45.—Enrollment of 3-, 4-, and 5-year-old children in preprimary programs, by level and control of program and by attendance status: October 1965 to October 1999," in *Digest of Education Statistics, 2000,* NCES 2001-034, U.S. Department of Education, National Center for Education Statistics, Washington, DC, January 2001

education and another 1.4 percent for higher education. Of the selected countries, Sweden spent the highest proportion (6.8 percent) of GDP on education, and Greece spent the lowest proportion (3.5 percent). For primary and secondary education, Sweden and New Zealand spent the highest proportion of GDP (4.7 percent each), and Greece the lowest (2.5 percent). Only Finland (1.7 percent) and Sweden (1.6 percent) spent a larger fraction of GDP on higher education than did the United States. The percentage of GDP that the U.S. spent on public education in 1997 was .5 percent higher than in 1985 (4.7 percent). No other country had a larger increase. (See Table 2.8.)

Another way to examine international expenditures for education is by comparing how much money countries spend per student in relation to GDP per capita. In general, those countries with the highest GDP per capita spent the most on education. The United States spent $5,718 per elementary student in 1997, and $7,230 per student at the secondary level. Mexico spent $935 per student at the elementary school level in that year, while Denmark spent $6,596. At the secondary school level, Mexico spent $1,726, while Switzerland spent $9,045 per student. For higher education, in 1997 the United States spent $17,466 per student, which was higher than all other selected countries. (See Figure 2.4.)

PRIVATE SCHOOLS

In 1999–2000 about 5.2 million students attended 27,223 private elementary and secondary schools throughout the country. (See Table 2.9.) Private schools served approximately 9 percent of all students. By 2010, enrollment is projected to be 5.9 million.

Characteristics

Most (60.7 percent) private schools in 1999–2000 existed at the elementary level, while 9.3 percent were high schools. About 30 percent were combined elementary and secondary schools. More than 78 percent were affiliated with a religion, and 21.6 percent were nonsectarian (not associated with a religion). (See Table 2.9.)

Catholic schools constituted 29.8 percent of all private schools in 1999–2000. Economic and social changes have caused a decline in Catholic school enrollment and in the number of Catholic schools. Despite these decreases, however, Catholic schools still accounted for nearly half (48.6 percent) of all students attending private schools. More than one-third (35.7 percent) of students attending private schools were enrolled in non-Catholic religious schools, and 15.7 percent attended nonsectarian schools. (See Table 2.9.)

FIGURE 2.2

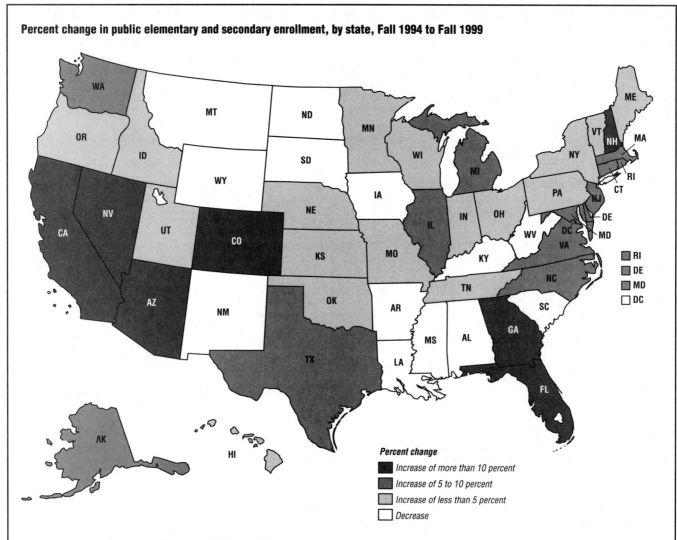

Percent change in public elementary and secondary enrollment, by state, Fall 1994 to Fall 1999

Percent change

- ■ Increase of more than 10 percent
- ▨ Increase of 5 to 10 percent
- ▧ Increase of less than 5 percent
- □ Decrease

SOURCE: Thomas D. Snyder and Charlene M. Hoffman, "Figure 9.—Percentage change in public elementary and secondary enrollment, by state: Fall 1994 to fall 1999," in *Digest of Education Statistics, 2000,* NCES 2001-034, U.S. Department of Education, National Center for Education Statistics, Washington, DC, January 2001

COMPARISONS OF PUBLIC AND PRIVATE SCHOOLS

Location, Teachers, and Size

In 1998–99 urban fringe areas and large towns contained 35,813 (39 percent) of the 90,874 public schools in the United States. Another 32,730 (36 percent) were located in rural communities and small towns, and 22,323 (25 percent) were in large central or mid-sized central cities. (See Table 2.10.) In 1999–2000 private school distribution was somewhat different. Nearly 11,000 private schools (39.8 percent) were in central cities, 10,359 (38.1 percent) were in urban fringe/large town areas, and 6,040 (22.2 percent) were in rural/small town communities. (See Table 2.9.)

In fall 1999 there were 2.9 million teachers and other faculty in public elementary and secondary schools and 397,000 in private schools. The average ratio of students to teachers was 16 pupils to every teacher. In general, the pupil-teacher ratio was higher in elementary schools (17.4) than in secondary schools (13.9). Public schools, on average, had higher pupil/teacher ratios (16.2) than private schools (15.0). These ratios were considerably lower in the 1990s than they were from the 1950s to the early 1980s. (See Table 2.11.)

In 1998–99 the average enrollment at public schools was 524 students per school—478 in elementary schools and 707 in secondary schools. Most (43 percent) public school students attended schools with enrollments of 500 students or more. Over a quarter (26 percent) were enrolled at schools of between 300 and 499 students, and 31 percent of public school students attended schools with enrollments below 300 students. (See Table 2.12.) Private schools in 1999–2000 tended to have lower enrollments.

TABLE 2.3

Enrollment in public elementary and secondary schools by race/ethnicity and state, Fall 1986 to Fall 1998

State or other area	Percent distribution, fall 1986						Percent distribution, fall 1998					
	Total	White[1]	Black[1]	Hispanic	Asian or Pacific Islander	American Indian/ Alaskan Native	Total	White[1]	Black[1]	Hispanic	Asian or Pacific Islander	American Indian/ Alaskan Native
United States	**100.0**	**70.4**	**16.1**	**9.9**	**2.8**	**0.9**	**100.0**	**62.9**	**17.1**	**15.0**	**3.9**	**1.1**
Alabama	100.0	62.0	37.0	0.1	0.4	0.5	100.0	61.5	36.2	0.9	0.7	0.7
Alaska	100.0	65.7	4.3	1.7	3.3	25.1	100.0	62.5	4.6	3.0	5.1	24.8
Arizona	100.0	62.2	4.0	26.4	1.3	6.1	100.0	55.0	4.5	31.7	1.9	6.9
Arkansas	100.0	74.7	24.2	0.4	0.6	0.2	100.0	72.8	23.5	2.5	0.8	0.4
California	100.0	53.7	9.0	27.5	9.1	0.7	100.0	37.9	8.7	41.4	11.1	0.9
Colorado	100.0	78.7	4.5	13.7	2.0	1.0	100.0	70.6	5.6	19.9	2.7	1.2
Connecticut	100.0	77.2	12.1	8.9	1.5	0.2	100.0	71.2	13.6	12.4	2.6	0.3
Delaware	100.0	68.3	27.7	2.5	1.4	0.2	100.0	62.4	30.4	4.9	2.0	0.2
District of Columbia	100.0	4.0	91.1	3.9	0.9	0.1	100.0	4.3	85.9	8.3	1.6	(2)
Florida	100.0	65.4	23.7	9.5	1.2	0.2	100.0	55.3	25.5	17.2	1.8	0.3
Georgia	100.0	60.7	37.9	0.6	0.8	(2)	100.0	56.4	38.1	3.4	2.0	0.1
Hawaii	100.0	23.5	2.3	2.2	71.7	0.3	100.0	20.8	2.4	4.6	71.7	0.4
Idaho	100.0	92.6	0.3	4.9	0.8	1.3	100.0	87.1	0.7	9.7	1.2	1.2
Illinois	100.0	69.8	18.7	9.2	2.3	0.1	100.0	61.4	21.4	13.9	3.2	0.2
Indiana	100.0	88.7	9.0	1.7	0.5	0.1	100.0	84.7	11.4	2.8	0.9	0.2
Iowa	100.0	94.6	3.0	0.9	1.2	0.3	100.0	91.4	3.6	2.8	1.7	0.5
Kansas	100.0	85.6	7.6	4.4	1.9	0.6	100.0	80.6	8.6	7.5	2.1	1.2
Kentucky	100.0	89.2	10.2	0.1	0.5	(2)	100.0	88.4	10.4	0.7	0.4	0.1
Louisiana	100.0	56.5	41.3	0.8	1.1	0.3	100.0	49.7	47.1	1.3	1.3	0.7
Maine	100.0	98.3	0.5	0.2	0.8	0.2	100.0	97.0	1.1	0.5	0.9	0.5
Maryland	100.0	59.7	35.3	1.7	3.1	0.2	100.0	55.0	36.6	4.0	4.0	0.3
Massachusetts	100.0	83.7	7.4	6.0	2.8	0.1	100.0	77.1	8.6	10.0	4.2	0.2
Michigan	100.0	76.4	19.8	1.8	1.2	0.8	100.0	74.7	19.5	3.0	1.7	1.0
Minnesota	100.0	93.9	2.1	0.9	1.7	1.5	100.0	85.6	5.6	2.5	4.4	2.0
Mississippi	100.0	43.9	55.5	0.1	0.4	0.1	100.0	47.7	51.0	0.5	0.6	0.1
Missouri	100.0	83.4	14.9	0.7	0.8	0.2	100.0	80.2	17.0	1.4	1.1	0.3
Montana	100.0	92.7	0.3	0.9	0.5	5.5	100.0	86.8	0.5	1.6	0.8	10.2
Nebraska	100.0	91.4	4.4	2.4	0.8	1.0	100.0	84.8	6.3	5.9	1.4	1.5
Nevada	100.0	77.4	9.6	7.5	3.2	2.3	100.0	61.2	9.9	22.0	5.1	1.8
New Hampshire	100.0	98.0	0.7	0.5	0.8	0.1	100.0	96.2	1.0	1.4	1.2	0.2
New Jersey	100.0	69.1	17.4	10.7	2.7	0.1	100.0	61.6	18.1	14.3	5.8	0.2
New Mexico	100.0	43.1	2.3	45.1	0.8	8.7	100.0	37.2	2.3	48.8	1.0	10.8
New York	100.0	68.4	16.5	12.3	2.7	0.2	100.0	55.6	20.4	18.1	5.6	0.4
North Carolina	100.0	68.4	28.9	0.4	0.6	1.7	100.0	62.5	31.2	3.1	1.7	1.5
North Dakota	100.0	92.4	0.6	1.1	0.8	5.0	100.0	89.9	1.0	1.2	0.7	7.3
Ohio	100.0	83.1	15.0	1.0	0.7	0.1	100.0	81.5	15.8	1.5	1.1	0.1
Oklahoma	100.0	79.0	7.8	1.6	1.0	10.6	100.0	67.0	10.7	4.9	1.4	16.0
Oregon	100.0	89.8	2.2	3.9	2.4	1.7	100.0	82.9	2.7	8.7	3.7	2.1
Pennsylvania	100.0	84.4	12.6	1.8	1.2	0.1	100.0	79.4	14.6	4.0	1.9	0.1
Rhode Island	100.0	87.9	5.6	3.7	2.4	0.3	100.0	76.4	7.6	12.3	3.3	0.5
South Carolina	100.0	54.6	44.5	0.2	0.6	0.1	100.0	55.7	42.0	1.2	0.9	0.2
South Dakota	100.0	90.6	0.5	0.6	0.7	7.6	100.0	87.5	1.0	1.0	0.9	9.6
Tennessee	100.0	76.5	22.6	0.2	0.6	(2)	100.0	73.6	23.9	1.2	1.1	0.1
Texas	100.0	51.0	14.4	32.5	2.0	0.2	100.0	44.1	14.4	38.6	2.5	0.3
Utah	100.0	93.7	0.4	3.0	1.5	1.5	100.0	87.9	0.8	7.2	2.5	1.5
Vermont	100.0	98.4	0.3	0.2	0.6	0.6	100.0	97.1	0.9	0.4	1.0	0.5
Virginia	100.0	72.6	23.7	1.0	2.6	0.1	100.0	64.9	27.2	3.9	3.7	0.2
Washington	100.0	84.5	4.2	3.8	5.1	2.3	100.0	76.1	5.1	9.1	7.1	2.6
West Virginia	100.0	95.9	3.7	0.1	0.3	(2)	100.0	94.9	4.2	0.5	0.3	0.1
Wisconsin	100.0	86.6	8.9	1.9	1.7	1.0	100.0	81.9	9.8	3.8	3.1	1.4
Wyoming	100.0	90.7	0.9	5.9	0.6	1.9	100.0	88.6	1.0	6.7	0.8	2.9
Outlying areas												
American Samoa	—	—	—	—	—	—	100.0	—	—	—	100.0	—
Guam	—	—	—	—	—	—	100.0	2.2	0.4	0.2	97.1	0.1
Northern Marianas	—	—	—	—	—	—	100.0	0.8	—	—	99.2	—
Puerto Rico	—	—	—	—	—	—	100.0	—	—	100.0	—	—
Virgin Islands	—	—	—	—	—	—	100.0	0.9	84.7	13.9	0.4	0.1

—Not available.
[1]Excludes persons of Hispanic origin.
[2]Less than 0.05 percent.
NOTE: The 1986–87 data were derived from the 1986 Elementary and Secondary School Civil Rights sample survey of public school districts. Detail may not sum to totals due to rounding.

SOURCE: Thomas D. Snyder and Charlene M. Hoffman, "Table 44.—Enrollment in public elementary and secondary schools, by race/ethnicity and state: Fall 1986 and fall 1998," in *Digest of Education Statistics, 2000,* NCES 2001-034, U.S. Department of Education, National Center for Education Statistics, Washington, DC, January 2001

TABLE 2.4

People and families in poverty by selected characteristics, 1993 and 2000

[Numbers in thousands.]

Characteristic	2000 below poverty				1993 below poverty				Change[1] 1993 to 2000			
	Number	90-pct. C.I. (±)	Percent	90-pct. C.I. (±)	Number	90-pct. C.I. (±)	Percent	90-pct. C.I. (±)	Number	90-pct. C.I. (±)	Percent	90-pct. C.I. (±)
PEOPLE												
Total	**31,139**	**880**	**11.3**	**0.3**	**39,260**	**933**	**15.1**	**0.4**	***−8,122**	**1,281**	***−3.9**	**0.5**
Family Status												
In families	22,088	755	9.6	0.3	29,927	829	13.6	0.4	*−7,839	1,122	*−4.0	0.5
Householder	6,226	227	8.6	0.3	8,393	263	12.3	0.4	*−2,167	347	*−3.7	0.5
Related children under 18	11,086	451	15.7	0.7	14,961	487	22.0	0.8	*−3,875	663	*−6.3	1.0
Related children under 6	3,931	283	16.9	1.3	6,097	331	25.6	1.5	*−2,166	434	*−8.7	2.0
In unrelated subfamilies	520	59	39.4	5.2	945	77	54.3	5.3	*−425	97	*−14.9	7.4
Reference person	198	36	37.5	7.9	367	48	51.6	8.0	*−168	59	*−14.1	11.2
Children under 18	314	82	41.8	12.3	554	105	57.2	12.7	*−239	133	−15.4	17.7
Unrelated individual	8,530	276	18.9	0.6	8,388	263	22.1	0.7	142	382	*−3.1	1.0
Male	3,458	161	16.0	0.8	3,281	151	18.1	0.9	176	220	*−2.1	1.2
Female	5,073	202	21.6	0.9	5,107	194	25.7	1.1	−34	280	*−4.1	1.4
Race[2] and Hispanic Origin												
White	21,291	742	9.4	0.3	26,226	783	12.2	0.4	*−4,935	1,079	*−2.8	0.5
Non-Hispanic	14,572	622	7.5	0.3	18,882	674	9.9	0.4	*−4,311	918	*−2.4	0.5
Black	7,901	416	22.1	1.2	10,877	443	33.1	1.3	*−2,975	607	*−10.9	1.8
Asian and Pacific Islander	1,226	178	10.8	1.6	1,134	165	15.3	2.2	92	242	*−4.5	2.7
Hispanic[3]	7,155	398	21.2	1.2	8,126	400	30.6	1.5	*−971	564	*−9.4	1.9
Age												
Under 18 years	11,633	461	16.2	0.6	15,727	495	22.7	0.7	*−4,095	676	*−6.5	1.0
18 to 64 years	16,146	648	9.4	0.4	19,783	681	12.4	0.4	*−3,637	941	*−3.0	0.6
18 to 24 years	3,893	192	14.4	0.7	4,854	204	19.1	0.8	*−961	281	*−4.6	1.1
25 to 34 years	3,892	199	10.4	0.5	5,804	230	13.8	0.5	*−1,912	303	*−3.4	0.8
35 to 44 years	3,678	192	8.2	0.4	4,415	202	10.6	0.5	*−737	280	*−2.4	0.6
45 to 54 years	2,441	158	6.4	0.4	2,522	155	8.5	0.5	−81	220	*−2.1	0.7
55 to 59 years	1,175	110	8.8	0.8	1,057	100	9.9	0.9	118	150	−1.0	1.3
60 to 64 years	1,066	105	10.2	1.0	1,129	105	11.3	1.0	−63	148	−1.1	1.5
65 years and over	3,360	179	10.2	0.5	3,755	181	12.2	0.6	*−395	253	*−2.0	0.8
Nativity												
Native	26,442	816	10.7	0.3	34,086	875	14.4	0.4	*−7,644	1,198	*−3.7	0.5
Foreign born	4,697	411	15.7	1.4	5,179	413	23.0	1.8	−482	582	*−7.3	2.3
Naturalized citizen	1,107	201	9.7	1.8	707	155	10.1	2.2	*400	253	−0.4	2.8
Not a citizen	3,590	360	19.4	1.9	4,472	385	28.7	2.5	*−882	526	*−9.3	3.1
Region												
Northeast	5,433	357	10.3	0.7	6,839	383	13.3	0.8	*−1,405	523	*−3.0	1.0
Midwest	5,971	411	9.5	0.7	8,172	459	13.4	0.8	*−2,201	617	*−3.9	1.0
South	12,205	595	12.5	0.6	15,375	637	17.1	0.7	*−3,170	870	*−4.6	0.9
West	7,530	474	11.9	0.8	8,879	492	15.6	0.9	*−1,349	683	*−3.7	1.2
Residence												
Inside metropolitan areas	24,296	788	10.8	0.4	29,615	826	14.6	0.4	*−5,319	1,142	*−3.8	0.5
Inside central cities	12,967	589	16.1	0.7	16,805	638	21.5	0.8	*−3,838	869	*−5.3	1.1
Outside central cities	11,329	553	7.8	0.4	12,810	561	10.3	0.5	*−1,481	788	*−2.4	0.6
Outside metropolitan areas	6,843	530	13.4	1.1	9,650	600	17.2	1.1	*−2,807	801	*−3.8	1.5
FAMILIES												
Total	**6,226**	**227**	**8.6**	**0.3**	**8,393**	**263**	**12.3**	**0.4**	***−2,167**	**347**	***−3.7**	**0.5**
White	4,153	179	6.9	0.3	5,452	202	9.4	0.4	*−1,299	270	*−2.5	0.5
Non-Hispanic	2,820	145	5.3	0.3	3,988	168	7.6	0.3	*−1,168	222	*−2.3	0.4
Black	1,686	109	19.1	1.3	2,499	130	31.3	1.7	*−813	169	*−12.1	2.2
Asian and Pacific Islander	235	39	8.8	1.5	235	378	13.5	2.3	−	54	*−4.7	2.7
Hispanic[3]	1,431	100	18.5	1.4	1,625	102	27.3	1.8	*−194	143	*−8.8	2.3
Type of Family												
Married-couple	2,638	140	4.7	0.3	3,481	156	6.5	0.3	*−843	209	*−1.8	0.4
White	2,163	125	4.4	0.3	2,757	137	5.8	0.3	*−595	186	*−1.4	0.4
Non-Hispanic	1,447	100	3.3	0.2	2,042	117	4.7	0.3	*−595	153	*−1.4	0.4
Black	260	41	6.1	1.0	458	53	12.3	1.5	*−199	67	*−6.3	1.8
Asian and Pacific Islander	169	33	7.7	1.6	177	33	12.4	2.4	−8	47	*−4.8	2.9
Hispanic[3]	742	71	14.1	1.4	770	69	19.1	1.8	−28	99	*−4.9	2.3
Female householder, no husband present	3,099	151	24.7	1.3	4,424	179	35.6	1.6	*−1,325	235	*−10.9	2.1
White	1,656	109	20.0	1.4	2,376	127	29.2	1.7	*−720	166	*−9.2	2.2
Non-Hispanic	1,127	89	16.9	1.4	1,699	105	25.0	1.7	*−571	137	*−8.1	2.2
Black	1,303	95	34.6	2.8	1,908	112	49.9	3.3	*−605	146	*−15.2	4.4
Asian and Pacific Islander	60	20	19.9	7.1	43	16	18.6	7.4	17	26	1.3	10.3
Hispanic[3]	597	64	34.2	4.0	772	69	51.6	5.4	*−175	94	*−17.4	6.8

− Represents zero. *Statistically significant at the 90-percent confidence level. CI = Confidence Interval

[1]As a result of rounding, some differences may appear to be slightly higher or lower than the differences of the reported rates.

[2]Data for American Indians and Alaska Natives are not shown separately.

[3]Hispanics may be of any race.

SOURCE: Joseph Dalaker, "Table A—4. "People and Families in Poverty by Selected Characteristics: 1993 and 2000," in *Poverty in the United States: 2000*, P60-214, U.S. Census Bureau, Economics and Statistics Administration, September 2001

FIGURE 2.3

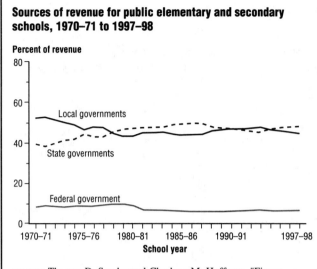

Sources of revenue for public elementary and secondary schools, 1970–71 to 1997–98

Percent of revenue

source: Thomas D. Snyder and Charlene M. Hoffman, "Figure 11.—Sources of revenue for public elementary and secondary schools: 1970–71 to 1997–98," in *Digest of Education Statistics, 2000,* NCES 2001-034, U.S. Department of Education, National Center for Education Statistics, Washington, DC, January 2001

TABLE 2.5

Strategies and results of state efforts to reduce funding gaps in school years 1991–92 and 1995–96

| | Strategy | | |
State	Strengthen equalization policies	Limit local tax effort	Result— funding gap reduced
Oregon	yes	yes	yes
Kansas	yes	yes	yes
Rhode Island	yes	no	no
Louisiana	yes	no	no

source: "Table 3.6: Strategies and Results of State Efforts to Reduce Funding Gaps in School Years 1991–92 and 1995–96," in *School Finance: State Efforts to Equalize Funding Between Wealthy and Poor School Districts,* GAO/HEHS-98-92, U.S. General Accounting Office, Health, Education, and Human Services Division, Washington, DC, June 1998

38 percent was for support services and noninstruction. New Jersey had the highest per student expenditure ($10,145) and Utah spent the least ($4,210) per student. (See Table 2.13.)

Prekindergarten and Kindergarten

Most public and private schools provide prekindergarten and kindergarten programs. According to *Key State Education Policies on K-12 Education* (Council of Chief State School Officers, Washington, DC, 2000), 26 states (52 percent) offered half-day kindergarten programs in 2000, 15 states (30 percent) offered full-day programs, and 9 states (18 percent) had no statewide policy. Kindergarten attendance is now nearly universal, and the majority of primary school children have had a least one organized group experience (day care center or nursery school) prior to starting first grade.

The U.S. Department of Education and U.S. Department of Justice, in *Working for Families and Children: Safe and Smart Afterschool Programs* (Washington, DC, April 2000) reported that six million school children participated in afterschool programs in 1999. According to *21st Century Learning Centers* (Andrea de Kanter, et al., U.S. Department of Education, Washington, DC, September 2000), in 1997 the supply of afterschool programs met only about 20 percent of the demand. Nearly three-quarters of the highest poverty schools (74 percent) offered before-school, after-school, or weekend instructional programs in 1997–98, but these programs served only 14 percent of all students. (See Figure 2.5.)

SCHOOL ATTENDANCE

Days in Attendance

According to the Council of Chief State School Officers, 34 states required 180 or more days per year of school in 2000, and 9 states required between 175 and 179 days.

The average enrollment for private schools was about 190 students per school. Over 80 percent of private school students were enrolled at schools with enrollments below 300 students. (See Table 2.9.)

In the 1998–99 school year nearly 70 percent of all schools were elementary schools, while 24 percent were secondary. Another 6 percent were combined elementary and secondary schools and special-purpose schools. Combined schools were more common in the private sector (30 percent) than in the public sector (4 percent).

Supportive Programs and Services

The type of supportive programs and services available to schools and school districts is one indicator of the access students have to educational opportunities. Although individual schools can apply directly for these programs and services, the school district (especially in public schools) usually decides whether the programs and services will be provided in its schools.

Schools offer a variety of student services, such as free or reduced-price lunches financed by public funds, services for disabled students, remedial programs, programs for gifted and talented students, programs under Chapter I (federal funds designated for special educational programs for disadvantaged children) of the Elementary and Secondary Education Act (PL 89-10), drug and alcohol prevention programs, English as a second language (ESL) programs, and bilingual programs.

Schools spent $6,508 per student in 1998–99. Most (62 percent) of this expenditure was for instruction, and

TABLE 2.6

Revenues for public elementary and secondary schools, by source and state, 1997–98

State or other area	Total, in thousands	Federal			State		Local and intermediate		Private [1]	
		Amount, in thousands	Per student	Percent of total	Amount, in thousands	Percent of total	Amount, in thousands	Percent of total	Amount, in thousands	Percent of total
United States	$325,976,011	$22,201,965	$481	6.8	$157,645,372	48.4	$137,798,615	42.3	$8,330,059	2.6
Alabama	4,146,629	389,242	520	9.4	2,589,826	62.5	960,799	23.2	206,762	5.0
Alaska	1,218,425	149,630	1,133	12.3	757,286	62.2	278,785	22.9	32,724	2.7
Arizona	4,731,675	482,748	593	10.2	2,096,739	44.3	2,045,829	43.2	106,360	2.2
Arkansas	2,600,655	280,682	615	10.8	1,500,334	57.7	674,943	26.0	144,697	5.6
California	38,142,613	3,120,793	538	8.2	22,963,395	60.2	11,655,935	30.6	402,490	1.1
Colorado	4,327,326	219,798	320	5.1	1,879,065	43.4	2,061,131	47.6	167,332	3.9
Connecticut	5,160,728	201,858	377	3.9	1,925,676	37.3	2,894,418	56.1	138,777	2.7
Delaware	913,616	69,240	618	7.6	588,211	64.4	243,784	26.7	12,380	1.4
District of Columbia	706,935	116,363	1,509	16.5	—	—	587,111	83.1	3,461	0.5
Florida	14,988,118	1,145,240	499	7.6	7,311,149	48.8	5,945,424	39.7	586,304	3.9
Georgia	9,041,434	616,455	448	6.8	4,625,560	51.2	3,625,225	40.1	174,194	1.9
Hawaii	1,282,702	110,725	583	8.6	1,141,002	89.0	6,229	0.5	24,746	1.9
Idaho	1,320,647	92,937	380	7.0	827,955	62.7	377,211	28.6	22,544	1.7
Illinois	14,194,654	957,788	479	6.7	4,033,015	28.4	8,844,102	62.3	359,750	2.5
Indiana	7,513,407	363,393	368	4.8	3,860,331	51.4	3,072,377	40.9	217,307	2.9
Iowa	3,346,481	177,460	354	5.3	1,715,706	51.3	1,278,597	38.2	174,719	5.2
Kansas	3,122,238	184,940	395	5.9	1,807,350	57.9	1,046,453	33.5	83,495	2.7
Kentucky	3,932,068	376,532	563	9.6	2,427,126	61.7	1,041,560	26.5	86,849	2.2
Louisiana	4,494,429	506,525	652	11.3	2,266,287	50.4	1,612,455	35.9	109,162	2.4
Maine	1,600,635	111,892	526	7.0	728,812	45.5	742,945	46.4	16,986	1.1
Maryland	6,454,696	337,791	407	5.2	2,514,141	39.0	3,401,284	52.7	201,480	3.1
Massachusetts	7,893,657	395,259	416	5.0	3,213,490	40.7	4,175,831	52.9	109,076	1.4
Michigan	14,329,715	950,569	558	6.6	9,459,203	66.0	3,641,277	25.4	278,665	1.9
Minnesota	6,529,420	320,513	375	4.9	3,418,033	52.3	2,537,752	38.9	253,122	3.9
Mississippi	2,407,954	339,316	672	14.1	1,333,568	55.4	653,106	27.1	81,964	3.4
Missouri	6,005,256	375,185	412	6.2	2,384,741	39.7	3,009,034	50.1	236,295	3.9
Montana	1,029,939	105,211	648	10.2	482,681	46.9	398,569	38.7	43,477	4.2
Nebraska	1,964,205	130,716	447	6.7	650,846	33.1	1,074,733	54.7	107,910	5.5
Nevada	1,910,794	87,580	295	4.6	607,846	31.8	1,149,020	60.1	66,347	3.5
New Hampshire	1,364,943	51,940	258	3.8	127,607	9.3	1,152,828	84.5	32,567	2.4
New Jersey	13,189,983	477,088	382	3.6	5,246,646	39.8	7,159,186	54.3	307,064	2.3
New Mexico	1,952,452	258,676	780	13.2	1,409,495	72.2	240,582	12.3	43,699	2.2
New York	27,782,468	1,512,286	528	5.4	11,038,714	39.7	14,970,650	53.9	260,818	0.9
North Carolina	7,188,615	520,907	421	7.2	4,838,150	67.3	1,631,999	22.7	197,558	2.7
North Dakota	682,419	84,339	711	12.4	280,238	41.1	280,742	41.1	37,100	5.4
Ohio	13,458,095	783,397	424	5.8	5,547,736	41.2	6,581,231	48.9	545,731	4.1
Oklahoma	3,416,296	295,299	473	8.6	2,103,243	61.6	837,037	24.5	180,716	5.3
Oregon	3,883,939	248,549	459	6.4	2,204,918	56.8	1,305,950	33.6	124,523	3.2
Pennsylvania	14,837,945	868,600	479	5.9	5,736,509	38.7	7,959,292	53.6	273,544	1.8
Rhode Island	1,264,156	68,680	448	5.4	507,377	40.1	671,445	53.1	16,653	1.3
South Carolina	4,055,072	343,673	521	8.5	2,087,806	51.5	1,448,682	35.7	174,911	4.3
South Dakota	794,256	79,522	558	10.0	282,518	35.6	408,047	51.4	24,168	3.0
Tennessee	4,815,833	425,768	477	8.8	2,299,491	47.7	1,751,162	36.4	339,411	7.0
Texas	24,179,060	1,845,074	474	7.6	10,675,578	44.2	11,070,763	45.8	587,646	2.4
Utah	2,305,397	159,879	331	6.9	1,406,577	61.0	681,185	29.5	57,756	2.5
Vermont	861,643	44,752	422	5.2	253,572	29.4	547,924	63.6	15,395	1.8
Virginia	7,757,954	405,791	365	5.2	2,432,370	31.4	4,671,063	60.2	248,731	3.2
Washington	6,895,693	442,455	446	6.4	4,548,851	66.0	1,682,908	24.4	221,480	3.2
West Virginia	2,216,984	204,827	680	9.2	1,389,076	62.7	593,409	26.8	29,671	1.3
Wisconsin	7,059,759	316,879	359	4.5	3,789,320	53.7	2,803,968	39.7	149,592	2.1
Wyoming	702,001	47,203	486	6.7	330,208	47.0	312,643	44.5	11,948	1.7
Outlying areas.										
American Samoa	49,677	38,669	2,542	77.8	10,897	21.9	28	0.1	82	0.2
Guam	173,339	18,100	558	10.4	—	—	151,023	87.1	4,216	2.4
Northern Marianas	58,239	15,242	1,648	26.2	42,796	73.5	132	0.2	70	0.1
Puerto Rico	2,094,025	572,495	928	27.3	1,520,398	72.6	320	(²)	811	(²)
Virgin Islands	152,499	27,719	1,252	18.2	—	—	124,635	81.7	146	0.1

—Not available.
[1]Includes revenues from gifts, and tuition and fees from patrons.
²Less than .05 percent.
NOTE: Data have been revised from previously published figures. Excludes revenues for state education agencies. Detail may not sum to totals due to rounding.

SOURCE: Thomas D. Snyder and Charlene M. Hoffman, "Table 159.—Revenues for public elementary and secondary schools, by source and state: 1997–98," in *Digest of Education Statistics, 2000,* NCES 2001-034, U.S. Department of Education, National Center for Education Statistics, Washington, DC, January 2001

Since 1998 Hawaii, Kansas, Mississippi, Oklahoma, and Texas have increased the number of days in the school year. The number of required hours per day ranged from three to seven, with 37 states requiring five or more hours per day.

Compulsory Attendance

Most industrialized Western nations require children to attend school for about 10 years. In 2000 all U.S. states required students to attend school starting between ages 5 and 8, and continuing through ages 16 to 18. Age 6 is the required age to start school in 21 states (42 percent). Students are required to attend school until age 16 in 28 states (56 percent).

GRADUATING FROM HIGH SCHOOL

In 1899–1900 only 6.4 percent of 17-year-olds had graduated from high school. By 1929–30 this proportion had risen to 29 percent, and by 1949–50, it had grown to 59 percent. The proportion peaked at about 77 percent in 1968–69 and then dropped to around 72 percent from 1978–79 through 1980–81. The proportion fluctuated between 71 and 73 percent throughout much of the 1980s and the early 1990s. At the end of the 1999–2000 school year, 2.8 million students graduated from high school, representing about 71 percent of all 17-year-olds. (See Table 2.14.) High school graduates are not the same as completers—students who finish their high school education through alternative programs, such as the General Educational Development (GED) program.

General Educational Development (GED) Diplomas

The General Educational Development (GED) diploma is an alternative way for young people who have left school to get equivalency credit for high school graduation. The number of those getting GED diplomas rose sharply from 342,000 in 1975 to 500,000 in 1981. The number gaining a GED diploma generally dropped during the 1980s, falling to 364,000 in 1989, but by 1999 it had again increased to 516,000. (See Table 2.15.) The GED Testing Service estimates that one in every seven high school graduates holds a GED high school credential.

TABLE 2.7

Current expediture per pupil in fall enrollment, 1979–80 to 1999–2000

School year	Unadjusted dollars	Constant dollars (1999–2000)[1]
1979–80	$2,088	$4,554
1985–86	3,479	5,413
1987–88	3,927	5,738
1989–90	4,643	6,190
1990–91	4,902	6,197
1991–92	5,023	6,153
1992–93	5,160	6,129
1993–94	5,327	6,168
1994–95	5,529	6,223
1995–96	5,689	6,234
1996–97	5,923	6,311
1997–98	6,189	6,478
1998–99[2]	6,408	6,593
1999–2000[2]	6,584	6,584

[1] Constant 1999–2000 dollars based on the Consumer Price Index, prepared by the Bureau of Labor Statistics, U.S. Department of Labor.
[2] Estimated.

SOURCE: Charlene M. Hoffman, "Table 34.—Current expenditures per pupil in fall enrollment: 1979–80 to 1999–2000," in *Mini-Digest of Education Statistics, 2000,* NCES 2001-046, U.S. Department of Education, National Center for Education Statistics, Washington, DC, August 2001

TABLE 2.8

Total public direct expenditures on education as a percentage of the gross domestic product, selected countries, 1985–97

Country	All institutions[1]					Primary and secondary institutions					Higher education institutions				
	1985	1990	1994	1995	1997[2]	1985	1990	1994	1995	1997[2]	1985	1990	1994	1995	1997[2]
Average for year	**5.3**	**4.9**	**5.0**	**4.9**	**5.1**	**3.7**	**3.5**	**3.5**	**3.4**	**3.6**	**1.1**	**1.0**	**1.0**	**0.9**	**1.0**
Average for countries reporting data for all years	**5.3**	**5.3**	**5.4**	**5.3**	**5.2**	**3.7**	**3.7**	**3.7**	**3.6**	**3.6**	**1.1**	**1.1**	**1.1**	**1.1**	**1.0**
Australia	5.4	4.3	4.4	4.5	4.3	3.5	3.2	3.2	3.2	3.3	1.7	1.0	1.1	1.2	1.0
Austria	5.6	5.2	—	5.3	6.0	3.7	3.6	—	3.8	4.2	1.0	1.0	—	0.9	1.3
Belgium[3]	6.3	4.8	5.5	5.0	4.8	4.0	3.4	3.8	3.4	3.3	1.0	0.8	1.0	0.9	0.8
Canada	6.1	5.4	6.0	5.8	5.4	4.1	3.7	4.2	4.0	4.0	2.0	1.5	1.6	1.5	1.2
Czech Republic	—	—	—	4.8	4.5	—	—	—	3.4	3.2	—	—	0.8	0.7	0.7
Denmark	6.2	6.2	6.5	6.5	6.5	4.7	4.4	4.3	4.2	4.3	1.2	1.3	1.4	1.3	1.1
Finland	5.8	6.4	6.6	6.6	6.3	—	4.3	4.4	4.2	3.8	—	1.2	1.5	1.7	1.7
France	—	5.1	5.6	5.8	5.8	—	3.7	4.0	4.1	4.1	—	0.8	0.9	1.0	1.0
Germany[4]	4.6	—	4.5	4.5	4.5	2.8	—	2.9	2.9	2.9	1.0	—	0.9	1.0	1.0
Greece	—	—	3.1	3.7	3.5	—	—	2.4	2.8	2.5	—	—	0.7	0.8	1.0
Hungary	—	5.0	5.7	4.9	4.5	—	3.5	3.9	3.3	2.9	—	0.8	0.9	0.8	0.8
Iceland	—	4.3	4.5	4.5	5.1	—	3.3	3.4	3.4	3.9	—	0.6	0.7	0.7	0.7
Ireland	5.6	4.7	5.1	4.7	4.5	4.0	3.3	3.6	3.3	3.4	0.9	0.9	1.0	0.9	1.0
Italy	4.7	5.8	4.6	4.5	4.6	3.2	4.1	3.3	3.2	3.4	0.6	1.0	0.7	0.7	0.6
Japan	—	3.6	3.8	3.6	3.6	—	2.9	2.9	2.8	2.8	—	0.4	0.5	0.4	0.5
Korea	—	—	3.6	3.6	4.4	—	—	2.9	3.0	3.4	—	—	0.3	0.3	0.5
Luxembourg	—	—	—	4.3	4.2	—	—	—	4.2	4.1	—	—	—	0.1	0.1
Mexico	—	3.2	4.5	4.6	4.5	—	2.2	3.2	3.4	3.3	—	0.7	0.9	0.8	0.8
Netherlands	6.2	5.7	4.5	4.6	4.3	4.1	3.6	3.0	3.0	2.9	1.5	1.6	1.2	1.1	1.1
New Zealand	—	5.5	5.4	5.3	6.1	—	3.9	3.9	3.8	4.7	—	1.2	1.1	1.1	1.0
Norway	5.1	6.2	6.9	6.8	6.6	4.0	4.1	4.1	4.1	4.4	0.7	1.1	1.4	1.5	1.3
Poland	—	—	—	5.2	5.8	—	—	—	3.3	3.8	—	—	—	0.8	1.2
Portugal	—	—	5.3	5.4	5.8	—	—	3.9	4.1	4.4	—	—	0.8	1.0	1.0
Russia	—	—	—	3.4	—	—	—	—	1.9	—	—	—	—	0.7	—
Spain	3.6	4.2	4.8	4.8	4.7	2.9	3.2	3.5	3.5	3.5	0.4	0.7	0.8	0.8	0.9
Sweden	—	5.3	6.6	6.6	6.8	—	4.4	4.5	4.4	4.7	—	1.0	1.5	1.6	1.6
Switzerland	4.9	5.0	5.5	5.5	5.4	4.0	3.7	4.1	4.1	4.0	0.9	1.0	1.1	1.1	1.1
Turkey	—	3.2	3.3	2.2	—	—	2.3	2.1	1.4	—	—	0.9	1.2	0.8	0.8
United Kingdom	4.9	4.3	4.6	4.6	4.6	3.1	3.5	3.8	3.8	3.4	1.0	0.7	0.7	0.7	0.7
United States	4.7	5.3	4.8	5.0	5.2	3.2	3.8	3.4	3.5	3.5	1.3	1.4	1.1	1.1	1.4

[1]Includes preprimary and other expenditures not classified by level.
[2]Due to the implementation of a new classification system post-1996 data are not comaparable with earlier data.
[3]Flemish Belgium data only.
[4]Data for 1985 refer to West Germany (Federal Republic of Germany before unification).
NOTE: Direct public expenditure on educational services includes both amounts spent directly by governments to hire educational personnel and to procure other resources, and amounts provided by governments to public or private institutions. Figures for 1985 also include transfers and payments to private entities, and thus are not strictly comparable with later figures.

SOURCE: Thomas D. Snyder and Charlene M. Hoffman, "Table 412.—Total public direct expenditures on education as a percentage of gross domestic product: Selected countries, 1985 to 1997," in *Digest of Education Statistics, 2000,* NCES 2001-034, U.S. Department of Education, National Center for Education Statistics, Washington, DC, January 2001

FIGURE 2.4

Educational expenditures per student in relation to GDP per capita, by level of education for selected OECD countries, 1997

Expenditures
per student

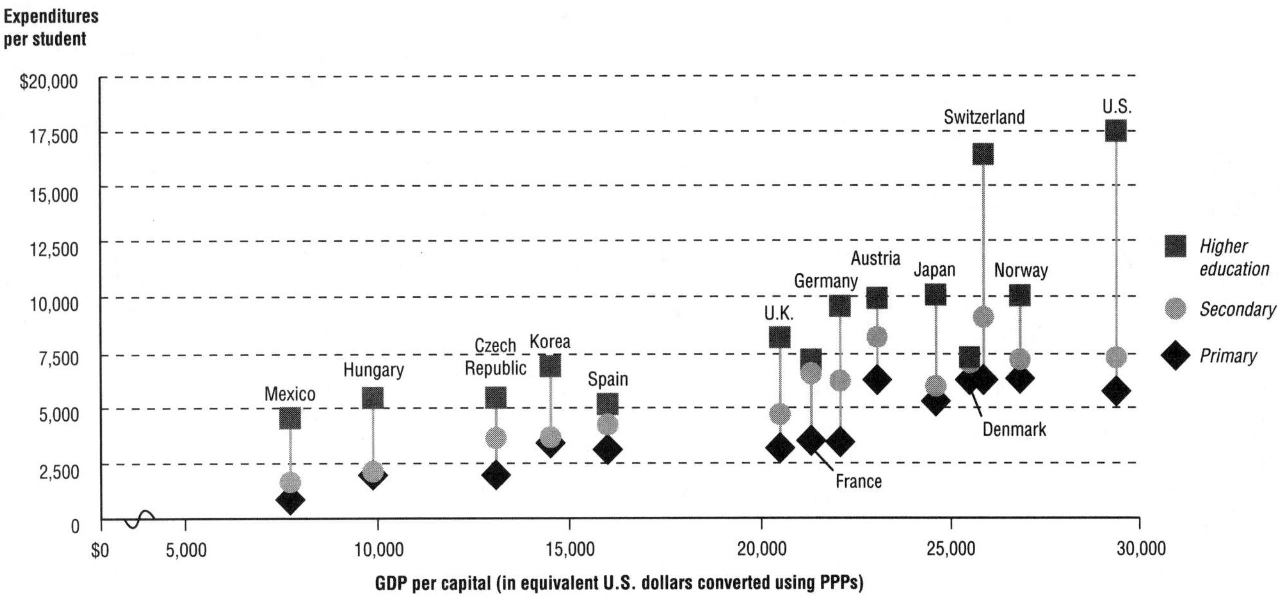

NOTE: Per student expenditures are calculated based on public and private full-time-equivalent (FTE) enrollment figures and expenditures from both public and private sources where data are available. Purchasing Power Parity (PPP) indices are used to convert other currencies to U.S. dollars. Within-country consumer price indices are used to adjust the PPP indices to account for inflation because the fiscal year has a different starting date in different countries.
GPD – gross domestic product
OECD – Organisation for Economic Co-Operation and Development

SOURCE: John Wirt, et al., "International Expenditures for Education: Educational expenditures per student in relation to GDP per capita, by level of education for selected OECD countries: 1997," in *The Condition of Education, 2001,* NCES 2001-072, U.S. Department of Education, National Center for Education Statistics, Washington, DC, June 2001

TABLE 2.9

Number and percentage distribution of private schools, students, and FTE teachers, by NCES typology and selected characteristics, 1999–2000

Selected characteristics	Schools		Students		FTE teachers	
	Number	Percent	Number	Percent	Number	Percent
Total	27,223	100.0	5,162,684	100.0	395,317	100.0
NCES typology						
Catholic	8,102	29.8	2,511,040	48.6	149,600	37.8
Parochial	4,607	16.9	1,307,461	25.3	72,497	18.3
Diocesan	2,598	9.5	835,327	16.2	49,415	12.5
Private	897	3.3	368,252	7.1	27,689	7.0
Other religious	13,232	48.6	1,843,580	35.7	152,915	38.7
Conservative Christian	4,989	18.3	773,237	15.0	60,481	15.3
Affiliated	3,531	13.0	553,530	10.7	47,433	12.0
Unaffiliated	4,712	17.3	516,813	10.0	45,001	11.4
Nonsectarian	5,889	21.6	808,063	15.7	92,801	23.5
Regular	2,494	9.2	546,649	10.6	58,279	14.7
Special emphasis	2,131	7.8	175,140	3.4	19,981	5.1
Special education	1,264	4.6	86,274	1.7	14,542	3.7
School level						
Elementary	16,530	60.7	2,831,372	54.8	187,833	47.5
Secondary	2,538	9.3	806,639	15.6	62,737	15.9
Combined	8,155	30.0	1,524,673	29.5	144,746	36.6
Program emphasis						
Regular elementary/ secondary	22,263	81.8	4,751,634	92.0	346,300	87.6
Montessori	1,190	4.4	77,264	1.5	8,462	2.1
Special program emphasis	606	2.2	111,219	2.2	10,949	2.8
Special education	1,409	5.2	95,261	1.9	15,978	4.0
Vocational/technical	—	—	—	—	—	—
Alternative	1,617	5.9	120,233	2.3	13,000	3.3
Early childhood	133	0.5	5,534	0.1	532	0.1
Size						
Less than 50	7,565	27.8	196,309	3.8	26,329	6.7
50–149	7,738	28.4	716,129	13.9	71,676	18.1
150–299	6,571	24.1	1,424,018	27.6	102,457	25.9
300–499	3,219	11.8	1,228,631	23.8	84,086	21.3
500–749	1,352	5.0	805,490	15.6	54,078	13.7
750 or more	778	2.9	792,106	15.3	56,691	14.3
Region						
Northeast	6,452	23.7	1,294,847	25.1	103,805	26.3
Midwest	6,991	25.7	1,345,446	26.1	91,444	23.1
South	8,240	30.3	1,575,784	30.5	131,192	33.2
West	5,540	20.4	946,608	18.3	68,876	17.4
Community type						
Central city	10,825	39.8	2,540,516	49.2	189,984	48.1
Urban fringe/large town	10,359	38.1	2,051,094	39.7	155,436	39.3
Rural/small town	6,040	22.2	571,074	11.1	49,897	12.6

— Too few sample cases for a reliable estimate.
NOTE: Details may not add to totals due to rounding or missing values in cells with too few sample cases.

SOURCE: Stephen P. Broughman and Lenore A. Colaciello, "Table 1.—Number and percentage distribution of private schools, students and FTE teachers, by NCES typology and selected characteristics: United States, 1999–2000," in *Private School Universe Survey: 1999–2000*, NCES 2001-330, U.S. Department of Education, National Center for Education Statistics, Washington, DC, August 2001

TABLE 2.10

Public elementary and secondary students, schools, pupil/teacher ratios, and finances by type of locale, 1997 and 1998

Characteristic	Total	Central city of large MSA[1]	Central city of mid-size MSA[2]	Urban fringe of large MSA[3]	Urban fringe of mid-size MSA[4]	Large town[5]	Small town[6]	Rural outside an MSA[7]	Rural within an MSA[8]
				Schools, enrollment, and teachers, 1998–99					
Enrollment, in thousands	46,387	7,070	6,443	15,291	5,545	624	4,928	4,198	2,288
Schools	90,874	10,847	11,476	24,206	10,302	1,305	12,124	15,820	4,786
Average school size[9]	524	693	575	643	549	495	418	271	483
Pupil/teacher ratio[10]	16.9	17.9	16.8	17.6	16.7	16.5	16.0	14.9	16.4
Enrollment (percentage distribution)	100.0	15.2	13.9	33.0	12.0	1.3	10.6	9.0	4.9
Schools (percent distribution)	100.0	11.9	12.6	26.6	11.3	1.4	13.3	17.4	5.3
				Revenues and expenditures, 1996–97 (in millions)					
Total revenue	$299,178	$48,530	$41,375	$101,754	$33,419	$3,591	$29,297	$26,266	$14,943
Federal[11]	21,391	5,282	3,540	4,809	2,046	305	2,441	2,356	612
Impact aid	717	41	80	153	72	10	92	258	11
Bilingual education	24	6	4	4	2	0	3	4	0
Indian education	47	3	4	5	2	2	11	20	0
Children with disabilites	2,411	474	359	714	263	33	271	193	104
Eisenhower science awards	170	37	27	46	17	3	19	15	5
Drug Free schools	296	69	49	85	28	4	29	22	10
Chapter 2 (block grants)	265	69	42	64	25	3	28	26	8
Vocational education	520	132	84	115	49	8	64	50	17
Title I	6,376	1,729	1,119	1,166	590	94	790	726	161
Other and unclassified	10,567	2,721	1,772	2,458	998	147	1,135	1,042	293
State	145,932	23,103	21,642	43,709	17,176	1,987	16,170	14,866	7,278
State school lunch programs	338	59	42	104	45	4	38	31	15
Local	131,854	20,145	16,194	53,235	14,197	1,300	10,685	9,045	7,053
Property tax[12]	89,936	11,499	10,347	39,272	9,501	922	7,737	6,304	4,356
Parent government contribution[12]	22,843	5,982	3,308	7,681	2,400	142	922	972	1,435
Lunch sales	4,483	390	546	1,635	606	59	510	452	286
Transportation	41	3	5	20	4	1	4	3	2
Other	14,552	2,272	1,988	4,628	1,687	176	1,513	1,314	974
Total revenue (percentage distribution)	100.0	100.0	100.0	100.0	100.0	100.0	100.0	100.0	100.0
Federal	7.2	10.9	8.6	4.7	6.1	8.5	8.3	9.0	4.1
State	48.8	47.6	52.3	43.0	51.4	55.3	55.2	56.6	48.7
Local	44.1	41.5	39.1	52.3	42.5	36.2	36.5	34.4	47.2
Total expenditures	$297,328	$48,018	$40,546	$102,142	$33,252	$3,533	$29,200	$25,602	$15,036
Current expenditures	263,927	42,839	36,622	90,154	29,097	3,205	26,146	22,960	12,903
Instruction	163,804	26,765	22,687	55,787	18,154	2,001	16,334	14,079	7,996
Operation and maintenance	25,685	4,357	3,584	8,945	2,740	321	2,413	2,130	1,196
Food service	11,068	1,837	1,561	3,166	1,323	149	1,311	1,219	501
Other	63,370	9,880	8,790	22,257	6,881	734	6,089	5,532	3,209
Interest on school debt	6,558	1,004	778	2,458	801	69	561	449	438
Capital outlay	26,843	4,176	3,146	9,529	3,353	258	2,493	2,193	1,695
Current expenditures (percentage distribution)	100.0	100.0	100.0	100.0	100.0	100.0	100.0	100.0	100.0
Instruction	62.1	62.5	61.9	61.9	62.4	62.4	62.5	61.3	62.0
Operation and maintenance	9.7	10.2	9.8	9.9	9.4	10.0	9.2	9.3	9.3
Food service	4.2	4.3	4.3	3.5	4.5	4.7	5.0	5.3	3.9
Other	24.0	23.1	24.0	24.7	23.6	22.9	23.3	24.1	24.9
Current expenditure per student	$5,690	$6,059	$5,684	$5,896	$5,247	$5,141	$5,305	$5,470	$5,640
Instruction expenditure per student	3,531	3,786	3,521	3,648	3,274	3,210	3,314	3,354	3,495

[1] Central city of metropolitan statistical area (MSA) with population of 400,000 or more or a population density of 6,000 or more persons per square mile.
[2] Central city of an MSA but not designated as a large central city.
[3] Place within the MSA of a large central city.
[4] Place within the MSA of a mid-size central city.
[5] Place not within an MSA but with population of 25,000 or more and defined as urban.
[6] Place not within an MSA with a population of at least 2,500, but less than 25,000.
[7] Place with a population of less than 2,500 outside an MSA.
[8] Place with a population of less than 2,500 within an MSA.
[9] Average for schools reporting enrollment.
[10] Ratio for schools reporting both FTE teachers and fall enrollment data.
[11] Federal revenue includes data for 1996 for California, Georgia, Massachusetts, and Ohio.
[12] Property tax and parent government contributions are determined on the basis of independence or dependence of the local school system and are mutually exclusive.
NOTE: Enrollment of schools were used to determine a classification for school districts. The locale classification of the predominate enrollment category was used for the entire school district.

SOURCE: Thomas D. Snyder and Charlene M. Hoffman, "Table 86.—Public elementary and secondary students, schools, pupil/teacher ratios, and finances, by type of locale: 1997 and 1998," in *Digest of Education Statistics, 2000*, NCES 2001-034, U.S. Department of Education, National Center for Education Statistics, Washington, DC, January 2001

TABLE 2.11

Public and private elementary and secondary teachers and pupil/teacher ratios, by level, fall 1955 to fall 1999

Year	Public and private elementary and secondary			Public elementary and secondary			Private elementary and secondary		
	Kindergarten to grade 12	Elementary	Secondary	Kindergarten to grade 12	Elementary	Secondary	Kindergarten to grade 12	Elementary	Secondary
	Number of teachers, in thousands								
1955	1,286	827	459	1,141	733	408	[1] 145	[1] 94	[1] 51
1960	1,600	991	609	1,408	858	550	[1] 192	[1] 133	[1] 59
1965	1,933	1,112	822	1,710	965	746	223	147	76
1970	2,292	1,283	1,009	2,059	1,130	929	233	153	80
1971	2,293	1,263	1,030	2,063	1,111	952	[1] 230	[1] 152	[1] 78
1972	2,337	1,296	1,041	2,106	1,142	964	[1] 231	[1] 154	[1] 77
1973	2,372	1,308	1,064	2,136	1,151	985	[1] 236	[1] 157	[1] 79
1974	2,410	1,330	1,079	2,165	1,166	998	[1] 245	[1] 164	[1] 81
1975	2,453	1,353	1,100	2,198	1,181	1,017	[1] 255	[1] 172	[1] 83
1976	2,457	1,351	1,106	2,189	1,168	1,021	268	183	85
1977	2,488	1,375	1,113	2,209	1,185	1,024	279	190	89
1978	2,479	1,376	1,103	2,207	1,191	1,016	272	185	87
1979	2,461	1,379	1,082	2,185	1,191	994	[1] 276	[1] 188	[1] 88
1980	2,485	1,401	1,084	2,184	1,189	995	301	212	89
1981	2,440	1,404	1,037	2,127	1,183	945	[1] 313	[1] 221	[1] 92
1982	2,458	1,413	1,045	2,133	1,182	951	[1] 325	[1] 231	[1] 94
1983	2,476	1,426	1,050	2,139	1,186	953	337	240	97
1984	2,508	1,451	1,057	2,168	1,208	960	[1] 340	[1] 243	[1] 97
1985	2,549	1,483	1,066	2,206	1,237	969	343	246	97
1986	2,592	1,521	1,071	2,244	1,271	973	[1] 348	[1] 250	[1] 98
1987	2,631	1,563	1,068	2,279	1,306	973	[1] 353	[1] 257	[1] 95
1988	2,668	1,604	1,064	2,323	1,353	970	[1] 345	[1] 251	[1] 94
1989	2,734	1,662	1,072	2,357	1,387	970	[1] 377	[1] 275	[1] 102
1990	2,753	1,683	1,070	2,398	1,429	969	[1] 355	[1] 254	[1] 101
1991	2,787	1,722	1,065	2,432	1,468	964	[1] 355	[1] 254	[1] 101
1992	2,822	1,752	1,070	2,459	1,492	967	[1] 363	[1] 260	[1] 103
1993	2,870	1,775	1,095	2,504	1,513	991	[1] 366	[1] 262	[1] 104
1994	2,926	1,791	1,135	2,552	1,525	1,027	[1] 374	[1] 266	[1] 108
1995	2,978	1,794	1,184	2,598	1,525	1,073	[1] 380	[1] 269	[1] 111
1996	3,054	1,856	1,198	2,667	1,582	1,085	[1] 387	[1] 274	[1] 113
1997	3,134	1,928	1,206	2,746	1,653	1,093	[2] 388	[2] 275	[2] 113
1998	3,217	1,978	1,239	2,826	1,701	1,125	[2] 391	[2] 277	[2] 114
1999 [2]	3,284	2,014	1,270	2,887	1,733	1,154	[2] 397	[2] 281	[2] 116
	Pupil/teacher ratios								
1955	27.4	31.4	20.3	26.9	30.2	20.9	[1] 31.7	[1] 40.4	[1] 15.7
1960	26.4	29.4	21.4	25.8	28.4	21.7	[1] 30.7	[1] 36.1	[1] 18.6
1965	25.1	28.4	20.6	24.7	27.6	20.8	28.3	33.3	18.4
1970	22.4	24.6	19.5	22.3	24.3	19.8	23.0	26.5	16.4
1971	22.4	25.0	19.1	22.3	24.9	19.3	[1] 22.6	[1] 25.7	[1] 16.7
1972	21.7	23.9	18.9	21.7	23.9	19.1	[1] 21.6	[1] 24.0	[1] 16.9
1973	21.3	23.0	19.1	21.3	23.0	19.3	[1] 21.2	[1] 23.6	[1] 16.5
1974	20.8	22.6	18.5	20.8	22.6	18.7	[1] 20.4	[1] 22.6	[1] 16.0
1975	20.3	21.7	18.6	20.4	21.7	18.8	[1] 19.6	[1] 21.5	[1] 15.7
1976	20.1	21.7	18.3	20.2	21.8	18.5	19.3	20.9	15.8
1977	19.6	20.9	17.9	19.7	21.1	18.2	18.4	20.0	15.1
1978	19.2	20.9	17.1	19.3	21.0	17.3	18.7	20.2	15.6
1979	19.0	20.5	17.0	19.1	20.6	17.2	[1] 18.1	[1] 19.7	[1] 14.8
1980	18.6	20.1	16.6	18.7	20.4	16.8	17.7	18.8	15.0
1981	18.7	20.0	16.8	18.8	20.3	16.9	[1] 17.6	[1] 18.6	[1] 15.2
1982	18.4	19.8	16.4	18.6	20.2	16.6	[1] 17.2	[1] 18.2	[1] 14.9
1983	18.2	19.6	16.2	18.4	19.9	16.4	17.0	18.0	14.4
1984	17.9	19.3	16.0	18.1	19.7	16.1	[1] 16.8	[1] 17.7	[1] 14.4
1985	17.6	19.1	15.6	17.9	19.5	15.8	16.2	17.1	14.0

TABLE 2.11

Public and private elementary and secondary teachers and pupil/teacher ratios, by level, fall 1955 to fall 1999 [CONTINUED]

Year	Public and private elementary and secondary			Public elementary and secondary			Private elementary and secondary		
	Kindergarten to grade 12	Elementary	Secondary	Kindergarten to grade 12	Elementary	Secondary	Kindergarten to grade 12	Elementary	Secondary
	Pupil/teacher ratios								
1986	17.4	18.8	15.5	17.7	19.3	15.7	[1]15.7	[1]16.5	[1]13.6
1987	17.3	18.8	15.0	17.6	19.3	15.2	[1]15.5	[1]16.5	[1]13.1
1988	17.0	18.6	14.7	17.3	19.0	14.9	[1]15.2	[1]16.1	[1]12.8
1989	16.8	18.4	14.3	17.2	19.0	14.6	[1]14.2	[1]15.1	[1]11.7
1990	16.9	18.5	14.3	17.2	18.9	14.6	[1]14.7	[1]16.1	[1]11.3
1991	17.0	18.4	14.6	17.3	18.8	15.0	[1]14.6	[1]16.0	[1]11.1
1992	17.1	18.4	14.8	17.4	18.8	15.2	[1]14.8	[1]16.2	[1]11.3
1993	17.1	18.5	14.7	17.4	18.9	15.1	[1]14.9	[1]16.3	[1]11.5
1994	17.0	18.6	14.4	17.3	19.0	14.8	[1]15.0	[1]16.4	[1]11.4
1995	17.0	18.9	14.0	17.3	19.3	14.4	[1]14.9	[1]16.6	[1]10.8
1996	16.8	18.4	14.2	17.1	18.9	14.4	[1]14.9	[1]16.4	[1]11.5
1997	16.6	18.1	14.2	16.8	18.3	14.5	[2]15.1	[2]16.6	[2]11.6
1998	16.3	17.8	14.0	16.5	18.0	14.2	[2]15.2	[2]16.6	[2]11.6
1999 [2]	16.0	17.4	13.9	16.2	17.6	14.1	[2]15.0	[2]16.4	[2]11.5

[1]Estimated.
[2]Projected.
NOTE: Data for teachers are expressed in full-time equivalents. Distribution of unclassified teachers by level is estimated. Distribution of elementary and secondary school teachers by level is determined by reporting units. Kindergarten includes a relatively small number of nursery school teachers and students. Some data have been revised from previously published figures. Detail may not sum to totals due to rounding.

SOURCE: Thomas D. Snyder and Charlene M. Hoffman, "Table 65.—Public and private elementary and secondary teachers and pupil/teacher ratios, by level: Fall 1955 to fall 1999," in *Digest of Education Statistics, 2000,* NCES 2001-034, U.S. Department of Education, National Center for Education Statistics, Washington, DC, January 2001

TABLE 2.12

Public elementary and secondary schools, by type and size of school, 1998–99

Enrollment size of school	Number of schools, by type						Enrollment, by type of school[1]					
			Secondary[4]		Combined				Secondary[4]		Combined	
	Total[2]	Elemen-tary[3]	All schools	Regular schools[6]	elementary/ secondary[5]	Other[2]	Total[2]	Elemen-tary[3]	All schools	Regular schools[6]	elementary/ secondary[5]	Other[2]
Total	91,062	63,574	22,103	18,571	3,770	1,615	46,398,360	30,299,964	15,031,195	14,538,776	993,968	73,233
Percent[7]	100.00	100.00	100.00	100.00	100.00	100.00	100.00	100.00	100.00	100.00	100.00	100.00
Under 100	10.14	6.23	15.37	8.62	41.96	60.77	0.89	0.63	0.99	0.60	5.89	19.36
100 to 199	9.50	8.70	10.57	9.69	16.45	18.42	2.72	2.76	2.20	1.82	8.20	19.00
200 to 299	11.17	12.22	8.31	8.45	9.53	10.31	5.38	6.48	2.92	2.68	8.11	18.77
300 to 399	13.11	15.41	7.44	7.89	7.01	5.34	8.75	11.28	3.66	3.50	8.41	13.76
400 to 499	13.17	15.75	7.05	7.72	5.17	2.39	11.29	14.80	4.47	4.40	7.98	7.75
500 to 599	11.52	13.69	6.33	7.00	5.29	1.29	12.05	15.68	4.92	4.90	9.96	5.12
600 to 699	8.48	9.69	5.76	6.38	4.30	0.00	10.47	13.09	5.28	5.25	9.54	0.00
700 to 799	6.20	6.78	5.25	5.83	2.45	0.18	8.84	10.57	5.56	5.55	6.31	1.07
800 to 999	7.10	6.86	8.65	9.74	3.04	0.55	12.05	12.69	10.98	11.11	9.40	3.48
1,000 to 1,499	6.11	4.09	12.76	14.44	3.07	0.37	13.92	9.94	22.12	22.50	12.31	3.59
1,500 to 1,999	2.07	0.49	6.98	7.92	1.08	0.00	6.76	1.71	16.99	17.32	6.24	0.00
2,000 to 2,999	1.19	0.07	4.68	5.33	0.38	0.18	5.36	0.34	15.62	15.98	3.19	2.83
3,000 or more	0.22	0.01	0.86	0.97	0.26	0.18	1.52	0.05	4.29	4.39	4.45	5.28
Average enrollment[7]	524	478	707	786	290	135	524	478	707	786	290	135

[1] These enrollment data should be regarded as approximations only. Totals differ from those reported in other tables because this table represents data reported by schools rather than by states or school districts. Percent distribution and average enrollment calculations exclude data for schools not reporting enrollment.

[2] Includes special education, alternative, and other schools not classified by grade span.

[3] Includes schools beginning with grade 6 or below and with no grade higher than 8.

[4] Includes schools with no grade lower than 7.

[5] Includes schools beginning with grade 6 or below and ending with grade 9 or above.

[6] Excludes special education schools, vocational schools, and alternative schools.

[7] Data are for schools reporting their enrollment size.

NOTE: Detail may not sum to totals due to rounding.

SOURCE: Thomas D. Snyder and Charlene M. Hoffman, "Table 94.—Public elementary and secondary schools, by type and size of school: 1998–99," in *Digest of Education Statistics, 2000,* NCES 2001-034, U.S. Department of Education, National Center for Education Statistics, Washington, DC, January 2001

TABLE 2.13

Student membership and current expenditures per pupil in membership for public elementary and secondary schools, by function and state, 1998–99

State	Fall 1998 student membership	Current expendiures per pupil in membership			
		Total	Instruction	Support services	Noninstruction
United States	[1]46,538,585	[1]$6,508	[1]$4,013	[1]$2,213	[1]$282
Alabama	[1]747,980	[1]5,188	[1]3,210	[1]1,618	[1]359
Alaska	135,373	8,404	[2]4,757	3,372	274
Arizona	848,262	4,672	[2]2,806	1,633	233
Arkansas	452,256	4,956	3,176	1,437	343
California	[1]5,926,037	[1]5,801	[1]3,539	[1]2,031	[1]232
Colorado	699,135	5,923	3,448	2,262	213
Connecticut	544,698	[1]9,318	5,922	2,941	[1]455
Delaware	113,262	7,706	4,716	2,634	356
District of Columbia	71,889	[1]9,650	[1]4,374	[2]4,887	389
Florida	2,337,633	5,790	3,390	2,116	284
Georgia	1,401,291	6,092	3,810	1,946	336
Hawaii	188,069	6,081	3,818	1,861	402
Idaho	244,722	5,066	3,138	1,707	221
Illinois	2,011,530	6,762	4,097	2,431	235
Indiana	989,001	6,772	4,230	2,254	288
Iowa	498,214	6,243	3,671	2,105	468
Kansas	472,353	6,015	3,456	2,258	301
Kentucky	655,687	5,560	3,431	1,816	313
Louisiana	768,734	[1]5,548	3,352	1,748	[1]448
Maine	211,051	7,155	4,813	2,093	249
Maryland	841,671	7,326	4,504	2,486	336
Massachusetts	962,317	8,260	5,503	2,500	256
Michigan	1,720,287	7,432	4,320	2,895	217
Minnesota	856,455	6,791	4,259	2,253	279
Mississippi	502,379	4,565	2,755	1,486	324
Missouri	913,494	5,855	3,605	1,999	250
Montana	159,988	5,974	3,736	1,994	243
Nebraska	291,140	6,256	[2]3,935	1,850	[2]471
Nevada	311,061	5,587	3,346	2,068	174
New Hampshire	204,713	6,433	[2]4,196	[2]2,013	[2]224
New Jersey	1,268,996	10,145	6,072	3,775	298
New Mexico	328,753	5,440	3,089	2,089	263
New York	2,877,143	9,344	6,335	2,756	253
North Carolina	1,254,821	5,656	3,553	1,770	334
North Dakota	114,927	5,442	3,325	1,674	443
Ohio	1,842,163	6,627	3,908	2,478	241
Oklahoma	628,492	5,303	3,183	1,777	343
Oregon	542,809	6,828	4,045	2,549	233
Pennsylvania	1,816,414	7,450	4,721	2,452	277
Rhode Island	154,785	8,294	5,503	2,564	227
South Carolina	[1]664,600	[1]5,656	[1]3,375	[1]1,944	[1]337
South Dakota	132,495	5,259	3,202	1,776	282
Tennessee	[1]905,454	[1]5,123	[1]3,350	[1]1,516	[1]258
Texas	3,945,367	5,685	3,440	1,944	301
Utah	481,176	4,210	2,762	1,194	254
Vermont	105,120	7,541	4,875	2,455	211
Virginia	1,124,022	[1]6,350	3,862	2,156	[1]332
Washington	998,053	[2]6,110	[2]3,654	2,159	297
West Virginia	297,530	6,677	4,137	2,147	393
Wisconsin	879,542	7,527	4,706	2,589	233
Wyoming	95,241	6,842	4,106	2,493	242
Outlying areas					
American Samoa	15,372	2,283	977	861	445
Guam	32,222	—	—	—	—
Northern Marianas	9,498	5,312	4,282	680	350
Puerto Rico	613,862	3,298	2,258	662	378
Virgin Islands	20,976	6,983	4,276	2,375	331

[1]Value contains imputation for missing data.
[2]Value affected by redistribution of reported expenditure values for missing data items.
— Data not available.
NOTE: Detail may not add to totals due to rounding. National figures do not include outlying areas.

SOURCE: Frank Johnson, "Table 5—Student membership and current expenditures per pupil in membership for public elementary and secondary schools, by function and state: School year 1998–99," in *Statistics in Brief: Revenues and Expenditures for Public Elementary and Secondary Education: School Year 1998–99*, NCES 2001-321, U.S. Department of Education, National Center for Education Statistics, March 2001

FIGURE 2.5

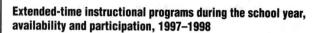

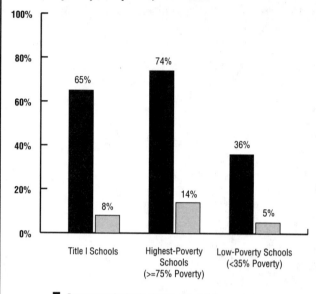

Extended-time instructional programs during the school year, availability and participation, 1997–1998

■ *Percentage of schools offering extended time programs*

□ *Percentage of students served in extended time programs*

NOTE: Nearly two-thirds of all Title I schools (65 percent) offered before-school, after-school, or weekend instructional programs, but these programs served only 8 percent of all students.

SOURCE: "Exhibit 25 Extended-Time Instructional Programs During the School Year: Availability and Participation, 1997–98," in *High Standards for All Students: A Report from the National Assessment of Title I on Progress and Challenges Since the 1994 Reauthorization,* U.S. Department of Education, Planning and Evaluation Service, Washington, DC, January 2001

TABLE 2.14

High school graduates compared with population 17 years of age, by sex and control of school, 1869–70 to 1999–2000

[Numbers in thousands]

School year	Population 17 years old[1]	High school graduates Total[2]	Sex Male	Sex Female	Control Public[3]	Control Private[4]	Graduates as a percent of 17-year-old population
1869–70	815	16	7	9	—	—	2.0
1879–80	946	24	11	13	—	—	2.5
1889–90	1,259	44	19	25	22	22	3.5
1899–1900	1,489	95	38	57	62	33	6.4
1909–10	1,786	156	64	93	111	45	8.8
1919–20	1,855	311	124	188	231	80	16.8
1929–30	2,296	667	300	367	592	75	29.0
1939–40	2,403	1,221	579	643	1,143	78	50.8
1947–48	2,261	1,190	563	627	1,073	117	52.6
1949–50	2,034	1,200	571	629	1,063	136	59.0
1951–52	2,086	1,197	569	627	1,056	141	57.4
1953–54	2,135	1,276	613	664	1,129	147	59.8
1955–56	2,242	1,415	680	735	1,252	163	63.1
1956–57	2,272	1,434	690	744	1,270	164	63.1
1957–58	2,325	1,506	725	781	1,332	174	64.8
1958–59	2,458	1,627	784	843	1,435	192	66.2
1959–60	2,672	1,858	895	963	1,627	231	69.5
1960–61	2,892	1,964	955	1,009	1,725	239	67.9
1961–62	2,768	1,918	938	980	1,678	240	69.3
1962–63	2,740	1,943	956	987	1,710	233	70.9
1963–64	2,978	2,283	1,120	1,163	2,008	275	76.7
1964–65	3,684	2,658	1,311	1,347	2,360	298	72.1
1965–66	3,489	2,665	1,323	1,342	2,367	298	76.4
1966–67	3,500	2,672	1,328	1,344	2,374	298	76.3
1967–68	3,532	2,695	1,338	1,357	2,395	300	76.3
1968–69	3,659	2,822	1,399	1,423	2,522	300	77.1
1969–70	3,757	2,889	1,430	1,459	2,589	300	76.9
1970–71	3,872	2,938	1,454	1,484	2,638	300	75.9
1971–72	3,973	3,002	1,487	1,515	2,700	302	75.6
1972–73	4,049	3,035	1,500	1,535	2,729	306	75.0
1973–74	4,132	3,073	1,512	1,561	2,763	310	74.4
1974–75	4,256	3,133	1,542	1,591	2,823	310	73.6
1975–76	4,272	3,148	1,552	1,596	2,837	311	73.7
1976–77	4,272	3,152	1,548	1,604	2,837	315	73.8
1977–78	4,286	3,127	1,531	1,596	2,825	302	73.0
1978–79	4,327	3,101	1,517	1,584	2,801	300	71.7
1979–80	4,262	3,043	1,491	1,552	2,748	295	71.4
1980–81	4,212	3,020	1,483	1,537	2,725	295	71.7
1981–82	4,134	2,995	1,471	1,524	2,705	290	72.4
1982–83	3,962	2,888	1,437	1,451	2,598	290	72.9
1983–84	3,784	2,767	—	—	2,495	272	73.1
1984–85	3,699	2,677	—	—	2,414	263	72.4
1985–86	3,670	2,643	—	—	2,383	260	72.0
1986–87	3,754	2,694	—	—	2,429	265	71.8
1987–88	3,849	2,773	—	—	2,500	273	72.1
1988–89	3,842	2,727	—	—	2,459	268	71.0
1989–90	3,505	2,586	—	—	2,320	266	73.8
1990–91	3,421	2,503	—	—	2,235	268	73.2
1991–92	3,391	2,482	—	—	2,226	256	73.2
1992–93	3,447	2,490	—	—	2,233	257	72.2
1993–94	3,459	2,479	—	—	2,221	258	71.7
1994–95	3,588	2,538	—	—	2,274	264	70.7
1995–96	3,641	2,540	—	—	2,273	267	69.8
1996–97	3,773	2,634	—	—	2,358	276	69.8
1997–98	3,930	2,724	—	—	2,440	284	69.3
1998–99[5]	3,965	2,775	—	—	2,485	290	70.0
1999–2000[5]	4,019	2,839	—	—	2,545	294	70.6

—Not available.

[1]Derived from *Current Population Reports,* Series P-25. 17-year-old population adjusted to reflect October 17-year-old population.

[2]Includes graduates of public and private schools.

[3]Data for 1929–30 and preceding years are from *Statistics of Public High Schools* and exclude graduates of high schools which failed to report to the Office of Education.

[4]For most years, private school data have been estimated based on periodic private school surveys.

[5]Public high school graduates based on state estimates.

NOTE: Includes graduates of regular day school programs. Excludes graduates of other programs, when separately reported, and recipients of high school equivalency certificates. Some data have been revised from previously published figures. Detail may not sum to totals due to rounding.

SOURCE: Thomas D. Snyder and Charlene M. Hoffman, "Table 101.—High school graduates compared with population 17 years of age, by sex and control of school: 1869–70 to 1999–2000," in *Digest of Education Statistics, 2000,* NCES 2001-034, U.S. Department of Education, National Center for Education Statistics, Washington, DC, January 2001

TABLE 2.15

General Educational Development (GED) credentials issued, and number and age of test takers, United States and outlying areas, 1971– 99

Year	Number of credentials issued, in thousands[1]	Number completing test battery, in thousands[2]	Number of test takers, in thousands[3]	Percentage distribution of test takers, by age				
				19 years old or less	20- to 24-year-olds	25- to 29-year-olds	30- to 34-year-olds	35 years old or over
1971	227	—	377	—	—	—	—	—
1975	342	507	652	33	26	14	9	18
1980	488	708	779	37	27	13	8	15
1981	500	701	770	37	27	13	8	15
1982	494	692	756	37	28	13	8	15
1983	477	678	740	34	29	14	9	15
1984	437	613	676	32	28	15	9	16
1985	427	622	685	33	26	15	10	16
1986	439	648	713	33	26	15	10	16
1987	458	662	729	33	24	15	10	18
1988	421	617	701	36	23	14	10	17
1989	364	554	645	36	24	13	10	16
1990	419	628	727	35	25	14	10	17
1991	471	672	770	33	27	14	10	17
1992	465	653	754	32	28	13	11	16
1993	476	652	757	33	27	14	11	16
1994	499	684	793	34	26	13	10	16
1995	513	698	803	37	25	13	10	15
1996	514	733	842	40	25	13	9	15
1997	471	697	802	41	25	12	8	14
1998	496	693	796	43	25	11	8	14
1999	516	723	831	43	25	11	8	14

—Not available.

[1]Number of people receiving high school equivalency credentials based on the GED tests.

[2]Number of people completing the entire GED battery of five tests.

[3]Number of people taking the GED tests (one or more subtests).

NOTE: Detail may not sum to totals due to rounding.

SOURCE: Thomas D. Snyder and Charlene M. Hoffman, "Table 104.—General Educational Development (GED) credentials issued, and number and age of test takers: United States and outlying areas, 1971 to 1996," in *Digest of Education Statistics, 2000,* NCES 2001-034, U.S. Department of Education, National Center for Education Statistics, Washington, DC, January 2001

CHAPTER 3

EDUCATION FOR SPECIAL SCHOOL POPULATIONS

The right to public education is guaranteed to all children in the United States. For many children, however, acquiring an education that fits their special needs is not always easy. For the mentally or physically disabled, gifted or talented, or significantly disadvantaged, preparation for adulthood requires extra effort on the part of both the children and the education system. In addition, many students need vocational education to prepare them to go straight from high school to work or to further occupational training.

DISABLED CHILDREN

In 1975 Congress passed the Education for All Handicapped Children Act (PL 94-142, amended in 1983 by PL 98-199), which required schools to develop programs for disabled children. In 1992 the act was renamed the Individuals with Disabilities Education Act (IDEA). The act defines disabled children as those who are

> ... mentally retarded, hard of hearing, deaf, orthopedically impaired, other health impaired, speech and language impaired, visually impaired, seriously emotionally disturbed, children with specific learning disabilities who, by reason thereof, require special education and related services (20 U.S.C. 1401 [a][1]).

In its 1993 report *To Assure the Free Appropriate Public Education of All Children with Disabilities,* the U.S. Department of Education Office of Special Education Programs stated the purposes of IDEA:

- To help states develop early intervention services for infants and toddlers with disabilities and their families.

- To assure a free appropriate public education to all children and youth with disabilities.

- To protect the rights of disabled children and youth from birth to age 21 and their families.

- To help provide early intervention services and the education of all children with disabilities.

- To assess and assure the effectiveness of efforts to provide early intervention services and education of children with disabilities.

Change in the Number Served

As a result of the Individuals with Disabilities Education Act, an increasing number and percentage of students have been served in programs for the disabled. During 1998–99, about 6 million disabled children and youth from birth through age 21 were served. From 1976–77 to 1999, the number of children served under these programs rose by more than 2.3 million, a 64 percent increase. (See Table 3.1.) From 1989–90 to 1998–99, there was an increase of 30.3 percent in the number of students ages 6 through 21 served under IDEA. The largest change was in the number of students with other health impairments (319 percent increase), followed by specific learning disabilities (37 percent increase). The number of deaf or blind students decreased by 1.5 percent. (See Table 3.2.) The U.S. Department of Education reported that the proportion of children and youth with disabilities, as a percentage of public school enrollment, has risen steadily from 8.3 percent in 1976–77 to 13 percent in 1998–99. Some of this increase may reflect more effective identification of persons with disabilities.

The majority of students with disabilities served in federally supported programs in 1998–99 were those identified as having specific learning disabilities (46 percent), speech or language impairments (17.6 percent), mental retardation (9.9 percent), or serious emotional disturbance (7.6 percent). Students with multiple disabilities, hearing impairments, orthopedic impairments, other health impairments, visual impairments, deaf-blindness, and autism each made up about 4 percent or less of students with disabilities. (See Table 3.1.)

Learning Disabilities

The Education for All Handicapped Children Act defines a learning disability (LD) as "a disorder in one or

TABLE 3.1

Children 0 to 21 years old served in federally supported programs for the disabled, by type of disability, 1976–77 to 1998–99

Type of disability	1976–77	1980–81	1986–87	1987–88	1988–89	1989–90	1990–91	1991–92	1992–93	1993–94	1994–95	1995–96	1996–97	1997–98	1998–99
	Number served,[1] in thousands														
All disabilities	**3,694**	**4,144**	**4,376**	**4,439**	**4,529**	**4,631**	**4,761**	**4,941**	**5,111**	**5,309**	**5,378**	**5,573**	**5,729**	**5,903**	**6,055**
Specific learning disabilities	796	1,462	1,914	1,928	1,984	2,047	2,129	2,232	2,351	2,408	2,489	2,579	2,649	2,725	2,789
Speech or language impairments	1,302	1,168	1,136	950	964	971	985	996	994	1,014	1,015	1,022	1,043	1,056	1,068
Mental retardation	961	830	644	580	560	547	535	537	518	536	555	570	579	589	597
Serious emotional disturbance	283	347	383	371	372	380	390	399	400	414	427	438	445	453	462
Hearing impairments	88	79	65	56	56	57	58	60	60	64	64	67	68	69	70
Orthopedic impairments	87	58	57	46	47	48	49	51	52	56	60	63	66	67	69
Other health impairments	141	98	52	45	50	52	55	58	65	82	106	133	160	190	221
Visual impairments	38	31	26	22	22	22	23	24	23	24	24	25	25	25	26
Multiple disabilities	—	68	97	77	83	86	96	97	102	108	88	93	98	106	106
Deaf-blindness	—	3	2	1	1	2	1	1	1	1	1	1	1	1	2
Autism and traumatic brain injury	—	—	—	—	—	—	—	5	19	24	29	39	44	54	67
Developmental delay	—	—	—	—	—	—	—	—	—	—	—	—	—	4	12
Preschool disabled [2]	196	231	263	332	357	381	390	416	450	487	519	544	552	564	568
Infants and toddlers	—	—	—	30	34	37	51	66	75	92	—	—	—	—	—
	Percentage distribution of children served														
All disabilities	**100.0**	**100.0**	**100.0**	**100.0**	**100.0**	**100.0**	**100.0**	**100.0**	**100.0**	**100.0**	**100.0**	**100.0**	**100.0**	**100.0**	**100.0**
Specific learning disabilities	21.5	35.3	43.7	43.4	43.8	44.2	44.7	45.2	46.0	45.4	46.3	46.3	46.2	46.2	46.0
Speech or language impairments	35.2	28.2	26.0	21.4	21.3	21.0	20.7	20.2	19.5	19.1	18.9	18.3	18.2	17.9	17.6
Mental retardation	26.0	20.0	14.7	13.1	12.4	11.8	11.2	10.9	10.1	10.1	10.3	10.2	10.1	10.0	9.9
Serious emotional disturbance	7.7	8.4	8.7	8.4	8.2	8.2	8.2	8.1	7.8	7.8	7.9	7.9	7.8	7.7	7.6
Hearing impairments	2.4	1.9	1.5	1.3	1.2	1.2	1.2	1.2	1.2	1.2	1.2	1.2	1.2	1.2	1.2
Orthopedic impairments	2.4	1.4	1.3	1.0	1.0	1.0	1.0	1.0	1.0	1.1	1.1	1.1	1.2	1.1	1.1
Other health impairments	3.8	2.4	1.2	1.0	1.1	1.1	1.2	1.2	1.3	1.5	2.0	2.4	2.8	3.2	3.6
Visual impairments	1.0	0.7	0.6	0.5	0.5	0.5	0.5	0.5	0.4	0.5	0.4	0.4	0.4	0.4	0.4
Multiple disabilities	—	1.6	2.2	1.7	1.8	1.9	2.0	2.0	2.0	2.0	1.6	1.7	1.7	1.8	1.8
Deaf-blindness	—	0.1	(3)	(3)	(3)	(3)	(3)	(3)	(3)	(3)	(3)	(3)	(3)	(3)	(3)
Autism and traumatic brain injury	—	—	—	—	—	—	—	0.1	0.4	0.5	0.5	0.7	0.8	0.9	1.1
Developmental delay	—	—	—	—	—	—	—	—	—	—	—	—	—	0.1	0.2
Preschool disabled [2]	5.3	5.6	6.0	7.5	7.9	8.2	8.2	8.4	8.8	9.2	9.7	9.8	9.6	9.6	9.4
Infants and toddlers	—	—	—	0.7	0.8	0.8	1.1	1.3	1.5	1.7	—	—	—	—	—
	Number served as a percent of total enrollment [4]														
All disabilities	**8.32**	**10.14**	**11.00**	**11.02**	**11.18**	**11.32**	**11.43**	**11.59**	**11.76**	**12.00**	**12.19**	**12.43**	**12.56**	**12.80**	**13.01**
Specific learning disabilities	1.80	3.58	4.81	4.82	4.94	5.05	5.17	5.31	5.49	5.54	5.64	5.75	5.81	5.91	5.99
Speech or language impairments	2.94	2.86	2.86	2.37	2.40	2.40	2.39	2.37	2.32	2.33	2.30	2.28	2.29	2.29	2.30
Mental retardation	2.17	2.03	1.62	1.45	1.39	1.35	1.30	1.28	1.21	1.23	1.26	1.27	1.27	1.28	1.28
Serious emotional disturbance	0.64	0.85	0.96	0.93	0.93	0.94	0.95	0.95	0.93	0.95	0.97	0.98	0.98	0.98	0.99
Hearing impairments	0.20	0.19	0.16	0.14	0.14	0.14	0.14	0.14	0.14	0.15	0.15	0.15	0.15	0.15	0.15
Orthopedic impairments	0.20	0.14	0.14	0.11	0.12	0.12	0.12	0.12	0.12	0.13	0.14	0.14	0.14	0.15	0.15
Other health impairments	0.32	0.24	0.13	0.11	0.12	0.13	0.13	0.14	0.15	0.19	0.24	0.30	0.35	0.41	0.47
Visual impairments	0.09	0.08	0.07	0.05	0.05	0.05	0.06	0.06	0.05	0.06	0.05	0.06	0.05	0.05	0.06
Multiple disabilities	—	0.17	0.24	0.19	0.21	0.21	0.23	0.23	0.24	0.25	0.20	0.21	0.21	0.23	0.23
Deaf-blindness	—	0.01	(5)	(5)	(5)	(5)	(5)	(5)	(5)	(5)	(5)	(5)	(5)	(5)	(5)
Autism and traumatic brain injury	—	—	—	—	—	—	—	0.01	0.04	0.06	0.07	0.09	0.10	0.12	0.14
Developmental delay	—	—	—	—	—	—	—	—	—	—	—	—	—	0.01	0.03
Preschool disabled [2]	0.44	0.57	0.66	0.83	0.89	0.94	0.95	0.99	1.05	1.12	1.18	1.21	1.21	1.22	1.22
Infants and toddlers	—	—	—	0.07	0.08	0.09	0.12	0.16	0.18	0.21	—	—	—	—	—

—Not available.

[1] Includes students served under Chapter I and Individuals with Disabilities Education Act (IDEA), formerly the Education of the Handicapped Act. Prior to October 1994, children and youth with disabilities were served under the Individuals with Disabilities Education Act, Part B, and Chapter 1 of the Elementary and Secondary Education Act. In October 1994, Congress passed the Improving America's Schools Act in which funding for children and youth with disabilities was consolidated under IDEA, Part B. Data reported in this table for years prior to 1993–94, include children ages 0–21 served under Chapter 1. Data reported in this table for years after 1993–94 reflect children ages 3–21 served under IDEA, Part B.

[2] Includes preschool children 3–5 years served under Chapter I and IDEA, Part B. Prior to 1987–88, these students were included in the counts by disability condition. Beginning in 1987–88, states were no longer required to report preschool children (0–5 years) by disability condition.

[3] Less than 0.05 percent.

[4] Based on the enrollment in public schools, kindergarten through 12th grade, including a relatively small number of prekindergarten students.

[5] Less than .005 percent.

NOTE: Counts are based on reports from the 50 states and District of Columbia only (i.e., figures from outlying areas are not included). Increases since 1987–88 are due in part to new legislation enacted fall 1986, which mandates public school special education services for all handicapped children ages 3 through 5. Some data have been revised from previously published figures.

SOURCE: Thomas D. Snyder and Charlene M. Hoffman, "Table 53.—Children 0 to 21 years old served in federally supported programs for the disabled, by type of disability: 1976–77 to 1998–99," in *Digest of Education Statistics, 2000,* NCES 2001-034, U.S. Department of Education, National Center for Education Statistics, Washington, DC, January 2001

more of the basic psychological processes involved in understanding or using language, spoken or written, which may manifest itself in an imperfect ability to listen, think, speak, read, write, or do mathematical calculations."

The law includes perceptual handicaps, brain injury, minimal brain dysfunction, dyslexia, and developmental aphasia (inability to use words) as learning disabilities. The LD category does not include learning problems that are primarily the result of visual, hearing, or motor handicaps; mental retardation; or environmental, cultural, or economic disadvantage. To be categorized as LD, a student must also show a severe discrepancy between potential, as measured by IQ (Intelligence Quotient), and current ability level, as measured by achievement tests. A student who has problems in school and needs remedial education but does not fit into any other category may be labeled as having a learning disability.

In 1998–99, 2.8 million students were classified with specific learning disabilities, three times the 796,000 students identified in 1976–77. In 1976–77, LD students made up fewer than one-quarter (22 percent) of all those with disabilities, compared to almost half (46 percent) in 1998–99 (Table 3.1.) Better understanding and diagnosis of learning disabilities may explain part of the increase. The growth also may reflect the problem of fitting students into a category, as mentioned above.

Characteristics of Special Education Students

Males are disproportionately represented among students in special education programs. More than two-thirds of all special education students are male. In 1998–99 males were 68.5 percent of all secondary school students with disabilities. Several theories have been proposed to explain the disproportion of males in various disability categories. Some evidence suggests that boys have a greater vulnerability than girls do to certain genetic maladies and are more prone to developmental lags because of physiological or maturational differences. Some researchers have reported a higher degree of reading disabilities in boys than in girls, although others failed to find similar problems among males in other countries. Still others have suggested sex bias in the diagnosis and classification of students with disabilities.

According to *22nd Annual Report to Congress on the Implementation of the Individuals with Disabilities Act,* (U.S. Department of Education, Washington, DC, 2000), 63.6 percent of the disabled population ages 6 through 21 in 1998–99 were white, 13.2 percent were Hispanic, 1.7 percent were Asian/Pacific Islander, and 1.3 percent were Native American. White students made up a smaller percentage of the special education population than their representation in the general population (66.2 percent), and the proportion of Hispanic students in special education was also less than their representation in the general pop-

TABLE 3.2

Number of students ages 6–21 served under IDEA[a] in the 1989–90 and 1998–99 school years

	1989-90	1998-99	Percent Change
Specific Learning Disabilities	2,062,076	2,817,148	36.6%
Speech and Language Impairments	974,256	1,074,548	10.3
Mental Retardation	563,902	611,076	8.4
Emotional Disturbance	381,639	463,262	21.4
Multiple Disabilities	87,957	107,763	22.5
Hearing Impairments	57,906	70,883	22.4
Orthopedic Impairments	48,050	69,495	44.6
Other Health Impairments	52,733	220,831	318.7
Visual Impairments	22,866	26,132	14.3
Autism	NA	53,576	b
Deaf-Blindness	1,633	1,609	-1.5
Traumatic Brain Injury	NA	12,933	
Developmental Delay	NA	11,910	c
All Disabilities	4,253,018	5,541,166	30.3

[a] Data from 1989-90 through 1993-94 include children with disabilities served under Chapter 1 of ESEA (SOP). Beginning in 1994-95, all services to students with disabilities were provided under IDEA only.

[b] Autism and traumatic brain injury were first required to be reported in 1992-93. The percentage increase for these disability categories between 1992-93 and 1998-99 was 243.9 percent and 226.6 percent, respectively.

[c] Developmental delay was first reported in 1997-98. The percentage increase between the two years was 214.1 percent.

SOURCE: "Table II—2 Number of Students Ages 6–21 Served Under IDEA, in the 1989–90 and 1998–99 School Year," in *22nd Annual Report to Congress on the Implementation of the Individuals with Disabilities Act,* U.S. Department of Education, Office of Special Education and Rehabilitative Services, Washington, DC, 2000

ulation (14.2 percent). Black students, who account for 14.8 percent of the general population, were 20.2 percent of the special education population. Black students' representation in the mental retardation (34.3 percent) and developmental delay (33.7 percent) categories was more than twice their national population estimates.

Mainstreaming and Inclusion Programs

A controversy has developed over where and how disabled students should be taught. For years, many disabled children were taught at home or in special classrooms or schools. Now, however, many parents, educators, and specialists believe that including disabled students in regular classrooms benefits both disabled and nondisabled students.

During the 1997–98 school year, 96 percent of disabled students ages 3 through 21 received most of their educational and related services in school settings with nondisabled students. Regular classrooms were the most common instructional environments (47 percent); an additional 27.2 percent received special education and related services in resource rooms, spending more than 21 percent of the school day outside of regular class; and 21.4 percent were served in separate classrooms within a regular education building. Almost 9 of every 10 speech or language impaired children (88 percent) were educated in

TABLE 3.3

Percentage of disabled persons 3 to 21 years old receiving education services for the disabled, by age group and educational environment, United States and outlying areas, 1997–98

Type of disability	All environments	Regular class[1]	Resource room[2]	Separate class[3]	Public separate school facility	Private separate school facility	Public residential facility	Private residential facility	Homebound/ hospital placement
All persons, 3 to 21 years old	**100.0**	**47.0**	**27.2**	**21.4**	**2.0**	**1.1**	**0.4**	**0.3**	**0.7**
3 to 5 years old	100.0	52.5	8.5	31.2	3.8	1.4	0.2	0.1	2.3
6 to 21 years old	100.0	46.4	29.0	20.4	1.8	1.0	0.4	0.3	0.5
Mental retardation	100.0	12.6	29.6	51.7	4.3	0.9	0.3	0.2	0.4
Speech or language impairments	100.0	87.8	7.3	4.4	0.2	0.1	—	—	0.1
Visual impairments	100.0	48.1	20.1	17.3	4.8	1.9	5.8	1.3	0.7
Serious emotional disturbance	100.0	24.9	23.3	33.5	7.4	5.7	1.6	2.0	1.6
Orthopedic impairments	100.0	46.6	21.3	26.2	2.9	0.8	0.2	0.1	2.0
Other health impairments	100.0	41.4	33.8	18.3	1.0	0.7	0.1	0.2	4.7
Specific learning disabilities	100.0	43.8	39.3	16.0	0.3	0.3	0.1	0.1	0.2
Deaf-blindness	100.0	13.6	11.3	39.0	14.9	5.0	11.0	3.8	1.5
Multiple disabilities	100.0	10.0	17.3	45.1	15.2	7.1	1.4	1.4	2.5
Hearing impairments	100.0	38.8	19.0	25.4	4.6	2.7	8.4	0.9	0.2
Autism	100.0	18.3	12.7	52.1	8.7	6.0	0.3	1.5	0.5
Traumatic brain injury	100.0	29.8	26.2	30.1	2.7	7.1	0.3	1.3	2.4

—Not available.

[1]Regular class is outside regular class less than 21 percent of the school day.

[2]Resource room is outside regular class more than 21 percent of the school day and less than 60 percent of the school day.

[3]Separate class is outside the regular class more than 60 percent of the school day.

NOTE: Data for 3- to 5-year-old children are not collected by disability condition. Disability data are only reported for 6- to 21-year-old students. Detail may not sum to totals due to rounding.

SOURCE: Thomas D. Snyder and Charlene M. Hoffman, "Table 54.—Percentage distribution of disabled persons 3 to 21 years old receiving education services for the disabled, by age group and educational environment: 1997–98," in *Digest of Education Statistics, 2000,* NCES 2001-034, U.S. Department of Education, National Center for Education Statistics, Washington, DC, January 2001

regular classrooms, and 83 percent of those with learning disabilities received special education in resource rooms or in regular classes. (See Table 3.3.)

In 2001 the National Center on Educational Outcomes surveyed state directors of special education. The state directors reported increased participation rates of students with disabilities in state assessments. They also reported seven positive and seven negative consequences of the participation of students with disabilities in state standards, assessments, and accountability systems.

Positive outcomes include increased access to the general curriculum (mentioned by 14 states), increased inclusion in accountability system (11 states), more rigorous education (10 states), increased participation in state assessments (9 states), increased academic expectations (6 states), improved performance on some state assessments (3 states), and increased general and special education networking (3 states). Negative consequences mention that state assessments are too difficult for some students (6 states), that students with disabilities make schools appear less effective (6 states), more paperwork and time (6 states), students with disabilities are traumatized by taking tests (5 states), too many students are identified for alternate assessments (3 states), students with disabilities may not graduate (3 states), and students with disabilities cannot access or reach standards (2 states). (See Figure 3.1 and Figure 3.2.)

Trends in Special Education

Two important trends in special education have emerged in recent years. First, children with handicaps are receiving educational services earlier. This builds the foundation for learning the skills they will need in elementary school. For many disabled children, early education programs can reduce or even eliminate the need for intensive services later.

Second, special education has helped to eliminate the myth that disabled individuals, even the severely disabled, are unwilling or unable to work. Schools are assessing the abilities and talents of students with handicaps and matching them with potential occupations. Disabled students are receiving more training in vocational skills, as well as in making the transition from school to community life and work.

Exiting from Special Education

In 1984–85, the Office of Special Education Programs began collecting data on students ages 14 and older who had left the education system. In 1997–98, about one-fourth (28.4 percent) of exiting students with disabilities graduated with diplomas, and 5.7 percent graduated with certificates. About 1 percent reached the maximum age for services, which varies by state. The remainder left the educational system for other reasons (including death). (See Table 3.4.)

FIGURE 3.1

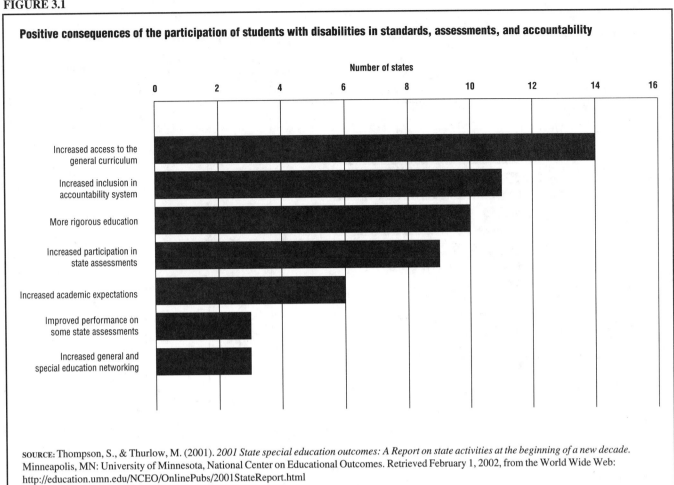

Positive consequences of the participation of students with disabilities in standards, assessments, and accountability

SOURCE: Thompson, S., & Thurlow, M. (2001). *2001 State special education outcomes: A Report on state activities at the beginning of a new decade.* Minneapolis, MN: University of Minnesota, National Center on Educational Outcomes. Retrieved February 1, 2002, from the World Wide Web: http://education.umn.edu/NCEO/OnlinePubs/2001StateReport.html

Youth with disabilities were significantly more likely than youth in general and somewhat more likely than youth with similar demographic characteristics to drop out of school. Disabled students who receive inadequate educational preparation are even more seriously disabled when they leave school; they have reached the legal age for independence but probably have not developed marketable job skills. Despite their efforts, high school programs sometimes fail to meet these students' needs.

GIFTED AND TALENTED STUDENTS

Defining Giftedness

For more than a century, researchers, scientists, and educators have tried to define the term "gifted." Historically, the term was closely associated with the concept of genius. After intelligence (IQ) tests were developed, people who scored poorly were labeled retarded, and those who scored extremely well were considered geniuses. Currently some observers criticize the use of IQ tests as a single measure of intelligence. They believe the tests are biased in favor of the white middle and upper classes and penalize those from different cultural backgrounds. Also, many researchers and educators believe that giftedness is more than high intellectual ability. It also involves creativity, memory, motivation, physical dexterity, social adeptness, and aesthetic sensitivity—qualities needed to succeed in life but not measured by IQ tests.

Researchers and educators generally agree that intelligence takes many forms and that multiple criteria are necessary for measurement. Educators are learning to identify outstanding talent by evaluating student abilities in different settings, rather than relying solely on test scores. The following definition, based on the definition in the Jacob K. Javits Gifted and Talented Student Education Act of 1988 (PL 100-297), reflects the current knowledge and thinking.

- Children and youth with outstanding talent perform or show the potential for performing at remarkably high levels of accomplishment when compared with others of their age, experience, or environment.

- These children and youth exhibit high performance capability in intellectual, creative, and/or artistic areas, possess an unusual leadership capacity, or excel in specific academic fields. They require services or activities not ordinarily provided by the schools.

FIGURE 3.2

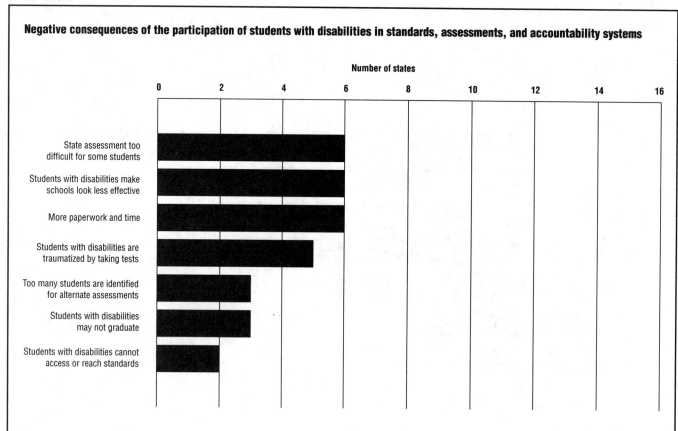

Negative consequences of the participation of students with disabilities in standards, assessments, and accountability systems

SOURCE: Thompson, S., & Thurlow, M. (2001). *2001 State special education outcomes: A report on state activities at the beginning of a new decade.* Minneapolis, MN: University of Minnesota, National Center on Educational Outcomes. Retrieved February 1, 2002, from the World Wide Web: http://education.umn.edu/NCEO/OnlinePubs/2001StateReport.html

- Outstanding talents are present in children and youth from all cultural groups, across all economic strata, and in all areas of human endeavor.

Identifying Gifted Students

Most states and localities have developed definitions of gifted and talented students based on the 1972 Marland Report to Congress. (See Table 3.5.) This definition identified a variety of abilities in addition to general intellectual ability and estimated that gifted students represent at least 3 to 5 percent of the student population. However, the methods used by most districts to identify gifted students lag far behind the Marland definition.

Serving Gifted Students

Not all states and localities collect data in the same way, so it is difficult to determine the exact number of students served in gifted and talented programs. According to the 1998–99 *State of the States Gifted and Talented Education Report* (Council of State Directors of Programs for the Gifted, Austin, TX, 1999), 30 states had state-mandated gifted and talented programs, and 12 states had discretionary programs (not set by law). This marks an improvement from 1980, when only 7 states had legislation and funding for gifted and talented programs.

The Jacob K. Javits Gifted and Talented Student Act of 1994 established a small federal contribution. This program supports grants, research, and the development of national leadership abilities. The act gives funding priority to programs that support gifted and talented students who are economically disadvantaged, speak limited English, or have disabilities. Since 1989, the Javits program has funded about 125 grants.

DISADVANTAGED STUDENTS

Children who are seriously disadvantaged economically and socially often lag behind their peers. Statistically, they start preschool education later or miss it entirely and thus are less ready to start school. They have more learning disabilities, are more likely to be held back a grade, and ultimately have higher dropout rates. Among the disadvantaged groups defined by educators and observers are children from families with very low incomes; children who are linguistically isolated (LI) or have limited English proficiency (LEP), usually because

TABLE 3.4

Students with diabilities exiting the educational system, by age, type of disability, and basis of exit, United States and outlying areas, 1996–97 and 1997–98

| | Number | | | | | | Percent | | | | | |
| | Graduated with diploma | | Graduated with certificate | | Reached maximum age | | Graduated with diploma | | Graduated with certificate | | Reached maximum age | |
Student characteristics	1996–97	1997–98	1996–97	1997–98	1996–97	1997–98	1996–97	1997–98	1996–97	1997–98	1996–97	1997–98
Age group												
14 to 21 (and over)	134,614	147,942	28,614	29,909	4,396	4,607	27.6	28.4	5.9	5.7	0.9	0.9
14	26	73	64	82	2	0	0.0	0.1	0.1	0.1	0.0	0.0
15	35	60	50	52	2	3	0.1	0.4	0.1	0.1	0.0	0.0
16	407	686	129	152	5	6	0.6	1.0	0.2	0.2	0.0	0.0
17	17,224	25,504	2,617	3,088	21	19	21.2	27.0	3.2	3.3	0.0	0.0
18	56,647	66,310	10,417	11,397	97	166	50.9	52.9	9.4	9.1	0.1	0.1
19	43,521	40,973	8,701	8,464	55	119	60.7	59.6	12.1	12.3	0.1	0.2
20	10,470	9,321	3,293	3,630	523	527	49.9	46.5	15.7	18.1	2.5	2.6
21 (and over)	6,284	5,015	3,343	3,044	3,691	3,767	35.6	33.6	18.9	20.4	20.9	25.2
Type of disability for 14- to 21-year-olds and over												
All disabilities	134,614	147,942	28,614	29,909	4,396	4,607	27.6	28.4	5.9	5.7	0.9	0.9
Specific learning disabilities	91,634	100,138	13,460	13,692	770	763	32.2	33.1	4.7	4.5	0.3	0.3
Mental retardation	14,352	15,292	10,067	10,538	2,091	2,210	24.4	24.8	17.1	17.1	3.6	3.6
Serious emotional disturbance	12,952	14,031	1,921	2,180	400	407	14.9	15.6	2.2	2.4	0.5	0.5
Speech or language impairments	3,847	4,137	503	525	73	73	18.5	17.5	2.4	2.2	0.4	0.3
Multiple disabilities	1,642	2,061	874	937	607	664	24.8	26.8	13.2	12.2	9.2	8.6
Other health impairments	3,605	5,102	461	542	57	64	28.8	30.5	3.7	3.2	0.5	0.4
Hearing impairments	2,642	2,774	467	545	58	68	43.4	43.3	7.7	8.5	1.0	1.1
Orthopedic impairments	1,861	2,051	363	361	126	125	33.3	35.7	6.5	6.3	2.3	2.2
Visual impairments	1,115	1,166	181	171	48	42	47.2	46.8	7.7	6.9	2.0	1.7
Autism	299	384	192	268	132	139	24.8	25.8	15.9	18.0	11.0	9.3
Deaf-blindness	39	132	26	18	7	17	29.1	55.7	19.4	7.6	5.2	7.2
Traumatic brain injury	626	674	99	132	27	35	43.3	42.3	6.8	8.3	1.9	2.2

NOTE: Reached maximum age figures reflect an estimate of those who were actually known to have dropped out and do not include youth who simply stopped coming to school or whose status was unknown.

SOURCE: Thomas D. Snyder and Charlene M. Hoffman, "Table 108.—Students with disabilities exiting the educational system, by age, type of disability, and basis of exit: The United States and outlying areas, 1996–97 and 1997–98," in *Digest of Education Statistics, 2000,* NCES 2001-034, U.S. Department of Education, National Center for Education Statistics, Washington, DC, January 2001

they are members of immigrant families; and children who change schools frequently—for example, children of seasonal farmworkers or homeless parents.

Table 3.6 shows the 1960–1999 dropout rates for 16- to 24-year-olds. (Status dropouts are those who were not enrolled in school but were not high school graduates.) In 1999 minority students (black, 12.6 percent; Hispanic, 28.6 percent) were more likely than white students (7.3 percent) to drop out. Although the proportion of students in all categories who dropped out of high school declined since 1972, in 2000 students from low income families still dropped out of high school more often than did students from middle or high income families. (See Figure 3.3.)

The Title I (formerly Chapter 1) education program is the major federal program designed to help states and schools meet the special educational needs of disadvantaged students. Title I originated as part of the Elementary and Secondary Education Act of 1965 (PL 89-10) and was amended by the Improving America's Schools Act of 1994 (PL 103-382). Title I provides about $8.6 billion per

TABLE 3.5

1972 Marland Definition (Public law 91-230. Section 806)

Gifted and talented children are those identified by professionally qualified persons, who by virtue of outstanding abilities are capable of high performance. These are children who require differentiated educational programs and/or services beyond those normally provided by the regular school program in order to realize their contribution to self and society .

Children capable of high performance include those with demonstrated achievement and/or potential ability in any of the following areas, singly or in combination:

1. general intellectual ability,
2. specific academic aptitude,
3. creative or productive thinking,
4. leadership ability,
5. visual and performing arts,
6. psychomotor ability,

It can be assumed that utilization of these criteria for identification of the gifted and talented will encompass a minimum of 3 to 5 percent of the school population.

SOURCE: Pat O'Connell Ross, "1972 Marland Definition (Public Law 91-20, section 806)," in *National Excellence: A Case for Developing America's Talent,* U.S. Department of Education, Office of Educational Research and Improvement, Washington, DC, October 1993

TABLE 3.6

Percent of high school dropouts (status dropouts) among persons 16 to 24 years old, by sex and race/ethnicity, April 1960–October 1999

	Total				Men				Women			
Year	All races	White, non-Hispanic	Black, non-Hispanic	Hispanic origin	All races	White, non-Hispanic	Black, non-Hispanic	Hispanic origin	All races	White, non-Hispanic	Black, non-Hispanic	Hispanic origin
1960[1]	27.2 —	— —	— —	— —	27.8 —	— —	— —	— —	26.7 —	— —	— —	— —
1970[2]	15.0 —	13.2 —	27.9 —	— —	14.2 —	12.2 —	29.4 —	— —	15.7 —	14.1 —	26.6 —	— —
1971[2]	14.7 —	13.4 —	23.7 —	— —	14.2 —	12.6 —	25.5 —	— —	15.2 —	14.2 —	22.1 —	— —
1972	14.6 (0.3)	12.3 (0.3)	21.3 (1.1)	34.3 (2.2)	14.1 (0.4)	11.6 (0.4)	22.3 (1.6)	33.7 (3.2)	15.1 (0.4)	12.8 (0.4)	20.5 (1.4)	34.8 (3.1)
1973	14.1 (0.3)	11.6 (0.3)	22.2 (1.1)	33.5 (2.2)	13.7 (0.4)	11.5 (0.4)	21.5 (1.5)	30.4 (3.2)	14.5 (0.4)	11.8 (0.4)	22.8 (1.5)	36.4 (3.2)
1974	14.3 (0.3)	11.9 (0.3)	21.2 (1.0)	33.0 (2.1)	14.2 (0.4)	12.0 (0.4)	20.1 (1.5)	33.8 (3.0)	14.3 (0.4)	11.8 (0.4)	22.1 (1.5)	32.2 (2.9)
1975	13.9 (0.3)	11.4 (0.3)	22.9 (1.1)	29.2 (2.0)	13.3 (0.4)	11.0 (0.4)	23.0 (1.6)	26.7 (2.8)	14.5 (0.4)	11.8 (0.4)	22.9 (1.4)	31.6 (2.9)
1976	14.1 (0.3)	12.0 (0.3)	20.5 (1.0)	31.4 (2.0)	14.1 (0.4)	12.1 (0.4)	21.2 (1.5)	30.3 (2.9)	14.2 (0.4)	11.8 (0.4)	19.9 (1.4)	32.3 (2.8)
1977	14.1 (0.3)	11.9 (0.3)	19.8 (1.0)	33.0 (2.0)	14.5 (0.4)	12.6 (0.4)	19.5 (1.5)	31.6 (2.9)	13.8 (0.4)	11.2 (0.4)	20.0 (1.4)	34.3 (2.8)
1978	14.2 (0.3)	11.9 (0.3)	20.2 (1.0)	33.3 (2.0)	14.6 (0.4)	12.2 (0.4)	22.5 (1.5)	33.6 (2.9)	13.9 (0.4)	11.6 (0.4)	18.3 (1.3)	33.1 (2.8)
1979	14.6 (0.3)	12.0 (0.3)	21.1 (1.0)	33.8 (2.0)	15.0 (0.4)	12.6 (0.4)	22.4 (1.5)	33.0 (2.8)	14.2 (0.4)	11.5 (0.4)	20.0 (1.3)	34.5 (2.8)
1980	14.1 (0.3)	11.4 (0.3)	19.1 (1.0)	35.2 (1.9)	15.1 (0.4)	12.3 (0.4)	20.8 (1.5)	37.2 (2.7)	13.1 (0.4)	10.5 (0.4)	17.7 (1.3)	33.2 (2.6)
1981	13.9 (0.3)	11.3 (0.3)	18.4 (0.9)	33.2 (1.8)	15.1 (0.4)	12.5 (0.4)	19.9 (1.4)	36.0 (2.6)	12.8 (0.4)	10.2 (0.4)	17.1 (1.2)	30.4 (2.5)
1982	13.9 (0.3)	11.4 (0.3)	18.4 (1.0)	31.7 (1.9)	14.5 (0.4)	12.0 (0.4)	21.2 (1.5)	30.5 (2.7)	13.3 (0.4)	10.8 (0.4)	15.9 (1.3)	32.8 (2.7)
1983	13.7 (0.3)	11.1 (0.3)	18.0 (1.0)	31.6 (1.9)	14.9 (0.4)	12.2 (0.4)	19.9 (1.5)	34.3 (2.8)	12.5 (0.4)	10.1 (0.4)	16.2 (1.3)	29.1 (2.6)
1984	13.1 (0.3)	11.0 (0.3)	15.5 (0.9)	29.8 (1.9)	14.0 (0.4)	11.9 (0.4)	16.8 (1.4)	30.6 (2.8)	12.3 (0.4)	10.1 (0.4)	14.3 (1.2)	29.0 (2.6)
1985	12.6 (0.3)	10.4 (0.3)	15.2 (0.9)	27.6 (1.9)	13.4 (0.4)	11.1 (0.4)	16.1 (1.4)	29.9 (2.8)	11.8 (0.4)	9.8 (0.4)	14.3 (1.2)	25.2 (2.7)
1986	12.2 (0.3)	9.7 (0.3)	14.2 (0.9)	30.1 (1.9)	13.1 (0.4)	10.3 (0.4)	15.0 (1.3)	32.8 (2.7)	11.4 (0.4)	9.1 (0.4)	13.5 (1.2)	27.2 (2.6)
1987	12.6 (0.3)	10.4 (0.3)	14.1 (0.9)	28.6 (1.8)	13.2 (0.4)	10.8 (0.4)	15.0 (1.3)	29.1 (2.6)	12.1 (0.4)	10.0 (0.4)	13.3 (1.2)	28.1 (2.6)
1988	12.9 (0.3)	9.6 (0.3)	14.5 (1.0)	35.8 (2.3)	13.5 (0.4)	10.3 (0.5)	15.0 (1.5)	36.0 (3.2)	12.2 (0.4)	8.9 (0.4)	14.0 (1.4)	35.4 (3.3)
1989	12.6 (0.3)	9.4 (0.3)	13.9 (1.0)	33.0 (2.2)	13.6 (0.5)	10.3 (0.5)	14.9 (1.5)	34.4 (3.1)	11.7 (0.4)	8.5 (0.4)	13.0 (1.3)	31.6 (3.1)
1990	12.1 (0.3)	9.0 (0.3)	13.2 (0.9)	32.4 (1.9)	12.3 (0.4)	9.3 (0.4)	11.9 (1.3)	34.3 (2.7)	11.8 (0.4)	8.7 (0.4)	14.4 (1.3)	30.3 (2.7)
1991	12.5 (0.3)	8.9 (0.3)	13.6 (0.9)	35.3 (1.9)	13.0 (0.4)	8.9 (0.4)	13.5 (1.4)	39.2 (2.7)	11.9 (0.4)	8.9 (0.4)	13.7 (1.3)	31.1 (2.7)
1992[3]	11.0 (0.3)	7.7 (0.3)	13.7 (0.9)	29.4 (1.9)	11.3 (0.4)	8.0 (0.4)	12.5 (1.3)	32.1 (2.7)	10.7 (0.4)	7.4 (0.4)	14.8 (1.4)	26.6 (2.6)
1993[3]	11.0 (0.3)	7.9 (0.3)	13.6 (0.9)	27.5 (1.8)	11.2 (0.4)	8.2 (0.4)	12.6 (1.3)	28.1 (2.5)	10.9 (0.4)	7.6 (0.4)	14.4 (1.3)	26.9 (2.5)
1994[3]	11.4 (0.3)	7.7 (0.3)	12.6 (0.8)	30.0 (1.2)	12.3 (0.4)	8.0 (0.4)	14.1 (1.1)	31.6 (1.6)	10.6 (0.4)	7.5 (0.4)	11.3 (1.0)	28.1 (1.7)
1995[3]	12.0 (0.3)	8.6 (0.3)	12.1 (0.7)	30.0 (1.1)	12.2 (0.4)	9.0 (0.4)	11.1 (1.0)	30.0 (1.6)	11.7 (0.4)	8.2 (0.4)	12.9 (1.1)	30.0 (1.7)
1996[3]	11.1 (0.3)	7.3 (0.3)	13.0 (0.8)	29.4 (1.2)	11.4 (0.4)	7.3 (0.4)	13.5 (1.2)	30.3 (1.7)	10.9 (0.4)	7.3 (0.4)	12.5 (1.1)	28.3 (1.7)
1997[3]	11.0 (0.3)	7.6 (0.3)	13.4 (0.8)	25.3 (1.1)	11.9 (0.4)	8.5 (0.4)	13.3 (1.2)	27.0 (1.6)	10.1 (0.4)	6.7 (0.4)	13.5 (1.1)	23.4 (1.6)
1998[3]	11.8 (0.3)	7.7 (0.3)	13.8 (0.8)	29.5 (1.1)	13.3 (0.4)	8.6 (0.4)	15.5 (1.2)	33.5 (1.6)	10.3 (0.4)	6.9 (0.4)	12.2 (1.1)	25.0 (1.6)
1999[3]	11.2 (0.3)	7.3 (0.3)	12.6 (0.8)	28.6 (1.1)	11.9 (0.4)	7.7 (0.4)	12.1 (1.1)	31.0 (1.6)	10.5 (0.4)	6.9 (0.4)	13.0 (1.1)	26.0 (1.5)

—Not available.

[1] Based on the April 1960 decennial census.

[2] White and black include persons of Hispanic origin.

[3] Because of changes in data collection procedures, data may not be comparable with figures for earlier years.

NOTE: "Status" dropouts are 16- to 24-year-olds who are not enrolled in school and who have not completed a high school program regardless of when they left school. People who have received GED credentials are counted as high school completers. All data except for 1960 are based on October counts. Data are based upon sample surveys of the civilian noninstitutionalized population. Standard errors appear in parentheses.

SOURCE: Thomas D. Snyder and Charlene M. Hoffman, "Table 106.—Percent of high school dropouts (status dropouts) among persons 16 to 24 years old, by sex and race/ethnicity: April 1960 to October 1999," in *Digest of Education Statistics, 2000*, NCES 2001-034, U.S. Department of Education, National Center for Education Statistics, Washington, DC, January 2001

year to fund programs and resources so that schools can improve learning for at-risk students, particularly schools with high concentrations of low-income children.

States and school districts can apply for Title I funds for a variety of programs aimed at improving the performance of disadvantaged students. Table 3.7 gives the appropriations for Title I and Title VI (formerly Chapter 2) programs by state for the 1999–99 and 1999–2000 school years. Typically states with higher rates of poor, immigrant, and/or migrant students, such as California, Florida, Illinois, Michigan, New York, Ohio, Pennsylvania, and Texas, apply for and receive more federal funds. (See Table 3.7.) Federal funding for special education increased by about 111 percent from 1994 to 2001, but funding for Title I increased only about 19 percent, from $7.2 billion to $8.6 billion. (See Figure 3.4.)

The number of Title I participants increased to 13.4 million in 1998–99. Most students who received services under three of the Title I programs (public targeted assistance, public schoolwide, and nonpublic) were at the elementary level. The Part A-Neglected program is for students who live in institutions for neglected children. Funding for this program is concentrated primarily at the secondary level. (See Figure 3.5.) Services offered in juvenile institutions for neglected and delinquent children include reading, mathematics, English as a Second Language, study skills, counseling, and social skills. (See Figure 3.6.)

Students on the Move

Children who move frequently during their school years are more likely to have emotional or behavioral

FIGURE 3.3

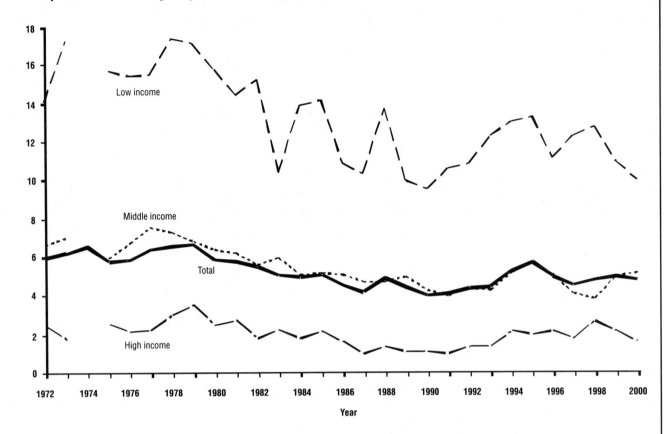

Event dropout rates of 15- through 24-year-olds who dropped out of grades 10–12, by family income*, October 1972–October 2000

*Low income is defined as the bottom 20 percent of all family incomes for the year; middle income is between 20 and 80 percent of all family incomes; and high income is the top 20 percent of all family incomes.

NOTE: Data on family income are missing for 1974. Numbers for years 1987 through 2000 reflect new editing procedures instituted by the U.S. Census Bureau for cases with missing data on school enrollment items. Numbers for years 1992 through 2000 reflect new wording of the educational attainment item in the CPS beginning in 1992. Numbers for years 1994 through 2000 reflect changes in the CPS due to newly instituted computer-assisted interviewing and the change in population controls used in the 1990 Census-based estimates, with adjustment for undercounting in the 1990 Census.

SOURCE: Philip Kaufman, Martha Naomi Alt, and Christopher D. Chapman, "Figure 1.—Event dropout rates of 15- to 24-year-olds who dropped out of grades 10-12, by family income:* October 1972 to October 2000," in *Dropout Rates in the United States: 2000*, NCES 2002-114, U.S. Department of Education, National Center for Education Statistics, November 2001

problems, to repeat a grade, or to be suspended or expelled from school. Experts theorize that these children experience stress in the loss of old friends and familiar surroundings. Children may not understand the reasons for moving or may see the moves as a loss of autonomy. In addition frequent moves may be a symptom of a stressed, chaotic family, a characteristic known to be related to emotional and school problems.

MIGRANT CHILDREN. With frequent moves, low incomes, and limited English skills, migrant children are at high risk for developing school problems. They often live in substandard housing and are frequently poverty-stricken and alienated from other children at school. They may experience exposure to harmful agricultural chemicals and receive inadequate health care. These factors can make getting an education very

difficult. The Title I Migrant Education Program (MEP), authorized under the Hawkins-Stafford Elementary and Secondary School Improvement Amendments of 1968 (PL 100-297), provides funding for state education agencies to meet the special needs of migratory children.

The term "migrant children" may refer to independent children who move often, perhaps from family to family, or to children of migratory workers who move frequently to secure jobs in farming, fishing, timber, or dairy industries. The MEP serves current and former (for up to three years) migrant children ages 3 through 21. Most migrant education programs include preschool services, testing, regular academic or remedial instruction, bilingual education, vocational education, guidance and counseling, and health services. In 1999–2000, the Title I

TABLE 3.7

Appropriations for Title I and Title VI, Elementary and Secondary Education Act (ESEA) of 1994, by state or other area and type of appropriation, 1998–99 and 1999–2000

[In thousands]

State or other area	Title I total, school year 1998–99[1]	Title I,[2] School year 1999–2000[3]							Title VI[4]	
		Total	Local education grants			Neglected and delinquent children	Migrant children	Other[5]	1998 appropriations for 1998–99	1999 appropriations for 1999–2000
			Total[6]	Basic grants	Concentration grants					
Total[7]	$8,005,135	$8,289,582	$7,732,397	$6,505,686	$1,147,377	$40,311	$354,689	$162,185	$350,000	$375,000
Alabama	132,936	133,972	128,530	107,868	20,662	552	2,792	2,098	5,224	5,520
Alaska	25,850	27,672	18,886	15,874	3,012	152	8,007	627	1,737	1,862
Arizona	124,486	130,818	121,033	101,096	19,937	917	6,681	2,186	5,403	6,408
Arkansas	82,293	85,004	78,656	67,024	11,633	284	4,729	1,334	3,243	3,443
California	954,281	1,065,523	940,850	801,202	139,648	3,297	103,467	17,909	41,044	44,575
Colorado	77,266	78,218	71,278	60,637	10,640	336	5,432	1,173	4,871	5,258
Connecticut	74,592	74,468	69,294	58,856	10,438	918	2,981	1,275	3,849	4,078
Delaware	19,818	22,269	21,088	16,264	4,823	125	322	734	1,737	1,862
District of Columbia	24,246	26,910	24,978	21,266	3,712	648	409	877	1,737	1,862
Florida	368,619	391,594	360,646	306,417	54,229	1,019	23,843	6,087	16,517	17,857
Georgia	206,111	218,637	207,638	178,180	29,458	2,065	5,587	3,348	9,376	10,131
Hawaii	21,147	21,021	20,120	17,285	2,835	74	195	633	1,737	1,862
Idaho	26,949	28,500	23,356	19,699	3,657	116	4,392	636	1,737	1,862
Illinois	340,733	337,019	326,648	278,734	47,914	1,832	1,758	6,780	15,005	16,090
Indiana	122,164	122,821	116,147	101,673	14,474	731	3,886	2,056	7,290	7,726
Iowa	54,939	55,659	53,276	47,038	6,238	361	935	1,086	3,597	3,838
Kansas	65,665	67,096	55,735	48,254	7,481	336	9,966	1,059	3,394	3,604
Kentucky	141,214	141,131	127,599	107,943	19,655	642	10,648	2,242	4,753	4,992
Louisiana	201,143	198,517	191,246	161,738	29,508	595	2,772	3,903	6,063	6,216
Maine	34,193	36,798	31,403	26,891	4,512	146	4,605	643	1,737	1,862
Maryland	104,482	105,879	102,233	87,393	14,840	1,392	449	1,806	6,203	6,531
Massachusetts	154,402	159,039	152,229	125,501	26,728	908	2,967	2,935	6,903	7,456
Michigan	347,722	351,442	333,880	277,681	56,199	905	11,055	5,601	12,489	13,123
Minnesota	93,438	92,688	87,876	76,790	11,086	283	2,600	1,929	6,230	6,625
Mississippi	130,165	128,450	124,768	106,119	18,649	297	1,109	2,276	3,696	3,907
Missouri	132,987	138,513	133,471	113,061	20,410	791	1,628	2,622	6,879	7,367
Montana	27,215	27,542	26,073	22,144	3,929	67	725	677	1,737	1,862
Nebraska	37,389	37,699	32,183	28,826	3,357	246	4,457	813	2,201	2,342
Nevada	23,528	23,883	22,832	20,042	2,789	147	268	636	1,962	2,217
New Hampshire	18,795	20,503	19,451	15,608	3,843	301	108	643	1,737	1,862
New Jersey	171,942	182,896	175,151	146,537	28,614	2,342	1,679	3,725	9,473	10,135
New Mexico	65,719	68,112	65,464	55,688	9,776	355	1,113	1,179	2,446	2,590
New York	715,928	751,931	725,738	615,375	110,362	2,696	7,987	15,511	21,549	23,004
North Carolina	149,100	155,311	146,133	126,192	19,941	884	5,891	2,404	8,843	9,598
North Dakota	19,234	20,736	19,639	16,264	3,375	40	356	700	1,737	1,862
Ohio	314,423	312,305	302,179	257,576	44,603	2,291	2,057	5,777	13,983	14,810
Oklahoma	91,560	99,005	95,179	81,363	13,816	209	2,079	1,538	4,373	4,622
Oregon	82,447	83,282	68,523	59,466	9,057	1,174	12,386	1,200	3,995	4,237
Pennsylvania	353,744	352,608	335,112	282,422	52,690	798	8,774	7,925	14,283	15,064
Rhode Island	26,343	25,943	24,638	21,211	3,426	357	119	830	1,737	1,862
South Carolina	98,461	101,870	98,915	84,498	14,418	893	471	1,592	4,579	4,972
South Dakota	21,095	21,417	19,730	16,672	3,058	242	776	669	1,737	1,862
Tennessee	133,238	137,269	134,264	112,127	22,137	531	338	2,136	6,414	6,822
Texas	698,148	727,313	661,699	563,304	98,395	2,610	51,493	11,511	25,904	28,121
Utah	35,799	38,152	35,295	29,501	5,794	772	1,436	649	3,284	3,489
Vermont	19,167	19,294	17,699	15,106	2,594	127	842	626	1,737	1,862
Virginia	115,031	119,224	115,970	100,401	15,569	593	746	1,916	7,880	8,445
Washington	124,778	125,513	108,934	93,160	15,774	761	13,965	1,853	7,036	7,571
West Virginia	75,971	75,111	73,471	61,841	11,630	315	118	1,208	2,110	2,184
Wisconsin	131,415	129,977	125,824	113,821	12,003	1,021	662	2,470	6,736	7,165
Wyoming	17,638	18,553	17,420	14,551	2,868	308	179	647	1,737	1,862

appropriation for migrant children was $355 million (see Table 3.7).

According to *The Federal Migrant Education Program: An Overview* (Patricia Osorio-O'Dea, Congressional Research Service, Washington, DC, 1998), about 83 percent of migrant students are Hispanic and include increasing numbers of immigrants. More than 40 percent are limited English proficient (LEP), and over two-thirds live in households with incomes below the poverty level. Migrant students experience more health problems, such as nutritional disease and respiratory infections, than other students.

California, Florida, Michigan, Texas, and Washington serve the majority of migrant students. Migrant families generally travel in three patterns of migration, called

TABLE 3.7

Appropriations for Title I and Title VI, Elementary and Secondary Education Act (ESEA) of 1994, by state or other area and type of appropriation, 1998–99 and 1999–2000 [CONTINUED]

[In thousands]

State or other area	Title I total, school year 1998–99[1]	Title I,[2] School year 1999–2000[3]							Title VI[4]	
		Total	Local education grants			Neglected and delinquent children	Migrant children	Other[5]	1998 appropriations for 1998–99	1999 appropriations for 1999–2000
			Total[6]	Basic grants	Concentration grants					
Other activities										
Bureau of Indian Affairs	47,834	50,205	49,390	0	0	0	0	815	0	0
Evaluation, Title VI	0	0	0	0	0	0	0	0	185	0
Migrant coordination activities	5,998	8,500	0	0	0	0	8,500	0	0	0
Even Start Migrant, Indian, and Territory setaside	6,200	6,200	0	0	0	0	0	6,200	0	0
Even Start Evaluation/ Technical Assistance	3,720	3,720	0	0	0	0	0	3,720	0	0
Even Start/State Literacy Initiative	1,000	1,000	0	0	0	0	0	1,000	0	0
Competitive grants	9,700	9,054	7,854	0	254	0	0	1,200	0	0
Outlying areas										
American Samoa	5,251	5,355	5,355	0	0	0	0	0	420	451
Guam	5,109	5,023	5,023	0	0	0	0	0	981	1,051
Northern Marianas	2,783	2,848	2,848	0	0	0	0	0	240	257
Puerto Rico	278,650	273,453	262,430	221,502	40,929	510	3,949	6,564	5,706	6,040
Virgin Islands	8,939	9,118	9,118	0	0	0	0	0	808	866

[1]Data are based on fiscal year 1999 budget authorizations. Excludes $6,977,000 for Title I evaluation.
[2]Formerly Chapter 1.
[3]Data are based on fiscal year 2000 budget authorizations. Excludes $6,977,000 for Title I evaluation.
[4]Formerly Chapter 2.
[5]Includes capital expenses, Even Start grants, and Comprehensive School Reform grants.
[6]Includes other programs not shown separately.
[7]Total includes other activities and outlying areas.
NOTE: Elementary and Secondary Education Act was most recently revised through the Improving America's Schools Act (IASA) of 1994. Detail may not sum to totals due to rounding.

SOURCE: Thomas D. Snyder and Charlene M. Hoffman, "Table 366.—Appropriations for Title I and Title VI, Elementary and Secondary Education Act (ESEA) of 1994, by state or other area: 1998–99 and 1999–2000," in *Digest of Education Statistics, 2000,* NCES 2001-034, U.S. Department of Education, National Center for Education Statistics, Washington, DC, January 2001

migrant streams: Texas and north through the Central Plains states; California to the Northwest and the western states; and Florida and north along the East Coast states. (See Figure 3.7.)

In the past, the Migrant Student Record Transfer System (MSRTS), a national computer network, was used to transfer education and health records of migratory workers' children across state lines and school districts. MSRTS data were used to locate and determine children who might be eligible for MEP services. Criticized for its high cost and alleged ineffectiveness, the MSRTS was not reauthorized by the 1994 Improving America's Schools Act (PL 103-382).

HOMELESS CHILDREN. Title VII of the Stewart B. McKinney Homeless Assistance Act (PL 100-77; 1987) provides funding to facilitate the enrollment, attendance, and success in school of homeless children and youth. Funding for the McKinney programs in 2001 was $35 million, an increase of 25 percent over the 2000 funding level.

According to *Education for Homeless Children and Youth Program Report to Congress* (U.S. Department of Education, Washington, DC, 1997), states estimated there were approximately 625,330 school-age homeless children in 1997. Of those, 521,610 (76 percent) were enrolled in school, but only 347,601 (55 percent) attended regularly.

Families who become homeless are often forced to move frequently. Because of length-of-stay restrictions in shelters, short stays with relatives and friends, and/or necessary relocation to find a job, homeless children may have a difficult time attending school regularly. Lack of transportation may also keep them from getting to school. Children who miss school frequently fall behind academically, losing the opportunity to acquire the skills needed to help them escape poverty.

Since the passage of the McKinney Act, states have been successful in removing some of the obstacles to the enrollment of homeless children and youth. Residency and school records requirements have been relaxed so that homeless children can enroll in school. However, guardianship and immunization still remain barriers to enrollment. According to the National Law Center on Poverty and Homelessness, access to special education programs and services, participation in afterschool events and extracurricular activities, availability of counseling

FIGURE 3.4

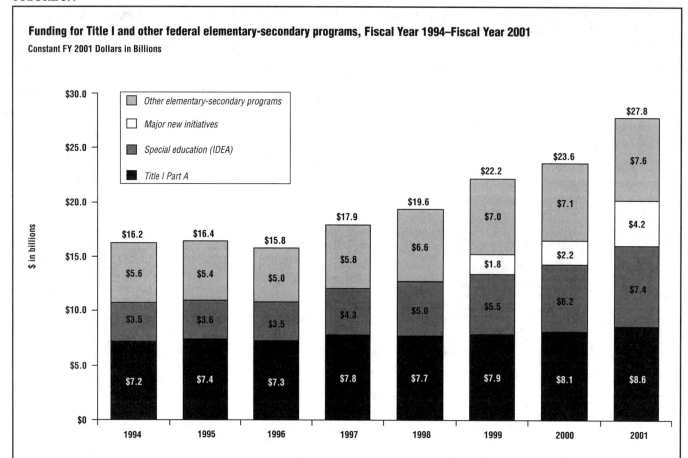

Funding for Title I and other federal elementary-secondary programs, Fiscal Year 1994–Fiscal Year 2001

Constant FY 2001 Dollars in Billions

Note: "Major New Initiatives" included in this exhibit are CSRD, REA, 21st Century Schools, Class Size Reduction, and School Renovation. Funds for Title I Accountability Grants are not included in "New Initiatives" because these are reserved from the Title I Part A appropriation.

SOURCE: "Exhibit 1 Funding for Title I and Other Federal Elementary-Secondary Programs, FY 1994 to FY 2001," in *High Standards for All Students: A Report from the National Assessment of Title I on Progress and Challenges Since the 1994 Reauthorization*, U.S. Department of Education, Planning and Evaluation Service, Washington, DC, January 2001

and psychological services, and access to care programs before and after school are still problems.

Head Start

The Head Start program, established as part of the Economic Opportunity Act of 1964 (PL 88-452), has been one of the most durable federal programs for at-risk children. Because disadvantaged children tend to be less ready for school, the Head Start program operates where it is needed most—in early childhood, infancy to five years. Most children enter the program at ages three or four. In the past, not many children under age three were served by Head Start projects. However, the Early Head Start (EHS) program was established by the 1994 reauthorization of Head Start (PL 103-252). The EHS program serves infants and toddlers, and in 1999, 7.5 percent of the total Head Start appropriation was set aside to fund this program. In 2000 most (56 percent) of enrollment in Head Start consisted of four-year-olds. (See Table 3.8.)

Head Start appropriations have increased substantially in recent years. Between 1980 and 1990, federal funding grew by 111 percent. Since 1990, Head Start appropriations have tripled, from $1.5 billion to nearly $4.5 billion in 1999. (See Table 3.9.)

In 2000 Head Start projects served 829,958 children. Black children (34.5 percent) accounted for the highest proportion of enrollees. White children comprised another 30.4 percent, Hispanic children made up 28.7 percent, 3.3 percent were Native Americans, and another 3 percent were Asian or Hawaiian/Pacific Islanders. (See Table 3.8.)

VOCATIONAL EDUCATION

Secondary Vocational Education

In the past, most high schools had a two-tiered educational system—a higher standards academic curriculum and a lower standards general track or vocational curriculum. Non-academic, vocational classes were for those who did not plan to attend college. However, today's high-skill job market requires all high school graduates to have both academic knowledge and workplace skills and training. Professional careers now demand technical skills and the ability to work in teams; technical careers require the ability to diagnose and analyze problems.

LEGISLATION. The 1990 Carl D. Perkins Vocational and Applied Technology Education Act (PL 101-392) mandated the integration of academic and vocational education, emphasizing a curriculum that makes connections between knowledge development and its application in the workplace. The 1998 renewal of the Perkins Act continued this commitment.

The School-to-Work Opportunities Act of 1994 (PL 103-239) further enhanced academic and vocational integration. School-to-work experiences prepare participants for both postsecondary education and employment and result in a variety of options following graduation from high school—four-year college, two-year college, technical training, skilled entry-level work on a career path, and pursuit of lifelong learning. The federal funding for the program was intended as seed money, and the legislation sunset in 2001. Many states have continued to fund School-to-Work activities.

FIGURE 3.5

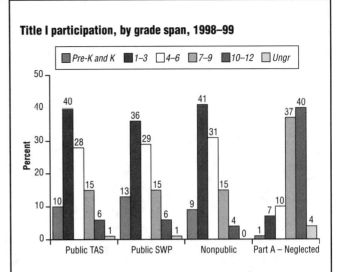

Title I participation, by grade span, 1998–99

Note: TAS=Targeted Assistance Schools and SWP=Schoolwide Program Schools

SOURCE: Beth Sinclair, "Figure 6 Title I Participation, by Grade Span, 1998-99," in *State ESEA Title I Participation Information for 1998-99: Final Summary Report,* prepared for the U.S. Department of Education, Office of the Deputy Secretary, Planning and Evaluation Service, Washington, DC, October 2001

FIGURE 3.6

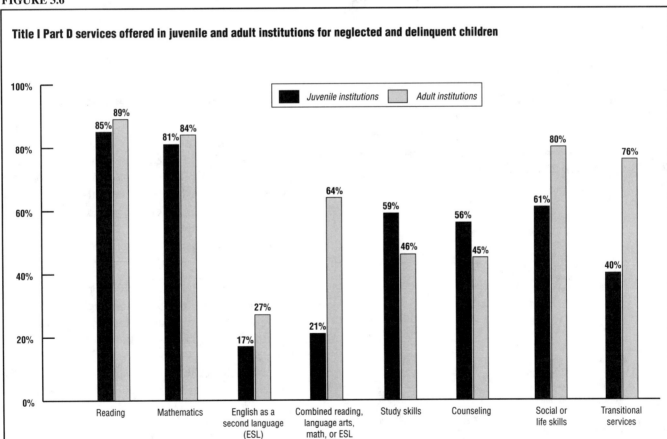

Title I Part D services offered in juvenile and adult institutions for neglected and delinquent children

SOURCE: "Exhibit 27 Title I Part D Services Offered in Juvenile and Adult Institutions for Neglected and Delinquent Children," in *High Standards for All Students: A Report from the National Assessment of Title I on Progress and Challenges Since the 1994 Reauthorization,* U.S. Department of Education, Planning and Evaluation Service, Washington, DC, January 2001

FIGURE 3.7

Traditional streams of migration

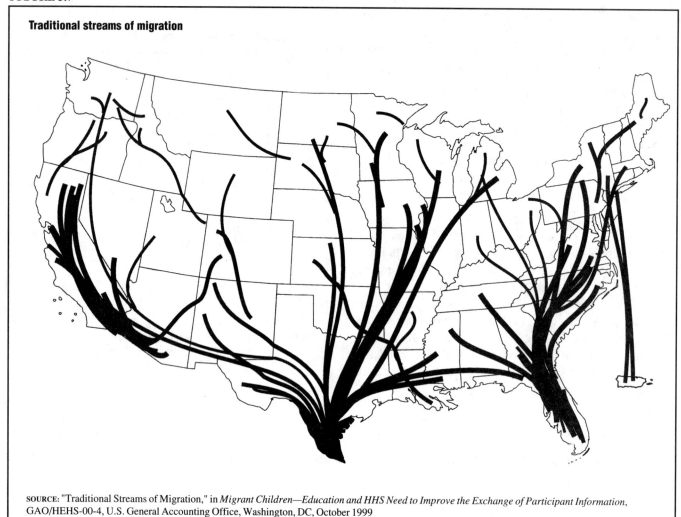

SOURCE: "Traditional Streams of Migration," in *Migrant Children—Education and HHS Need to Improve the Exchange of Participant Information*, GAO/HEHS-00-4, U.S. General Accounting Office, Washington, DC, October 1999

TABLE 3.8

Head Start Fiscal Year 2000 data

Enrollment	857,664
Ages:	
Number of 5 year olds and older	5%
Number of 4 year olds	56%
Number of 3 year olds	33%
Number under 3 years of age	6%
Racial/Ethnic Composition	
American Indian	3.3%
Hispanic	28.7%
Black	34.5%
White	30.4%
Asian	2.0%
Hawaiian/Pacific Islander	1.0%
Number of Grantees	1,525
Number of Classrooms	46,225
Number of Centers	18,200
Average Cost Per Child	$5,951
Paid Staff	180,400
Volunteers	1,252,000

SOURCE: "Head Start Facts FY–2000 Data," in *Head Start Fact Sheet*, U.S. Department of Health and Human Services, The Administration for Children and Families [Online] http://www2.acf.dhhs.gov/programs/hsb/about/fact2001.htm [accessed November 7, 2001]

STUDENT PARTICIPATION IN VOCATIONAL EDUCATION. In 1998 students earned an average of 18.3 academic Carnegie units, which is 4.0 more academic credits than students earned in 1982. Students also earned more total credits in 1998 (25.1 credits) than in 1982 (21.6 credits). Students earned .7 fewer credits in vocational curriculum in 1998 (4 credits) than in 1982 (4.7 credits). (See Figure 3.8.)

A vocational concentration is three or more credits in a single occupational program area (such as business). Most vocational areas did not experience a decline from 1982 to 1998. The two largest vocational areas—trade and industry, and business—experienced declines in enrollment, but health care, technology and communications, food service and hospitality, and child care and education had higher enrollments in 1998 than in 1982.

VOCATIONAL EDUCATION PROGRAMS CHANGING. According to the Office of Vocational and Adult Education, a division of the Department of Education, vocational-technical education has been changing in the following ways:

TABLE 3.9

U.S. Department of Health and Human Services allocations for Head Start and enrollment in Head Start, by state or other area, fiscal years 1996–1999

(in thousands of current dollars)

State or other area	1996 Head Start allocations (in thousands)	1996 Head Start enrollment[1]	1997 Head Start allocations (in thousands)	1997 Head Start enrollment[2]	1998 Head Start allocations (in thousands)	1998 Head Start enrollment[3]	1999 Head Start allocations (in thousands)	1999 Head Start enrollment[4]
Total	$3,438,268	752,077	$3,876,707	793,809	$4,232,433	822,316	$4,502,423	829,958
Alabama	58,265	14,429	65,970	14,979	67,517	15,118	71,983	15,263
Alaska	6,748	1,299	7,581	1,212	8,209	1,261	8,786	1,281
Arizona	47,617	9,818	53,478	10,561	59,017	11,055	62,444	11,127
Arkansas	33,153	9,193	36,396	9,637	39,367	9,893	43,449	10,097
California	392,965	72,606	458,841	79,929	528,339	86,368	554,366	86,459
Colorado	36,364	8,647	40,902	8,952	42,368	8,863	46,602	9,135
Connecticut	27,382	5,567	32,985	6,190	35,244	6,476	37,906	6,825
Delaware	6,239	1,455	8,314	2,077	8,446	2,114	8,873	2,126
District of Columbia	14,530	3,339	17,361	3,273	18,276	3,295	19,201	3,279
Florida	127,325	27,535	144,663	29,523	159,055	30,285	169,996	30,792
Georgia	86,596	19,563	96,295	20,505	105,423	21,195	112,040	21,121
Hawaii	10,981	2,517	12,632	2,539	13,983	2,769	15,786	2,799
Idaho	10,043	1,869	12,529	2,213	13,058	2,231	14,121	2,266
Illinois	148,915	31,817	170,193	33,924	182,050	34,871	192,580	35,211
Indiana	49,804	11,847	55,293	12,415	61,337	12,930	65,226	13,057
Iowa	25,968	6,178	28,458	6,341	33,451	6,922	36,038	7,003
Kansas	25,129	6,074	28,815	6,355	31,299	7,175	32,958	7,000
Kentucky	58,935	14,447	65,587	14,828	71,283	15,163	76,409	15,281
Louisiana	79,596	19,344	87,261	19,998	94,565	20,402	100,196	20,703
Maine	13,734	10,816	15,536	3,392	17,233	3,537	18,695	3,618
Maryland	42,461	8,915	47,688	9,514	51,664	9,507	54,966	9,626
Massachusetts	61,742	3,466	68,913	11,499	73,664	11,877	78,544	12,094
Michigan	135,349	31,198	150,074	32,440	162,316	33,316	171,121	33,422
Minnesota	38,812	8,641	43,536	9,117	48,909	9,545	51,740	9,630
Mississippi	97,001	24,081	103,523	24,693	110,564	24,953	117,375	25,091
Missouri	59,241	14,035	66,763	14,899	73,482	15,415	78,622	16,191
Montana	10,048	2,304	11,500	2,510	12,292	2,555	13,839	2,678
Nebraska	15,890	3,800	19,037	4,088	21,318	4,335	23,890	4,518
Nevada	8,213	1,823	9,942	2,019	11,280	2,035	11,484	2,035
New Hampshire	6,558	1,235	7,430	1,267	8,512	1,382	9,114	1,425
New Jersey	75,151	13,085	82,650	13,746	89,319	14,201	94,945	14,443
New Mexico	27,731	6,587	33,971	7,187	32,470	7,012	35,363	7,108
New York	228,243	40,365	261,541	43,716	286,961	45,608	304,283	45,040
North Carolina	72,594	16,002	80,559	16,825	87,978	17,221	93,979	17,394
North Dakota	7,206	1,874	8,733	2,121	9,721	1,966	10,561	2,002
Ohio	141,607	33,919	155,354	35,441	168,724	36,300	178,271	36,454
Oklahoma	41,397	11,165	45,865	11,631	50,997	12,142	54,422	12,217
Oregon	29,460	4,695	34,466	5,222	37,909	5,400	40,118	5,480
Pennsylvania	127,086	26,198	142,973	27,515	154,046	28,902	165,674	29,124
Rhode Island	10,549	2,567	13,135	2,676	13,901	2,778	15,330	2,817
South Carolina	44,540	10,164	51,714	10,822	52,826	11,110	56,280	11,207
South Dakota	8,480	2,258	10,139	2,374	11,088	2,355	12,708	2,485
Tennessee	62,163	14,291	69,365	14,553	76,803	14,748	81,387	14,753
Texas	224,923	52,107	253,186	54,624	279,640	57,281	299,891	58,173
Utah	18,219	4,201	20,132	4,419	21,728	4,654	23,185	4,679
Vermont	7,811	1,531	8,433	1,379	8,900	1,404	9,691	1,438
Virginia	49,706	11,028	54,571	11,480	61,960	12,053	66,246	12,243
Washington	52,311	8,878	59,644	9,387	64,841	9,682	69,601	9,831
West Virginia	28,125	6,515	31,064	6,858	33,349	6,876	36,062	7,043
Wisconsin	54,013	12,283	58,550	12,556	63,218	12,905	67,582	13,113
Wyoming	5,195	1,279	5,814	1,395	6,421	1,452	7,546	1,500
Migrant programs	139,438	35,117	153,788	36,458	162,206	37,116	178,122	38,132
American Indian/Alaskan Native programs	96,836	19,071	113,920	21,019	121,272	21,612	130,191	21,237

- Vocational-technical education now incorporates both school-based and work-based learning.

- Business partnerships are key to successful programs.

- For most occupations, postsecondary education is essential.

- Vocational-technical education now encompasses postsecondary institutions up to and including universities.

- Vocational-technical education uses more and higher technology.

- Vocational-technical education uses cyberspace as a resource.

SKILLS AND COMPETENCIES. In 1999 public secondary schools that offered at least one occupational program reported using five procedures to ensure job skills were

TABLE 3.9

U.S. Department of Health and Human Services allocations for Head Start and enrollment in Head Start, by state or other area, fiscal years 1996–1999 [CONTINUED]

(in thousands of current dollars)

State or other area	1996 Head Start allocations (in thousands)	Head Start enrollment[1]	1997 Head Start allocations (in thousands)	Head Start enrollment[2]	1998 Head Start allocations (in thousands)	Head Start enrollment[3]	1999 Head Start allocations (in thousands)	Head Start enrollment[4]
Special projects	—	—	—	—	—	—	—	—
Outlying areas
Puerto Rico	134,072	31,744	143,121	32,221	155,526	33,273	155,526	33,470
Pacific Territories	9,541	5,849	9,963	5,849	10,297	5,989	10,297	5,989
Virgin Islands	6,267	1,446	6,560	1,446	6,811	1,430	6,811	1,430

—Not available.

[1] The distribution of enrollment by age was: 6 percent were 5 years old and over; 62 percent were 4-year-olds; 29 percent were 3-year-olds; and 4 percent were under 3 years of age. Handicapped children accounted for 12.8 percent in Head Start programs. The racial/ethnic composition was: American Indian/Alaskan Native, 3.5 percent; Hispanic, 25.2 percent; black, 36 percent; white, 32.3 percent; and Asian, 3 percent.

[2] The distribution of enrollment by age was: 6 percent were 5 years old and over; 60 percent were 4-year-olds; 30 percent were 3-year-olds; and 4 percent were under 3 years of age. Handicapped children accounted for 13 percent in Head Start programs. The racial/ethnic composition was: American Indian/Alaskan Native, 4 percent; Hispanic, 26 percent; black, 36 percent; white, 31 percent; and Asian, 3 percent.

[3] The distribution of enrollment by age was: 6 percent were 5 years old and over; 59 percent were 4-year-olds; 31 percent were 3-year-olds; and 4 percent were under 3 years of age. Handicapped children accounted for 13 percent in Head Start programs. The racial/ethnic composition was: American Indian/Alaskan Native, 3 percent; Hispanic, 26 percent; black, 36 percent; white, 32 percent; and Asian, 3 percent.

[4] The distribution of enrollment by age was: 6 percent were 5 years old and over; 59 percent were 4-year-olds; 31 percent were 3-year-olds; and 4 percent were under 3 years of age. Handicapped children accounted for 13 percent in Head Start programs. The racial/ethnic composition was: American Indian/Alaskan Native, 3 percent; Hispanic, 27 percent; black, 35 percent; white, 31 percent; and Asian, 3 percent.

NOTE: Detail may not sum to totals due to rounding.

SOURCE: Thomas D. Snyder and Charlene M. Hoffman, "Table 371. U.S. Department of Health and Human Services allocations for Head Start and enrollment in Head Start, by state or other area: Fiscal years 1996 to 1999," in *Digest of Education Statistics, 2000,* NCES 2001-034, U.S. Department of Education, National Center for Education Statistics, Washington, DC, January 2001

FIGURE 3.8

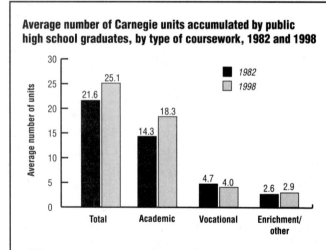

Average number of Carnegie units accumulated by public high school graduates, by type of coursework, 1982 and 1998

■ 1982
□ 1998

Average number of units

Total: 21.6 (1982), 25.1 (1998)
Academic: 14.3 (1982), 18.3 (1998)
Vocational: 4.7 (1982), 4.0 (1998)
Enrichment/other: 2.6 (1982), 2.9 (1998)

NOTE: In secondary education, one Carnegie unit is awarded for the completion of a course that meets one period per day for one year, or the equivalent.

SOURCE: David Hurst and Lisa Hudson, "Figure 1. Average number of Carnegie units accumulated by public high school graduates, by type of coursework: 1982 and 1998," in *Changes in High School Vocational Coursetaking in a Larger Perspective*, NCES 2001-026, U.S. Department of Education, National Center for Education Statistics, Washington, DC, December 2000

taught. Student work experiences were offered at 83 percent of vocational schools, and at 70 percent of comprehensive high schools. Follow-up surveys of graduates were conducted by 88 percent of vocational high schools, and by 69 percent of comprehensive schools. Employer surveys were completed by 73 percent of vocational schools, and by 66 percent of comprehensive high schools. An advisory committee made up of industry was utilized at 91 percent of vocational schools, and at 65 percent of comprehensive high schools. Least common were faculty externships, which were offered by 58 percent of vocational schools, and by 46 percent of comprehensive high schools. (See Figure 3.9.)

Vocational educators sometimes utilize skill competencies to measure the progress of students toward meeting a defined set of outcomes that the curriculum is supposed to convey. These skills should match those needed by employers in the field. In 1999 public secondary schools that offered at least one occupational program reported using different approaches to involving educators and industry representatives to develop or adopt skill competency lists. Course instructors or groups of educators developed the skill competencies exclusively at 35 percent of comprehensive and 19 percent of vocational high schools. Educators relied on some input from industry at 53 percent of comprehensive high schools, and 62 percent of vocational schools. Equal input from educators and industry was reported by 31 percent of comprehensive and 49 percent of vocational high schools. The least common approach was leaving the task primarily or exclusively to industry, which was done by 5 percent of comprehensive high schools and 9 percent of vocational schools. (See Figure 3.10.)

FIGURE 3.9

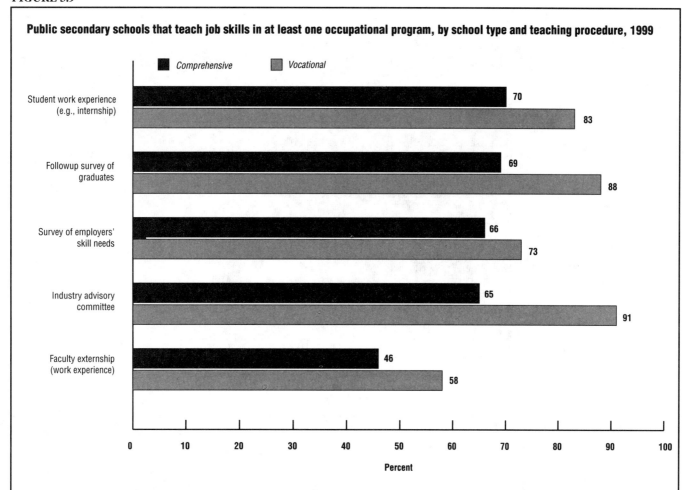

Public secondary schools that teach job skills in at least one occupational program, by school type and teaching procedure, 1999

NOTE: Data are presented for public secondary schools that offer one or more of the listed occupational programs. Estimates are based on public secondary schools with 11th and 12th grades.

SOURCE: Richard P. Phelps, Basmat Parsad, Elizabeth Farris, et al., "Figure 7. Percent of public secondary schools offering at least one listed occupational program that report using each of five procedures to ensure they teach job skills in at least one program, by school type: 1999," in *Features of Occupational Programs at the Secondary and Postsecondary Levels*, NCES 2001-018, U.S. Department of Education, National Center for Education Statistics, Washington, DC, June 2001

Tech Prep Education

The Perkins Act and the School-to-Work Opportunities Act both emphasized Tech Prep education, a 4+2, 3+2, or a 2+2 (depending on the number of years spent in the high school program) organized sequence of study in a technical field. The sequence, begun as early as ninth grade, extends through two years of postsecondary occupational education or an apprenticeship program of at least two years past high school. The program culminates in an associate degree or certificate.

States receive federal funds to implement Tech Prep programs. In addition to receiving an associate degree or certificate, students will receive technical preparation in at least one field: engineering technology; applied science; mechanical, industrial, or practical art or trade; or agriculture, health or business. Outcomes also include employment.

Postsecondary Vocational Education

In 1999 less-than-four-year postsecondary institutions with occupational programs reported offering mechanical occupations, building trades, technical occupations, business and marketing occupations, health/life sciences occupations, and service occupations. Most programs are offered by two-year institutions, although service occupations are common at less-than-two-year institutions. (See Figure 3.11.)

Postsecondary institutions use different methods to link vocational curriculum with skill benchmarks. Of those institutions offering occupational programs, 89 percent of two-year and 87 percent of less-than-two-year schools reported using periodic internal review to ensure the teaching of job skills in 1999. Industry advisory committees were utilized by 89 percent of two-year, and 84 percent of less-than-two-year, institutions. Follow-up surveys of

FIGURE 3.10

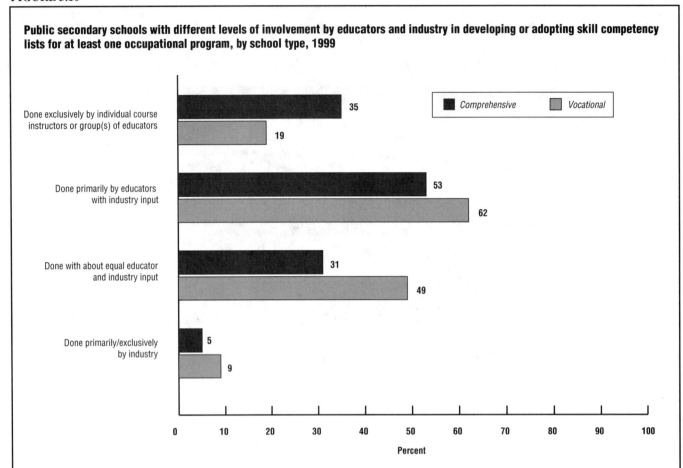

Public secondary schools with different levels of involvement by educators and industry in developing or adopting skill competency lists for at least one occupational program, by school type, 1999

NOTE: Data are presented for public secondary schools that offer one or more of the listed occupational programs. Estimates are based on public secondary schools with 11th and 12th grades.

SOURCE: Richard P. Phelps, Basmat Parsad, Elizabeth Farris, et al., "Figure 11. Percent of public secondary schools offering at least one listed occupational program that report different levels of involvement by educators and industry in developing or adopting skill competency lists for at least one program, by school type: 1999," in *Features of Occupational Programs at the Secondary and Postsecondary Levels,* NCES 2001-018, U.S. Department of Education, National Center for Education Statistics, Washington, DC, June 2001

graduates were conducted by 88 percent of two-year institutions, and by 89 percent of less-than-two-year institutions. Surveys of employers' skill needs were done by 82 percent of two-year institutions, and by 84 percent of less-than-two-year institutions. Slightly more than half of these institutions provided mechanisms for faculty to get recent work experience—53 percent of two-year and 56 percent of less-than-two-year institutions. (See Figure 3.12.)

In 1999 postsecondary institutions that offered at least one occupational program reported varying levels of involvement by educators and industry in developing or adopting skill competency lists. Twelve percent of two-year and 15 percent of less-than-two-year institutions reported that their skill competency lists were developed or adopted exclusively by educators. Educators utilized some industry input in their curricula at 52 percent of two-year institutions, and 33 percent of less-than-two-year institutions. Educators and industry representatives

had about equal input at 38 percent of two-year, and 34 percent of less-than-two-year postsecondary institutions. Only 11 percent of two-year institutions and 5 percent of less-than-two-year institutions reported allowing competencies to be developed primarily or exclusively by industry. (See Figure 3.13.)

Postsecondary institutions offer different types of credentials to completers of vocational programs. In 1999 an institutional certificate or diploma was the most common, with 86 percent of two-year and 89 percent of less-than-two-year institutions offering this credential. Not surprisingly, 86 percent of two-year institutions offered an associate's degree, but only 8 percent of less-than-two-year institutions granted this degree. State registration, license, or certificate was offered by 65 percent of two-year and by 72 percent of less-than-two-year institutions. An industry or trade certificate or diploma was available at more than one-third (38 percent) of two-year

FIGURE 3.11

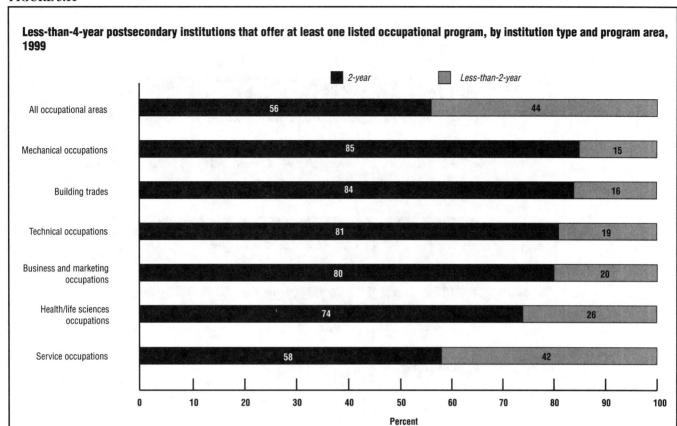

Less-than-4-year postsecondary institutions that offer at least one listed occupational program, by institution type and program area, 1999

Note: Data presented in "All occupational areas" bar represent the distribution for all less-than-4-year postsecondary institutions that offer one or more of the listed occupational programs. Data presented in each of the other bars are based on the number of less-than-4-year postsecondary institutions that offer one or more of the listed occupational programs in that broad program area. Estimates are based on 2-year and less-than-2-year postsecondary institutions with Title IV eligibility.

SOURCE: Richard P. Phelps, Basmat Parsad, Elizabeth Farris, et al., "Figure 5. Percentage distribution of types of less-than-4-year postsecondary institutions that offer at least one listed occupational program, for all program areas, and in each broad program area: 1999," in *Features of Occupational Programs at the Secondary and Postsecondary Levels*, NCES 2001-018, U.S. Department of Education, National Center for Education Statistics, Washington, DC, June 2001

institutions, and at one-quarter (25 percent) of less-than-two-year institutions. A company certificate was a creden-tial offered by 23 percent of two-year and by 9 percent of less-than-two-year institutions. (See Figure 3.14.)

FIGURE 3.12

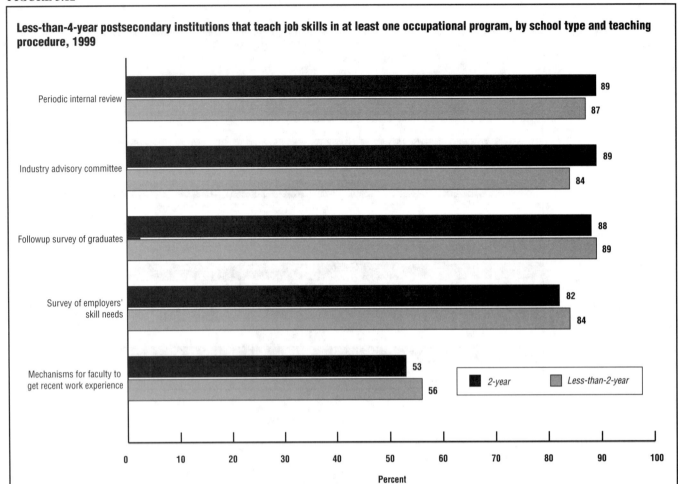

Less-than-4-year postsecondary institutions that teach job skills in at least one occupational program, by school type and teaching procedure, 1999

NOTE: Data are presented for less-than-4-year postsecondary institutions that offer one or more of the listed occupational programs. Estimates are based on 2-year and less-than-2-year postsecondary institutions with Title IV eligibility.

SOURCE: Richard P. Phelps, Basmat Parsad, Elizabeth Farris, et al., "Figure 8. Percent of less-than-4-year postsecondary institutions offering at least one listed occupational program that report using each of five procedures to ensure they teach job skills, by type of institution: 1999," in *Features of Occupational Programs at the Secondary and Postsecondary Levels*, NCES 2001-018, U.S. Department of Education, National Center for Education Statistics, Washington, DC, June 2001

FIGURE 3.13

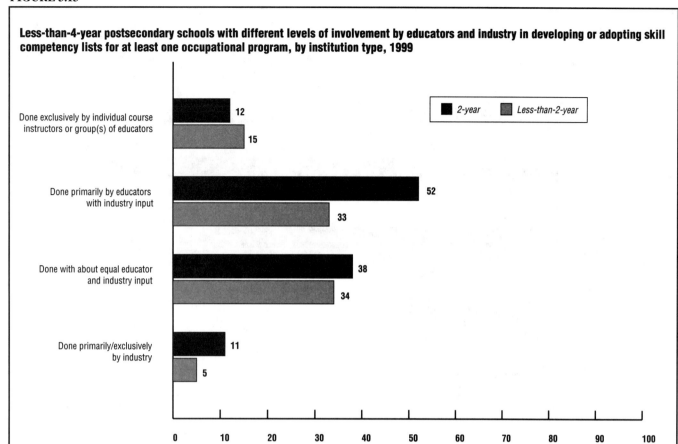

Less-than-4-year postsecondary schools with different levels of involvement by educators and industry in developing or adopting skill competency lists for at least one occupational program, by institution type, 1999

NOTE: Data are presented for less-than-4-year postsecondary institutions that offer one or more of the listed occupational programs. Estimates are based on 2-year and less-than-2-year postsecondary insititutions with Title IV eligibility.

SOURCE: Richard P. Phelps, Basmat Parsad, Elizabeth Farris, et al., "Figure 12. Percent of less-than-4-year postsecondary institutions offering at least one listed occupational program that report different levels of involvement by educators and industry in developing or adopting skill competency lists for at least one program, by type of institution: 1999," in *Features of Occupational Programs at the Secondary and Postsecondary Levels,* NCES 2001-018, U.S. Department of Education, National Center for Education Statistics, Washington, DC, June 2001

FIGURE 3.14

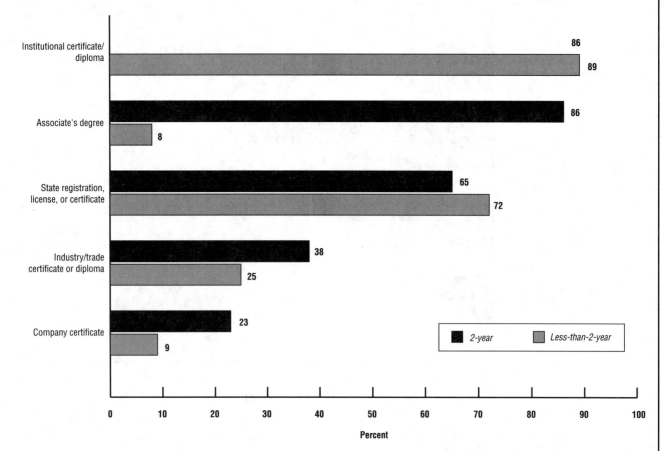

Less-than-4-year postsecondary schools offering credentials for at least one occupational program, by type of institution and credential, 1999

NOTE: Data are presented for less-than-4-year postsecondary institutions that offer one or more of the listed occupational programs. Estimates are based on 2-year and less-than-2-year postsecondary institutions with Title IV eligibility.

SOURCE: Richard P. Phelps, Basmat Parsad, Elizabeth Farris, et al., "Figure 13. Percent of less-than-4-year postsecondary institutions offering at least one occupational program, that offer each type of credential for at least one program, by type of institution: 1999," in *Features of Occupational Programs at the Secondary and Postsecondary Levels,* NCES 2001-018, U.S. Department of Education, National Center for Education Statistics, Washington, DC, June 2001

CHAPTER 4
TESTING AND ACHIEVEMENT

STANDARDS AND ASSESSMENTS

Content standards provide a framework for the knowledge and skills that students are expected to acquire. Performance standards determine how well students should be able to perform relative to the content standards. Assessments provide information regarding the attainment of standards. Elementary, secondary, and special education programs rely on state standards-based assessment systems to evaluate the effectiveness of federal programs. According to federal expectations for Title I (the federal program that helps states and schools meet special education needs), academic standards must be rigorous, and exceed minimum competencies. They must be fair, valid, and reliable, and include all students. Assessment results should be reported for schools and districts, and they must include demographic categories (gender, race and ethnicity, English proficiency, disability, migrant status, and low-income status). Title I legislation specifies that performance standards must provide information for at least three levels of performance.

In 2000 50 states and the District of Columbia had content standards in place, while 28 states had performance standards for mathematics and reading/language arts. (See Figure 4.1.) In 1999–2000, 48 states included reading and mathematics in their statewide assessment, 34 assessed science, 31 measured writing ability, and 29 included social studies in their assessment system. (See Figure 4.2.)

FIGURE 4.1

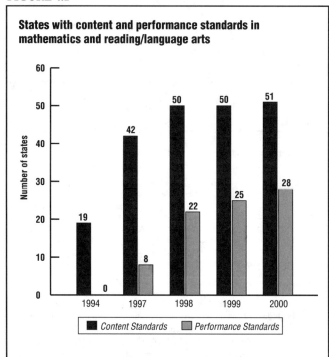

SOURCE: "Exhibit 14. States with Content and Performance Standards in Mathematics and Reading/Language Arts," in *High Standards for All Students: A Report from the National Assessment of Title I on Progress and Challenges Since the 1994 Reauthorization,* U.S. Department of Education, January 2001

FIGURE 4.2

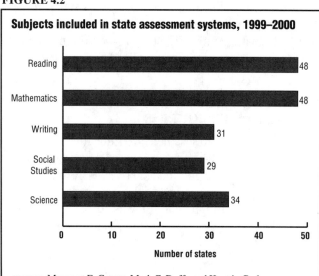

SOURCE: Margaret E. Goertz, Mark C. Duffy and Kerstin Carlson Le Floch, "Figure 1. Subjects Included in State Assessment Systems, 1999–2000," in *Assessment and Accountability Systems in the United States: 1999–2000*, University of Pennsylvania, Graduate School of Education, Consortium for Policy Research in Education, March 2001

TABLE 4.1

Opinion about achievement testing in public schools

	National Totals			Public School Parents		
	'01 %	'00 %	'97 %	'01 %	'00 %	'97 %
Too much emphasis on testing	31	30	20	36	34	19
Not enough emphasis	22	23	28	20	19	26
Just the right amount of emphasis	44	43	48	43	46	54
Don't know	3	4	4	1	1	1

SOURCE: Lowell C. Rose and Alec M. Gallup, "In your opinion, is there too much emphasis on achievement testing in the public schools in your community, not enough emphasis on testing, or about the right amount?" in "The 33rd Annual Phi Delta Kappa/Gallup Poll of the Public's Attitude Toward the Public Schools," Phi Delta Kappan, vol. 83, no. 1, September 2001

"The 33rd Annual Phi Delta Kappa/Gallup Poll of the Public's Attitude Toward the Public Schools" asked the public for opinions about standardized testing. The results were mixed. In 2001 less than half (44 percent) of Americans believed there was just the right amount of emphasis on achievement testing in public schools. Less than one-third (31 percent) felt there was too much emphasis on testing, while 22 percent said there was not enough emphasis on achievement testing in public schools. (See Table 4.1.) Americans favor using classroom work and homework (63 percent) over test scores (31 percent) as the best way to measure student achievement. (See Figure 4.3.)

Besides test achievement, other measures of student and school performance are often collected by the states. In 39 states attendance rates were included in assessments in 1999–2000. Enrollment was included in 38 states' reports, dropout rates were included by 37 states. Other states measured graduation rates (27 states), promotion/ retention rates (12 states), and student mobility/transfer (11 states).

NATIONAL ASSESSMENT OF EDUCATIONAL PROGRESS

The National Assessment of Educational Progress (NAEP) has conducted assessments of American students since 1969. The federally funded NAEP is the only regular national survey of educational achievement at the elementary, middle, and high school levels. It is authorized by Congress and administered by the National Center for Education Statistics (NCES). The Augustus F. Hawkins-Robert T. Stafford Elementary and Secondary School Improvement Amendments of 1988 (P.L. 100-290) established the National Assessment Governing Board (NAGB) to formulate policy guidelines for NAEP. The National Assessment Governing Board (NAGP) determines which subjects will be assessed and how they will be assessed.

FIGURE 4.3

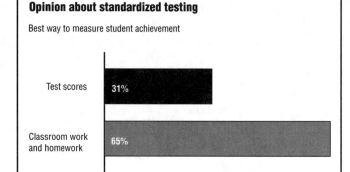

Opinion about standardized testing

Best way to measure student achievement

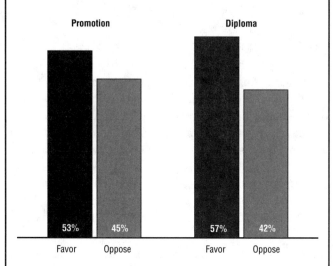

Use a single standardized test to decide

SOURCE: Lowell C. Rose and Alec M. Gallup, "Figure 12. Opinions Regarding Standardized Testing," in "The 33rd Annual Phi Delta Kappa/ Gallup Poll of the Public's Attitude Toward the Public Schools," Phi Delta Kappan, vol. 83, no. 1, September 2001

FIGURE 4.4

Academic achievement level definitions

Basic   This level denotes partial mastery of prerequisite knowledge and skills that are fundamental for proficient work at each grade.

Proficient   This level represents solid academic performance for each grade assessed. Students reaching this level have demonstrated competency over challenging subject matter, including subject-matter knowledge, application of such knowledge to real-world situations, and analytical skills appropriate to the subject matter.

Advanced   This level signifies superior performance.

SOURCE: Patricia L. Donahue, Robert J. Finnegan, Anthony D. Lutkus, et al., "Figure i.3. Achievement Levels," in The Nation's Report Card: Fourth Grade Reading 2000, NCES 2001-499, U.S. Department of Education, National Center for Education Statistics, Washington, DC, April 2001

TABLE 4.2

Average student proficiency in reading, by age and selected characteristics of students, 1971–99

Selected characteristics of students	1971	1975	1980	1984	1988	1990	1992	1994	1996	1999
9-year-olds[1]										
Total	207.6 (1.0)	210.0 (0.7)	215.0 (1.0)	210.9 (0.7)	211.8 (1.1)	209.2 (1.2)	210.5 (0.9)	211.0 (1.2)	212.5 (1.0)	211.7 (1.3)
Male	201.2 (1.1)	204.3 (0.8)	210.0 (1.1)	207.5 (0.8)	207.5 (1.4)	204.0 (1.7)	205.9 (1.3)	207.3 (1.3)	207.0 (1.4)	208.5 (1.6)
Female	213.9 (1.0)	215.8 (0.8)	220.1 (1.1)	214.2 (0.8)	216.3 (1.3)	214.5 (1.2)	215.4 (0.9)	214.7 (1.4)	217.8 (1.1)	214.8 (1.5)
Race/ethnicity										
White, non-Hispanic	214.0 (0.9)	216.6 (0.7)	221.3 (0.8)	218.2 (0.8)	217.7 (1.4)	217.0 (1.3)	217.9 (1.0)	218.0 (1.3)	219.6 (1.2)	221.0 (1.6)
Black, non-Hispanic	170.1 (1.7)	181.2 (1.2)	189.3 (1.8)	185.7 (1.1)	188.5 (2.4)	181.8 (2.9)	184.5 (2.2)	185.4 (2.3)	190.9 (2.6)	185.5 (2.3)
Hispanic	(2)—	182.7 (2.2)	190.2 (2.3)	187.2 (2.1)	193.7 (3.5)	189.4 (2.3)	191.7 (3.1)	185.9 (3.9)	194.8 (3.4)	193.0 (2.7)
Parental education										
Not high school graduate	188.6 (1.5)	189.9 (1.3)	194.3 (1.6)	195.1 (1.4)	192.5 (4.9)	192.6 (3.2)	194.9 (4.5)	189.1 (4.0)	197.3 (3.4)	199.1 (3.9)
Graduated high school	207.8 (1.2)	211.3 (0.9)	213.0 (1.3)	208.9 (1.0)	210.8 (2.2)	209.1 (1.8)	207.4 (1.5)	207.1 (2.6)	206.8 (2.0)	206.2 (2.0)
Post high school	223.9 (1.1)	221.5 (0.9)	226.0 (1.1)	222.9 (0.9)	220.0 (1.7)	217.7 (2.0)	219.5 (1.4)	221.0 (1.3)	219.4 (1.4)	219.7 (1.7)
Control of school										
Public	——	——	213.5 (1.1)	209.4 (0.8)	210.2 (1.2)	207.5 (1.4)	208.6 (1.0)	209.4 (1.4)	210.2 (1.0)	209.9 (1.3)
Private	——	——	227.0 (1.8)	222.8 (1.6)	223.4 (3.0)	228.3 (3.3)	224.7 (2.3)	225.0 (2.7)	226.6 (3.0)	225.7 (3.3)
Region										
Northeast	213.0 (1.7)	214.8 (1.3)	221.1 (2.1)	215.7 (1.7)	215.2 (2.6)	217.4 (2.2)	217.6 (2.6)	217.4 (2.9)	220.0 (1.8)	222.0 (3.5)
Southeast	193.9 (2.9)	201.1 (1.2)	210.3 (2.3)	204.3 (1.6)	207.2 (2.1)	197.4 (3.2)	199.3 (2.0)	208.4 (3.0)	206.0 (2.8)	205.0 (2.3)
Central	214.9 (1.2)	215.5 (1.2)	216.7 (1.4)	215.3 (1.5)	218.2 (2.2)	212.7 (2.0)	215.8 (1.6)	214.3 (2.3)	215.0 (2.6)	215.0 (3.9)
West	205.0 (2.0)	207.0 (2.0)	212.8 (1.8)	207.8 (1.5)	207.9 (2.6)	209.6 (2.8)	209.3 (2.3)	205.1 (2.8)	210.0 (1.9)	206.0 (1.8)
13-year-olds[1]										
Total	255.2 (0.9)	255.9 (0.8)	258.5 (0.9)	257.1 (0.5)	257.5 (1.0)	256.8 (0.8)	259.8 (1.2)	257.9 (0.9)	257.9 (1.0)	259.4 (1.0)
Male	249.6 (1.0)	249.6 (0.8)	254.3 (1.1)	252.6 (0.6)	251.8 (1.3)	250.5 (1.1)	254.1 (1.7)	250.6 (1.2)	251.1 (1.2)	253.5 (1.3)
Female	260.8 (0.9)	262.3 (0.9)	262.6 (0.9)	261.7 (0.6)	263.0 (1.0)	263.1 (1.1)	265.3 (1.2)	265.7 (1.2)	264.3 (1.2)	265.2 (1.2)
Race/ethnicity										
White, non-Hispanic	260.9 (0.7)	262.1 (0.7)	264.4 (0.7)	262.6 (0.6)	261.3 (1.1)	262.3 (0.9)	266.4 (1.2)	265.1 (1.1)	265.9 (1.0)	266.7 (1.2)
Black, non-Hispanic	222.4 (1.2)	225.7 (1.2)	232.8 (1.5)	236.3 (1.0)	242.9 (2.4)	241.5 (2.2)	237.6 (2.3)	234.3 (2.4)	234.0 (2.6)	238.2 (2.4)
Hispanic	(2)—	232.5 (3.0)	237.2 (2.0)	239.6 (1.7)	240.1 (3.5)	237.8 (2.3)	239.2 (3.5)	235.1 (1.9)	238.3 (2.9)	243.8 (2.9)
Parental education										
Not high school graduate	238.4 (1.3)	238.7 (1.2)	238.5 (1.1)	240.0 (0.9)	246.5 (2.1)	240.8 (1.8)	239.2 (2.6)	236.7 (2.4)	239.3 (2.8)	237.9 (3.4)
Graduated high school	255.5 (0.8)	254.6 (0.7)	253.5 (0.9)	253.4 (0.7)	252.7 (1.2)	251.4 (0.9)	252.1 (1.7)	251.4 (1.4)	250.9 (1.5)	251.4 (1.8)
Post high school	270.2 (0.8)	269.8 (0.8)	270.9 (0.8)	267.6 (0.7)	265.3 (1.4)	266.9 (1.0)	269.9 (1.4)	268.5 (1.2)	268.7 (1.2)	269.6 (1.1)
Control of school										
Public	——	——	256.9 (1.1)	255.2 (0.6)	256.1 (1.0)	255.0 (0.8)	257.2 (1.3)	255.6 (1.0)	256.0 (1.1)	256.9 (1.4)
Private	——	——	270.6 (1.5)	271.2 (1.7)	268.3 (2.8)	269.7 (2.9)	276.3 (2.6)	275.8 (3.4)	273.0 (3.4)	276.4 (3.4)
Region										
Northeast	261.1 (2.0)	258.5 (1.8)	260.0 (1.8)	260.4 (0.6)	258.6 (2.4)	258.9 (1.8)	264.6 (3.2)	269.0 (2.0)	259.0 (2.6)	263.0 (2.9)
Southeast	244.7 (1.7)	249.3 (1.5)	252.6 (1.6)	254.4 (1.5)	257.6 (2.2)	255.5 (2.2)	253.8 (2.5)	252.7 (2.5)	251.0 (3.3)	254.0 (2.4)
Central	260.1 (1.8)	261.5 (1.4)	264.5 (1.4)	258.8 (1.0)	255.9 (2.0)	257.4 (1.5)	263.5 (3.0)	259.3 (3.3)	267.0 (1.8)	261.0 (1.9)
West	253.6 (1.3)	253.2 (1.7)	256.4 (2.0)	253.8 (0.9)	257.9 (2.1)	255.6 (1.6)	257.5 (1.6)	252.9 (2.1)	257.0 (1.7)	259.0 (2.2)
17-year-olds[1]										
Total	285.2 (1.2)	285.6 (0.8)	285.5 (1.2)	288.8 (0.6)	290.1 (1.0)	290.2 (1.1)	289.7 (1.1)	288.1 (1.3)	287.6 (1.1)	287.8 (1.3)
Male	278.9 (1.2)	279.7 (1.0)	281.8 (1.3)	283.8 (0.6)	286.0 (1.5)	284.0 (1.6)	284.2 (1.6)	281.7 (2.2)	280.6 (1.3)	281.5 (1.6)
Female	291.3 (1.3)	291.2 (1.0)	289.2 (1.2)	293.9 (0.8)	293.8 (1.5)	296.5 (1.2)	295.7 (1.1)	294.7 (1.5)	295.1 (1.2)	294.6 (1.4)
Race/ethnicity										
White, non-Hispanic	291.4 (1.0)	293.0 (0.6)	292.8 (0.9)	295.2 (0.7)	294.7 (1.2)	296.6 (1.2)	297.4 (1.4)	295.7 (1.5)	295.1 (1.2)	294.6 (1.4)
Black, non-Hispanic	238.7 (1.7)	240.6 (2.0)	243.1 (1.8)	264.3 (1.0)	274.4 (2.4)	267.3 (2.3)	260.6 (2.1)	266.2 (3.9)	266.1 (2.7)	263.9 (1.7)
Hispanic	(2)—	252.4 (3.6)	261.4 (2.7)	268.1 (2.2)	270.8 (4.3)	274.8 (3.6)	271.2 (3.7)	263.2 (4.9)	265.4 (4.1)	270.7 (3.9)
Parental education										
Not high school graduate	261.3 (1.5)	262.5 (1.3)	262.1 (1.5)	269.4 (1.1)	267.4 (2.0)	269.7 (2.8)	270.8 (3.9)	267.9 (2.7)	267.3 (3.2)	264.8 (3.6)
Graduated high school	283.0 (1.2)	281.4 (1.1)	277.5 (1.0)	281.2 (0.7)	282.0 (1.3)	282.9 (1.4)	280.5 (1.6)	276.1 (1.9)	273.4 (1.7)	273.9 (2.1)
Post high school	302.2 (1.0)	300.6 (0.7)	298.9 (1.0)	301.2 (0.7)	299.5 (1.3)	299.9 (1.1)	298.6 (1.4)	298.5 (1.4)	297.7 (1.2)	297.5 (1.2)
Control of school										
Public	——	——	284.4 (1.2)	287.2 (0.6)	288.7 (1.0)	288.6 (1.1)	287.8 (1.0)	286.0 (1.5)	287.0 (1.1)	285.6 (1.3)
Private	——	——	298.4 (2.7)	303.0 (2.0)	299.6 (3.8)	311.0 (4.2)	309.6 (4.2)	306.1 (5.8)	294.2 (5.7)	307.2 (3.5)
Region										
Northeast	291.3 (2.8)	289.1 (1.7)	285.9 (2.4)	292.2 (1.9)	294.8 (2.9)	295.7 (1.8)	297.3 (3.2)	296.8 (4.2)	292.0 (2.8)	295.0 (4.0)
Southeast	270.5 (2.4)	276.5 (1.4)	280.1 (2.2)	284.7 (1.6)	285.2 (2.1)	285.1 (2.5)	278.4 (2.9)	283.5 (2.8)	279.0 (2.6)	279.0 (2.4)
Central	290.7 (2.1)	291.8 (1.4)	287.4 (2.2)	290.0 (1.4)	291.2 (1.9)	293.5 (2.4)	293.8 (2.1)	285.7 (3.7)	293.0 (2.1)	292.0 (1.5)
West	283.7 (1.8)	281.6 (1.9)	287.3 (2.1)	288.4 (1.1)	289.0 (1.8)	286.8 (2.6)	290.4 (2.3)	287.8 (2.8)	287.0 (2.4)	286.0 (3.0)

— Not available.

[1]Excludes persons not enrolled in school.

[2]Test scores of Hispanics were not tabulated separately.

NOTE: These test scores are from the National Assessment of Educational Progress (NAEP). The NAEP scores have been evaluated at certain performance levels. A score of 300 implies an ability to find, understand, summarize, and explain relatively complicated literary and informational material. A score of 250 implies an ability to search for specific information, interrelate ideas, and make generalizations about literature, science, and social studies materials. A score of 200 implies an ability to understand, combine ideas, and make inferences based on short uncomplicated passages about specific or sequentially related information. A score of 150 implies an ability to follow brief written directions and carry out simple, discrete reading tasks. Scale ranges from 0 to 500. Some data have been revised from previously published figures. Standard errors appear in parentheses.

SOURCE: Thomas D. Snyder and Charlene M. Hoffman, "Table 110.—Average student proficiency in reading, by age and selected characteristics of students: 1971 to 1999," in *Digest of Education Statistics, 2000*, NCES 2001-034, U.S. Department of Education, National Center for Education Statistics, Washington, DC, January 2001

FIGURE 4.5

Reading achievement level descriptions for grade 4

Basic (208)   Fourth-grade students performing at the *Basic* level should demonstrate an understanding of the overall meaning of what they read. When reading text appropriate for fourth-graders, they should be able to make relatively obvious connections between the text and their own experiences and extend the ideas in the text by making simple inferences.

For example, when reading **literary text**, students should be able to tell what the story is generally about—providing details to support their understanding—and be able to connect aspects of the stories to their own experiences.

When reading **informational text**, *Basic*-level fourth-graders should be able to tell what the selection is generally about or identify the purpose for reading it, provide details to support their understanding, and connect ideas from the text to their background knowledge and experiences.

Proficient (238)   Fourth-grade students performing at the *Proficient* level should be able to demonstrate an overall understanding of the text, providing inferential as well as literal information. When reading text appropriate to fourth grade, they should be able to extend the ideas in the text by making inferences, drawing conclusions, and making connections to their own experiences. The connection between the text and what the student infers should be clear.

For example, when reading **literary text**, *Proficient*-level fourth-graders should be able to summarize the story, draw conclusions about the characters or plot, and recognize relationships such as cause and effect.

When reading **informational text**, *Proficient*-level students should be able to summarize the information and identify the author's intent or purpose. They should be able to draw reasonable conclusions from the text, recognize relationships such as cause and effect or similarities and differences, and identify the meaning of the selection's key concepts.

Advanced (268)   Fourth-grade students performing at the *Advanced* level should be able to generalize about topics in the reading selection and demonstrate an awareness of how authors compose and use literary devices. When reading text appropriate to fourth grade, they should be able to judge text critically and, in general, give thorough answers that indicate careful thought.

For example, when reading **literary text**, *Advanced*-level students should be able to make generalizations about the point of the story and extend its meaning by integrating personal experiences and other readings with the ideas suggested by the text. They should be able to identify literary devices such as figurative language.

When reading **informational text**, *Advanced*-level fourth-graders should be able to explain the author's intent by using supporting material from the text. They should be able to make critical judgments of the form and content of the text and explain their judgments clearly.

SOURCE: Patricia L. Donahue, Robert J. Finnegan, Anthony D. Lutkus, et al., "Figure 1.3. Reading Achievement Levels," in *The Nation's Report Card: Fourth Grade Reading 2000*, NCES 2001-499, U.S. Department of Education, National Center for Education Statistics, Washington, DC, April 2001

Designed as a measure of the nation's educational system, the NAEP is a series of reading, writing, mathematics, science, history, civics, and geography tests. The tests are given periodically to randomly selected samples of youth ages 9, 13, and 17 attending both public and private schools. Student performance in all grade levels is measured on a proficiency scale of 0 to 500. This allows a comparison of younger students with older ones, as well as an assessment of progress from year to year.

Beginning with the 1990 assessments, the NAGB also developed achievement levels for each subject at each grade level in an effort to measure the match between students' actual achievement and their desired achievement. A panel of teachers, education specialists, and other members of the general public categorized these levels into Basic, Proficient, and Advanced. (See Figure 4.4.) Achievement levels provide another way to report assessment results, allowing comparisons between percentages of students who achieve a particular level on one assessment with the percentage who achieve that level the next time that subject is assessed. They are also used to make comparisons between states and the nation.

Reading Performance

U.S. Secretary of Education Rod Paige noted in a 2001 *Back To School Address* for the National Press Club that "nearly 70 percent of inner city and rural fourth graders can't read at a basic level. There is a persistent achievement gap between disadvantaged and minority students and their peers. Reading scores have been flat for the past eight years." (Washington, DC, September 2001.)

The ability to read is fundamental to virtually all aspects of the education process. If students cannot read well, they usually cannot succeed in other subject areas. Eventually, they may have additional problems in a society that requires increasingly sophisticated job skills. The NAEP assesses reading proficiency on five levels, ranging from simple, discrete (separate) reading tasks to learning from specialized reading materials. Performance is also described in terms of the percentage of students attaining the three achievement levels—Basic, Proficient, and Advanced. (See Figure 4.5.)

In 2000 NAEP released reading scale scores for grade four. They showed overall stability in student performance. (See Figure 4.6.) In 1999 the average reading score for 9-year-olds was 211.7 out of a possible 500 (a 300 score indicates relative proficiency in understanding complicated literary and informational material). For 13-year-olds it was 259.4, and for 17-year-olds it was 287.8. (See Table 4.2.)

AVERAGE READING PROFICIENCY SCORES BY REGION, TYPE AND POVERTY LEVEL OF SCHOOL. In 1999 students in the Northeast and Central regions attained higher average scores than those in the Southeast and West. At all three grade levels, public school students tended to have lower scores than nonpublic school students. (See Table 4.2.)

Third-grade students at high-poverty public schools (those where 76 to 100 percent of students were eligible for free or reduced-price lunch) had lower reading scores between 1988 and 1999 than students at low-poverty schools (those where up to 25 percent of students were eligible for free or reduced-price lunch). The average scale scores of nine-year-old students at high poverty schools declined from 190 in 1988 to 186 in 1999. (See Figure 4.7.)

AVERAGE READING PROFICIENCY SCORES BY RACE AND GENDER. For all grade levels in 1999, the average reading scores for white students were higher than for black and Hispanic students. From 1992 to 2000, fourth-grade Asian/Pacific Islander students significantly increased their reading scale scores. (See Figure 4.8.) At the eighth-grade level, white, black and Hispanic students increased their scores from 1996 to 1999. Twelfth-grade Hispanic students raised their average reading scores between 1996 and 1999. (See Table 4.2.) Female students consistently scored higher reading proficiency averages than male students. Scores for both males and females in all three grade levels have been stable. (See Table 4.2 and Figure 4.9.)

READING ACTIVITIES IN FAMILIES. Children whose family members read to them eventually demonstrate higher reading performance and do better in school. In 1999 the majority (92 percent) of preschool children were read to by a relative three or more times per week. With the exception of learning songs or music, children with multiple risk factors (defined as having a race/ethnicity other than white, having a mother whose home language is other than English, having a mother whose highest education is less than high school, being a member of a family with no parent or only one parent in the household, and being a member of a family whose poverty status is below the poverty threshold) were less likely to participate in home literacy activities than those with one or no risk factors. (See Figure 4.10.)

Mathematics Performance

Since 1978, the NAEP has assessed the mathematics performance of 9-, 13-, and 17-year-olds. Figure 4.11 describes the requirements for basic, proficient, and advanced achievement levels for fourth graders.

Results from the 2000 NAEP assessment indicate that mathematics performance has improved nationally since 1990. In 2000 average mathematics scale scores for fourth grade students were 15 points higher than in 1990. For

FIGURE 4.6

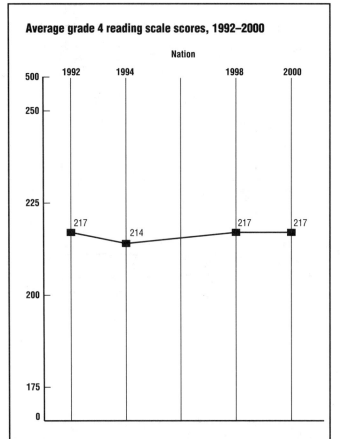

Average grade 4 reading scale scores, 1992–2000

SOURCE: Patricia L. Donahue, Robert J. Finnegan, Anthony D. Lutkus, et al., "Figure 1.1. Scale Score Results," in *The Nation's Report Card: Fourth Grade Reading 2000*, NCES 2001-499, U.S. Department of Education, National Center for Education Statistics, Washington, DC, April 2001

eighth grade students, scores had increased by 12 points, and for twelfth graders scores were 7 points higher than they were in 1990. (See Figure 4.12.)

AVERAGE MATHEMATICS PROFICIENCY SCORES BY TYPE AND POVERTY LEVEL OF SCHOOL. Public school students at all age levels tended to have lower math scores than nonpublic school students. In 1999 more than three-quarters (78 percent) of twelfth-grade students in private schools were at or above the "moderately complex procedures and reasoning" (scale score of 300 or above) proficiency level in mathematics, compared to 59 percent of their public school peers. Among private school eighth graders, 90 percent had mastered "numerical operations and beginning problem solving" (scale score of 250 or above), while 77 percent of that age group in public school were at that same level. "Beginning skills and understanding" (scale score of 200 or above) had been attained by 90 percent of private school third graders, and by 81 percent of public school students in third grade. (See Table 4.3.)

Third grade students at high-poverty public schools had lower mathematics scores than students at low-poverty

FIGURE 4.7

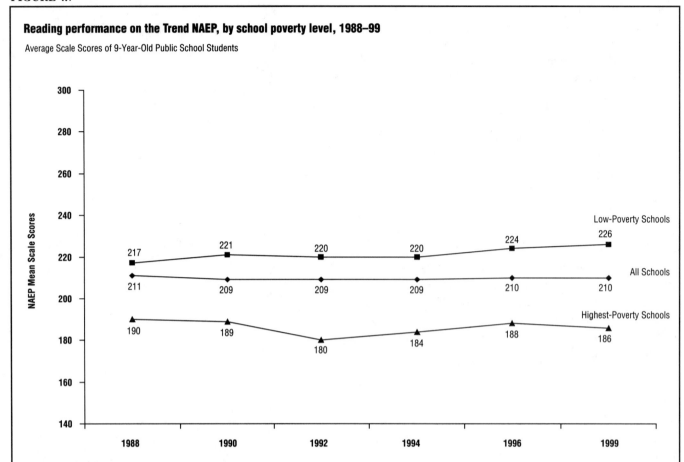

Reading performance on the Trend NAEP, by school poverty level, 1988–99

Average Scale Scores of 9-Year-Old Public School Students

Highest-poverty schools = 76% to 100% of students eligible for free or reduced-price lunch.
Low-poverty schools = 0% to 25% of students eligible for free or reduced-price lunch.
Scale scores are 0-500.

SOURCE: "Exhibit 10 Reading Performance on the Trend NAEP, by School Poverty Level, 1988 to 1999," in *High Standards for All Students: A Report from the National Assessment of Title I on Progress and Challenges Since the 1994 Reauthorization,* U.S. Department of Education, Planning and Evaluation Service, Washington, DC, January 2001

schools from 1986 to 1999, but the average scale scores of 9-year-old students at high-poverty schools increased from 208 in 1986 to 212 in 1999. (See Figure 4.13.)

AVERAGE MATHEMATICS PROFICIENCY SCORES BY RACE AND GENDER. Over the years, white students have consistently averaged higher in mathematics scores than black and Hispanic students. Black and Hispanic scores, however, have increased significantly since 1978. The proportion of both males and females who have attained selected mathematics proficiency levels have increased from 1978 to 1999. Male students in the twelfth grade tend to receive higher mathematics scale scores, and this trend continued in 1999. (See Table 4.3).

Science Performance

Since 1977 the NAEP has assessed the science perfor-mance of students ages 9, 13, and 17. Table 4.4 describes each level, from "partial mastery of prerequisite knowledge and skills that are fundamental for proficient work at each

grade" to "superior performance." In general, the 2000 NAEP assessment indicated that science performance has remained stable since 1996. High-performing eighth grade students increased their science scale scores from 1996 to 2000, while those of middle-performing twelfth graders decreased. (See Figure 4.14.)

AVERAGE SCIENCE PROFICIENCY SCORES BY RACE AND GENDER. In general, average scores on the NAEP sci-ence assessment were not significantly different in 2000 than they were in 1996, although eighth grade American Indian students and twelfth grade white students both had lower scores in 2000 than they did in 1996. (See Figure 4.15.) White students have consistently achieved higher NAEP science scores than blacks and Hispanics. White and black 9- and 13-year-olds scored slightly higher in 1999 than they did in 1970, but 17-year-olds of both races scored lower in 1999 than in 1970. The scores of Hispanic students of all three ages, despite some fluctuations, rose between 1977 and 1999. (See Table 4.5.)

FIGURE 4.8

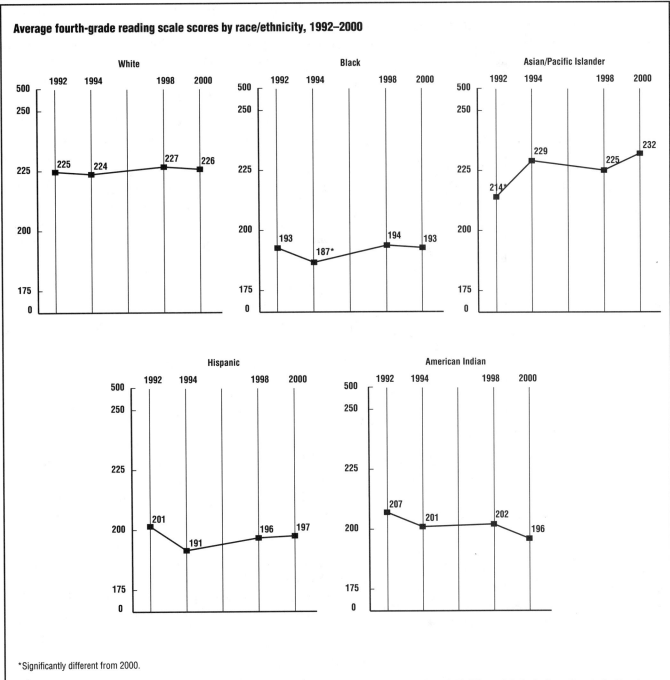

Average fourth-grade reading scale scores by race/ethnicity, 1992–2000

*Significantly different from 2000.

SOURCE: Patricia L. Donahue, Robert J. Finnegan, Anthony D. Lutkus, Nancy L. Allen and Jay R. Campbell, "Figure 2.3. Scale Score Results by Race/Ethnicity," in The Nation's Report Card: Fourth Grade Reading 2000, NCES 2001-499, U.S. Department of Education, National Center for Education Statistics, Washington, DC, April 2001

In 2000 eighth grade male students' average science score was higher than it was in 1996, but twelfth grade males scored lower in 2000, on average, than they had in 1996. (See Figure 4.16.) Among both male and female 17-year-olds, average science scores declined between 1970 and 1999. For 9- and 13-year-olds, scores fluctuated between 1970 and 1999, but the scores in 1999 had recovered and were at or above the 1970 levels. Male students at all age levels achieved higher average science proficiency scores than did female students. (See Table 4.6.)

Writing Performance

In 1998, NAEP administered a writing assessment to students at grades four, eight, and twelve, measuring performance on three types of writing: narrative, informative, and persuasive. Responses were evaluated using scoring guides developed for each grade level and purpose of writing. Student performance was reported in two ways: scale scores and achievement levels.

When the 1998 results were released, Gary W. Phillips, Acting Commissioner for the National Center for Educa-

FIGURE 4.9

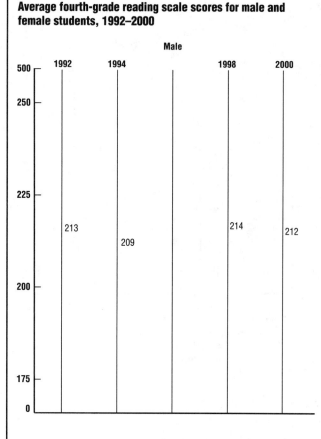

Average fourth-grade reading scale scores for male and female students, 1992–2000

Male

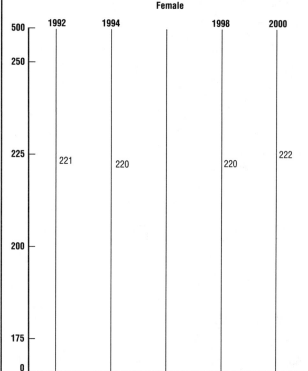

Female

SOURCE: Patricia L. Donahue, Robert J. Finnegan, Anthony D. Lutkus, Nancy L. Allen and Jay R. Campbell, "Figure 2.1. Scale Score Results by Gender," in *The Nation's Report Card: Fourth Grade Reading 2000*, NCES 2001-499, U.S. Department of Education, National Center for Education Statistics, Washington, DC, April 2001

tion Statistics, said, "The average, or typical, American student is not a proficient writer. Instead, students show only partial mastery of the knowledge and skills needed for solid academic performance in writing." Only about one-fourth or less of the students in each grade level assessed performed at the "Proficient" level, and only 1 percent performed at the "Advanced" level. (See Table 4.7.)

WRITING PERFORMANCE BY RACE AND GENDER. Writing scores at each grade level ranged from 0 to 300, with a national average of 150. Fourth-grade Asian/Pacific Islander students had higher average writing scores than white students; white fourth graders had higher scores than black, Hispanic, and American Indian students. At grades eight and twelve, Asian/Pacific Islander and white students had higher scores than black, Hispanic, and American Indian students. (See Table 4.8.) Around 10 percent of black, Hispanic, and American Indian students reached or exceeded the "Proficient" level, compared to between one-fourth and one-third of white students and Asian/Pacific Islander students.

At all three grade levels, females had higher average writing scores than males. (See Table 4.9.) Across the three grades, between 29 and 36 percent of female students were at or above the "Proficient" level, while between 14 and 17 percent of male students attained this level.

READING MATERIALS IN THE HOME. The *NAEP 1998 Writing Report Card for the States* (National Center for Education Statistics, Washington, DC, 1998) stated that "previous NAEP assessments in a variety of subjects and recent research have consistently shown that certain home factors are related to student achievement." Students in all three grades were asked a series of questions about reading materials in their homes. Students at all grade levels who reported having more types of reading materials (a newspaper, an encyclopedia, magazines, and more than 25 books) in their home achieved higher scale scores in writing. (See Figure 4.17.)

NAEP Assessment of Civics

In 1998, NAEP conducted an assessment of civics for fourth-, eighth-, and twelfth-grade students. It was based on a newly developed civics framework with the goal of measuring how well American youth are being prepared to meet their citizenship responsibilities. The assessment included both multiple-choice and essay items.

About two-thirds of the students at each grade performed at or above the "Basic" level, and about one-fourth performed at or above the "Proficient" level. Between 30 and 35 percent of the students performed below the "Basic" level.

In general, eighth- and twelfth-grade girls scored higher than boys in civics. White and Asian/Pacific Islander students outscored American Indian, black, and

FIGURE 4.10

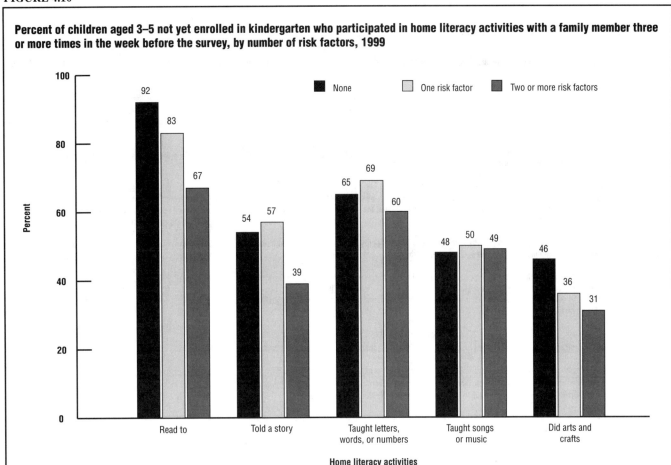

Percent of children aged 3–5 not yet enrolled in kindergarten who participated in home literacy activities with a family member three or more times in the week before the survey, by number of risk factors, 1999

SOURCE: John Wirt, Susan Choy, Debra Gerald, Stephen Provasnik, Patrick Rooney, Satoshi Watanabe, Richard Tobin, and Mark Glander, "Preschool Reading Activities: Percentage of 3- to 5-year-old children not yet enrolled in kindergarten who participated in home literacy activities with a family member three or more times in the week before the survey, by number of risk factors: 1999," in *The Condition of Education, 2001*, NCES 2001-072, U.S. Department of Education, National Center for Education Statistics, Washington, DC, June 2001

Hispanic students. Students in the Northeast and Central regions generally scored higher than those in the Southeast and West. At all three grades, scores were higher among nonpublic school students than among public school students. Scores tended to increase with parents' level of education.

INTERNATIONAL COMPARISONS

Student Performance in Mathematics and Science

The Third International Mathematics and Science Study (TIMSS) compared the mathematics and science skills of a half-million fourth-, eighth-, and twelfth-grade students in countries around the world. This comparison with students in other countries allows the U.S. to monitor its progress toward the National Education Goal of being first in the world in mathematics and science achievement.

For the twelve nations that participated in both the 1995 and 1999 TIMSS, the average 1999 achievement scores of students in the eighth grade were 529 for mathe-

matics and 534 for science, a slight increase over 1995, when they were 528 and 530, respectively. U.S. students scored considerably below both averages, although scores in the U.S. increased 10 points in mathematics and 2 points in science from 1995 to 1999. In mathematics, U.S. students scored lower than students in eight countries, outperforming students in only three countries. In science, U.S. eighth graders scored below students in nine countries and scored higher than students in two countries. (See Table 4.10.)

According to *Education at a Glance: OECD Indicators,* (Organisation for Economic Co-operation and Development, Paris, France, 2001), gender differences exist in mathematics and science in most of the 12 countries, but they are larger and more likely to be statistically significant in the science field. In 1999 boys in the United States scored higher than did girls in both mathematics (by 7 points) and science (by 19 points). The Czech Republic and England had larger gender gaps in both sub-

FIGURE 4.11

NAEP mathematics achievement levels, Grade 4

Basic (214)	**Fourth-grade students performing at the *Basic* level should show some evidence of understanding the mathematical concepts and procedures in the five NAEP content strands.**
	Fourth-graders performing at the *Basic* level should be able to estimate and use basic facts to perform simple computations with whole numbers; show some understanding of fractions and decimals; and solve some simple real-world problems in all NAEP content strands. Students at this level should be able to use — though not always accurately — four-function calculators, rulers, and geometric shapes. Their written responses are often minimal and presented without supporting information.
Proficient (249)	**Fourth-grade students performing at the *Proficient* level should consistently apply integrated procedural knowledge and conceptual understanding to problem solving in the five NAEP content strands.**
	Fourth-graders performing at the *Proficient* level should be able to use whole numbers to estimate, compute, and determine whether results are reasonable. They should have a conceptual understanding of fractions and decimals; be able to solve real-world problems in all NAEP content strands; and use four-function calculators, rulers, and geometric shapes appropriately. Students performing at the *Proficient* level should employ problem-solving strategies such as identifying and using appropriate information. Their written solutions should be organized and presented both with supporting information and explanations of how they were achieved.
Advanced (282)	**Fourth-grade students performing at the *Advanced* level should apply integrated procedural knowledge and conceptual understanding to complex and nonroutine real-world problem solving in the five NAEP content strands.**
	Fourth-graders performing at the *Advanced* level should be able to solve complex and nonroutine real-world problems in all NAEP content strands. They should display mastery in the use of four-function calculators, rulers, and geometric shapes. These students are expected to draw logical conclusions and justify answers and solution processes by explaining why, as well as how, they were achieved. They should go beyond the obvious in their interpretations and be able to communicate their thoughts clearly and concisely.

Note: The scores in parentheses indicate the cutpoint on the scale at which the achievement level range begins.

SOURCE: James S. Braswell, Anthony D. Lutkus, Wendy S. Grigg, Shari L. Santapau, Brenda Tay-Lim and Matthew Johnson, "Figure 1.4. NAEP mathematics achievement levels: Grade 4," in *The Nation's Report Card: Fourth Grade Mathematics 2000*, NCES 2001-517, U.S. Department of Education, National Center for Education Statistics, Washington, DC, August 2001

jects than the United States. Italy and Japan had larger gender gaps in mathematics, and Hungary and Korea had larger gender gaps in science.

The 1999 TIMSS results show that 28 percent of U.S. students were in eighth grade mathematics classes that emphasized arithmetic, which was more than three times the international average. For science, 28 percent of American students were in a class that emphasized earth science, while only 5 percent of eighth graders were studying physics or chemistry. Among international students, about one-quarter were in a physics or chemistry class. Most American high school students stop taking mathematics courses before getting to calculus. Although state requirements for challenging mathematics and science courses have increased, there is still a great need for improvement. In 1987, no state required four years of mathematics and science courses in high school; by 2000 that number had increased to four states.

Educational Attainment

Among a group of 28 countries, the United States in 1999 had the highest proportion (87 percent) of the population aged 25 to 64 that has completed secondary school. This is well above the average proportion for all countries, which was 62 percent. Mexico had the lowest proportion (20 percent) of secondary school completers. (See Figure 4.18.)

Males aged 25 to 64 in the 28 nations were more likely to have completed secondary school in 1999 (63 percent) than were females (58 percent). In the United States, 86 percent of males and 87 percent of females have completed at least secondary school. Korea, where 75 percent of males and 58 percent of females age 25 to 64 finished secondary school in 1999, had the largest gender gap. The average proportion of U.S. males aged 25 to 64 who had postsecondary education in 1999 was 37 percent. For American females, 35 percent had a college degree. Both are above the average proportion among the 28 countries, which was 23 percent for males and 21 percent for females. Canada had a higher proportion of female graduates of postsecondary school than the U.S. (41 percent), but the proportion of males (37 percent) was the same as in the U.S. Poland had the smallest proportion of males (8 percent) while Turkey had the smallest proportion of female postsecondary completers (6 percent).

CARNEGIE UNITS

In response to the recommendations of the National Education Goals Panel, many state legislatures, local school boards, and departments of education have attempted to strengthen high school graduation requirements. While state-mandated standards cannot necessarily measure activities in the classroom, they tend to indicate a state's desire to improve its schools.

The District of Columbia and most states have established minimum Carnegie units (one unit equals an academic year course of two semesters) required for high school graduation. As of 2000, according to *Key State Education Policies on K-12 Education,* (Council of Chief State School Officers, Washington, DC, 2000), 36 states required 4 credits in English, 25 states required 2.5 or more credits in mathematics, 20 states required more than 2.5 credits in science, and 35 states required 2.5 or more credits in social studies. Table 4.11 shows the average Carnegie units earned by high school graduates in various subject fields from 1982 to 1998. The average number of Carnegie units earned by public high school graduates in 1998 was just over 25.

HIGH SCHOOL EXIT EXAMS

In recent years, school accountability has been a major issue of school reform. Many states have mandated what children should learn in each grade, developed assessments to measure student achievement, designed school report cards, rated their schools and publicly identified failing schools, assisted low-performing schools with additional funding, and even closed or taken over failing schools. Included in the various accountability measures is the high school exit examination.

According to *Key State Education Policies on K-12 Education,* 28 states were either using high school exit exams or were in the process of developing such tests in 2000. In most states, students must pass an exit test to receive a high school diploma. A few states differentiate the diplomas according to whether the test was passed or not. Most states initially administer the exit exam in tenth or eleventh grade. This allows time for remediation or other interventions to be provided for students who fail the test the first time. All states with high school exit exams allow students to take the test multiple times.

Proponents of high school exit exams believe that standardized tests are the best way to ensure high standards and accountability. They maintain that tests can communicate what is expected of students and teachers and assess whether progress is being made. If tests are aligned to a rigorous curriculum, they are the best chance that low-performing students have to get the education they need and to narrow the minority achievement gap.

Those who oppose these tests point out that a single test is not an accurate measure of a student's performance. Opponents claim that these tests put poor and minority students at a disadvantage. A further criticism of "high-stakes" tests is that they push teachers to "teach to" the test, taking too much time away from classroom practices that support true learning.

The 33rd Annual Phi Delta Kappa/Gallup Poll asked participants if they favored or opposed using a single

FIGURE 4.12

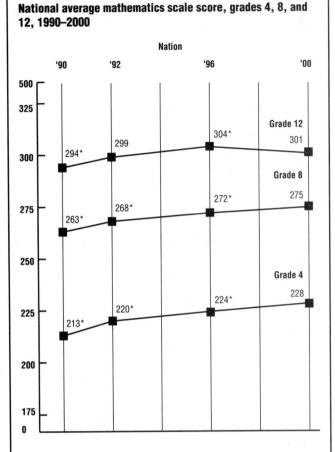

National average mathematics scale score, grades 4, 8, and 12, 1990–2000

*Significantly different from 2000.

SOURCE: James S. Braswell, Anthony D. Lutkus, Wendy S. Grigg, Shari L. Santapau, Brenda Tay-Lim and Matthew Johnson, "Figure 2.1 National Scale Score Results," in *The Nation's Report Card: Fourth Grade Mathematics 2000,* NCES 2001-517, U.S. Department of Education, National Center for Education Statistics, Washington, DC, August 2001

standard test in the public schools in the community to determine whether a student should be promoted from grade to grade. Respondents were also asked if they favored or opposed using a single standard test to determine whether a student should receive a high school diploma. In 2001 more than half (53 for promotion and 57 for graduation, respectively) of those surveyed favored the tests, while 45 percent opposed using a single test for promotion, and 42 percent opposed using a test to determine high school graduation.

SCORES ON COLLEGE ENTRANCE TESTS

Students wishing to enter most colleges and universities in the United States generally take either the Scholastic Assessment Test (SAT®) or the American College Test (ACT) as part of their admission requirements. The SAT is the primary admissions test for 22 states, mostly in the East and on the West Coast. The ACT is more popular in 28

TABLE 4.3

Students at or above selected mathematics proficiency levels, by sex, race/ethnicity, type of school, and age, selected years, 1978 to 1999

Sex, race/ethnicity, control, and year	9-year-olds[1]				13-year-olds[2]				17-year-olds[2]			
	Simple arithmetic facts[3]	Beginning skills and understanding[4]	Numerical operations and beginning problem solving[5]	Moderately complex procedures and reasoning[6]	Beginning skills and understanding[4]	Numerical operations and beginning problem solving[5]	Moderately complex procedures and reasoning[6]	Multi-step problem solving and algebra[7]	Beginning skills and understanding[4]	Numerical operations and beginning problem solving[5]	Moderately complex procedures and reasoning[6]	Multi-step problem solving and algebra[7]
Total												
1978	96.7 (0.3)	70.4 (0.9)	19.6 (0.7)	0.8 (0.1)	94.6 (0.5)	64.9 (1.2)	18.0 (0.7)	1.0 (0.2)	99.8 (0.1)	92.0 (0.5)	51.5 (1.1)	7.3 (0.4)
1982	97.1 (0.3)	71.4 (1.2)	18.8 (1.0)	0.6 (0.1)	97.7 (0.4)	71.4 (1.2)	17.4 (0.9)	0.5 (0.1)	99.9 (0.0)	93.0 (0.5)	48.5 (1.3)	5.5 (0.4)
1986	97.9 (0.3)	74.1 (1.2)	20.7 (0.9)	0.6 (0.2)	98.6 (0.2)	73.3 (1.6)	15.8 (1.0)	0.4 (0.1)	99.9 —	95.6 (0.5)	51.7 (1.4)	6.5 (0.5)
1990	99.1 (0.2)	81.5 (1.0)	27.7 (0.9)	1.2 (0.3)	98.5 (0.2)	74.7 (1.0)	17.3 (1.0)	0.4 (0.2)	100.0 —	96.0 (0.5)	56.1 (1.4)	7.2 (0.6)
1992	99.0 (0.2)	81.4 (0.8)	27.8 (0.9)	1.2 (0.3)	98.7 (0.3)	77.7 (1.1)	18.9 (1.0)	0.6 (0.2)	100.0 —	96.6 (0.5)	59.1 (1.3)	7.2 (0.6)
1994	99.0 (0.2)	82.0 (0.7)	29.9 (1.1)	1.3 (0.4)	98.5 (0.3)	78.1 (1.1)	21.3 (1.4)	0.6 (0.1)	100.0 —	96.5 (0.5)	58.6 (1.4)	7.4 (0.8)
1996	99.1 (0.2)	81.5 (0.8)	29.7 (1.0)	1.6 (0.3)	98.8 (0.2)	78.6 (0.9)	20.6 (1.2)	0.6 (0.1)	100.0 —	96.8 (0.4)	60.1 (1.7)	7.4 (0.8)
1999	98.9 (0.2)	82.5 (0.8)	30.9 (1.1)	1.7 (0.3)	98.7 (0.2)	78.8 (1.0)	23.2 (1.0)	0.9 (0.2)	100.0 —	96.8 (0.5)	60.7 (1.6)	8.4 (0.8)
Male												
1978	96.2 (0.5)	68.9 (1.0)	19.2 (0.6)	0.7 (0.2)	93.9 (0.5)	63.9 (1.3)	18.4 (0.9)	1.1 (0.2)	99.9 (0.1)	93.0 (0.5)	55.1 (1.2)	9.5 (0.6)
1982	96.5 (0.5)	68.8 (1.3)	18.1 (1.1)	0.6 (0.1)	97.5 (0.6)	71.3 (1.4)	18.9 (1.2)	0.7 (0.2)	99.9 (0.0)	93.9 (0.6)	51.9 (1.5)	6.9 (0.7)
1986	98.0 (0.5)	74.0 (1.4)	20.9 (1.1)	0.7 (0.3)	98.5 (0.3)	73.8 (1.8)	17.6 (1.1)	0.5 (0.2)	99.9 —	96.1 (0.6)	54.6 (1.8)	8.4 (0.9)
1990	99.0 (0.3)	80.6 (1.0)	27.5 (1.0)	1.3 (0.4)	98.2 (0.3)	75.1 (1.8)	19.0 (1.2)	0.5 (0.2)	100.0 —	95.8 (0.8)	57.6 (1.4)	8.8 (0.8)
1992	99.0 (0.3)	81.9 (1.0)	29.4 (1.2)	1.4 (0.3)	98.8 (0.4)	78.1 (1.6)	20.7 (1.1)	0.8 (0.3)	100.0 —	96.9 (0.6)	60.5 (1.8)	9.1 (0.7)
1994	99.1 (0.3)	82.3 (0.9)	31.5 (1.6)	1.4 (0.4)	98.3 (0.4)	78.9 (1.5)	23.9 (1.6)	0.8 (0.2)	100.0 —	97.3 (0.6)	60.2 (2.1)	9.3 (1.0)
1996	99.1 (0.2)	82.5 (1.1)	32.7 (1.7)	2.0 (0.5)	98.7 (0.3)	79.8 (1.4)	23.0 (1.6)	1.0 (0.2)	100.0 —	97.0 (0.7)	62.7 (1.8)	9.5 (1.3)
1999	99.0 (0.3)	83.0 (0.9)	32.0 (1.3)	2.0 (0.4)	99.0 (0.3)	79.0 (1.1)	25.0 (1.2)	1.0 (0.3)	100.0 —	96.0 (0.8)	63.0 (2.1)	10.0 (1.1)
Female												
1978	97.2 (0.3)	72.0 (1.1)	19.9 (1.0)	0.8 (0.2)	95.2 (0.5)	65.9 (1.2)	17.5 (0.7)	0.9 (0.2)	99.7 (0.1)	91.0 (0.6)	48.2 (1.3)	5.2 (0.7)
1982	97.6 (0.3)	74.0 (1.3)	19.6 (1.1)	0.5 (0.1)	98.0 (0.3)	71.4 (1.3)	15.9 (1.0)	0.4 (0.2)	99.9 (0.0)	92.1 (0.6)	45.3 (1.4)	4.1 (0.4)
1986	97.8 (0.4)	74.3 (1.3)	20.6 (1.3)	0.6 (0.3)	98.6 (0.3)	72.7 (1.9)	14.1 (1.3)	0.3 (0.1)	100.0 —	95.1 (0.7)	48.9 (1.7)	4.7 (0.6)
1990	99.1 (0.3)	82.3 (1.3)	27.9 (1.3)	1.0 (0.3)	98.9 (0.2)	74.4 (1.3)	15.7 (1.0)	0.2 (0.1)	100.0 —	96.2 (0.8)	54.7 (1.8)	5.6 (0.8)
1992	99.0 (0.3)	80.9 (1.1)	26.3 (1.5)	1.0 (0.4)	98.6 (0.2)	77.7 (1.1)	17.2 (1.4)	0.3 —	100.0 —	96.3 (0.8)	57.7 (1.6)	5.2 (0.8)
1994	98.9 (0.3)	81.7 (0.9)	28.3 (1.3)	1.1 (0.4)	98.7 (0.3)	77.3 (1.0)	18.7 (1.4)	0.5 (0.3)	100.0 —	96.0 (0.6)	57.2 (1.4)	5.5 (0.9)
1996	99.1 (0.4)	80.7 (0.9)	26.7 (1.1)	1.2 (0.4)	98.8 (0.3)	77.4 (1.1)	18.4 (1.5)	0.5 (0.2)	100.0 —	96.7 (0.6)	57.6 (2.2)	5.3 (0.8)
1999	99.0 (0.2)	82.0 (1.2)	29.0 (1.4)	2.0 (0.4)	99.0 (0.4)	78.0 (1.2)	21.0 (1.4)	1.0 (0.3)	100.0 —	97.0 (0.4)	58.0 (1.9)	7.0 (1.1)
White, non-Hispanic												
1978	98.3 (0.2)	76.3 (1.0)	22.9 (0.9)	0.9 (0.2)	97.6 (0.3)	72.9 (0.9)	21.4 (0.7)	1.2 (0.2)	100.0	95.6 (0.3)	57.6 (1.1)	8.5 (0.5)
1982	98.5 (0.3)	76.8 (1.2)	21.8 (1.1)	0.6 (0.1)	99.1 (0.1)	78.3 (0.9)	20.5 (1.0)	0.6 (0.1)	100.0	96.2 (0.3)	54.7 (1.4)	6.4 (0.5)
1986	98.8 (0.2)	79.6 (1.3)	24.6 (1.0)	0.8 (0.3)	99.3 (0.3)	78.9 (1.7)	18.6 (1.2)	0.4 (0.1)	100.0	98.0 (0.4)	59.1 (1.7)	7.9 (0.7)
1990	99.6 (0.2)	86.9 (0.9)	32.7 (1.0)	1.5 (0.4)	99.4 (0.1)	82.0 (1.0)	21.0 (1.2)	0.4 (0.2)	100.0	97.6 (0.3)	63.2 (1.6)	8.3 (0.7)
1992	99.6 (0.1)	86.9 (0.7)	32.4 (1.0)	1.4 (0.3)	99.6 (0.2)	84.9 (1.1)	22.8 (1.3)	0.4 (0.2)	100.0	98.3 (0.4)	66.4 (1.4)	8.7 (0.9)
1994	99.6 (0.2)	87.0 (0.8)	35.3 (1.3)	1.5 (0.4)	99.3 (0.2)	85.5 (0.9)	25.6 (1.6)	0.7 (0.3)	100.0	98.4 (0.4)	67.0 (1.4)	9.4 (1.1)
1996	99.6 (0.1)	86.6 (0.8)	35.7 (1.4)	2.0 (0.4)	99.6 (0.2)	86.4 (1.0)	25.4 (1.5)	0.8 (0.2)	100.0	98.7 (0.4)	68.7 (2.2)	9.2 (1.0)
1999	100.0 (0.1)	89.0 (0.8)	37.0 (1.4)	2.0 (0.4)	99.0 (0.3)	87.0 (0.9)	29.0 (1.3)	1.0 (0.3)	100.0	99.0 (0.4)	70.0 (2.0)	10.0 (1.1)
Black, non-Hispanic												
1978	88.4 (1.0)	42.0 (1.4)	4.1 (0.6)	0.0 —	79.7 (1.5)	28.7 (2.1)	2.3 (0.5)	0.0 —	98.8 (0.3)	70.7 (1.7)	16.8 (1.6)	0.5 (0.2)
1982	90.2 (1.0)	46.1 (2.4)	4.4 (0.8)	0.0 —	90.2 (1.6)	37.9 (2.5)	2.9 (1.0)	0.0 —	99.7 (0.2)	76.4 (1.5)	17.1 (1.5)	0.5 (0.3)
1986	93.9 (1.4)	53.4 (2.5)	5.6 (0.9)	0.1 —	95.4 (0.9)	49.0 (3.7)	4.0 (1.4)	0.1 —	100.0 —	85.6 (2.5)	20.8 (2.8)	0.2 —
1990	96.9 (0.9)	60.0 (2.8)	9.4 (1.7)	0.1 —	95.4 (1.1)	48.7 (3.6)	3.9 (1.6)	0.1 —	99.9 —	92.4 (2.2)	32.8 (4.5)	2.0 (1.0)

TABLE 4.3

Students at or above selected mathematics proficiency levels, by sex, race/ethnicity, type of school, and age, selected years, 1978 to 1999 [CONTINUED]

Sex, race/ethnicity, control, and year	9-year-olds[1]				13-year-olds[2]				17-year-olds[2]			
	Simple arithmetic facts[3]	Beginning skills and understanding[4]	Numerical operations and beginning problem solving[5]	Moderately complex procedures and reasoning[6]	Beginning skills and understanding[4]	Numerical operations and beginning problem solving[5]	Moderately complex procedures and reasoning[6]	Multi-step problem solving and algebra[7]	Beginning skills and understanding[4]	Numerical operations and beginning problem solving[5]	Moderately complex procedures and reasoning[6]	Multi-step problem solving and algebra[7]
Black, non-Hispanic [CONTINUED]												
1992	96.6 (1.1)	59.8 (2.8)	9.6 (1.4)	0.1	95.0 (1.4)	51.0 (2.7)	4.0 (0.7)	0.1	100.0 —	89.6 (2.5)	29.8 (3.9)	0.9 —
1994	97.4 (1.0)	65.9 (2.6)	11.1 (1.7)	0.0	95.6 (1.6)	51.0 (3.9)	6.4 (2.4)	0.3	100.0 —	90.6 (1.8)	29.8 (3.4)	0.4 —
1996	97.3 (0.8)	65.3 (2.4)	10.0 (1.2)	0.1	96.2 (1.3)	53.7 (2.6)	4.8 (1.1)	0.1	100.0 —	90.6 (1.3)	31.2 (2.5)	0.9 —
1999	96.0 (0.6)	63.0 (2.1)	12.0 (1.5)	0.0	97.0 (1.1)	51.0 (4.0)	4.0 (1.4)	0.0	100.0 —	89.0 (2.0)	27.0 (2.7)	1.0 —
Hispanic												
1978	93.0 (1.2)	54.2 (2.8)	9.2 (2.5)	0.2	86.4 (0.9)	36.0 (2.9)	4.0 (1.0)	0.1	99.3 (0.4)	78.3 (2.3)	23.4 (2.7)	1.4 (0.6)
1982	94.3 (1.2)	55.7 (2.3)	7.8 (1.7)	0.0	95.9 (0.9)	52.2 (2.5)	6.3 (1.0)	0.2	99.8 —	81.4 (1.9)	21.6 (2.2)	0.7 (0.4)
1986	96.4 (1.3)	57.6 (2.9)	7.3 (2.8)	0.1	96.9 (1.4)	56.6 (5.0)	5.5 (1.1)	0.1	99.4 —	89.3 (2.5)	26.5 (4.5)	1.1 —
1990	98.0 (0.8)	68.4 (3.0)	11.3 (3.5)	0.2	96.8 (1.1)	56.7 (3.3)	6.4 (1.7)	0.1	99.6 —	85.8 (4.2)	30.1 (3.1)	1.9 (0.8)
1992	97.2 (1.3)	65.0 (2.9)	11.7 (2.5)	0.1	98.1 (0.7)	63.3 (2.7)	7.0 (1.2)	0.0	100.0 —	94.1 (2.2)	39.2 (4.9)	1.2 —
1994	97.2 (1.2)	63.5 (3.1)	9.7 (1.8)	0.0	97.1 (1.3)	59.2 (2.2)	6.4 (1.8)	0.0	100.0 —	91.8 (3.6)	38.3 (5.5)	1.4 —
1996	98.1 (0.7)	67.1 (2.1)	13.8 (2.3)	0.2	96.2 (0.8)	58.3 (2.3)	6.7 (1.2)	0.0	99.9 —	92.2 (2.2)	40.1 (3.5)	1.8 —
1999	98.0 (0.7)	68.0 (2.5)	11.0 (1.6)	0.0	97.0 (0.6)	63.0 (2.5)	8.0 (1.4)	0.0	100.0 —	94.0 (2.2)	38.0 (4.1)	3.0 (1.1)
Public												
1978	96.4 (0.3)	68.8 (0.9)	18.5 (0.7)	0.7 (0.2)	94.1 (0.5)	63.3 (1.2)	17.0 (0.8)	0.9 (0.2)	99.8 (0.1)	91.7 (0.5)	50.6 (1.2)	7.0 (0.4)
1982	96.8 (0.4)	69.4 (1.2)	17.3 (0.9)	0.5 (0.1)	97.5 (0.4)	69.7 (1.3)	16.4 (1.0)	0.5 (0.1)	99.9 (0.0)	92.5 (0.6)	46.9 (1.3)	5.2 (0.4)
1986	97.7 (0.3)	72.7 (1.4)	19.1 (1.1)	0.6 (0.2)	98.5 (0.3)	72.9 (1.7)	15.6 (1.0)	0.4 (0.1)	99.9 —	95.5 (0.5)	50.7 (1.6)	6.1 (0.5)
1990	99.0 (0.2)	80.5 (1.1)	26.8 (1.0)	1.1 (0.3)	98.4 (0.2)	73.3 (1.2)	16.7 (1.1)	0.3 (0.2)	100.0 —	95.8 (0.6)	55.0 (1.3)	6.5 (0.5)
1992	98.8 (0.3)	79.7 (0.9)	26.1 (0.9)	1.1 (0.3)	98.5 (0.3)	76.3 (1.2)	18.0 (0.3)	0.3 (0.2)	100.0 —	96.3 (0.6)	56.9 (1.2)	6.7 (0.7)
1994	98.9 (0.3)	80.6 (0.8)	27.9 (1.2)	1.1 (0.4)	98.5 (0.3)	76.7 (1.2)	20.0 (1.4)	0.6 (0.2)	100.0 —	96.2 (0.5)	56.2 (1.3)	6.4 (0.7)
1996	99.0 (0.2)	80.7 (0.8)	28.3 (1.1)	1.5 (0.3)	98.6 (0.2)	77.2 (0.9)	19.2 (1.3)	0.6 (0.1)	100.0 —	96.7 (0.5)	59.0 (1.8)	7.1 (0.7)
1999	99.0 (0.2)	81.0 (1.0)	29.0 (1.2)	2.0 (0.3)	99.0 (0.2)	77.0 (1.3)	22.0 (1.3)	1.0 (0.2)	100.0 —	96.0 (0.5)	59.0 (1.6)	8.0 (0.7)
Private												
1978	99.0 —	83.3 (1.9)	28.4 (2.0)	1.2 (0.4)	99.0 (0.4)	80.8 (1.7)	26.9 (1.8)	1.4 (0.4)	100.0 —	97.1 (0.6)	67.7 (3.3)	12.9 (2.7)
1982	99.0 (0.4)	84.3 (2.1)	28.6 (2.6)	1.0 (0.6)	99.5 (0.3)	85.1 (1.6)	26.3 (3.1)	1.0 (0.3)	100.0 —	98.1 (0.5)	66.3 (2.4)	8.2 (1.4)
1986	98.7 (0.8)	81.8 (2.3)	28.9 (2.7)	1.1 (0.6)	98.9 (0.6)	81.9 (3.3)	22.0 (6.8)	0.1 —	100.0 —	99.4 —	75.1 (10.6)	16.3 (9.1)
1990	99.7 —	89.3 (1.8)	35.2 (3.3)	1.8 (1.2)	99.7 —	87.0 (2.0)	23.2 (2.5)	0.7 (0.4)	100.0 —	98.2 (1.2)	71.0 (7.9)	15.7 (5.3)
1992	99.8 (0.1)	92.2 (1.2)	38.6 (2.7)	1.9 (0.7)	99.9 —	89.7 (2.1)	25.9 (3.7)	0.7 (0.4)	100.0 —	99.5 —	79.5 (3.7)	12.2 (2.7)
1994	99.8 —	92.3 (1.3)	44.4 (4.0)	2.2 (0.8)	98.7 —	88.5 (2.6)	30.7 (3.7)	1.0 —	100.0 —	98.8 (0.6)	75.7 (4.3)	14.5 (3.5)
1996	99.6 —	87.1 (1.5)	38.7 (3.0)	2.1 (1.1)	99.6 —	89.3 (3.5)	31.6 (4.8)	1.0 (0.6)	100.0 —	98.5 (0.8)	71.5 (6.4)	10.4 (4.0)
1999	100.0 —	90.0 (1.6)	41.0 (2.9)	3.0 (0.9)	99.0 —	90.0 (2.6)	35.0 (3.1)	2.0 (0.8)	100.0 —	100.0 —	78.0 (6.1)	13.0 (4.6)

—Not available.

[1] Virtually no students were able to perform multi-step problems and algebra.

[2] Virtually all students knew simple arithmetic facts. Data are only for students enrolled in school.

[3] Scale score of 150 or above.   [6] Scale score of 300 or above.

[4] Scale score of 200 or above.   [7] Scale score of 350 or above.

[5] Scale score of 250 or above.

NOTE: Mathematics proficiency levels measured by the National Assessment of Educational Progress (NAEP). Characteristics data for 1999 rounded to full percentage points. Standard errors appear in parentheses.

SOURCE: Thomas D. Snyder and Charlene M. Hoffman, "Table 123. Percent of students at or above selected mathematics proficiency levels, by sex, race/ethnicity, control of school, and age: 1978 to 1999," in *Digest of Education Statistics, 2000*, NCES 2001-034, U.S. Department of Education, National Center for Education Statistics, Washington, DC, January 2001

FIGURE 4.13

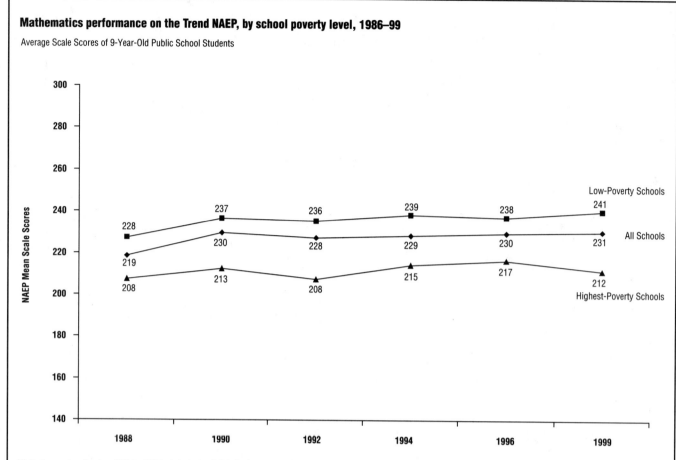

Mathematics performance on the Trend NAEP, by school poverty level, 1986–99

Average Scale Scores of 9-Year-Old Public School Students

Highest-poverty schools = 76% to 100% of students eligible for free or reduced-price lunch.
Low-poverty schools = 0% to 25% of students eligible for free or reduced-price lunch.
Scale scores are 0-500.

SOURCE: "Exhibit 11 Mathematics Performance on the Trend NAEP, by School Poverty Level, 1986 to 1999: Average Scale Scores of 9-Year-Old Public School Students," in *High Standards for All Students: A Report from the National Assessment of Title I on Progress and Challenges Since the 1994 Reauthorization,* U.S. Department of Education, Planning and Evaluation Service, Washington, DC, January 2001

TABLE 4.4

Achievement levels

Basic: This level denotes partial mastery of prerequisite knowledge and skills that are fundamental for proficient work at each grade.

Proficient: This level represents solid academic performance for each grade assessed. Students reaching this level have demonstrated competency over challenging subject matter, including subject-matter knowledge, application of such knowledge to real-world situations, and analytical skills appropriate to the subject matter.

Advanced: This level signifies superior performance.

SOURCE: "Achievement Levels," in *The Nation's Report Card: Science Highlights 2000,* NCES 2002-452, U.S. Department of Education, Office of Educational Research and Improvement, National Center for Education Statistics, Washington, DC, November 2000

states in the Midwest, South, and West, where a large percentage of students attend public colleges and universities. Most colleges will accept either the SAT or the ACT. In addition, some schools require three SAT II subject tests.

These two college entrance tests are standardized, three-hour tests intended as an assessment of readiness for college. The SAT measures students' mathematical and verbal reasoning abilities. The ACT is curriculum-based and tests four areas: English, mathematics, reading comprehension, and science reasoning. Students who elect to take these tests usually plan to continue their education beyond high school; therefore, these tests do not profile all high school students.

Performance on the SAT is measured on a scale of 200 to 800. The mean SAT scores for 2001 were 506 for the verbal section and 514 for the mathematics section. (See Table 4.12.) The verbal score was well below the 1972 level, while the mathematics score was a bit higher than in 1972. (Note that the score scale was recalculated in April 1995, so the data shown in Table 4.12 may differ from earlier reports of SAT scores. Scores for earlier years in Table 4.12 have been estimated on the new scale.)

FIGURE 4.14

Percentile scores, grades 4, 8, and 12, 1996–2000

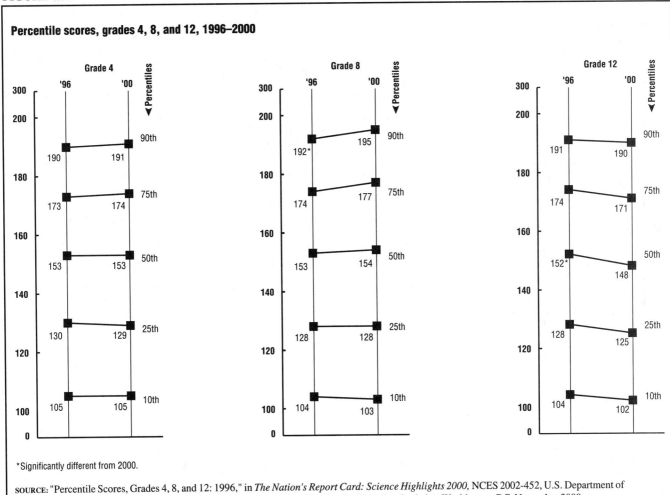

*Significantly different from 2000.

SOURCE: "Percentile Scores, Grades 4, 8, and 12: 1996," in *The Nation's Report Card: Science Highlights 2000,* NCES 2002-452, U.S. Department of Education, Office of Educational Research and Improvement, National Center for Education Statistics, Washington, DC, November 2000

The ACT results are measured on a scale of 1 to 36. The 2001 average composite ACT score was 22, unchanged since 1997. (See Table 4.13, which also includes scores for English, mathematics, reading, and science reasoning.)

About 1.3 million college-bound seniors took the SAT in 2001 and more than 1 million students took the ACT. The number of students taking both the SAT and ACT has grown steadily, especially over the past few years. In general, the more students taking the tests, the lower the scores will be, because the higher number of test-takers will likely include students who are less academically accomplished.

Are Scores Rising?

As shown in Table 4.12, SAT test scores dropped in the 1970s, 1980s, and early 1990s. Observers have attributed the decline in college entrance examination scores to the increase in the number of students from lower scholastic achievement levels taking the tests in recent years. While that may explain the initial drop, a major

part of the decrease also resulted from a decline in performance among the kinds of students who had previously done well in these tests. Although verbal scores have remained unchanged, mathematics scores increased slightly starting in the 1990s, leading some officials to be cautiously optimistic.

Gender of Test-Takers

In 2001 females accounted for the majority (54 percent) of students taking the SAT. Females have historically scored lower than males on college entrance examinations. The SAT was found to over-predict male college grades and under-predict female grades, so in 1995 the SAT was revised, partly to reduce "gender-related prediction differences."

In 2001, females' mean verbal SAT score was 502, compared to 509 for males, and females' mathematics score was 498, compared to 533 for males. (See Table 4.12.) Among ACT-takers, females' 2001 average composite score was 20.9, compared to 21.1 for males. While females scored slightly higher in English and reading,

FIGURE 4.15

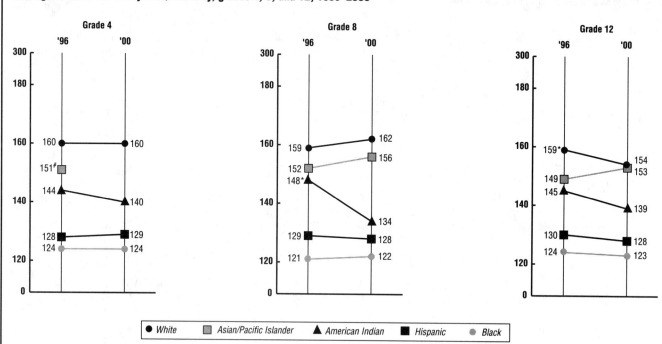

Average science scores by race/ethnicity, grades 4, 8, and 12, 1996–2000

*Significantly different from 2000.

#Special analyses raised concerns about the accuracy and precision of national grade 4 Asian/Pacific Islander results in 2000. As a result, they are omitted here.

SOURCE: "Average Science Scores by Race/Ethnicity, Grades 4, 8, and 12: 1996–2000," in *The Nation's Report Card: Science Highlights 2000,* NCES 2002-452, U.S. Department of Education, Office of Educational Research and Improvement, National Center for Education Statistics, Washington, DC, November 2000

TABLE 4.5

Average science scale scores, by race/ethnicity and age, 1970–99

Year	White			Black			Hispanic		
	Age 9	Age 13	Age 17	Age 9	Age 13	Age 17	Age 9	Age 13	Age 17
1970	*236	*263	*312	*179	*215	258	—	—	—
1973	*231	*259	304	*177	*205	250	—	—	—
1977	*230	*256	*298	*175	*208	*240	*192	*213	*262
1982	*229	*257	*293	*187	*217	*235	*189	225	*249
1986	*232	*259	*298	196	222	253	199	226	*259
1990	237	264	*301	196	226	253	206	232	*261
1992	239	267	304	200	224	256	205	*238	270
1994	240	267	306	201	224	257	201	232	261
1996	239	266	307	202	226	260	207	232	269
1999	240	266	306	199	227	254	206	227	276

—Not available.
*Significantly different from 1999.
NOTE: The NAEP (National Assessment of Educational Progress) in science was first administered to 17-year-olds in 1969 and to 9- and 13-year-olds in 1970. Although Hispanic students participated in the initial assessments, their scores were not reported separately until 1977.

SOURCE: John Wirt, Susan Choy, Debra Gerald, Stephen Provasnik, Patrick Rooney, Satoshi Watanabe, Richard Tobin, and Mark Glander, "Table 13—1. Average science scale scores, by race/ethnicity and age: 1970–1999," in *The Condition of Education, 2001,* NCES 2001-072, U.S. Department of Education, National Center for Education Statistics, Washington, DC, June 2001

FIGURE 4.16

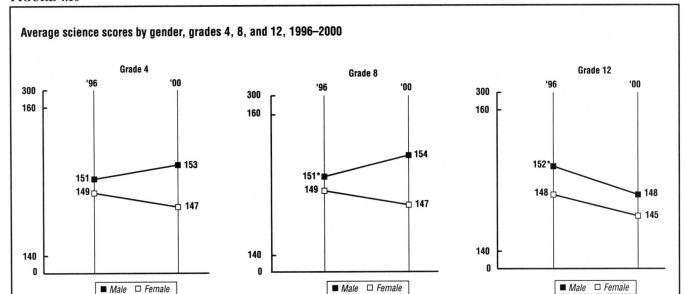

Average science scores by gender, grades 4, 8, and 12, 1996–2000

*Significantly different from 2000.

SOURCE: "Average Science Scores by Gender, Grades 4, 8, and 12: 1996–2000," in The Nation's Report Card: Science Highlights 2000, NCES 2002-452, U.S. Department of Education, Office of Educational Research and Improvement, National Center for Education Statistics, Washington, DC, November 2000

TABLE 4.6

Average science scores, by sex and age, 1970–99

Year	Total			Male			Female		
	Age 9	Age 13	Age 17	Age 9	Age 13	Age 17	Age 9	Age 13	Age 17
1970	*225	255	*305	228	257	*314	*223	253	*297
1973	*220	*250	296	*223	*252	304	*218	*247	288
1977	*220	*247	290	*222	251	297	*218	*244	282
1982	*221	*250	*283	*221	256	*292	*221	*245	*275
1986	*224	*251	*288	227	256	*295	*221	*247	*282
1990	229	255	*290	230	259	*296	227	252	*285
1992	231	*258	294	*235	260	299	227	*256	289
1994	231	257	294	232	259	300	230	254	289
1996	230	256	296	231	260	300	228	252	292
1999	229	256	295	231	259	300	228	253	291

*Significantly different from 1999.
NOTE: The NAEP (National Asessment of Educational Progress) in science was first administered to 17-year-olds in 1969 and to 9- and 13-year-olds in 1970.

SOURCE: John Wirt, Susan Choy, Debra Gerald, Stephen Provasnik, Patrick Rooney, Satoshi Watanabe, Richard Tobin, and Mark Glander, "Table 13—3. Average science scale scores, by sex and age: 1970–1999," in The Condition of Education, 2001, NCES 2001-072, U.S. Department of Education, National Center for Education Statistics, Washington, DC, June 2001

males scored higher averages on mathematics and science reasoning. (See Table 4.14.)

Race and Ethnicity of Test-Takers

In 2001 white students accounted for two-thirds (66 percent) of those taking the SAT, although the proportion of minority test-takers has risen steadily from 13 percent in 1973 to 34 percent in 2001. African American students made up 11 percent; Asian American/Pacific

Islanders, 10 percent; Hispanic, 9 percent; and Native American, 1 percent. Two percent classified themselves as "other."

Gains have been made since 1991, but overall SAT scores for minorities (with the exception of Asian American students) still lagged behind the scores of white students. White students averaged 529 on the verbal section and 531 on the mathematics section in 2001, an increase of 11 points and 18 points, respectively, since 1991.

TABLE 4.7

Percentage of students at or above the writing achievement levels for the nation, 1998

	Below Basic	At or above Basic	At or above Proficient	Advanced
Grade 4	16	84	23	1
Grade 8	16	84	27	1
Grade 12	22	78	22	1

SOURCE: Elissa Greenwald, Hilary R. Persky, Jay R. Campbell, John Mazzeo, Frank Jenkins, and Bruce Kaplan, "Table 1.2. Percentage of students at or above the writing achievement levels for the nation: 1998," in *NAEP 1998 Writing Report Card for the Nation and the States*, NCES 1999-462, U.S. Department of Education, National Center for Education Statistics, Washington, DC, September 1999

TABLE 4.9

Average writing scale scores by gender, 1998

	Percentage of students	Average scale score
Grade 4		
Male	51	142
Female	49	158
Grade 8		
Male	51	140
Female	49	160
Grade 12		
Male	48	140
Female	52	159

NOTE: Percentages may not add to 100 due to rounding.

SOURCE: Elissa Greenwald, Hilary R. Persky, Jay R. Campbell, John Mazzeo, Frank Jenkins, and Bruce Kaplan, "Table 2.1. Average writing scale scores by gender: 1998," in *NAEP 1998 Writing Report Card for the Nation and the States*, NCES 1999-462, U.S. Department of Education, National Center for Education Statistics, Washington, DC, September 1999

TABLE 4.8

Average writing scale scores by race/ethnicity, 1998

	Percentage of students	Average scale score
Grade 4		
White	67	157
Black	15	131
Hispanic	13	134
Asian/Pacific Islander	2	164
American Indian	2	138
Grade 8		
White	67	158
Black	14	131
Hispanic	14	131
Asian/Pacific Islander	3	159
American Indian	1	132
Grade 12		
White	69	156
Black	14	134
Hispanic	12	135
Asian/Pacific Islander	4	152
American Indian	1	129

NOTE: Percentages may not add to 100 due to rounding.

SOURCE: Elissa Greenwald, Hilary R. Persky, Jay R. Campbell, John Mazzeo, Frank Jenkins, and Bruce Kaplan, "Table 2.2. Average writing scale scores by race/ethnicity: 1998," in *NAEP 1998 Writing Report Card for the Nation and the States*, NCES 1999-462, U.S. Department of Education, National Center for Education Statistics, Washington, DC, September 1999

1991. In 2001 the average scores of Hispanic, Latino, Mexican American and Puerto Rican students ranged from 451 to 460 on the verbal section and from 451 to 465 on the mathematics section, up from 1991 scores of 436 to 454 and 439 to 462.

For those taking the ACT in 2001, the racial and ethnic proportions were similar to those taking the SAT. Whites (Caucasians) made up 72 percent of ACT test-takers; African Americans, 10 percent. Smaller proportions of Hispanics (Mexican American and Puerto Rican/Hispanic, 5 percent), Asian-Americans (3 percent), and American Indians (1 percent) took the ACT. The mean composite score of white students was 21.8. For Asian-American students it was 21.7, followed by Hispanics (18.5 to 19.4), American Indians (18.8), and African Americans (16.9). (See Table 4.15.)

African American students scored 433 on the verbal component and 426 on the mathematics. These scores were 6 points and 7 points higher, respectively, than those of

FIGURE 4.17

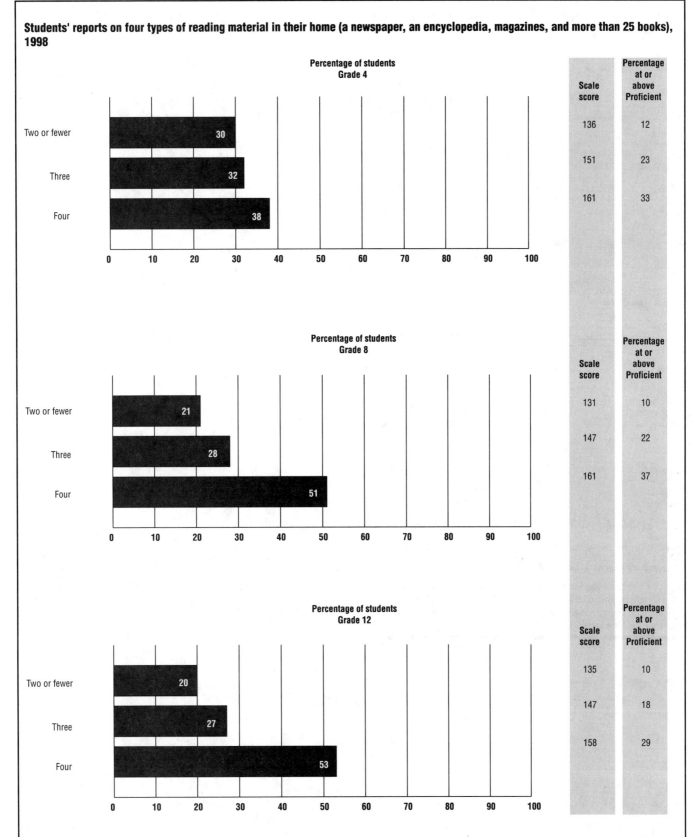

Students' reports on four types of reading material in their home (a newspaper, an encyclopedia, magazines, and more than 25 books), 1998

Note: Percentages may not add to 100 due to rounding.

SOURCE: Elissa Greenwald, Hilary R. Persky, Jay R. Campbell, John Mazzeo, Frank Jenkins, and Bruce Kaplan, "Figure 4.9. Students' reports on the presence of four types of reading materials in their home (a newspaper, an encyclopedia, magazines, and more than 25 books): 1998," in *NAEP 1998 Writing Report Card for the Nation and the States,* NCES 1999-462, U.S. Department of Education, National Center for Education Statistics, Washington, DC, September 1999

TABLE 4.10

Trends in mean achievement scores in the 8th grade, by subject, selected countries, 1995 and 1999

Mathematics achievement

	1995 Mean scale score	1999 Mean scale score	1995-1999 Difference in means
Australia	519 (3.8)	524 (4.8)	6 (6.1)
Belgium (Fl.)[1]	550 (5.9)	558 (3.3)	8 (6.8)
Canada	521 (2.2)	531 (2.5)	10 (3.2)
Czech Republic	546 (4.5)	520 (4.2)	-26 (6.1)
England[1]	498 (3.0)	496 (4.1)	-1 (5.2)
Hungary	527 (3.2)	532 (3.7)	5 (4.9)
Italy*	491 (3.4)	485 (4.8)	-6 (6.0)
Japan	581 (1.6)	579 (1.7)	-2 (2.2)
Korea	581 (2.0)	587 (2.0)	6 (2.8)
Netherlands[1]	529 (6.1)	540 (7.1)	11 (9.5)
New Zealand	501 (4.7)	491 (5.2)	-10 (7.1)
United States	492 (4.7)	502 (4.0)	9 (6.2)
Country mean	**528 (3.8)**	**529 (4.0)**	**1 (5.5)**

Science achievement

	1995 Mean scale score	1999 Mean scale score	1995-1999 Difference in means
Australia	527 (4.0)	540 (4.4)	14 (6.0)
Belgium (Fl.)[1]	533 (6.4)	535 (3.1)	2 (7.1)
Canada	514 (2.6)	533 (2.1)	19 (3.3)
Czech Republic	555 (4.5)	539 (4.2)	-16 (6.1)
England[1]	533 (3.6)	538 (4.8)	5 (5.8)
Hungary	537 (3.1)	552 (3.7)	16 (4.9)
Italy*	497 (3.6)	498 (4.8)	1 (5.9)
Japan	554 (1.8)	550 (2.2)	-5 (3.0)
Korea	546 (2.0)	549 (2.6)	3 (3.4)
Netherlands[1]	541 (6.0)	545 (6.9)	3 (9.1)
New Zealand	511 (4.9)	510 (4.9)	-1 (6.9)
United States	513 (5.6)	515 (4.6)	2 (7.2)
Country mean	**530 (4.0)**	**534 (4.0)**	**4 (5.7)**

NOTE: Data presented for 1995 have been re-scaled in order to allow comparison with 1999 data.
[1]Guidelines for sample participation rates were met only after replacement schools were included.
() Standard errors appear in parentheses.

SOURCE: Centre for Educational Research and Innovation, "Table F.1. Trends in mean achievement scores in the 8th grade, by subject (1995 and 1999)," in *Education at a Glance: OECD Indicators*, Organisation for Economic Co-operation and Development, Paris, France, 2001

FIGURE 4.18

Educational attainment of the population, selected countries, 1999

Distribution of the population 25 to 64 years of age, by level of educational attainment

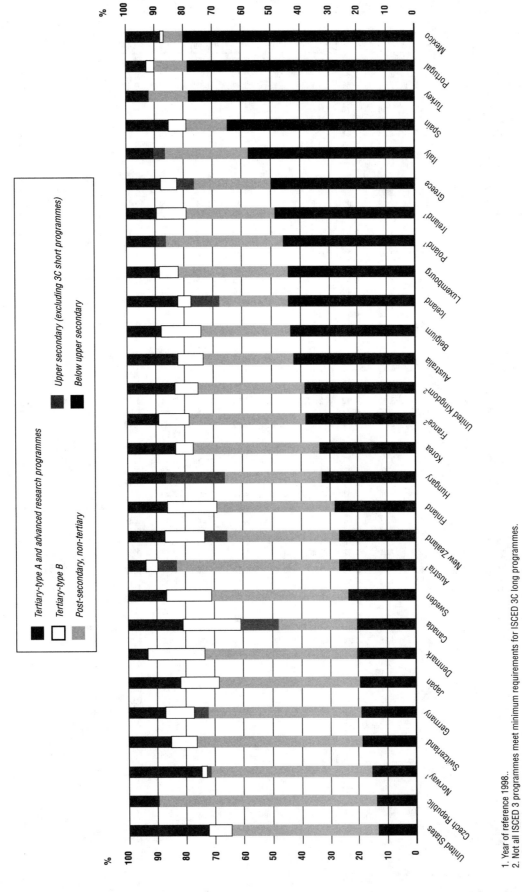

1. Year of reference 1998..
2. Not all ISCED 3 programmes meet minimum requirements for ISCED 3C long programmes.

Countries are ranked in descending order of the percentage of the population who have completed at least upper secondary education

SOURCE: Centre for Educational Research and Innovation, "Chart A2.1. Educational attainment of the population (1999)," in *Education at a Glance: OECD Indicators*, Organisation for Economic Co-operation and Development, Paris, France, 2001

TABLE 4.11

Average number of Carnegie units earned by public high school graduates in various subject fields, by student characteristics, 1982–98

Student characteristics	Total	English	History/ social studies	Mathematics			Science					Foreign languages	Arts	Vocational education[1]	Personal use[2]	Computer science[3]
				Total	Less than algebra	Algebra or higher	Total	General science	Biology	Chemistry	Physics					
1982 graduates	**21.58**	**3.93**	**3.16**	**2.63**	**0.90**	**1.74**	**2.20**	**0.73**	**0.94**	**0.34**	**0.17**	**0.99**	**1.47**	**4.62**	**2.58**	**0.12**
Male	21.40	3.88	3.16	2.71	0.94	1.77	2.27	0.76	0.91	0.36	0.23	0.80	1.29	4.60	2.69	0.14
Female	21.75	3.98	3.15	2.57	0.86	1.71	2.13	0.71	0.97	0.33	0.12	1.17	1.63	4.64	2.48	0.11
Race/ethnicity																
White	21.69	3.90	3.19	2.68	0.77	1.91	2.27	0.73	0.97	0.38	0.20	1.06	1.53	4.53	2.52	0.13
Black	21.15	4.08	3.08	2.61	1.36	1.25	2.06	0.81	0.90	0.26	0.09	0.72	1.26	4.75	2.60	0.12
Hispanic	21.23	3.94	3.00	2.33	1.21	1.12	1.80	0.75	0.81	0.16	0.07	0.77	1.29	5.22	2.87	0.08
Asian	22.46	4.01	3.16	3.15	0.71	2.44	2.64	0.51	1.11	0.61	0.42	1.79	1.31	3.34	3.05	0.22
American Indian	21.45	3.98	3.25	2.35	1.23	1.12	2.04	0.67	0.84	0.42	0.12	0.48	1.72	4.77	2.84	0.06
Academic track																
Academic[4]	21.75	4.11	3.32	3.04	0.73	2.30	2.65	0.73	1.13	0.53	0.26	1.54	1.91	2.55	2.62	0.10
Vocational[5]	20.21	3.44	2.63	1.80	1.09	0.71	1.32	0.69	0.57	0.04	0.02	0.18	0.59	7.74	2.51	0.12
Both[6]	22.89	4.04	3.33	2.69	1.02	1.67	2.17	0.79	0.94	0.29	0.14	0.75	1.41	6.03	2.47	0.18
Neither[7]	18.73	3.58	2.70	1.73	1.08	0.65	1.33	0.69	0.59	0.03	0.02	0.22	0.85	5.23	3.06	0.05
1987 graduates	**23.00**	**4.12**	**3.32**	**3.01**	**0.86**	**2.15**	**2.54**	**0.76**	**1.10**	**0.47**	**0.21**	**1.35**	**1.44**	**4.55**	**2.67**	**0.47**
Male	22.88	4.08	3.29	3.05	0.91	2.14	2.57	0.79	1.05	0.47	0.26	1.16	1.24	4.64	2.83	0.47
Female	23.12	4.15	3.35	2.97	0.82	2.15	2.52	0.74	1.14	0.47	0.17	1.53	1.63	4.47	2.51	0.47
Race/ethnicity																
White	23.11	4.08	3.29	3.01	0.74	2.27	2.61	0.75	1.12	0.50	0.23	1.38	1.50	4.65	2.60	0.49
Black	22.40	4.22	3.34	2.99	1.40	1.59	2.32	0.90	1.01	0.31	0.10	1.08	1.20	4.52	2.73	0.39
Hispanic	22.84	4.30	3.22	2.81	1.30	1.50	2.24	0.78	1.07	0.29	0.10	1.25	1.34	4.49	3.19	0.42
Asian	24.47	4.37	3.65	3.72	0.53	3.18	3.13	0.59	1.17	0.87	0.50	2.07	1.18	3.11	3.23	0.58
American Indian	23.23	4.22	3.18	2.98	1.35	1.63	2.44	0.81	1.22	0.32	0.09	0.75	1.68	4.92	3.06	0.39
Academic track																
Academic[4]	23.20	4.26	3.55	3.33	0.65	2.68	2.97	0.73	1.23	0.68	0.32	1.92	1.87	2.57	2.73	0.38
Vocational[5]	21.07	3.62	2.59	2.00	1.29	0.71	1.48	0.74	0.70	0.03	0.01	0.18	0.47	8.07	2.67	0.39
Both[6]	23.53	4.11	3.29	2.93	0.97	1.96	2.37	0.81	1.07	0.35	0.14	1.01	1.20	6.09	2.53	0.64
Neither[7]	19.56	3.55	2.45	2.11	1.62	0.49	1.47	0.84	0.59	0.03	0.00	0.18	0.76	5.10	3.93	0.17
1990 graduates	**23.53**	**4.19**	**3.47**	**3.15**	**0.90**	**2.25**	**2.75**	**0.85**	**1.14**	**0.53**	**0.23**	**1.54**	**1.55**	**4.19**	**2.68**	**0.54**
Male	23.35	4.13	3.45	3.16	0.96	2.20	2.78	0.88	1.11	0.52	0.28	1.33	1.31	4.32	2.87	0.50
Female	23.69	4.25	3.50	3.14	0.85	2.29	2.73	0.83	1.17	0.53	0.19	1.72	1.76	4.08	2.51	0.57
Race/ethnicity																
White	23.54	4.12	3.46	3.13	0.80	2.33	2.80	0.84	1.15	0.55	0.25	1.58	1.61	4.22	2.61	0.52
Black	23.40	4.34	3.49	3.20	1.25	1.95	2.68	0.98	1.11	0.42	0.16	1.20	1.34	4.41	2.74	0.60
Hispanic	23.83	4.51	3.42	3.13	1.30	1.83	2.50	0.83	1.10	0.42	0.14	1.57	1.48	4.12	3.10	0.58
Asian	24.07	4.50	3.70	3.52	0.70	2.82	2.97	0.68	1.12	0.74	0.42	2.06	1.29	3.07	2.96	0.54
American Indian	22.64	4.08	3.34	3.04	1.03	2.01	2.48	0.83	1.09	0.42	0.15	1.15	1.11	4.62	2.81	0.60
Academic track																
Academic[4]	23.53	4.30	3.65	3.37	0.68	2.70	3.06	0.81	1.23	0.70	0.32	2.02	1.93	2.41	2.78	0.42
Vocational[5]	21.73	3.60	2.58	2.07	1.54	0.53	1.62	0.87	0.71	0.03	0.01	0.17	0.42	8.68	2.59	0.46
Both[6]	23.92	4.14	3.38	3.02	1.12	1.90	2.51	0.92	1.09	0.36	0.14	1.07	1.17	6.10	2.53	0.73
Neither[7]	19.81	3.63	2.59	2.01	1.57	0.44	1.47	0.79	0.60	0.04	0.03	0.21	0.79	5.81	3.29	0.36
1994 graduates	**24.17**	**4.29**	**3.55**	**3.33**	**0.76**	**2.57**	**3.04**	**0.88**	**1.26**	**0.62**	**0.28**	**1.71**	**1.66**	**3.96**	**2.63**	**0.64**
Male	24.00	4.26	3.51	3.32	0.85	2.48	3.03	0.91	1.20	0.59	0.32	1.49	1.43	4.13	2.83	0.63
Female	24.34	4.32	3.59	3.34	0.68	2.66	3.06	0.86	1.31	0.64	0.24	1.93	1.87	3.80	2.44	0.65
Race/ethnicity																
White	24.33	4.23	3.56	3.36	0.70	2.66	3.13	0.89	1.29	0.65	0.30	1.76	1.74	3.96	2.61	0.63
Black	23.59	4.36	3.51	3.23	1.09	2.14	2.80	0.92	1.21	0.49	0.17	1.35	1.36	4.29	2.69	0.64
Hispanic	24.06	4.61	3.45	3.28	0.96	2.32	2.69	0.83	1.19	0.49	0.17	1.73	1.51	3.87	2.93	0.76
Asian	24.47	4.60	3.66	3.66	0.67	2.98	3.35	0.80	1.22	0.81	0.48	2.09	1.32	3.01	2.78	0.71
American Indian	24.47	4.27	3.57	3.11	0.94	2.17	2.82	0.91	1.28	0.50	0.13	1.30	2.01	4.27	3.12	0.53
Academic track																
Academic[4]	24.07	4.37	3.69	3.52	0.58	2.94	3.32	0.83	1.34	0.77	0.37	2.14	2.05	2.28	2.71	0.50
Vocational[5]	21.60	3.70	2.49	2.20	1.56	0.64	1.69	0.80	0.83	0.03	0.02	0.14	0.34	8.64	2.41	0.55
Both[6]	24.61	4.23	3.45	3.17	0.96	2.21	2.78	0.96	1.19	0.45	0.17	1.24	1.21	6.01	2.52	0.85
Neither[7]	21.28	3.54	2.24	2.25	1.71	0.54	1.53	0.82	0.63	0.05	0.02	0.19	0.56	6.51	4.47	0.33

TABLE 4.11

Average number of Carnegie units earned by public high school graduates in various subject fields, by student characteristics, 1982–98
[CONTINUED]

Student characteristics	Total	English	History/ social studies	Mathematics Total	Less than algebra	Alge- bra or higher	Science Total	General science	Biology	Chem- istry	Physics	Foreign lan- guages	Arts	Vocational educa- tion [1]	Per- sonal use [2]	Computer science [3]
1998 graduates	**25.14**	**4.25**	**3.74**	**3.40**	**0.67**	**2.73**	**3.12**	**0.89**	**1.26**	**0.66**	**0.31**	**1.85**	**1.90**	**3.99**	**2.89**	**0.74**
Male	24.93	4.19	3.68	3.37	0.74	2.64	3.09	0.93	1.20	0.62	0.33	1.62	1.61	4.25	3.12	0.78
Female	25.36	4.31	3.80	3.42	0.62	2.80	3.17	0.87	1.32	0.70	0.28	2.06	2.15	3.77	2.67	0.71
Race/ethnicity																
White	25.21	4.19	3.77	3.40	0.57	2.84	3.18	0.87	1.28	0.69	0.33	1.90	2.00	3.97	2.80	0.73
Black	24.83	4.28	3.69	3.42	0.90	2.53	3.03	0.97	1.24	0.58	0.22	1.58	1.57	4.33	2.94	0.84
Hispanic	25.08	4.51	3.60	3.28	1.05	2.23	2.81	0.97	1.13	0.50	0.20	1.78	1.78	3.97	3.36	0.71
Asian	25.23	4.37	3.92	3.62	0.65	2.97	3.43	0.81	1.26	0.83	0.51	2.29	1.52	3.15	2.95	0.67
American Indian	24.43	4.18	3.67	3.10	0.90	2.20	2.68	0.98	1.07	0.49	0.15	1.45	1.94	4.02	3.40	0.67
Academic track																
Academic[4]	24.91	4.33	3.87	3.54	0.53	3.00	3.34	0.84	1.33	0.78	0.38	2.24	2.41	2.22	2.97	0.52
Vocational[5]	22.60	3.46	2.55	2.17	1.30	0.87	1.69	1.05	0.59	0.03	0.01	0.14	0.47	9.12	3.01	0.81
Both[6]	25.64	4.20	3.66	3.30	0.81	2.49	2.94	0.96	1.20	0.54	0.23	1.45	1.31	6.06	2.73	1.03
Neither[7]	21.50	3.21	2.32	2.19	1.59	0.60	1.58	0.88	0.58	0.04	0.08	0.20	0.55	5.64	5.82	0.51

[1] Includes nonoccupational vocational education, vocational general introduction, agriculture, business, marketing, health, occupational home economics, trade and industry, and technical courses.
[2] Includes personal and social courses, religion and theology, and courses not included in the other subject fields.
[3] Computer courses are included in mathematics and vocational categories.
[4] Includes students who complete at least 12 Carnegie units in academic courses, but less than 3 Carnegie units in any specific labor market preparation field.
[5] Includes students who complete at least 3 Carnegie units in a specific labor market preparation field, but less than 12 Carnegie units in academic courses.
[6] Includes students who complete at least 12 Carnegie units in academic courses and at least 3 Carnegie units in a specific labor market preparation field.
[7] Includes students who complete less than 12 Carnegie units in academic courses and less than 3 Carnegie units in a specific labor market preparation field.
NOTE: The Carnegie unit is a standard of measurement that represents one credit for the completion of a 1–year course.

SOURCE: Thomas D. Snyder and Charlene M. Hoffman, "Table 138.—Average number of Carnegie units earned by public high school graduates in various subject fields, by student characteristics: 1982 to 1998," in *Digest of Education Statistics, 2000,* NCES 2001-034, U.S. Department of Education, National Center for Education Statistics, Washington, DC, January 2001

TABLE 4.12

The average SAT scores of entering college classes, 1967–2001*

Year	Male Verbal	Male Math	Female Verbal	Female Math	All Verbal	All Math
1967	540	535	545	495	543	516
1968	541	533	543	497	543	516
1969	536	534	543	498	540	517
1970	536	531	538	493	537	512
1971	531	529	534	494	532	513
1972	531	527	529	489	530	509
1973	523	525	521	489	523	506
1974	524	524	520	488	521	505
1975	515	518	509	479	512	498
1976	511	520	508	475	509	497
1977	509	520	505	474	507	496
1978	511	517	503	474	507	494
1979	509	516	501	473	505	493
1980	506	515	498	473	502	492
1981	508	516	496	473	502	492
1982	509	516	499	473	504	493
1983	508	516	498	474	503	494
1984	511	518	498	478	504	497
1985	514	522	503	480	509	500
1986	515	523	504	479	509	500
1987	512	523	502	481	507	501
1988	512	521	499	483	505	501
1989	510	523	498	482	504	502
1990	505	521	496	483	500	501
1991	503	520	495	482	499	500
1992	504	521	496	484	500	501
1993	504	524	497	484	500	503
1994	501	523	497	487	499	504
1995	505	525	502	490	504	506
1996	507	527	503	492	505	508
1997	507	530	503	494	505	511
1998	509	531	502	496	505	512
1999	509	531	502	495	505	511
2000	507	533	504	498	505	514
2001	509	533	502	498	506	514

*When the SAT was renormed in April 1995, mean scores were set at or near the midpoint of 500 of the 200-800 score scale, a process called "recentering." All scores in this table reflect that process. Means after 1996 are recentered, and those for 1996 are based on recentered scores plus scores converted from the original to the new scale. Means for 1987-1995 were recomputed after individual scores were converted from the original to the new scale; means for 1972-1986 were converted to the new scale after a formula was applied to the original mean and standard deviation; and means before 1972 are based on estimates.

TABLE 4.13

Average ACT scores by level of academic preparation, 1997–2001

Year	Number of Students Core*	Number of Students Less*	Percent Core/Less	English Core/Less	Math Core/Less	Reading Core/Less	Sci. Reas. Core/Less	Composite Core/Less
1997	566,141	361,947	59/38	21.5/18.6	21.8/18.7	22.5/19.7	22.1/19.6	22.1/19.3
1998	606,406	354,306	61/36	21.5/18.6	22.0/18.9	22.4/19.7	22.0/19.6	22.1/19.3
1999	615,545	367,537	60/36	21.6/18.7	21.8/18.9	22.4/19.8	21.9/19.6	22.0/19.4
2000	645,513	376,645	61/35	21.5/18.8	21.8/19.0	22.4/19.8	21.9/19.7	22.0/19.5
2001	645,258	369,921	60/35	21.5/18.8	21.7/19.0	22.2/19.8	21.8/19.8	21.9/19.5

*Core = students who reported completing or planning to complete the recommended core college-preparatory curriculum
Less = those who did not
Note: State departments of education may have a different definition of the college preparatory courses and may, therefore, publish reports showing slightly different data.

SOURCE: The American College Testing Program, "Average ACT Scores by Level of Academic Preparation," in *2001 ACT National and State Scores,* [Online] http://www.act.org/research/ [accessed November 5, 2001]

TABLE 4.14

Average ACT scores and standard deviation for males and females, 2001

Group	No.	English Avg.	English S.D.	Mathematics Avg.	Mathematics S.D.	Reading Avg.	Reading S.D.	Science Reasoning Avg.	Science Reasoning S.D.	Composite Avg.	Composite S.D.
Males	459,547	20.0	5.6	21.4	5.2	21.1	6.1	21.6	4.9	21.1	4.9
Females	604,808	20.8	5.6	20.2	4.7	21.5	6.0	20.6	4.3	20.9	4.6
No Gender Reported	5,417	19.8	5.5	20.3	4.7	21.0	6.0	20.6	4.4	20.6	4.6

	Percentages of Students in Standards for Transition Score Intervals by Gender									
	English		Mathematics		Reading		Science Reasoning		Composite	
Score Interval	M	F	M	F	M	F	M	F	M	F
33–36	1	2	2	1	4	4	2	1	1	1
28–32	9	11	12	7	13	13	10	6	10	8
24–27	16	19	20	17	17	18	21	17	20	20
20–23	25	26	23	23	24	26	33	35	29	31
16–19	26	24	31	36	20	20	24	30	27	29
01–15	22	18	12	15	22	19	9	11	13	12

S.D. = Standard Deviation

SOURCE: The American College Testing Program, "Table 6: Average ACT Scores and Standard Deviations for Males and Females," in *2001 ACT National and State Scores,* [Online] http://www.act.org/research/ [accessed November 5, 2001]

TABLE 4.15

Average ACT scores by academic preparation for different ethnic groups, 2001

	African American Average	American Indian Average	Caucasian Average	Mexican American Average	Asian American Average	Puerto Rican/ Hispanic Average
Total Group	(N = 112,924)	(N = 11,386)	(N = 763,377)	(N = 42,414)	(N = 36,267)	(N = 17,302)
English	16.2	17.8	21.3	17.5	20.7	18.6
Usage/Mechanics	7.7	8.6	10.7	8.5	10.5	9.2
Rhetorical Skills	8.4	9.3	11.0	9.0	10.6	9.6
Mathematics	16.8	18.4	21.3	18.7	23.1	19.4
Pre/Elementary Algebra	8.2	9.3	11.3	9.5	12.2	10.0
Algebra/Coordinate Geometry	8.2	9.0	10.5	9.2	11.6	9.6
Plane Geometry/Trigonometry	8.3	9.4	10.9	9.5	11.8	9.9
Reading	16.9	19.2	22.2	18.6	21.1	19.7
Social Studies/Science	8.4	9.6	11.2	9.2	10.7	9.8
Arts/Literature	8.4	9.7	11.5	9.5	10.7	10.1
Science Reasoning	17.2	19.3	21.8	18.8	21.5	19.5
Composite	16.9	18.8	21.8	18.5	21.7	19.4
Core or More*	(N = 64,555)	(N = 5,589)	(N = 469,616)	(N = 25,107)	(N = 24,802)	(N = 9,984)
English	17.1	19.4	22.3	18.3	21.4	19.7
Usage/Mechanics	8.3	9.5	11.3	9.0	10.9	9.8
Rhetorical Skills	8.9	10.1	11.5	9.4	10.9	10.1
Mathematics	17.5	19.7	22.3	19.4	23.7	20.3
Pre/Elementary Algebra	8.8	10.3	12.0	10.1	12.6	10.7
Algebra/Coordinate Geometry	8.6	9.7	11.0	9.6	11.9	10.1
Plane Geometry/Trigonometry	8.6	10.1	11.4	9.9	12.1	10.3
Reading	17.6	20.6	23.1	19.3	21.8	20.7
Social Studies/Science	8.8	10.4	11.7	9.5	11.0	10.3
Arts/Literature	8.8	10.6	12.0	9.9	11.1	10.7
Science Reasoning	17.8	20.5	22.5	19.4	22.0	20.3
Composite	17.6	20.2	22.7	19.2	22.3	20.3
Less Than Core	(N = 43,515)	(N = 4,941)	(N = 261,332)	(N = 15,438)	(N = 9,538)	(N = 5,620)
English	14.9	16.4	19.6	16.4	18.9	17.2
Usage/Mechanics	7.0	7.7	9.7	7.8	9.4	8.3
Rhetorical Skills	7.8	8.6	10.1	8.5	9.7	8.9
Mathematics	15.9	17.0	19.6	17.5	21.5	18.0
Pre/Elementary Algebra	7.4	8.3	10.2	8.7	11.1	9.0
Algebra/Coordinate Geometry	7.7	8.3	9.6	8.5	10.8	8.8
Plane Geometry/Trigonometry	7.8	8.7	10.0	8.9	11.0	9.1
Reading	15.9	17.9	20.6	17.6	19.6	18.4
Social Studies/Science	7.8	8.9	10.4	8.7	9.9	9.1
Arts/Literature	7.7	9.0	10.6	8.8	9.8	9.2
Science Reasoning	16.4	18.2	20.5	17.9	20.3	18.4
Composite	15.9	17.5	20.2	17.5	20.2	18.1
No Response	(N = 4,854)	(N = 856)	(N = 32,429)	(N = 1,869)	(N = 1,927)	(N = 1,698)

* Core = at least four years of English and three years each of mathematics (algebra and above), social sciences, and natural sciences

SOURCE: The American College Testing Program, "Table 1: Average ACT Scores by Academic Preparation for Different Ethnic Groups," in *2001 ACT National and State Scores,* [Online] http://www.act.org/research/ [accessed November 5, 2001]

CHAPTER 5
NATIONAL GOALS FOR IMPROVEMENT

A CALL TO REFORM

A Nation at Risk (Washington, DC, 1983), a report prepared by the National Commission on Excellence in Education, proved to be a "wake-up call" to the nation on the state of its educational system. It warned of a "rising tide of mediocrity that threatens our very future as a nation and as a people." As a result, educators, lawmakers, and governors began earnest efforts to improve schools. The report recommended, among other things, a longer school year, a tougher curriculum, and stronger teacher-training programs. It specifically expressed alarm at the deterioration of academics at the secondary school level.

To improve the situation, the report recommended that no student should graduate from high school without completing four years of English; three years each of mathematics, science, and social studies; one-half year of computer science; and for college-bound students, two years of a foreign language.

NATIONAL EDUCATION GOALS

At the first Education Summit held in Charlottesville, Virginia in 1989, President George Bush and the nation's state governors established six National Education Goals to be achieved by the year 2000. The bipartisan National Education Goals Panel was created in 1990 to oversee and report on the progress toward these national goals. The panel is made up of eight governors, four members of Congress, four state legislators, and two members appointed by the President. Expressing the continued concern of the nation, Congress passed the Goals 2000: Educate America Act (PL 103-227), signed on March 31, 1994, by President Bill Clinton. The Act reemphasized the National Education Goals and added two more goals.

The eight goals call for greater levels of student achievement, high school completion, teacher education and professional development, parental participation in the schools, and adult literacy and lifelong learning. They also include safe, disciplined, and alcohol- and drug-free schools, preparing children so they are ready to learn by the time they start school, and ensuring that U.S. students are first in the world in mathematics and science. Figure 5.1 lists the goals and a brief explanation for each.

MODEST GAINS AND UNEVEN PROGRESS

How Close Are We to Reaching the Goals?

While many schools responded to the challenge, the Goals panel reported in its 1992 report that any gains had been modest. In its November 1995 report, the panel noted that results had been disappointing. Although the nation was halfway to the target year (2000), it was far from reaching its education goals. In its 1999 report, the panel found that, of the 27 indicators established to measure progress, 12 areas showed improvement, 11 were unchanged, and 5 had worsened. The remaining indicators were either not measured or only showed baseline (current status) measurements. In 2000 and 2001 the panel released reports that examined, for selected indicators in each goal, which states were showing progress, which were not changing, and which had declined.

Goal 1: Ready to Learn

Much improvement has been made in preparing youngsters to enter school ready to learn. Birth defects declined somewhat, to 33 percent in 1997 compared to 37 percent in 1990. The proportion of two-year-olds immunized against childhood diseases grew from 75 percent in 1994 to 78 percent in 1997. Reading to preschool children, an important aid to learning readiness, grew from 66 percent in 1993 to 72 percent in 1996, although it dropped to 69 percent in 1999. Between 1991 and 1999, improvement in preschool participation was particularly significant, reducing the gap between three- to five-year-olds from high- and low-income families by more than half

FIGURE 5.1

The National Education Goals

Goal 1: Ready to learn

By the year 2000, all children in America will start school ready to learn.

Goal 2: School completion

By the year 2000, the high school graduation rate will increase to at least 90 percent.

Goal 3: Student achievement and citizenship

By the year 2000, all students will leave grades 4, 8, and 12 having demonstrated competency over challenging subject matter including English, mathematics, science, foreign languages, civics and government, economics, arts, history, and geography, and every school in America will ensure that all students learn to use their minds well, so they may be prepared for responsible citizenship, further learning, and productive employment in our Nation's modern economy.

Goal 4: Teacher education and professional development

By the year 2000, the Nation's teaching force will have access to programs for the continued improvement of their professional skills and the opportunity to acquire the knowledge and skills needed to instruct and prepare all American students for the next century.

Goal 5: Mathematics and science

By the year 2000, United States students will be first in the world in mathematics and science achievement

Goal 6: Adult literacy and lifelong learning

By the year 2000, every adult American will be literate and will possess the knowledge and skills necessary to compete in a global economy and exercise the rights and responsibilities of citizenship.

Goal 7: Safe, disciplined, and alcohol- and drug-free schools

By the year 2000, every school in the United States will be free of drugs, violence, and the unauthorized presence of firearms and alcohol and will offer a disciplined environment conducive to learning.

Goal 8: Parental participation

By the year 2000, every school will promote partnerships that will increase parental involvement and participation in promoting the social, emotional, and academic growth of children.

SOURCE: Cynthia Price, "The National Education Goals," in *The National Educational Goals Report: Building a Nation of Learners, 1999*, National Education Goals Panel, Washington, DC, 1999

(53.6 percent). (See Table 5.1. Note the legend showing progress: an arrow pointing up indicates improvement.)

From 1990 to 1998, most states reduced the percentage of infants born with one or more of four health risks, which translates to an improvement in the "Children's Health Index" of Goal 1 in 39 states. Eight states had no change in this indicator, and two states were worse. The District of Columbia, Massachusetts, Arizona, Florida, and Rhode Island showed the most improvement. (See Table 5.2.)

Goal 2: School Completion

The goal for high school completion among 18- to 24-year-olds was 90 percent by 2000. However, the proportion of high school graduates was virtually unchanged, dropping slightly from 86 percent in 1990 to 85 percent in 1998. (See Table 5.3).

Iowa, Maine, Massachusetts, New York, North Dakota, and Wisconsin had the lowest high school dropout rates among the states, and 13 states improved their graduation rates from 1992 to 1997. No change was seen during this five-year period in 3 states, and 11 had graduation rates that dropped from 1992 to 1997. (See Table 5.4.)

Goal 3: Student Achievement and Citizenship

Progress toward student achievement and citizenship has been uneven. For most indicators, only baseline data were released in the 1999 NAGP report. Mathematics performance improved at all grades between 1990 and 1996, but the percentage of fourth-grade and twelfth-grade students who met the panel's reading standards between 1992 and 1998 was statistically unchanged. The reading performance of eighth graders increased 4 percent. (See Table 5.5.)

The National Educational Goals intend to increase student academic achievement overall, and also to diminish the gaps in achievement that exist between high and low performers. From 1992 to 1996 eight states reduced the gap in performance between students in the top and bottom quartiles of achievement. Two states reduced the gap that exists in performance between whites and minorities. There were 28 states where there was no change in the quartile achievement gap, and 37 that failed to alter the white/minority achievement gap. The quartile achievement gap increased in two states, but in no state did the white/minority gap worsen between 1992 and 1996. (See Table 5.6).

Between 1991 and 2000 all states in the nation increased one indicator, the number of Advanced Placement examinations receiving a grade of three or higher. Biggest gains were seen in the District of Columbia, Connecticut, Massachusetts, New York and Virginia. (See Table 5.7.)

Goal 4: Teacher Education and Development

Between 1991 and 1994, the percentage of teachers with a degree in their primary teaching assignment declined from 66 percent to 63 percent. The baseline measurement for professional development, 85 percent, was established in 1994, and this area has not been updated since. (See Table 5.8.)

One indicator, the proportion of new teachers who reported that they participated in a formal mentoring program by being assigned to a master teacher, saw improvement in 17 states. In 33 states, there was no change in this area, and in one state, the proportion declined. North Carolina, Pennsylvania, Kentucky, New York, Indiana, and Virginia saw the most improvement. (See Table 5.9.)

Goal 5: Mathematics and Science

The purpose of this goal is to provide future workers for the high-technology labor market. Many observers claim that, without an adequate supply of persons trained in mathematics and science, the United States will not be able to participate successfully in the global economy. Table 5.10 shows the status of the indicators that support this goal. It is encouraging to note that the proportion of college degrees in mathematics and science increased between 1991 and 1996.

Fifteen states showed an increase in the average scores of fourth graders in mathematics between 1992 and 1996. Three states had declines, and 21 states experienced no changes. Seven states had increases in the proportion of students scoring at or above the proficient level, and 32

TABLE 5.1

Goal 1: Ready to learn

	Baseline	Update	Progress?
Children's Health Index: Has the U.S. reduced the percentage of infants born with 1 or more of 4 health risks? (1990 vs. 1997)	37%	33%	↑
Immunizations: Has the U.S. increased the percentage of 2-year-olds who have been fully immunized against preventable childhood diseases? (1994 vs. 1997)	75%	78%	↑
Family-Child Reading and Storytelling: Has the U.S. increased the percentage of 3- to 5-year-olds whose parents read to them or tell them stories regularly? (1993 vs. 1999)	66%	69%	↑
Preschool Participation: Has the U.S. reduced the gap (in percentage points) in preschool participation between 3- to 5-year-olds from high- and low-income families? (1991 vs. 1999)	28 points	13 points	↑

SOURCE: Cynthia Price, "Goal 1," in *The National Educational Goals Report: Building a Nation of Learners,* National Education Goals Panel, Washington, DC, 1999

states saw no change. No state saw declining percentages of fourth-grade students scoring at the proficient level in mathematics. Between 1990 and 1996, 26 states increased the number of eighth-grade students scoring at the proficient level, 28 states improved upon the average scores of those students, six states demonstrated no change in the proportion who scored proficient, and four states showed no change in average scores. No state experienced a decline in performance in those years. (See Table 5.11 and Table 5.12).

Average fourth-grade reading scores remained unchanged in 26 states, and in three states they declined from 1992 to 1998. Seven states saw an increase in reading scores. The proportion of students scoring at the proficient level increased in eight states, it remained unchanged in 28 states, and in no state did the percentage of students achieving at or above the proficient level in fourth grade reading decline. (See Table 5.13.)

One indicator of progress towards Goal 5—making U.S. students first in science and math—is to increase "percentages of public school eighth graders whose mathematics teachers report that they have computers available in their mathematics classrooms." No trend data has been reported, but in 1996, Alaska, the District of Columbia, Tennessee, Vermont and Wyoming had the highest percentages of eighth-grade students whose mathematics teachers reported having computers in their classrooms. (See Table 5.14.)

TABLE 5.2

Goal 1: Ready to learn / children's health index

Children's Health Index

Have states[1] reduced the percentages of infants born with one or more of four health risks?[2]

↑	Better	39 states and the U.S.
↔	No Change	8 states
↓	Worse	2 states

Improvement over time

Between 1990 and 1998, the U.S. and 39 states (out of 49) significantly reduced the percentages of infants born with one or more of four health risks:

1. Alabama	11. Illinois	21. Nebraska	31. South Carolina
2. Arizona	12. Iowa	22. Nevada	32. Tennessee
3. Arkansas	13. Kentucky	23. New Hampshire	33. Texas
4. Colorado	14. Louisiana	24. New Mexico	34. Vermont
5. Delaware	15. Maryland	25. North Carolina	35. Virginia
6. District of Columbia	16. Massachusetts	26. Ohio	36. Washington
7. Florida	17. Michigan	27. Oklahoma	37. West Virginia
8. Georgia	18. Minnesota	28. Oregon	38. Wisconsin
9. Hawaii	19. Mississippi	29. Pennsylvania	39. Puerto Rico
10. Idaho	20. Missouri	30. Rhode Island	

Highest-performing states*

States with the lowest percentages of infants born with one or more of four health risks:

	(1998)		(1998)
Connecticut	25%	Georgia	31%
Hawaii	25%	Massachusetts	31%
Maryland	28%	Virginia	31%
Utah	28%	Washington	31%
Texas	29%	Idaho	32%
Rhode Island	29%	Kansas	32%
Arizona	30%	Nevada	32%
Colorado	30%	New Hampshire	32%
Florida	30%		
Minnesota	30%	**U.S.**	**33%**

* States that had a significantly lower percentage than the U.S. average.

Most-improved states

States that made the greatest reductions in the percentages of infants born with one or more of four health risks:

	(1990)	(1998)	Change*
District of Columbia	48%	34%	-14
Massachusetts	42%	31%	-11
Arizona	37%	30%	-7
Florida	37%	30%	-7
Rhode Island	36%	29%	-7

* Differences between the first two columns may differ slightly from the figures reported in the change column due to rounding.

[1] The term state is used to refer to the 50 states, the District of Columbia, and the outlying areas.

[2] Risks are: late (in third trimester) or no prenatal care; low maternal weight gain (less than 21 pounds); mother smoked during pregnancy; or mother drank alcohol during pregnancy.

SOURCE: "Goal 1: Ready to Learn," in *Promising Practices: Progress Toward the Goals 2000*, National Education Goals Panel, Washington, DC, December 2000

TABLE 5.3

Goal 2: School completion

	Baseline	Update	Progress?
High School Completion: Has the U.S. increased the percentage of 18- to 24-year-olds who have a high school credential? (1990 vs. 1998)	86%	85%	↔

SOURCE: Cynthia Price, "Goal 2," in *The National Educational Goals Report: Building a Nation of Learners, 1999*, National Education Goals Panel, Washington, DC, 1999

Goal 6: Adult Literacy and Learning

Adult literacy and lifelong learning is another area in which the lack of progress has been disappointing. Level three prose literacy requires a person to make low-level inferences from text or to match information in text with task directions. In 1992, only 52 percent of adult Americans could successfully perform this task. The gap in adult education participation between those with a high school diploma or less and those who have postsecondary education has remained statistically unchanged. In addition, the ratio of white and minority college attendance and completion has not statistically improved. (See Table 5.15.)

In 39 states the proportion of high school graduates who immediately enroll in postsecondary school increased from 1992 to 1996. One state experienced no change, and 11 states had a decrease in this indicator. The District of Columbia, California, South Carolina, Massachusetts, and Delaware made the greatest gains. (See Table 5.16.)

TABLE 5.4

Goal 2: School completion / High school dropout rates

High School Dropout Rates

Have states[1] reduced the percentages of students in Grades 9-12 who leave school without completing a recognized secondary program?

↑	Better	13 states
↔	No Change	3 states
↓	Worse	11 states

Improvement over time

Between 1992 and 1997, 13 states (out of 27) significantly reduced the percentages of students in Grades 9-12 who left school without completing a recognized secodary program:

1.	Arizona	5.	Iowa	9.	Ohio	13.	Puerto Rico
2.	Connecticut	6.	Missouri	10.	Rhode Island		
3.	District of Columbia	7.	Montana	11.	West Virginia		
4.	Georgia	8.	New York	12.	Wyoming		

Highest-performing states*

States with the lowest percentages of students in Grades 9-12 who left school without completing a recognized secondary program:

	(1997)
Iowa	3%
Maine	3%
Massachusetts	3%
New York	3%
North Dakota	3%
Wisconsin	3%

No comparable national data available.

* Top 6 states (out of 39)

Most-improved states

States that made the greatest reductions in the percentages of students in Grades 9-12 who left school without completing a recognized secondary program:

	(1992)	(1997)	Change*
Arizona	11%	10%	-1
Connecticut**	5%	4%	-1
District of Columbia**	12%	11%	-1
Georgia**	9%	8%	-1
Montana**	6%	5%	-1
Puerto Rico**	2%	2%	-1
Wyoming**	7%	6%	-1

* Differences between the first two columns may differ slightly from the figure reported in the change colun due to rounding.
** Data for the District of Columbia were collected in 1992 and 1995.
Data for Connecticut were collected in 1993 and 1997.
Data for Georgia were collected in 1994 and 1997.
Data for Puerto Rico were collected in 1995 and 1996.
Data for Wyoming were collected in 1995 and 1997.
Data for Montana were collected in 1996 and 1997.

[1] The term state is used to refer to the 50 states, the District of Columbia, and the outlying areas.

SOURCE: "Goal 2: School Completion," in *Promising Practices: Progress Toward the Goals 2000*, National Education Goals Panel, Washington, DC, December 2000

Goal 7: Safe, Disciplined, and Alcohol- and Drug-Free Schools

Almost no progress has been made toward reaching the goal of safe, disciplined, and alcohol- and drug-free schools. The only encouraging sign is that fewer tenth graders (33 percent) reported being threatened or injured at school than in 1991 (40 percent). On the other hand, more public-school teachers were threatened or injured in 1994 (15 percent) than in 1991 (10 percent). All other indicators were either unchanged or had declined. (See Table 5.17.)

From 1991 to 1994 no state reduced the proportion of public secondary school teachers reporting that student disruptions interfered with teaching, while 14 states experienced no change. In 37 states, more teachers reported disruptions in 1994 than in 1991. In 1994 Montana, North Dakota, Oklahoma, and Wyoming had the lowest percentages of public secondary school teachers reporting that student disruptions interfered with teaching. (See Table 5.18.)

Goal 8: Parental Participation

The Goals panel's 1998 report found that 78 percent of K-8 public schools had more than one-half of their parents involved in parent-teacher conferences in 1996. On the other hand, only 41 percent of K-8 public schools considered parent input when making policy decisions in three or more areas. The proportion of parents who had participated in two or more activities at their children's schools was unchanged from 1993 to 1999. (See Table 5.19.)

Between 1991 and 1994, 17 states increased the percentage of public school principals reporting that the parent association in their schools had influence in selected areas of school policy. No states reported a decline in the proportion, and 34 states showed no change in this area. The highest performing states in 1994 were Alaska, California, Colorado, Kentucky, and New Mexico. (See Table 5.20.)

TABLE 5.5

Goal 3: Student achievement and citizenship

	Baseline	Update	Progress?
Reading Achievement:			
Has the U.S. increased the percentage of students scoring at or above Proficient in readng? (1992 vs. 1998)			
• Grade 4	29%	31%[ns]	←→
• Grade 8	29%	33%	↑
• Grade 12	40%	40%	←→
Writing Achievement:			
Has the U.S. increased the percentage of students scoring at or above Proficient in writing? (1998)			
• Grade 4	23%	—	
• Grade 8	27%	—	
• Grade 12	22%	—	
Mathematics Achievement:			
Has the U.S. increased the percentage of students scoring at or above Proficient in mathematics? (1990 vs. 1996)			
• Grade 4	13%	21%	↑
• Grade 8	15%	24%	↑
• Grade 12	12%	16%	↑
Science Achievement:			
Has the U.S. increased the percentage of students scoring at or above Proficient in science? (1996)			
• Grade 4	29%	—	
• Grade 8	29%	—	
• Grade 12	21%	—	
Civics Achievement:			
Has the U.S. increased the percentage of students scoring at or above Proficient in civics? (1998)			
• Grade 4	23%	—	
• Grade 8	22%	—	
• Grade 12	26%	—	
History Achievement:			
Has the U.S. increased the percentage of students scoring at or above Proficient in U.S. history? (1994)			
• Grade 4	17%	—	
• Grade 8	14%	—	
• Grade 12	11%	—	
Geography Achievement:			
Has the U.S. increased the percentage of students scoring at or above Proficient in geography? (1994)			
• Grade 4	22%	—	
• Grade 8	28%	—	
• Grade 12	27%	—	

— Data not available.
[ns] Interpret with caution. Change was not statistically significant.

SOURCE: Cynthia Price, "Goal 3," in *The National Educational Goals Report: Building a Nation of Learners,* National Education Goals Panel, Washington, DC, 1999

Goals Not Considered a Failure

In spite of the inability of America's schools to reach any of the eight National Education Goals, both Republican and Democratic politicians credited the goals with setting high standards. The Goals panel recognized 12 states—Connecticut, Indiana, Maine, Maryland, Michi-

TABLE 5.6

State trends in closing achievement gaps, 1990s

Gap closing	4th Grade mathematics (of 39 states)	8th Grade mathematics (of 32 states)	4th Grade reading (of 36 states)
States Improving by narrowing the:			
* Quartile Gap	8	5	1
* White/Minority Gap	2	0	1
States Unchanged:			
* Quartile Gap	28	25	19
* White/Minority Gap	37	29	28
States Declining by increasing the:			
* Quartile Gap	2	2	16
* White/Minority Gap	0	2	6

SOURCE: Paul E. Barton, "Gap Closing," in *Raising Achievement and Reducing Gaps: Reporting Progress Toward Goals for Academic Achievement,* National Education Goals Panel, Washington, DC, March 2001

gan, Minnesota, North Carolina, North Dakota, Oklahoma, Texas, Washington, and Wisconsin—for making outstanding progress toward the goals over the past decade.

NATIONAL URBAN EDUCATION GOALS

The Council of the Great City Schools (GCS), representing 56 of the nation's largest urban public school districts, revised and adapted the National Education Goals to the needs of urban schools. The National Urban Education Goals are:

• Readiness to learn—All urban children will start school ready to learn.

• Increased graduation rates—Urban schools will increase their graduation rates so they are at least comparable to the national average.

• Improvement in academic achievement—Schools and communities will demonstrate high expectations for all learners so that urban students will attain a level of achievement that will allow them to successfully compete with students nationally and internationally in our global community.

• Quality teachers—Urban schools will be adequately staffed with qualified teachers who are culturally and racially sensitive and who reflect the racial characteristics of their students.

• Postsecondary opportunities—Urban school graduates will be fully prepared to enter and successfully complete higher education, experience successful employment, and exercise their responsibilities as citizens.

• Safe and caring environment—Urban schools will be free of drugs and alcohol, students will be healthy and well nourished, and schools will be well maintained and safe.

TABLE 5.7

Goal 3: Student achievement and citizenship / advanced placement performance

Advanced Placement Performance

Have states[1] increased the number of Advanced Placement examinations receiving a grade of 3 or higher (per 1,000 11th and 12th graders)?

↑	Better	51 states and the U.S.
↔	No Change	0 states
↓	Worse	0 states

Improvement over time

Between 1991 and 2000, the U.S. and 51 states (out of 51) significantly increased the numbers of Advanced Placement examinations receiving a grade of 3 or higher (per 1,000 11th and 12th graders):

1. Alabama	14. Illinois	27. Montana	40. Rhode Island
2. Alaska	15. Indiana	28. Nebraska	41. South Carolina
3. Arizona	16. Iowa	29. Nevada	42. South Dakota
4. Arkansas	17. Kansas	30. New Hampshire	43. Tennessee
5. California	18. Kentucky	31. New Jersey	44. Texas
6. Colorado	19. Louisiana	32. New Mexico	45. Utah
7. Connecticut	20. Maine	33. New York	46. Vermont
8. Delaware	21. Maryland	34. North Carolina	47. Virginia
9. District of Columbia	22. Massachusetts	35. North Dakota	48. Washington
10. Florida	23. Michigan	36. Ohio	49. West Virginia
11. Georgia	24. Minnesota	37. Oklahoma	50. Wisconsin
12. Hawaii	25. Mississippi	38. Oregon	51. Wyoming
13. Idaho	26. Missouri	39. Pennsylvania	

Highest-performing states*

States with the highest numbers of Advanced Placement examinations receiving a grade of 3 or higher (per 1,000 11th and 12th graders):

	(2000)
District of Columbia	271
Virginia	177
New York	173
Connecticut	167
Massachusetts	158
U.S.	**104**

* Top 5 states (out of 51)

Most-improved states

States that made the greatest reductions in the percentages of students in Grades 9-12 who left school without completing a recognized secondary program:

	(1991)	(2000)	Change*
District of Columbia	177	271	+94
Connecticut	83	167	+84
Massachusetts	82	158	+76
New York	97	173	+76
Virginia	102	177	+75

*Differences between the first two columns may differ slightly from the figures reported in the change column due to rounding.

[1] The term state is used to refer to the 50 states, the District of Columbia, and the outlying areas.

SOURCE: "Goal 3: Student Achievement and Citizenship," in *Promising Practices: Progress Toward the Goals 2000*, National Education Goals Panel, Washington, DC, December 2000

- Equitable and adequate funding—America's urban schools will be funded equitably and adequately by all levels of government to enable urban students to meet the Urban Goals.

- Increased parental involvement—All parents/guardians of urban school children will be involved in the education of their children, and urban schools will have programs to encourage and reinforce that activity.

Urban Student Performance

The 56 GCS districts enrolled 14 percent of all K-12 public-school children in 2000. This proportion has stayed relatively constant since 1982–83. In 2000 about 61 percent of GCS students were eligible to receive free/reduced-price lunches, compared to 38 percent nationally. Twenty-two percent were English language learners, compared to 8 percent of students in the nation. About 70 percent of GCS students were African American or Hispanic, compared with 32 percent nationally.

In *Beating the Odds* (Council of Great City Schools, Washington, DC, May 2001), the Council reported that 92 percent of city school districts had improved mathematics scores and 80 percent had improved reading scores in more than half the grade levels tested in 2000. However, despite significant gains in mathematics and reading achievement, urban schools still score below national averages.

TABLE 5.8

Goal 4: Teacher education and professional development

	Baseline	Update	Progress?
Teacher Preparation: Has the U.S. increased the percentage of secondary teachers who hold an undergraduate or graduate degree in their main teaching assignment? (1991 vs. 1994)	66%	63%	↓
Teacher Professional Development: Has the U.S. increased the percentage of teachers reporting that they participated in professional development programs on 1 or more topics since the end of the previous school year? (1994)	85%	—	

— Data not available.
ns Interpret with caution. Change was not statistically significant.

SOURCE: Cynthia Price, "Goal 4," in *The National Educational Goals Report: Building a Nation of Learners,* National Education Goals Panel, Washington, DC, 1999

TABLE 5.9

Goal 4: Teacher education and professional development / teacher support

Teacher Support

Have states[1] increased the percentages of public school teachers who report that during their first year of teaching they participated in a formal teacher induction program to help beginning teachers by assigning them to a master or mentor teacher?

↑	Better	17 states and the U.S.
↔	No Change	33 states
↓	Worse	1 state

Improvement over time

Between 1991 and 1994, the U.S. and 17 states (out of 51) significantly increased the percentages of public school teachers who reported that during their first year of teaching they participated in a formal teacher induction program to help beginning teachers by assigning them to a master or mentor teacher:

1. Arizona	6. Idaho	10. New York	14. Texas
2. California	7. Indiana	11. North Carolina	15. Utah
3. Connecticut	8. Kentucky	12. Pennsylvania	16. Virginia
4. Delaware	9. Missouri	13. South Carolina	17. Wisconsin
5. Florida			

Highest-performing states*

States with the highest percentages of public school teachers who reported that during their first year of teaching they participated in a formal teacher induction program to help beginning teachers by assigning them to a master or mentor teacher:

	(1994)
Florida	48%
Oklahoma	45%
Utah	40%
District of Columbia	39%
North Carolina	36%
California	35%
Kentucky	34%
Hawaii	33%
U.S.	**27%** **

Most-improved states

States that made the greatest gains in the percentages of public school teachers who reported that during their first year of teaching they participated in a formal teacher induction program to help beginning teachers by assigning them to a master or mentor teacher:

	(1991)	(1994)	Change*
North Carolina	24%	36%	+12
Pennsylvania	20%	31%	+11
Kentucky	24%	34%	+10
New York	21%	31%	+10
Indiana	14%	22%	+9
Virginia	21%	30%	+9

*Differences between the first two columns may differ slightly from the figures reported in the change column due to rounding.

* States that had a significantly higher percentage than the U.S. average.
** Percentage shown for the U.S. includes both public and nonpublic school data.

[1] The term state is used to refer to the 50 states, the District of Columbia, and the outlying areas.

SOURCE: "Goal 4: Teacher Education and Professional Development," in *Promising Practices: Progress Toward the Goals 2000*, National Education Goals Panel, Washington, DC, December 2000

TABLE 5.10

Goal 5: Mathematics and science

	Baseline	Update	Progress?
International Mathematics Achievement: Has the U.S. improved its standing on international mathematics assessments? (1995)			
• Grade 4	7 out of 25 countries scored above the U.S.		
• Grade 8	20 out of 40 countries scored above the U.S.		
• Grade 12	14 out of 20 countries scored above the U.S.		
International Science Achievement: Has the U.S. improved its standing on international science assessments? (1995)			
• Grade 4	1 out of 25 countries scored above the U.S.		
• Grade 8	9 out of 40 countries scored above the U.S.		
• Grade 12	11 out of 20 countries scored above the U.S.		
Mathematics and Science Degrees: Has the U.S increased mathematics and science degrees (as a percentage of all degrees) awarded to:			
• all students (1991 vs. 1996)	39%	43%	↑
• minorities (Blacks, Hispanics, American Indians/ Alaskan Natives)? (1991 vs. 1996)	39%	40%	↑
• females? (1991 vs. 1996)	35%	41%	↑

— Data not available.

ns Interpret with caution. Change was not statistically significant.

SOURCE: Cynthia Price, "Goal 5," in *The National Educational Goals Report: Building a Nation of Learners,* National Education Goals Panel, Washington, DC, 1999

TABLE 5.11

Changes in fourth grade mathematics achievement scores between 1992 and 1996

4ᵗʰ Grade Math	Average score	Bottom Quartile	Top Quartile	% scoring Proficient
States Improving	15	20	16	7
States Unchanged	21	17	19	32
States Declining	3	2	4	0

SOURCE: Paul E. Barton, "4th Grade Math," in *Raising Achievement and Reducing Gaps: Reporting Progress Toward Goals for Academic Achievement*, National Education Goals Panel, Washington, DC, March 2001

TABLE 5.12

Changes in eighth grade mathematics achievement scores between 1990 and 1996

8ᵗʰ Grade Math	Average score	Bottom Quartile	Top Quartile	% scoring Proficient
States Improving	28	24	30	26
States Unchanged	4	8	2	6
States Declining	0	0	0	0

SOURCE: Paul E. Barton, "8th Grade Math," in *Raising Achievement and Reducing Gaps: Reporting Progress Toward Goals for Academic Achievement*, National Education Goals Panel, Washington, DC, March 2001

TABLE 5.13

Changes in fourth grade reading achievement scores from 1992 to 1998

4ᵗʰ Grade Reading	Average score	Bottom Quartile	Top Quartile	% scoring Proficient
States Improving	7	3	12	8
States Unchanged	26	15	24	28
States Declining	3	18	0	0

SOURCE: Paul E. Barton, "4th Grade Reading," in *Raising Achievement and Reducing Gaps: Reporting Progress Toward Goals for Academic Achievement*, National Education Goals Panel, Washington, DC, March 2001

TABLE 5.14

Goal 5: Mathematics and science / mathematics resources—computers

Have states[1] increased the percentages of public school 8th graders whose mathematics teachers report that they have computers available in their classrooms?

Improvement over time

Improvement over time cannot be determined yet because this information has been collected only once at the state level since 1990. The Goals Panel wil report state improvements when this information is collected again in 2000.

Highest-performing states*

States with the highest percentages of public school 8th graders whose mathematics teachers reported that they had computers available in their mathematics classroom:

	(1996)
Tennessee	54%
Alaska	50%
Vermont	44%
District of Columbia	42%
Wyoming	41%
U.S.	**30%****

* States that had a significantly higher percentage than the U.S. average.
** Percentage shown for the U.S. includes both public and nonpublic school data.

[1] The term state is used to refer to the 50 states, the District of Columbia, and the outlying areas.

SOURCE: "Goal 5: Mathematics and Science," in *Promising Practices: Progress Toward the Goals 2000*, National Education Goals Panel, Washington, DC, December 2000

Most-improved states

States that made the greatest gains in the percentages of public school 8th graders whose mathematics teachers reported that they had computers available in their mathematics classrooms:

The states that made the greatest improvements over time cannot be identified yet because this information has been collected only once at the state level since 1990. The Goals Panel will recognize the most-improved states when this information is collected again in 2000.

TABLE 5.15

Goal 6: Adult literacy and lifelong learning

	Baseline	Update	Progress?
Adult Literacy: Has the U.S. increased the percentage of adults who score at the three highest levels in prose literacy? (1992)	52%	—	
Participation in Adult Education: Has the U.S. reduced the gap (in percentage points) in adult education participation between adults who have a high school diploma or less, and those who have additional postsecondary education or technical training? (1991 vs. 1999)	27 points	29 points[ns]	←→
Participation in Higher Education: Has the U.S. reduced the gap (in percentage points) between White and Black high school graduates who:			
• enroll in college? (1990 vs. 1997)	14 points	9 points[ns]	←→
• complete a college degree? (1992 vs. 1998)	16 points	19 points[ns]	←→
Has the U.S. reduced the gap (in percentage points) between White and Hispanic high school graduates who:			
• enroll in college? (1990 vs. 1997)	11 points	13 points[ns]	
• complete a college degree? (1992 vs. 1998)	15 points	19 points[ns]	

— Data not available.

[ns] Interpret with caution. Change was not statistically significant.

SOURCE: Cynthia Price, "Goal 6," in *The National Educational Goals Report: Building a Nation of Learners,* National Education Goals Panel, Washington, DC, 1999

TABLE 5.16

Goal 6: Adult literacy and lifelong learning / participation in higher education

Have states[1] increased the percentages of high school graduates who immediately enroll in 2-year or 4-year colleges in any state?

↑	Better	39 states and the U.S.
↔	No Change	1 state
↓	Worse	11 states

Improvement over time

Between 1992 and 1996, the U.S. and 39 states (out of 51) significantly increased the percentages of high school graduates who immediately enroll in 2-year or 4-year colleges in any state:

1. Alabama	11. Georgia	21. Mississippi	31. Ohio
2. Alaska	12. Hawaii	22. Missouri	32. Pennsylvania
3. Arizona	13. Indiana	23. Montana	33. Rhode Island
4. Arkansas	14. Kansas	24. Nevada	34. South Carolina
5. California	15. Kentucky	25. New Hampshire	35. Tennessee
6. Colorado	16. Maine	26. New Jersey	36. Texas
7. Connecticut	17. Maryland	27. New Mexico	37. Virginia
8. Delaware	18. Massachusetts	28. New York	38. West Virginia
9. District of Columbia	19. Michigan	29. North Carolina	39. Wyoming
10. Florida	20. Minnesota	30. North Dakota	

Highest-performing states*

States with the highest percentages of high school graduates who immediately enrolled in 2-year or 4-year colleges in any state:

	(1996)
Massachusetts	73%
New York	71%
North Dakota	71%
Delaware	67%
California	66%
Rhode Island	66%

Indicators are not the same at the national and state levels.

* Top 6 states (out of 51).

[1] The term state is used to refer to the 50 states, the District of Columbia, and the outlying areas.

Most-improved states

States that made the greatest gains in the percentages of high school graduates who immediately enrolled in 2-year or 4-year colleges in any state:

	(1992)	(1996)	Change*
District of Columbia	33%	58%	+25
California	50%	66%	+16
South Carolina	43%	59%	+16
Massachusetts	60%	73%	+14
Delaware	57%	67%	+10

* Differences between the first two columns may differ slightly from the figures reported in the change column due to rounding.

SOURCE: "Goal 6: Adult Literacy and Lifelong Learning," in *Promising Practices: Progress Toward the Goals 2000*, National Education Goals Panel, Washington, DC, December 2000

TABLE 5.17

Goal 7: Safe, disciplined, and alcohol- and drug-free schools

	Baseline	Update	Progress?
Overall Student Drug and Alcohol Use: Has the U.S. reduced the percentage of 10th graders reporting doing the following during the previous year:			
• using any illicit drug? (1991 vs. 1998)	24%	37%	↓
• using alcohol? (1993 vs. 1998)	63%	63%	←→
Sale of Drugs at School: Has the U.S. reduced the percentage of 10th graders reporting that someone offered to sell or give them an illegal drug at school during the previous year? (1992 vs. 1998)	18%	29%	↓
Student and Teacher Victimization: Has the U.S. reduced the percentage of students and teachers reporting that they were threatened or injured at school during the previous year?			
• 10th grade students (1991 vs. 1998)	40%	33%	↑
• public school teachers (1991 vs. 1994)	10%	15%	↓
Disruptions in Class by Students: Has the U.S. reduced the percentage of students and teachers reporting that student disruptions interfere with teaching and learning?			
• 10th grade students (1992 vs. 1998)	17%	16%[ns]	←→
• secondary school teachers (1991 vs. 1994)	37%	46%	↓

— Data not available.

[ns] Interpret with caution. Change was not statistically significant.

SOURCE: Cynthia Price, "Goal 7," in *The National Educational Goals Report: Building a Nation of Learners,* National Education Goals Panel, Washington, DC, 1999

TABLE 5.18

Goal 7: Safe, disciplined, and alcohol- and drug- free schools / disruptions in class by students

Have states[1] reduced the percentages of public secondary school teachers reporting that student disruptions interfere with teaching?

	Better	0 states
↕	No Change	14 states
↓	Worse	37 states

Improvement over time

Between 1991 and 1994, no state (out of 51) significantly reduced the percentage of public secondary school teachers reporting that student disruptions interfere with teaching.

Highest-performing states*

States with the lowest percentages of public secondary school teachers reporting that student disruptions interfere with teaching:

	(1994)
Montana	33%
North Dakota	33%
Oklahoma	39%
Wyoming	39%
U.S.	**46%****

Most-improved states

States that made the greatest reductions in the percentages of public secondary school teachers reporting that student disruptions interfere with teaching:

No state made a significant improvement between 1991 and 1994.

* States that had a significantly lower percentage than the U.S. average.
** Percentage shown for the U.S. includes both public and nonpublic school data.

[1] The term state is used to refer to the 50 states, the District of Columbia, and the outlying areas.

SOURCE: "Goal 7: Safe, Disciplined and Alcohol- and Drug-Free Schools," in *Promising Practices: Progress Toward the Goals 2000*, National Education Goals Panel, Washington, DC, December 2000

TABLE 5.19

Goal 8: Parental participation

	Baseline	Update	Progress?
Schools' Reports of Parent Attendance at Parent-Teacher Conferences: Has the U.S. increased the percentage of K-8 public schools which reported that more than half of their parents attended parent-teacher conferences during the school year? (1996)	78%	—	
Schools' Reports of Parent Involvement in School Policy Decisions: Has the U.S. increased the percentage of K-8 public schools which reported that parent input is considered when making policy decisions in three or more areas? (1996)	41%	—	
Parents' Reports of Their Involvement in School Activities: Has the U.S. increased the percentage of students in Grades 3 to 12 whose parents reported that they participated in two or more activities in their child's school during the current school year? (1993 vs. 1999)	63%	62%[ns]	↔

— Data not available.
[ns] Interpret with caution. Change was not statistically significant.

SOURCE: Cynthia Price, "Goal 8," in *The National Educational Goals Report: Building a Nation of Learners*, National Education Goals Panel, Washington, DC, 1999

TABLE 5.20

Goal 8: Parental participation / influence of parent associations

Have states[1] increased the percentages of public school principals reportin that the parent associations in their schools have influence in one or more of three areas of school policy?

↑	Better	17 states
↔	No Change	34 states
↓	Worse	0 states

Improvement over time

Between 1991 and 1994, the U.S. and 17 states (out of 51) significantly increased the percentages of public school principals reporting that the parent associations in their schools have influence in one or more of three areas of school policy:

1. Alaska	6. Kentucky	10. New York	14. Texas
2. Arizona	7. Massachusetts	11. Oklahoma	15. Utah
3. Colorado	8. Nevada	12. Pennsylvania	16. Vermont
4. Idaho	9. New Mexico	13. Rhode Island	17. Wisconsin
5. Iowa			

Highest-performing states*

States with the highest percentages of public school principals reporting that the parent associations in their schools have influence in one or more of three areas of school policy:

	(1994)
Colorado	50%
Alaska	43%
New Mexico	40%
Kentucky	37%
California	36%

Indicators are not the same at the national and state levels.

* Top 5 states (out of 51)

Most-improved states

States that made the greatest gains in the percentages of public school principals reporting that the parent associations in their schools have influence in one or more of three areas of school policy:

	(1991)	(1994)	Change*
Colorado	28%	50%	+22
Kentucky	17%	37%	+20
Pennsylvania	10%	28%	+18
Vermont	8%	24%	+17
Alaska	27%	43%	+16
New York	18%	34%	+16
Utah	17%	33%	+16

*Differences between the first two columns may differ slightly from the figures reported in the change column due to rounding.

[1] The term state is used to refer to the 50 states, the District of Columbia, and the outlying areas.

SOURCE: "Goal 8: Parental Participation," in *Promising Practices: Progress Toward the Goals 2000*, National Education Goals Panel, Washington, DC, December 2000

CHAPTER 6
STUDENTS AT RISK

WHAT DOES "AT RISK" MEAN?

In 1997 the U. S. Bureau of the Census identified six indicators of risk to children's welfare. These included poverty, welfare dependence, absent parents, one-parent families, having an unwed mother and having parents who have not completed high school.

Children who grow up with one or more of these conditions may be statistically at greater risk of dropping out of school, being unemployed, or, for girls, becoming teenage mothers. About 16 percent of 16- and 17-year-olds with three or more risk factors were not in school. In contrast, only 1 percent of students with no risk factors, 4 percent with one risk factor, and 10 percent with two risk factors had left school.

The relationship between these risk factors and teenage motherhood was similar: 15 percent of 16- and 17-year-old girls who experienced three or more risk factors had given birth. Fewer than 1 percent for those with no risk factors, 2 percent with only one factor, and 4 percent with two factors had become mothers.

AT-RISK CHILDREN

In school, at-risk children are those who face significant obstacles, such as poverty or cultural and language barriers, that make it difficult for them to succeed academically. In 2000 the poverty threshold for a family of four was $17,463. The poverty rate for children under age 18 was 16 percent in 2000. The proportion of poor varied by race and ethnicity. In 2000 the poverty rate for blacks (22 percent) and Hispanics (21 percent) was far greater than the rates for non-Hispanic whites (7.5 percent) and Asian and Pacific Islanders (11 percent). (See Figure 6.1.)

Parents, educators, and government officials generally agree that disadvantaged children often need special help to prepare them for school, and both public and private services are available. In 1999 about half (52 percent) of disadvantaged children ages three to five were enrolled in Head Start and other early childhood programs. (See Table 6.1.)

Language Barriers

At-risk students with language barriers are classified either as "linguistically isolated" (LI) or as "limited English proficiency" (LEP). LI students are those in homes where no person over 13 years of age speaks proficient English. LEP indicates those who have difficulty reading, writing, or understanding English. The majority of LEP students are Hispanic.

MIDDLE SCHOOL AND JUNIOR HIGH— HIGH-RISK YEARS

The Carnegie Council on Adolescent Development published *Turning Points* (Report of the Task Force on Education and Youth Adolescents, New York) in 1989, which highlighted the importance of children's transition during the middle grades. It has sparked debate and additional research on the middle school years, including *Great Transitions: Preparing Adolescents for a New Century* (Carnegie Council on Adolescent Development, New York, 1995). These publications and other research pointed out that the organization and curriculum of middle and junior high schools are often inconsistent with students' intellectual, emotional, and interpersonal needs. For many young people, this change means leaving the neighborhood elementary school to be thrust into a much larger, possibly more impersonal environment some distance from home.

The Carnegie Council concluded that the middle school curriculum does not encourage critical, complex thinking, and they encouraged the creation of learning teams, a core academic curriculum, the elimination of tracking, and the hiring of teachers who have been specifically trained to teach in the middle grades. In 1999 the

FIGURE 6.1

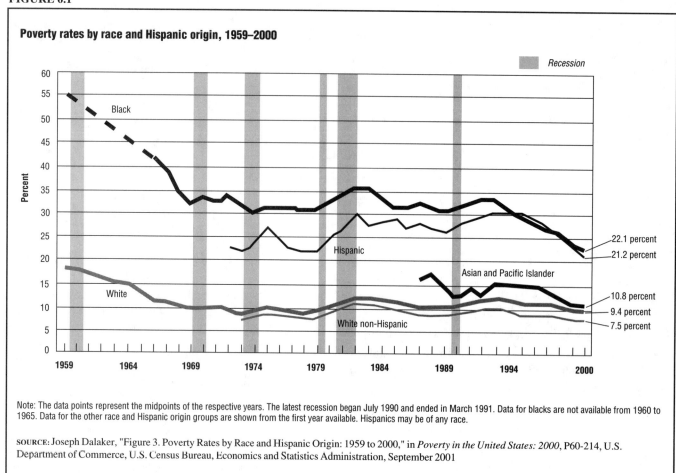

Poverty rates by race and Hispanic origin, 1959–2000

Note: The data points represent the midpoints of the respective years. The latest recession began July 1990 and ended in March 1991. Data for blacks are not available from 1960 to 1965. Data for the other race and Hispanic origin groups are shown from the first year available. Hispanics may be of any race.

SOURCE: Joseph Dalaker, "Figure 3. Poverty Rates by Race and Hispanic Origin: 1959 to 2000," in *Poverty in the United States: 2000*, P60-214, U.S. Department of Commerce, U.S. Census Bureau, Economics and Statistics Administration, September 2001

U.S. Department of Education awarded grants to seven organizations to develop models of school reform. This support, along with funding from private foundations, has meant research continued on the issue. In *Turning Points 2000* (Teacher's College Press, New York, 2000), Anthony Jackson and Gayle Davis examined the progress being made and the experiences of middle school teachers and administrators.

DROPPING OUT

Trends in Dropout Rates

In general high school dropout rates have declined since 1960. The total status-dropout rate for persons 16 through 24 years of age was 27.2 percent in 1960, 14.1 percent in 1980, 12.1 percent in 1990, and 11.2 percent in 1999. (Status dropouts are persons who are not enrolled in school and who are not high school graduates or holders of General Educational Development [GED] diplomas.) (See Table 6.2.)

Historically, Hispanic students have had significantly higher dropout rates than either whites or African Americans. In 1980, white students had a dropout rate of 11.4 percent; black students, 19.1 percent; and Hispanic stu-

dents, 35.2 percent. By 1999 the estimated white rate was 7.3 percent, the black rate was 12.6 percent, and the Hispanic rate was 28.6 percent. (See Table 6.2.)

Data from *Dropout Rates in the United States* (Phillip Kaufman, Martha Naomi Alt, and Christopher D. Chapman, National Center for Education Statistics, Washington, DC, September 2001) showed that in October 2000 more than one-quarter (27.8) of all dropouts were Hispanic. The high Hispanic dropout rate can be partly attributed to the fact that more Hispanics than non-Hispanics ages 16 to 24 were born outside the United States.

Among the foreign-born group, the dropout rate (44.2 percent) was considerably higher than it was among first-generation (14.6 percent) and later-generation Hispanics (15.9 percent). More than half of the foreign-born Hispanic dropouts had never enrolled in a U.S. school. They may have entered the United States at an age beyond high school age or may have come to this country for employment, not education. In addition, language may be a barrier.

The Costs of Dropping Out

Young people who drop out before finishing high school usually pay a high price. Dropouts have a much harder time making the transition from school to work and economic independence. The employment rates of high school graduates and GED holders have consistently been higher than those of dropouts. In 1999 the proportion of females ages 16 to 24 who did not complete high school and were unemployed was 16.6 percent, compared to 9.8 percent of high school graduates and 4 percent of college graduates. For male dropouts, 15.6 percent were unemployed, compared to 9.7 percent of high school graduates and about 5 percent of college graduates. (See Table 6.3.)

Minority students who drop out are at even higher economic risk. In 1999 the proportion of black high school dropouts who were unemployed was 31.2 percent, while about 16 percent of Hispanic dropouts ages 16 to 24 were unemployed. In comparison, 13.7 percent of white dropouts in the same age range were not working. (See Table 6.3.)

Persons without high school diplomas tend to earn considerably less than those with more education. In 1999 the median income (half earned more; half earned less) of males ages 25 to 34 who attended high school but did not graduate was $18,582, which is 69 percent of the annual median earnings of male high school graduates ($26,842). Females with less than a high school education earned $10,174, just 61 percent of the earnings of females who finished high school ($16,770). (See Table 6.4.)

As might be expected from the unemployment and income data, non-graduates were more likely than graduates to be on welfare. In 1995 those without a high school diploma were more than twice as likely as high school graduates to receive food stamps, to be on Medicaid, and to receive housing assistance. (See Table 6.5.)

Many significant consequences of dropping out of school cannot be measured statistically. Some of those who drop out may likely experience lifelong poverty. Some who are poorly prepared to compete in society may turn to crime or substance abuse. Some become teenage parents without the ability to offer their children more than they had, possibly contributing to a cycle of dependence. Furthermore, the U.S. economy is deprived of the literate, technically trained, and dedicated workers it needs to compete internationally. Finally, those without a high school diploma generally do not have the opportunities available to the more highly educated.

Reasons for Dropping Out

Prepared by the National Center for Education Statistics, the *National Education Longitudinal Study of 1988* (NELS: 88) studied students from the eighth grade through their high school years and beyond. Follow-up surveys were done in 1990, 1992, 1994 and 2000.

The survey revealed that students who dropped out of school were more likely to give school-related than job-

TABLE 6.1

Percent of children ages 3 to 5[a] years old who are enrolled in center-based early childhood care and education programs[b], selected years 1991–99

Characteristic	1991	1993	1995	1996	1999
Total	53	53	55	55	60
Gender					
Male	52	53	55	55	61
Female	53	53	55	55	59
Race and Hispanic origin					
White, non-Hispanic	54	54	57	57	60
Black, non-Hispanic	58	57	60	65	73
Hispanic[c]	39	43	37	39	44
Other	53	51	57	45	66
Poverty status[d]					
Below poverty	44	49	45	44	52
At or above poverty	56	53	59	59	62
Family type					
Two parents	50	52	55	54	59
One or no parent	54	54	56	58	62
Mother's highest level of education[e]					
Less than high school graduate	32	33	35	37	40
High school graduate/GED	46	43	48	49	52
Vocational/technical or some college	60	60	57	58	63
College graduate	72	73	75	73	74
Mother's employment status[e]					
Worked 35 hours or more per week	59	61	60	63	65
Worked less than 35 hours per week	58	57	62	64	64
Looking for work	43	48	52	47	55
Not in labor force	45	44	47	43	52

[a] Estimates are based on children who have yet to enter kindergarten.
[b] Center-based programs include day care centers, Head Start programs, preschool, nursery school, prekindergarten, and other early childhood programs.
[c] Persons of Hispanic origin may be of any race.
[d] Poverty estimates for 1991 and 1993 are not comparable to later years because respondents were not asked exact household income.
[e] Children without mothers in the home are not included in estimates dealing with mother's education or mother's employment status.

SOURCE: "Table ED2. Early childhood care and education: Percentage of children ages 3 to 5 who are enrolled in center-based early childhood care and education programs by child and family characteristics, selected years 1991–99," in *America's Children: Key National Indicators of Well-Being, 2001*, Federal Interagency Forum on Child and Family Statistics, Washington, DC, July 2001

related or family-related reasons. Less than half of those who dropped out between the tenth and twelfth grades reported that they "did not like school." Nearly as many reported that they were failing in school. Almost equal proportions of female and male students complained that they left because they "could not get along with teachers." Male students were more likely than females to report school expulsion and suspension as reasons for leaving school.

Female dropouts were more likely than males to cite family-related reasons. More females than males left school because they became parents. More than one-quarter of female dropouts said they left school because of pregnancy. African American dropouts were the least likely to mention "got married" as a reason for leaving school prematurely. Over one-fourth of dropouts left school because they "found a job."

TABLE 6.2

Percent of high school dropouts (status dropouts) among persons 16 to 24 years old, by sex and race/ethnicity: April 1960–October 1999

Year	Total				Men				Women			
	All races	White, non-Hispanic	Black, non-Hispanic	Hispanic origin	All races	White, non-Hispanic	Black, non-Hispanic	Hispanic origin	All races	White, non-Hispanic	Black, non-Hispanic	Hispanic origin
1960[1]	27.2 —	——	——	——	27.8 —	——	——	——	26.7 —	——	——	——
1970[2]	15.0 —	13.2 —	27.9 —	——	14.2 —	12.2 —	29.4 —	——	15.7 —	14.1 —	26.6 —	——
1971[2]	14.7 —	13.4 —	23.7 —	——	14.2 —	12.6 —	25.5 —	——	15.2 —	14.2 —	22.1 —	——
1972	14.6 (0.3)	12.3 (0.3)	21.3 (1.1)	34.3 (2.2)	14.1 (0.4)	11.6 (0.4)	22.3 (1.6)	33.7 (3.2)	15.1 (0.4)	12.8 (0.4)	20.5 (1.4)	34.8 (3.1)
1973	14.1 (0.3)	11.6 (0.3)	22.2 (1.1)	33.5 (2.2)	13.7 (0.4)	11.5 (0.4)	21.5 (1.5)	30.4 (3.2)	14.5 (0.4)	11.8 (0.4)	22.8 (1.5)	36.4 (3.2)
1974	14.3 (0.3)	11.9 (0.3)	21.2 (1.0)	33.0 (2.1)	14.2 (0.4)	12.0 (0.4)	20.1 (1.5)	33.8 (3.0)	14.3 (0.4)	11.8 (0.4)	22.1 (1.5)	32.2 (2.9)
1975	13.9 (0.3)	11.4 (0.3)	22.9 (1.1)	29.2 (2.0)	13.3 (0.4)	11.0 (0.4)	23.0 (1.6)	26.7 (2.8)	14.5 (0.4)	11.8 (0.4)	22.9 (1.4)	31.6 (2.9)
1976	14.1 (0.3)	12.0 (0.3)	20.5 (1.0)	31.4 (2.0)	14.1 (0.4)	12.1 (0.4)	21.2 (1.5)	30.3 (2.9)	14.2 (0.4)	11.8 (0.4)	19.9 (1.4)	32.3 (2.8)
1977	14.1 (0.3)	11.9 (0.3)	19.8 (1.0)	33.0 (2.0)	14.5 (0.4)	12.6 (0.4)	19.5 (1.5)	31.6 (2.9)	13.8 (0.4)	11.2 (0.4)	20.0 (1.4)	34.3 (2.8)
1978	14.2 (0.3)	11.9 (0.3)	20.2 (1.0)	33.3 (2.0)	14.6 (0.4)	12.2 (0.4)	22.5 (1.5)	33.6 (2.9)	13.9 (0.4)	11.6 (0.4)	18.3 (1.3)	33.1 (2.8)
1979	14.6 (0.3)	12.0 (0.3)	21.1 (1.0)	33.8 (2.0)	15.0 (0.4)	12.6 (0.4)	22.4 (1.5)	33.0 (2.8)	14.2 (0.4)	11.5 (0.4)	20.0 (1.3)	34.5 (2.8)
1980	14.1 (0.3)	11.4 (0.3)	19.1 (1.0)	35.2 (1.9)	15.1 (0.4)	12.3 (0.4)	20.8 (1.5)	37.2 (2.7)	13.1 (0.4)	10.5 (0.4)	17.7 (1.3)	33.2 (2.6)
1981	13.9 (0.3)	11.3 (0.3)	18.4 (0.9)	33.2 (1.8)	15.1 (0.4)	12.5 (0.4)	19.9 (1.4)	36.0 (2.6)	12.8 (0.4)	10.2 (0.4)	17.1 (1.2)	30.4 (2.5)
1982	13.9 (0.3)	11.4 (0.3)	18.4 (1.0)	31.7 (1.9)	14.5 (0.4)	12.0 (0.4)	21.2 (1.5)	30.5 (2.7)	13.3 (0.4)	10.8 (0.4)	15.9 (1.3)	32.8 (2.7)
1983	13.7 (0.3)	11.1 (0.3)	18.0 (1.0)	31.6 (1.9)	14.9 (0.4)	12.2 (0.4)	19.9 (1.5)	34.3 (2.8)	12.5 (0.4)	10.1 (0.4)	16.2 (1.3)	29.1 (2.6)
1984	13.1 (0.3)	11.0 (0.3)	15.5 (0.9)	29.8 (1.9)	14.0 (0.4)	11.9 (0.4)	16.8 (1.4)	30.6 (2.8)	12.3 (0.4)	10.1 (0.4)	14.3 (1.2)	29.0 (2.6)
1985	12.6 (0.3)	10.4 (0.3)	15.2 (0.9)	27.6 (1.9)	13.4 (0.4)	11.1 (0.4)	16.1 (1.4)	29.9 (2.8)	11.8 (0.4)	9.8 (0.4)	14.3 (1.2)	25.2 (2.7)
1986	12.2 (0.3)	9.7 (0.3)	14.2 (0.9)	30.1 (1.9)	13.1 (0.4)	10.3 (0.4)	15.0 (1.3)	32.8 (2.7)	11.4 (0.4)	9.1 (0.4)	13.5 (1.2)	27.2 (2.6)
1987	12.6 (0.3)	10.4 (0.3)	14.1 (0.9)	28.6 (1.8)	13.2 (0.4)	10.8 (0.4)	15.0 (1.3)	29.1 (2.6)	12.1 (0.4)	10.0 (0.4)	13.3 (1.2)	28.1 (2.6)
1988	12.9 (0.3)	9.6 (0.3)	14.5 (1.0)	35.8 (2.3)	13.5 (0.4)	10.3 (0.5)	15.0 (1.5)	36.0 (3.2)	12.2 (0.4)	8.9 (0.4)	14.0 (1.4)	35.4 (3.3)
1989	12.6 (0.3)	9.4 (0.3)	13.9 (1.0)	33.0 (2.2)	13.6 (0.5)	10.3 (0.5)	14.9 (1.5)	34.4 (3.1)	11.7 (0.4)	8.5 (0.4)	13.0 (1.3)	31.6 (3.1)
1990	12.1 (0.3)	9.0 (0.3)	13.2 (0.9)	32.4 (1.9)	12.3 (0.4)	9.3 (0.4)	11.9 (1.3)	34.3 (2.7)	11.8 (0.4)	8.7 (0.4)	14.4 (1.3)	30.3 (2.7)
1991	12.5 (0.3)	8.9 (0.3)	13.6 (0.9)	35.3 (1.9)	13.0 (0.4)	8.9 (0.4)	13.5 (1.4)	39.2 (2.7)	11.9 (0.4)	8.9 (0.4)	13.7 (1.3)	31.1 (2.7)
1992[3]	11.0 (0.3)	7.7 (0.3)	13.7 (0.9)	29.4 (1.9)	11.3 (0.4)	8.0 (0.4)	12.5 (1.3)	32.1 (2.7)	10.7 (0.4)	7.4 (0.4)	14.8 (1.4)	26.6 (2.6)
1993[3]	11.0 (0.3)	7.9 (0.3)	13.6 (0.9)	27.5 (1.8)	11.2 (0.4)	8.2 (0.4)	12.6 (1.3)	28.1 (2.5)	10.9 (0.4)	7.6 (0.4)	14.4 (1.3)	26.9 (2.5)
1994[3]	11.4 (0.3)	7.7 (0.3)	12.6 (0.8)	30.0 (1.2)	12.3 (0.4)	8.0 (0.4)	14.1 (1.1)	31.6 (1.6)	10.6 (0.4)	7.5 (0.4)	11.3 (1.0)	28.1 (1.7)
1995[3]	12.0 (0.3)	8.6 (0.3)	12.1 (0.7)	30.0 (1.1)	12.2 (0.4)	9.0 (0.4)	11.1 (1.0)	30.0 (1.6)	11.7 (0.4)	8.2 (0.4)	12.9 (1.1)	30.0 (1.7)
1996[3]	11.1 (0.3)	7.3 (0.3)	13.0 (0.8)	29.4 (1.2)	11.4 (0.4)	7.3 (0.4)	13.5 (1.2)	30.3 (1.7)	10.9 (0.4)	7.3 (0.4)	12.5 (1.1)	28.3 (1.7)
1997[3]	11.0 (0.3)	7.6 (0.3)	13.4 (0.8)	25.3 (1.1)	11.9 (0.4)	8.5 (0.4)	13.3 (1.2)	27.0 (1.6)	10.1 (0.4)	6.7 (0.4)	13.5 (1.1)	23.4 (1.6)
1998[3]	11.8 (0.3)	7.7 (0.3)	13.8 (0.8)	29.5 (1.1)	13.3 (0.4)	8.6 (0.4)	15.5 (1.2)	33.5 (1.6)	10.3 (0.4)	6.9 (0.4)	12.2 (1.1)	25.0 (1.6)
1999[3]	11.2 (0.3)	7.3 (0.3)	12.6 (0.8)	28.6 (1.1)	11.9 (0.4)	7.7 (0.4)	12.1 (1.1)	31.0 (1.6)	10.5 (0.4)	6.9 (0.4)	13.0 (1.1)	26.0 (1.5)

—Not available.

[1]Based on the April 1960 decennial census.

[2]White and black include persons of Hispanic origin.

[3]Because of changes in data collection procedures, data may not be comparable with figures for earlier years.

NOTE: "Status" dropouts are 16- to 24-year-olds who are not enrolled in school and who have not completed a high school program regardless of when they left school. People who have received GED credentials are counted as high school completers. All data except for 1960 are based on October counts. Data are based upon sample surveys of the civilian noninstitutionalized population. Standard errors appear in parentheses.

SOURCE: Thomas D. Snyder and Charlene M. Hoffman, "Table 106.—Percent of high school dropouts (status dropouts) among persons 16 to 24 years old, by sex and race/ethnicity: April 1960 to October 1999," in *Digest of Education Statistics, 2000*, NCES 2001-034, U.S. Department of Education, National Center for Education Statistics, Washington, DC, January 2001

"DETACHED YOUTH"

Some young people drop out not only from school, but also from work. The Federal Interagency Forum on Child and Family Statistics applies the term "detached youth" to persons ages 16 to 19 "who are neither enrolled in school nor working." The proportion of youth who fit this description is one measure of the amount of young people who are at risk. Since 1980 this has been a persistent problem; however, the proportion has been declining since 1991, when 11 percent of youth ages 16 to 19 were not enrolled in school or working. By 2000 the proportion had fallen to 8 percent. Females (9 percent) tend to be more likely to be detached from school and work activities than males (7 percent), although the decrease in detached youth from 1984 to 2000 occurred mostly because of a decline in the proportion of young women

who fit this description. African American youths (13 percent) were more likely than white youths (6 percent) to be detached. Nearly 13 percent of Hispanic youths were not in school and not working. However, both African American and Hispanic youth were less likely to be "detached" in 2000 than they had been in 1984. (See Figure 6.2.)

NATIONAL STUDIES ON ADOLESCENT HEALTH

The behavioral choices teens make can put their health and success in life at risk. Both the Adolescent Health Program at the University of Minnesota (Minneapolis) and the Centers for Disease Control and Prevention (CDC) monitor teen risk behaviors. The Adolescent Health Program conducts the "National Longitudinal Study on Adolescent Health" (Add Health), and the CDC prepares the annual "Youth Risk Behavior Surveillance" study.

TABLE 6.3

Unemployment rate of persons 16 years old and over, by age, sex, race/ethnicity, and highest degree attained, 1997–99

Sex, race/ethnicity, and highest degree attained	Percent unemployed, 1997[1]				Percent unemployed, 1998[1]				Percent unemployed, 1999[1]			
	16- to 24-year-olds[2]			25 years old and over	16- to 24-year-olds[2]			25 years old and over	16- to 24-year-olds[2]			25 years old and over
	Total	16 to 19 years	20 to 24 years		Total	16 to 19 years	20 to 24 years		Total	16 to 19 years	20 to 24 years	
All persons												
All education levels	11.3	16.0	8.5	3.8	10.4	14.6	7.9	3.4	9.9	13.9	7.5	3.1
Less than a high school graduate	18.4	18.9	17.1	8.1	14.0	13.2	16.1	7.1	16.0	16.5	14.6	6.7
High school graduate, no college	11.0	14.0	9.6	4.3	10.1	12.5	9.1	4.0	9.7	12.3	8.6	3.5
Some college, no degree	7.1	8.5	6.7	3.5	6.3	7.7	5.9	3.2	5.9	7.3	5.4	3.0
Associate degree	4.5	—	4.3	2.7	4.3	—	4.1	2.5	4.7	6.7	4.6	2.5
Bachelor's degree or higher	3.7	—	3.7	2.0	4.0	—	4.1	1.8	4.7	—	4.8	1.8
Men												
All education levels	11.8	16.9	8.9	3.6	11.1	16.2	8.1	3.2	10.3	14.7	7.7	3.0
Less than a high school graduate	18.3	19.7	15.1	7.2	17.4	18.7	14.2	6.1	15.6	17.0	12.2	5.8
High school graduate, no college	10.8	13.9	9.6	4.2	10.0	13.6	8.5	3.9	9.7	12.3	8.6	3.3
Some college, no degree	7.5	9.2	7.1	3.3	6.7	8.7	6.2	3.0	6.2	8.2	5.7	2.8
Associate degree	—	—	—	2.6	4.2	—	—	2.3	5.3	9.1	5.2	2.5
Bachelor's degree or higher	4.2	—	4.3	1.9	4.3	—	4.3	1.6	5.6	—	5.7	1.8
Women												
All education levels	10.7	15.0	8.1	3.9	9.8	12.9	7.8	3.6	9.5	13.2	7.2	3.3
Less than a high school graduate	18.6	17.9	21.2	9.6	16.6	15.8	20.0	8.6	16.6	15.9	19.1	8.2
High school graduate, no college	11.2	14.2	9.7	4.3	10.3	11.4	9.8	4.1	9.8	12.3	8.6	3.7
Some college, no degree	6.7	8.0	6.3	3.7	5.9	7.0	5.6	3.4	5.6	6.8	5.2	3.2
Associate degree	4.8	—	4.5	2.8	4.5	—	4.2	2.7	4.2	5.3	4.2	2.5
Bachelor's degree or higher	3.2	—	3.3	2.2	3.8	—	3.9	2.0	4.1	—	4.1	1.8
White[3]												
All education levels	9.4	13.6	6.9	3.3	8.8	12.6	6.5	3.0	8.5	12.0	6.3	2.8
Less than a high school graduate	15.5	16.2	13.5	7.2	14.3	14.9	12.6	6.3	13.7	14.3	12.1	5.9
High school graduate, no college	9.1	11.6	7.9	3.6	8.4	10.8	7.2	3.4	8.0	10.3	7.0	3.0
Some college, no degree	5.9	7.1	5.6	3.0	5.5	6.9	5.1	2.8	5.0	6.4	4.6	2.7
Associate degree	3.6	—	3.4	2.5	3.9	—	3.7	2.2	4.4	8.0	4.2	2.3
Bachelor's degree or higher	3.1	—	3.2	1.8	3.9	—	3.9	1.7	4.6	—	4.6	1.7
Black[3]												
All education levels	23.2	32.4	18.3	7.3	20.7	27.6	16.8	6.4	19.2	27.9	14.6	5.7
Less than a high school graduate	36.3	36.4	35.8	13.1	33.1	33.1	33.2	11.6	31.2	32.3	28.7	11.6
High school graduate, no college	20.9	28.1	18.4	8.1	19.5	22.8	18.2	7.4	18.6	24.6	16.4	6.3
Some college, no degree	15.1	21.0	14.0	6.1	11.2	14.0	10.6	5.5	10.8	15.4	10.0	4.7
Associate degree	—	—	—	—	8.1	—	—	4.0	8.0	20.0	7.4	3.8
Bachelor's degree or higher	6.5	—	6.4	3.6	4.6	—	4.6	2.9	5.7	—	5.7	2.7
Hispanic origin[4]												
All education levels	13.8	21.6	10.3	6.1	13.2	21.3	9.3	5.5	11.8	18.7	8.3	5.0
Less than a high school graduate	18.8	25.7	13.0	8.5	17.9	24.3	11.9	7.2	16.1	21.3	11.1	7.1
High school graduate, no college	11.4	15.7	9.9	5.7	11.6	17.3	9.6	5.5	10.2	15.4	8.3	4.7
Some college, no degree	8.9	11.3	8.4	4.1	7.9	12.4	7.0	4.0	7.2	11.4	6.1	3.4
Associate degree	—	—	—	—	—	—	—	3.4	4.3	—	4.4	3.1
Bachelor's degree or higher	—	—	—	3.5	—	—	—	3.2	4.1	—	4.1	2.5

—Not available.

[1]The unemployment rate is the percent of individuals in the labor force who are not working and who made specific efforts to find employment sometime during the prior 4 weeks. The labor force includes both employed and unemployed persons.

[2]Excludes persons enrolled in school.

[3]Includes persons of Hispanic origin.

[4]Persons of Hispanic origin may be of any race.

SOURCE: Thomas D. Snyder and Charlene M. Hoffman, "Table 378.—Unemployment rate of persons 16 years old and over, by age, sex, race/ethnicity, and highest degree attained: 1997, 1998, and 1999," in *Digest of Education Statistics, 2000,* NCES 2001-034, U.S. Department of Education, National Center for Education Statistics, Washington, DC, January 2001

The Add Health study, as reported in the *Journal of the American Medical Association* (Michael D. Resnick et al., "Protecting Adolescents from Harm," vol. 278, no. 10, September 10, 1997), found certain home conditions statistically associated with risk behaviors. For example, access to guns in the home was linked to suicidal tendencies and violence, and access to substances at home was related to teens' use of cigarettes, alcohol, and marijuana. Working 20 hours or more a week was linked to emotional distress and use of cigarettes, alcohol, and marijuana.

On the other hand, adolescents who felt strongly connected to family and school were protected to some extent against health-risk behaviors. Parental disapproval of early sexual activity was associated with later onset of sexual

TABLE 6.4

Median annual earnings of all wage and salary workers ages 25–34, by sex and educational attainment level, March 1970–99
(in constant U.S. dollars)

Year	Male				Female			
	Grades 9–11	High school diploma or equivalent	Some college including vocational/ technical	Bachelor's degree or higher	Grades 9–11	High school diploma or equivalent	Some college including vocational/ technical	Bachelor's degree or higher
1970	$30,346	$36,726	$40,074	$45,484	$8,925	$15,166	$18,150	$27,656
1971	31,039	36,935	38,947	45,219	10,045	15,656	17,942	29,345
1972	30,845	38,951	39,342	46,065	10,235	16,217	19,188	29,047
1973	32,579	39,326	39,118	45,610	11,122	15,929	20,301	28,401
1974	29,965	37,122	37,765	42,491	9,833	15,815	18,885	27,463
1975	26,882	34,318	36,681	40,089	10,161	15,810	19,594	27,249
1976	27,191	34,740	35,920	41,279	10,080	16,544	18,815	26,170
1977	26,970	34,968	35,779	41,175	10,527	16,820	20,613	25,757
1978	26,928	35,197	36,802	41,422	8,839	16,424	19,139	25,460
1979	26,214	34,533	36,455	40,033	11,687	16,585	19,788	25,770
1980	23,575	32,100	33,459	38,242	10,624	16,469	20,454	25,042
1981	21,939	29,898	31,849	38,691	9,842	16,055	19,776	24,777
1982	19,773	27,785	31,030	37,253	10,427	15,680	18,905	25,551
1983	19,598	27,945	31,622	37,809	10,542	15,857	19,662	26,438
1984	18,111	28,622	32,995	38,864	9,341	16,564	20,072	26,702
1985	19,395	27,536	32,707	41,276	10,415	16,618	19,582	28,053
1986	19,204	27,660	32,602	41,608	10,690	16,534	20,075	29,437
1987	20,305	28,082	31,804	41,743	11,404	16,932	21,171	30,164
1988	19,469	28,759	31,570	40,720	9,305	16,640	21,780	30,131
1989	19,559	28,040	31,479	40,656	10,037	16,020	21,118	30,889
1990	18,628	26,259	30,051	38,770	9,139	15,872	21,223	30,503
1991	16,471	25,563	29,161	39,019	9,910	15,539	20,534	29,516
1992	16,596	24,389	27,668	39,070	11,724	15,339	20,575	30,684
1993	16,201	24,231	27,218	38,014	8,905	15,172	19,909	30,245
1994	16,588	24,589	28,149	37,437	9,248	15,993	19,244	29,822
1995	17,847	24,213	26,891	37,553	9,436	15,346	19,603	29,328
1996	16,926	24,663	28,233	38,593	9,789	15,366	19,579	28,940
1997	18,191	25,618	28,453	38,410	10,279	16,276	19,817	31,024
1998	18,569	26,717	31,118	41,695	10,989	15,863	20,736	31,789
1999	18,582	26,842	31,208	42,341	10,174	16,770	21,008	32,145

NOTE: The Current Population Survey (CPS) questions used to obtain educational attainment were changed in 1992. In 1994, the survey methodology for the CPS was changed and weights were adjusted.

SOURCE: John Wirt, et al., "Table 18—1 Median annual earnings (in constant 2000 dollars of all wage and salary workers ages 25-34, by sex and educational attainment level: March 1970–99," in *The Condition of Education, 2001,* NCES 2001-072, U.S. Department of Education, National Center for Education Statistics, Washington, DC, June 2001

activity, and parental expectations of school achievement were linked to lower levels of risk behavior. The presence of parents before school, after school, at dinner, and at bedtime was associated with lower levels of emotional distress, suicidal thoughts, and suicide attempts. Feeling "connected" at school also was associated with lower levels of these behaviors.

THE MONITORING THE FUTURE AND "YOUTH RISK BEHAVIOR SURVEILLANCE" STUDIES

Funded by the National Institute on Drug Abuse (NIDA) in Washington, DC, the Institute for Social Research at the University of Michigan conducts an annual survey of substance use among students. The 2000 *Monitoring the Future* study (Lloyd D. Johnson, Patrick M. O'Malley, and Jerald G. Bachman, National Institute on Drug Abuse, Bethesda, MD, August 2001) found that the use of illegal drugs has declined among eighth graders

and, for the fourth consecutive year, remained level for tenth and twelfth graders.

In *Youth Risk Behavior Surveillance—United States, 1999* (Laura Kann, et al., *CDC Surveillance Summaries,* vol. 49, no. SS-5, June 9, 2000), the CDC reported on risk behaviors among young people.

Attitudes Toward Drugs

In 2000 fewer students considered substance use extremely dangerous than in 1991. The proportions of those who saw great risk in the use of marijuana decreased significantly in all grades between 1991 and 2000; only 13.7 percent of 2000 seniors said that trying marijuana once or twice was very risky, down from 27.1 percent in 1991. In 2000 the proportion (73.1 percent) of seniors who saw great risk in smoking one or more packs of cigarettes a day increased slightly since 1991, when it was 69.4 percent. All students in 2000 perceived daily

TABLE 6.5

Average monthly program participation rates for any means-tested programs by selected characteristics, 1993–95

	Program participation rates (in percent)					
	Any major means-tested programs[1]					
Characteristics	1993	Standard error	1994	Standard error	1995	Standard error
Total number of recipients[2]	39,162	670	39,514	669	38,995	682
As percent of the population	15.2	0.3	15.2	0.3	14.9	0.3
Race and Hispanic Origin[3]						
White	11.7	0.3	11.8	0.3	11.6	0.3
Not of Hispanic origin	9.4	0.3	9.4	0.3	9.2	0.6
Black	36.6	0.9	36.0	0.9	35.0	0.4
Hispanic origin	32.3	1.1	31.7	1.1	30.6	1.1
Not of Hispanic origin	0.0	13.2	0.3	12.6	0.3	
Age						
Under 18 years	26.2	0.6	26.5	0.6	26.1	0.6
18 to 64 years	11.0	0.3	10.8	0.3	10.6	0.3
65 years and over	12.0	0.7	11.7	0.7	11.6	0.7
Sex						
Men	13.0	0.4	13.0	0.4	12.5	0.4
Women	17.2	0.4	17.3	0.4	17.1	0.4
Educational Attainment (people 18 years and over)						
Less than 4 years of high school	25.8	0.9	25.6	0.9	24.8	0.9
High school graduate, no college	10.5	0.4	10.5	0.4	10.3	0.4
1 or more years of college	4.6	0.3	4.5	0.3	4.5	0.3
Disability Status (people 15 to 64 years old)						
With a work disability	25.0	1.0	25.5	1.0	25.3	1.0
With no work disability	8.7	0.3	8.5	0.3	8.3	0.3
Residence						
Metropolitan	14.7	0.3	14.7	0.3	14.5	0.3
Central city	23.0	0.6	22.4	0.6	22.0	0.6
Noncentral city	9.3	0.3	9.5	0.3	9.2	0.3
Nonmetropolitan	17.0	0.6	16.6	0.6	16.1	0.6
Region						
Northeast	14.8	0.6	14.6	0.6	14.5	0.6
Midwest	12.5	0.5	12.6	0.5	12.2	0.5
South	16.5	0.5	16.4	0.5	16.0	0.5
West	16.7	0.6	16.8	0.6	16.5	0.6
Family Status						
In families	15.6	0.3	15.6	0.3	15.3	0.3
In married-couple families	9.1	0.3	8.9	0.3	8.6	0.3
In families with a female householder, no spouse present	44.3	1.0	44.3	0.9	44.2	1.0
Unrelated individuals	12.8	0.7	12.4	0.7	12.3	0.4
Employment and Labor Force Status (people 18 years and over)						
Employed full-time	4.0	0.2	3.8	0.2	3.7	0.2
Employed part-time	8.6	0.7	9.2	0.7	9.3	0.8
Unemployed	26.6	1.9	26.9	2.2	25.7	2.3
Not in labor force	21.3	0.6	21.3	0.6	21.0	0.6
Marital Status (people 18 years and over)						
Married	6.6	0.3	6.2	0.3	5.9	0.3
Separated, divorced, or widowed	19.6	0.8	19.6	0.8	19.1	0.8
Never married	15.6	0.7	15.6	0.7	15.6	0.7
Family Income-to-Poverty Ratio						
Under 1.00	60.5	0.9	60.3	0.9	60.2	1.0
1.00 and over	6.7	0.2	7.0	0.2	6.9	0.2

[1] Major means-tested programs include Aid to Families with Dependent Children (AFDC), General Assistance, Supplemental Security Income, food stamps, medicaid, and housing assistance.
[2] In thousands.
[3] People of Hispanic origin may be of any race.

SOURCE: Jan Tim and Charita Castro, "Table A—1. Average Monthly Program Participation Rates for Any Means-Tested Programs by Selected Characteristics: 1993–95," in *Dynamics of Economic Well-Being: Program Participation, 1993 to 1995, Who Gets Assistance?* Bureau of the Census, Washington, DC, September 2001

drinking and binge drinking as less risky than they did in 1991, while 2000 seniors considered daily drinking far less risky than 1991 seniors. One encouraging sign was that a slightly higher proportion of eighth-grade students considered using heroin dangerous in 2000 than in 1995, when heroin was first added to the survey. (See Table 6.6.)

FIGURE 6.2

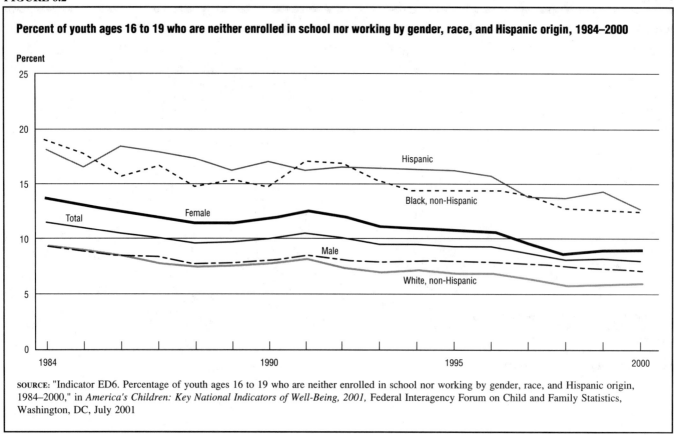

Percent of youth ages 16 to 19 who are neither enrolled in school nor working by gender, race, and Hispanic origin, 1984–2000

SOURCE: "Indicator ED6. Percentage of youth ages 16 to 19 who are neither enrolled in school nor working by gender, race, and Hispanic origin, 1984–2000," in *America's Children: Key National Indicators of Well-Being, 2001,* Federal Interagency Forum on Child and Family Statistics, Washington, DC, July 2001

Generally, with a few exceptions, personal disapproval of drug use also declined from 1991 to 1999. In 2000 about half (52.5 percent) of seniors disapproved of trying marijuana once or twice, compared to 68.7 percent in 1991. Only three-fifths (65.8 percent) disapproved of occasional use, while 79.4 percent of seniors in 1991 did. In general students disapproved most strongly of heroin (more than 90 percent), crack (at least 87.5 percent), cocaine (at least 84 percent), and LSD (at least 82 percent), and disapproved least of trying alcohol (25.5 percent).

Marijuana

In 2000 the proportion of eighth-grade students who reported having used marijuana at least once during the 12 months before the survey was 15.6 percent, with 32.2 percent of tenth graders and 36.5 percent of twelfth graders reporting this same behavior. These rates represented increases from 1991, when 6.2 percent of eighth graders, 16.5 percent of tenth graders, and 23.9 percent of twelfth graders said they had used marijuana at least once in the past year. Among high-school seniors, current use of marijuana (any use within 30 days of the survey) was down from a peak of 37 percent in 1979 to 21.6 percent in 2000, but the rate had been as low as 11.9 percent in 1992. (See Table 6.7.) About 6 percent of seniors reported using marijuana daily in 2000, up significantly from 1991 (2 percent), but still far below the almost 11 percent in 1978.

The most alarming news is that the proportion of eighth graders using marijuana in the month preceding the survey nearly tripled, from 3.2 percent in 1991 to 9.1 percent in 2000. At the same time, the proportion of tenth-grade users more than doubled, from 8.7 percent in 1991 to 19.7 percent in 2000, and twelfth-grade users increased from 13.8 percent in 1991 to 21.6 percent in 2000. (See Table 6.7.)

White youth (45.9 percent) were slightly less likely to report lifetime marijuana use than either black (48.6 percent) or Hispanic (51 percent) students. Students of all races were about equally likely to have used marijuana in the past 30 days—whites, 26.4 percent; blacks, 26.4 percent; and Hispanics, 28.2 percent. A lower percentage of females (22.6 percent) than males (30.8 percent) were current users in 1999. (See Table 6.8.)

Inhalants

The proportion of eighth, tenth, and twelfth graders who used inhalants, such as glues, solvents, and aerosols, peaked in 1995 and then began to decline. Inhalants are most often used in the earlier grade levels. For example, 9.4 percent of eighth graders reported using an inhalant during the previous year, compared to 7.3 percent of tenth graders and 5.9 percent of twelfth graders in 2000. (See Table 6.7). Because most inhalants are common household products, young people may not understand that they are potentially lethal.

TABLE 6.6

Trends in harmfulness of drugs as perceived by eighth and tenth graders, 1991–2000

Percentage saying "great risk"[a]

Q. How much do you think people risk harming themselves (physically or in other ways), if they . . .	8th Grade											10th Grade										
	1991	1992	1993	1994	1995	1996	1997	1998	1999	2000	'99–'00 change	1991	1992	1993	1994	1995	1996	1997	1998	1999	2000	'99–'00 change
Try marijuana once or twice	40.4	39.1	36.2	31.6	28.9	27.9	25.3	28.1	28.0	29.0	+0.9	30.0	31.9	29.7	24.4	21.5	20.0	18.8	19.6	19.2	18.5	-0.7
Smoke marijuana occasionally	57.9	56.3	53.8	48.6	45.9	44.3	43.1	45.0	45.7	47.4	+1.8	48.6	48.9	46.1	38.9	35.4	32.8	31.9	32.5	33.5	32.4	-1.1
Smoke marijuana regularly	83.8	82.0	79.6	74.3	73.0	70.9	72.7	73.0	73.3	74.8	+1.4	82.1	81.1	78.5	71.3	67.9	65.9	65.9	65.8	65.9	64.7	-1.2
Try inhalants once or twice[b]	35.9	37.0	36.5	37.9	36.4	40.8	40.1	38.9	40.8	41.2	+0.3	37.8	38.7	40.9	42.7	41.6	47.2	47.5	45.8	48.2	46.6	-1.6
Try inhalants regularly[b]	65.6	64.4	64.6	65.5	64.8	68.2	68.7	67.2	68.8	69.9	+1.1	69.8	67.9	69.6	71.5	71.8	75.8	74.5	73.3	76.3	75.0	-1.3
Take LSD once or twice[c]	—	—	42.1	38.3	36.7	36.5	37.0	34.9	34.1	34.0	-0.2	—	—	48.7	46.5	44.7	45.1	44.5	43.5	45.0	43.0	-2.1
Take LSD regularly[c]	—	—	68.3	65.8	64.4	63.6	64.1	59.6	58.8	57.5	-1.3	—	—	78.9	75.9	75.5	75.3	73.8	72.3	73.9	72.0	-1.9
Try crack once or twice[b]	62.8	61.2	57.2	54.4	50.8	51.0	49.9	49.3	48.7	48.5	-0.2	70.4	69.6	66.6	64.7	60.9	60.9	59.2	58.0	57.8	56.1	-1.7
Take crack occasionally[b]	82.2	79.6	76.8	74.4	72.1	71.6	71.2	70.6	70.6	70.1	-0.5	87.4	86.4	84.4	83.1	81.2	80.3	78.7	77.5	79.1	76.9	-2.2s
Try cocaine powder once or twice[b]	55.5	54.1	50.7	48.4	44.9	45.2	45.0	44.0	43.3	43.3	0.0	59.1	59.2	57.5	56.4	53.5	53.6	52.2	50.9	51.6	48.8	-2.8ss
Take cocaine powder occasionally[b]	77.0	74.3	71.8	69.1	66.4	65.7	65.8	65.2	65.4	65.5	+0.1	82.2	80.1	79.1	77.8	75.6	75.0	73.9	71.8	73.6	70.9	-2.7ss
Try heroin once or twice without using a needle[c]	—	—	—	—	60.1	61.3	63.0	62.8	63.0	62.0	-1.0	—	—	—	—	70.7	72.1	73.1	71.7	73.7	71.7	-1.9
Take heroin occasionally without using a needle[c]	—	—	—	—	76.8	76.6	79.2	79.0	78.9	78.6	-0.3	—	—	—	—	85.1	85.8	86.5	84.9	86.5	85.2	-1.3
Try one or two drinks of an alcoholic beverage (beer, wine, liquor)	11.0	12.1	12.4	11.6	11.6	11.8	10.4	12.1	11.6	11.9	+0.3	9.0	10.1	10.9	9.4	9.3	8.9	9.0	10.1	10.5	9.6	-1.0
Take one or two drinks nearly every day	31.8	32.4	32.6	29.9	30.5	28.6	29.1	30.3	29.7	30.4	+0.7	36.1	36.8	35.9	32.5	31.7	31.2	31.8	31.9	32.9	32.3	-0.6
Have five or more drinks once or twice each weekend	59.1	58.0	57.7	54.7	54.1	51.8	55.6	56.0	55.3	55.9	+0.6	54.7	55.9	54.9	52.9	52.0	50.9	51.8	52.5	51.9	51.0	-0.9
Smoke one or more packs of cigarettes per day[d]	51.6	50.8	52.7	50.8	49.8	50.4	52.6	54.3	54.8	58.8	+4.0ss	60.3	59.3	60.7	59.0	57.0	57.9	59.9	61.9	62.7	65.9	+3.3s
Use smokeless tobacco regularly	35.1	35.1	36.9	35.5	33.5	34.0	35.2	36.5	37.1	39.0	+1.9	40.3	39.6	44.2	42.2	38.2	41.0	42.2	42.8	44.2	46.7	+2.5s
Take steroids[e]	64.2	69.5	70.2	67.6	—	—	—	—	—	—	—	67.1	72.7	73.4	72.5	—	—	—	—	—	—	—
Approx. N (in thousands) =	17.4	18.7	18.4	17.4	17.5	17.9	18.8	18.1	16.7	16.7		14.7	14.8	15.3	15.9	17.0	15.7	15.6	15.0	13.6	14.3	

NOTES: Level of significance of difference between the two most recent classes: s = .05, ss = .01, sss = .001. '—' indicates data not available. Any apparent inconsistency between the change estimate and the prevalence of use estimates for the two most recent classes is due to rounding error.

[a] Answer alternatives were: (1) No risk, (2) Slight risk, (3) Moderate risk, (4) Great risk, and (5) Can't say, drug unfamiliar.
[b] Beginning in 1997, data based on two-thirds of N indicated due to changes in questionnaire forms.
[c] Data based on one of two forms in 1993–96; N is one-half of N indicated. Beginning in 1997, data based on one-third of N indicated due to changes in questionnaire forms.
[d] Beginning in 1999, data based on two-thirds of N indicated due to changes in questionnaire forms.
[e] Data based on one of two forms in 1991 and 1992. Data based on one of two forms in 1993 and 1994; N is one-half of N indicated.

SOURCE: Lloyd D. Johnson, Patrick M. O'Malley, and Jerald G. Bachman, "Table 8—1 Trends in Harmfulness of Drugs as Perceived by Eighth and Tenth Graders, 1991–2000," in *Monitoring the Future: National Survey Results on Drug Use 1975–2000, Volume I: Secondary School Students*, NIH Publication No. 01-4924, National Institute on Drug Abuse, Bethesda, MD, August 2001

TABLE 6.7

Trends in prevalence of use of various drugs for eighth, tenth, and twelfth graders, 1991–2000

(Entries are percentages)

	Lifetime											Annual											30-Day										
	1991	1992	1993	1994	1995	1996	1997	1998	1999	2000	'99-'00 change	1991	1992	1993	1994	1995	1996	1997	1998	1999	2000	'99-'00 change	1991	1992	1993	1994	1995	1996	1997	1998	1999	2000	'99-'00 change
Marijuana/Hashish																																	
8th Grade	10.2	11.2	12.6	16.7	19.9	23.1	22.6	22.2	22.0	20.3	-1.8	6.2	7.2	9.2	13.0	15.8	18.3	17.7	16.9	16.5	15.6	-0.9	3.2	3.7	5.1	7.8	9.1	11.3	10.2	9.7	9.7	9.1	-0.6
10th Grade	23.4	21.4	24.4	30.4	34.1	39.8	42.3	39.6	40.9	40.3	-0.7	16.5	15.2	19.2	25.2	28.7	33.6	34.8	31.1	32.1	32.2	+0.2	8.7	8.1	10.9	15.8	17.2	20.4	20.5	18.7	19.4	19.7	+0.3
12th Grade	36.7	32.6	35.3	38.2	41.7	44.9	49.6	49.1	49.7	48.8	-0.9	23.9	21.9	26.0	30.7	34.7	35.8	38.5	37.5	37.8	36.5	-1.3	13.8	11.9	15.5	19.0	21.2	21.9	23.7	22.8	23.1	21.6	-1.6
Inhalants[a,b]																																	
8th Grade	17.6	17.4	19.4	19.9	21.6	21.2	21.0	20.5	19.7	17.9	-1.8s	9.0	9.5	11.0	11.7	12.8	12.2	11.8	11.1	10.3	9.4	-0.9	4.4	4.7	5.4	5.6	6.1	5.8	5.6	4.8	5.0	4.5	-0.5
10th Grade	15.7	16.6	17.5	18.0	19.0	19.3	18.3	18.3	17.0	16.6	-0.4	7.1	7.5	8.4	9.1	9.6	9.5	8.7	8.0	7.2	7.3	+0.1	2.7	2.7	3.3	3.6	3.5	3.3	3.0	2.9	2.6	2.6	0.0
12th Grade	17.6	16.6	17.4	17.7	17.4	16.6	16.1	15.2	15.4	14.2	-1.2	6.6	6.2	7.0	7.7	8.0	7.6	6.7	6.2	5.6	5.9	+0.3	2.4	2.3	2.5	2.7	3.2	2.5	2.5	2.3	2.0	2.2	+0.2
Nitrites[c]																																	
8th Grade	—	—	—	—	—	—	—	—	—	—	—	—	—	—	—	—	—	—	—	—	—	—	—	—	—	—	—	—	—	—	—	—	—
10th Grade	—	—	—	—	—	—	—	—	—	—	—	—	—	—	—	—	—	—	—	—	—	—	—	—	—	—	—	—	—	—	—	—	—
12th Grade	1.6	1.5	1.4	1.7	1.5	1.8	2.0	2.7	1.7	0.8	-0.8	0.9	0.5	0.9	1.1	1.1	1.6	1.2	1.4	0.9	0.6	-0.3	0.4	0.3	0.6	0.4	0.4	0.7	0.7	1.0	0.4	0.3	-0.1
Hallucinogens[b]																																	
8th Grade	3.2	3.8	3.9	4.3	5.2	5.9	5.4	4.9	4.8	4.6	-0.1	1.9	2.5	2.6	2.7	3.6	4.1	3.7	3.4	2.9	2.8	-0.1	0.8	1.1	1.2	1.3	1.7	1.9	1.8	1.4	1.3	1.2	-0.1
10th Grade	6.1	6.4	6.8	8.1	9.3	10.5	10.5	9.8	9.7	8.9	-0.8	4.0	4.3	4.7	5.8	7.2	7.8	7.6	6.9	6.9	6.1	-0.9	1.6	1.8	1.9	2.4	3.3	2.8	3.3	3.2	2.9	2.3	-0.6s
12th Grade	9.6	9.2	10.9	11.4	12.7	14.0	15.1	14.1	13.7	13.0	-0.7	5.8	5.9	7.4	7.6	9.3	10.1	9.8	9.0	9.4	8.1	-1.3s	2.2	2.1	2.7	3.1	4.4	3.5	3.9	3.8	3.5	2.6	-0.9ss
LSD																																	
8th Grade	2.7	3.2	3.5	3.7	4.4	5.1	4.7	4.1	4.1	3.9	-0.2	1.7	2.1	2.3	2.4	3.2	3.5	3.2	2.8	2.4	2.4	+0.1	0.6	0.9	1.0	1.1	1.4	1.5	1.5	1.1	1.1	1.0	-0.1
10th Grade	5.6	5.8	6.2	7.2	8.4	9.4	9.5	8.5	8.5	7.6	-1.0	3.7	4.0	4.2	5.2	6.5	6.9	6.7	5.9	6.0	5.1	-0.9	1.5	1.6	1.6	2.0	3.0	2.4	2.8	2.7	2.3	1.6	-0.7ss
12th Grade	8.8	8.6	10.3	10.5	11.7	12.6	13.6	12.6	12.2	11.1	-1.1	5.2	5.6	6.8	6.9	8.4	8.8	8.4	7.6	8.1	6.6	-1.5s	1.9	2.0	2.4	2.6	4.0	2.5	3.1	3.2	2.7	1.6	-1.2sss
Hallucinogens Other Than LSD																																	
8th Grade	1.4	1.7	1.7	2.2	2.5	3.0	2.6	2.5	2.4	2.3	-0.1	0.7	1.1	1.0	1.3	1.7	2.0	1.8	1.6	1.5	1.4	-0.1	0.3	0.4	0.5	0.7	0.8	0.9	0.7	0.7	0.6	0.6	+0.1
10th Grade	2.2	2.5	2.8	3.8	3.9	4.7	4.8	5.0	4.7	4.8	+0.1	1.3	1.4	1.9	2.4	2.8	3.3	3.3	3.4	3.2	3.1	-0.1	0.4	0.5	0.7	1.0	1.0	1.0	1.2	1.4	1.2	1.2	0.0
12th Grade	3.7	3.3	3.9	4.9	5.4	6.8	7.5	7.1	6.7	6.9	+0.2	2.0	1.7	2.2	3.1	3.8	4.4	4.6	4.6	4.3	4.4	+0.1	0.7	0.5	0.8	1.2	1.3	1.6	1.7	1.6	1.6	1.7	+0.1
PCP[c]																																	
8th Grade	—	—	—	—	—	—	—	—	—	—	—	—	—	—	—	—	—	—	—	—	—	—	—	—	—	—	—	—	—	—	—	—	—
10th Grade	—	—	—	—	—	—	—	—	—	—	—	—	—	—	—	—	—	—	—	—	—	—	—	—	—	—	—	—	—	—	—	—	—
12th Grade	2.9	2.4	2.9	2.8	2.7	4.0	3.9	3.9	3.4	3.4	-0.1	1.4	1.4	1.4	1.6	1.8	2.6	2.3	2.1	1.8	2.3	+0.5	0.5	0.6	1.0	0.7	0.6	1.3	0.7	1.0	0.8	0.9	+0.1
MDMA (Ecstasy)[c,d]																																	
8th Grade	—	—	—	—	—	3.4	3.2	2.7	2.7	4.3	+1.6ss	—	—	—	—	—	2.3	2.3	1.8	1.7	3.1	+1.4ss	—	—	—	—	—	1.0	1.0	0.9	0.8	1.4	+0.7ss
10th Grade	—	—	—	—	—	5.6	5.7	5.1	6.0	7.3	+1.3	—	—	—	—	—	4.6	3.9	3.3	4.4	5.4	+1.0	—	—	—	—	—	1.8	1.3	1.3	1.8	2.6	+0.8s
12th Grade	—	—	—	—	—	6.1	6.9	5.8	8.0	11.0	+3.0s	—	—	—	—	—	4.6	4.0	3.6	5.6	8.2	+2.6ss	—	—	—	—	—	2.0	1.6	1.5	2.5	3.6	+1.1
Cocaine																																	
8th Grade	2.3	2.9	2.9	3.6	4.2	4.5	4.4	4.6	4.7	4.5	-0.2	1.1	1.5	1.7	2.1	2.6	3.0	2.8	3.1	2.7	2.6	-0.1	0.5	0.7	0.7	1.0	1.2	1.3	1.1	1.4	1.3	1.2	-0.1
10th Grade	4.1	3.3	3.6	4.3	5.0	6.5	7.1	7.2	7.7	6.9	-0.9	2.2	1.9	2.1	2.8	3.5	4.2	4.7	4.7	4.9	4.4	-0.5	0.7	0.7	0.9	1.2	1.7	1.7	2.0	2.1	1.8	1.8	-0.1
12th Grade	7.8	6.1	6.1	5.9	6.0	7.1	8.7	9.3	9.8	8.6	-1.2	3.5	3.1	3.3	3.6	4.0	4.9	5.5	5.7	6.2	5.0	-1.3s	1.4	1.3	1.3	1.5	1.8	2.0	2.3	2.4	2.6	2.1	-0.5
Crack																																	
8th Grade	1.3	1.6	1.7	2.4	2.7	2.9	2.7	3.2	3.1	3.1	0.0	0.7	0.9	1.0	1.3	1.6	1.8	1.7	2.1	1.8	1.8	0.0	0.3	0.5	0.5	0.7	0.7	0.8	0.7	0.9	0.8	0.8	-0.1
10th Grade	1.7	1.5	1.8	2.1	2.8	3.3	3.6	3.9	4.0	3.7	-0.3	0.9	0.9	1.1	1.4	1.8	2.1	2.2	2.5	2.4	2.2	-0.2	0.3	0.4	0.5	0.6	0.9	0.8	0.9	1.1	0.8	0.9	+0.1
12th Grade	3.1	2.6	2.6	3.0	3.0	3.3	3.9	4.4	4.6	3.9	-0.7s	1.5	1.5	1.5	1.9	2.1	2.4	2.3	2.5	2.7	2.2	-0.5s	0.7	0.6	0.7	0.8	1.0	1.0	0.9	1.0	1.1	1.0	-0.1
Other Cocaine[e]																																	
8th Grade	2.0	2.4	2.4	3.0	3.4	3.8	3.5	3.7	3.8	3.5	-0.3	1.0	1.2	1.3	1.7	2.1	2.5	2.2	2.4	2.3	1.9	-0.4	0.5	0.5	0.6	0.9	1.0	1.0	0.8	1.0	1.1	0.9	-0.2
10th Grade	3.8	3.0	3.3	3.8	4.4	5.5	6.1	6.4	6.8	6.0	-0.8	2.1	1.7	1.8	2.4	3.0	3.5	4.1	4.0	4.4	3.8	-0.6	0.6	0.6	0.7	1.0	1.4	1.3	1.6	1.8	1.6	1.6	0.0
12th Grade	7.0	5.3	5.4	5.2	5.1	6.4	8.2	8.4	8.8	7.7	-1.1	3.2	2.6	2.9	3.0	3.4	4.2	5.0	4.9	5.8	4.5	-1.4s	1.2	1.0	1.2	1.3	1.3	1.6	2.0	2.0	2.5	1.7	-0.7s

TABLE 6.7

Trends in prevalence of use of various drugs for eighth, tenth, and twelfth graders, 1991–2000 [CONTINUED]

(Entries are percentages)

	Lifetime											Annual											30-Day										
	1991	1992	1993	1994	1995	1996	1997	1998	1999	2000	'99–'00 change	1991	1992	1993	1994	1995	1996	1997	1998	1999	2000	'99–'00 change	1991	1992	1993	1994	1995	1996	1997	1998	1999	2000	'99–'00 change
Heroin[f]																																	
8th Grade	1.2	1.4	1.4	2.0	2.3	2.4	2.1	2.3	2.3	1.9	-0.4	0.7	0.7	0.7	1.2	1.4	1.6	1.3	1.3	1.4	1.1	-0.3s	0.2	0.4	0.4	0.6	0.6	0.7	0.6	0.6	0.6	0.5	-0.2
10th Grade	1.2	1.2	1.3	1.5	1.7	2.1	2.1	2.3	2.3	2.2	-0.1	0.5	0.6	0.7	0.9	1.1	1.2	1.4	1.4	1.4	1.4	0.0	0.2	0.2	0.3	0.4	0.6	0.5	0.6	0.7	0.7	0.5	-0.2
12th Grade	0.9	1.2	1.1	1.2	1.6	1.8	2.1	2.0	2.0	2.4	+0.4	0.4	0.6	0.5	0.6	1.1	1.0	1.2	1.0	1.1	1.5	+0.4s	0.2	0.3	0.2	0.3	0.6	0.5	0.5	0.5	0.5	0.7	+0.2
With a needle[g]																																	
8th Grade	—	—	—	—	1.5	1.6	1.3	1.4	1.6	1.1	-0.5ss	—	—	—	—	0.9	1.0	0.8	0.8	0.9	0.6	-0.3ss	—	—	—	—	0.4	0.5	0.4	0.5	0.4	0.3	-0.1
10th Grade	—	—	—	—	1.0	1.1	1.1	1.2	1.3	1.0	-0.2	—	—	—	—	0.6	0.7	0.7	0.8	0.6	0.5	-0.1	—	—	—	—	0.3	0.3	0.3	0.4	0.3	0.3	-0.1
12th Grade	—	—	—	—	0.7	0.8	0.9	0.8	0.9	0.8	-0.1	—	—	—	—	0.5	0.5	0.5	0.4	0.4	0.4	0.0	—	—	—	—	0.3	0.4	0.3	0.2	0.2	0.2	0.0
Without a needle[g]																																	
8th Grade	—	—	—	—	1.5	1.6	1.4	1.5	1.4	1.3	-0.1	—	—	—	—	0.8	1.0	0.8	0.8	0.9	0.7	-0.2	—	—	—	—	0.3	0.4	0.4	0.3	0.4	0.3	-0.1
10th Grade	—	—	—	—	1.1	1.7	1.7	1.7	1.6	1.7	0.0	—	—	—	—	0.8	0.9	1.1	1.0	1.1	1.1	0.0	—	—	—	—	0.3	0.3	0.4	0.5	0.5	0.4	-0.2
12th Grade	—	—	—	—	1.4	1.7	2.1	1.6	1.8	2.4	+0.6	—	—	—	—	1.0	1.0	1.2	0.8	1.0	1.6	+0.6ss	—	—	—	—	0.6	0.4	0.6	0.4	0.4	0.7	+0.3
Other Narcotics[h]																																	
8th Grade	—	—	—	—	—	—	—	—	—	—	—	—	—	—	—	—	—	—	—	—	—	—	—	—	—	—	—	—	—	—	—	—	—
10th Grade	—	—	—	—	—	—	—	—	—	—	—	—	—	—	—	—	—	—	—	—	—	—	—	—	—	—	—	—	—	—	—	—	—
12th Grade	6.6	6.1	6.4	6.6	7.2	8.2	9.7	9.8	10.2	10.6	+0.4	3.5	3.3	3.6	3.8	4.7	5.4	6.2	6.3	6.7	7.0	+0.3	1.1	1.2	1.3	1.5	1.8	2.0	2.3	2.4	2.6	2.9	+0.3
Amphetamines[h]																																	
8th Grade	10.5	10.8	11.8	12.3	13.1	13.5	12.3	11.3	10.7	9.9	-0.8	6.2	6.5	7.2	7.9	8.7	9.1	8.1	7.2	6.9	6.5	-0.4	2.6	3.3	3.6	3.6	4.2	4.6	3.8	3.3	3.4	3.4	+0.1
10th Grade	13.2	13.1	14.9	15.1	17.4	17.7	17.0	16.0	15.7	15.7	+0.1	8.2	8.2	9.6	10.2	11.9	12.4	12.1	10.7	10.4	11.1	+0.7	3.3	3.6	4.3	4.5	5.3	5.5	5.1	5.1	5.0	5.4	+0.5
12th Grade	15.4	13.9	15.1	15.7	15.3	15.3	16.5	16.4	16.3	15.6	-0.7	8.2	7.1	8.4	9.4	9.3	9.5	10.2	10.1	10.2	10.5	+0.3	3.2	2.8	3.7	4.0	4.0	4.1	4.8	4.6	4.5	5.0	+0.5
Methamphetamine[i,j]																																	
8th Grade	—	—	—	—	—	—	—	—	4.5	4.2	-0.3	—	—	—	—	—	—	—	—	3.2	2.5	-0.7	—	—	—	—	—	—	—	—	1.1	0.8	-0.3
10th Grade	—	—	—	—	—	—	—	—	7.3	6.9	-0.5	—	—	—	—	—	—	—	—	4.6	4.0	-0.6	—	—	—	—	—	—	—	—	1.8	2.0	+0.2
12th Grade	—	—	—	—	—	—	—	—	8.2	7.9	-0.3	—	—	—	—	—	—	—	—	4.7	4.3	-0.3	—	—	—	—	—	—	—	—	1.7	1.9	+0.2
Ice[j]																																	
8th Grade	—	—	—	—	—	—	—	—	—	—	—	—	—	—	—	—	—	—	—	—	—	—	—	—	—	—	—	—	—	—	—	—	—
10th Grade	—	—	—	—	—	—	—	—	—	—	—	—	—	—	—	—	—	—	—	—	—	—	—	—	—	—	—	—	—	—	—	—	—
12th Grade	3.3	2.9	3.1	3.4	3.9	4.4	4.4	5.3	4.8	4.0	-0.8	1.4	1.3	1.7	1.8	2.4	2.8	2.3	3.0	1.9	2.2	-0.8	0.6	0.4	0.6	0.7	1.1	1.1	0.8	1.2	0.8	1.0	+0.2
Barbiturates[h]																																	
8th Grade	—	—	—	—	—	—	—	—	—	—	—	—	—	—	—	—	—	—	—	—	—	—	—	—	—	—	—	—	—	—	—	—	—
10th Grade	—	—	—	—	—	—	—	—	—	—	—	—	—	—	—	—	—	—	—	—	—	—	—	—	—	—	—	—	—	—	—	—	—
12th Grade	6.2	5.5	6.3	7.0	7.4	7.6	8.1	8.7	8.9	9.2	+0.2	3.4	2.8	3.4	4.1	4.7	4.9	5.1	5.5	5.8	6.2	+0.4	1.4	1.3	1.7	1.7	2.2	2.1	2.1	2.6	2.6	3.0	+0.4
Methaqualone[c,h]																																	
8th Grade	—	—	—	—	—	—	—	—	—	—	—	—	—	—	—	—	—	—	—	—	—	—	—	—	—	—	—	—	—	—	—	—	—
10th Grade	—	—	—	—	—	—	—	—	—	—	—	—	—	—	—	—	—	—	—	—	—	—	—	—	—	—	—	—	—	—	—	—	—
12th Grade	1.3	1.6	0.8	1.4	1.2	2.0	1.7	1.6	1.8	0.8	-1.0s	0.5	0.6	0.2	0.8	0.7	1.1	1.0	1.1	1.1	0.3	-0.8ss	0.2	0.4	0.1	0.4	0.4	0.6	0.3	0.6	0.4	0.2	-0.3
Tranquilizers[h]																																	
8th Grade	3.8	4.1	4.4	4.6	4.5	5.3	4.8	4.6	4.4	4.4	0.0	1.8	2.0	2.1	2.4	2.7	3.3	2.9	2.6	2.5	2.6	+0.2	0.8	0.8	0.9	1.1	1.2	1.5	1.2	1.2	1.1	1.4	+0.3
10th Grade	5.8	5.9	5.7	5.4	6.0	7.1	7.3	7.8	7.9	8.0	+0.1	3.2	3.5	3.3	3.3	4.0	4.6	4.9	5.1	5.4	5.6	+0.2	1.2	1.5	1.1	1.5	1.7	1.7	2.2	2.2	2.2	2.5	+0.4
12th Grade	7.2	6.0	6.4	6.6	7.1	7.2	7.8	8.5	9.3	8.9	-0.5	3.6	2.8	3.5	3.7	4.4	4.6	4.7	5.5	5.8	5.7	-0.1	1.4	1.0	1.2	1.4	1.8	2.0	1.8	2.4	2.5	2.6	+0.1
Rohypnol[j,k]																																	
8th Grade	—	—	—	—	—	1.5	1.1	1.4	1.3	1.0	-0.3	—	—	—	—	—	1.0	0.8	0.8	0.5	0.5	+0.1	—	—	—	—	—	0.5	0.3	0.4	0.3	0.3	0.0
10th Grade	—	—	—	—	—	1.5	1.7	2.0	1.8	1.3	-0.5	—	—	—	—	—	1.1	1.3	1.2	1.0	0.8	-0.3	—	—	—	—	—	0.5	0.5	0.4	0.5	0.4	-0.2
12th Grade	—	—	—	—	—	1.2	1.8	3.0	2.0	1.5	-0.6	—	—	—	—	—	1.1	1.2	1.4	1.0	0.8	-0.2	—	—	—	—	—	0.5	0.3	0.3	0.3	0.4	+0.1

TABLE 6.7

Trends in prevalence of use of various drugs for eighth, tenth, and twelfth graders, 1991–2000 [CONTINUED]

(Entries are percentages)

	Lifetime											Annual											30-Day										
	1991	1992	1993	1994	1995	1996	1997	1998	1999	2000	'99–'00 change	1991	1992	1993	1994	1995	1996	1997	1998	1999	2000	'99–'00 change	1991	1992	1993	1994	1995	1996	1997	1998	1999	2000	'99–'00 change
GHB[i,j]																																	
8th Grade	—	—	—	—	—	—	—	—	—	—	—	—	—	—	—	—	—	—	—	—	—	—	—	—	—	—	—	—	—	—	—	1.2	—
10th Grade	—	—	—	—	—	—	—	—	—	—	—	—	—	—	—	—	—	—	—	—	—	—	—	—	—	—	—	—	—	—	—	1.1	—
12th Grade	—	—	—	—	—	—	—	—	—	—	—	—	—	—	—	—	—	—	—	—	—	—	—	—	—	—	—	—	—	—	—	1.9	—
Ketamine[i,j]																																	
8th Grade	—	—	—	—	—	—	—	—	—	—	—	—	—	—	—	—	—	—	—	—	—	—	—	—	—	—	—	—	—	—	—	1.6	—
10th Grade	—	—	—	—	—	—	—	—	—	—	—	—	—	—	—	—	—	—	—	—	—	—	—	—	—	—	—	—	—	—	—	2.1	—
12th Grade	—	—	—	—	—	—	—	—	—	—	—	—	—	—	—	—	—	—	—	—	—	—	—	—	—	—	—	—	—	—	—	2.5	—
Alcohol[i]																																	
Any use																																	
8th Grade	70.1	69.3	67.1 / 55.7	55.8	54.5	55.3	53.8	52.5	52.1	51.7	-0.4	54.0	53.7	51.6 / 45.4	46.8	45.3	46.5	45.5	43.7	43.5	43.1	-0.4	25.1	26.1	26.2 / 24.3	25.5	24.6	26.2	24.5	23.0	24.0	22.4	-1.7
10th Grade	83.8	82.3	80.8 / 71.6	71.1	70.5	71.8	72.0	69.8	70.6	71.4	+0.9	72.3	70.2	69.3 / 63.4	63.9	63.5	65.0	65.2	62.7	63.7	65.3	+1.6	42.8	39.9	41.5 / 38.2	39.2	38.8	40.4	40.1	38.8	40.0	41.0	+0.9
12th Grade	88.0	87.5	87.0 / 80.0	80.4	80.7	79.2	81.7	81.4	80.0	80.3	+0.2	77.7	76.8	76.0 / 72.7	73.0	73.7	72.5	74.8	74.3	73.8	73.2	-0.6	54.0	51.3	51.0 / 48.6	50.1	51.3	50.8	52.7	52.0	51.0	50.0	-1.0
Been Drunk[i]																																	
8th Grade	26.7	26.8	25.9	25.9	25.3	26.8	25.2	24.8	24.8	25.1	+0.3	17.5	18.3	18.2	18.2	18.4	19.8	18.4	17.9	18.5	18.5	0.0	7.6	7.5	7.8	8.7	8.3	9.6	8.2	8.4	9.4	8.3	-1.1
10th Grade	50.0	47.7	47.9 / 47.2	47.2	46.9	48.5	49.4	46.7	48.9	49.3	+0.4	40.1	37.0	37.8 / 38.0	38.0	38.5	40.1	40.7	38.3	40.9	41.6	+0.7	20.5	18.1	19.8	20.3	20.8	21.3	22.4	21.1	22.5	23.5	+1.0
12th Grade	65.4	63.4	62.5 / 62.9	62.9	63.2	61.8	64.2	62.4	62.3	62.3	0.0	52.7	50.3	49.6 / 51.7	51.7	52.5	51.9	53.2	52.0	53.2	51.8	-1.4	31.6	29.9	28.9	30.8	33.2	31.3	34.2	32.9	32.9	32.3	-0.6
Cigarettes																																	
Any use																																	
8th Grade	44.0	45.2	45.3	46.1	46.4	49.2	47.3	45.7	44.1	40.5	-3.6ss	—	—	—	—	—	—	—	—	—	—	—	14.3	15.5	16.7	18.6	19.1	21.0	19.4	19.1	17.5	14.6	-2.8ss
10th Grade	55.1	53.5	56.3	56.9	57.6	61.2	60.2	57.7	57.6	55.1	-2.5s	—	—	—	—	—	—	—	—	—	—	—	20.8	21.5	24.7	25.4	27.9	30.4	29.8	27.6	25.7	23.9	-1.8
12th Grade	63.1	61.8	61.9	62.0	64.2	63.5	65.4	65.3	64.6	62.5	-2.1	—	—	—	—	—	—	—	—	—	—	—	28.3	27.8	29.9	31.2	33.5	34.0	36.5	35.1	34.6	31.4	-3.2ss
Bidis[i,j]																																	
8th Grade	—	—	—	—	—	—	—	—	—	—	—	—	—	—	—	—	—	—	—	—	3.9	—	—	—	—	—	—	—	—	—	—	—	—
10th Grade	—	—	—	—	—	—	—	—	—	—	—	—	—	—	—	—	—	—	—	—	6.4	—	—	—	—	—	—	—	—	—	—	—	—
12th Grade	—	—	—	—	—	—	—	—	—	—	—	—	—	—	—	—	—	—	—	—	9.2	—	—	—	—	—	—	—	—	—	—	—	—
Smokeless Tobacco[c,d]																																	
8th Grade	22.2	20.7	18.7	19.9	20.0	20.4	16.8	15.0	14.4	12.8	-1.6	—	—	—	—	—	—	—	—	—	—	—	6.9	7.0	6.6	7.7	7.1	7.1	5.5	4.8	4.5	4.2	-0.3
10th Grade	28.2	26.6	28.1	29.2	27.6	27.4	26.3	22.7	20.4	19.1	-1.3	—	—	—	—	—	—	—	—	—	—	—	10.0	9.6	10.4	10.5	9.7	8.6	8.9	7.5	6.5	6.1	-0.5
12th Grade	—	32.4	31.0	30.7	30.9	29.8	25.3	26.2	23.4	23.1	-0.4	—	—	—	—	—	—	—	—	—	—	—	—	11.4	10.7	11.1	12.2	9.8	9.7	8.8	8.4	7.6	-0.7
Steroids[j]																																	
8th Grade	1.9	1.7	1.6	2.0	2.0	1.8	1.8	2.3	2.7	3.0	+0.3	1.0	1.1	0.9	1.2	1.0	0.9	1.0	1.2	1.7	1.7	0.0	0.4	0.5	0.5	0.5	0.6	0.4	0.5	0.5	0.7	0.8	+0.1
10th Grade	1.8	1.7	1.7	2.0	2.0	1.8	2.0	2.0	2.7	3.5	+0.8ss	1.1	1.1	1.0	1.1	1.2	1.2	1.2	1.2	1.7	2.2	+0.5s	0.6	0.6	0.5	0.6	0.6	0.5	0.6	0.6	0.9	1.0	0.0
12th Grade	2.1	2.1	2.0	2.4	2.3	1.9	2.4	2.7	2.9	2.5	-0.4	1.4	1.1	1.2	1.3	1.5	1.4	1.4	1.7	1.8	1.7	-0.1	0.8	0.6	0.7	0.9	0.7	0.7	1.0	1.1	0.9	0.8	-0.1

TABLE 6.7

Trends in prevalence of use of various drugs for eighth, tenth, and twelfth graders, 1991–2000 [CONTINUED]

(Entries are percentages)

NOTES: Level of significance of difference between the two most recent classes: s = .05, ss = .01, sss = .001.
'—' indicates data not available. '*' indicates less than .05 percent but greater than 0 percent.
Any apparent inconsistency between the change estimate and the prevalence of use estimates for the two most recent classes is due to rounding error.

Approximate Weighted Ns	1991	1992	1993	1994	1995	1996	1997	1998	1999	2000
8th Graders	17,500	18,600	18,300	17,300	17,500	17,800	18,600	18,100	16,700	16,700
10th Graders	14,800	14,800	15,300	15,800	17,000	15,600	15,500	15,000	13,600	14,300
12th Graders	15,000	15,800	16,300	15,400	15,400	14,300	15,400	15,200	13,600	12,800

[a] 12th grade only: Data based on five of six forms in 1991–98; N is five-sixths of N indicated. Data based on three of six forms beginning in 1999; N is three-sixths of N indicated.

[b] 12th grade only: Unadjusted for underreporting of certain drugs.

[c] 12th grade only: Data based on one of six forms; N is one-sixth of N indicated.

[d] 8th and 10th grade only: MDMA data based one of two forms in 1996; N is one-half of N indicated. Beginning in 1997, data based on one-third of N indicated due to changes in the questionnaire forms. Smokeless tobacco data based on one of two forms for 1991–96 and on two of four forms beginning in 1997; N is one-half of N indicated.

[e] 12th grade only: Data based on four of six forms; N is four-sixths of N indicated.

[f] In 1995, the heroin question was changed in three of six forms for 12th graders and in one of two forms for 8th and 10th graders. Separate questions were asked for use with injection and without injection. Data presented here represent the combined data from all forms. In 1996, the heroin question was changed in all remaining 8th and 10th grade forms.

[g] For 8th and 10th graders only: Data based on one of two forms in 1995; N is one-half of N indicated. For 12th graders only: Data based on three of six forms; N is three-sixths of N indicated.

[h] 12th grade only: Only drug use which was not under a doctor's orders is included here.

[i] For 8th and 10th graders only: Data based on one of four forms; N is one-third of N indicated.

[j] 12th grade only: Data based on two of six forms; N is two-sixths of N indicated.

[k] For 8th and 10th graders only: Data based on one of two forms in 1996; N is one-half of N indicated. Data based on three of four forms in 1997–98; N is two-thirds of N indicated. Data based on two of four forms beginning in 1999; N is one-third of N indicated.

[l] In 1993, the question text was changed slightly in some forms to indicate that a "drink" meant "more than a few sips." The data in the upper line for alcohol came from forms using the old wording, while the data in the lower line came from forms using the revised wording. For 1993 only: Data based on one of two forms for 8th and 10th grades and on three of six forms for 12th grade. N is one-half of N indicated. In 1994–99, data were based on all forms for all grades.

SOURCE: Lloyd D. Johnson, Patrick M. O'Malley, and Jerald G. Bachman, "Table 5—5a Trends in Prevalence of Use of Various Drugs for Eighth, Tenth, and Twelfth Graders," in *Monitoring the Future: National Survey Results on Drug Use 1975–2000, Volume I: Secondary School Students*, NIH Publication No. 01-4924, National Institute on Drug Abuse, Bethesda, MD, August 2001

TABLE 6.8

Percent of high school students who drank alcohol and used marijuana, by sex, race/ethnicity, and grade, 1999

Category	Lifetime alcohol use[1]			Current alcohol use[2]			Episodic heavy drinking[3]			Lifetime marijuana use[4]			Current marijuana use[5]		
	Female	Male	Total	Female	Male	Total	Female	Male	Total	Female	Male	Total	Female	Male	Total
Race/Ethnicity															
White[6]	82.3	81.8	**82.0**	49.8	54.9	**52.5**	32.2	39.1	**35.8**	42.3	49.2	**45.9**	22.9	29.6	**26.4**
	(±3.0)[7]	(±3.3)	**(±3.0)**	(±4.8)	(±4.0)	**(±3.1)**	(±3.1)	(±3.4)	**(±2.0)**	(±3.1)	(±5.8)	**(±3.7)**	(±2.6)	(±4.8)	**(±3.1)**
Black[6]	75.8	73.8	**74.8**	40.7	39.1	**39.9**	14.7	17.4	**16.0**	42.7	54.8	**48.6**	21.9	31.2	**26.4**
	(±6.4)	(±4.3)	**(±4.7)**	(±7.6)	(±9.2)	**(±8.0)**	(±5.4)	(±5.3)	**(±5.1)**	(±5.3)	(±11.5)	**(±7.2)**	(±5.6)	(±9.3)	**(±6.9)**
Hispanic	84.8	82.2	**83.4**	49.3	56.3	**52.8**	26.8	37.5	**32.1**	46.4	55.8	**51.0**	21.8	34.8	**28.2**
	(±3.2)	(±4.2)	**(±2.6)**	(±5.4)	(±5.7)	**(±4.5)**	(±4.5)	(±4.9)	**(±4.2)**	(±5.7)	(±6.1)	**(±5.0)**	(±3.9)	(±6.8)	**(±4.4)**
Grade															
9	74.5	72.3	**73.4**	41.0	40.2	**40.6**	20.2	21.7	**21.1**	28.7	40.7	**34.8**	18.6	24.7	**21.7**
	(±5.9)	(±5.0)	**(±4.6)**	(±5.9)	(±4.5)	**(±4.4)**	(±3.2)	(±3.8)	**(±2.3)**	(±5.4)	(±6.6)	**(±5.0)**	(±3.9)	(±5.1)	**(±3.7)**
10	84.0	82.4	**83.2**	46.8	52.7	**49.7**	31.1	33.4	**32.2**	46.7	51.6	**49.1**	24.3	31.4	**27.8**
	(±3.5)	(±4.5)	**(±3.6)**	(±3.4)	(±5.8)	**(±3.7)**	(±3.7)	(±5.5)	**(±3.1)**	(±4.2)	(±8.3)	**(±4.1)**	(±4.4)	(±6.4)	**(±4.1)**
11	82.2	79.5	**80.8**	48.3	53.5	**50.9**	29.0	38.8	**34.0**	48.5	51.0	**49.7**	22.1	31.1	**26.7**
	(±4.2)	(±4.5)	**(±3.8)**	(±5.1)	(±5.9)	**(±3.8)**	(±4.8)	(±5.8)	**(±2.9)**	(±4.2)	(±6.2)	**(±4.5)**	(±4.5)	(±6.4)	**(±4.8)**
12	87.0	89.6	**88.3**	56.9	66.6	**61.7**	33.9	49.5	**41.6**	53.2	63.8	**58.4**	26.3	36.9	**31.5**
	(±2.9)	(±3.2)	**(±2.2)**	(±5.8)	(±4.6)	**(±4.4)**	(±5.7)	(±5.6)	**(±5.3)**	(±6.7)	(±4.7)	**(±4.6)**	(±5.7)	(±7.1)	**(±5.6)**
Total	**81.7**	**80.4**	**81.0**	**47.7**	**52.3**	**50.0**	**28.1**	**34.9**	**31.5**	**43.4**	**51.0**	**47.2**	**22.6**	**30.8**	**26.7**
	(±2.2)	**(±2.5)**	**(±2.0)**	**(±2.8)**	**(±2.9)**	**(±2.5)**	**(±2.1)**	**(±2.7)**	**(±1.9)**	**(±2.3)**	**(±4.2)**	**(±2.6)**	**(±1.8)**	**(±3.8)**	**(±2.5)**

[1]Ever had ≥1 drinks of alcohol.
[2]Drank alcohol on ≥1 of the 30 days preceding the survey.
[3]Drank ≥5 drinks of alcohol on ≥1 occasions on ≥1 of the 30 days preceding the survey.
[4]Ever used marijuana.
[5]Used marijuana ≥1 times during the 30 days preceding the survey.
[6]Non-Hispanic.
[7]Ninety-five percent confidence interval.

SOURCE: Laura Kann, Steven A. Kinchen, Barbara I. Williams, James G. Ross, Richard Lowry, Jo Anne Grunbaum, and Lloyd J. Kolbe, "Table 20. Percentage of high school students who drank alcohol and used marijuana, by sex, race/ethnicity, and grade - United States, Youth Risk Behavior Survey, 1999," in "Youth Risk Behavior Surveillance - United States, 1999," in *CDC Surveillance Summaries,* MMWR 2000, vol. 49, No. SS-5, June 9, 2000

Alcohol

In 2000 the proportion of eighth graders who reported having tried alcohol in their lifetimes was 51.7 percent, with 71.4 percent of tenth graders and 80.3 percent of twelfth graders reporting this same behavior. During the month prior to the survey, 22.4 percent of eighth graders, 41 percent of tenth graders, and 50 percent of twelfth graders had used alcohol. When asked if they had been drunk in the month prior to the survey, 8.3 percent of eighth graders, 23.5 percent of tenth graders, and 32.3 percent of twelfth graders reported that they had. (See Table 6.7.)

In 1999 black high school students (39.9 percent) reported lower levels of current alcohol use than either white (52.5 percent) or Hispanic students (52.8 percent). Black teenagers (16 percent) were also less likely to report binge drinking (five or more drinks in a row on at least one occasion during the month preceding the survey) than were white (35.8 percent) or Hispanic students (32.1 percent). Female students were slightly less likely than males to be current drinkers and considerably less likely to be binge drinkers. (See Table 6.8.)

Tobacco Use Among American Middle And High School Students

Cigarette smoking among high school students declined slowly but steadily from 1975 to the early 1990s,

but the rates grew during the mid-1990s. Since then they have declined slightly. The proportion of students who reported smoking during the month preceding the survey were 14.6 percent for eighth graders, 23.9 for tenth graders, and 31.4 percent for seniors in 2000. (See Table 6.7.)

In 2000 about one-half to two-thirds of students believed that smoking one or more packs of cigarettes a day represented a great risk, virtually unchanged since 1991. (See Figure 6.3). Students in the younger grades were somewhat more likely than seniors to disapprove of daily cigarette smoking. (See Figure 6.4.)

In "Youth Tobacco Surveillance: United States, 1998–99" (CDC Surveillance Summaries, vol. 49, no. SS-10, October 13, 2000) the Centers for Disease Control and Prevention (CDC) reported on the prevalence of tobacco use among middle school and high school students across the country. In 1999 nearly 13 percent of middle school students and 35 percent of high school students used some type of tobacco (See Table 6.9.)

Among middle school students (grades six through eight), cigarettes (9.2 percent) and cigars (6.1 percent) were the most prevalent type of tobacco used. Cigarette smoking rates were similar among males and females and among racial/ethnic groups. Black students (8.8 percent) were significantly more likely than white students (4.9

FIGURE 6.3

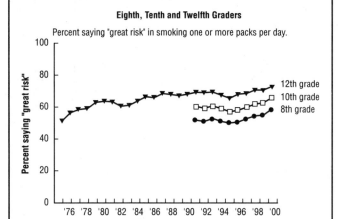

Trends in perceived harmfulness of smoking one or more packs of cigarettes per day for eighth, tenth, and twelfth graders, 1975–2000

Eighth, Tenth and Twelfth Graders

Percent saying "great risk" in smoking one or more packs per day.

SOURCE: Lloyd D. Johnson, Patrick M. O'Malley, and Jerald G. Bachman, "Figure 8—10a Trends in Perceived Harmfulness of Smoking One or More Packs of Cigarettes per Day for Eighth, Tenth, and Twelfth Graders," in *Monitoring the Future: National Survey Results on Drug Use 1975–2000, Volume I: Secondary School Students*, NIH Publication No. 01-4924, National Institute on Drug Abuse, Bethesda, MD, August 2001

FIGURE 6.4

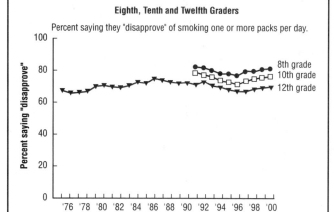

Trends in disapproval of smoking one or more packs of cigarettes per day for eighth, tenth, and twelfth graders, 1975–2000

Eighth, Tenth and Twelfth Graders

Percent saying they "disapprove" of smoking one or more packs per day.

SOURCE: Lloyd D. Johnson, Patrick M. O'Malley, and Jerald G. Bachman, "Figure 8—10b Trends in Disapproval of Smoking One or More Packs of Cigarettes per Day for Eighth, Tenth, and Twelfth Graders," in *Monitoring the Future: National Survey Results on Drug Use 1975–2000, Volume I: Secondary School Students*, NIH Publication No. 01-4924, National Institute on Drug Abuse, Bethesda, MD, August 2001

TABLE 6.9

Percentage of middle and high school students who were current users of any tobacco product, by sex and race/ethnicity, National Youth Tobacco Survey, 1999

	Any tobacco[1]	Cigarettes	Cigars	Smokeless tobacco	Pipes	Bidis	Kreteks
Middle school							
Sex							
Male	14.2 (±2.2)[2]	9.6 (±1.7)	7.8 (±1.3)	4.2 (±1.3)	3.5 (±0.8)	3.1 (±0.8)	2.2 (±0.6)
Female	11.3 (±2.2)	8.9 (±1.7)	4.4 (±1.3)	1.3 (±0.5)	1.4 (±0.6)	1.8 (±0.6)	1.7 (±0.7)
Race/ethnicity							
White	11.6 (±2.3)	8.8 (±2.0)	4.9 (±1.0)	3.0 (±1.1)	2.0 (±0.6)	1.8 (±0.5)	1.7 (±0.7)
Black	14.4 (±2.7)	9.0 (±1.8)	8.9 (±2.3)	1.9 (±0.9)	2.0 (±0.9)	2.8 (±1.3)	1.7 (±0.8)
Hispanic	15.2 (±5.2)	11.0 (±4.1)	7.6 (±2.9)	2.2 (±0.9)	3.8 (±1.7)	3.5 (±1.6)	2.1 (±0.6)
Total, middle school	**12.8 (±2.0)**	**9.2 (±1.6)**	**6.1 (±1.1)**	**2.7 (±0.7)**	**2.4 (±0.5)**	**2.5 (±0.6)**	**1.9 (±0.5)**
High school							
Sex							
Male	38.1 (±3.2)	28.7 (±2.8)	20.3 (±1.9)	11.7 (±2.8)	4.2 (±0.9)	6.1 (±1.0)	6.2 (±1.1)
Female	31.4 (±3.1)	28.2 (±3.3)	10.2 (±1.6)	1.5 (±0.6)	1.4 (±0.5)	3.8 (±1.0)	5.3 (±1.5)
Race/ethnicity							
White	39.4 (±3.2)	32.9 (±3.1)	16.0 (±1.6)	8.7 (±2.1)	2.6 (±0.6)	4.4 (±0.9)	6.5 (±1.5)
Black	24.0 (±4.2)	15.9 (±3.8)	14.8 (±3.5)	2.4 (±1.3)	1.9 (±0.9)	5.8 (±2.1)	2.8 (±1.5)
Hispanic	30.7 (±4.4)	25.8 (±4.7)	13.4 (±2.9)	3.7 (±1.6)	3.8 (±1.4)	5.6 (±2.1)	5.5 (±1.9)
Total, high school	**34.8 (±2.6)**	**28.5 (±2.6)**	**15.3 (±1.4)**	**6.6 (±1.6)**	**2.8 (±0.5)**	**5.0 (±0.8)**	**5.8 (±1.2)**

[1] Current use of cigarettes *or* cigars *or* smokeless tobacco *or* pipes *or* bidis *or* kreteks on ≥1 of the 30 days preceding the survey.
[2] Ninety-five percent confidence interval.

SOURCE: "Table 4. Percentage of middle school and high school students who were current users of any tobacco product, cigarettes, cigars, smokeless tobacco, pipes, bidis, or kreteks, by sex and race/ethnicity," in "Youth Tobacco Surveillance: United States, 1998–99," *CDC Surveillance Summaries*, Center for Disease Control and Prevention, MMWR 2000 vol. 49, no. SS-10, October 13, 2000

percent) to smoke cigars. Boys were more likely than girls to use smokeless tobacco, smoke cigars, and smoke tobacco in a pipe. (See Table 6.9.)

High school students (grades nine through twelve) were most likely to smoke cigarettes (28.5 percent) and cigars (15.3 percent). White (32.8 percent) and Hispanic

TABLE 6.10

Percent of high school students who have used tobacco, by sex, race/ethnicity, and grade, 1999

Category	Lifetime cigarette use[1]			Lifetime daily cigarette use[2]			Current cigarette use[3]			Current frequent cigarette use[4]			Smoked>10 cigarettes/day[5]		
	Female	Male	Total	Female	Male	Total	Female	Male	Total	Female	Male	Total	Female	Male	Total
Race/Ethnicity															
White[6]	70.9	70.8	**70.9**	29.2	29.3	**29.3**	39.1	38.2	**38.6**	19.4	20.9	**20.2**	4.9	8.4	**6.6**
	(±3.6)[7]	(±5.3)	(**±4.1**)	(±3.5)	(±3.5)	(**±3.2**)	(±3.5)	(±3.7)	(**±3.2**)	(±3.7)	(±3.2)	(**±3.0**)	(±1.4)	(±1.6)	(**±1.2**)
Black[6]	68.9	69.0	**68.9**	8.0	14.6	**11.2**	17.7	21.8	**19.7**	5.0	9.1	**7.0**	1.0	0.8	**0.9**
	(±6.8)	(±7.9)	(**±6.7**)	(±3.3)	(±11.9)	(**±6.9**)	(±3.5)	(±7.1)	(**±4.1**)	(±3.1)	(±4.4)	(**±3.4**)	(±0.9)	(±0.5)	(**±0.6**)
Hispanic	71.1	74.9	**72.9**	18.2	21.1	**19.6**	31.5	34.0	**32.7**	8.5	12.5	**10.4**	2.0	3.5	**2.7**
	(±4.1)	(±3.9)	(**±3.2**)	(±3.7)	(±5.0)	(**±3.2**)	(±4.6)	(±4.5)	(**±3.8**)	(±3.1)	(±4.6)	(**±2.7**)	(±1.6)	(±1.5)	(**±1.1**)
Grade															
9	60.3	63.1	**61.8**	17.3	19.7	**18.5**	29.2	26.1	**27.6**	11.0	11.4	**11.2**	3.0	3.5	**3.3**
	(±7.2)	(±5.4)	(**±5.6**)	(±4.4)	(±4.3)	(**±3.4**)	(±4.8)	(±6.1)	(**±4.0**)	(±2.8)	(±3.1)	(**±2.6**)	(±1.2)	(±1.9)	(**±1.2**)
10	75.1	72.7	**73.9**	27.7	26.3	**27.0**	35.7	33.6	**34.7**	15.3	15.0	**15.2**	3.0	5.2	**4.1**
	(±2.7)	(±6.8)	(**±4.1**)	(±3.2)	(±4.8)	(**±2.9**)	(±4.1)	(±2.8)	(**±2.5**)	(±4.0)	(±3.9)	(**±3.5**)	(±1.5)	(±2.5)	(**±1.2**)
11	71.8	68.1	**69.9**	26.9	24.4	**25.7**	35.6	36.4	**36.0**	17.1	20.4	**18.7**	3.8	6.1	**4.9**
	(±2.8)	(±5.2)	(**±3.2**)	(±4.0)	(±5.3)	(**±3.1**)	(±5.2)	(±5.9)	(**±3.0**)	(±3.0)	(±5.7)	(**±2.7**)	(±1.5)	(±2.7)	(**±1.6**)
12	75.5	80.5	**78.0**	28.8	34.3	**31.5**	40.5	45.2	**42.8**	20.3	26.1	**23.1**	7.2	10.8	**8.9**
	(±5.4)	(±3.4)	(**±4.0**)	(±6.0)	(±8.6)	(**±6.5**)	(±5.9)	(±6.7)	(**±5.5**)	(±6.0)	(±10.1)	(**±6.7**)	(±3.5)	(±5.2)	(**±4.1**)
Total	70.2	70.5	**70.4**	24.8	25.8	**25.3**	34.9	34.7	**34.8**	15.6	17.9	**16.8**	4.1	6.3	**5.2**
	(**±2.9**)	(**±3.8**)	(**±3.0**)	(**±2.4**)	(**±3.1**)	(**±2.6**)	(**±2.6**)	(**±3.0**)	(**±2.5**)	(**±2.6**)	(**±3.2**)	(**±2.5**)	(**±1.2**)	(**±1.4**)	(**±1.2**)

[1]Ever tried cigarette smoking, even one or two puffs.
[2]Ever smoked ≥1 cigarettes every day for 30 days.
[3]Smoked cigarettes on ≥1 of the 30 days preceding the survey.
[4]Smoked cigarettes on ≥20 of the 30 days preceding the survey.
[5]Smoked >10 cigarettes/day on the days smoked during the 30 days preceding the survey.
[6]Non-Hispanic.
[7]Ninety-five percent confidence interval.

SOURCE: Laura Kann, Steven A. Kinchen, Barbara I. Williams, James G. Ross, Richard Lowry, Jo Anne Grunbaum, and Lloyd J. Kolbe, "Table 14. Percentage of high school students who used tobacco by sex, race/ethnicity, and grade - United States, Youth Risk Behavior Survey, 1999," in "Youth Risk Behavior Surveillance - United States, 1999," in *CDC Surveillance Summaries, MMWR* 2000, vol. 49, no. SS-5, June 9, 2000

(25.8 percent) students were significantly more likely than black students (15.8 percent) to smoke cigarettes. White students (8.7 percent) were significantly more likely than black (2.4 percent) and Hispanic (3.7 percent) students to use smokeless tobacco. Boys were far more likely to use smokeless tobacco, smoke cigars, and smoke tobacco in a pipe than girls. (See Table 6.9.)

The proportions of middle school students and high school students who smoked bidis in 1999 were 2.4 percent and 5 percent, respectively (See Table 6.9). A *bidi,* imported primarily from India, is a small, hand-rolled cigarette wrapped in herb leaves. The tobacco is available in a variety of flavors, such as strawberry, chocolate, and mint. The CDC reports that *bidis* contain as much as seven times the nicotine as regular cigarettes.

About 2 percent of middle school students and 5.8 percent of high school students smoked *Kreteks* (See Table 6.9). *Kreteks* are clove cigarettes, a mixture of tobacco and clove spice rolled into a cigarette. Most are imported from Indonesia. Many clove cigarettes have a mint flavor added to the paper around the filter.

In 1999 white students (38.6 percent) and Hispanic students (32.7 percent) were more likely than black teens (19.7 percent) to have smoked cigarettes at least once in

the 30 days preceding the survey. White students were also more likely to be frequent cigarette smokers (20.2 percent). (See Table 6.10.)

Not surprisingly, seniors were most likely to be current (42.8 percent) and frequent (23.1 percent) smokers. Males and females were almost equally likely to be frequent smokers in ninth and tenth grades, but in eleventh and twelfth grades, males were more likely to smoke frequently. (See Table 6.10.)

Sexual Activity

Great Transitions: Preparing Adolescents for a New Century (Carnegie Council on Adolescent Development, New York, 1995) pointed out that the age of first intercourse has declined over the past 30 years. In its "1999 Youth Risk Behavior Surveillance" (cited earlier), the CDC reported that about 4.4 percent of females and 12.2 percent of males had first experienced sexual intercourse before age 13. Over one-third (36 percent) of both high school females and males claimed they were currently sexually active. The proportion of females who reported that they had had four or more sexual partners was about 13 percent, and for males, the percentage was 19.3. Nearly one-quarter (23.9 percent) of high school females and

TABLE 6.11

Percent of high school seniors who engaged in sexual behaviors, by sex, race/ethnicity, and grade, 1999

Category	Ever had sexual intercourse			First sexual intercourse before age 13			Four or more sex partners during lifetime			Currently sexually active[1]			Currently abstinent[2]		
	Female	Male	Total	Female	Male	Total	Female	Male	Total	Female	Male	Total	Female	Male	Total
Race/Ethnicity															
White[3]	44.8	45.4	**45.1**	3.5	7.5	**5.5**	12.7	12.1	**12.4**	34.7	31.3	**33.0**	22.4	31.3	**27.0**
	(±4.5)[4]	(±4.6)	**(±4.2)**	(±0.7)	(±1.1)	**(±0.8)**	(±2.4)	(±2.9)	**(±2.2)**	(±4.6)	(±4.2)	**(±3.5)**	(±4.0)	(±4.9)	**(±2.5)**
Black[3]	66.9	75.7	**71.2**	11.4	29.9	**20.5**	21.3	48.1	**34.4**	50.3	55.8	**53.0**	24.9	25.8	**25.3**
	(±11.3)	(±6.5)	**(±8.2)**	(±5.4)	(±5.9)	**(±4.8)**	(±8.8)	(±12.8)	**(±10.4)**	(±9.1)	(±10.1)	**(±9.0)**	(±5.0)	(±9.6)	**(±5.9)**
Hispanic	45.5	62.9	**54.1**	4.4	14.2	**9.2**	10.5	23.0	**16.6**	34.0	38.5	**36.3**	25.3	38.4	**32.7**
	(±6.2)	(±5.5)	**(±5.0)**	(±1.5)	(±2.6)	**(±1.5)**	(±3.7)	(±6.4)	**(±4.5)**	(±4.7)	(±6.2)	**(±4.4)**	(±4.2)	(±7.4)	**(±5.0)**
Grade															
9	32.5	44.5	**38.6**	5.5	17.7	**11.7**	7.9	15.6	**11.8**	24.0	29.1	**26.6**	26.7	34.7	**31.3**
	(±7.6)	(±6.1)	**(±6.2)**	(±1.7)	(±3.1)	**(±1.8)**	(±2.3)	(±3.4)	**(±2.4)**	(±7.2)	(±5.2)	**(±5.8)**	(±7.2)	(±6.8)	**(±6.1)**
10	42.6	51.1	**46.8**	5.1	13.9	**9.4**	10.1	21.4	**15.6**	32.0	33.9	**33.0**	24.8	33.1	**29.2**
	(±5.0)	(±7.6)	**(±5.8)**	(±2.5)	(±3.9)	**(±3.0)**	(±2.7)	(±8.1)	**(±5.1)**	(±4.9)	(±7.9)	**(±5.2)**	(±4.8)	(±7.9)	**(±4.0)**
11	53.8	51.4	**52.5**	4.5	7.8	**6.2**	15.1	19.4	**17.3**	39.5	35.4	**37.5**	26.5	30.9	**28.6**
	(±4.5)	(±5.8)	**(±4.3)**	(±2.4)	(±2.1)	**(±1.6)**	(±4.7)	(±5.5)	**(±4.3)**	(±3.8)	(±5.2)	**(±3.7)**	(±3.8)	(±6.0)	**(±3.5)**
12	65.8	63.9	**64.9**	2.1	7.6	**4.8**	20.6	20.6	**20.6**	53.0	48.1	**50.6**	19.5	24.6	**22.0**
	(±7.6)	(±6.3)	**(±5.0)**	(±1.6)	(±2.3)	**(±1.2)**	(±5.4)	(±3.9)	**(±3.0)**	(±8.6)	(±5.7)	**(±5.2)**	(±5.6)	(±4.1)	**(±3.8)**
Total	**47.7**	**52.2**	**49.9**	**4.4**	**12.2**	**8.3**	**13.1**	**19.3**	**16.2**	**36.3**	**36.2**	**36.3**	**23.9**	**30.5**	**27.3**
	(±4.2)	**(±4.5)**	**(±4.0)**	**(±1.1)**	**(±1.9)**	**(±1.3)**	**(±2.3)**	**(±3.8)**	**(±2.8)**	**(±4.2)**	**(±4.1)**	**(±3.7)**	**(±3.0)**	**(±3.5)**	**(±2.4)**

[1] Sexual intercourse during the 3 months preceding the survey.
[2] Among those who have ever had sexual intercourse, no sexual intercourse during the 3 months preceding the survey.
[3] Non-Hispanic.
[4] Ninety-five percent confidence interval.

SOURCE: Laura Kann, Steven A. Kinchen, Barbara I. Williams, James G. Ross, Richard Lowry, Jo Anne Grunbaum, and Lloyd J. Kolbe, "Table 30. Percentage of high school students who engaged in sexual behaviors, by sex, race/ethnicity, and grade - United States, Youth Risk Behavior Survey, 1999," in "Youth Risk Behavior Surveillance - United States, 1999," in *CDC Surveillance Summaries*, MMWR 2000, vol. 49, no. SS-5, June 9, 2000

TABLE 6.12

Teen birth rate, 1960–2000
(Births per 1,000 females aged 15-19, 15-17, and 18-19)

Ages:	1960	1970	1980	1986	1990	1991	1995	1996	1997	1998	1999	2000
15-19	89.1	68.3	53.0	50.2	59.9	62.1	56.8	54.4	52.3	51.1	49.6	48.7
15-17	43.9	38.8	32.5	30.5	37.5	38.7	36.0	33.8	32.1	30.4	28.7	27.5
18-19	166.7	114.7	82.1	79.6	88.6	94.4	89.1	86.0	83.6	82.0	80.3	79.5

SOURCE: Kristin Anderson Moore, Jennifer Manlove, Elizabeth Terry-Humen, Stephanie Williams, Angela Romano Papillo, and Juliet Scarpa, "Teen Birth Rate (Births per 1,000 Females Ages 15-19, 15-17, and 18-19)," in *CTS Facts at a Glance*, Child Trends, Washington, DC, August 2001

30.5 percent of high school males reported that they were currently abstinent. (See Table 6.11.)

Older students tended to be more sexually active than younger students. Black students (53 percent) were more likely than white (33 percent) or Hispanic (36.3 percent) students to be sexually active. More than one-fifth (21 percent) of black students had first experienced sexual intercourse before age 13, and 34 percent reported four or more partners. (See Table 6.11.)

In 1999 more than half (58 percent) of sexually active students reported using condoms during their last sexual encounters, and one-fifth (20.4 percent) of the female students used birth control pills. Black students (70 percent) were significantly more likely than white (55 percent) and Hispanic (55.2 percent) students to report using condoms. About 8 percent of the females surveyed reported having been pregnant, and 5 percent of the males stated that they had gotten someone pregnant.

TEENAGE PREGNANCY. From 1960 through 1986, the number of live births per 1,000 females ages 15 to 17 generally declined, but the rate increased during the late 1980s and early 1990s. The National Center for Health Statistics reported that in 2000 there were 27.5 live births per 1,000 females ages 15 to 17. (See Table 6.12.)

In 2000 mothers under age 20 accounted for a total of 479,067 live births. Non-Hispanic white teenagers had a birth rate of 33 births per 1,000 females ages 15 through 19, while Hispanic females experienced a birth rate of 94

FIGURE 6.5

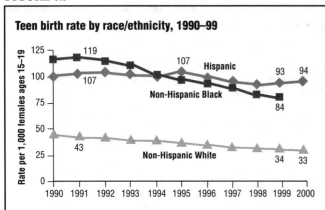

Teen birth rate by race/ethnicity, 1990–99

SOURCE: Kristin Anderson Moore, Jennifer Manlove, Elizabeth Terry-Humen, Stephanie Williams, Angela Romano Papillo, and Juliet Scarpa, "U.S. Teen Birth Rate by Race/Ethnicity 1990–1999," in *CTS Facts at a Glance*, Child Trends, Washington, DC, August 2001

births per 1,000 females in the same age group. The birth rate for non-Hispanic black teenage mothers was not available for 2000, but in 1999 it was 84 births per 1,000 females ages 15 through 19. (See Figure 6.5.)

Most teenage mothers are unmarried and lack the resources to give their children adequate care. The National Center for Health Statistics reported that in 1999 about 79 percent of all teen births occurred outside of marriage. In 1999 the non-marital birth rate of females ages 15 through 19 was 40 per 1,000 females. (See Table 6.13.)

AIDS AND OTHER SEXUALLY TRANSMITTED DISEASES. The Centers for Disease Control and Prevention (CDC) identifies certain diseases as "notifiable," meaning that state and local medical authorities must report each occurrence to the CDC. Sexually transmitted diseases (STDs) are included in the notifiable disease list. Human immunodeficiency virus (HIV, the virus that causes AIDS [acquired immunodeficiency syndrome]) is probably the best known STD, but it is not the most common. Syphilis, chlamydia, and gonorrhea are the three most common STDs reported to the CDC.

According to *STD Surveillance* (Center for Disease Control and Prevention, Atlanta, GA, September 2000),

adolescents and young adults are at a higher risk for acquiring STDs than older adults. In 2000 the highest rates of chlamydia and gonorrhea occurred in those ages 15 through 19. Although antibiotics can cure many STDs, they can still have serious health consequences, including an increase in a victim's risk of contracting HIV if exposed.

HIV/AIDS remains the most dangerous STD. Young people who are sexually active and/or inject drugs are at great risk of contracting the virus. Through December 2000 the CDC reported that a cumulative total of 4,061 AIDS cases had been diagnosed in youths 13 to 19 years of age. More males (2,366 cases) were diagnosed than were females (1,695 cases). (See Table 6.14.) Countless more are infected with HIV, the virus that causes AIDS. Because of the long incubation period from the time of infection and the onset of symptoms, many people who develop AIDS in their early twenties were probably infected with HIV as teenagers.

VIOLENCE IN SCHOOL

At the end of the twentieth century, the issue of violence in schools received attention because of several incidents that garnered tremendous attention, including the Columbine massacre in 1999, when two students murdered a dozen of their classmates and a teacher at their Littleton, Colorado high school.

Violence in school—threats, physical fights, weapons at school, and the feeling of being unsafe—has increased since 1980. Nonetheless, most students and teachers still report that they feel safe at school. In its 1999 "Youth Risk Behavior Surveillance," the CDC found that more than five percent of the students surveyed had missed at least one school day during the 30 days before the survey because they felt too unsafe to go to school. About 4 percent of white students felt too unsafe to go to school, compared to 6 percent of black and 11.2 percent of Hispanic students. Students in ninth grade (7 percent) were almost twice as likely as twelfth graders (3.9 percent) to fear going to school. (See Table 6.15.)

TABLE 6.13

Marital and non-marital birth rate, 1960–99
(Births per 1,000 females)

Marital Status and Age:	1960	1970	1980	1986	1990	1991	1992	1993	1994	1995	1996	1997	1998	1999
Marital, ages 15-19	531	444	350	352	420	410	398	388	351	362	344	323	322	311
Non-marital, ages 15-19	15	22	28	32	43	45	45	45	46	44	43	42	42	40
Non-marital, ages 20-24	40	38	41	49	65	68	69	69	72	70	71	71	72	73
Non-marital, ages 15-44	22	26	29	34	44	45	45	45	47	45	45	44	44	44

SOURCE: Kristin Anderson Moore, Jennifer Manlove, Elizabeth Terry-Humen, Stephanie Williams, Angela Romano Papillo, and Juliet Scarpa, "Marital and Non-marital Birth Rate (Births per 1,000 Females)," in *CTS Facts at a Glance*, Child Trends, Washington, DC, August 2001

TABLE 6.14

AIDS cases by sex, age at diagnosis, and race/ethnicity, reported through December 2000

Male Age at diagnosis (years)	White, not Hispanic		Black, not Hispanic		Hispanic		Asian/Pacific Islander		American Indian/ Alaska Native		Total[1]	
	No.	(%)	No.	(%)	No.	(%)	No.	(%)	No.	(%)	No.	(%)
Under 5	524	(0)	2,129	(1)	768	(1)	17	(0)	12	(1)	3,454	(1)
5-12	341	(0)	475	(0)	282	(0)	10	(0)	6	(0)	1,117	(0)
13-19	874	(0)	919	(0)	523	(0)	25	(1)	22	(1)	2,366	(0)
20-24	7,761	(3)	7,160	(3)	4,297	(4)	174	(3)	81	(4)	19,499	(3)
25-29	38,283	(13)	25,564	(12)	16,507	(14)	626	(13)	334	(18)	81,411	(13)
30-34	69,614	(23)	44,093	(21)	27,268	(24)	1,085	(22)	497	(26)	142,702	(22)
35-39	69,257	(23)	48,397	(23)	25,680	(22)	1,089	(22)	425	(22)	145,053	(23)
40-44	50,497	(17)	38,662	(18)	18,124	(16)	860	(17)	281	(15)	108,580	(17)
45-49	30,632	(10)	22,833	(11)	10,206	(9)	529	(11)	119	(6)	64,411	(10)
50-54	16,650	(6)	11,778	(5)	5,442	(5)	281	(6)	54	(3)	34,258	(5)
55-59	8,923	(3)	6,420	(3)	2,989	(3)	162	(3)	34	(2)	18,557	(3)
60-64	4,916	(2)	3,510	(2)	1,649	(1)	69	(1)	18	(1)	10,174	(2)
65 or older	4,051	(1)	2,957	(1)	1,334	(1)	70	(1)	14	(1)	8,439	(1)
Male subtotal	**302,323**	**(100)**	**214,898**	**(100)**	**115,069**	**(100)**	**4,997**	**(100)**	**1,897**	**(100)**	**640,022**	**(100)**
Female **Age at diagnosis (years)**												
Under 5	496	(2)	2,126	(3)	763	(3)	15	(2)	13	(3)	3,418	(3)
5-12	187	(1)	501	(1)	219	(1)	9	(1)			919	(1)
13-19	273	(1)	1,122	(1)	286	(1)	8	(1)	4	(1)	1,695	(1)
20-24	1,671	(6)	4,443	(6)	1,536	(6)	41	(6)	34	(8)	7,733	(6)
25-29	4,633	(16)	11,108	(14)	4,157	(16)	102	(14)	62	(14)	20,083	(15)
30-34	6,464	(22)	16,777	(22)	6,077	(23)	136	(19)	100	(23)	29,608	(22)
35-39	5,812	(20)	16,914	(22)	5,475	(21)	133	(18)	85	(19)	28,459	(21)
40-44	3,848	(13)	11,949	(15)	3,613	(14)	109	(15)	57	(13)	19,597	(15)
45-49	2,072	(7)	6,079	(8)	2,028	(8)	72	(10)	40	(9)	10,313	(8)
50-54	1,183	(4)	3,016	(4)	1,114	(4)	29	(4)	20	(5)	5,367	(4)
55-59	756	(3)	1,649	(2)	682	(3)	25	(3)	15	(3)	3,128	(2)
60-64	480	(2)	973	(1)	363	(1)	26	(4)	5	(1)	1,849	(1)
65 or older	959	(3)	967	(1)	312	(1)	26	(4)	4	(1)	2,272	(2)
Female subtotal	**28,834**	**(100)**	**77,624**	**(100)**	**26,625**	**(100)**	**731**	**(100)**	**439**	**(100)**	**134,441**	**(100)**
Total[2]	**331,160**		**292,522**		**141,694**		**5,728**		**2,337**		**774,467**	

[1]Includes 838 males and 187 females whose race/ethnicity is unknown.
[2]Includes 1 male whose age at diagnosis is unknown, and 4 persons whose sex is unknown.

SOURCE: "Table 7. AIDS cases by sex, age at diagnosis, and race/ethnicity, reported through December 2000, United States," in *HIV/AIDS Surveillance Report,* vol. 12, no. 2, 2000

Juvenile Offenders

The American Youth Policy Forum (Richard Mendel, *Less Hype, More Help: Reducing Juvenile Crime, What Works - and What Doesn't,* Washington DC, 2000), reported that youths are far more likely to be victimized by violence than to commit violence. According to the U.S. Department of Justice, serious violent crimes committed by juvenile offenders declined 33 percent between 1993 and 1997. In 1997 juveniles under age 18 made up 19 percent of all arrests. Based on their proportion, juveniles were disproportionately involved in arrests for arson (50 percent), vandalism (43 percent), motor vehicle theft (40 percent), burglary (37 percent), larceny-theft (34 percent), robbery (30 percent), and weapons law violations (24 percent).

Young people who commit violent crimes are likely to be sent to juvenile detention facilities or even adult prisons and jails. In any of these facilities, they are much less likely to complete their high school education.

FIGHTS AND GANGS. The CDC asked high school students whether they had been in a fight on school property. In 1999 about 14 percent of the students surveyed were in at least one physical fight on school property during the 12 months preceding the survey. Male students (18.5 percent) were almost twice as likely as females (9.8 percent) to have been in a fight. Black (18.7 percent) and Hispanic (15.7 percent) students were more likely than white students (12.3 percent) to have been in a fight. (See Table 6.15.) The Office of Juvenile Justice and Delinquency Prevention reports that in 1999 more than one-third of students said there was a gang presence at their school.

CARRYING A WEAPON. Weapons brought to school have included guns, knives, clubs, brass knuckles, razor

TABLE 6.15

Percentage of high school students who engaged in violence and in behaviors resulting from violence on school property by sex, race/ethnicity, and grade, 1999

Category	Felt too unsafe to go to school[1]			Carried a weapon on school property[1,2]			Threatened or injured with a weapon on school property[3]			Engaged in a physical fight on school property[3]		
	Female	Male	Total	Female	Male	Total	Female	Male	Total	Female	Male	Total
Race/Ethnicity												
White[4]	4.3	3.6	**3.9**	1.6	11.0	**6.4**	5.2	7.9	**6.6**	7.1	17.2	**12.3**
	(±1.7)[5]	(±1.7)	**(±1.3)**	(±0.6)	(±3.1)	**(±1.7)**	(±1.9)	(±1.5)	**(±0.7)**	(±2.3)	(±2.0)	**(±1.7)**
Black[4]	7.1	4.9	**6.0**	4.8	5.3	**5.0**	6.4	9.0	**7.6**	18.4	19.0	**18.7**
	(±2.5)	(±1.4)	**(±1.2)**	(±2.4)	(±2.1)	**(±1.0)**	(±2.2)	(±2.5)	**(±1.7)**	(±7.1)	(±2.9)	**(±2.9)**
Hispanic	10.2	12.3	**11.2**	3.7	12.3	**7.9**	6.6	13.1	**9.8**	10.8	20.6	**15.7**
	(±3.9)	(±3.8)	**(±3.2)**	(±2.0)	(±2.3)	**(±1.5)**	(±1.7)	(±3.1)	**(±2.1)**	(±2.1)	(±3.3)	**(±2.0)**
Grade												
9	7.9	6.2	**7.0**	3.0	11.4	**7.2**	8.4	12.6	**10.5**	12.7	24.3	**18.6**
	(±2.7)	(±1.9)	**(±1.7)**	(±1.7)	(±3.7)	**(±2.1)**	(±2.6)	(±3.2)	**(±1.9)**	(±2.5)	(±3.1)	**(±2.0)**
10	5.2	4.4	**4.8**	2.8	10.5	**6.6**	5.4	10.9	**8.2**	12.1	22.3	**17.2**
	(±1.9)	(±2.4)	**(±1.4)**	(±1.0)	(±3.1)	**(±1.6)**	(±1.5)	(±3.4)	**(±1.8)**	(±3.4)	(±3.3)	**(±2.4)**
11	4.3	4.6	**4.5**	2.9	11.1	**7.0**	5.1	7.0	**6.1**	7.1	14.4	**10.8**
	(±1.8)	(±2.3)	**(±1.8)**	(±1.4)	(±1.9)	**(±1.1)**	(±2.3)	(±1.5)	**(±1.0)**	(±2.3)	(±3.1)	**(±2.0)**
12	4.5	3.4	**3.9**	2.3	10.1	**6.2**	3.5	6.6	**5.1**	6.0	10.2	**8.1**
	(±2.2)	(±1.8)	**(±1.5)**	(±1.9)	(±2.8)	**(±1.6)**	(±1.8)	(±2.5)	**(±1.5)**	(±3.1)	(±2.5)	**(±1.9)**
Total	**5.7**	**4.8**	**5.2**	**2.8**	**11.0**	**6.9**	**5.8**	**9.5**	**7.7**	**9.8**	**18.5**	**14.2**
	(±1.5)	**(±1.6)**	**(±1.3)**	**(±0.7)**	**(±2.1)**	**(±1.2)**	**(±1.2)**	**(±1.6)**	**(±0.8)**	**(±1.9)**	**(±1.4)**	**(±1.3)**

[1] On ≥1 of the 30 days preceding the survey.
[2] For example, a gun, knife, or club.
[3] One or more times during the 12 months preceding the survey.
[4] Non-Hispanic.
[5] Ninety-five percent confidence interval.

SOURCE: Laura Kann, Steven A. Kinchen, Barbara I. Williams, James G. Ross, Richard Lowry, Jo Anne Grunbaum, and Lloyd J. Kolbe, "Table 10. Percentage of high school students who engaged in violence and in behaviors resulting from violence on school property, by sex, race/ethnicity, and grade - United States, Youth Risk Behavior Survey, 1999," in "Youth Risk Behavior Surveillance - United States, 1999 ," in *CDC Surveillance Summaries,* MMWR 2000, vol. 49, no. SS-5, June 9, 2000

blades, spiked jewelry, and other objects capable of inflicting harm. The 1999 "Youth Risk Behavior Surveillance" found that about 6.9 percent of students reported carrying a weapon of some type on school property during the 30 days before the survey. Males (11 percent) were far more likely than females (2.8 percent) to carry weapons at school. (See Table 6.15.)

In the *Report on State Implementation of the Gun-Free Schools Act 1998–99* (Karen Gray and Beth Sinclair, Westat, Rockville, MD, October 2000), the U.S. Department of Education found that fewer students were expelled for taking guns to school in 1998–99 than in the previous school year. Expulsions dropped by over 10 percent, from 3,930 in 1997–98 to 3,523 in 1998–99. Over half (57 percent) of the expulsions were at high schools, 33 percent were at junior high schools, and 10 percent were at elementary schools.

The U.S. Departments of Education and Justice report that during the late 1990s there was a steady decline in the proportion of high school students who reported carrying a weapon to school on one or more days during the previous month. Theft, vandalism, and physical fighting that did not involve a weapon were more common in schools than were more serious incidents.

Juvenile Victims

Youth ages 16 to 19 are in the highest risk categories for becoming victims of violent crimes. In 2000 persons in this age range were twice as likely as those ages 25 to 34 to be victims and three times as likely as persons ages 35 to 49. The Bureau of Justice publication *Criminal Victimization 2000* (Callie May Rennison, Washington, DC, June 2001) reported that 60.1 of every 1,000 12- to 15-year-olds were victims of violent crimes (excluding murder and manslaughter), as were 64.3 of every 1,000 16- to 19-year-olds. These rates were significantly higher than in older age groups (See Table 6.16).

In 1999 nearly 8 percent of the students surveyed reported that they had been threatened or injured with a weapon at school one or more times in the past 12 months. Males (9.5 percent) were more likely than females (5.8 percent) to report this behavior. More ninth graders (10.5 percent) than tenth graders (8.2 percent), eleventh graders (6.1 percent), and twelfth graders (5.1 percent) reported threats and injuries with weapons. (See Table 6.15.)

According to *Indicators of School Crime and Safety,* (Phillip Kaufman, et al., National Center for Education Statistics and U.S. Department of Justice, Washington,

TABLE 6.16

Rates of violent crime and personal theft, by gender, age, race, and Hispanic origin, 2000

[Victimizations per 1,000 persons age 12 or older]

Characteristic of victim	Population	Violent crimes						Per-sonal theft
		All	Rape/ sexual assault	Robbery	Assault			
					Total	Aggra-vated	Simple	
Gender								
Male	109,816,970	32.9	0.1*	4.5	28.3	8.3	19.9	1.0
Female	116,987,650	23.2	2.1	2.0	19.0	3.2	15.8	1.4
Age								
12-15	16,064,090	60.1	2.1	4.2	53.8	9.9	43.9	1.8
16-19	16,001,650	64.3	4.3	7.3	52.7	14.3	38.3	3.0
20-24	18,587,790	49.4	2.1	6.2	41.2	10.9	30.3	1.1*
25-34	37,757,070	34.8	1.3	3.9	29.5	6.8	22.7	1.5
35-49	64,927,820	21.8	0.8	2.7	18.4	4.7	13.7	0.9
50-64	40,764,000	13.7	0.4*	2.1	11.1	2.8	8.4	0.5*
65 or older	32,702,210	3.7	0.1*	0.7*	2.9	0.9	2.0	1.2
Race								
White	189,308,050	27.1	1.1	2.7	23.3	5.4	17.9	1.1
Black	27,978,180	35.3	1.2	7.2	26.9	7.7	19.2	1.9
Other	9,518,390	20.7	1.1*	2.8	16.7	5.2	11.5	1.8*
Hispanic origin								
Hispanic	24,513,290	28.4	0.5*	5.0	23.0	5.6	17.4	2.4
Non-Hispanic	200,294,810	27.7	1.2	3.0	23.5	5.7	17.8	1.1

NOTE: The National Crime Victimization Survey includes as violent crime rape, sexual assault, robbery, and assault. Because the NCVS interviews persons about their victimizations, murder and manslaughter cannot be included.
* Based on 10 or fewer sample cases.

SOURCE: Callie Marie Rennison, "Table 2. Rates of violent crime and personal theft, by gender, age, race, and Hispanic origin, 2000," in *Criminal Victimization 2000: Changes 1999–2000 with Trends 1993–2000*, U.S. Department of Justice, Bureau of Justice Statistics, Washington, DC, June 2001

DC, October 2001), students ages 12 to 18 were victims of more than 2.5 million total crimes at school. About one-third of high school students said that someone stole or deliberately damaged their property on school grounds during the last year, and nearly 5 percent of students ages 12 to 18 reported that they had been bullied at school in the six months before they were surveyed. However, the proportion of students who reported avoiding at least one place at school for their own safety dropped from 9 percent to 5 percent during the 1990s, and students were two times as likely to be victims of serious violent crime while away from school than while at school.

CHAPTER 7

ISSUES IN EDUCATION

Schools, like other institutions, face various issues as they grow and attempt to meet the needs of an ever-changing population. In the nineteenth century the common school movement sought to establish education for all, to be paid for by property taxes. In the early twentieth century, school advocates debated questions of whether school should be compulsory, whether teachers should use corporal punishment, the best way to train teachers, and centralization. During the post-World War II "baby boom," concerns included building enough schools and educating enough teachers to fill the need. During the 1960s and beyond, schools faced the challenges of integration and busing. Later came sex and drug education and the role of religion in the classroom.

Today, our schools continue to face enduring problems and new challenges. Some of the topics under discussion are diversity, school facilities, higher standards, assessment, accountability, school governance, school-choice programs, school funding, safety, discipline, and the role of educational technology. There is no clear consensus on how to approach these and other issues, but voters do believe educational topics are important.

SCHOOL-REFORM MOVEMENTS

In 1957 the "space race" began when the Soviet Union launched Sputnik I, the first satellite sent into space. To prevent the nation from falling behind in the technology competition, American leaders called for improved educational techniques and student performance. In 1983, the Ronald Reagan Administration released *A Nation at Risk* (National Commission on Excellence in Education, Washington, DC), a report on education in the United States. Instead of responding to the 1957 challenge to raise standards, the report claimed that American education had produced students who actually were scoring lower on performance tests than in 1957. The writers of the report feared that the nation would become less competitive in world markets, causing the economy to suffer.

The report recommended that American education, especially in high school, should primarily focus on academic achievement, with students spending more time in school and working on homework. As a result, most states raised graduation requirements, revised programs of testing and evaluation, and improved teacher preparation standards.

Demands for reform continued in 1986 with eight new reports on the state of American education, including *Time for Results* (National Governors' Association, Washington, DC), *A Nation Prepared: Teachers for the 21st Century* (Carnegie Forum on Education and the Economy, Washington, DC), and *What Next? More Leverage for Teachers* (Education Commission of the States, Denver, CO). These publications focused on strategies to improve education including teacher training and salaries, state initiatives to reform education, and school choice. The states followed many of the reports' recommendations, especially in the areas of recruiting and preparing teachers, and in restructuring the organization and management of their school systems.

At the Education Summit held in Charlottesville, Virginia, in 1989, President George Bush and the state governors established six National Education Goals to be met by the year 2000. In 1994 Congress passed the Goals 2000: Educate America Act (PL 103-227), reemphasizing the National Education Goals and adding two more goals. These goals presented a broad approach to education reform, including more parental involvement, improvement in nutrition and health care for preschool children, and improved adult education. Progress toward the goals has been slow.

Four years later, Congress passed the Charter School Expansion Act of 1998 (PL 105-278), which authorizes

TABLE 7.1

Source of primary control for various charter school decisions and operations, by area of control

| Area of control | Source of primary control | | | |
	School	District/charter granting agency	Both	Other
	Percentage of schools (%)			
Budget	72.9	19.4	0.3	7.4
Purchase of supplies/equipment	87.8	7.6	0.2	4.5
School calendar	76.8	19.6	0.1	3.5
Daily schedule	94.8	2.9	0.2	2.2
Student assessment policies	71.5	19.7	0.6	8.2
Student admissions policies	59.4	27.8	0.7	12.0
Student discipline	87.3	9.0	0.1	3.6
Establishment of curriculum	83.2	11.3	0.2	5.3
Hiring of teaching staff	87.5	7.4	0.3	4.8

NOTE: These data are based on responses from between 972 and 975 of the 975 open charter schools that responded to the survey. Schools were asked to rate each of these items separately, resulting in the range of responses. Up to three schools answered "don't know" for certain items. Most responses in the "other" category include the management company, the state legislature, and parents.

SOURCE: Beryl Nelson, Paul Berman, John Ericson, et al., "Estimated Percentage of Charter Schools by Source of Primary Control for Various School Decisions and Operations," in *The State of Charter Schools 2000: Fourth-Year Report*, U.S. Department of Education, Office of Educational Research and Improvement, Washington, DC, January 2000

state educational agencies (SEAs) to use federal funds for planning, designing, and implementing public charter schools, and requires local education agencies (LEAs) to use innovative assistance funds for the same purpose. Funding priorities are based on a state's progress in increasing its number of high quality charter schools. The act extends the authorization of appropriations for fiscal years (FY) 1999 through 2003.

The Education Flexibility Partnership Act of 1999 (PL 106-25) gives states more freedom in how they spend federal education dollars. To participate in the Ed-Flex Partnership program, states must apply to the Secretary of Education for a waiver from the normal requirements for obtaining federal funds. They may then set up their own programs under which they would be held accountable for improved educational results in order to receive continued funding. For example, schools could use federal money intended for science and mathematics teachers on reading programs to boost progress in that area.

The following sections describe some of the approaches developed in recent years with the intent of improving education.

CHARTER SCHOOLS

In 1991 only one charter school existed in the United States. By 2001 nearly three-quarters (37) of the states, the District of Columbia and Puerto Rico had authorized charter schools. In charter schools, teachers, parents, administrators, community groups, or private corporations design and operate a local school under charter (written contract) from a school district, state education agency, or other public institution. These local schools often have a specific focus, such as mathematics, arts, or science. In some cases, charter schools are nearly autonomous (self-directing) and are exempt from many state and district education rules. In other cases, the schools operate much like traditional public schools and must apply for certain exemptions, which may or may not be granted.

In 1998–99, according to *The State of Charter Schools 2000* (Beryl Nelson, et al., U.S. Department of Education, Washington, DC, 2000), most charter schools had primary control over administrative operations, such as purchase of supplies and equipment (87.7 percent), hiring of teachers (87.5 percent), and budget (72.9 percent). In addition, the majority had primary control over their education programs: daily schedule (94.8 percent), discipline (87.3 percent), curriculum (83.2 percent), school calendar (76.8 percent), and student assessment policies (71.5 percent). A lower percentage, yet still a majority (59.4 percent), of charter schools reported primary control over their student admissions policies. When charter schools were not given primary control, the district, the charter-granting agency, or another source had primary authority. (See Table 7.1.)

Many states find charter schools appealing. Four common reasons noted for considering alternatives such as charter schools are overcrowded classrooms, district mismanagement or disorganization, low scores on standardized tests, and a high number of students at risk of dropping out of school. In Arizona, charter schools on Indian reservations use the system to maintain their native languages and customs.

Charter schools are held accountable for school and student outcomes. Because state legislation and regulatory

FIGURE 7.1

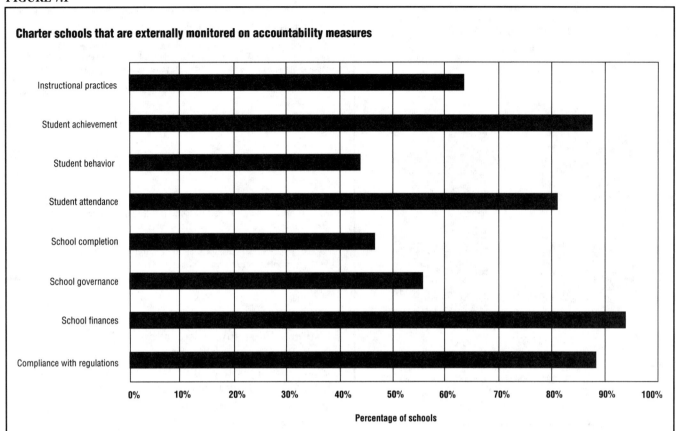

Charter schools that are externally monitored on accountability measures

Percentage of schools

SOURCE: Beryl Nelson, Paul Berman, John Ericson, et al., "Estimated Percentage of Charter Schools that are Externally Monitored on Accountability Measures," in *The State of Charter Schools 2000: Fourth-Year Report,* U.S. Department of Education, Office of Educational Research and Improvement, Washington, DC, January 2000

practices differ greatly by state, charter schools report varying amounts of external monitoring. According to *The State of Charter Schools 2000,* the schools surveyed received external monitoring in the areas of school finance (94 percent), compliance with state or federal regulations (88 percent), student achievement (87 percent), and school attendance (81 percent). In other areas such as student behavior and school governance, there was a wider variation in monitoring among the states. (See Figure 7.1.)

Charter schools that target special populations such as at-risk students are increasingly popular. These schools may focus on nontraditional teaching and learning experiences, such as combining academics with work experience or changing the class structure. Some states require a specific number of charter schools to serve this special population.

Funding for charter schools varies widely, ranging from direct state funding to funding through the local school district. In fiscal year 1998 the federal budget appropriated $80 million for charter schools. In 2001 Secretary of Education Rod Paige announced $182 million to support charter school programs. Nearly half ($89 mil-

lion) was awarded in new three-year charter school grants for Arizona, California, Colorado, Georgia, Indiana, Louisiana, Massachusetts, Michigan, Minnesota, Missouri, Nevada, Ohio, Rhode Island, and Texas.

Impact of Charter Schools on Districts

Challenge and Opportunity: The Impact of Charter Schools on School Districts (John Ericson, et al., U.S. Department of Education, Washington, DC, June 2001) presented the results of a study of 274 charter schools in Arizona, California, Colorado, Massachusetts, and Michigan. About half (47 percent) of district leaders reported that charter schools had no impact on the district budget, and half (45 percent) said charter schools had a negative impact. Eight percent of district leaders perceived a positive impact, noting that although enrollment revenues were lost, costs to the district were also less.

Nearly all (94 percent) participants reported that charter schools affected the district's central office. Activities included student tracking and increased customer service. Some reported downsizing due to decreased revenues. The majority (62 percent) of districts said they had made

FIGURE 7.2

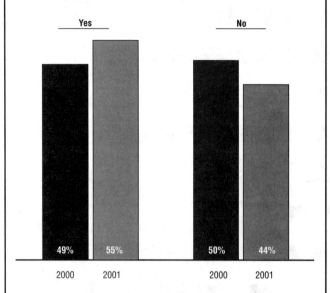

Public awareness of charter schools, 2000–01

Percent answering "yes" or "no" when asked whether they had read or heard about charter schools

Yes	No
2000	2001	2000	2001
49%	55%	50%	44%

SOURCE: Lowell C. Rose and Alec M. Gallup, "Figure 4. Awareness of Charter Schools," in "The 33rd Annual Phi Delta Kappa/Gallup Poll of the Public's Attitude Toward the Public Schools," *Phi Delta Kappan*, vol. 83, no. 1, September 2001

TABLE 7.2

Opinion about the idea of charter schools, 2000–01

As you may know, charter schools operate under a charter or contract that frees them from many of the state regulations imposed on public schools and permits them to operate independently. Do you favor or oppose the idea of charter schools?

| | National totals | | Public school parents | |
	'01 %	'00 %	'01 %	'00 %
Favor	42	42	43	40
Oppose	49	47	47	47
Don't know	9	11	10	13

SOURCE: Lowell C. Rose and Alec M. Gallup, "As you may know, charter schools operate under a charter or contract that frees them from many of the state regulations imposed on public schools and permits them to operate independently. Do you favor or oppose the idea of charter schools?" in "The 33rd Annual Phi Delta Kappa/Gallup Poll of the Public's Attitude Toward the Public Schools," *Phi Delta Kappan*, vol. 83, no. 1, September 2001

changes in the educational offerings in response to the presence of charter schools, including adding new programs and changing curriculum structure.

The Public Has Mixed Feelings

In the "33rd Annual Phi Delta Kappa/Gallup Poll of the Public's Attitude Toward the Public Schools," survey respondents were asked if they had read or heard about charter schools. More than half (55 percent) of those surveyed in 2001 said they had, which was an increase of about 6 percent over the 2000 results. (See Figure 7.2.) When asked whether they supported or opposed the idea of charter schools, about half (49 percent) of the public opposed the idea of charter schools in 2001, while 42 percent favored the idea, and 9 percent were uncertain. (See Table 7.2.)

For-Profit Schools

In some cases school boards and state education offices have turned to "privatizing" their schools, contracting with private corporations to administer one or more local schools. In 2001 the state of Pennsylvania passed a school reform plan to take control of Philadelphia's public schools, privatize the district's leadership positions, and place school operations in the hands of church, business and other community groups.

Contracts for privatizing services are usually awarded based on bids submitted by the education companies. In general, teachers' unions oppose privatizing schools. The National Education Association (NEA) stated in their 2000–01 resolutions that they opposed education for profit, because there is an inherent conflict between serving the needs of children and serving the needs of stockholders in an educational setting.

The Edison Project

Private, for-profit companies run an estimated 10 percent of all charter schools. By 2001 the Edison Project, the largest private manager of public schools in the country, operated 136 schools in 22 states, with an enrollment of over 75,000 students. Its program is based on extensive use of high technology, a longer school day and year, and a full-day kindergarten that has an academic program.

In the *Fourth Annual Report on School Performance* (Edison schools, New York, September 2001), the company states that 84 percent of Edison schools were performing at a higher level than before they were privatized. During the 2000–01 school year, 64 percent of students at Edison Schools were African American, 17 percent were Hispanic, and 16 percent were white. Most (70 percent) were eligible for free or reduced-price lunch. Edison parents were satisfied with their schools. The turnover of teachers was 17 percent in 2000–01.

Are For-Profit Schools Improving Student Performance?

In the 1998 AFT (American Federation of Teachers) *Report on Student Achievement in the Edison Schools* (Washington, DC), researchers studied Edison schools in 1997–98. They reported that the Edison schools utilized a widely admired reading program for elementary students, that they tended to have motivated parents involved, and that they attracted donations from outside organizations in addition to public funding. However, they also contended that class size and teacher turnover rates tend to be high and that years of teaching experience tend to be low. In addition, the report noted that Edison does not measure or report performance in the same way that regular public schools do, but instead presents only the most favorable comparisons and test score gains.

In *A Guide to Recent Studies of School Effectiveness by the Edison Project and the American Federation of Teachers* (Harvard University, Cambridge, MA, May 1998), Paul E. Peterson conducted a review of Edison's 1997 *Annual Report,* as well as the AFT report. He stated that the evidence, although not definitive, supported Edison's claims that they were providing more effective schools than were available otherwise to students in those communities.

Gary Miron and Brooks Applegate compared students at 10 Edison Schools with a group of similar students at other schools in *An Evaluation of Student Achievement at Edison Schools Opened in 1995 and 1996* (Western Michigan University, Kalamazoo, MI, December 2000). They concluded that the trends in achievement scores were mixed. The majority of Edison students were achieving at the levels no different than students in the comparison group.

SCHOOL CHOICE AND VOUCHERS

"School choice" allows students to attend schools other than the designated neighborhood school. Families who can afford to move to an area with high-performing schools or send their children to private schools already have school choice; less wealthy families generally do not. The major debate over school choice is whether or not parents should receive some kind of financial assistance from the state or local government to pay school fees if they elect to send their children to private schools.

Should Parents Choose Schools?

Parents generally influence which schools their children attend, often locating in an area known for excellent schools. The U.S. Supreme Court, in *Pierce v. Society of Sisters* (286 U.S. 510, 1925), upheld parents' constitutional right to select a church- affiliated or private school. Because "the child is not the mere creature of the state," parents cannot be forced to send their children to public schools. A family is free to choose private education or to leave one school district for another in which it believes the public schools are better. In reality many people are limited by financial and social restrictions, and moving to another district or enrolling their children in private school may not be possible without financial help.

Minnesota introduced the first school-choice program in 1987. Since then, about three-fifths of the states have instituted "choice" plans of one sort or another. The plans usually follow one of three models:

- The *district-wide* model allows parents to select a public school within their district. Often, the district establishes specialty or "magnet" schools (those offering an emphasis on a particular subject area, such as business, science, or the arts) to attract students to different schools.

- The *statewide* model permits students to attend public schools outside their home districts, depending on available space, desegregation requirements, and the students' ability to travel. Typically, when a school district loses students, it also loses state funding, so this plan may not appeal to many school districts.

- The *private school* model, known as the voucher or scholarship plan, is the most controversial. This model allows parents to use public funds to send their children to private schools. Presently only a few school districts offer a voucher plan.

Vouchers—Pro and Con

Since about 1990 voucher plans have become a hotly debated political issue. Those favoring voucher programs consider them an equitable means of helping low-income families provide their children with better education. Voucher programs emphasize educational choices rather than requirements dictated by the government. In addition many believe increased competition will cause public schools to improve or face closure.

Those opposing vouchers believe the plans would only help a few students, leaving most low-income students behind in schools with reduced community commitment. Critics maintain that vouchers weaken public schools by diverting resources from them. The debate becomes even more heated when voucher supporters advocate allowing students to attend religious schools with public voucher funds. A major dimension of that debate concerns whether the use of vouchers at religiously affiliated private schools would violate the First Amendment by directly supporting religious institutions, or whether vouchers avoid such violations by supporting only the children.

Vouchers and the Law

State-enacted voucher programs exist in Milwaukee, Cleveland, and Florida, and all three have undergone or are still involved in court challenges. In June 2001 Florida lawmakers approved a plan to give students in the state's lowest performing schools taxpayer-funded tuition payments to attend qualified public, private, or religious schools.

The Court of Appeals for the 6th circuit in Ohio concluded in December 2000 there was probable cause that the Cleveland voucher program, which gives low-income students scholarships to attend private secular or religious schools, violated the constitutional separation of church

TABLE 7.3

Private school choice at public expense

Do you favor or oppose allowing students and parents to choose a private school to attend at public expense?

	National Totals						
	'01 %	'00 %	'99 %	'98 %	'97 %	'96 %	'95 %
Favor	34	39	41	44	44	36	33
Oppose	62	56	55	50	52	61	65
Don't know	4	5	4	6	4	3	2

SOURCE: Lowell C. Rose and Alec M. Gallup, "Do you favor or oppose allowing students and parents to choose a private school to attend at public expense?," in "The 33rd Annual Phi Delta Kappa/Gallup Poll of the Public's Attitude Toward the Public Schools," in *Phi Delta Kappan*, September 2001

TABLE 7.4

Adoption of the voucher system

In the voucher system, parents are given a voucher which can be used to pay all the tuition for attendance at a private or church-related school. Parents can then choose any private school, church-related school, or public school for their child. If a parent chooses a public school, the voucher would not apply. Would you favor or oppose the adoption of the voucher system in your state?

	Teachers %	Public %
Favor	17	47
Oppose	76	48
Don't know	7	5

SOURCE: Carol A. Langdon and Nick Vesper, "In the voucher system, parents are given a voucher which can be used to pay all the tuition for attendance at a private or church-related school. Parents can then choose any private school, church-related school, or public school for their child. If a parent chooses a public school, the voucher would not apply. Would you favor or oppose the use of the voucher program in your state?," in "The Sixth Phi Delta Kappa Poll of Teachers' Attitudes Toward the Public Schools, in *Phi Delta Kappan*, vol. 81, no. 8, April 2000

and state and would be found unconstitutional. The court rejected arguments that the Cleveland vouchers were a neutral form of aid to parents that only indirectly benefited religious schools. The ruling was appealed to the U.S. Supreme Court by the state of Ohio as well as by a group of voucher parents and by several religious schools participating in the program, which has continued to operate pending the further appeals. The court accepted all three petitions for review but said it would treat them as one case. A decision is expected by July 2002.

The Wisconsin Supreme Court, in *Jackson v. Benson* (218 Wis.2d 835, 578 N.W.2d 602), ruled that inclusion of religious schools in the Milwaukee Parental Choice Program does not violate U.S. federal or Wisconsin state constitutional prohibitions against government support of religion. The U.S Supreme Court declined to review the case (119 S. Ct. 467, 1998).

In two related cases (*Bagley v. Raymond School Department*, 1999 Me. 60 and *Strout v. Albanese*, No. 98-1986, 1999) brought by parents who wanted reimbursement for the cost of religious schools, the Supreme Judicial Court of Maine and the U.S. Court of Appeals for the 1st Circuit ruled that inclusion of religious schools in the tuitioning program would be unconstitutional. Maine's "tuitioning" law allows reimbursements to families that send their children from districts lacking public schools to secular private schools. Appeals to the U.S. Supreme Court were filed in both cases. In October 1999 the Court declined without comment or a recorded vote to review either case.

The Arizona Supreme Court, in *Kotterman v. Killian* (972 P.2d 606), upheld the state program allowing a tax credit of up to $500 for individuals making charitable contributions to "school tuition organizations" that provide scholarships to private schools, including religious schools. In October 1999 the U.S. Supreme Court denied review (68 LW 3232).

Do Americans Support School Choice?

The 33rd Annual Phi Delta Kappa/Gallup Poll asked if respondents favored or opposed allowing students and parents to choose a private school at public expense. The poll found that most (62 percent) Americans do not support allowing parents to choose private schools and receive financial assistance from public funds in order to do so. In 2001 more than one-third (34 percent) of the survey respondents favored publicly supported school choice. (See Table 7.3.) "The Sixth Phi Delta Kappa Poll of Teachers' Attitudes Toward the Public Schools," conducted in 2000, found that when asked if they favored a voucher program that covered tuition for attendance at any private, church-related, or public school, more than three-quarters (76 percent) of teachers opposed vouchers. Among the general public, results were mixed. About half (48 percent) opposed the adoption of a voucher system in their state, and the remaining half (47 percent) favored the idea. (See Table 7.4.)

HOME SCHOOLING

In the 1970s a number of parents, unhappy with public schools, began teaching their children at home. In 1990 the Home School Legal Defense Association (HSLDA) in Paeonian Springs, Virginia, estimated that about 474,000 school-aged children were being taught at home. (The HSLDA provides legal counsel for home-schooling families.) According to *Homeschooling in the United States* (Stacey Bielick, Kathryn Chandler and Stephen P. Broughman, U.S. Department of Education, Washington, DC, July 2001), about 850,000 students in the United States were being home-schooled in 1999, which is about 1.7 percent of American children.

State Requirements

Home schools are now legal in all 50 states, but states vary widely in the way they govern home schooling.

FIGURE 7.3

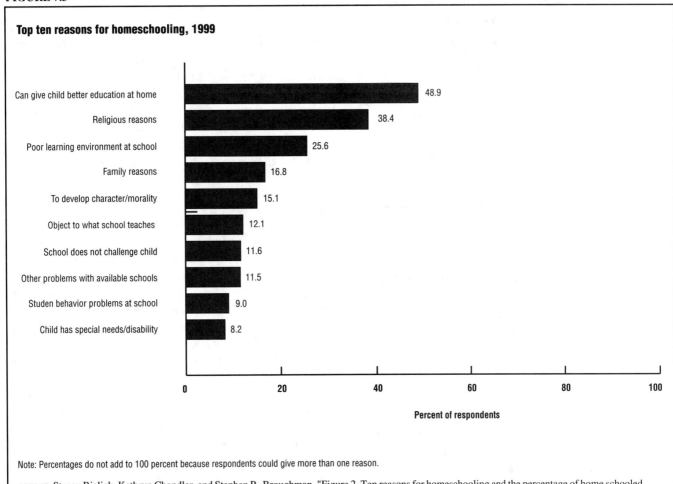

Top ten reasons for homeschooling, 1999

Reason	Percent
Can give child better education at home	48.9
Religious reasons	38.4
Poor learning environment at school	25.6
Family reasons	16.8
To develop character/morality	15.1
Object to what school teaches	12.1
School does not challenge child	11.6
Other problems with available schools	11.5
Studen behavior problems at school	9.0
Child has special needs/disability	8.2

Percent of respondents

Note: Percentages do not add to 100 percent because respondents could give more than one reason.

SOURCE: Stacey Bielick, Kathryn Chandler, and Stephen P. Broughman, "Figure 2. Ten reasons for homeschooling and the percentage of home schooled students whose parents gave each reason," in *Homeschooling in the United States: 1999* NCES 2001-033, U.S. Department of Education, National Center for Educational Statistics, Washington, DC, July 2001

Because all states' laws require school attendance, the states have jurisdiction over home schools. Some states have set up elaborate requirements for home schools, while others have taken a "hands-off" approach.

Three states—New York, Ohio, and Texas—illustrate the wide variance in home school requirements.

NEW YORK. New York has established extensive requirements for home schools. Elementary-age students must spend 900 hours per year in class, and those in grades seven through twelve must be in class 990 hours per year. The teacher must be "competent" (no specific credentials required), and each year, the superintendent of local schools must receive advance notice of the intent to home-school. Records of attendance and assessment (including standardized tests) must be filed with the superintendent at specified times. Curriculum is specified by grade level and includes the basics, plus eight other subjects, such as American and New York history, music and art, health, and physical education. Students instructed at home are not awarded high school diplomas.

OHIO. Ohio requires students to spend 900 hours per year in class, and the home-school teacher must have a high school diploma or equivalent. Each year, advance notice of intent to home-school and assessment of student performance must be filed with the superintendent of schools. The assessment can be standardized test scores, a written description of progress, or another approved form of assessment. No attendance records are required. The state specifies which subjects must be taught, including the basics and other topics, such as first aid, fine arts, health, and government.

TEXAS. Texas has very few requirements for home schools, considering them private schools (which are not regulated by the state). The state requires no teacher certification, no advance notice, and no testing or attendance records. The only specified subjects are reading, spelling, grammar, mathematics, and good citizenship. Texas does not award diplomas to students that are home-schooled.

Reasons for Home Schooling

Parents give many reasons for home schooling their children. *Homeschooling in the United States,* citing

TABLE 7.5

State and national assessment testing of home-schooled children

Would you favor or oppose requiring children who are schooled at home to take all the state and national assessment tests that public school students are required to take?

	Teachers %	Public %
Favor	94	92
Oppose	4	7
Don't know	2	1

SOURCE: Carol A. Langdon and Nick Vesper, "Would you favor or oppose requiring children who are schooled at home to take all the state and national assessment tests that public school students are required to take?," in "The Sixth Phi Delta Kappa Poll of Teachers' Attitudes Toward the Public Schools, in *Phi Delta Kappan,* vol. 81, no. 8, April 2000

results from the Parent Survey of the National Household Education Surveys Program, reported that almost half (49 percent) of parents who home-schooled their children believed they could provide a better education at home, 38 percent did it for religious reasons, and more than one-quarter (25.6 percent) felt there was a poor learning environment at school. (See Figure 7.3.)

Profile of Average Home School Family

According to *Homeschooling in the United States,* in 1999 the average home school student was more likely to live with two or more siblings in a two-parent family with only one parent working outside the home. A greater proportion of home school parents had college degrees, although their incomes were about the same as other parents.

Public Opinion About Home Schools

Americans are somewhat uncertain about home schools, although opposition has been decreasing. The Phi Delta Kappa/Gallup Poll first asked about home schools in 1985 and found that 73 percent of those polled felt home schools were a bad thing. By 2001 opposition had declined to 59 percent. In 2000 the majority (92 percent) of those polled believed that home schooled students should take all the state and national assessment tests that public school students are required to take. (See Table 7.5.) Responses to other questions were more divided. Half of the public believed that home schooling did not contribute to raising academic standards, while 43 percent thought that it did. Nearly half (49 percent) believed home schooling did not promote good citizenship; 46 percent believed that it did.

RELIGION IN PUBLIC SCHOOLS

The First Amendment issue of the separation of church and state is one of the most widely debated constitutional issues. During the past two decades, controversy has swirled around school prayer, religious baccalaureate services, and other exercises of religious belief within public schools.

The church/state separation clause in the First Amendment was intended to prohibit the establishment of a state religion or the coercion of citizens to belong to a particular group, either religious or anti-religious. Contrary to popular belief, the Supreme Court's interpretations of First Amendment rights do not prohibit the private expression of religion in the public school. They do not prevent students from praying at school or in the classroom, so long as these activities do not disrupt the school's normal order or instruction. A student may pray either silently or quietly aloud whenever he or she is not actively participating in school activities, such as recitation in class. For example, students may not decide to pray aloud just as the teacher calls on them for an answer in class.

On the other hand, a student may not attempt to turn a class or meeting into a captive audience for a religious service. Public school officials may not legally require prayers during the school day, make them a part of graduation exercises, or organize religious baccalaureate services. Teachers and school administrators may not participate in, encourage, or insist upon student religious or anti-religious activities while they are acting in their capacities as representatives of the state. Doing so could be interpreted as coercion or as the establishment of a particular group as a state-sanctioned religion, something that violates the First Amendment. Teachers and other school personnel may exercise private religious activity within the boundaries of the First Amendment in faculty lounges or private offices.

Public schools may teach about religion, but they cannot give religious instruction. The study of the Bible and other religious scriptures is permissible as part of literature, history, and social studies classes so that students can understand the contribution of religious ideas and groups to the nation's culture. Students may express their personal religious beliefs in reports, homework, or artwork so long as these meet the goals of the assignments and are appropriate to the topics assigned.

The separation of church and state is very clear in some areas, but can be very ambiguous in others. For example, one of the biggest issues surrounding school vouchers is whether or not state funds, generated from taxes, can be used to pay tuition at parochial schools. The Wisconsin State Supreme Court, among others, has ruled that doing so would be an unconstitutional mingling of church and state. However, the U.S. Supreme Court seems to have changed its stance on the necessity for a rigid barrier between public schools and parochial schools. Five justices criticized a 1985 finding in *Aguilar v. Felton* (473 U.S. 402), which ruled that sending public school teachers to parochial schools to conduct remedial classes was unconstitutional.

In 1997 the Court reheard the case, a most unusual procedure. A 5-4 divided U.S. Supreme Court, in *Agosti-*

TABLE 7.6

Opinion about faith-based or religious organizations receiving public tax money for providing after-school programs designed to improve students' academic performance, May–June 2001

	National Totals %	No Children In School %	Public School Parents %
Yes, should	62	58	70
No, should not	35	39	29
Don't know	3	3	1

SOURCE: Lowell C. Rose and Alec M. Gallup, "In your opinion, should faith-based or religious organizations receive public tax money for providing after-school programs designed to improve students' academic performance?" in "The 33rd Annual Phi Delta Kappa/Gallup Poll of the Public's Attitude Toward the Public Schools," *Phi Delta Kappan*, vol. 83, no. 1, September 2001

ni v. Felton (65 LW 4524, 1997), ruled that "*Aguilar* [is] no longer good law." In reversing *Aguilar,* the court declared that

> A federally funded program providing supplemental, remedial instruction to disadvantaged children on a neutral basis is not invalid under the Establishment Clause when such instruction is given on the premises of sectarian schools by government employees pursuant to a program containing safeguards ... this carefully constrained program also cannot reasonably be viewed as an endorsement of religion.... The mere circumstance that [an aid recipient] has chosen to use neutrally available state aid to help pay for [a] religious education [does not] confer any message of state endorsement of religion.

Specifically, the Court decided that Title I instructional services may be provided by public school teachers in private schools. Some observers believe the decision may help define future cases concerning state and religion, especially those involving vouchers that could be used to pay for tuition at religion-oriented schools.

A Constitutional Amendment on School Prayer?

Many U.S. Congressmen have proposed legislation to amend the constitution specifically to allow prayer in public schools. To date, none of the proposals has passed, but some legislators continue trying. In June 1998 the U.S. House voted for the first time since 1971 on a constitutional amendment to restore voluntary school prayer. The measure, the Religious Freedom Amendment, had a majority of voters but not the two-thirds needed to amend the Constitution.

Most Americans support the idea of a constitutional amendment. In a 2001 Gallup poll, 78 percent favored a constitutional amendment to permit prayer in the public schools. When asked about their preferences in terms of types of prayer, 16 percent favored spoken prayer, 50 percent preferred a moment of silence or silent prayer, 21 percent supported both, and 12 percent supported neither.

Support for Faith-Based Organizations Providing Services

As part of his education agenda, President George W. Bush proposed using tax dollars to support afterschool programs designed to improve academic performance, provided by faith-based and religious organizations. When asked by the 33rd Annual Phi Delta Kappa/Gallup Poll, the majority (62 percent) of the public favored the idea. This proposal enjoys even stronger support among public school parents (70 percent). (See Table 7.6.)

TECHNOLOGY IN AMERICAN SCHOOLS

Computers have become common in American schools. According to the U.S. Department of Education, in 1999 the majority of public elementary (92 percent) and secondary (80 percent) teachers reported that students used computers at school. More than three-quarters (78 percent) of teachers indicated that students used computers in a lab or media center at school, and over two-thirds (69 percent) reported students had computers in the classroom, although only about one-quarter (28 percent and 26 percent, respectively) described student use in these settings as occurring "often" or "sometimes," while 13 to 14 percent characterized it as happening "rarely." (See Figure 7.4.)

Home Computers for Teachers and Other Adults

From 1994 to 1998 more schoolteachers than adults in other occupations reported having computers at home, but there were significant increases in home computer use among both groups. In 1994 more than half (54 percent) of teachers reported having a home computer, while just over one-quarter (28 percent) of adults in other occupations had a computer in their homes. These proportions increased to 74 percent for teachers and 46 percent for other adults in 1998. (See Figure 7.5.)

Internet Access at School

From 1994 to 1999 there were large increases in the proportion of schools with Internet access. In 1994 over one-third (35 percent) of public schools had Internet access; by 1999 this proportion had increased to 95 percent. (See Figure 7.6.)

More than half (56 percent) of elementary teachers, and nearly three-quarters (72 percent) of secondary teachers indicated that students used the Internet while at school in 1999. About one-third (34 percent) of teachers reported that students used the Internet while in the classroom, while 55 percent of teachers described students' Internet use as taking place in the library or a computer lab. (See Figure 7.4.)

Distance Learning for Elementary and Secondary Students

According to "Florida Clicks Into The Future, Offers An Online High School" (Susan Ferrechio, *The*

FIGURE 7.4

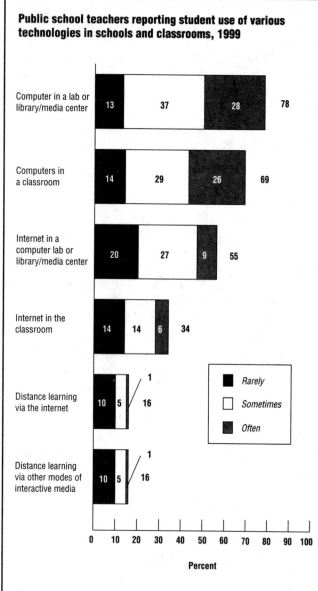

Public school teachers reporting student use of various technologies in schools and classrooms, 1999

Computer in a lab or library/media center — 13 | 37 | 28 | 78

Computers in a classroom — 14 | 29 | 26 | 69

Internet in a computer lab or library/media center — 20 | 27 | 9 | 55

Internet in the classroom — 14 | 14 | 6 | 34

Distance learning via the internet — 10 | 5 | 1 | 16

Distance learning via other modes of interactive media — 10 | 5 | 1 | 16

■ Rarely
□ Sometimes
■ Often

Percent

Note: Teachers who reported that computers were not available to them in the classroom were excluded from the analyses presented in this figure. Detail may not sum to totals due to rounding.

SOURCE: Becky Smerdon, Stephanie Cronen, Lawrence Lanahan, et al., "Figure 4.8. Percent of Public School Teachers Reporting Student Use of Various Technologies in Schools and Classrooms: 1999," in *Teachers' Tools for the 21st Century: A Report on Teachers' Use of Technology,* NCES 2000-102, U.S. Department of Education, National Center for Education Statistics, Washington, DC, September 2000

Miami Herald, April 15, 2001, p. 1BR), in 2001 nine states—California, Florida, Indiana, Kentucky, Massachusetts, Nebraska, Hawaii, Colorado, and Utah—offered some online courses for high school students. However, only about 16 percent of teachers surveyed by the U.S. Department of Education reported that students participated in distance learning via the Internet or other modes of interactive media, and 10 percent described student distance learning activities as occurring "rarely." (See Figure 7.4.)

The 33rd Annual Phi Delta Kappa/Gallup Poll asked whether respondents approved of earning high school credits over the Internet. More than two-thirds (67 percent) disapproved of this sort of instruction in cyberspace.

BILINGUAL EDUCATION

In 1997-98 four states—California, Florida, New York, and Texas—had greater than 200,000 students with limited English proficiency. Two others, Illinois and New Mexico, enrolled between 100,000 and 200,000 students who are considered limited English proficient (LEP) in public schools. (See Figure 7.7.) When first adopted, bilingual education was intended to offer better education to students (usually poor and recently immigrated to this country) who did not speak English. By instructing these students in their native languages—and teaching them English at the same time—they would overcome the language barriers to successful school achievement. Many observers still believe that children in bilingual programs acquire English at least as well as, and usually better than, children in all-English programs. In recent years, however, bilingual education has come under fire for failing to deliver the expected benefits.

While it is difficult to measure the effectiveness of bilingual education, some observers suggest that students in bilingual classes do not learn English more quickly and do not achieve better test scores. Some students do not participate in bilingual education, even when it is offered. And in many school districts, there is a shortage of bilingual teachers. In California, only 30 percent of its LEP (limited English proficient) students were in bilingual classes due to a shortage of bilingual teachers.

California Ends Bilingual Education Programs

The debate as to the effectiveness of bilingual education has led many critics to propose ending bilingual programs. In June 1998 California voters passed Proposition 227, which requires that public school students who cannot speak English be placed in a one-year English immersion course instead of in bilingual education. About 1.4 million of California's 5 million public school students are limited English proficient (LEP), nearly half (45 percent) the total number of LEP students in the United States.

Los Angeles teachers soon began reporting that their LEP students were learning English more quickly than anticipated after the ban on bilingual education. However, they questioned whether these students had acquired the language skills necessary to understand mathematics, reading, or history lessons taught in English. They also worried that these students would not be ready to enter mainstream English classes within one year.

When California reported its standardized testing scores in August 1999, the scores of English learners had

FIGURE 7.5

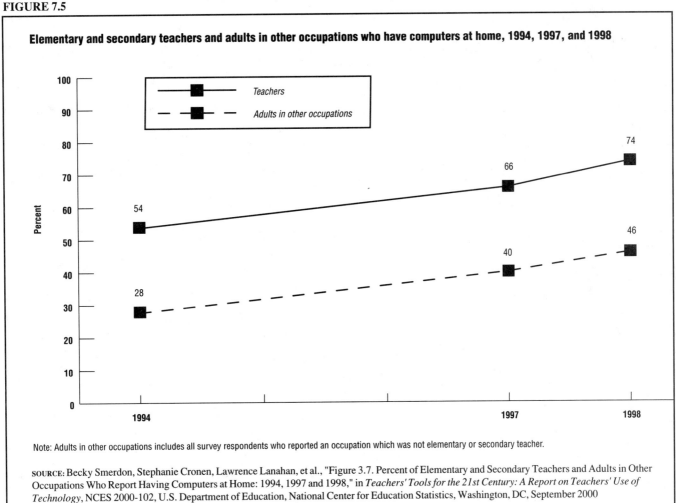

Elementary and secondary teachers and adults in other occupations who have computers at home, 1994, 1997, and 1998

Note: Adults in other occupations includes all survey respondents who reported an occupation which was not elementary or secondary teacher.

SOURCE: Becky Smerdon, Stephanie Cronen, Lawrence Lanahan, et al., "Figure 3.7. Percent of Elementary and Secondary Teachers and Adults in Other Occupations Who Report Having Computers at Home: 1994, 1997 and 1998," in *Teachers' Tools for the 21st Century: A Report on Teachers' Use of Technology*, NCES 2000-102, U.S. Department of Education, National Center for Education Statistics, Washington, DC, September 2000

risen 18 percent in reading, 21 percent in mathematics, 15 percent in language, 21 percent in spelling, and 19 percent overall during the past year. In a few school districts, some of the score improvements had been as much as 93 percent.

SITE-BASED MANAGEMENT

Site-based management (SBM; also called school-based management) moves control and decision-making from those in the central offices of a school system to those most closely involved with a school and its students—principals, teachers, parents, and other interested citizens. Acting as a school council, these individuals can develop their school's goals, allocate funds received from the system's budget, hire personnel, and set curriculum and discipline policies. SBM advocates claim that SBM can eliminate the cost and inefficiency of excessive bureaucracy, as well as increase accountability.

Proponents of SBM maintain the system improves teacher morale and permits more parent and community involvement in schools. Critics worry that SBM removes the decision-making power from capable administrators and gives it to a group of inexperienced, often adversarial

members. The real measure is whether or not site-based management actually improves school performance.

The *Assessment of School-Based Management* (Pricilla Wohlstetter and Susan Albers Mohrman, U.S. Department of Education, Washington, DC, 1996), a study of 27 schools in three U.S. school districts, one Canadian district and one Australian district, reported that there was "scant evidence that schools get better just because decisions are made by those closer to the classroom."

However, SBM can be a successful part of other reforms that produce local school efforts to improve teaching and learning. Wohlstetter and Mohrman recommended establishing teacher-led decision-making subcommittees, focusing on continuous improvement through professional development, creating a system for sharing school-related information within the school and in the community, developing ways to reward staff behavior directed toward achieving school goals, selecting leaders who can facilitate and manage change, and using district, state and/or national guidelines to focus reform efforts and to target changes in curriculum and instruction.

FIGURE 7.6

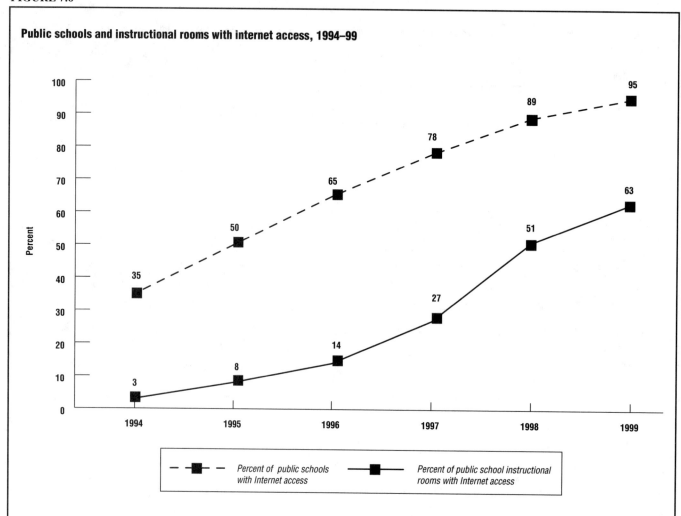

Public schools and instructional rooms with internet access, 1994–99

SOURCE: Becky Smerdon, Stephanie Cronen, Lawrence Lanahan, et al., "Figure 3.4. Percent of Public Schools and Instructional Rooms with Internet Access: 1994 to 1999," in *Teachers' Tools for the 21st Century: A Report on Teachers' Use of Technology*, NCES 2000-102, U.S. Department of Education, National Center for Education Statistics, Washington, DC, September 2000

AN AGING INFRASTRUCTURE

The poor physical condition of American schools is a growing national problem. The average age of the country's K-12 schools is 43 years. In *Condition of America's Public School Facilities* (National Center for Education Statistics, Washington, DC, June 2000), the U.S. Department of Education reported that one-half of all schools nationwide had at least one building feature in less than adequate condition in 1999. Features included roofs, windows, plumbing, and electric power. The most common problem was heating, ventilation and air conditioning systems, which were found inadequate in 29 percent of school buildings. (See Table 7.7.)

In 1999 about 60 percent of overcrowded schools had at least one building feature in inadequate condition, and from 46 to 57 percent had at least one environmental fac-

tor in unsatisfactory condition. Heating and ventilation fell into the environmental category. (See Table 7.8.)

Cost Matters

Lack of funds is a major cause of delaying vital repairs and maintenance from one year to the next (or beyond). Most states use a combination of state and local funding for school repair and construction. In 1998, 8,243 contracts were awarded for public school construction projects, which included both new schools and renovations of existing schools. Elementary schools accounted for about half of these awards. Costs amounted to about $18 billion in 1998.

In 2001 more than two-thirds (68 percent) of respondents to the 33rd Annual Phi Delta Kappa/Gallup Poll felt that funding affects education quality a great deal. (See Figure 7.8.)

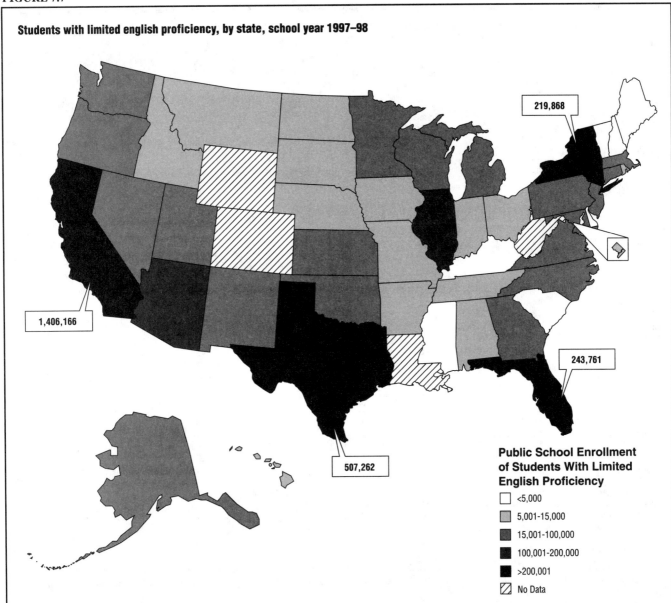

FIGURE 7.7

Students with limited english proficiency, by state, school year 1997–98

219,868

1,406,166

243,761

507,262

Public School Enrollment of Students With Limited English Proficiency

☐ <5,000

▨ 5,001-15,000

▨ 15,001-100,000

■ 100,001-200,000

■ >200,001

▨ No Data

SOURCE: Karen Whiten and Suzanne Lofhjelm, "Figure 2: Concentration of Students With Limited English Proficiency in the United States, School Year 1997–98," in *Bilingual Education: Four Overlapping Programs Could Be Consolidated*, GAO-01-657, U.S. General Accounting Office, Washington, DC, May 2001

TABLE 7.7

Public schools rating the condition of building features as less than adequate, by school characteristics, 1999

[Percent]

School characteristic	At least one building feature is in less than adequate condition	Roofs	Framing, floors, foundations	Exterior walls, finishes, windows, doors	Interior finishes, trim	Plumbing	Heating, ventilation, air conditioning	Electric power	Electrical lighting	Life safety features
All public schools	50	22	14	24	17	25	29	22	17	20
School instructional level										
Elementary school	49	22	14	23	17	24	28	21	17	19
High school	56	26	16	27	20	28	34	25	19	22
Combined	54	18	15	31	14	25	34	20	20	29
School enrollment size										
Less than 300	55	24	19	31	20	28	29	23	19	26
300 to 599	50	22	12	21	16	27	32	21	17	21
600 or more	49	22	14	23	18	20	26	22	16	16
Locale										
Central city	56	23	12	27	20	28	30	26	18	21
Urban fringe/large town	44	19	13	21	16	21	27	21	15	17
Rural/small town	52	25	17	25	17	26	31	19	20	23
Region										
Northeast	39	16	10	18	14	19	22	14	10	11
Midwest	51	20	15	28	15	25	27	19	15	19
South	51	25	15	22	16	24	28	22	20	22
West	57	27	16	26	25	32	40	32	22	27
Percent minority enrollment										
5 percent or less	48	21	15	26	14	22	28	18	16	18
6 to 20 percent	49	25	15	23	17	26	29	18	16	22
21 to 50 percent	46	17	12	17	14	23	25	19	15	18
More than 50 percent	59	28	14	29	24	29	34	32	23	24
Percent of students in school eligible for free or reduced-price school lunch										
Less than 20 percent	45	18	14	21	17	23	28	18	14	16
20 to 39 percent	45	21	11	21	14	23	26	20	15	18
40 to 69 percent	53	22	16	25	14	23	29	21	18	22
70 percent or more	63	32	17	30	26	32	35	30	24	27

NOTE: Ratings of less than adequate encompass the ratings of fair, poor, and replace.

SOURCE: Laurie Lewis, Kyle Snow, Elizabeth Farris, et al.,"Table 4. Percent of public schools rating the condition of building features as less than adequate, by school characteristics: 1999," in *Condition of American's Public School Facilities: 1999,* NCES 2000-032, U.S. Department of Education, National Center for Educational Statistics, June 2000

TABLE 7.8

Public schools with an inadequate or unsatisfactory physical infrastructure, by condition and enrollment levels, 1999

[percent]

Condition of facility[1]	Underenrolled			Overcrowded	
	More than 25 percent under capacity	6–25 percent under capacity	Within 5 percent of capacity	6–25 percent over capacity	More than 25 percent over capacity
At least one type of onsite building in less than adequate condition[2]	17	19	19	43	45
At least one building feature in less than adequate condition[3]	50	46	48	61	59
At least one environmental factor in unsatisfactory condition[4]	42	41	39	57	46

[1] Categories for condition are not mutually exclusive.
[2] The condition of all onsite buildings is computed across original buildings, permanent additions, and temporary buildings. Ratings of "less than adequate" encompass the ratings of "fair," "poor," and "replace."
[3] The condition of all building features is computed across nine building features (e.g., roofs, plumbing). Ratings of "less than adequate" encompass the ratings of "fair," "poor," and "replace."
[4] The condition of all environmental factors is computed across six environmental factors (e.g., heating, ventilation). Ratings of "unsatisfactory" include the ratings of "unsatisfactory" and "very unsatisfactory."

SOURCE: John Wirt, Susan Choy, Debra Gerald, et al., "Table 45–1. Percentage of public schools with an inadequate or unsatisfactory building, building feature, or environmental feature, by categories of under-enrolled and overcrowded: 1999," in *The Condition of Education 2001*, NCES 2001-072, U.S. Department of Education, National Center for Education Statistics, Washington, DC, June 2001

FIGURE 7.8

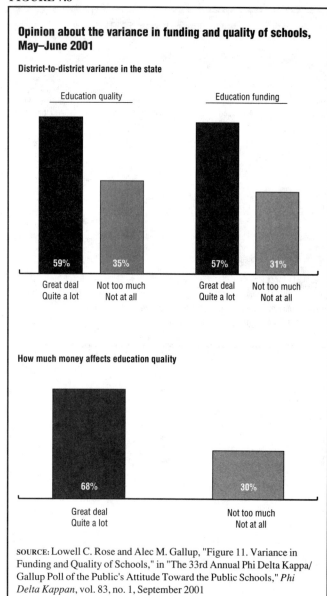

Opinion about the variance in funding and quality of schools, May–June 2001

District-to-district variance in the state

Education quality   Education funding

59%   35%   57%   31%

Great deal   Not too much   Great deal   Not too much
Quite a lot   Not at all   Quite a lot   Not at all

How much money affects education quality

68%   30%

Great deal   Not too much
Quite a lot   Not at all

SOURCE: Lowell C. Rose and Alec M. Gallup, "Figure 11. Variance in Funding and Quality of Schools," in "The 33rd Annual Phi Delta Kappa/ Gallup Poll of the Public's Attitude Toward the Public Schools," *Phi Delta Kappan*, vol. 83, no. 1, September 2001

CHAPTER 8

TEACHERS

Teachers are the foundation of the education process. A well-designed, challenging curriculum, a first-class facility, and state-of-the-art equipment need motivated and well-trained teachers to complete the equation. Teachers are usually the first to come under fire when test scores and achievement are less than satisfactory, and among the last to be rewarded when things go well. Overall their salaries are considerably lower than those of similarly educated professionals.

A growing number of teachers face situations that would have been inconceivable a generation ago, ranging from lack of respect from students to outright physical attacks. Teachers in inner-city schools particularly bear the brunt of many "school" problems that are often a reflection of society's problems. Despite these challenges, however, the number of teachers is increasing, and a clear majority of teachers are pleased with what they do.

TRENDS IN TEACHER SUPPLY AND DEMAND

The number of classroom teachers in elementary and secondary schools has increased steadily, reaching 3.3 million in 1999, an increase of 27 percent from 1986. The National Center for Education Statistics (NCES) projects the number of classroom teachers to increase to 3.6 million by the year 2011, a 10 percent increase from 1999. (See Figure 8.1 and Table 8.1.)

A Teacher Shortage?

In 1999 the American Association for Employment in Education (AAEE) surveyed 1,262 career services directors, deans, and directors of teacher education at colleges and universities. The association reported, in *Educator Supply and Demand in the United States* (AAEE, Columbus, OH, 2001), that there were considerable shortages in physics, bilingual education, and in some areas of special education. There were 18 other subjects (including mathematics, chemistry, speech pathology, computer science,

Spanish, and technology) that had some shortage. No education field had a large surplus of practitioners, but three (physical education, health education, and social studies) had some surplus.

Teacher retirement, the region of the country, student enrollment, class size, subject area shortages, turnover rates, the reserve pool of teachers who have already been trained, and school reform impact teacher supply and demand. Following a survey of personnel officers in the nations's 200 largest school districts, the American Federation of Teachers (AFT) reported in *Survey and Analysis of Teacher Salary Trends 1998* (F. Howard Nelson and Krista Schneider, Washington, DC) that while some states are experiencing considerable shortages, others produce more certified teachers than they can hire.

FIGURE 8.1

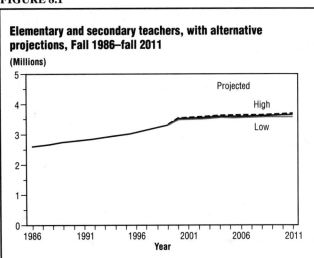

Elementary and secondary teachers, with alternative projections, Fall 1986–fall 2011

SOURCE: Debra E. Gerald and William J. Hussar, "Figure 45.—Elementary and secondary teachers, with alternative projections: Fall 1986 to fall 2011," in *Projections of Education Statistics to 2011*, NCES 2001-083, U.S. Department of Education, National Center for Education Statistics, Washington, DC, October 2001

TABLE 8.1

Elementary and secondary teachers, by control of institution and organizational level, with alternative projections, fall 1986– fall 2011

(In thousands)

Year	Total			Public			Private		
	K-12	Elementary	Secondary	K-12	Elementary	Secondary	K-12	Elementary	Secondary
1986[1]	2,592	1,521	1,071	2,244	1,271	973	348	250	98
1987[1]	2,631	1,563	1,068	2,279	1,306	973	352	257	95
1988[1]	2,668	1,604	1,064	2,323	1,353	970	345	251	94
1989[2]	2,734	1,662	1,072	2,357	1,387	970	377	275	102
1990[2]	2,753	1,683	1,070	2,398	1,429	969	355	254	101
1991[2]	2,787	1,722	1,065	2,432	1,468	964	355	254	101
1992[2]	2,822	1,752	1,070	2,459	1,492	967	363	260	103
1993[2]	2,870	1,775	1,095	2,504	1,513	991	366	262	104
1994[2]	2,926	1,791	1,135	2,552	1,525	1,027	374	266	108
1995[3]	2,978	1,794	1,184	2,598	1,525	1,073	380	269	111
1996[3]	3,054	1,856	1,198	2,667	1,582	1,085	387	274	113
1997[3]	3,134	1,928	1,206	2,746	1,653	1,093	388	275	113
1998[3]	3,221	1,978	1,243	2,830	1,701	1,129	391	277	114
1999[3]	3,304	2,029	1,275	2,907	1,748	1,159	397	281	116
				Middle alternative projections					
2000	3,507	2,192	1,315	3,080	1,885	1,194	428	307	121
2001	3,551	2,208	1,343	3,119	1,899	1,220	432	309	123
2002	3,541	2,180	1,361	3,111	1,875	1,236	430	305	125
2003	3,564	2,184	1,381	3,132	1,878	1,254	432	306	127
2004	3,590	2,188	1,402	3,155	1,881	1,274	435	306	129
2005	3,576	2,188	1,388	3,142	1,881	1,261	434	306	127
2006	3,594	2,196	1,398	3,159	1,889	1,270	436	308	128
2007	3,600	2,195	1,406	3,164	1,887	1,277	436	307	129
2008	3,600	2,195	1,405	3,164	1,888	1,276	436	307	129
2009	3,619	2,209	1,410	3,180	1,900	1,280	439	309	129
2010	3,633	2,228	1,405	3,192	1,916	1,276	441	312	129
2011	3,649	2,246	1,403	3,206	1,932	1,274	443	315	129
				Low alternative projections					
2000	3,507	2,192	1,315	3,080	1,885	1,194	428	307	121
2001	3,553	2,210	1,343	3,120	1,900	1,220	433	309	123
2002	3,537	2,176	1,361	3,108	1,871	1,236	430	305	125
2003	3,566	2,185	1,381	3,134	1,879	1,254	433	306	127
2004	3,604	2,201	1,403	3,167	1,893	1,275	437	308	129
2005	3,585	2,200	1,385	3,150	1,892	1,258	435	308	127
2006	3,593	2,193	1,400	3,157	1,886	1,272	435	307	128
2007	3,595	2,179	1,417	3,160	1,873	1,287	435	305	130
2008	3,588	2,173	1,415	3,154	1,869	1,285	434	304	130
2009	3,591	2,184	1,407	3,156	1,878	1,278	435	306	129
2010	3,593	2,201	1,392	3,157	1,893	1,264	436	308	128
2011	3,607	2,222	1,385	3,169	1,911	1,258	438	311	127
				High alternative projections					
2000	3,507	2,192	1,315	3,080	1,885	1,194	428	307	121
2001	3,552	2,209	1,343	3,119	1,899	1,220	432	309	123
2002	3,545	2,184	1,361	3,114	1,878	1,236	431	306	125
2003	3,581	2,200	1,381	3,146	1,892	1,254	435	308	127
2004	3,605	2,202	1,403	3,168	1,894	1,274	437	308	129
2005	3,588	2,196	1,392	3,152	1,888	1,264	435	308	128
2006	3,619	2,207	1,412	3,180	1,898	1,282	439	309	129
2007	3,625	2,207	1,418	3,186	1,898	1,288	439	309	130
2008	3,620	2,208	1,412	3,181	1,899	1,282	439	309	129
2009	3,642	2,223	1,418	3,200	1,912	1,288	441	311	130
2010	3,661	2,245	1,415	3,216	1,931	1,285	444	314	130
2011	3,681	2,268	1,413	3,234	1,950	1,284	447	318	130

[1]Private school numbers are estimated on the basis on past data.
[2]Private school numbers are from the Early Estimates survey.
[3]Private school numbers are projected.
NOTE: The numbers of elementary and secondary teachers reported separately by the National Education Association were prorated to the NCES totals for each year. Some data have been revised from previously published figures. Projections are based on data through 1998. Because of rounding, details may not add to totals.

SOURCE: Debra E. Gerald and William J. Hussar, "Table 31.—"Elementary and secondary teachers, by control of institution and organizational level, with alternative projections: Fall 1986 to fall 2011," in *Projections of Education Statistics to 2011*, NCES 2001-083, U.S. Department of Education, National Center for Education Statistics, Washington, DC, October 2001

Significant differences exist even within states. Though some school districts have hundreds of applicants for every job, others in less desirable areas and with lower pay scales may have none.

Elizabeth F. Fideler, Elizabeth D. Foster, and Shirley Schwartz studied teacher supply and demand in the Great City School Districts. In *The Urban Teacher Challenge: Teacher Demand and Supply in the Great City Schools*

(Urban Teacher Collaborative, Belmont, MA, January 2000), the researchers report that there is immediate demand for science, special education, mathematics, bilingual education, English as a Second Language, and educational technology teachers.

One consequence of teacher shortages is the increased hiring of uncertified teachers. According to *Solving the Dilemmas of Teacher Supply, Demand, and Standards: How We Can Ensure a Competent, Caring, and Qualified Teacher for Every Child* (Linda Darling-Hammond, National Commission on Teaching and America's Future, New York, 2000), demand for teachers is estimated to be 200,000 per year. Although 63 percent of newly hired teachers in this study had regular or advanced licenses, more than one-fourth (27 percent) had not fully met the state licensing standards, 16 percent held a substandard license, 11 percent were hired with no license at all, and an additional 10 percent held probationary licenses.

In 2001 the public was asked the best way to address the expected teacher shortage by "The 33rd Annual Phi Delta Kappa/Gallup Poll of the Public's Attitude Toward the Public Schools." Respondents supported raising teacher salaries (88 percent) and between-state transfer of benefits (89 percent), over changing college (31 percent) and state (17 percent) requirements for teacher preparation.

Pupil-Teacher Ratio

Educators prefer a low ratio of students per teacher, which allows teachers to spend more time with each pupil. From 1986 to 1999 the pupil-teacher ratio in elementary schools declined slightly from 17.4 to 16.0 students per teacher. The NCES projects that this ratio will decline to 14.5 in 2011. (See Table 8.2.)

Table 8.3 shows the number of teachers and students and the average pupil-teacher ratios in public elementary and secondary schools by state. In fall 1998, Maine and Vermont reported the lowest average pupil-teacher ratio (13.2 and 12.8, respectively), while Utah and California reported the highest (22.4 and 21.0, respectively). Some states have laws limiting class sizes, especially in elementary schools. Several other states are involved in or considering similar laws. In 1998, Congress passed the 1999 Omnibus Appropriations Act (PL 105-277), allocating $1.1 billion for reducing class sizes and hiring more teachers in grades one through three.

SELECTED CHARACTERISTICS OF TEACHERS

According to the U.S. Department of Education, in 1996, women made up about three-quarters (74.4 percent) of public school teachers. The vast majority (90.7 percent) of teachers were white. Most teachers (75.9 percent) were married. The median age (half were over, half were under) was 44. Over half (54.5 percent) of public school teachers

TABLE 8.2

Pupil/teacher ratios in elementary and secondary schools, by control of institution, with alternative projections, fall 1986–fall 2011

Year	Total	Public	Private
1986[1]	17.4	17.7	15.7
1987[1]	17.3	17.6	15.6
1988[1]	17.0	17.3	15.2
1989[2]	16.7	17.2	13.8
1990[2]	16.9	17.2	14.7
1991[2]	17.0	17.3	14.9
1992[2]	17.1	17.4	14.7
1993[2]	17.0	17.4	14.6
1994[2]	17.0	17.3	14.7
1995[3]	17.0	17.3	14.9
1996[3]	16.8	17.1	14.5
1997[3]	16.5	16.8	14.2
1998[3]	16.2	16.4	14.8
1999[3]	16.0	16.1	15.2
Middle alternative projections			
2000	15.1	15.3	13.7
2001	14.9	15.1	13.5
2002	15.0	15.2	13.6
2003	15.0	15.1	13.6
2004	14.9	15.1	13.5
2005	14.9	15.1	13.5
2006	14.9	15.0	13.4
2007	14.8	15.0	13.4
2008	14.8	14.9	13.4
2009	14.6	14.8	13.3
2010	14.6	14.8	13.2
2011	14.5	14.7	13.2
Low alternative projections			
(Based on high alternative projections of teachers)			
2000	15.1	15.3	13.7
2001	14.9	15.1	13.5
2002	15.0	15.2	13.6
2003	14.9	15.1	13.5
2004	14.8	15.0	13.4
2005	14.9	15.1	13.5
2006	14.7	14.9	13.3
2007	14.7	14.9	13.3
2008	14.7	14.9	13.3
2009	14.6	14.7	13.2
2010	14.5	14.7	13.2
2011	14.4	14.6	13.1
High alternative projections			
(Based on low alternative projections of teachers)			
2000	15.1	15.3	13.7
2001	14.9	15.1	13.5
2002	15.0	15.2	13.6
2003	14.9	15.1	13.5
2004	14.8	15.0	13.4
2005	14.9	15.1	13.5
2006	14.9	15.1	13.5
2007	14.8	15.0	13.4
2008	14.8	15.0	13.5
2009	14.8	14.9	13.4
2010	14.7	14.9	13.4
2011	14.7	14.9	13.4

[1]Private school numbers are estimated on the basis on past data.
[2]Private school teacher numbers are from the Early Estimates survey and private school enrollment numbers are from the Private School Universe Survey.
[3]Private school numbers are projected or interpolated.
NOTE: Projections are based on data through 1999.

SOURCE: Debra E. Gerald and William J. Hussar, "Table 32.—Pupil/teacher ratios in elementary and secondary teachers, by control of institution, with alternative projections: Fall 1986 to fall 2011," in *Projections of Education Statistics to 2011*, NCES 2001-083, U.S. Department of Education, National Center for Education Statistics, Washington, DC, October 2001

TABLE 8.3

Teachers, enrollment, and pupil/teacher ratios in public elementary and secondary schools, by state, fall 1993–fall 1998

State or other area	Pupil/ teacher ratio, fall 1993	Pupil/ teacher ratio, fall 1994	Pupil/ teacher ratio, fall 1995	Fall 1996			Fall 1997[1]			Fall 1998		
				Teachers	Enrollment	Pupil/ teacher ratio	Teachers	Enrollment	Pupil/ teacher ratio	Teachers	Enrollment	Pupil/ teacher ratio
United States	**17.4**	**17.3**	**17.3**	[2]**2,667,419**	[2]**45,611,046**	**17.1**	[2]**2,746,157**	[2]**46,126,897**	[2]**16.8**	[2]**2,826,146**	[2]**46,534,687**	[2]**16.5**
Alabama	17.1	17.2	16.9	[2]45,035	[2]747,932	16.6	[2]45,967	[2]749,207	[2]16.3	[2]47,753	[2]747,970	[2]15.7
Alaska	17.5	17.6	17.3	7,418	129,919	17.5	7,625	132,123	17.3	8,118	135,373	16.7
Arizona	18.9	19.3	19.6	40,521	799,250	19.7	41,129	814,113	19.8	42,352	848,262	20.0
Arkansas	17.1	17.1	17.1	[2]26,681	457,349	17.1	[2]26,931	456,497	[2]17.0	27,953	452,256	16.2
California	24.0	24.0	24.0	[2]248,818	[2]5,686,198	22.9	[2]268,535	[2]5,803,887	[2]21.6	[2]281,686	[2]5,925,964	[2]21.0
Colorado	18.6	18.4	18.5	36,398	673,438	18.5	37,840	687,167	18.2	39,434	699,135	17.7
Connecticut	14.4	14.4	14.4	36,551	527,129	14.4	37,658	535,164	14.2	38,772	544,698	14.0
Delaware	16.5	16.6	16.8	6,642	110,549	16.6	6,850	111,960	16.3	7,074	113,262	16.0
District of Columbia	13.3	13.2	15.0	5,288	78,648	14.9	[3]4,388	77,111	17.6	5,187	71,889	13.9
Florida	18.4	19.1	18.9	120,471	2,242,212	18.6	124,473	2,294,077	18.4	126,796	2,337,633	18.4
Georgia	16.7	16.3	16.5	81,795	1,346,761	16.5	86,244	1,375,980	16.0	88,658	1,401,291	15.8
Hawaii	17.8	17.9	17.8	10,576	187,653	17.7	10,653	189,887	17.8	10,639	188,069	17.7
Idaho	19.7	19.1	19.0	13,078	245,252	18.8	13,207	244,403	18.5	13,426	244,722	18.2
Illinois	17.1	17.3	17.1	116,274	1,973,040	17.0	118,734	1,998,289	16.8	121,758	2,011,530	16.5
Indiana	17.5	17.5	17.5	56,708	982,876	17.3	57,371	986,836	17.2	58,084	988,094	17.0
Iowa	15.8	15.8	15.5	32,593	502,941	15.4	32,700	501,054	15.3	32,822	498,214	15.2
Kansas	15.1	15.1	15.1	30,875	466,293	15.1	31,527	468,687	14.9	32,003	472,353	14.8
Kentucky	17.6	17.0	16.9	39,331	656,089	16.7	40,488	669,322	16.5	40,803	655,687	16.1
Louisiana	17.1	16.8	17.0	47,334	793,296	16.8	48,599	776,813	16.6	49,124	768,734	16.6
Maine	14.1	13.8	13.9	15,551	213,593	13.7	15,700	212,579	13.5	15,890	210,503	13.2
Maryland	17.5	17.0	16.8	47,943	818,583	17.1	48,318	830,744	17.2	49,840	841,671	16.9
Massachusetts	14.9	14.8	14.6	64,574	933,898	14.5	67,170	949,006	14.1	69,752	962,317	13.8
Michigan	19.9	20.1	19.7	88,051	1,685,714	19.1	90,529	1,702,717	18.8	93,220	[2]1,720,266	[2]18.5
Minnesota	17.3	17.5	17.8	48,245	847,204	17.6	51,998	853,621	16.4	50,565	855,119	16.9
Mississippi	17.8	17.5	17.5	29,293	503,967	17.2	29,441	504,792	17.1	31,140	502,379	16.1
Missouri	15.8	15.5	15.4	59,428	900,517	15.2	60,889	910,613	15.0	62,222	912,445	14.7
Montana	16.4	16.3	16.4	10,268	164,627	16.0	10,228	162,335	15.9	10,221	159,988	15.7
Nebraska	14.5	14.5	14.5	20,174	291,967	14.5	20,065	292,681	14.6	20,310	291,140	14.3
Nevada	18.7	18.7	19.1	14,805	282,131	19.1	16,053	296,621	18.5	16,415	311,061	18.9
New Hampshire	15.5	15.6	15.7	12,692	198,308	15.6	12,931	201,629	15.6	13,290	204,713	15.4
New Jersey	13.6	13.8	13.8	87,642	1,227,832	14.0	89,671	1,250,276	13.9	92,264	1,268,996	13.8
New Mexico	17.5	17.2	17.0	19,971	332,632	16.7	19,647	331,673	16.9	19,981	328,753	16.5
New York	15.2	15.2	15.5	185,104	2,843,131	15.4	190,874	2,861,823	15.0	197,253	2,877,143	14.6
North Carolina	16.3	16.2	16.2	75,239	1,210,108	16.1	77,785	1,236,083	15.9	79,531	1,254,821	15.8
North Dakota	15.4	15.3	15.9	7,892	120,123	15.2	8,070	118,572	14.7	7,974	114,597	14.4
Ohio	16.8	16.6	17.1	108,515	1,844,698	17.0	110,761	1,847,114	16.7	113,986	1,842,559	16.2
Oklahoma	15.5	15.5	15.7	39,568	620,695	15.7	40,215	623,681	15.5	40,886	628,492	15.4
Oregon	19.5	19.9	19.8	26,757	537,854	20.1	26,935	541,346	20.1	27,152	542,809	20.0
Pennsylvania	17.2	17.1	17.0	106,432	1,804,256	17.0	108,014	1,815,151	16.8	111,065	1,816,414	16.4
Rhode Island	14.8	14.7	14.3	10,656	151,324	14.2	10,598	153,321	14.5	11,124	154,785	13.9
South Carolina	16.7	16.4	16.2	41,463	[2]652,816	15.7	42,336	[2]659,273	[2]15.6	43,689	[2]664,592	[2]15.2
South Dakota	14.9	14.4	15.0	9,625	143,331	14.9	9,282	142,443	15.3	9,273	132,495	14.3
Tennessee	18.8	18.6	16.7	54,790	[2]904,818	16.5	54,142	[2]893,044	[2]16.5	59,258	[2]905,442	[2]15.3
Texas	16.0	15.7	15.6	247,650	3,828,975	15.5	254,557	3,891,877	15.3	259,739	3,945,367	15.2
Utah	24.7	24.3	23.8	19,734	481,812	24.4	21,115	482,957	22.9	21,501	481,176	22.4
Vermont	14.0	13.8	13.8	7,751	106,341	13.7	7,909	105,984	13.4	8,221	105,120	12.8
Virginia	14.8	14.6	14.4	[2]74,526	1,096,093	14.7	[2]77,575	1,110,815	[2]14.3	[2]79,393	1,124,022	[2]14.2
Washington	20.1	20.2	20.4	48,307	974,504	20.2	49,074	991,235	20.2	49,671	998,053	20.1
West Virginia	14.9	14.8	14.6	20,888	304,052	14.6	20,947	301,419	14.4	20,989	297,530	14.2
Wisconsin	16.0	15.9	15.8	54,769	879,259	16.1	55,732	881,780	15.8	61,176	879,542	14.4
Wyoming	15.4	14.9	14.8	6,729	99,058	14.7	6,677	97,115	14.5	6,713	95,241	14.2
Outlying areas												
American Samoa	22.1	20.7	20.0	734	14,766	20.1	762	15,214	20.0	764	15,372	20.1
Guam	18.8	17.6	18.3	1,416	33,393	23.6	1,363	32,444	23.8	1,052	32,222	30.6
Northern Marianas	19.0	20.8	20.9	592	9,041	15.3	483	9,246	19.1	496	9,498	19.1
Puerto Rico	15.9	15.6	16.0	36,498	618,861	17.0	38,953	617,157	15.8	39,781	613,862	15.4
Virgin Islands	14.5	15.1	14.0	4,763	22,385	4.7	1,559	22,136	14.2	1,567	20,976	13.4

[1] Data revised from previously published data.
[2] Includes imputations for underreporting.
[3] Data imputed by the National Center for Education Statistics based on previous year's data.
NOTE: Teachers reported in full-time equivalents.

SOURCE: Thomas D. Snyder and Charlene M. Hoffman, "Table 67.—Teachers, enrollment, and pupil/teacher ratios in public elementary and secondary schools, by state: Fall 1993 to fall 1998," in *Digest of Education Statistics, 2000*, NCES 2001-034, U.S. Department of Education, National Center for Education Statistics, Washington, DC, January 2001

had a master's or specialist degree, while less than 2 percent had a doctoral degree. The American Federation of Teachers reports that the average teacher had an estimated 16.1 years of experience in 1999–2000.

Shortage of Minority Teachers

The American Association for Employment in Education found that in 1999 there was a slight increase in the number of minority teachers in preparation programs, but the increase was not enough to fulfill the demand for minority candidates.

In *The Urban Teacher Challenge: Teacher Demand and Supply in the Great City Schools*, the Urban Teacher Collaborative found that nearly three-quarters (72.5 percent) of districts in the Great City School Districts had an immediate need for teachers of color in 2000. Nearly as many (70 percent) had special recruitment efforts underway to attract minority teachers.

The difference between the proportion of minority students and the proportion of minority teachers is likely to continue to increase. The minority student population is growing rapidly, while the minority teaching force is not. Educators are concerned about the scarcity of minority teachers. It is also becoming harder to recruit minority teachers, as many minority college students elect to enter other, more lucrative professions.

SALARIES

The past two decades have been marked by fluctuations in teachers' salaries. As school enrollments fell in the late 1970s and early 1980s , average teachers' salaries (in constant 1997–98 dollars, adjusted for inflation) also declined. In 1980–81, teachers' salaries averaged $33,514. From 1982–83 to 1990–91, salaries rose steadily to $40,650, a 21 percent increase. From 1990–91 to 1998–99, salaries remained comparatively stable. (See Table 8.4.) Private schools tend to pay their teachers less than public schools.

In 1998–99, the average teacher salary was $40,582. Connecticut, at $51,584, had the highest average salary in the nation. Other states with the highest average teacher salaries were New Jersey ($51,193), Michigan ($48,207), New York ($49,437), and Pennsylvania ($48,457). The lowest average salaries were paid in South Dakota ($28,552), North Dakota, ($28,976), Mississippi ($29,530), Oklahoma ($31,149) and Montana ($31,356). (See Table 8.5.)

Comparisons to Other Selected White-Collar Workers

The average teacher's salary tends to be considerably less than the salaries of other professionals with comparable years of education and experience (F. Howard Nelson, Rachel Drown, and Jewell C. Gould, American Federation

TABLE 8.4

Average annual salary for public elementary and secondary school teachers, 1970–71 to 1998–99
[In constant 1998–99 dollars]*

Year	All teachers	Elementary teachers	Secondary teachers
1970–71	$38,388	$37,365	$39,631
1975–76	37,384	36,434	38,384
1980–81	33,514	32,728	34,460
1982–83	34,694	33,909	35,693
1984–85	36,715	36,092	37,628
1985–86	38,103	37,376	39,082
1986–87	39,302	38,545	40,301
1988–89	40,139	39,403	41,027
1990–91	40,650	39,920	41,648
1995–96	40,155	39,699	40,866
1997–98	40,137	39,822	40,712
1998–99	40,582	40,293	41,155

*Constant 1998–99 dollars based on the Consumer Price Index, prepared by the Bureau of Labor Statistics, U.S. Department of Labor.

SOURCE: Charlene M. Hoffman, "Table 16.—Average annual salary for public elementary and secondary schools (sic) teachers: 1970–71 to 1998–99 (in constant 1998–99 dollars)*," in *Mini-Digest of Education Statistics, 2000*, NCES 2001-046, U.S. Department of Education, National Center for Education Statistics, Washington, DC, August 2001

of Teachers, *Survey and Analysis of Teacher Salary Trends: 2000*, Washington, DC). Table 8.6 compares average teachers' salaries to the average salaries of other selected white-collar professionals. The American Federation of Teachers (AFT) found that, in inflation-adjusted 2000 dollars, teachers earned 80 percent of accountants' earnings, 73 percent of the salaries of buyers and contract specialists, 63 percent as much as computer systems analysts, 58 percent of engineers' salaries, and 54 percent of the earnings of attorneys. In 2000 beginning teachers, on average, earned only 70 percent of the earnings of new college graduates in other fields.

TEACHER TURNOVER

Richard M. Ingersoll reports in *Teaching Quality Policy Briefs: A Different Approach to Solving the Teaching Shortage Problem* (Center for the Study of Teaching and Policy, Seattle, WA, January 2001) that turnover averages about 13.2 percent for teachers, compared to 11 percent for employees in all professions. Schools with high poverty rates also have higher teacher turnover rates (15.2 percent) than schools with low poverty rates (10.5 percent). Private schools (18.9 percent) have higher turnover rates than public schools (12.4 percent), and small private schools (22.8 percent) have higher turnover rates than large private schools (9.8 percent). (See Figure 8.2.)

Reasons for Teacher Turnover

Teachers who move to other schools do not represent a loss to the profession, but they are a loss to the schools from which they move. Their departures cause a decrease

TABLE 8.5

Estimated average annual salary of teachers in public elementary and secondary schools, by state, 1969–70 to 1998–99

State	Current dollars							Constant 1998–99 dollars						Percent change, 1989–90 to 1998–99 in constant dollars
	1969–70	1979–80	1989–90	1995–96	1996–97	1997–98	1998–99	1969–70	1979–80	1989–90	1995–96	1996–97	1997–98	
United States	$8,626	$15,970	$31,367	$37,704	$38,536	$39,454	$40,582	$37,574	$33,848	$40,647	$40,155	$39,902	$40,137	–0.2
Alabama	6,818	13,060	24,828	31,313	32,549	32,818	35,820	29,698	27,680	32,174	33,348	33,703	33,386	11.3
Alaska	10,560	27,210	43,153	49,171	50,647	47,601	46,845	45,998	57,671	55,920	52,367	52,443	48,425	–16.2
Arizona	8,711	15,054	29,402	32,483	33,685	34,411	35,025	37,944	31,907	38,101	34,594	34,879	35,007	–8.1
Arkansas	6,307	12,299	22,352	29,533	30,578	31,592	32,350	27,472	26,068	28,965	31,453	31,662	32,139	11.7
California	10,315	18,020	37,998	42,259	42,992	44,585	45,400	44,931	38,193	49,240	45,006	44,516	45,357	–7.8
Colorado	7,761	16,205	30,758	35,364	36,271	37,240	38,025	33,806	34,346	39,858	37,663	37,557	37,885	–4.6
Connecticut	9,262	16,229	40,461	50,254	50,426	50,730	51,584	40,344	34,397	52,432	53,520	52,214	51,608	–1.6
Delaware	9,015	16,148	33,377	40,533	41,436	42,439	43,164	39,268	34,225	43,252	43,168	42,905	43,174	–0.2
District of Columbia	10,285	22,190	38,402	43,700	45,012	46,350	47,150	44,800	47,031	49,764	46,540	46,608	47,152	–5.3
Florida	8,412	14,149	28,803	33,330	33,889	34,475	35,196	36,641	29,989	37,325	35,496	35,091	35,072	–5.7
Georgia	7,276	13,853	28,006	34,002	35,596	37,569	39,675	31,693	29,361	36,292	36,212	36,858	38,219	9.3
Hawaii	9,453	19,920	32,047	35,807	35,842	38,377	40,377	41,176	42,220	41,528	38,134	37,113	39,041	–2.8
Idaho	6,890	13,611	23,861	30,892	31,820	32,834	34,063	30,012	28,848	30,921	32,900	32,948	33,402	10.2
Illinois	9,569	17,601	32,794	40,919	42,125	43,690	45,569	41,681	37,305	42,496	43,579	43,619	44,446	7.2
Indiana	8,833	15,599	30,902	37,675	38,845	39,750	41,163	38,475	33,062	40,045	40,124	40,222	40,438	2.8
Iowa	8,355	15,203	26,747	32,372	33,272	34,084	34,927	36,393	32,223	34,660	34,476	34,452	34,674	0.8
Kansas	7,612	13,690	28,744	35,023	35,739	36,811	37,405	33,157	29,016	37,248	37,299	37,006	37,448	0.4
Kentucky	6,953	14,520	26,292	33,080	33,949	34,613	35,526	30,286	30,775	34,071	35,230	35,153	35,212	4.3
Louisiana	7,028	13,760	24,300	27,530	29,025	30,090	32,510	30,613	29,164	31,489	29,319	30,054	30,611	3.2
Maine	7,572	13,071	26,881	32,869	33,676	34,349	34,906	32,982	27,704	34,834	35,005	34,870	34,944	0.2
Maryland	9,383	17,558	36,319	41,160	41,148	41,739	42,526	40,871	37,214	47,064	43,835	42,607	42,462	–9.6
Massachusetts	8,764	17,253	34,712	41,408	42,650	43,930	45,075	38,175	36,567	44,982	44,099	44,162	44,690	0.2
Michigan	9,826	19,663	37,072	46,832	47,181	47,500	48,207	42,801	41,675	48,040	49,876	48,854	48,322	0.3
Minnesota	8,658	15,912	32,190	36,922	38,115	37,932	39,458	37,713	33,725	41,714	39,322	39,466	38,589	–5.4
Mississippi	5,798	11,850	24,292	27,692	27,720	28,692	29,530	25,255	25,116	31,479	29,492	28,703	29,189	–6.2
Missouri	7,799	13,682	27,094	32,322	33,155	33,946	34,746	33,971	28,999	35,110	34,423	34,330	34,534	–1.0
Montana	7,606	14,537	25,081	29,364	29,958	30,620	31,356	33,131	30,811	32,501	31,273	31,020	31,150	–3.5
Nebraska	7,375	13,516	25,522	31,496	31,768	32,668	32,880	32,124	28,647	33,073	33,543	32,894	33,234	–0.6
Nevada	9,215	16,295	30,590	36,167	37,340	37,094	38,883	40,139	34,537	39,640	38,518	38,664	37,736	–1.9
New Hampshire	7,771	13,017	28,986	35,792	36,029	36,663	37,405	33,849	27,589	37,562	38,118	37,306	37,298	–0.4
New Jersey	9,130	17,161	35,676	48,751	49,786	50,442	51,193	39,769	36,372	46,231	51,920	51,551	51,315	10.7
New Mexico	7,796	14,887	24,756	29,074	30,131	30,152	32,398	33,958	31,553	32,080	30,964	31,199	30,674	1.0
New York	10,336	19,812	38,925	48,115	48,000	48,712	49,437	45,022	41,991	50,441	51,242	49,702	49,555	–2.0
North Carolina	7,494	14,117	27,883	30,411	31,167	33,129	36,098	32,643	29,921	36,133	32,388	32,272	33,703	–0.1
North Dakota	6,696	13,263	23,016	26,969	27,711	28,230	28,976	29,167	28,111	29,826	28,722	28,693	28,719	–2.8
Ohio	8,300	15,269	31,218	37,835	38,676	38,985	40,566	36,154	32,362	40,454	40,294	40,047	39,660	0.3
Oklahoma	6,882	13,107	23,070	28,404	30,369	30,692	31,149	29,977	27,780	29,896	30,250	31,446	31,223	4.2
Oregon	8,818	16,266	30,840	39,706	40,960	42,200	42,833	38,410	34,476	39,964	42,287	42,412	42,931	7.2
Pennsylvania	8,858	16,515	33,338	46,087	47,148	47,542	48,457	38,584	35,003	43,201	49,083	48,820	48,365	12.2
Rhode Island	8,776	18,002	36,057	41,765	43,019	45,650	45,650	38,227	38,155	46,725	44,480	44,544	45,067	–2.3
South Carolina	6,927	13,063	27,217	31,622	32,830	33,697	34,506	30,173	27,687	35,269	33,677	33,994	34,280	–2.2
South Dakota	6,403	12,348	21,300	26,346	26,764	27,875	28,552	27,890	26,171	27,602	28,058	27,713	28,358	3.4
Tennessee	7,050	13,972	27,052	33,126	34,222	35,340	36,500	30,709	29,613	35,056	35,279	35,435	35,952	4.1
Texas	7,255	14,132	27,496	32,001	33,038	34,133	35,041	31,602	29,953	35,631	34,081	34,209	34,724	–1.7
Utah	7,644	14,909	23,686	30,588	31,867	32,394	32,950	33,296	31,599	30,694	32,576	32,997	32,955	7.4
Vermont	7,968	12,484	29,012	36,295	36,053	36,299	36,800	34,707	26,460	37,596	38,654	37,331	36,927	–2.1
Virginia	8,070	14,060	30,938	34,792	35,536	36,654	37,475	35,152	29,800	40,091	37,053	36,796	37,289	–6.5
Washington	9,225	18,820	30,457	37,853	37,815	38,765	38,692	40,183	39,889	39,468	40,313	39,156	39,436	–2.0
West Virginia	7,650	13,710	22,842	32,155	33,250	33,397	34,244	33,322	29,058	29,600	34,245	34,429	33,975	15.7
Wisconsin	8,963	16,006	31,921	38,182	39,057	39,357	40,657	39,041	33,924	41,365	40,664	40,442	40,038	–1.7
Wyoming	8,232	16,012	28,141	31,571	31,715	32,022	33,500	35,857	33,937	36,467	33,623	32,839	32,576	–8.1

NOTE: Constant 1998–99 dollars based on the Consumer Price Index prepared by the Bureau of Labor Statistics, U.S. Department of Labor. Price index does not account for different rates of change in the cost of living among states. Some data have been revised from previously published figures.

SOURCE: Thomas D. Snyder and Charlene M. Hoffman, "Table 76.—Estimated average annual salary of teachers in public elementary and secondary schools, by state: 1969–70 to 1998–99," in *Digest of Education Statistics, 2000*, NCES 2001-034, U.S. Department of Education, National Center for Education Statistics, Washington, DC, January 2001. Data from National Education Association, *Rankings & Estimates: Rankings of the States 1999 and Estimates of School Statistics 2000* (© 2000, NEA, Washington, D.C. All rights reserved.); and Rankings and Estimates Database (© 2000, NEA, Washington, D.C. All rights reserved.)

TABLE 8.6

Trends in teacher salaries compared to the average annual salaries of selected white-collar occupations, 1962–2000

	Mean Teacher Salary	Accountant III	Buyer/ Contract Specialist III	Attorney III	Computer Systems Analyst III	Engineer IV	Full Prof. Public Doctoral	Assistant Prof. Public Comprehensive
2000 *	$41,820	$52,323	$57,035	$77,150	$66,849	$72,427	$82,535	$43,362
1999 *	40,540	49,257	57,392	69,104	66,782	68,294	78,830	41,940
1998 *	39,360	45,919	54,625	71,530	63,072	64,489	75,150	40,760
1997 *	38,415	42,921	51,323	67,980	59,031	62,259	72,220	40,170
1996	37,594	42,172	46,592	66,560	57,772	60,684	69,760	39,000
1994	35,764	39,884	44,616	64,532	54,548	56,368	64,860	37,220
1992	34,027	37,648	41,392	65,884	53,300	53,404	61,950	35,730
1990	31,347	35,489	38,385	59,087	47,958	49,365	57,520	32,730
1988	28,071	33,028	36,040	55,407	45,093	45,680	51,080	28,380
1986	25,260	31,143	33,580	50,119	41,548	42,667	45,600	26,000
1984	21,974	28,721	30,610	44,743	38,057	39,005	39,800	23,000
1982	18,945	25,673	27,424	39,649	na	34,443	35,700	20,800
1980	16,100	21,299	22,904	33,034	na	28,486	30,100	17,800
1978	14,207	18,115	19,590	27,738	na	23,972	26,400	15,900
1976	12,591	15,428	17,122	24,205	na	20,749	24,200	14,600
1974	10,778	13,285	14,659	21,082	na	17,929	21,600	13,100
1972	9,705	11,879	13,117	18,392	na	16,159	19,800	11,800
1970	8,635	10,686	11,665	16,884	na	14,695	18,100	10,800
1968	7,423	9,367	10,260	15,283	na	13,095	16,100	9,500
1966	6,485	8,328	9,252	14,052	na	11,784	14,100	8,300
1964	5,995	7,908	na	12,816	na	11,016	12,500	7,700
1962	$5,515	$7,416	na	$11,844	na	$10,248	na	na
(2000 DOLLARS)								
2000 *	$41,820	$52,323	$57,035	$77,150	$66,849	$72,427	$82,535	$43,362
1999 *	41,913	50,926	59,336	71,444	69,044	70,607	81,500	43,360
1998 *	41,760	48,719	57,956	75,891	66,918	68,421	79,732	43,245
1997 *	41,388	46,244	55,295	73,242	63,600	67,077	77,810	43,279
1996	41,244	46,267	51,116	73,023	63,382	66,576	76,534	42,787
1994	41,569	46,358	51,858	75,007	63,402	65,518	75,388	43,262
1992	41,724	46,165	50,756	80,788	65,357	65,485	75,964	43,813
1990	40,765	46,152	49,918	76,840	62,367	64,197	74,802	42,564
1988	40,534	47,692	52,041	80,007	65,114	65,961	73,759	40,980
1986	39,776	49,040	52,877	78,920	65,424	67,186	71,805	40,941
1984	36,310	47,459	50,581	73,934	62,886	64,453	65,766	38,006
1982	33,775	45,769	48,891	70,686	na	61,405	63,645	37,082
1980	32,461	42,944	46,180	66,604	na	57,434	60,688	35,889
1978	36,514	46,558	50,349	71,291	na	61,612	67,852	40,866
1976	37,643	46,125	51,189	72,365	na	62,033	72,351	43,649
1974	36,134	44,539	49,146	70,680	na	60,109	72,416	43,919
1972	39,733	48,634	53,703	75,299	na	66,157	81,064	48,311
1970	37,751	46,718	50,998	73,814	na	64,244	79,131	47,216
1968	36,383	45,911	50,288	74,908	na	64,184	78,913	46,563
1966	34,298	44,045	48,932	74,318	na	62,323	74,571	43,897
1964	33,434	44,102	na	71,474	na	61,435	69,712	42,942
1962	$31,566	$42,447	na	$67,791	na	$58,656	na	na
RATIO OF SALARIES IN OTHER OCCUPATIONS TO TEACHER SALARIES								
2000	1.00	1.25	1.36	1.84	1.60	1.73	1.97	1.04
1999 *	1.00	1.22	1.42	1.70	1.65	1.68	1.94	1.03
1998 *	1.00	1.17	1.39	1.82	1.60	1.64	1.91	1.04
1997 *	1.00	1.12	1.34	1.77	1.54	1.62	1.88	1.05
1996	1.00	1.12	1.24	1.77	1.54	1.61	1.86	1.04
1994	1.00	1.12	1.25	1.80	1.53	1.58	1.81	1.04
1992	1.00	1.11	1.22	1.94	1.57	1.57	1.82	1.05
1990	1.00	1.13	1.22	1.88	1.53	1.57	1.83	1.04
1988	1.00	1.18	1.28	1.97	1.61	1.63	1.82	1.01
1986	1.00	1.23	1.33	1.98	1.64	1.69	1.81	1.03
1984	1.00	1.31	1.39	2.04	1.73	1.78	1.81	1.05
1982	1.00	1.36	1.45	2.09	na	1.82	1.88	1.10
1980	1.00	1.32	1.42	2.05	na	1.77	1.87	1.11
1978	1.00	1.28	1.38	1.95	na	1.69	1.86	1.12
1976	1.00	1.23	1.36	1.92	na	1.65	1.92	1.16
1974	1.00	1.23	1.36	1.96	na	1.66	2.00	1.22
1972	1.00	1.22	1.35	1.90	na	1.67	2.04	1.22
1970	1.00	1.24	1.35	1.96	na	1.70	2.10	1.25
1968	1.00	1.26	1.38	2.06	na	1.76	2.17	1.28
1966	1.00	1.28	1.43	2.17	na	1.82	2.17	1.28
1964	1.00	1.32	na	2.14	na	1.84	2.09	1.28
1962	1.00	1.34	na	2.15	na	1.86	na	na

TABLE 8.6

Trends in teacher salaries compared to the average annual salaries of selected white-collar occupations, 1962–2000 [CONTINUED]

	Mean Teacher Salary	Accountant III	Buyer/ Contract Specialist III	Attorney III	Computer Systems Analyst III	Engineer IV	Full Prof. Public Doctoral	Assistant Prof. Public Comprehensive
				PERCENT INCREASE FROM PREVIOUS YEAR				
2000 *	3.2%	6.2%	-0.6%	11.6%	0.1%	6.1%	4.7%	3.4%
1999 *	3.0%	7.3%	5.1%	-3.4%	5.9%	5.9%	4.9%	2.9%
1998 *	2.5%	7.0%	6.4%	5.2%	6.8%	3.6%	4.1%	1.5%
1997 *	2.2%	1.8%	10.2%	2.1%	2.2%	2.6%	3.5%	3.0%
1996	2.3%	1.8%	2.4%	2.5%	1.7%	1.6%	3.3%	1.7%
1994	2.2%	2.7%	3.6%	-5.9%	-0.2%	1.9%	2.5%	2.9%
1992	3.2%	2.0%	2.6%	7.0%	6.6%	4.1%	2.5%	3.7%
1990	5.8%	4.0%	3.1%	3.3%	4.5%	4.4%	6.0%	5.9%
1988	5.5%	3.0%	3.5%	6.2%	3.4%	3.0%	4.8%	3.1%
1986	7.2%	3.7%	5.7%	5.0%	4.8%	4.1%	7.0%	6.6%
1984	6.9%	5.0%	5.4%	5.8%	na	6.2%	4.2%	4.5%
1982	9.1%	9.0%	8.8%	9.0%	na	9.9%	8.5%	7.8%
1980	7.5%	9.4%	8.0%	11.4%	na	9.6%	6.7%	7.2%
1978	6.4%	9.5%	8.7%	8.9%	na	8.6%	4.8%	1.3%
1976	7.7%	6.7%	7.0%	7.3%	na	6.7%	6.6%	5.0%
1974	5.9%	6.5%	6.0%	7.8%	na	5.3%	5.4%	4.8%
1972	4.7%	4.4%	4.2%	5.0%	na	4.0%	3.1%	3.5%
1970	8.6%	6.6%	6.6%	6.3%	na	5.8%	5.8%	6.9%
1968	8.7%	5.5%	4.5%	6.0%	na	5.4%	7.3%	10.5%
1966	4.7%	2.5%	na	3.0%	na	3.6%	6.8%	5.1%
1964	4.6%	3.1%	na	4.2%	na	2.7%	5.9%	2.7%
1962	na	na	na	na	na	na	na	na

*AFT estimates based on average weekly pay increase in U.S. Department of Labor, Employment and Earnings, various years, January issues.

SOURCE: "Survey and Analysis of Teacher Salary Trends 2000." Research & Information Services, American Federation of Teachers, AFL-CIO, Washington, D.C.

in staff, which usually must be replaced. Ingersoll found that teachers leave due to personal reasons (such as caring for family members), school staffing actions (layoffs, school closings, and reorganization), dissatisfaction with teaching, job change (to nonteaching jobs in education or to jobs outside the field of education), and retirement.

Personal reasons, such as departures for family moves, for pregnancy and child rearing, or for health problems, accounted for 33 percent of migration ("movers" leaving a teaching job at one school for another) and 45 percent of attrition ("leavers" giving up the teaching profession entirely). Teachers in small private schools were more likely to leave teaching because of personal reasons. Similar proportions of all movers and leavers reported departing to pursue a better job or other career opportunities.

Far more turnover in small private schools was linked to job dissatisfaction than in high-poverty, urban public schools. Teachers cited two major reasons for their departure—poor salary and inadequate administrative support. About three-quarters of those departing small private schools because of job dissatisfaction cited poor salaries as the reason. Salaries of private school teachers were significantly lower than salaries of public school teachers, and private school teachers were far more likely to change to public school jobs than public school teachers to private school jobs.

TEACHERS' FEELINGS OF PREPAREDNESS

According to *Teacher Quality: A Report on the Preparation and Qualifications of Public School Teachers* (National Center for Education Statistics, Washington, DC, 1999), less than half of America's teachers reported feeling "very well prepared" for their jobs. Only 20 percent felt well prepared to integrate educational technology into classroom instruction. Twenty percent reported feeling well prepared to meet the needs of limited English-proficient students, culturally diverse students, or students with disabilities. Twenty-eight percent felt well prepared to use student performance assessment techniques. Thirty-six percent said they were well prepared to implement state or district curriculum and performance standards. Forty-one percent reported feeling well prepared to implement new teaching methods. In most areas the more professional development hours teachers received, the more likely they were to feel well prepared.

Teachers' Tools for the 21st Century: A Report on Teachers' Use of Technology, (Becky Smerdon, et al., U.S. Department of Education, Washington, DC, September 2000) reports that the majority of public school teachers felt prepared to use computers or the Internet to create instructional materials (78 percent) and to gather information for lesson plans (59 percent). Only 12 to 17 percent, however, felt prepared to use computers or the Internet to communicate with students and to post assignments.

About half said they were prepared to use computers or the Internet for record keeping and to communicate with colleagues, while one-quarter reported being prepared to use technology for communicating with parents. (See Figure 8.3 for percentages of teachers prepared to use the Internet as it relates to years of teaching experience.)

THE PHI DELTA KAPPA POLL OF TEACHERS' ATTITUDES

Periodically, Phi Delta Kappa International, the professional education fraternity, contracts with the Gallup Organization to survey American teachers on education issues. "The Sixth Phi Delta Kappa Poll of Teachers' Attitudes Toward the Public Schools" (Carol A. Langdon and Nick Vesper, *Phi Delta Kappan*, April 2000) found that while teachers definitely see much room for improvement, they are generally optimistic about the performance of the nation's educational systems.

Most teachers (64 percent) gave their communities' schools a grade of A or B in 2000, but the public tended to grade community schools lower than teachers did. (See Table 8.7.) The public and teachers alike rated the public schools in the nation as a whole as substandard. In 2000 a majority of teachers (60 percent) and the public (62 percent) would assign a C or a D to the nation's education system.

When asked by the Sixth Phi Delta Kappa Poll which educational skills local public schools should emphasize, about half (48 percent) of teachers believed the focus should be the academic skills of students, and 44 percent felt the ability of students to take responsibility was most important. The remaining 8 percent believed the focus of school should be on the ability of students to work with others. When the public was asked this same question, 39 percent of survey respondents indicated that the academic skills of students should be the main emphasis of schools, while 46 percent felt it should be on the ability of students to take responsibility. The ability of students to work with others was considered most important by 13 percent of the public.

Attracting and Retaining Good Teachers

The Sixth Phi Delta Kappa Poll asked teachers and the public whether they favored or opposed selected ways for attracting and retaining teachers. In 2000 teachers favored school-financed professional development activities (91 percent), increased pay for all teachers (89 percent), and loans and scholarships for prospective teachers (85 percent). About half (53 percent) supported increased pay for teachers who demonstrate high performance, and 39 percent favored tax credits for teachers who demonstrate high performance. Among the public, the majority favored increased pay for teachers who demonstrate high performance (90 percent), loans and scholarships for prospective teachers (86 percent), and school-financed

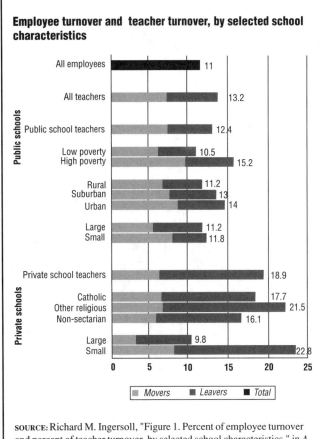

FIGURE 8.2

Employee turnover and teacher turnover, by selected school characteristics

SOURCE: Richard M. Ingersoll, "Figure 1. Percent of employee turnover and percent of teacher turnover, by selected school characteristics," in *A Different Approach to Solving the Teaching Shortage Problem*, Center for the Study of Teaching and Policy, Seattle, WA, January 2001

professional development activities (85 percent). Tax credits (63 percent) and increased pay for all teachers (62 percent) also had considerable support. (See Table 8.8.)

What Should Determine Salary?

Most (62 percent) surveyed teachers believed that years of teaching experience should be very important in determining a public school teacher's salary. More than half (52 percent) of the public felt the same way. Very few teachers (3 percent) believed that the standardized test scores of the teacher's students should be very important in determining a teacher's salary, but nearly half (47 percent) of the public felt test scores should be considered "very important." The level of academic degree earned by the teacher should be a very important determinant of a teacher salary, according to 60 percent of the public and 54 percent of teachers.

TEACHERS' OPINIONS ABOUT SCHOOLS

The Sixth Phi Delta Kappa Poll asked teachers to rate the importance of 12 factors in choosing a public school. All teachers and the public selected the quality of the

FIGURE 8.3

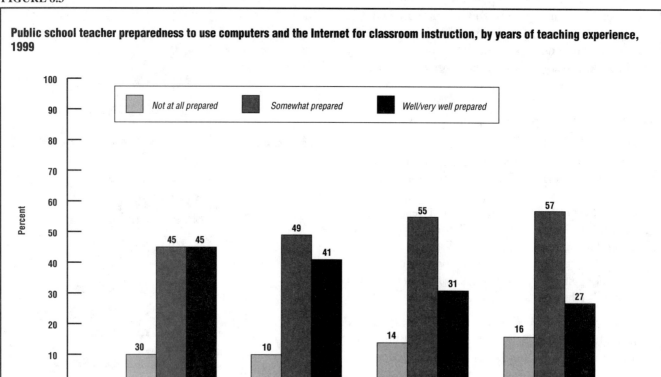

Public school teacher preparedness to use computers and the Internet for classroom instruction, by years of teaching experience, 1999

Legend: Not at all prepared | Somewhat prepared | Well/very well prepared

Years of teaching experience:
- 3 or fewer: 30, 45, 45
- 4 to 9: 10, 49, 41
- 10 to 19: 14, 55, 31
- 20 or more: 16, 57, 27

SOURCE: Becky Smerdon, Stephanie Cronen, Lawrence Lanahan, et al., "Table 5.1. Percent of public school teachers reporting feeling not at all, somewhat, or well/very well prepared to use computers and the internet for classroom instruction, by years of teaching experience: 1999," in *Teachers' Tools for the 21st Century: A Report on Teachers' Use of Technology,* NCES 2000-102, U.S. Department of Education, National Center for Education Statistics, Washington, DC, September 2000

TABLE 8.7

Grading of public schools

Students are often given the grades A, B, C, D, and FAIL to denote the quality of their work. Suppose the public schools themselves, in this community, were graded in the same way. What grade would you give the public schools here — A, B, C, D, or FAIL?

	Teachers %	Public %
A & B	64	49
A	14	11
B	50	38
C	25	31
D	7	9
FAIL	1	5
Don't know	3	6

SOURCE: Carol A. Langdon and Nick Vesper, "Students are often given the grades A, B, C, D, and FAIL to denote the quality of their work. Suppose the public schools themselves, in this community, were graded in the same way. What grade would you give the public schools here -- A, B, C, D, or FAIL?," in "The Sixth Phi Delta Kappa Poll of Teachers' Attitudes Toward the Public Schools, in *Phi Delta Kappan,* vol. 81, no. 8, April 2000

teaching staff as very or fairly important. Maintenance of student discipline was considered important by 100 percent of teachers and 99 percent of the public. The curricu-

lum was selected as important by 99 percent of both teachers and the public. Teachers (99 percent) and the public (94 percent) considered class size to be important in choosing a public school. Proximity to home, extracurricular activities, school size, exposing children to a diverse student body, and reputation were considered important by a majority of both teachers and the public, but the public considered proximity to parent's work and the athletic program more important than teachers did. (See Table 8.9.)

Teachers most often cited lack of free time to learn, practice and plan as the barrier (82 percent) to their use of computers or the Internet for instruction. Seventy-eight percent of teachers felt that the lack of computers was a barrier. Eight percent saw lack of time in the schedule for students to use computers in class as a barrier, and lack of good software was cited by 71 percent. Lack of administrative support was considered a barrier by 43 percent of teachers; only 9 percent listed this as a great barrier. (See Figure 8.4.)

In *The Metropolitan Life Survey of The American Teacher, 1998* (Louis Harris and Associates, Inc., New York, New York, 1998), public school teachers were asked several

TABLE 8.8

Opinion on attracting and retaining good public school teachers, 1999

Here are some ways that have been suggested for attracting and retaining good public school teachers. As you read each suggestion, would you indicate whether you favor it or oppose it as a way to attract and retain good teachers?

	Favor		Oppose		Don't Know	
	Teachers %	Public %	Teachers %	Public %	Teachers %	Public %
School-financed professional development opportunities	91	85	4	12	5	3
Increased pay for all teachers	89	62	7	37	4	1
Loans and scholarships for prospective teachers	85	86	5	12	10	2
Increased pay for teachers who demonstrate high performance	53	90	33	9	14	1
Tax credits for teachers who demonstrate high performance	39	63	39	37	22	*

*Less than one-half of 1%.

SOURCE: Carol A. Langdon and Nick Vesper, "Here are some ways that have been suggested for attracting and retaining good public school teachers. As you read each suggestion, would you indicate whether you favor it or oppose it as a way to attract and retain good teachers?" in "The Sixth Phi Delta Kappa Poll of Teachers' Attitudes Toward the Public Schools," in *Phi Delta Kappan*, vol. 81, no. 8, April 2000

TABLE 8.9

Factors affecting choice of a public school, 1999

Here are different factors that might be considered in choosing a public school for a child, assuming free choice of public and private schools were allowed in this community. As you read each of these factors, would you indicate whether you consider it very important, fairly important, not too important, or not at all important in choosing a local school?

	Very or Fairly Important	
	Teachers %	Public %
Quality of the teaching staff	100	100
Maintenance of student discipline	100	99
Curriculum (i.e., the courses offered)	99	99
Size of class	99	94
Proximity to home	85	87
Extracurricular activities, such as band/orchestra, theater, clubs	84	91
Size of the school (number of students)	81	79
Having your child exposed to a more diverse student body	69	79
Reputation or prestige of the school	59	80
Athletic program	50	80
Proximity to the parent's workplace	42	60
Having your child exposed to a less diverse student body	12	45

SOURCE: Carol A. Langdon and Nick Vesper, "Here are different factors that might be considered in choosing a public school for a child, assuming free choice of public and private schools were allowed in this community. As you read each of these factors, would you indicate whether you consider it very important, fairly important, not too important, or not at all important in choosing a local school?" in "The Sixth Phi Delta Kappa Poll of Teachers' Attitudes Toward the Public Schools," in *Phi Delta Kappan*, vol. 81, no. 8, April 2000

questions about their schools. In 1997, 95 percent said the qualifications and competence of teachers in their schools were either excellent or good. While only 13 percent felt the relations between parents and teachers were excellent, 58 percent reported the relations were good. About one-quarter, however, felt the relations were either fair or poor.

When asked about the availability and responsiveness of parents when teachers needed to make contact, nearly two-thirds (63 percent) of teachers surveyed said it was excellent or good. Ten percent of the teachers felt parent availability and responsiveness was poor. While two-thirds (63 percent) also thought parent support for the school was excellent or good, 28 percent replied "fair," and 10 percent said parents showed poor support.

The overwhelming majority of teachers (92 percent) reported that the quality of education students received at their school was excellent or good. Seven percent said the quality was fair. Teachers in urban schools were nearly twice as likely to say the overall quality of education students received at their school was fair or poor than teachers in rural-area schools, and three to four times as likely as teachers in suburban and small-town schools.

Teachers' Perceptions of Problems In Schools

In the Sixth Phi Delta Kappa Poll, teachers and the public were asked about the seriousness of the following problems in their communities—parents' lack of support, pupils' lack of interest, funding, discipline, overcrowding, drugs, violence, and morals/sexual activity/teen pregnancy. The public considered five (discipline, overcrowding, drugs, violence, and morals/sexual activity/teen pregnancy) of the problems to be more serious than did the teachers. Teachers were more concerned about parental involvement and pupils' lack of interest, while both teachers and the public were equally concerned about funding. (See Table 8.10.)

Teachers and the public were also asked who or what was the main obstacle to improving public schools in their communities. The largest proportion—21 percent of teachers and 13 percent of the public—felt that a lack of finances hindered school improvement. Lack of parental involvement was selected by 17 percent of teachers and 12 percent of the public. Ten percent of the public blamed the government, while only 3 percent of teachers agreed. The board of education and superintendent were considered the main obstacle to school improvement by 8 percent of the public and 7 percent of teachers. (See Table 8.11.)

Only 4 percent of teachers reported that their schools were not very or not at all safe and orderly, while 10 percent of the public believed schools in their community were not safe and orderly. (See Table 8.12.)

FIGURE 8.4

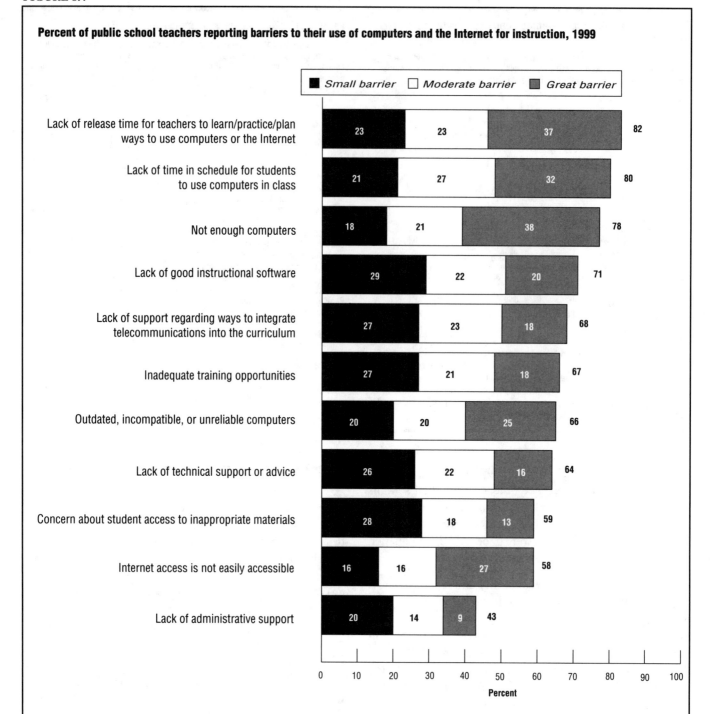

Percent of public school teachers reporting barriers to their use of computers and the Internet for instruction, 1999

■ *Small barrier* □ *Moderate barrier* ▨ *Great barrier*

Barrier	Small	Moderate	Great	Total
Lack of release time for teachers to learn/practice/plan ways to use computers or the Internet	23	23	37	82
Lack of time in schedule for students to use computers in class	21	27	32	80
Not enough computers	18	21	38	78
Lack of good instructional software	29	22	20	71
Lack of support regarding ways to integrate telecommunications into the curriculum	27	23	18	68
Inadequate training opportunities	27	21	18	67
Outdated, incompatible, or unreliable computers	20	20	25	66
Lack of technical support or advice	26	22	16	64
Concern about student access to inappropriate materials	28	18	13	59
Internet access is not easily accessible	16	16	27	58
Lack of administrative support	20	14	9	43

Percent: 0 10 20 30 40 50 60 70 80 90 100

Note: Teachers who reported that computers were not available to them anywhere in the school were excluded from the analyses presented in this figure. Detail may not sum to totals due to rounding.

SOURCE: Becky Smerdon, Stephanie Cronen, Lawrence Lanahan, et al., "Figure 6.1. Percent of Public School Teachers Reporting Small, Moderate, or Great Barriers to Their Use of Computers and the Internet for Instruction: 1999," in *Teachers' Tools for the 21st Century: A Report on Teachers' Use of Technology*, NCES 2000-102, U.S. Department of Education, National Center for Education Statistics, Washington, DC, September 2000

TABLE 8.10

Opinion on the biggest problem of public schools, selected years 1984–99

What do you think are the biggest problems with which the public schools of this community must deal?

	1999 Teachers %	1996 Teachers %	1989 Teachers %	1984 Teachers %	1999 Public %
Parents' lack of support/interest	18	22 (1T)	34 (1)	31 (1)	4 (6T)
Pupils' lack of interest/attitudes/ truancy	13	16 (3)	26 (3)	20 (3)	2 (7T)
Lack of financial support/funding/ money	9	22 (1T)	27 (2)	21 (2)	9 (3)
Lack of discipline/ more control	7	20 (2)	25 (4T)	19 (4)	18 (1)
Lack of family structure/problems of home life (one-parent households '84 &'89)	6	15 (4)	8 (8)	4 (13)	-
Overcrowded schools	4	7 (5T)	7 (9T)	4 (10)	8 (4T)
Use of drugs/dope	2	7 (5T)	13 (7)	5 (7)	8 (4T)
Fighting/violence/gangs	1	7 (5T)	-	-	11 (2)
Moral standards/dress code/sex/pregnancy	*	7	4 (15T)	2 (22)	2 (7T)

*Less than one-half of 1%.

(Figures add to more than 100% because of multiple answers except 1999 figures for teachers, which add to less than 100% because all answers are not reported.)

Rankings for the 1984, 1989, and 1996 teacher surveys and for the 1999 public survey appear in parentheses. "T" means that a response tied for a given rank.

SOURCE: Carol A. Langdon and Nick Vesper, "What do you think are the biggest problems with which the public schools must deal?" in "The Sixth Phi Delta Kappa Poll of Teachers' Attitudes Toward the Public Schools," in *Phi Delta Kappan*, vol. 81, no. 8, April 2000

TABLE 8.11

Opinion on obstacles to public school improvement, 1999

In your opinion who or what is the main obstacle to improving the public schools in your community?

	Teachers %	Public %
Finances/funding	21	13
Parents/lack of parent involvement	17	12
Board of education/superintendent	7	8
Politics/politicians	6	4
Taxpayers/general public	6	4
Government	3	10
Administration/administrators	3	2
Lack of discipline/teachers can't discipline	2	3
Better teachers	*	5
Unions/teacher unions/NEA	*	3
Students/kids	*	2

*Less than one-half of 1%.

SOURCE: Carol A. Langdon and Nick Vesper, "In your opinion who or what is the main obstacle to improving the public schools in your community?" in "The Sixth Phi Delta Kappa Poll of Teachers' Attitudes Toward the Public Schools," in *Phi Delta Kappan*, vol. 81, no. 8, April 2000

TABLE 8.12

Opinion on public school learning environment, 1999

Thinking about the public schools in your community, how would you describe the learning environment for students in those schools - very safe and orderly, somewhat safe and orderly, not very safe and orderly, or not at all safe and orderly?

	Teachers %	Public %
Very safe and orderly	43	24
Somewhat safe and orderly	53	62
Not very safe and orderly	3	7
Not at all safe and orderly	1	3
Don't know	*	4

*This option was not presented to teachers.

SOURCE: Carol A. Langdon and Nick Vesper, "Thinking about the public schools in your community, how would you describe the learning environment for students in those schools - very safe and orderly, somewhat safe and orderly, not very safe and orderly, or not at all safe and orderly?" in "The Sixth Phi Delta Kappa Poll of Teachers' Attitudes Toward the Public Schools," in *Phi Delta Kappan*, vol. 81, no. 8, April 2000

CHAPTER 9
COLLEGES AND UNIVERSITIES

ENROLLMENT IN COLLEGE

The last half of the twentieth century saw a dramatic increase in the number of high school graduates going on to college. In 1960 only 45 percent of high school graduates enrolled in college; by 1999, 63 percent enrolled. The enrollment rates have fluctuated from year to year, but the trend has generally been upward.

Between 1970 and 2000 enrollment in degree-granting higher education institutions increased, and this trend is expected to continue. (See Figure 9.1.) In fall 1999 an estimated 14.8 million students were enrolled in American colleges and universities. The 1999 enrollment was 18 percent more than the 12.5 million students in 1986. The National Center for Education Statistics (NCES) projects that college enrollments will reach 17.7 million by 2011. (See Table 9.1.)

Tuition at most public degree-granting institutions is generally lower than tuition at private institutions. In 1999 far more students were enrolled in public institutions (11.3 million) than in private institutions (3.5 million). (See Table 9.1.)

Between 1986 and 1999 full-time enrollment grew by 23 percent, while part-time enrollment increased by 12 percent. In 1970 about one-third (32 percent) of college students were part-time. By 1999 more than 2 of every 5 students (41 percent) attended part-time. Increased female enrollment has also contributed to the growth in college enrollment. From 1986 to 1999 male enrollment increased by 10 percent, but the number of females enrolled rose by 25 percent. (See Table 9.1.)

More than half (56 percent) of college students in fall 1998 were attending four-year institutions, with the remainder (44 percent) enrolled in two-year colleges. About 12.5 million were enrolled in undergraduate institutions, 1.8 million in graduate schools, and 302,555 in first-professional institutions (such as theological, dental, medical, and law schools).

Older Students

During the late 1980s enrollment of nontraditional students (those over 30 years in age) in degree-granting institutions increased faster than enrollment of students under age 22. (See Figure 9.1.) Between 1991 and 2001 the number of older students attending colleges grew almost as fast as the number of younger students. During that period, enrollment of students under age 25 increased by 13 percent, while enrollment of persons 35 and over increased by 11 percent. However from 2001 to 2011, the NCES projects an 18 percent increase for students less than 25 years of age, while enrollment of students age 35 and older is expected to stay about the same. (See Figure 9.2.)

In 1996 almost 2.8 million students age 35 years or older and about 8.2 million students under age 25 pursued

FIGURE 9.1

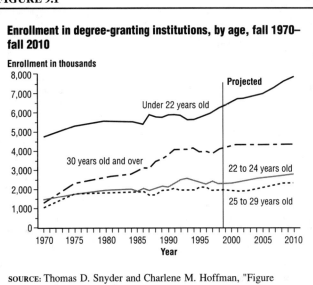

Enrollment in degree-granting institutions, by age, fall 1970– fall 2010

SOURCE: Thomas D. Snyder and Charlene M. Hoffman, "Figure 15.—Enrollment in degree-granting institutions, by age: Fall 1970 to fall 2010," in *Digest of Education Statistics, 2000,* NCES 2001-034, U.S. Department of Education, National Center for Education Statistics, Washington, DC, January 2001

TABLE 9.1

Total enrollment in all degree-granting institutions, by sex, attendance status, and control of institution, with alternative projections, fall 1986–fall 2011

(In thousands)

Year	Total	Sex		Attendance status		Control	
		Men	Women	Full-time	Part-time	Public	Private
1986	12,505	5,885	6,620	7,120	5,384	9,715	2,790
1987	12,767	5,932	6,835	7,231	5,536	9,973	2,793
1988	13,055	6,002	7,053	7,437	5,618	10,161	2,894
1989	13,539	6,190	7,349	7,661	5,878	10,578	2,961
1990	13,819	6,284	7,535	7,821	5,998	10,845	2,974
1991	14,359	6,502	7,857	8,115	6,244	11,310	3,049
1992	14,486	6,524	7,963	8,161	6,325	11,385	3,103
1993	14,305	6,427	7,877	8,128	6,177	11,189	3,116
1994	14,279	6,372	7,907	8,138	6,141	11,134	3,145
1995	14,262	6,343	7,919	8,129	6,133	11,092	3,169
1996	14,368	6,353	8,015	8,303	6,065	11,120	3,247
1997	14,502	6,396	8,106	8,438	6,064	11,196	3,306
1998	14,507	6,369	8,138	8,563	5,944	11,138	3,369
1999	14,791	6,491	8,301	8,786	6,005	11,309	3,482
Middle alternative projections							
2000	14,979	6,538	8,441	8,797	6,182	11,535	3,444
2001	15,300	6,644	8,656	9,035	6,265	11,775	3,525
2002	15,527	6,708	8,819	9,170	6,357	11,947	3,580
2003	15,812	6,786	9,026	9,366	6,446	12,161	3,651
2004	16,074	6,862	9,212	9,544	6,530	12,360	3,714
2005	16,296	6,922	9,374	9,696	6,600	12,527	3,769
2006	16,533	6,991	9,542	9,869	6,664	12,706	3,827
2007	16,754	7,066	9,688	10,039	6,715	12,872	3,881
2008	17,005	7,159	9,846	10,239	6,766	13,063	3,943
2009	17,249	7,252	9,997	10,432	6,816	13,246	4,002
2010	17,457	7,325	10,132	10,586	6,871	13,402	4,055
2011	17,688	7,401	10,287	10,747	6,942	13,573	4,115
Low alternative projections							
2000	14,829	6,473	8,357	8,709	6,120	11,420	3,410
2001	15,162	6,584	8,578	8,954	6,209	11,669	3,493
2002	15,387	6,648	8,740	9,087	6,300	11,839	3,548
2003	15,638	6,711	8,927	9,263	6,375	12,027	3,611
2004	15,720	6,711	9,009	9,334	6,386	12,088	3,632
2005	15,807	6,714	9,093	9,405	6,402	12,151	3,656
2006	16,037	6,781	9,256	9,573	6,464	12,325	3,712
2007	16,251	6,854	9,397	9,738	6,514	12,486	3,765
2008	16,495	6,944	9,551	9,932	6,563	12,671	3,825
2009	16,732	7,034	9,697	10,119	6,612	12,849	3,882
2010	16,933	7,105	9,828	10,268	6,665	13,000	3,933
2011	17,157	7,179	9,978	10,425	6,734	13,166	3,992
High alternative projections							
2000	15,129	6,603	8,525	8,885	6,244	11,650	3,478
2001	15,438	6,704	8,734	9,116	6,321	11,881	3,557
2002	15,667	6,768	8,898	9,253	6,414	12,055	3,612
2003	15,986	6,861	9,125	9,469	6,517	12,295	3,691
2004	16,428	7,013	9,415	9,754	6,674	12,632	3,796
2005	16,785	7,130	9,655	9,987	6,798	12,903	3,882
2006	17,029	7,201	9,828	10,165	6,864	13,087	3,942
2007	17,257	7,278	9,979	10,340	6,916	13,258	3,997
2008	17,515	7,374	10,141	10,546	6,969	13,455	4,061
2009	17,766	7,470	10,297	10,745	7,020	13,643	4,122
2010	17,981	7,545	10,436	10,904	7,077	13,804	4,177
2011	18,219	7,623	10,596	11,069	7,150	13,980	4,238

NOTE: Some data have been revised from previously published figures. Data for 1999 were imputed using alternative procedures. Detail may not sum to totals due to rounding.

SOURCE: Debra E. Gerald and William J. Hussar, "Table 10.—Total enrollment in all degree-granting institutions, by sex, attendance status, and control of institution, with alternative projections: Fall 1986 to fall 2011," in *Projections of Education Statistics to 2011*, NCES 2001-083, U.S. Department of Education, National Center for Education Statistics, Washington, DC, October 2001

degrees. Observers attribute the increased enrollment of older students to the higher education levels required by many occupations and the growing number of students who leave school to work and return later. The main reasons older students begin or return to degree programs are career transitions and the need for updated skills to obtain new jobs.

In 1996 most (80 percent) older students were part-time students, and 63 percent were women. Older students tend to study computer science, education, library science, mechanics/transportation, and public administration/social work more than any other subjects. Colleges have eagerly courted older students in order to maintain enrollments that otherwise would have decreased because of the decline in high school graduates after the baby boom.

Minority Enrollment

The enrollment of minority students (non-Hispanic African Americans, Hispanics, Asians or Pacific Islanders, and Native Americans) in higher education has been rising steadily. In 1976 only 15.4 percent of college students were from minority groups, compared to 26 percent in 1997. Much of the increase can be traced to larger numbers of Hispanic and Asian or Pacific Islander students.

While white students still comprise the large majority of college students, the trend is toward more racial and ethnic diversity on campuses. In 1976 white students made up 84.3 percent of higher education enrollment. In 1997 whites accounted for 73.2 percent of those attending college; blacks, 11 percent; Hispanics, 8.6 percent; Asians or Pacific Islanders, 6.1 percent; and American Indians/Alaskan Natives, 1 percent. Between 1976 and 1997 the number of white students grew by 12 percent and the number of black students by 48 percent. Other minority groups increased by even higher proportions: American Indians/Alaskan Natives by 82 percent, Hispanics by 213 percent, and Asians or Pacific Islanders by 330 percent. (See Table 9.2.)

In 2000 African American and Hispanic students were underrepresented in attaining college degrees, although there was improvement since 1971. In 1971 the proportion of 25- to 29-year-olds who had completed a bachelor's degree was 23 percent for whites, 12 percent for African Americans, and 11 percent for Hispanics. In 2000 the percentages had increased to 36 percent for whites, 21 percent for African Americans, and 15 percent for Hispanics.

Disabled Students

During the 1995–96 school year about 5 percent of all undergraduate students and 3 percent of all graduate-level students were classified as disabled. The reported disabilities included visual and hearing impairments, health impairments, speech or specific learning disabilities, and orthopedic handicaps. Disabled students tended to be older than other undergraduate students; 54 percent of the disabled undergraduates were age 24 or older, compared to 44.5 percent of nondisabled undergraduates.

About three-fifths of disabled undergraduate students lived independently, and 29.8 percent not only lived independently, but also had dependents of their own. Most (62.7 percent) lived off-campus, but not with their parents. About 61 percent were part-time students, and 27.7 percent were majoring in business or the humanities. In

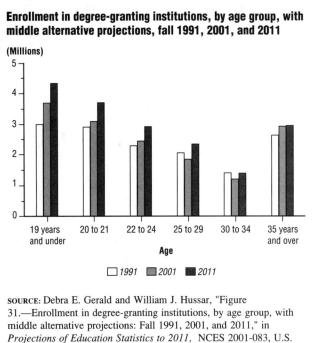

FIGURE 9.2

Enrollment in degree-granting institutions, by age group, with middle alternative projections, fall 1991, 2001, and 2011

(Millions)

Age: 19 years and under, 20 to 21, 22 to 24, 25 to 29, 30 to 34, 35 years and over

□ 1991 ▨ 2001 ■ 2011

SOURCE: Debra E. Gerald and William J. Hussar, "Figure 31.—Enrollment in degree-granting institutions, by age group, with middle alternative projections: Fall 1991, 2001, and 2011," in *Projections of Education Statistics to 2011*, NCES 2001-083, U.S. Department of Education, National Center for Education Statistics, Washington, DC, October 2001

general disabled undergraduates chose the same fields of study that nondisabled students did.

International Students

In 1999–2000, 514,723 international students attended institutions of higher learning in this country. Students from Asia accounted for more than half (54 percent) of the total international student population in the United States. About 11 percent of international students were from China (54,466), 9 percent from Japan (46,872), 8 percent each from India (42,337) and Korea (41,191), and nearly 6 percent from Taiwan (29,234). European students (15 percent) were the second largest group of international students. Students from Canada, Mexico, and Brazil accounted for more than 49 percent of the international student enrollment from the Western Hemisphere and 8 percent of all enrollments worldwide.

Studying Abroad

Many college students from the United States participate in study abroad programs. In 1999–2000 the countries with the largest numbers of Americans enrolled in institutions of higher learning included Britain (29,282), Spain (13,972), Italy (12,930), France (11,924), and Mexico (7,374). Canada and Argentina experienced the most growth (57.6 percent and 34.7 percent, respectively) in American students, and Denmark and Russia had the largest decreases (-9.5 percent and -7.8 percent) from 1998–99 to 1999–2000.

TABLE 9.2

Total fall enrollment in degree-granting institutions, by level of study, sex, and race/ethnicity of student, 1976–97

Level of study, sex, and race/ethnicity of student	Institutions of higher education, in thousands[1]						Degree-granting institutions, in thousands[2]		Percentage distribution of students[3] Institutions of higher education[1]						Degree-granting institutions[2]	
	1976	1980	1990	1995	1996	1997	1996	1997	1976	1980	1990	1995	1996	1997	1996	1997
All students																
Total	10,985.6	12,086.8	13,818.6	14,261.8	14,300.3	14,345.4	14,367.5	14,502.3	100.0	100.0	100.0	100.0	100.0	100.0	100.0	100.0
White, non-Hispanic	9,076.1	9,833.0	10,722.5	10,311.2	10,226.0	10,160.9	10,263.9	10,266.1	84.3	83.5	79.9	74.7	73.9	73.2	73.8	73.1
Total minority	1,690.8	1,948.8	2,704.7	3,496.2	3,609.3	3,723.2	3,637.4	3,771.2	15.7	16.5	20.1	25.3	26.1	26.8	26.2	26.9
Black, non-Hispanic	1,033.0	1,106.8	1,247.0	1,473.7	1,499.4	1,532.8	1,505.6	1,551.0	9.6	9.4	9.3	10.7	10.8	11.0	10.8	11.0
Hispanic	383.8	471.7	782.4	1,093.8	1,152.2	1,200.1	1,166.1	1,218.5	3.6	4.0	5.8	7.9	8.3	8.6	8.4	8.7
Asian or Pacific Islander	197.9	286.4	572.4	797.4	823.6	851.5	828.2	859.2	1.8	2.4	4.3	5.8	6.0	6.1	6.0	6.1
American Indian/ Alaskan Native	76.1	83.9	102.8	131.3	134.0	138.8	137.6	142.5	0.7	0.7	0.8	1.0	1.0	1.0	1.0	1.0
Nonresident alien	218.7	305.0	391.5	454.4	464.9	461.3	466.3	465.0	(4)	(4)	(4)	(4)	(4)	(4)	(4)	(4)
Men	5,794.4	5,868.1	6,283.9	6,342.5	6,344.0	6,330.0	6,352.8	6,396.0	100.0	100.0	100.0	100.0	100.0	100.0	100.0	100.0
White, non-Hispanic	4,813.7	4,772.9	4,861.0	4,594.1	4,553.0	4,504.8	4,552.2	4,548.8	85.3	84.4	80.5	75.6	74.9	74.3	74.8	74.2
Total minority	826.6	884.4	1,176.6	1,484.2	1,524.3	1,562.2	1,533.4	1,582.3	14.7	15.6	19.5	24.4	25.1	25.7	25.2	25.8
Black, non-Hispanic	469.6	463.7	484.7	555.9	563.6	572.5	564.1	579.8	8.3	8.2	8.0	9.1	9.3	9.4	9.3	9.5
Hispanic	209.7	231.6	353.9	480.2	501.3	518.1	506.6	525.8	3.7	4.1	5.9	7.9	8.2	8.5	8.3	8.6
Asian or Pacific Islander	108.4	151.3	294.9	393.3	403.6	414.0	405.5	417.7	1.9	2.7	4.9	6.5	6.6	6.8	6.7	6.8
American Indian/ Alaskan Native	38.5	37.8	43.1	54.8	55.7	57.6	57.2	59.0	0.7	0.7	0.7	0.9	0.9	0.9	0.9	1.0
Nonresident alien	154.1	210.8	246.3	264.3	266.7	262.9	267.2	264.9	(4)	(4)	(4)	(4)	(4)	(4)	(4)	(4)
Women	5,191.2	6,218.7	7,534.7	7,919.2	7,956.3	8,015.5	8,014.7	8,106.3	100.0	100.0	100.0	100.0	100.0	100.0	100.0	100.0
White, non-Hispanic	4,262.4	5,060.1	5,861.5	5,717.2	5,673.1	5,656.1	5,711.7	5,717.4	83.1	82.6	79.3	74.0	73.1	72.4	73.1	72.3
Total minority	864.2	1,064.4	1,528.1	2,012.0	2,085.0	2,161.0	2,104.0	2,188.9	16.9	17.4	20.7	26.0	26.9	27.6	26.9	27.7
Black, non-Hispanic	563.1	643.0	762.3	917.8	935.8	960.2	941.4	971.3	11.0	10.5	10.3	11.9	12.1	12.3	12.0	12.3
Hispanic	174.1	240.1	428.5	613.7	650.9	682.0	659.5	692.7	3.4	3.9	5.8	7.9	8.4	8.7	8.4	8.8
Asian or Pacific Islander	89.4	135.2	277.5	404.1	420.0	437.4	422.6	441.5	1.7	2.2	3.8	5.2	5.4	5.6	5.4	5.6
American Indian/ Alaskan Native	37.6	46.1	59.7	76.5	78.2	81.3	80.4	83.4	0.7	0.8	0.8	1.0	1.0	1.0	1.0	1.1
Nonresident alien	64.6	94.2	145.2	190.1	198.2	198.4	199.0	200.1	(4)	(4)	(4)	(4)	(4)	(4)	(4)	(4)
Full-time	6,703.6	7,088.9	7,821.0	8,128.8	8,213.5	8,322.4	8,303.0	8,438.1	100.0	100.0	100.0	100.0	100.0	100.0	100.0	100.0
White, non-Hispanic	5,512.6	5,717.0	6,016.5	5,833.8	5,847.5	5,886.7	5,906.1	5,960.1	84.2	83.4	79.9	74.9	74.4	73.9	74.3	73.8
Total minority	1,030.9	1,137.5	1,514.9	1,955.3	2,017.2	2,079.8	2,046.8	2,118.7	15.8	16.6	20.1	25.1	25.6	26.1	25.7	26.2
Black, non-Hispanic	659.2	685.6	718.3	840.4	861.0	880.7	871.9	896.6	10.1	10.0	9.5	10.8	10.9	11.1	11.0	11.1
Hispanic	211.1	247.0	394.7	553.2	577.1	599.6	588.8	614.0	3.2	3.6	5.2	7.1	7.3	7.5	7.4	7.6
Asian or Pacific Islander	117.7	162.0	347.4	488.7	503.9	520.6	508.5	526.6	1.8	2.4	4.6	6.3	6.4	6.5	6.4	6.5
American Indian/ Alaskan Native	43.0	43.0	54.4	73.0	75.2	79.0	77.5	81.5	0.7	0.6	0.7	0.9	1.0	1.0	1.0	1.0
Nonresident alien	160.0	234.4	289.6	339.7	348.7	355.9	350.1	359.2	(4)	(4)	(4)	(4)	(4)	(4)	(4)	(4)
Part-time	4,282.1	4,997.9	5,997.7	6,133.0	6,086.8	6,023.1	6,064.6	6,064.3	100.0	100.0	100.0	100.0	100.0	100.0	100.0	100.0
White, non-Hispanic	3,563.5	4,116.0	4,706.0	4,477.4	4,378.5	4,274.3	4,357.8	4,306.0	84.4	83.5	79.8	74.4	73.3	72.2	73.3	72.3
Total minority	659.9	811.3	1,189.8	1,540.9	1,592.1	1,643.4	1,590.6	1,652.5	15.6	16.5	20.2	25.6	26.7	27.8	26.7	27.7
Black, non-Hispanic	373.8	421.2	528.7	633.3	638.4	652.1	633.6	654.5	8.9	8.6	9.0	10.5	10.7	11.0	10.7	11.0
Hispanic	172.7	224.8	387.7	540.7	575.1	600.6	577.3	604.5	4.1	4.6	6.6	9.0	9.6	10.1	9.7	10.1
Asian or Pacific Islander	80.2	124.4	225.1	308.6	319.7	330.9	319.6	332.6	1.9	2.5	3.8	5.1	5.4	5.6	5.4	5.6
American Indian/ Alaskan Native	33.1	40.9	48.4	58.3	58.8	59.9	60.0	61.0	0.8	0.8	0.8	1.0	1.0	1.0	1.0	1.0
Nonresident alien	58.7	70.6	101.8	114.7	116.2	105.4	116.2	105.8	(4)	(4)	(4)	(4)	(4)	(4)	(4)	(4)
Undergraduate																
Total	9,419.0	10,469.1	11,959.1	12,231.7	12,259.4	12,298.3	12,326.9	12,450.6	100.0	100.0	100.0	100.0	100.0	100.0	100.0	100.0
White, non-Hispanic	7,740.5	8,480.7	9,272.6	8,805.6	8,730.9	8,681.8	8,769.5	8,783.9	83.4	82.7	79.0	73.6	72.8	72.1	72.8	72.1
Total minority	1,535.3	1,778.5	2,467.7	3,158.5	3,254.4	3,351.5	3,282.1	3,398.5	16.6	17.3	21.0	26.4	27.2	27.9	27.2	27.9
Black, non-Hispanic	943.4	1,018.8	1,147.2	1,333.6	1,352.6	1,379.9	1,358.6	1,398.1	10.2	9.9	9.8	11.1	11.3	11.5	11.3	11.5
Hispanic	352.9	433.1	724.6	1,012.0	1,065.6	1,107.8	1,079.4	1,125.9	3.8	4.2	6.2	8.5	8.9	9.2	9.0	9.2
Asian or Pacific Islander	169.3	248.7	500.5	692.2	713.2	736.6	717.6	743.7	1.8	2.4	4.3	5.8	6.0	6.1	6.0	6.1
American Indian/ Alaskan Native	69.7	77.9	95.5	120.7	122.9	127.2	126.5	130.8	0.8	0.8	0.8	1.0	1.0	1.1	1.0	1.1
Nonresident alien	143.2	209.9	218.7	267.6	274.1	265.0	275.3	268.2	(4)	(4)	(4)	(4)	(4)	(4)	(4)	(4)
Men	4,896.8	4,997.4	5,379.8	5,401.1	5,411.1	5,405.4	5,420.7	5,468.5	100.0	100.0	100.0	100.0	100.0	100.0	100.0	100.0
White, non-Hispanic	4,052.2	4,054.9	4,184.0	3,918.1	3,890.7	3,857.3	3,890.8	3,899.3	84.4	83.5	79.6	74.5	73.9	73.3	73.8	73.2
Total minority	748.2	802.7	1,069.3	1,339.3	1,375.0	1,408.4	1,384.1	1,427.9	15.6	16.5	20.4	25.5	26.1	26.7	26.2	26.8
Black, non-Hispanic	430.7	428.2	448.0	506.8	513.1	520.6	513.6	527.7	9.0	8.8	8.5	9.6	9.7	9.9	9.7	9.9
Hispanic	191.7	211.2	326.9	444.2	464.0	479.1	469.2	486.7	4.0	4.3	6.2	8.4	8.8	9.1	8.9	9.1
Asian or Pacific Islander	91.1	128.5	254.5	338.1	346.9	356.1	348.8	359.4	1.9	2.6	4.8	6.4	6.6	6.8	6.6	6.7
American Indian/ Alaskan Native	34.8	34.8	39.9	50.2	51.0	52.6	52.4	54.1	0.7	0.7	0.8	1.0	1.0	1.0	1.0	1.0
Nonresident alien	96.4	139.8	126.1	143.8	145.3	139.6	145.8	141.4	(4)	(4)	(4)	(4)	(4)	(4)	(4)	(4)

TABLE 9.2

Total fall enrollment in degree-granting institutions, by level of study, sex, and race/ethnicity of student, 1976–97 [CONTINUED]

| Level of study, sex, and race/ethnicity of student | Institutions of higher education, in thousands[1] | | | | | | Degree-granting institutions, in thousands[2] | | Percentage distribution of students[3] | | | | | | | |
| | | | | | | | | | Institutions of higher education[1] | | | | | | Degree-granting institutions[2] | |
	1976	1980	1990	1995	1996	1997	1996	1997	1976	1980	1990	1995	1996	1997	1996	1997
Women	4,522.1	5,471.7	6,579.3	6,830.6	6,848.4	6,892.9	6,906.3	6,982.1	100.0	100.0	100.0	100.0	100.0	100.0	100.0	100.0
White, non-Hispanic	3,688.3	4,425.8	5,088.2	4,887.5	4,840.2	4,824.5	4,878.7	4,884.6	82.4	81.9	78.4	72.9	72.0	71.3	72.0	71.3
Total minority	787.0	975.8	1,398.5	1,819.2	1,879.3	1,943.0	1,898.1	1,970.6	17.6	18.1	21.6	27.1	28.0	28.7	28.0	28.7
Black, non-Hispanic	512.7	590.6	699.2	826.9	839.5	859.3	845.0	870.3	11.5	10.9	10.8	12.3	12.5	12.7	12.5	12.7
Hispanic	161.2	221.8	397.6	567.8	601.6	628.7	610.1	639.3	3.6	4.1	6.1	8.5	9.0	9.3	9.0	9.3
Asian or Pacific Islander	78.2	120.2	246.0	354.1	366.3	380.5	368.8	384.4	1.7	2.2	3.8	5.3	5.5	5.6	5.4	5.6
American Indian/ Alaskan Native	34.9	43.1	55.5	70.5	71.9	74.5	74.1	76.7	0.8	0.8	0.9	1.1	1.1	1.1	1.1	1.1
Nonresident alien	46.8	70.1	92.6	123.8	128.8	125.4	129.5	126.8	(4)	(4)	(4)	(4)	(4)	(4)	(4)	(4)
Graduate																
Total	1,322.5	1,340.9	1,586.2	1,732.5	1,743.1	1,750.6	1,742.3	1,753.5	100.0	100.0	100.0	100.0	100.0	100.0	100.0	100.0
White, non-Hispanic	1,115.6	1,104.7	1228.4	1,282.3	1,273.9	1,260.2	1,272.6	1,261.8	89.2	88.5	86.6	82.6	81.7	80.7	81.6	80.7
Total minority	134.5	144.0	190.5	270.7	286.0	301.6	286.3	302.3	10.8	11.5	13.4	17.4	18.3	19.3	18.4	19.3
Black, non-Hispanic	78.5	75.1	83.9	118.6	125.5	131.7	125.5	131.6	6.3	6.0	5.9	7.6	8.0	8.4	8.0	8.4
Hispanic	26.4	32.1	47.2	68.0	72.7	78.4	72.8	78.7	2.1	2.6	3.3	4.4	4.7	5.0	4.7	5.0
Asian or Pacific Islander	24.5	31.6	53.2	75.6	79.0	82.1	79.1	82.6	2.0	2.5	3.8	4.9	5.1	5.3	5.1	5.3
American Indian/ Alaskan Native	5.1	5.2	6.2	8.5	8.9	9.4	8.9	9.4	0.4	0.4	0.4	0.5	0.6	0.6	0.6	0.6
Nonresident alien	72.4	92.2	167.3	179.5	183.2	188.8	183.3	189.4	(4)	(4)	(4)	(4)	(4)	(4)	(4)	(4)
Men	707.9	672.2	737.4	767.5	760.5	756.1	759.4	757.9	100.0	100.0	100.0	100.0	100.0	100.0	100.0	100.0
White, non-Hispanic	589.1	538.5	538.8	541.6	530.2	519.5	529.0	520.4	90.2	89.2	86.8	83.1	82.3	81.5	82.3	81.4
Total minority	63.7	65.0	82.1	110.4	113.9	118.2	114.0	118.8	9.8	10.8	13.2	16.9	17.7	18.5	17.7	18.6
Black, non-Hispanic	32.0	28.2	29.3	39.8	41.2	42.8	41.2	42.8	4.9	4.7	4.7	6.1	6.4	6.7	6.4	6.7
Hispanic	14.6	15.7	20.6	28.2	29.5	31.3	29.6	31.5	2.2	2.6	3.3	4.3	4.6	4.9	4.6	4.9
Asian or Pacific Islander	14.4	18.6	29.7	39.0	39.7	40.4	39.7	40.7	2.2	3.1	4.8	6.0	6.2	6.3	6.2	6.4
American Indian/ Alaskan Native	2.7	2.5	2.6	3.4	3.6	3.7	3.6	3.7	0.4	0.4	0.4	0.5	0.6	0.6	0.6	0.6
Nonresident alien	55.1	68.7	116.4	115.6	116.3	118.4	116.4	118.7	(4)	(4)	(4)	(4)	(4)	(4)	(4)	(4)
Women	614.6	668.7	848.8	965.0	982.6	994.5	982.8	995.6	100.0	100.0	100.0	100.0	100.0	100.0	100.0	100.0
White, non-Hispanic	526.5	566.2	689.5	740.7	743.7	740.7	743.6	741.4	88.1	87.8	86.4	82.2	81.2	80.2	81.2	80.2
Total minority	70.8	79.0	108.3	160.3	172.1	183.3	172.3	183.5	11.9	12.2	13.6	17.8	18.8	19.8	18.8	19.8
Black, non-Hispanic	46.5	46.9	54.6	78.8	84.3	88.8	84.3	88.8	7.8	7.3	6.8	8.7	9.2	9.6	9.2	9.6
Hispanic	11.8	16.4	26.6	39.9	43.1	47.1	43.2	47.2	2.0	2.5	3.3	4.4	4.7	5.1	4.7	5.1
Asian or Pacific Islander	10.1	13.0	23.6	36.6	39.3	41.7	39.4	41.8	1.7	2.0	3.0	4.1	4.3	4.5	4.3	4.5
American Indian/ Alaskan Native	2.4	2.7	3.6	5.0	5.3	5.7	5.3	5.7	0.4	0.4	0.5	0.6	0.6	0.6	0.6	0.6
Nonresident alien	17.3	23.5	50.9	63.9	66.9	70.4	66.9	70.7	(4)	(4)	(4)	(4)	(4)	(4)	(4)	(4)
First-professional																
Total	244.1	276.8	273.4	297.6	297.7	296.5	298.3	298.3	100.0	100.0	100.0	100.0	100.0	100.0	100.0	100.0
White, non-Hispanic	220.0	247.7	221.5	223.3	221.2	218.9	221.7	220.4	91.3	90.4	82.6	76.9	76.2	75.7	76.3	75.8
Total minority	21.1	26.3	46.5	67.0	68.9	70.1	69.0	70.4	8.7	9.6	17.4	23.1	23.8	24.3	23.7	24.2
Black, non-Hispanic	11.2	12.8	15.9	21.4	21.4	21.2	21.5	21.4	4.6	4.7	5.9	7.4	7.4	7.3	7.4	7.3
Hispanic	4.5	6.5	10.7	13.8	14.0	13.9	13.9	13.9	1.9	2.4	4.0	4.8	4.8	4.8	4.8	4.8
Asian or Pacific Islander	4.1	6.1	18.7	29.6	31.4	32.8	31.4	32.9	1.7	2.2	7.0	10.2	10.8	11.4	10.8	11.3
American Indian/ Alaskan Native	1.3	0.8	1.1	2.1	2.2	2.3	2.2	2.3	0.5	0.3	0.4	0.7	0.7	0.8	0.7	0.8
Nonresident alien	3.1	2.9	5.4	7.3	7.7	7.5	7.6	7.5	(4)	(4)	(4)	(4)	(4)	(4)	(4)	(4)
Men	189.6	198.5	166.8	173.9	172.5	168.4	172.7	169.6	100.0	100.0	100.0	100.0	100.0	100.0	100.0	100.0
White, non-Hispanic	172.4	179.5	137.8	134.4	132.0	128.0	132.3	129.1	92.1	91.5	84.5	79.5	78.9	78.3	78.9	78.3
Total minority	14.7	16.7	25.3	34.6	35.3	35.5	35.4	35.7	7.9	8.5	15.5	20.5	21.1	21.7	21.1	21.7
Black, non-Hispanic	7.2	7.4	7.4	9.4	9.4	9.1	9.4	9.2	3.9	3.8	4.5	5.5	5.6	5.6	5.6	5.6
Hispanic	3.5	4.6	6.4	7.8	7.8	7.6	7.7	7.6	1.9	2.4	3.9	4.6	4.6	4.7	4.6	4.6
Asian or Pacific Islander	2.9	4.1	10.8	16.2	17.0	17.6	17.1	17.6	1.6	2.1	6.6	9.6	10.2	10.7	10.2	10.7
American Indian/ Alaskan Native	1.0	0.5	0.6	1.2	1.2	1.2	1.2	1.2	0.6	0.3	0.4	0.7	0.7	0.7	0.7	0.7
Nonresident alien	2.5	2.3	3.8	4.9	5.1	4.9	5.1	4.9	(4)	(4)	(4)	(4)	(4)	(4)	(4)	(4)

READINESS FOR COLLEGE

Mathematics and reading are considered "gatekeeper" courses for college graduation; students who require remedial coursework in these two subjects often are not as successful in college as are students who are better prepared in those subjects. Students who must enroll in remedial courses in reading graduate from college only about 61 percent as often as students who need to take no remedial coursework in college. Students who need to take one or two remedial courses in mathematics graduate 80 percent as often as students who do not place in remedial mathematics courses. (See Table 9.3.) More two-year college students (63 percent) than four-year college students (40 percent) take remedial courses.

TABLE 9.2

Total fall enrollment in degree-granting institutions, by level of study, sex, and race/ethnicity of student, 1976–97 [CONTINUED]

Level of study, sex, and race/ethnicity of student	Institutions of higher education, in thousands[1]						Degree-granting institutions, in thousands[2]		Percentage distribution of students[3]							
									Institutions of higher education[1]						Degree-granting institutions[2]	
	1976	1980	1990	1995	1996	1997	1996	1997	1976	1980	1990	1995	1996	1997	1996	1997
Women	54.5	78.4	106.6	123.7	125.3	128.1	125.6	128.6	100.0	100.0	100.0	100.0	100.0	100.0	100.0	100.0
White, non-Hispanic	47.6	68.1	83.7	88.9	89.1	90.9	89.4	91.3	88.2	87.6	79.7	73.3	72.6	72.4	72.7	72.5
Total minority	6.4	9.6	21.3	32.4	33.6	34.6	33.6	34.7	11.8	12.4	20.3	26.7	27.4	27.6	27.3	27.5
Black, non-Hispanic	3.9	5.5	8.5	12.1	12.0	12.0	12.1	12.1	7.3	7.0	8.1	10.0	9.8	9.6	9.8	9.6
Hispanic	1.0	1.9	4.3	6.0	6.2	6.2	6.2	6.2	1.9	2.4	4.1	5.0	5.1	5.0	5.0	4.9
Asian or Pacific Islander	1.1	2.0	7.9	13.4	14.4	15.3	14.4	15.3	2.1	2.6	7.6	11.0	11.7	12.2	11.7	12.1
American Indian/ Alaskan Native	0.2	0.3	0.5	0.9	1.0	1.1	1.0	1.1	0.4	0.3	0.5	0.8	0.8	0.8	0.8	0.8
Nonresident alien	0.5	0.6	1.6	2.4	2.6	2.6	2.6	2.6	(4)	(4)	(4)	(4)	(4)	(4)	(4)	(4)

[1]Institutions that were accredited by an agency or association that was recognized by the U.S. Department of Education, or recognized directly by the Secretary of Education.
[2]Four-year and 2-year degree-granting institutions that were participating in Title IV federal financial aid programs.
[3]Distribution for U.S. citizens only.
[4]Not applicable.
NOTE: Because of underreporting and nonreporting of racial/ethnic data, some figures are slightly lower than corresponding data in other tables. Detail may not sum to totals due to rounding.

SOURCE: Thomas D. Snyder and Charlene M. Hoffman, "Table 208.—Total enrollment in degree-granting institutions, by level of study, sex, and race/ethnicity of student: 1976 to 1997," in *Digest of Education Statistics, 2000*, NCES 2001-034, U.S. Department of Education, National Center for Education Statistics, Washington, DC, January 2001

From 1987 to 1999 academic preparation rose among all college-bound high school students. In 1999 nearly three-quarters of students from high-income (above $100,000) families completed college preparatory core courses, up from under half (47.2 percent) in 1987. Among students from low income (between $12,000 and $18,000) families, more than half (53.1 percent) completed college preparatory core courses in 1999, a 20 percent increase over 1987, when about one-third (32.7 percent) completed the core courses. (See Table 9.4.)

NUMBER OF SCHOOLS

In 1998–99 there were 4,070 degree-granting institutions in the United States—1,688 public and 2,382 private. About 61 percent (2,343) were four-year institutions, and 39 percent (1,727) were two-year schools. While most four-year schools were private (1,730, compared to 613 public institutions), most two-year schools were public (1,075, compared to 652 private schools). (See Table 9.5.)

Since 1969–70, 472 degree-granting institutions, including branch campuses, have shut down. The majority (91 percent) were private institutions, and more than half (54 percent) were two-year public and private colleges. Nearly 42 percent closed between 1990 and 1999, when 197 institutions closed their doors.

SCHOOL SIZE

Most students go to large colleges and universities. Although about 40 percent of higher education institutions have enrollments that are under 1,000 students, enrollment at small institutions accounts for less than 5 percent of total college students in the United States. About 50 percent of all college students in the United States attend the 10 percent of the higher education institutions in the country that have enrollments over 10,000. In fall 1998 the schools with the largest enrollments were the University of Texas at Austin (48,906), Ohio State University, Main Campus (48,511), Miami-Dade Community College (48,222), University of Minnesota, Twin Cities (46,973), and Arizona State University, Main Campus (43,732).

COLLEGES THAT SERVE SPECIFIC POPULATIONS

Women's Colleges

During fall 1998 there were 112,523 students attending women's colleges, and 92 percent of these students were females. Part-time enrollment among men accounted for 65 percent of total male enrollment at women's institutions. In 1997–98 these colleges awarded 1,166 associate degrees, 15,978 bachelor's degrees, 5,760 master's degrees, and 121 doctorates to women.

Historically Black Colleges and Universities

Historically black colleges and universities (HBCUs) are accredited institutions of higher learning established before 1964, whose principal mission was to educate African Americans. The first HBCU was Cheyney University in Pennsylvania, established in 1837, well before the Civil War (1860–1865). At that time, most African Americans in the nation were still slaves, and the prevailing practice was to limit or prohibit their education.

Richard Humphreys, a Philadelphia Quaker, founded Cheyney University. It began as a high school and then

TABLE 9.3

College graduation rates of students taking remedial courses as a percent of students taking no remedial courses, 2000

Number of Remedial Courses Taken	Graduation Rate
One (not mathematics or reading)	98%
Two or more (no reading)	77%
Two or fewer (mathematics only)	80%
Any remedial reading	61%

SOURCE: "Figure 16: Graduation Rates of Students Taking Remedial Courses as a Percent of Students Taking No Remedial Courses," in *Access Denied: Restoring the Nation's Commitment to Equal Educational Opportunity,* Advisory Committee on Student Financial Assisstance, Washington, DC, February 2001

TABLE 9.4

Completion of college preparatory core courses by college-bound high school seniors, 1987–99

Income Range	1987	1990	1995	1999
$12,000 - $18,000	32.7%	42.2%	52.4%	53.1%
$30,000 - $36,000	38.2	48.0	58.0	59.7
$50,000 - $60,000	44.0	54.1	63.2	65.0
$100,000 - above	47.2	58.4	68.2	72.9

SOURCE: "Figure 13: College Preparatory Core Course Completion for College-Bound High School Seniors," in *Access Denied: Restoring the Nation's Commitment to Equal Educational Opportunity,* Advisory Committee on Student Financial Assisstance, Washington, DC, February 2001

became a college (Cheyney State College), awarding its first baccalaureate degree almost 100 years later in the 1930s. Two HBCUs were established in the 1850s: Lincoln University in Pennsylvania (1854) and Wilberforce College in Ohio (1856). Both of these colleges were founded by African Americans to promote education for African Americans.

Another institution whose beginnings go back to the 1850s is now known as the University of the District of Columbia. Miner Normal School was started in 1851 by Myrtilla Miner as a school to train African American women as teachers. In 1955 this institution united with Wilson Normal School to become D.C. Teachers College. In 1976 D.C. Teachers College, Federal City College, and Washington Technical Institute merged to form today's University of the District of Columbia.

Following the Civil War, educating the freed slaves became a top priority of the federal government, the African American community, and private philanthropic groups. Public support in the various states generally came in the form of land grants for schools buildings. Many of the HBCUs founded during this time were religious schools, such as Edward Waters College in Florida (1866), Fisk University in Tennessee (1867), and Talledega College in Alabama (1867). Howard University in Washington, DC was also founded in 1867 by an act of the U.S. Congress. The university was established as a coeducational and multiracial private school.

In 1998, 273,472 students were enrolled in the 102 historically black colleges and universities in the United States. In 1998 full-time students outnumbered part-time students by more than three to one. Women made up a majority (60 percent) of all students at these institutions. Most HCBU students were black—83 percent of the women and 80 percent of the men. (See Table 9.6.)

Hispanic Serving Institutions

Hispanic Serving Institutions (HSIs) are institutions that have a minimum of 25 percent Hispanic student enrollment. Total enrollment in fall 1997 at higher education institutions that served Hispanics was 1.4 million students, but less than half (47 percent) of the students enrolled were Hispanics. Hispanic students received 25,226 associate degrees, 27,230 bachelor's degrees, 5,003 master's degrees, 206 doctoral degrees, and 807 first professional degrees from these institutions in 1997–98.

Native American Colleges

Although Native American and tribal colleges and universities differ widely in their stages of development, they share some similarities. The governing boards of most are made up primarily of Native Americans and Alaskan Natives, as are their student bodies. Located in 12 states, most of the tribal colleges are in isolated areas of the nation.

In 1998 these colleges served about 13,271 full- and part-time students. Most of the colleges are two-year institutions, but four offer bachelor's degrees, and two offer master's degrees. In 1997–98 Native American colleges awarded 1,105 associate's degrees, 48 bachelor's degrees, and 2 master's degrees. One of the major thrusts of the Native American schools is to reinforce traditional cultures and transmit them to the coming generation. Their curricula are primarily practical and geared to local needs. Many of them are strongly oriented toward community service.

Most funding for these schools has come from the federal government under the Tribally Controlled College or University Assistance Act (PL 95-471). In 1999 the government paid Native American colleges about $3,000 for each Indian student, almost 40 percent less than what the average community college receives per student from federal, state, and local sources. Tribal colleges typically do not receive state support because they have been established by sovereign nations and are usually located on federal trust land.

TABLE 9.5

Degree-granting institutions, by control and type of institution, 1949–50 to 1998–99

Year	All institutions			Public			Private		
	Total	4-year	2-year	Total	4-year	2-year	Total	4-year	2-year
	Institutions of higher education[1]								
Excluding branch campuses									
1949–50	1,851	1,327	524	641	344	297	1,210	983	227
1950–51	1,852	1,312	540	636	341	295	1,216	971	245
1951–52	1,832	1,326	506	641	350	291	1,191	976	215
1952–53	1,882	1,355	527	639	349	290	1,243	1,006	237
1953–54	1,863	1,345	518	662	369	293	1,201	976	225
1954–55	1,849	1,333	516	648	353	295	1,201	980	221
1955–56	1,850	1,347	503	650	360	290	1,200	987	213
1956–57	1,878	1,355	523	656	359	297	1,222	996	226
1957–58	1,930	1,390	540	666	366	300	1,264	1,024	240
1958–59	1,947	1,394	553	673	366	307	1,274	1,028	246
1959–60	2,004	1,422	582	695	367	328	1,309	1,055	254
1960–61	2,021	1,431	590	700	368	332	1,321	1,063	258
1961–62	2,033	1,443	590	718	374	344	1,315	1,069	246
1962–63	2,093	1,468	625	740	376	364	1,353	1,092	261
1963–64	2,132	1,499	633	760	386	374	1,372	1,113	259
1964–65	2,175	1,521	654	799	393	406	1,376	1,128	248
1965–66	2,230	1,551	679	821	401	420	1,409	1,150	259
1966–67	2,329	1,577	752	880	403	477	1,449	1,174	275
1967–68	2,374	1,588	786	934	414	520	1,440	1,174	266
1968–69	2,483	1,619	864	1,011	417	594	1,472	1,202	270
1969–70	2,525	1,639	886	1,060	426	634	1,465	1,213	252
1970–71	2,556	1,665	891	1,089	435	654	1,467	1,230	237
1971–72	2,606	1,675	931	1,137	440	697	1,469	1,235	234
1972–73	2,665	1,701	964	1,182	449	733	1,483	1,252	231
1973–74	2,720	1,717	1,003	1,200	440	760	1,520	1,277	243
1974–75	2,747	1,744	1,003	1,214	447	767	1,533	1,297	236
1975–76	2,765	1,767	998	1,219	447	772	1,546	1,320	226
1976–77	2,785	1,783	1,002	1,231	452	779	1,554	1,331	223
1977–78	2,826	1,808	1,018	1,241	454	787	1,585	1,354	231
1978–79	2,954	1,843	1,111	1,308	463	845	1,646	1,380	266
1979–80	2,975	1,863	1,112	1,310	464	846	1,665	1,399	266
1980–81	3,056	1,861	1,195	1,334	465	869	1,722	1,396	[2]326
1981–82	3,083	1,883	1,200	1,340	471	869	1,743	1,412	[2]331
1982–83	3,111	1,887	1,224	1,336	472	864	1,775	1,415	[2]360
1983–84	3,117	1,914	1,203	1,325	474	851	1,792	1,440	352
1984–85	3,146	1,911	1,235	1,329	461	868	1,817	1,450	367
1985–86	3,155	1,915	1,240	1,326	461	865	1,829	1,454	375
Including branch campuses									
1974–75	3,004	1,866	1,138	1,433	537	896	1,571	1,329	242
1975–76	3,026	1,898	1,128	1,442	545	897	1,584	1,353	231
1976–77	3,046	1,913	1,133	1,455	550	905	1,591	1,363	228
1977–78	3,095	1,938	1,157	1,473	552	921	1,622	1,386	236
1978–79	3,134	1,941	1,193	1,474	550	924	1,660	1,391	269
1979–80	3,152	1,957	1,195	1,475	549	926	1,677	1,408	269
1980–81	3,231	1,957	1,274	1,497	552	945	1,734	1,405	[2]329
1981–82	3,253	1,979	1,274	1,498	558	940	1,755	1,421	[2]334
1982–83	3,280	1,984	1,296	1,493	560	933	1,787	1,424	[2]363
1983–84	3,284	2,013	1,271	1,481	565	916	1,803	1,448	355
1984–85	3,331	2,025	1,306	1,501	566	935	1,830	1,459	371
1985–86	3,340	2,029	1,311	1,498	566	932	1,842	1,463	379
1986–87[3]	3,406	2,070	1,336	1,533	573	960	1,873	1,497	376
1987–88[3]	3,587	2,135	1,452	1,591	599	992	1,996	1,536	460
1988–89[3]	3,565	2,129	1,436	1,582	598	984	1,983	1,531	452
1989–90[3]	3,535	2,127	1,408	1,563	595	968	1,972	1,532	440
1990–91[3]	3,559	2,141	1,418	1,567	595	972	1,992	1,546	446
1991–92[3]	3,601	2,157	1,444	1,598	599	999	2,003	1,558	445
1992–93[3]	3,638	2,169	1,469	1,624	600	1,024	2,014	1,569	445
1993–94[3]	3,632	2,190	1,442	1,625	604	1,021	2,007	1,586	421
1994–95[3]	3,688	2,215	1,473	1,641	605	1,036	2,047	1,610	437
1995–96[3]	3,706	2,244	1,462	1,655	608	1,047	2,051	1,636	415

Alliance for Equity in Higher Education

The Alliance for Equity in Higher Education is made up of the Hispanic Association of Colleges and Universities (HACU), the American Indian Higher Education Consortium (AIHEC), and the National Association for Equal Opportunity in Higher Education (NAFEO). It is coordinated by the Institute for Higher Education Policy, a Washington, D.C.-based non-profit education group. The Alliance represents more than 300 Hispanic-Serving Institutions (HSIs), Historically Black Colleges and

TABLE 9.5

Degree-granting institutions, by control and type of institution, 1949–50 to 1998–99 [CONTINUED]

Year	All institutions			Public			Private		
	Total	4-year	2-year	Total	4-year	2-year	Total	4-year	2-year
	Degree-granting institutions[4]								
1996–97	4,009	2,267	1,742	1,702	614	1,088	2,307	1,653	654
1997–98	4,064	2,309	1,755	1,707	615	1,092	2,357	1,694	663
1998–99	4,070	2,343	1,727	1,688	613	1,075	2,382	1,730	652

[1] Institutions that were accredited by an agency or association that was recognized by the U.S. Department of Education, or recognized directly by the Secretary of Education.
[2] Large increases are due to the addition of schools accredited by the Accrediting Commission of Career Schools and Colleges of Technology.
[3] Because of revised survey procedures, data are not entirely comparable with figures for earlier years. The number of branch campuses reporting separately has increased since 1986–87.
[4] Data are for 4-year and 2-year degree-granting institutions that were eligible to participate in Title IV federal financial aid programs.

Thomas D. Snyder and Charlene M. Hoffman, "Table 245.—Degree-granting institutions, by control and type of institution: 1949–50 to 1998–99," in *Digest of Education Statistics, 2000*, NCES 2001-034, U.S. Department of Education, National Center for Education Statistics, Washington, DC, January 2001

Universities (HBCUs), other predominately African American institutions, and Tribal Colleges and Universities. These colleges educate 42 percent of all Hispanic students, 24 percent of African American students, and 16 percent of Native American students. However, member institutions serve students of all races and ethnicities; nearly one-quarter of students at NAFEO institutions are non-African American, over half of students at HACU institutions are non-Hispanic, and almost two in five students at AIHEC institutions are non-Native American.

The Alliance member colleges provide greater access to low-income and underserved populations, striving to keep tuitions affordable. These colleges tend to have higher student success rates among minority students than do traditional colleges. In 1996 they awarded almost 188,000 degrees.

TRENDS IN DEGREES

Trends in Enrollment by Degree Levels

Undergraduate enrollment grew from 10.8 million in 1986 to 12.7 million in 1999, a 17 percent increase. Women outnumbered men 56 percent to 44 percent. By 2011, enrollment is projected to reach about 15.3 million. (See Table 9.7.)

Between 1986 and 1999, graduate enrollment increased 26 percent, from 1.4 million to 1.8 million. By 2011 enrollment is projected to reach over 2 million, increasing about 13 percent from 1999. The number of women (over 1 million) enrolled in graduate programs in 1999 was higher than the number of men (766,000). (See Table 9.8.)

Enrollment in first-professional degree programs (medicine, law, dentistry, theology, etc.) increased 12 percent between 1986 and 1999, from 270,000 to 303,000. In 1999 more men (166,000) than women (138,000) were enrolled in first-professional degree programs. Proportionally, however, the enrollment of women increased from 36 percent in 1986 to 46 percent in 1999. Total enrollment is projected to be 342,000 by 2011, of which 47 percent will be women. (See Table 9.9.)

Trends in Degrees Conferred

Between school years 1988–89 and 1998–99, the number of associate, bachelor's, master's, first professional, and doctoral degrees conferred rose—by 28 percent, 16 percent, 30 percent, 13 percent, and 27 percent, respectively. In 1998–99, students earned 561,000 associate degrees, 1.2 million bachelor's degrees, 405,000 master's degrees, 80,300 first-professional degrees, and 45,900 doctorates. (See Table 9.10.) Table 9.11 shows the number, level, and disciplines of degrees conferred during 1997–98.

Associate Degrees

In 1997–98, 558,555 associate degrees were earned. (See Table 9.12.) Public institutions accounted for 81 percent of all associate degrees in 1997–98. At public institutions, liberal arts/general studies, health professions, and business management/administration were the most popular areas of study. At private institutions, in addition to these three areas, engineering-related technology was a popular degree program. (See Table 9.11.)

Bachelor's Degrees

In 1997–98 students earned almost 1.2 million bachelor's degrees. Since 1981–82 more bachelor's degrees have been awarded to women than to men. Of the 1.2 million degrees awarded in 1997–98, women earned 664,450 or 56 percent. (See Table 9.10.) The largest numbers of degrees conferred were in business management/administration, social sciences and history, education, health and related sciences, psychology, and engineering. (See Table 9.11.)

Master's Degrees

The annual number of master's degrees awarded declined during the late 1970s and the early 1980s but began to rise again in the 1984–85 academic year. In

TABLE 9.6

Selected statistics on degree-granting historically black colleges and universities, 1980, 1990, 1997, and 1998

Item	Total	Public		Private	
		4-year	2-year	4-year	2-year
Number of institutions, fall 1998	**102**	**41**	**11**	**48**	**2**
Total enrollment, fall 1980	233,557	155,085	13,132	62,924	2,416
Men	106,387	70,236	6,758	28,352	1,041
Men, black	81,818	53,654	2,781	24,412	971
Women	127,170	84,849	6,374	34,572	1,375
Women, black	109,171	70,582	4,644	32,589	1,356
Total enrollment, fall 1990	257,152	171,969	15,077	68,528	1,578
Men	105,157	70,220	6,321	28,054	562
Men, black	82,897	54,041	3,214	25,198	444
Women	151,995	101,749	8,756	40,474	1,016
Women, black	125,785	80,883	6,066	38,115	721
Total enrollment, fall 1998	273,472	174,776	23,827	74,155	714
Men	108,752	68,990	9,907	29,627	228
Men, black	87,163	55,970	3,961	27,026	206
Women	164,720	105,786	13,920	44,528	486
Women, black	136,582	87,015	7,298	41,811	458
Full-time enrollment, fall 1998	209,135	130,293	11,527	66,830	485
Men	85,247	53,714	4,700	26,639	194
Women	123,888	76,579	6,827	40,191	291
Part-time enrollment, fall 1998	64,337	44,483	12,300	7,325	229
Men	23,505	15,276	5,207	2,988	34
Women	40,832	29,207	7,093	4,337	195
Earned degrees conferred, 1997–98					
Associate	3,407	1,097	2,098	154	58
Men	1,170	397	701	55	17
Men, black	485	160	266	45	14
Women	2,237	700	1,397	99	41
Women, black	1,118	271	720	90	37
Bachelor's	29,780	20,290	—	9,490	—
Men	10,759	7,466	—	3,293	—
Men, black	8,980	5,877	—	3,103	—
Women	19,021	12,824	—	6,197	—
Women, black	16,526	10,624	—	5,902	—
Master's	6,411	5,261	—	1,150	—
Men	1,993	1,617	—	376	—
Men, black	1,253	986	—	267	—
Women	4,418	3,644	—	774	—
Women, black	3,135	2,474	—	661	—
Doctor's	377	142	—	235	—
Men	181	59	—	122	—
Men, black	122	28	—	94	—
Women	196	83	—	113	—
Women, black	138	42	—	96	—
First-professional	1,348	491	—	857	—
Men	621	236	—	385	—
Men, black	406	124	—	282	—
Women	727	255	—	472	—
Women, black	537	169	—	368	—
Financial statistics, 1996–97, in thousands of dollars					
Current-fund revenues	—	$2,173,308	$99,880	—	—
Tuition and fees	—	446,451	18,981	—	—
Federal government	—	366,229	16,601	—	—
State governments	—	894,660	51,076	—	—
Local governments	—	79,080	8,000	—	—
Private gifts, grants, and contracts	—	38,235	209	—	—
Endowment income	—	3,604	3	—	—
Sales and services	—	10,087	102	—	—
Other sources	—	334,962	4,908	—	—
Current-fund expenditures	—	2,136,616	98,176	—	—
Educational and general expenditures	—	1,851,522	93,863	—	—
Auxiliary enterprises	—	285,093	4,313	—	—
Hospitals	—	0	0	—	—
Independent operations	—	0	0	—	—

— Not available.

NOTE: Historically black colleges and universities are degree-granting institutions established prior to 1964 with the principal mission of educating black Americans. Federal regulations, 20 U.S. Code, Section 1061 (2), allow for certain exceptions to the founding date. Most institutions are in the southern and border states and were established prior to 1954. Federal, state, and local governments revenue includes appropriations, grants, contracts, and independent operations. Detail may not sum to totals due to rounding.

SOURCE: Thomas D. Snyder and Charlene M. Hoffman, "Table 223.—Selected statistics on degree-granting historically black colleges and universities: 1980, 1990, 1997 and 1998," in *Digest of Education Statistics, 2000*, NCES 2001-034, U.S. Department of Education, National Center for Education Statistics, Washington, DC, January 2001

TABLE 9.7

Total undergraduate enrollment in all degree-granting institutions, by sex, attendance status, and control of institution, with alternative projections, Fall 1986–fall 2011

(In thousands)

Year	Total	Sex		Attendance status		Control	
		Men	Women	Full-time	Part-time	Public	Private
1986	10,799	5,018	5,781	6,353	4,446	8,661	2,137
1987	11,046	5,069	5,978	6,463	4,584	8,919	2,128
1988	11,317	5,137	6,179	6,642	4,674	9,103	2,213
1989	11,743	5,311	6,431	6,841	4,901	9,488	2,255
1990	11,959	5,380	6,579	6,976	4,983	9,710	2,250
1991	12,439	5,571	6,868	7,222	5,217	10,148	2,291
1992	12,537	5,582	6,954	7,243	5,293	10,216	2,320
1993	12,324	5,484	6,840	7,179	5,145	10,012	2,312
1994	12,263	5,423	6,840	7,169	5,094	9,945	2,317
1995	12,232	5,402	6,831	7,146	5,087	9,904	2,328
1996	12,327	5,421	6,907	7,299	5,029	9,935	2,392
1997	12,451	5,469	6,982	7,419	5,032	10,007	2,443
1998	12,437	5,446	6,991	7,539	4,898	9,950	2,487
1999	12,681	5,560	7,122	7,735	4,947	10,110	2,571

Middle alternative projections

Year	Total	Sex		Attendance status		Control	
		Men	Women	Full-time	Part-time	Public	Private
2000	12,894	5,617	7,277	7,785	5,109	10,334	2,561
2001	13,182	5,715	7,467	8,012	5,170	10,554	2,628
2002	13,378	5,773	7,605	8,136	5,242	10,708	2,670
2003	13,628	5,845	7,784	8,316	5,313	10,902	2,726
2004	13,855	5,912	7,942	8,474	5,380	11,080	2,775
2005	14,048	5,966	8,083	8,611	5,438	11,231	2,818
2006	14,261	6,031	8,231	8,772	5,490	11,395	2,866
2007	14,461	6,099	8,361	8,927	5,533	11,549	2,911
2008	14,694	6,187	8,508	9,115	5,580	11,729	2,965
2009	14,922	6,274	8,648	9,296	5,626	11,904	3,018
2010	15,111	6,341	8,771	9,438	5,674	12,049	3,062
2011	15,305	6,404	8,902	9,574	5,732	12,199	3,106

Low alternative projections

Year	Total	Sex		Attendance status		Control	
		Men	Women	Full-time	Part-time	Public	Private
2000	12,765	5,561	7,204	7,707	5,058	10,231	2,535
2001	13,063	5,664	7,400	7,940	5,123	10,459	2,604
2002	13,258	5,721	7,537	8,063	5,195	10,612	2,646
2003	13,478	5,781	7,698	8,225	5,255	10,782	2,696
2004	13,550	5,782	7,767	8,288	5,262	10,836	2,714
2005	13,627	5,787	7,841	8,353	5,275	10,894	2,733
2006	13,833	5,850	7,984	8,509	5,325	11,053	2,780
2007	14,027	5,916	8,110	8,659	5,367	11,203	2,824
2008	14,253	6,001	8,253	8,842	5,413	11,377	2,876
2009	14,474	6,086	8,389	9,017	5,457	11,547	2,927
2010	14,658	6,151	8,508	9,155	5,504	11,688	2,970
2011	14,846	6,212	8,635	9,287	5,560	11,833	3,013

1997–98 the number reached 430,164. The proportion earned by women has steadily increased. In 1970–71, women earned 40 percent of all master's degrees; in 1997–98 the proportion rose to 57 percent and is projected to remain well above 50 percent through 2009–10. (See Table 9.10.) The fields with the greatest numbers of degrees awarded were education and business management/administration. (See Table 9.11.)

Doctoral Degrees

The number of doctorates conferred remained virtually unchanged at around 33,000 throughout most of the 1970s and 1980s. Since 1984–85, the number has increased slightly each year, reaching 46,010 in 1997–98. Generally, men receiving doctor's degrees far outnumbered women, but the number of women earning doctorates has more than doubled since the late 1970s. In 1997–98 women earned 42 percent of all doctor's degrees conferred. The NCES projects that through 2009–10 the proportion will remain about the same. (See Table 9.10.) The majority of doctorates earned in 1997–98 were in education and technical fields such as engineering, the biological/life sciences, and physical science. (See Table 9.11.)

TABLE 9.7

Total undergraduate enrollment in all degree-granting institutions, by sex, attendance status, and control of institution, with alternative projections, Fall 1986–fall 2011 [CONTINUED]

(In thousands)

High alternative projections

Year	Total	Sex		Attendance status		Control	
		Men	Women	Full-time	Part-time	Public	Private
2000	13,023	5,673	7,350	7,863	5,160	10,437	2,587
2001	13,301	5,766	7,534	8,084	5,217	10,649	2,652
2002	13,498	5,825	7,673	8,209	5,289	10,804	2,694
2003	13,778	5,909	7,870	8,407	5,371	11,022	2,756
2004	14,160	6,042	8,117	8,660	5,498	11,324	2,836
2005	14,469	6,145	8,325	8,869	5,601	11,568	2,903
2006	14,689	6,212	8,478	9,035	5,655	11,737	2,952
2007	14,895	6,282	8,612	9,195	5,699	11,895	2,998
2008	15,135	6,373	8,763	9,388	5,747	12,081	3,054
2009	15,370	6,462	8,907	9,575	5,795	12,261	3,109
2010	15,564	6,531	9,034	9,721	5,844	12,410	3,154
2011	15,764	6,596	9,169	9,861	5,904	12,565	3,199

NOTE: Some data have been revised. Data for 1999 were imputed using alternative procedures. Detail may not sum to totals due to rounding.

SOURCE: Debra E. Gerald and William J. Hussar, "Table 19—Total undergraduate enrollment in all degree-granting institutions, by sex, attendance status, and control of institution, with alternative projections: Fall 1986 to fall 2011," in *Projections of Education Statistics to 2011*, NCES 2001-083, U.S. Department of Education, National Center for Education Statistics, Washington, DC, October 2001

First Professional Degrees

There have been large changes in the total number of first-professional degrees (dentistry, medicine, law, etc.) awarded to women. There was an almost 700 percent increase from 1970–71 to 1980–81. (The increase for men during the same period was 49 percent.) By 1997–98 first-professional degrees earned by women had increased an additional 81 percent. Women still lagged behind men, however, earning 43 percent of all first-professional degrees in 1997–98. (See Table 9.10.) Women received 38 percent of dental degrees, 42 percent of medical degrees, and 44 percent of all law degrees in 1997–98. (See Table 9.12.)

FACULTY

In fall 1997, 2.8 million people were involved in operating the nation's colleges and universities. About 67 percent were professional staff, including executives, administrators, and instructors. About 33 percent were nonprofessional, such as clerical or secretarial staff, paraprofessionals, and skilled staff, including building maintenance and groundskeepers.

Instructional and research faculty filled 989,813 positions; 222,724 research and instruction assistants were also employed. Almost 80 percent were full-time employees. Seventy percent worked in public institutions.

In fall 1997 men accounted for 64 percent of the 568,719 full-time instructional faculty members. Far more men (80 percent) than women (20 percent) were full professors. Nearly three-quarters (74 percent) of full-time faculty members were professors, associate professors, or assistant professors. The remainder was instructors, lecturers, or other faculty. (See Table 9.13.)

Race/Ethnicity

Members of ethnic and racial minority groups are underrepresented among full-time college faculty. In 1997 non-Hispanic whites made up 84 percent of all full-time faculty members, down slightly from 88 percent in 1991. Non-Hispanic blacks accounted for about 5 percent of full-time faculty; Hispanics, 2.5 percent; Asians or Pacific Islanders, 5 percent; and American Indians/Alaskan Natives, less than 1 percent. Nonresident aliens made up about 2 percent. (See Table 9.13.)

Salaries

Salaries for instructional faculty have increased slowly but steadily since 1980. In 1970–71 the average faculty member earned $12,710; in 1996–97 the average salary was $50,829. Taking inflation into account, however, the 1996–97 average salary was about the same as in 1970–71 ($50,841 in constant 1996–97 dollars).

According to the American Association of University Professors ("The Annual Report on the Economic Status of the Profession," *Academe*, March/April 2001, vol. 87, no. 2) average faculty salary increased 3.5 percent from 1999–2000 to 2000–01, an increase of .1 percent when adjusted for inflation. In 2000–01 the average salary of a full professor was $80,860. For associate and assistant professors, the average salaries were $58,941 and $49,015, respectively, while instructors earned an average of $36,198 and lecturers earned $41,486.

Male full professors received an average salary of $80,860, while female full professors received about 12 percent less ($71,419). At the associate and assistant

TABLE 9.8

Total graduate enrollment in all degree-granting institutions, by sex, attendance status, and control of institution, with alternate projections, fall 1986–fall 2011

(In thousands)

Year	Total	Sex		Attendance status		Control	
		Men	Women	Full-time	Part-time	Public	Private
1986	1,435	693	742	522	913	941	494
1987	1,452	694	758	527	925	945	507
1988	1,472	697	775	553	919	949	522
1989	1,522	710	811	572	949	978	544
1990	1,586	737	849	599	987	1,023	563
1991	1,639	760	878	641	997	1,050	589
1992	1,669	772	896	665	1,003	1,058	611
1993	1,688	771	918	689	1,000	1,064	625
1994	1,721	776	945	706	1,015	1,075	647
1995	1,732	768	964	717	1,015	1,074	659
1996	1,742	759	983	737	1,005	1,069	674
1997	1,753	758	996	753	1,001	1,070	683
1998	1,768	754	1,013	753	1,014	1,067	701
1999	1,807	766	1,041	781	1,026	1,077	730
Middle alternative projections							
2000	1,787	758	1,028	747	1,039	1,082	705
2001	1,816	764	1,053	756	1,061	1,100	716
2002	1,844	768	1,077	764	1,081	1,118	727
2003	1,875	773	1,101	775	1,099	1,137	738
2004	1,905	780	1,125	790	1,115	1,155	750
2005	1,929	784	1,145	801	1,128	1,170	760
2006	1,950	788	1,162	811	1,139	1,182	768
2007	1,967	793	1,174	821	1,146	1,193	774
2008	1,982	797	1,185	830	1,152	1,202	780
2009	1,994	801	1,194	840	1,155	1,209	785
2010	2,010	806	1,205	849	1,162	1,219	792
2011	2,041	815	1,225	867	1,173	1,237	804
Low alternative projections							
2000	1,769	750	1,018	740	1,029	1,071	698
2001	1,800	757	1,044	749	1,051	1,090	710
2002	1,827	761	1,067	757	1,071	1,108	720
2003	1,854	764	1,089	766	1,087	1,124	730
2004	1,863	763	1,100	773	1,090	1,130	734
2005	1,871	760	1,111	777	1,094	1,135	737
2006	1,892	764	1,127	787	1,105	1,147	745
2007	1,908	769	1,139	796	1,112	1,157	751
2008	1,923	773	1,149	805	1,117	1,166	757
2009	1,934	777	1,158	815	1,120	1,173	761
2010	1,950	782	1,169	824	1,127	1,182	768
2011	1,980	791	1,188	841	1,138	1,200	780
High alternative projections							
2000	1,805	766	1,038	754	1,049	1,093	712
2001	1,832	771	1,062	763	1,071	1,110	722
2002	1,861	775	1,087	771	1,091	1,128	734
2003	1,896	782	1,113	784	1,111	1,150	746
2004	1,947	797	1,150	807	1,140	1,180	767
2005	1,987	808	1,179	825	1,162	1,205	783
2006	2,009	812	1,197	835	1,173	1,217	791
2007	2,026	817	1,209	846	1,180	1,229	797
2008	2,041	821	1,221	855	1,187	1,238	803
2009	2,054	825	1,230	865	1,190	1,245	809
2010	2,070	830	1,241	874	1,197	1,256	816
2011	2,102	839	1,262	893	1,208	1,274	828

NOTE: Some data have been revised from previously published figures. Data for 1999 were imputed using alternative procedures. Detail may not sum to totals due to rounding.

SOURCE: Debra E. Gerald and William J. Hussar, "Table 20.—Total graduate enrollment in all degree-granting institutions, by sex, attendance status, and control of institution, with alternative projections: Fall 1986 to fall 2011," in *Projections of Education Statistics to 2011,* NCES 2001-083, U.S. Department of Education, National Center for Education Statistics, Washington, DC, October 2001

levels, the gap was 7 percent; at the instructor level it was 4 percent; and at the lecturer level, the gap in earnings between males and females was 10 percent. Men earn 6.5 percent more than women in public institutions, 5.9 percent more in independent (private) colleges and 10 percent more in research (doctoral) universities.

THE RISING COST OF A COLLEGE EDUCATION

The cost of a college education has been increasing dramatically. Overall costs for all institutions have quadrupled since 1976–77. Costs were considerably less for students attending a state-supported school within their state of residence. In 1996–97, the estimated average

TABLE 9.9

Total first-professional enrollment in all degree-granting institutions, by sex, attendance status, and control of institution, with alternative projections, fall 1986–fall 2011

(In thousands)

Year	Total	Sex		Attendance status		Control	
		Men	Women	Full-time	Part-time	Public	Private
1986	270	174	96	246	24	112	158
1987	268	170	98	242	26	110	158
1988	267	167	100	241	26	109	158
1989	274	169	105	248	26	113	162
1990	273	167	107	246	28	112	162
1991	281	170	111	252	29	111	169
1992	281	169	112	252	29	111	170
1993	292	173	120	260	33	114	179
1994	295	174	120	263	31	114	181
1995	298	174	123	266	31	115	183
1996	298	173	125	267	31	117	182
1997	298	169	129	267	31	118	180
1998	302	168	134	271	31	121	182
1999	303	166	138	271	33	123	180
Middle alternative projections							
2000	298	164	135	266	33	119	179
2001	301	165	136	268	33	120	181
2002	305	166	138	271	33	121	183
2003	309	168	142	276	34	123	186
2004	314	169	144	279	34	125	189
2005	318	171	147	284	34	127	191
2006	322	172	149	287	34	129	193
2007	326	173	152	290	35	130	195
2008	329	175	154	294	35	132	197
2009	332	176	155	296	35	133	199
2010	336	179	157	300	36	134	201
2011	342	182	161	307	36	137	205
Low alternative projections							
2000	295	162	134	263	33	118	177
2001	298	164	135	266	33	119	179
2002	302	165	137	269	33	120	181
2003	306	166	140	273	34	122	184
2004	307	165	141	273	33	122	185
2005	308	166	143	275	33	123	185
2006	312	167	145	278	33	125	187
2007	316	168	147	281	34	126	189
2008	319	170	149	285	34	128	191
2009	322	171	150	287	34	129	193
2010	326	174	152	291	35	130	195
2011	332	177	156	298	35	133	199
High alternative projections							
2000	301	166	136	269	33	120	181
2001	304	166	137	270	33	121	183
2002	308	167	139	273	33	122	185
2003	312	170	144	279	34	124	188
2004	321	173	147	285	35	128	193
2005	328	176	151	293	35	131	197
2006	332	177	153	296	35	133	199
2007	336	178	157	299	36	134	201
2008	339	180	159	303	36	136	203
2009	342	181	160	305	36	137	205
2010	346	184	162	309	37	138	207
2011	352	187	166	316	37	141	211

NOTE: Some data have been revised from previously published figures. Data for 1999 were imputed using alternative procedures. Detail may not sum to totals due to rounding.

SOURCE: Debra E. Gerald and William J. Hussar, "Table 21.—Total first-professional enrollment in all degree-granting institutions, by sex, attendance status, and control of institution, with alternative projections: Fall 1986 to fall 2011," in *Projections of Education Statistics to 2011*, NCES 2001-083, U.S. Department of Education, National Center for Education Statistics, Washington, DC, October 2001

annual cost for undergraduate tuition, room and board, and fees was $6,530 for a public institution and $18,039 for a private college.

In 2000–2001, the average residential student paid $11,338 in total costs if he or she attended an in-state, four-year public college. At a four-year private college, total costs were $24,946. The West had the lowest tuition rate for public four-year institutions, the Southwest had the lowest tuition rate for private four-year institutions, while New England had the highest rates for both. (See Table 9.14.)

TABLE 9.10

Earned degrees conferred by degree-granting institutions, by level of degree and sex of student, 1869–70 to 2009–10

Year	Associate degrees			Bachelor's degrees			Master's degrees			First-professional degrees			Doctor's degrees[1]		
	Total	Men	Women	Total	Men	Women	Total	Men	Women	Total	Men	Women	Total	Men	Women
1869–70	—	—	—	[2]9,371	[2]7,993	[2]1,378	0	0	0	[3]	[3]	[3]	1	1	0
1879–80	—	—	—	[2]12,896	[2]10,411	[2]2,485	879	868	11	[3]	[3]	[3]	54	51	3
1889–90	—	—	—	[2]15,539	[2]12,857	[2]2,682	1,015	821	194	[3]	[3]	[3]	149	147	2
1899–1900	—	—	—	[2]27,410	[2]22,173	[2]5,237	1,583	1,280	303	[3]	[3]	[3]	382	359	23
1909–10	—	—	—	[2]37,199	[2]28,762	[2]8,437	2,113	1,555	558	[3]	[3]	[3]	443	399	44
1919–20	—	—	—	[2]48,622	[2]31,980	[2]16,642	4,279	2,985	1,294	[3]	[3]	[3]	615	522	93
1929–30	—	—	—	[2]122,484	[2]73,615	[2]48,869	14,969	8,925	6,044	[3]	[3]	[3]	2,299	1,946	353
1939–40	—	—	—	[2]186,500	[2]109,546	[2]76,954	26,731	16,508	10,223	[3]	[3]	[3]	3,290	2,861	429
1949–50	—	—	—	[2]432,058	[2]328,841	[2]103,217	58,183	41,220	16,963	[3]	[3]	[3]	6,420	5,804	616
1959–60	—	—	—	[2]392,440	[2]254,063	[2]138,377	74,435	50,898	23,537	[3]	[3]	[3]	9,829	8,801	1,028
1960–61	—	—	—	365,174	224,538	140,636	84,609	57,830	26,779	25,253	24,577	676	10,575	9,463	1,112
1961–62	—	—	—	383,961	230,456	153,505	91,418	62,603	28,815	25,607	24,836	771	11,622	10,377	1,245
1962–63	—	—	—	411,420	241,309	170,111	98,684	67,302	31,382	26,590	25,753	837	12,822	11,448	1,374
1963–64	—	—	—	461,266	265,349	195,917	109,183	73,850	35,333	27,209	26,357	852	14,490	12,955	1,535
1964–65	—	—	—	493,757	282,173	211,584	121,167	81,319	39,848	28,290	27,283	1,007	16,467	14,692	1,775
1965–66	111,607	63,779	47,828	520,115	299,287	220,828	140,602	93,081	47,521	30,124	28,982	1,142	18,237	16,121	2,116
1966–67	139,183	78,356	60,827	558,534	322,711	235,823	157,726	103,109	54,617	31,695	30,401	1,294	20,617	18,163	2,454
1967–68	159,441	90,317	69,124	632,289	357,682	274,607	176,749	113,552	63,197	33,939	32,402	1,537	23,089	20,183	2,906
1968–69	183,279	105,661	77,618	728,845	410,595	318,250	193,756	121,531	72,225	35,114	33,595	1,519	26,158	22,722	3,436
1969–70	206,023	117,432	88,591	792,316	451,097	341,219	208,291	125,624	82,667	34,918	33,077	1,841	29,866	25,890	3,976
1970–71	252,311	144,144	108,167	839,730	475,594	364,136	230,509	138,146	92,363	37,946	35,544	2,402	32,107	27,530	4,577
1971–72	292,014	166,227	125,787	887,273	500,590	386,683	251,633	149,550	102,083	43,411	40,723	2,688	33,363	28,090	5,273
1972–73	316,174	175,413	140,761	922,362	518,191	404,171	263,371	154,468	108,903	50,018	46,489	3,529	34,777	28,571	6,206
1973–74	343,924	188,591	155,333	945,776	527,313	418,463	277,033	157,842	119,191	53,816	48,530	5,286	33,816	27,365	6,451
1974–75	360,171	191,017	169,154	922,933	504,841	418,092	292,450	161,570	130,880	55,916	48,956	6,960	34,083	26,817	7,266
1975–76	391,454	209,996	181,458	925,746	504,925	420,821	311,771	167,248	144,523	62,649	52,892	9,757	34,064	26,267	7,797
1976–77	406,377	210,842	195,535	919,549	495,545	424,004	317,164	167,783	149,381	64,359	52,374	11,985	33,232	25,142	8,090
1977–78	412,246	204,718	207,528	921,204	487,347	433,857	311,620	161,212	150,408	66,581	52,270	14,311	32,131	23,658	8,473
1978–79	402,702	192,091	210,611	921,390	477,344	444,046	301,079	153,370	147,709	68,848	52,652	16,196	32,730	23,541	9,189
1979–80	400,910	183,737	217,173	929,417	473,611	455,806	298,081	150,749	147,332	70,131	52,716	17,415	32,615	22,943	9,672
1980–81	416,377	188,638	227,739	935,140	469,883	465,257	295,739	147,043	148,696	71,956	52,792	19,164	32,958	22,711	10,247
1981–82	434,526	196,944	237,582	952,998	473,364	479,634	295,546	145,532	150,014	72,032	52,223	19,809	32,707	22,224	10,483
1982–83	449,620	203,991	245,629	969,510	479,140	490,370	289,921	144,697	145,224	73,054	51,250	21,804	32,775	21,902	10,873
1983–84	452,240	202,704	249,536	974,309	482,319	491,990	284,263	143,595	140,668	74,468	51,378	23,090	33,209	22,064	11,145
1984–85	454,712	202,932	251,780	979,477	482,528	496,949	286,251	143,390	142,861	75,063	50,455	24,608	32,943	21,700	11,243
1985–86	446,047	196,166	249,881	987,823	485,923	501,900	288,567	143,508	145,059	73,910	49,261	24,649	33,653	21,819	11,834
1986–87	436,304	190,839	245,465	991,264	480,782	510,482	289,349	141,269	148,080	71,617	46,523	25,094	34,041	22,061	11,980
1987–88	435,085	190,047	245,038	994,829	477,203	517,626	299,317	145,163	154,154	70,735	45,484	25,251	34,870	22,615	12,255
1988–89	436,764	186,316	250,448	1,018,755	483,346	535,409	310,621	149,354	161,267	70,856	45,046	25,810	35,720	22,648	13,072
1989–90	455,102	191,195	263,907	1,051,344	491,696	559,648	324,301	153,653	170,648	70,988	43,961	27,027	38,371	24,401	13,970
1990–91	481,720	198,634	283,086	1,094,538	504,045	590,493	337,168	156,482	180,686	71,948	43,846	28,102	39,294	24,756	14,538
1991–92	504,231	207,481	296,750	1,136,553	520,811	615,742	352,838	161,842	190,996	74,146	45,071	29,075	40,659	25,557	15,102
1992–93	514,756	211,964	302,792	1,165,178	532,881	632,297	369,585	169,258	200,327	75,387	45,153	30,234	42,132	26,073	16,059
1993–94	530,632	215,261	315,371	1,169,275	532,422	636,853	387,070	176,085	210,985	75,418	44,707	30,711	43,185	26,552	16,633
1994–95	539,691	218,352	321,339	1,160,134	526,131	634,003	397,629	178,598	219,031	75,800	44,853	30,947	44,446	26,916	17,530
1995–96	555,216	219,514	335,702	1,164,792	522,454	642,338	406,301	179,081	227,220	76,734	44,748	31,986	44,652	26,841	17,811
1996–97	571,226	223,948	347,278	1,172,879	520,515	652,364	419,401	180,947	238,454	78,730	45,564	33,166	45,876	27,146	18,730
1997–98	558,555	217,613	340,942	1,184,406	519,956	664,450	430,164	184,375	245,789	78,598	44,911	33,687	46,010	26,664	19,346
1998–99[4]	561,000	218,000	343,000	1,178,000	517,000	661,000	405,000	172,000	233,000	80,300	45,600	34,700	45,900	27,300	18,600
1999–2000[4]	559,000	216,000	342,000	1,185,000	517,000	668,000	398,000	168,000	230,000	78,400	44,700	33,600	45,200	26,700	18,500
2000–01[4]	569,000	215,000	354,000	1,194,000	515,000	678,000	396,000	166,000	230,000	76,500	43,200	33,300	45,000	26,500	18,500
2001–02[4]	571,000	216,000	355,000	1,210,000	516,000	694,000	396,000	165,000	231,000	75,400	42,100	33,300	44,900	26,400	18,500
2002–03[4]	577,000	217,000	359,000	1,220,000	522,000	697,000	399,000	165,000	233,000	75,200	41,600	33,600	45,000	26,400	18,600
2003–04[4]	581,000	218,000	363,000	1,240,000	527,000	712,000	402,000	166,000	236,000	75,400	41,500	33,900	45,100	26,400	18,700
2004–05[4]	583,000	218,000	364,000	1,253,000	529,000	725,000	406,000	167,000	239,000	75,900	41,500	34,400	45,300	26,500	18,800
2005–06[4]	587,000	219,000	367,000	1,264,000	533,000	731,000	411,000	168,000	243,000	76,700	41,800	35,000	45,600	26,600	19,000
2006–07[4]	591,000	220,000	371,000	1,277,000	536,000	741,000	417,000	169,000	248,000	77,700	42,100	35,600	46,000	26,700	19,300
2007–08[4]	596,000	221,000	374,000	1,290,000	538,000	751,000	425,000	171,000	254,000	78,700	42,300	36,400	46,400	26,800	19,600
2008–09[4]	603,000	223,000	380,000	1,304,000	542,000	761,000	432,000	173,000	260,000	80,100	42,700	37,400	46,800	27,000	19,800
2009–10[4]	611,000	224,000	387,000	1,324,000	547,000	776,000	439,000	175,000	264,000	81,600	43,200	38,400	47,100	27,100	20,000

— Not available.

[1]Includes Ph.D., Ed.D., and comparable degrees at the doctoral level. Excludes first-professional degrees, such as M.D., D.D.S., and law degrees.
[2]Includes first-professional degrees.
[3]First-professional degrees are included with bachelor's degrees.
[4]Projected data for higher education institutions.

NOTE: Data for 1869–70 to 1994–95 and 1998–99 to 2009–10 are for institutions of higher education. Institutions of higher education were accredited by an agency or association that was recognized by the U.S. Department of Education, or recognized directly by the Secretary of Education. The new degree-granting classification is very similar to the earlier higher education classification, except that it includes some additional institutions, primarily 2-year colleges, and excludes a few higher education institutions that did not award associate or higher degrees. Some data have been revised from previously published figures. Detail may not sum to totals due to rounding.

SOURCE: Thomas D. Snyder and Charlene M. Hoffman, "Table 248.—Earned degrees conferred by degree-granting institutions, by level of degree and sex of student: 1869–70 to 2009–10," in *Digest of Education Statistics, 2000*, NCES 2001-034, U.S. Department of Education, National Center for Education Statistics, Washington, DC, January 2001

TABLE 9.11

Degrees conferred by degree-granting institutions, by control of institution, level of degree, and discipline division, 1997–98

Discipline division	Public institutions				Private institutions			
	Associate degrees	Bachelor's degrees	Master's degrees	Doctor's degrees[1]	Associate degrees	Bachelor's degrees	Master's degrees	Doctor's degrees[1]
Total	**455,084**	**784,296**	**235,922**	**29,715**	**103,471**	**400,110**	**194,242**	**16,295**
Agriculture and natural resources[2]	6,309	21,337	3,857	1,275	364	1,947	618	27
Architecture and related programs	170	5,727	2,989	90	95	1,925	1,358	41
Area, ethnic, and cultural studies	86	3,438	878	98	18	2,715	739	83
Biological sciences/life sciences	2,033	43,130	4,438	3,412	80	22,738	1,823	1,549
Business[3]	71,884	136,394	39,880	843	32,775	96,725	62,291	447
Communications	1,499	34,276	2,858	291	869	15,109	2,753	63
Communications technologies	1,299	439	102	0	303	290	462	5
Computer and information sciences	8,233	16,408	6,412	521	5,637	10,444	4,834	337
Construction trades	1,801	67	4	0	371	115	12	0
Education	8,002	78,448	70,570	5,065	1,276	27,520	44,121	1,664
Engineering	1,692	45,140	17,442	4,230	457	14,770	8,494	1,750
Engineering-related technologies	18,576	10,090	916	11	14,172	3,637	220	3
English language and literature/letters	1,527	33,688	5,816	1,166	82	16,020	1,979	473
Foreign languages and literatures	495	9,368	2,230	563	48	5,083	697	396
Health professions and related sciences	76,803	55,064	21,811	1,550	15,228	29,315	17,449	934
Home economics and vocational home economics	7,884	14,852	1,613	265	408	2,444	1,301	159
Law and legal studies	4,989	1,144	635	9	2,808	873	2,593	57
Liberal arts and sciences, general studies, and humanities	176,627	21,706	1,107	44	9,621	11,496	1,694	43
Library science	91	70	3,909	47	5	3	962	1
Mathematics	817	8,045	2,766	896	27	4,283	877	363
Mechanics and repairers	8,114	16	0	0	2,502	75	0	0
Multi/interdisciplinary studies	9,284	20,081	1,678	232	117	6,082	999	276
Parks, recreation, leisure, and fitness studies	757	12,778	1,688	122	138	4,003	336	7
Philosophy and religion	47	3,351	452	228	47	4,856	855	357
Physical sciences and science technologies	2,195	12,658	3,942	3,217	91	6,758	1,419	1,354
Precision production trades	6,928	340	5	0	4,157	67	10	0
Protective services	17,963	19,513	1,192	39	1,039	5,563	808	0
Psychology	1,609	49,330	5,764	1,957	156	24,642	7,983	2,116
Public administration and services	3,806	14,427	15,629	290	350	5,981	9,515	209
R.O.T.C. and military technologies	22	3	0	0	0	0	0	0
Social sciences and history	3,859	81,894	9,415	2,505	337	43,146	5,523	1,622
Theological studies/religious vocations	1	0	0	0	569	5,903	4,692	1,460
Transportation and material moving workers	659	1,478	97	0	350	1,728	639	0
Visual and performing arts	6,772	29,596	5,827	749	8,208	22,481	5,318	414
Not classified by field of study	2,251	0	0	0	766	1,373	868	85

[1]Includes Ph.D., Ed.D., and comparable degrees at the doctoral level. Excludes first-professional degrees, such as M.D., D.D.S., and law degrees.
[2]Includes "Agricultural business and production," "Agricultural sciences," and "Conservation and renewable natural resources."
[3]Includes "Business management and administrative services," "Marketing operations/ marketing and distribution," and "Consumer and personal services."

SOURCE: Thomas D. Snyder and Charlene M. Hoffman, "Table 259.—Degrees conferred by degree-granting institutions, by control of institution, level of degree and discipline division: 1997–98," in *Digest of Education Statistics, 2000*, NCES 2001-034, U.S. Department of Education, National Center for Education Statistics, Washington, DC, January 2001

Between 1976–77 and 1999–2000, charges at public colleges rose by more than 300 percent, and those at private colleges increased by more than 400 percent. Many factors have contributed to the increase in costs at public schools, including declines in government appropriations, increases in instructional and student services costs, and increases in research expenditures. Many states have raised room and board and tuition costs at once-inexpensive state schools to compensate for declining federal aid. Public schools still remain significantly less expensive than private schools, but they are not quite as much the educational bargains that they once were. Private schools attribute the increases to mounting expenses on several factors, including higher student aid, increases in salaries and benefits for faculty and staff, higher energy costs, and maintenance of their academic programs and libraries.

In 1964 a family in the twentieth percentile (lowest) of income could expect to spend 29 percent of its total annual income on public college tuition, room, and board. A family at the mid-point of income levels would have spent 14.4 percent of its income, and a family at the eightieth percentile (highest) would have had to expend only 9.2 percent of its income on public college costs. In 1995 these expenditures had risen to 32.2 percent of the income of the low-income family; the costs for families at the fiftieth (middle income) and eightieth percentiles were about the same proportion as in 1964.

TABLE 9.12

First professional degrees conferred by degree-granting institutions in dentistry, medicine, and law, by sex, and number of institutions conferring degress, 1949–50 to 1997–98

	Dentistry (D.D.S. or D.M.D.)				Medicine (M.D.)				Law (LL.B. or J.D.)			
	Number of institutions conferring degrees	Degrees conferred			Number of institutions conferring degrees	Degrees conferred			Number of institutions conferring degrees	Degrees conferred		
Year		Total	Men	Women		Total	Men	Women		Total	Men	Women
1949–50	40	2,579	2,561	18	72	5,612	5,028	584	(¹)	(¹)	(¹)	(¹)
1951–52	41	2,918	2,895	23	72	6,201	5,871	330	(¹)	(¹)	(¹)	(¹)
1953–54	42	3,102	3,063	39	73	6,712	6,377	335	(¹)	(¹)	(¹)	(¹)
1955–56	42	3,009	2,975	34	73	6,810	6,464	346	131	8,262	7,974	288
1957–58	43	3,065	3,031	34	75	6,816	6,469	347	131	9,394	9,122	272
1959–60	45	3,247	3,221	26	79	7,032	6,645	387	134	9,240	9,010	230
1961–62	46	3,183	3,166	17	81	7,138	6,749	389	134	9,364	9,091	273
1963–64	46	3,180	3,168	12	82	7,303	6,878	425	133	10,679	10,372	307
1965–66	47	3,178	3,146	32	84	7,673	7,170	503	136	13,246	12,776	470
1967–68	48	3,422	3,375	47	85	7,944	7,318	626	138	16,454	15,805	649
1969–70	48	3,718	3,684	34	86	8,314	7,615	699	145	14,916	14,115	801
1970–71	48	3,745	3,703	42	89	8,919	8,110	809	147	17,421	16,181	1,240
1971–72	48	3,862	3,819	43	92	9,253	8,423	830	147	21,764	20,266	1,498
1972–73	51	4,047	3,992	55	97	10,307	9,388	919	152	27,205	25,037	2,168
1973–74	52	4,440	4,355	85	99	11,356	10,093	1,263	151	29,326	25,986	3,340
1974–75	52	4,773	4,627	146	104	12,447	10,818	1,629	154	29,296	24,881	4,415
1975–76	56	5,425	5,187	238	107	13,426	11,252	2,174	166	32,293	26,085	6,208
1976–77	57	5,138	4,764	374	109	13,461	10,891	2,570	169	34,104	26,447	7,657
1977–78	57	5,189	4,623	566	109	14,279	11,210	3,069	169	34,402	25,457	8,945
1978–79	58	5,434	4,794	640	109	14,786	11,381	3,405	175	35,206	25,180	10,026
1979–80	58	5,258	4,558	700	112	14,902	11,416	3,486	179	35,647	24,893	10,754
1980–81	58	5,460	4,672	788	116	15,505	11,672	3,833	176	36,331	24,563	11,768
1981–82	59	5,282	4,467	815	119	15,814	11,867	3,947	180	35,991	23,965	12,026
1982–83	59	5,585	4,631	954	118	15,484	11,350	4,134	177	36,853	23,550	13,303
1983–84	60	5,353	4,302	1,051	119	15,813	11,359	4,454	179	37,012	23,382	13,630
1984–85	59	5,339	4,233	1,106	120	16,041	11,167	4,874	181	37,491	23,070	14,421
1985–86	59	5,046	3,907	1,139	120	15,938	11,022	4,916	181	35,844	21,874	13,970
1986–87	58	4,741	3,603	1,138	121	15,428	10,431	4,997	179	36,056	21,561	14,495
1987–88	57	4,477	3,300	1,177	122	15,358	10,278	5,080	180	35,397	21,067	14,330
1988–89	58	4,265	3,124	1,141	124	15,460	10,310	5,150	182	35,634	21,069	14,565
1989–90	57	4,100	2,834	1,266	124	15,075	9,923	5,152	182	36,485	21,079	15,406
1990–91	55	3,699	2,510	1,189	121	15,043	9,629	5,414	179	37,945	21,643	16,302
1991–92	52	3,593	2,431	1,162	120	15,243	9,796	5,447	177	38,848	22,260	16,588
1992–93	55	3,605	2,383	1,222	122	15,531	9,679	5,852	184	40,302	23,182	17,120
1993–94	53	3,787	2,330	1,457	121	15,368	9,544	5,824	185	40,044	22,826	17,218
1994–95	53	3,897	2,480	1,417	119	15,537	9,507	6,030	183	39,349	22,592	16,757
1995–96	53	3,697	2,374	1,323	119	15,341	9,061	6,280	183	39,828	22,508	17,320
1996–97	52	3,784	2,387	1,397	118	15,571	9,121	6,450	184	40,079	22,548	17,531
1997–98	53	4,032	2,490	1,542	117	15,424	9,006	6,418	185	39,331	21,876	17,455

¹ Law degree data prior to 1955–56 are not shown because they lack comparability with the figures for subsequent years.

SOURCE: Thomas D. Snyder and Charlene M. Hoffman, "Table 261.—First-professional degrees conferred by degree-granting institutions in dentistry, medicine, and law, by sex, and number of institutions conferring degrees: 1949–50 to 1997–98," in *Digest of Education Statistics, 2000,* NCES 2001-034, U.S. Department of Education, National Center for Education Statistics, Washington, DC, January 2001

At private institutions of higher learning, the increase in tuition, room, and board escalated even more rapidly. By 1995 a family at the twentieth percentile of income would have had to spend 88.5 percent of its annual income for one year of private college, far above the 1964 level of 58.3 percent. The proportions for fiftieth- and eightieth-percentile families increased by 45 percent and 26 percent, respectively.

Nonetheless, the investment in higher education offers impressive returns. In 1997 median annual income for households headed by workers with a bachelor's degree or more was nearly twice as much as median annual income among households headed by workers who were high school graduates. (See Figure 9.3.)

Financial Assistance For Students

In 1995–96 half of all undergraduate students received some type of financial support. Almost two-fifths received federal support (36.6 percent), and almost one-third (32 percent) received nonfederal assistance, usually from the state. About 39 percent received grants (which do not have to be paid back), 25.6 percent got loans (which do have to be paid back), and about 5 percent were on work-study programs. A full-time

TABLE 9.13

Full-time instructional faculty in degree-granting institutions, by race/ethnicity, academic rank, and sex, fall 1997

Academic rank and sex	Total	White, non-Hispanic	Minority		Black, non-Hispanic	Hispanic	Asian or Pacific Islander	American Indian/ Alaskan Native	Non-resident alien	Race/ ethnicity unknown
			Number	Percent						
Men and women, all ranks	**568,719**	**477,130**	**76,041**	**13.7**	**27,723**	**14,768**	**31,259**	**2,291**	**12,968**	**2,580**
Professors	163,632	145,025	17,082	10.5	5,240	2,921	8,508	413	1,090	435
Associate professors	128,262	110,047	16,469	13.0	6,047	2,979	7,067	376	1,373	373
Assistant professors	128,329	101,620	21,443	17.4	8,046	3,951	8,900	546	4,494	772
Instructors	68,329	56,395	10,304	15.4	4,575	2,654	2,612	463	973	657
Lecturers	14,342	11,556	2,076	15.2	805	553	655	63	628	82
Other faculty	65,825	52,487	8,667	14.2	3,010	1,710	3,517	430	4,410	261
Men, all ranks	363,925	306,270	46,495	13.2	14,059	8,792	22,323	1,321	9,580	1,580
Professors	131,279	116,918	13,056	10.0	3,316	2,154	7,265	321	963	342
Associate professors	84,740	72,461	10,929	13.1	3,373	1,891	5,434	231	1,110	240
Assistant professors	70,975	55,235	12,004	17.9	3,758	2,198	5,787	261	3,292	444
Instructors	33,595	27,598	4,981	15.3	1,985	1,385	1,348	263	653	363
Lecturers	6,733	5,367	953	15.1	367	251	301	34	373	40
Other faculty	36,603	28,691	4,572	13.7	1,260	913	2,188	211	3,189	151
Women, all ranks	204,794	170,860	29,546	14.7	13,664	5,976	8,936	970	3,388	1,000
Professors	32,353	28,107	4,026	12.5	1,924	767	1,243	92	127	93
Associate professors	43,522	37,586	5,540	12.8	2,674	1,088	1,633	145	263	133
Assistant professors	57,354	46,385	9,439	16.9	4,288	1,753	3,113	285	1,202	328
Instructors	34,734	28,797	5,323	15.6	2,590	1,269	1,264	200	320	294
Lecturers	7,609	6,189	1,123	15.4	438	302	354	29	255	42
Other faculty	29,222	23,796	4,095	14.7	1,750	797	1,329	219	1,221	110

NOTE: Percents are based on the number of faculty members who were U.S. citizens and who were reported by race/ethnicity. Data exclude faculty employed by system offices. Totals may differ from figures reported in other tables because of varying survey methodologies.

SOURCE: Thomas D. Snyder and Charlene M. Hoffman, "Table 230.—Full-time instructional faculty in degree-granting institutions, by race/ethnicity, academic rank, and sex: Fall 1997," in *Digest of Education Statistics, 2000*, NCES 2001-034, U.S. Department of Education, National Center for Education Statistics, Washington, DC, January 2001

undergraduate student received an average of $6,832 per year.

Federal assistance that goes directly to students includes Pell Grants (the maximum was $3,000 in 1998–99), the Stafford Student Loan Program (a maximum loan of $17,250 for four years), and Supplemental Education Opportunity Grants (a maximum of $4,000). Colleges or universities receive assistance, which they in turn pay out to students, through Campus-Based Programs and Perkins Loans. In general, the federal government has shifted its spending from grants to loans. Loan aid has more than doubled between 1988–89 and 1998–99, from 17.9 billion to 37.2 billion, while grant aid has increased by about two-thirds, from 15.8 billion to 25.9 billion over the same period.

The Pell Grant maximum has fallen as a percentage of the cost of college attendance. In 1975–76 the Pell Grant covered 84 percent of public four-year college costs, but it declined to 39 percent in 1999–2000. (See Table 9.15.) At the same time, the proportion of student grant aid that is merit-based, rather than need-based, nearly doubled from 1982 to 1998.

In *Access Denied: Restoring the Nation's Commitment to Equal Educational Opportunity* (Washington, DC, February 2001) the Advisory Committee on Student Financial Assistance defines unmet need as the residual educational cost after all aid, including loans, is awarded. On average, the lowest-income students have $3,200 of unmet need at two-year public institutions, and $3,800 at four-year public institutions. (See Table 9.16.) About 44 percent of low-income (those with family incomes below $30,000) students enroll in a four-year institution, while 62 percent of high-income (those with family incomes above $60,000) students attend a four-year institution.

AID FOR MIDDLE CLASS STUDENTS. In 1992 President George Bush signed legislation increasing college assistance for middle-income families. In an attempt to help those caught in the middle—too much income to qualify for Pell Grants and too little income to meet the spiraling college costs—the new law dropped the previous practice of calculating assets by including a family's equity in a home or farm and college-savings accounts.

Students from families of four with annual incomes of up to $42,000 could now qualify for grants; the previous maximum income was $30,000. The bill also established a new unsubsidized (not guaranteed by the government) loan program for students and families who do not qualify for subsidized loans because of income. Unsubsidized borrowing by students (Stafford Unsubsidized) and parents

TABLE 9.14

Average student expenses, by College Board Region, 2000–01

	Tuition & Fees	Out-of-State Tuition	Books & Supplies	Residential Room and Board	Trans.	Other Costs	Commuter Board Only	Trans.	Other Costs
NATIONAL									
2-yr public	1,705	3,237	663	—	—	—	2,426	1,035	1,195
2-yr private	7,458		661	4,736	679	1,145	2,032	980	1,088
4-yr public	3,510	5,510	704	4,960	643	1,521	2,444	1,014	1,557
4-yr private	16,332		730	6,209	573	1,102	2,495	926	1,221
New England									
2-yr public	2,150	3,959	635	—	—	—	2,197	1,008	1,241
2-yr private	14,854		754	6,969	1,041	1,077	2,143	739	910
4-yr public	4,748	5,796	660	5,393	456	1,266	2,249	923	1,222
4-yr private	21,215		727	7,544	505	1,097	2,385	1,008	1,109
Middle States									
2-yr public	2,653	2,899	637	—	—	—	2,295	996	1,071
2-yr private	9,334		578	—	—	—	1,793	1,030	1,336
4-yr public	4,686	4,693	700	5,642	508	1,293	2,465	961	1,476
4-yr private	17,547		695	7,108	460	998	2,364	933	1,122
South									
2-yr public	1,327	3,245	655	—	—	—	2,529	1,180	1,137
2-yr private	8,697		715	4,494	611	1,345	*1,666*	1,010	909
4-yr public	2,906	5,954	719	4,387	772	1,540	2,514	1,159	1,619
4-yr private	13,912		727	5,415	725	1,168	2,445	982	1,202
Midwest									
2-yr public	1,878	3,507	681	—	—	—	*2,806*	1,070	1,199
2-yr private	8,541		593	4,199	425	991	1,881	1,148	1,130
4-yr public	3,992	5,221	654	4,715	525	1,502	2,182	966	1,497
4-yr private	15,299		728	5,231	531	1,019	2,805	804	1,241
Southwest									
2-yr public	1,133	1,661	681	*2,803*	*755*	*1,093*	2,086	*1,097*	1,165
2-yr private	6,315		706	4,074	940	1,425	1,681	1,492	1,242
4-yr public	2,925	5,029	672	4,351	832	1,637	2,611	1,232	1,630
4-yr private	11,965		708	4,843	724	1,315	2,308	1,166	1,370
West									
2-yr public	—	3,773	—	—	—	—	—	—	—
2-yr private	*4,089*		—	—	—	—	2,226	*892*	*1,025*
4-yr public	2,747	6,883	779	5,909	742	1,810	2,592	859	1,638
4-yr private	15,878		838	6,382	654	1,375	2,490	893	1,417

NOTE: Averages in *italicized* type indicate that while the number of institutions reporting data on this item was large enough to support an analysis, the sample size was marginal. Dashes indicate that the sample was too small to provide meaningful information. Data are enrollment weighted.

SOURCE: "Table 4. Average Student Expenses, by College Board Region, 2000-2001." *Trends in College Pricing*, (2000):6. Copyright © 2000 by College Entrance Examination Board. Reprinted with permission. All rights reserved. www.collegboard.com.

(Parent Loans to Undergraduate Students; PLUS) currently accounts for about 45 percent of federal education loans.

The Higher Education Amendments of 1998 (PL 105-244) continued the authorization level for the maximum individual Pell Grant at $4,500 for the 1999–2000 academic year, increasing by $300 for each of the next three years and by $400 in 2003–04. The actual appropriation (amount funded by the federal budget), however, was less than the authorized amount. In 1998–99, the maximum Pell Grant was $3,000. The Higher Education Amendments also increased the amount of money that independent and working dependent students may earn before it is counted against their eligibility to receive federal grant aid, including Pell Grants. For those eligible, the act doubled the amount of a Pell Grant for the first two years of undergraduate study for students who graduate in the top 10 percent of their high school class.

In 1997 President Bill Clinton signed legislation that established new incentives to help middle class taxpayers save for college, pay tuition bills, and repay student loans. The major provisions of the Taxpayers Relief Act of 1997 (PL 105-34) include Hope scholarships, lifetime learning credits (LLC), and education Individual Retirement Accounts (IRAs).

The Hope scholarship provides a tax credit against tuition of up to $1,500 per year per student for the first two years of postsecondary education. This benefit phases out—beginning at an $80,000 yearly income for a couple ($40,000 for single taxpayers) and ending entirely at annual incomes of $100,000 for a couple ($50,000 for single taxpayers).

The lifetime learning credit offers a tax credit of up to $1,000 per year for tuition after the first two years. It may be taken for an unlimited number of years. The income phase-outs are the same as for Hope scholarships.

FIGURE 9.3

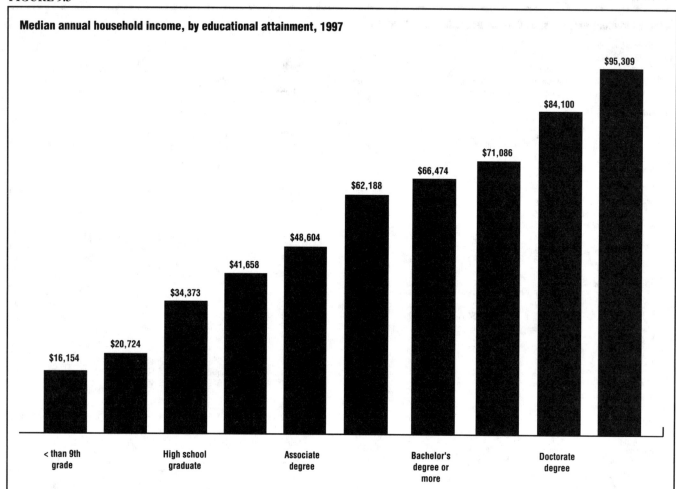

Median annual household income, by educational attainment, 1997

$95,309

$84,100

$71,086

$66,474

$62,188

$48,604

$41,658

$34,373

$20,724

$16,154

< than 9th grade   High school graduate   Associate degree   Bachelor's degree or more   Doctorate degree

Note: While data in the report are the most recent and authoritative, sources vary as do the years and definitions of low-income.

SOURCE: "Figure 1: Median Annual Household Income by Educational Attainment of Householder, 1997," in *Access Denied: Restoring the Nation's Commitment to Equal Educational Opportunity*, Advisory Committee on Student Financial Assisstance, Washington, DC, February 2001

TABLE 9.15

Pell Grant maximum award as a percentage of institutional cost of attendance, 1975–2001

| Year | Institution Type | |
	Public 4-year	Private 4-year
1975-76	84%	38%
1985-86	57%	26%
1995-96	34%	13%
1999-2000	39%	15%
2000-01	39%	15%

SOURCE: "Figure 7: Pell Grant Maximum Award as a Percentage of Institutional Cost of Attendance," in *Access Denied: Restoring the Nation's Commitment to Equal Educational Opportunity*, Advisory Committee on Student Financial Assisstance, Washington, DC, February 2001

TABLE 9.16

Unmet need by institution type and family income, 1999

| Institution Type | Family Income | | |
	Low	Middle	High
Public Two Year	$3,200	$1,650	$100
Public Four Year	$3,800	$2,250	$400
Private Four Year	$6,200	$4,700	$3,000

SOURCE: "Figure 10: Unmet Need by Institution Type and Family Income," in *Access Denied: Restoring the Nation's Commitment to Equal Educational Opportunity*, Advisory Committee on Student Financial Assisstance, Washington, DC, February 2001

Education IRAs permit tax-free withdrawals for tuition, fees, room and board, and books and supplies for elementary, secondary, undergraduate and graduate education, as well as technical training. In 2002 taxpayers may contribute up to $2,000 per child per year in a designated education IRA account. Contributions are not tax-deductible, but the interest earned on the account is tax-free. No new contributions can be made once the beneficiary reaches age 18. When the money is used for education, no tax is owed as long as the withdrawal is less

TABLE 9.17

New sources of higher education

- New stand-alone, degree-granting online colleges and universities
- Degree-granting online consortia
- Non-degree-granting online consortia
- Corporate universities
- Unaffiliated online programs and courses

SOURCE: Judith S. Eaton, "'New Providers' of Higher Education. . ." in *Distance Learning: Academic and Political Challenges for Higher Education Accreditation,* Council for Higher Education Accreditation, CHEA Monograph Series 2001 Number 1, Washington, DC, 2001

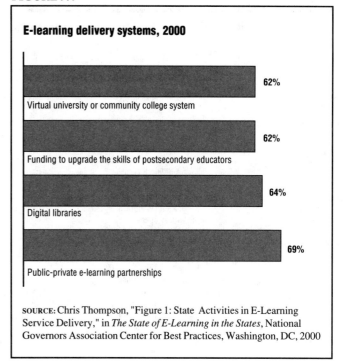

FIGURE 9.4

E-learning delivery systems, 2000

Virtual university or community college system — 62%
Funding to upgrade the skills of postsecondary educators — 62%
Digital libraries — 64%
Public-private e-learning partnerships — 69%

SOURCE: Chris Thompson, "Figure 1: State Activities in E-Learning Service Delivery," in *The State of E-Learning in the States*, National Governors Association Center for Best Practices, Washington, DC, 2000

than or equal to the higher education expenses. This benefit phases out at higher income levels.

WORKING STUDENTS

As might be expected in this time of rising education costs, many college students must find employment in order to help pay their way through school. In 1970 about one-third (34 percent) of full-time students worked. In 1999 the proportion had increased to almost one-half (46 percent). White students (49 percent) and Hispanic students (44 percent) were more likely to work than were African American students (32 percent).

Typically, part-time students were much more likely to work while attending school, as were students at two-year institutions. Men (47 percent) and women (45 percent) were about equally likely to work.

DISTANCE EDUCATION

Distance education is not a new concept. It started with classes taken by mail (correspondence courses) and by watching teachers' lectures on videos or cable television. Now, according to *Distance Education at Postsecondary Education Institutions: 1997–98* (U.S. Department of Education, National Center for Education Statistics, Washington, DC, 1999), the term refers to "education or training courses delivered to remote (off-campus) location(s) via audio, video (live or prerecorded), or computer technologies ...." Distance learning can be used to describe various types of courses, programs, providers, and delivery systems. Table 9.17 summarizes some of these new providers of higher education.

The State of E-Learning in the States (Chris Thompson, National Governor's Association Center for Best Practices, Washington, DC, 2000) presented the results of a 2000 survey of distance learning policies and programs in the 50 states. The states reported that they most frequently enlisted in public-private e-learning partnerships (69 percent). Other popular e-learning models included digital libraries (64 percent of responding states), providing funding to upgrade the computer skills of postsec-

ondary educators, and establishing virtual universities or community college systems (62 percent of responding states). (See Figure 9.4.)

Distance education is growing rapidly. Many colleges and universities offer online/distance education programs, including Cornell, the University of Illinois, the State University of New York (SUNY), and Temple University. Enrollment, number of courses, and degrees offered are increasing. (See Table 9.18.) These schools usually team up with course management system vendors, such as Blackboard and WebCT, which provide the software platforms for online courses. (See Table 9.19.) Other schools enter into corporate-university joint ventures run by hybrid content providers, such as Unext.com and Universitas 21, that offer courses and programs in affiliation with universities (Columbia, Chicago, Stanford, etc.), or that were designed by individual faculty members at universities (Williams, Brown, Yale, etc.). (See Table 9.20). Pure "virtual" universities include Capella University, University of Phoenix Online, and Western Governor's University. Generally, these distance education providers offer undergraduate and graduate degrees, and enrollment ranges from slightly more than 200 to 23,000 students. (See Table 9.21.)

Distance education can provide access to postsecondary education where otherwise it might not be available due to distance, work schedules, disability, and family responsibilities. Increased access to certificate and degree programs may encourage students to undertake these programs or to complete them more quickly. However, some observers question the effectiveness of online

TABLE 9.18

Some colleges and universities that offer online/distance education programs, 2001

Institution	Characteristics	Number and Type of DE Programs	DE Enrollment	Accreditation
e-Cornell	For-profit spin off; no courses offered yet	Will offer certificates, not degree programs	NA	Not accredited as a separate entity
NYU Online	For-profit spin off primarily for corporate market	Two graduate; many corporate programs	166 (in graduate programs)*	Not accredited as a separate entity
University of Illinois Online	Umbrella organization for different U. of Illinois campuses	One professional degree; 10 master's; bachelor's completion program	6,000 courses taken online	North Central
University of Maryland University College	Claims online program is world's largest online university	14 bachelor; 10 graduate	7,955;* UMUC now claims enrollment of 40,000	Middle States
Rio Salado Community College	One of the first and largest online community college programs	Six associate degree; 12 certificate	200 online courses; 8,000 students per semester	North Central
SUNY Learning Network	One of the three largest DE programs in the country (with Phoenix and UMUC)	1,500 courses from accounting to Web design	Approximately 10,000 course enrollments per semester	Middle States
Virtual Temple	For-profit spin off; no courses offered yet	NA	NA	Not accredited as a separate entity

* Figures for 1999-2000, US Department of Education, *Report to Congress on the Distance Education Demonstration Programs*, January 2001. Other statistics reported directly by institutions.

SOURCE: Thomas J. Kriger, "Table 1. A Sampling of Colleges and Universities that Offer Online/Distance Education Programs," in *A Virtual Revolution: Trends in the Expansion of Distance Education*, American Federation of Teachers, Washington, DC, May 2001

TABLE 9.19

Corporate-university joint ventures: course management system vendors

Institution	Characteristics	Number and Type of DE Programs	Affiliations	Accreditation
Blackboard	Software for online "learning environments"	NA	Used by more than 1,900 institutions, according to estimates	NA
Campus Pipeline	Provides Web platform for higher education	NA	List of nearly 600 campus licensees	NA
eCollege	Provides online campuses for universities; competes with Blackboard, Web CT	NA	Clients include Univ. of Colorado, Johns Hopkins, Seton Hall, DeVry	NA
Web CT	Provides campuses platform for distance education	NA	Estimated in use at 2,600 institutions	NA

SOURCE: Thomas J. Kriger, "Table 2. Corporate-University Joint Ventures: Course Management System Vendors," *A Virtual Revolution: Trends in the Expansion of Distance Education*, American Federation of Teachers, Washington, DC, May 2001

college courses, and there are concerns that not all providers offer equal quality. Distance learning is an area of much debate and study among educational researchers.

In fall 1998 nearly all (97 percent) college faculty had access to the Internet, 69 percent used e-mail to communicate with students, and 40 percent had a course website. Faculty at four-year doctoral institutions were more likely to use e-mail (77 percent) and a course website (45 per-

cent) than were faculty at two-year colleges (48 percent and 34 percent, respectively).

SUBSTANCE ABUSE AMONG COLLEGE STUDENTS

Illicit Drug Use

Monitoring the Future: National Survey Results on Drug Use 1975–2000, Volume II: College Students & Adults

TABLE 9.20

Corporate-university joint ventures: distance education hybrid course or content providers

Institution	Characteristics	Number & Type of DE Programs	Affiliations	Accreditation
Cardean University/ UNext.com	Creates courses in collaboration with prestigious business schools; problem-solving based curriculum	MBA program and 80 courses offered	Columbia, Chicago, Stanford, Carnegie Mellon, and the London School of Economics	DETC
Cenquest	Offers graduate business degrees and training	1 certificate 2 masters' program	Partnered with Babson, U. of Texas, Oregon Institute, Adelaide University, Monterrey Institute of Technology	No
Fathom	Columbia's for-profit spin-off; niche is to provide high-quality content; courses to include arts and humanities	600 courses listed; 75,000 registered users; several hundred students enrolled in online courses	13 member institutions including Univ. Of Chicago, American Film Institute, London School of Economics, NY Public Library	No
Global Education Network	Brainchild of Williams professor Mark Taylor and investment banker Herbert Allen; trying to attract faculty with star power; will offer core curriculum including arts and humanities	3 or 4 courses currently in development; no degree programs available	Courses by individual faculty from Williams, Wellesley, Brown, Amherst, Yale	Seeking accreditation
Quisic (formerly University Access)	Offers under-graduate, graduate business courses, training; original focus undergraduate DE	Clients include Cisco, United, Citigroup, Lexus, IBM	200 corporate clients; university partners include Dartmouth, London School of Economics, North Carolina, USC	No
Universitas 21	Global network of 18 institutions world-wide; joint venture with Thomson Learning	In planning stages	Seeking U.S. institutional participants	No

SOURCE: Thomas J. Kriger, "Table 3. Corporate-University Joint Ventures: Hybrid Course or Content Providers," *A Virtual Revolution: Trends in the Expansion of Distance Education,* American Federation of Teachers, Washington, DC, May 2001

Ages 19–40 (National Institute on Drug Abuse, Bethesda, MD, August 2001) was prepared by Lloyd D. Johnson, Patrick M. O'Malley, and Jerald G. Bachman at the University of Michigan. The survey of drug use among college students covers full-time students, one to four years out of high school, who were enrolled in two- or four-year institutions.

Compared to their nonstudent peers, college students showed a somewhat higher annual prevalence of illicit drug use, (36.1 percent, compared to 30.8 percent for young adults ages 19–28). College students also reported a higher 30-day prevalence than did their peers (21.5 percent versus 18.1 percent). Annual prevalence means using a drug at any time within the year preceding the survey; 30-day prevalence refers to using a drug in the 30 days prior to the survey. Drug use among college students has generally increased since 1991. (See Table 9.22.)

In 2000 more than one-third of college students (34 percent) reported that they had used marijuana at some time during the previous year, compared to 27.9 percent of nonstudents. Fewer students used cocaine than did their nonstudent peers. Use of cocaine within the past year increased slightly for college students, while it stayed about the same among young people not in college. While heroin use was still under 1 percent among both students and nonstudents, the annual use of heroin increased for college students in 2000. (See Table 9.22.)

Alcohol Use

College students who responded to the 2000 survey were about as likely to have used alcohol in the past year as their nonstudent peers (83.2 percent, compared to 84 percent). (See Table 9.22.) The high incidence of heavy or "binge" drinking (five or more drinks in a row in the past two weeks) among college students has been an important issue in recent years. In 2000 nearly two in five (39.3 percent) college students reported bouts of heavy drinking in the last two weeks, compared to 34.7 percent of

TABLE 9.21

Virtual Universities

Institution	Characteristics	Number and Type of DE Programs	DE Enrollment	Accreditation
Andrew Jackson University	Correspondence school offering textbook study	3 bachelor's; 3 graduate	400-450	DETC
Capella University	Offers traditional courses and corporate training; partners include Honeywell, Lawson Software	36 certificate; 1 bachelor's; 11 graduate*	1,049*	North Central
Jones International University	First fully accredited online university	21 certificate; 1 bachelor's; 2 graduate	1,500	North Central
Kennedy-Western University	Markets to "mid-career professionals"	13 bachelor's; 12 graduate; 12 Ph.D.	23,000	Not regionally accredited; licensed by Wyoming State Dept. of Ed.
University of Phoenix Online	Fastest growing for-profit university; Now 25% online	8 bachelor's; 10 master's; 1 Ph.D.; developing certificate programs	18,500	North Central
Western Governors University	Private university offering menu of courses from other institutions and corporations	3 certificate; 4 bachelor's; 1 graduate*	208*	Candidate for IRAC accreditation

* Figures for 1999-2000, U.S. Department of Education, *Report to Congress on the Distance Education Demonstration Programs,* January 2001. Other statistics reported directly by institutions.

SOURCE: Thomas J. Kriger, "Table 4. Virtual Universities," *A Virtual Revolution: Trends in the Expansion of Distance Education,* American Federation of Teachers, Washington, DC, May 2001

nonstudent young adults. Binge drinking has not fluctuated much among either group since 1991. (See Table 9.23.)

Tobacco Use

Recent studies have shown that full-time college students were less likely than other persons of the same age group to be regular smokers. In 2000, 17.8 percent of college students reported daily smoking, down from 19.3 percent in 1999. Over 10 percent reported smoking half a pack or more per day. About 22 percent of nonstudents in the same age group reported daily smoking, while 15 percent said they smoked half a pack or more a day. (See Table 9.23.)

TABLE 9.22

Trends in annual and 30-day prevalence of use of various drugs for eighth, tenth, and twelfth graders, college students, and young adults, 1991–2000

	Annual											30-Day										
	1991	1992	1993	1994	1995	1996	1997	1998	1999	2000	'99–'00 change	1991	1992	1993	1994	1995	1996	1997	1998	1999	2000	'99–'00 change
Any Illicit Drug[a]																						
8th Grade	11.3	12.9	15.1	18.5	21.4	23.6	22.1	21.0	20.5	19.5	-1.1	5.7	6.8	8.4	10.9	12.4	14.6	12.9	12.1	12.2	11.9	-0.4
10th Grade	21.4	20.4	24.7	30.0	33.3	37.5	38.5	35.0	35.9	36.4	+0.5	11.6	11.0	14.0	18.5	20.2	23.2	23.0	21.5	22.1	22.5	+0.4
12th Grade	29.4	27.1	31.0	35.8	39.0	40.2	42.4	41.4	42.1	40.9	-1.2	16.4	14.4	18.3	21.9	23.8	24.6	26.2	25.6	25.9	24.9	-1.0
College Students	29.2	30.6	30.6	31.4	33.5	34.2	34.1	37.8	36.9	36.1	-0.9	15.2	16.1	15.1	16.0	19.1	17.6	19.2	19.7	21.6	21.5	-0.1
Young Adults	27.0	28.3	28.4	28.4	29.8	29.2	29.2	29.9	30.3	30.8	+0.5	15.1	14.8	14.9	15.3	15.8	15.8	16.4	16.1	17.1	18.1	+1.0
Any Illicit Drug Other Than Marijuana[a]																						
8th Grade	8.4	9.3	10.4	11.3	12.6	13.1	11.8	11.0	10.5	10.2	-0.4	3.8	4.7	5.3	5.6	6.5	6.9	6.0	5.5	5.5	5.6	+0.1
10th Grade	12.2	12.3	13.9	15.2	17.5	18.4	18.2	16.6	16.7	16.7	0.0	5.5	5.7	6.5	7.1	8.9	8.9	8.8	8.6	8.6	8.5	-0.1
12th Grade	16.2	14.9	17.1	18.0	19.4	19.8	20.7	20.2	20.7	20.4	-0.3	7.1	6.3	7.9	8.8	10.0	9.5	10.7	10.7	10.4	10.4	0.0
College Students	13.2	13.1	12.5	12.2	15.9	12.8	15.8	14.0	15.4	15.6	+0.2	4.3	4.6	5.4	4.6	6.3	4.5	6.8	6.1	6.4	6.9	+0.6
Young Adults	14.3	14.1	13.0	13.0	13.8	13.2	13.6	13.2	13.7	14.9	+1.2	5.4	5.5	4.9	5.3	5.7	4.7	5.5	5.5	6.0	6.4	+0.4
Any Illicit Drug Including Inhalants[a,b]																						
8th Grade	16.7	18.2	21.1	24.2	27.1	28.7	27.2	26.2	25.3	24.0	-1.4	8.8	10.0	12.0	14.3	16.1	17.5	16.0	14.9	15.1	14.4	-0.7
10th Grade	23.9	23.5	27.4	32.5	35.6	39.6	40.3	37.1	37.7	38.0	+0.3	13.1	12.6	15.5	20.0	21.6	24.5	24.1	22.5	23.1	23.6	+0.5
12th Grade	31.2	28.8	32.5	37.6	40.2	41.9	43.3	42.4	42.8	42.5	-0.3	17.8	15.5	19.3	23.0	24.8	25.5	26.9	26.6	26.4	26.4	0.0
College Students	29.8	31.1	31.7	31.9	33.7	35.1	35.5	39.1	37.4	37.0	-0.5	15.1	16.5	15.7	16.4	19.6	18.0	19.6	21.0	21.8	22.6	+0.8
Young Adults	27.8	29.2	28.9	29.2	30.4	30.2	30.1	30.6	30.6	31.2	+0.6	15.4	15.3	15.1	16.1	16.1	16.4	16.9	16.7	17.4	18.8	+1.4
Marijuana/Hashish																						
8th Grade	6.2	7.2	9.2	13.0	15.8	18.3	17.7	16.9	16.5	15.6	-0.9	3.2	3.7	5.1	7.8	9.1	11.3	10.2	9.7	9.7	9.1	-0.6
10th Grade	16.5	15.2	19.2	25.2	28.7	33.6	34.8	31.1	32.1	32.2	+0.2	8.7	8.1	10.9	15.8	17.2	20.4	20.5	18.7	19.4	19.7	+0.3
12th Grade	23.9	21.9	26.0	30.7	34.7	35.8	38.5	37.5	37.8	36.5	-1.3	13.8	11.9	15.5	19.0	21.2	21.9	23.7	22.8	23.1	21.6	-1.6
College Students	26.5	27.7	27.9	29.3	31.2	33.1	31.6	35.9	35.2	34.0	-1.2	14.1	14.6	14.2	15.1	18.6	17.5	17.7	18.6	20.7	20.0	-0.6
Young Adults	23.8	25.2	25.1	25.5	26.5	27.0	26.8	27.4	27.6	27.9	+0.3	13.5	13.3	13.4	14.1	14.0	15.1	15.0	14.9	15.6	16.1	+0.5
Inhalants[b,c]																						
8th Grade	9.0	9.5	11.0	11.7	12.8	12.2	11.8	11.1	10.3	9.4	-0.9	4.4	4.7	5.4	5.6	6.1	5.8	5.6	4.8	5.0	4.5	-0.5
10th Grade	7.1	7.5	8.4	9.1	9.6	9.5	8.7	8.0	7.2	7.3	+0.1	2.7	2.7	3.3	3.6	3.5	3.3	3.0	2.9	2.6	2.6	0.0
12th Grade	6.6	6.2	7.0	7.7	8.0	7.6	6.7	6.2	5.6	5.9	+0.3	2.4	2.3	2.5	2.7	3.2	2.5	2.5	2.3	2.0	2.2	+0.2
College Students	3.5	3.1	3.8	3.0	3.9	3.6	4.1	3.0	3.2	2.9	-0.3	0.9	1.1	1.3	0.6	1.6	0.8	0.8	0.6	1.5	0.9	-0.6
Young Adults	2.0	1.9	2.1	2.1	2.4	2.2	2.3	2.1	2.3	2.1	-0.1	0.5	0.6	0.7	0.5	0.7	0.5	0.5	0.7	0.8	0.5	-0.3
Nitrites[d]																						
8th Grade	—	—	—	—	—	—	—	—	—	—	—	—	—	—	—	—	—	—	—	—	—	—
10th Grade	—	—	—	—	—	—	—	—	—	—	—	—	—	—	—	—	—	—	—	—	—	—
12th Grade	0.9	0.5	0.9	1.1	1.1	1.6	1.2	1.4	0.9	0.6	-0.3	0.4	0.3	0.6	0.4	0.4	0.7	0.7	1.0	0.4	0.3	-0.1
College Students	—	—	—	—	—	—	—	—	—	—	—	—	—	—	—	—	—	—	—	—	—	—
Young Adults	0.2	0.1	0.4	0.3	—	—	—	—	—	—	—	*	0.1	0.2	0.1	—	—	—	—	—	—	—
Hallucinogens[c]																						
8th Grade	1.9	2.5	2.6	2.7	3.6	4.1	3.7	3.4	2.9	2.8	0.0	0.8	1.1	1.2	1.3	1.7	1.9	1.8	1.4	1.3	1.2	-0.1
10th Grade	4.0	4.3	4.7	5.8	7.2	7.8	7.6	6.9	6.9	6.1	-0.9	1.6	1.8	1.9	2.4	3.3	2.8	3.3	3.2	2.9	2.3	-0.6s
12th Grade	5.8	5.9	7.4	7.6	9.3	10.1	9.8	9.0	9.4	8.1	-1.3s	2.2	2.1	2.7	3.1	4.4	3.5	3.9	3.8	3.5	2.6	-0.9ss
College Students	6.3	6.8	6.0	6.2	8.2	6.9	7.7	7.2	7.8	6.7	-1.2	1.2	2.3	2.5	2.1	3.3	1.9	2.1	2.1	2.0	1.4	-0.5
Young Adults	4.5	5.0	4.5	4.8	5.6	5.6	5.9	5.2	5.4	5.4	0.0	1.1	1.5	1.2	1.4	1.7	1.2	1.5	1.4	1.3	1.2	-0.1
LSD																						
8th Grade	1.7	2.1	2.3	2.4	3.2	3.5	3.2	2.8	2.4	2.4	+0.1	0.6	0.9	1.0	1.1	1.4	1.5	1.5	1.1	1.1	1.0	-0.1
10th Grade	3.7	4.0	4.2	5.2	6.5	6.9	6.7	5.9	6.0	5.1	-0.9	1.5	1.6	1.6	2.0	3.0	2.4	2.8	2.7	2.3	1.6	-0.7ss
12th Grade	5.2	5.6	6.8	6.9	8.4	8.8	8.4	7.6	8.1	6.6	-1.5s	1.9	2.0	2.4	2.6	4.0	2.5	3.1	3.2	2.7	1.6	-1.2sss
College Students	5.1	5.7	5.1	5.2	6.9	5.2	5.0	4.4	5.4	4.3	-1.0	0.8	1.8	1.6	1.8	2.5	0.9	1.1	1.5	1.2	0.9	-0.2
Young Adults	3.8	4.3	3.8	4.0	4.6	4.5	4.4	3.5	4.0	3.7	-0.3	0.8	1.1	0.8	1.1	1.3	0.7	0.9	1.0	0.8	0.8	-0.1
Hallucinogens Other Than LSD																						
8th Grade	0.7	1.1	1.0	1.3	1.7	2.0	1.8	1.6	1.5	1.4	-0.1	0.3	0.4	0.5	0.7	0.8	0.9	0.7	0.7	0.6	0.6	+0.1
10th Grade	1.3	1.4	1.9	2.4	2.8	3.3	3.3	3.4	3.2	3.1	-0.1	0.4	0.5	0.7	1.0	1.0	1.0	1.2	1.4	1.2	1.2	0.0
12th Grade	2.0	1.7	2.2	3.1	3.8	4.4	4.6	4.6	4.3	4.4	+0.1	0.7	0.5	0.8	1.2	1.3	1.6	1.7	1.6	1.6	1.7	+0.1
College Students	3.1	2.6	2.7	2.8	4.0	4.1	4.9	4.4	4.5	4.4	-0.1	0.6	0.7	1.1	0.8	1.6	1.2	1.2	0.7	1.2	0.8	-0.4
Young Adults	1.7	1.9	1.9	2.0	2.5	2.8	3.1	3.0	3.0	3.4	+0.4	0.3	0.5	0.6	0.6	0.6	0.6	0.7	0.5	0.6	0.7	+0.1
PCP[d]																						
8th Grade	—	—	—	—	—	—	—	—	—	—	—	—	—	—	—	—	—	—	—	—	—	—
10th Grade	—	—	—	—	—	—	—	—	—	—	—	—	—	—	—	—	—	—	—	—	—	—
12th Grade	1.4	1.4	1.4	1.6	1.8	2.6	2.3	2.1	1.8	2.3	+0.5	0.5	0.6	1.0	0.7	0.6	1.3	0.7	1.0	0.8	0.9	+0.1
College Students	—	—	—	—	—	—	—	—	—	—	—	—	—	—	—	—	—	—	—	—	—	—
Young Adults	0.3	0.3	0.2	0.3	0.3	0.2	0.5	0.6	0.6	0.3	-0.3	0.1	0.2	0.2	0.1	0.0	0.1	0.1	0.2	0.2	0.0	-0.2

TABLE 9.22

Trends in annual and 30-day prevalence of use of various drugs for eighth, tenth, and twelfth graders, college students, and young adults, 1991–2000 [CONTINUED]

	Annual											30-Day										
	1991	1992	1993	1994	1995	1996	1997	1998	1999	2000	'99–'00 change	1991	1992	1993	1994	1995	1996	1997	1998	1999	2000	'99–'00 change
MDMA (Ecstasy)d,e																						
8th Grade	—	—	—	—	—	2.3	2.3	1.8	1.7	3.1	+1.4sss	—	—	—	—	—	1.0	1.0	0.9	0.8	1.4	+0.7ss
10th Grade	—	—	—	—	—	4.6	3.9	3.3	4.4	5.4	+1.0	—	—	—	—	—	1.8	1.3	1.3	1.8	2.6	+0.8s
12th Grade	—	—	—	—	—	4.6	4.0	3.6	5.6	8.2	+2.6ss	—	—	—	—	—	2.0	1.6	1.5	2.5	3.6	+1.1
College Students	0.9	2.0	0.8	0.5	2.4	2.8	2.4	3.9	5.5	9.1	+3.6s	0.2	0.4	0.3	0.2	0.7	0.7	0.8	0.8	2.1	2.5	+0.4
Young Adults	0.8	1.0	0.8	0.7	1.6	1.7	2.1	2.9	3.6	7.2	+3.6sss	0.1	0.3	0.3	0.2	0.4	0.3	0.6	0.8	1.3	1.9	+0.5
Cocaine																						
8th Grade	1.1	1.5	1.7	2.1	2.6	3.0	2.8	3.1	2.7	2.6	-0.1	0.5	0.7	0.7	1.0	1.2	1.3	1.1	1.4	1.3	1.2	-0.1
10th Grade	2.2	1.9	2.1	2.8	3.5	4.2	4.7	4.7	4.9	4.4	-0.5	0.7	0.7	0.9	1.2	1.7	1.7	2.0	2.1	1.8	1.8	-0.1
12th Grade	3.5	3.1	3.3	3.6	4.0	4.9	5.5	5.7	6.2	5.0	-1.3s	1.4	1.3	1.3	1.5	1.8	2.0	2.3	2.4	2.6	2.1	-0.5
College Students	3.6	3.0	2.7	2.0	3.6	2.9	3.4	4.6	4.6	4.8	+0.2	1.0	1.0	0.7	0.6	0.7	0.8	1.6	1.6	1.2	1.4	+0.2
Young Adults	6.2	5.7	4.7	4.3	4.4	4.1	4.7	4.9	5.4	5.4	0.0	2.0	1.8	1.4	1.3	1.5	1.2	1.6	1.7	1.9	1.7	-0.3
Crack																						
8th Grade	0.7	0.9	1.0	1.3	1.6	1.8	1.7	2.1	1.8	1.8	0.0	0.3	0.5	0.4	0.7	0.7	0.8	0.7	0.9	0.8	0.8	-0.1
10th Grade	0.9	0.9	1.1	1.4	1.8	2.1	2.2	2.5	2.4	2.2	-0.2	0.3	0.4	0.5	0.6	0.9	0.8	0.9	1.1	0.8	0.9	+0.1
12th Grade	1.5	1.5	1.5	1.9	2.1	2.1	2.4	2.5	2.7	2.2	-0.5s	0.7	0.6	0.7	0.8	1.0	1.0	0.9	1.0	1.1	1.0	-0.1
College Students	0.5	0.4	0.6	0.5	1.1	0.6	0.4	1.0	0.9	0.9	0.0	0.3	0.1	0.1	0.1	0.1	0.1	0.2	0.2	0.3	0.3	0.0
Young Adults	1.2	1.4	1.3	1.1	1.1	1.1	1.0	1.1	1.4	1.2	-0.2	0.4	0.4	0.4	0.3	0.2	0.3	0.3	0.4	0.4	0.4	-0.1
Other Cocainef																						
8th Grade	1.0	1.2	1.3	1.7	2.1	2.5	2.2	2.4	2.3	1.9	-0.4	0.5	0.5	0.6	0.9	1.0	1.0	0.8	1.0	1.1	0.9	-0.2
10th Grade	2.1	1.7	1.8	2.4	3.0	3.5	4.1	4.0	4.4	3.8	-0.6	0.6	0.6	0.7	1.0	1.4	1.3	1.6	1.8	1.6	1.6	0.0
12th Grade	3.2	2.6	2.9	3.0	3.4	4.2	5.0	4.9	5.8	4.5	-1.4s	1.2	1.0	1.2	1.3	1.3	1.6	2.0	2.0	2.5	1.7	-0.7s
College Students	3.2	2.4	2.5	1.8	3.3	2.3	3.0	4.2	4.2	4.1	-0.1	1.0	0.9	0.6	0.3	0.8	0.6	1.3	1.5	1.0	0.9	-0.1
Young Adults	5.4	5.1	3.9	3.6	3.9	3.8	4.3	4.5	4.8	4.8	0.0	1.8	1.7	1.1	1.0	1.3	1.1	1.5	1.5	1.6	1.5	-0.2
Heroing																						
8th Grade	0.7	0.7	0.7	1.2	1.4	1.6	1.3	1.3	1.4	1.1	-0.3s	0.3	0.4	0.4	0.6	0.6	0.7	0.6	0.6	0.6	0.5	-0.2
10th Grade	0.5	0.6	0.7	0.9	1.1	1.2	1.4	1.4	1.4	1.4	0.0	0.2	0.2	0.3	0.4	0.6	0.5	0.6	0.7	0.7	0.5	-0.2
12th Grade	0.4	0.6	0.5	0.6	1.1	1.0	1.2	1.0	1.1	1.5	+0.4s	0.2	0.3	0.2	0.3	0.6	0.5	0.5	0.5	0.5	0.7	+0.2
College Students	0.1	0.1	0.1	0.1	0.3	0.4	0.3	0.6	0.2	0.5	+0.3	0.1	0.0	*	0.0	0.1	*	0.2	0.1	0.1	0.2	+0.1
Young Adults	0.1	0.2	0.2	0.1	0.4	0.4	0.3	0.4	0.4	0.4	0.0	*	0.1	0.1	0.1	0.1	0.1	0.1	0.1	0.1	0.1	0.0
With a needleh																						
8th Grade	—	—	—	—	0.9	1.0	0.8	0.8	0.9	0.6	-0.3ss	—	—	—	—	0.4	0.5	0.4	0.5	0.4	0.3	-0.1
10th Grade	—	—	—	—	0.6	0.7	0.7	0.8	0.6	0.5	-0.1	—	—	—	—	0.3	0.3	0.3	0.4	0.3	0.3	-0.1
12th Grade	—	—	—	—	0.5	0.5	0.5	0.4	0.4	0.4	0.0	—	—	—	—	0.3	0.4	0.3	0.2	0.2	0.2	0.0
College Students	—	—	—	—	0.1	0.0	0.1	0.2	0.1	0.1	0.0	—	—	—	—	0.0	0.0	0.1	0.0	0.1	0.1	0.0
Young Adults	—	—	—	—	0.1	0.1	0.1	0.1	0.1	*	-0.1	—	—	—	—	0.0	0.0	0.1	*	0.1	*	0.0
Without a needleh																						
8th Grade	—	—	—	—	0.8	1.0	0.8	0.8	0.9	0.7	-0.2	—	—	—	—	0.3	0.4	0.4	0.3	0.4	0.3	-0.1
10th Grade	—	—	—	—	0.8	0.9	1.1	1.0	1.1	1.1	0.0	—	—	—	—	0.3	0.3	0.4	0.5	0.5	0.4	-0.2
12th Grade	—	—	—	—	1.0	1.0	1.2	0.8	1.0	1.6	+0.6ss	—	—	—	—	0.6	0.4	0.6	0.4	0.4	0.7	+0.3
College Students	—	—	—	—	0.0	0.8	0.4	0.9	0.3	0.8	+0.5	—	—	—	—	0.0	0.1	0.2	0.2	0.3	0.4	+0.1
Young Adults	—	—	—	—	0.3	0.4	0.4	0.7	0.6	0.5	-0.1	—	—	—	—	0.1	*	0.1	0.2	0.2	0.2	-0.1
Other Narcoticsi																						
8th Grade	—	—	—	—	—	—	—	—	—	—	—	—	—	—	—	—	—	—	—	—	—	—
10th Grade	—	—	—	—	—	—	—	—	—	—	—	—	—	—	—	—	—	—	—	—	—	—
12th Grade	3.5	3.3	3.6	3.8	4.7	5.4	6.2	6.3	6.7	7.0	+0.3	1.1	1.2	1.3	1.5	1.8	2.0	2.3	2.4	2.6	2.9	+0.3
College Students	2.7	2.7	2.5	2.4	3.8	3.1	4.2	4.2	4.3	4.5	+0.2	0.6	1.0	0.7	0.4	1.2	0.7	1.3	1.1	1.0	1.7	+0.7
Young Adults	2.5	2.5	2.2	2.5	3.0	2.9	3.3	3.4	3.8	4.1	+0.4	0.6	0.7	0.7	0.6	0.9	0.7	0.9	0.9	1.2	1.4	+0.2
Amphetaminesi																						
8th Grade	6.2	6.5	7.2	7.9	8.7	9.1	8.1	7.2	6.9	6.5	-0.4	2.6	3.3	3.6	3.6	4.2	4.6	3.8	3.3	3.4	3.4	+0.1
10th Grade	8.2	8.2	9.6	10.2	11.9	12.4	12.1	10.7	10.4	11.1	+0.7	3.3	3.6	4.3	4.5	5.3	5.5	5.1	5.1	5.0	5.4	+0.5
12th Grade	8.2	7.1	8.4	9.4	9.3	9.5	10.2	10.1	10.2	10.5	+0.3	3.2	2.8	3.7	4.0	4.0	4.1	4.8	4.6	4.5	5.0	+0.5
College Students	3.9	3.6	4.2	4.2	5.4	4.2	5.7	5.1	5.8	6.6	+0.8	1.0	1.1	1.5	1.5	2.2	0.9	2.1	1.7	2.3	2.9	+0.6
Young Adults	4.3	4.1	4.0	4.5	4.6	4.2	4.6	4.5	4.7	5.4	+0.7	1.5	1.5	1.5	1.7	1.7	1.5	1.7	1.7	1.9	2.3	+0.4
Methamphetaminei,k																						
8th Grade	—	—	—	—	—	—	—	—	3.2	2.5	-0.7	—	—	—	—	—	—	—	—	1.1	0.8	-0.3
10th Grade	—	—	—	—	—	—	—	—	4.6	4.0	-0.6	—	—	—	—	—	—	—	—	1.8	2.0	+0.2
12th Grade	—	—	—	—	—	—	—	—	4.7	4.3	-0.3	—	—	—	—	—	—	—	—	1.7	1.9	+0.2
College Students	—	—	—	—	—	—	—	—	3.3	1.6	-1.7	—	—	—	—	—	—	—	—	1.2	0.2	-1.0
Young Adults	—	—	—	—	—	—	—	—	2.8	2.5	-0.3	—	—	—	—	—	—	—	—	0.8	0.7	-0.1
Icek																						
8th Grade	—	—	—	—	—	—	—	—	—	—	—	—	—	—	—	—	—	—	—	—	—	—
10th Grade	—	—	—	—	—	—	—	—	—	—	—	—	—	—	—	—	—	—	—	—	—	—
12th Grade	1.4	1.3	1.7	1.8	2.4	2.8	2.3	3.0	1.9	2.2	+0.3	0.6	0.5	0.6	0.7	1.1	1.1	0.8	1.2	0.8	1.0	+0.2
College Students	0.1	0.2	0.7	0.8	1.1	0.3	0.8	1.0	0.5	0.5	0.0	0.0	0.0	0.3	0.5	0.3	0.1	0.2	0.3	0.0	0.0	0.0
Young Adults	0.3	0.4	0.8	0.9	1.2	0.9	0.9	1.1	0.9	1.2	+0.3	*	0.1	0.3	0.5	0.3	0.3	0.3	0.3	0.4	0.4	+0.1

TABLE 9.22

Trends in annual and 30-day prevalence of use of various drugs for eighth, tenth, and twelfth graders, college students, and young adults, 1991–2000 [CONTINUED]

	Annual											30-Day										
	1991	1992	1993	1994	1995	1996	1997	1998	1999	2000	'99–'00 change	1991	1992	1993	1994	1995	1996	1997	1998	1999	2000	'99–'00 change
Barbiturates^i																						
8th Grade	—	—	—	—	—	—	—	—	—	—	—	—	—	—	—	—	—	—	—	—	—	—
10th Grade	—	—	—	—	—	—	—	—	—	—	—	—	—	—	—	—	—	—	—	—	—	—
12th Grade	3.4	2.8	3.4	4.1	4.7	4.9	5.1	5.5	5.8	6.2	+0.4	1.4	1.1	1.3	1.7	2.2	2.1	2.1	2.6	2.6	3.0	+0.4
College Students	1.2	1.4	1.5	1.2	2.0	2.3	3.0	2.5	3.2	3.7	+0.5	0.3	0.7	0.4	0.4	0.5	0.8	1.2	1.1	1.1	1.1	0.0
Young Adults	1.8	1.6	1.9	1.8	2.1	2.2	2.4	2.5	2.8	3.4	+0.6s	0.5	0.5	0.6	0.6	0.8	0.8	0.9	0.9	1.1	1.3	+0.2
Tranquilizers^i																						
8th Grade	1.8	2.0	2.1	2.4	2.7	3.3	2.9	2.6	2.5	2.6	+0.2	0.8	0.8	0.9	1.1	1.2	1.5	1.2	1.2	1.1	1.4	+0.3
10th Grade	3.2	3.5	3.3	3.3	4.0	4.6	4.9	5.1	5.4	5.6	+0.2	1.2	1.5	1.1	1.5	1.7	1.7	2.2	2.2	2.2	2.5	+0.4
12th Grade	3.6	2.8	3.5	3.7	4.4	4.6	4.7	5.5	5.8	5.7	-0.1	1.4	1.0	1.2	1.4	1.8	2.0	1.8	2.4	2.5	2.6	+0.1
College Students	2.4	2.9	2.4	1.8	2.9	2.8	3.8	3.9	3.8	4.2	+0.4	0.6	0.6	0.4	0.4	0.5	0.7	1.2	1.3	1.1	2.0	+0.9s
Young Adults	3.5	3.4	3.1	2.9	3.4	3.2	3.1	3.8	3.7	4.6	+0.9s	0.9	1.0	1.0	0.8	1.1	0.7	1.1	1.2	1.3	1.8	+0.5s
Rohypnol^d,l																						
8th Grade	—	—	—	—	—	1.0	0.8	0.8	0.5	0.5	+0.1	—	—	—	—	—	0.5	0.3	0.4	0.3	0.3	0.0
10th Grade	—	—	—	—	—	1.1	1.3	1.2	1.0	0.8	-0.3	—	—	—	—	—	0.5	0.5	0.4	0.5	0.4	-0.2
12th Grade	—	—	—	—	—	1.1	1.2	1.4	1.0	0.8	-0.2	—	—	—	—	—	0.5	0.3	0.3	0.3	0.4	+0.1
College Students	—	—	—	—	—	—	—	—	—	—	—	—	—	—	—	—	—	—	—	—	—	—
Young Adults	—	—	—	—	—	—	—	—	—	—	—	—	—	—	—	—	—	—	—	—	—	—
GHB^j,k																						
8th Grade	—	—	—	—	—	—	—	—	—	1.2	—	—	—	—	—	—	—	—	—	—	—	—
10th Grade	—	—	—	—	—	—	—	—	—	1.1	—	—	—	—	—	—	—	—	—	—	—	—
12th Grade	—	—	—	—	—	—	—	—	—	1.9	—	—	—	—	—	—	—	—	—	—	—	—
College Students	—	—	—	—	—	—	—	—	—	—	—	—	—	—	—	—	—	—	—	—	—	—
Young Adults	—	—	—	—	—	—	—	—	—	—	—	—	—	—	—	—	—	—	—	—	—	—
Ketamine^j,k																						
8th Grade	—	—	—	—	—	—	—	—	—	1.6	—	—	—	—	—	—	—	—	—	—	—	—
10th Grade	—	—	—	—	—	—	—	—	—	2.1	—	—	—	—	—	—	—	—	—	—	—	—
12th Grade	—	—	—	—	—	—	—	—	—	2.5	—	—	—	—	—	—	—	—	—	—	—	—
College Students	—	—	—	—	—	—	—	—	—	—	—	—	—	—	—	—	—	—	—	—	—	—
Young Adults	—	—	—	—	—	—	—	—	—	—	—	—	—	—	—	—	—	—	—	—	—	—
Alcohol^m																						
Any use																						
8th Grade	54.0	53.7	51.6	—	—	—	—	—	—	—	—	25.1	26.1	26.2	—	—	—	—	—	—	—	—
8th Grade	—	—	45.4	46.8	45.3	46.5	45.5	43.7	43.5	43.1	-0.4	—	—	24.3	25.5	24.6	26.2	24.5	23.0	24.0	22.4	-1.7
10th Grade	72.3	70.2	69.3	—	—	—	—	—	—	—	—	42.8	39.9	41.5	—	—	—	—	—	—	—	—
10th Grade	—	—	63.4	63.9	63.5	65.0	65.2	62.7	63.7	65.3	+1.6	—	—	38.2	39.2	38.8	40.4	40.1	38.8	40.0	41.0	+0.9
12th Grade	77.7	76.8	76.0	—	—	—	—	—	—	—	—	54.0	51.3	51.0	—	—	—	—	—	—	—	—
12th Grade	—	—	72.7	73.0	73.7	72.5	74.8	74.3	73.8	73.2	-0.6	—	—	48.6	50.1	51.3	50.8	52.7	52.0	51.0	50.0	-1.0
College Students	88.3	86.9	85.1	82.7	83.2	82.9	82.4	84.6	83.6	83.2	-0.3	74.7	71.4	70.1	67.8	67.5	67.0	65.8	68.1	69.6	67.4	-2.2
Young Adults	86.9	86.2	85.3	83.7	84.7	84.0	84.3	84.0	84.1	84.0	-0.1	70.6	69.0	68.3	67.7	68.1	66.7	67.5	66.9	68.2	66.8	-1.4
Been Drunk^k																						
8th Grade	17.5	18.3	18.2	18.2	18.4	19.8	18.4	17.9	18.5	18.5	0.0	7.6	7.5	7.8	8.7	8.3	9.6	8.2	8.4	9.4	8.3	-1.1
10th Grade	40.1	37.0	37.8	38.0	38.5	40.1	40.7	38.3	40.9	41.6	+0.7	20.5	18.1	19.8	20.3	20.8	21.3	22.4	21.1	22.5	23.5	+1.0
12th Grade	52.7	50.3	49.6	51.7	52.5	51.9	53.2	52.0	53.2	51.8	-1.4	31.6	29.9	28.9	30.8	33.2	31.3	34.2	32.9	32.9	32.3	-0.6
College Students	—	—	—	—	—	—	—	—	—	—	—	—	—	—	—	—	—	—	—	—	—	—
Young Adults	—	—	—	—	—	—	—	—	—	—	—	—	—	—	—	—	—	—	—	—	—	—
Cigarettes																						
Any use																						
8th Grade	—	—	—	—	—	—	—	—	—	—	—	14.3	15.5	16.7	18.6	19.1	21.0	19.4	19.1	17.5	14.6	-2.8sss
10th Grade	—	—	—	—	—	—	—	—	—	—	—	20.8	21.5	24.7	25.4	27.9	30.4	29.8	27.6	25.7	23.9	-1.8
12th Grade	—	—	—	—	—	—	—	—	—	—	—	28.3	27.8	29.9	31.2	33.5	34.0	36.5	35.1	34.6	31.4	-3.2ss
College Students	35.6	37.3	38.8	37.6	39.3	41.4	43.6	44.3	44.5	41.3	-3.2	23.2	23.5	24.5	23.5	26.8	27.9	28.3	30.0	30.6	28.2	-2.4
Young Adults	37.7	37.9	37.8	38.3	38.8	40.3	41.8	41.6	41.1	40.9	-0.2	28.2	28.3	28.0	28.0	29.2	30.1	29.9	30.9	30.3	30.1	-0.3
Bidis^j,k																						
8th Grade	—	—	—	—	—	—	—	—	—	3.9	—	—	—	—	—	—	—	—	—	—	—	—
10th Grade	—	—	—	—	—	—	—	—	—	6.4	—	—	—	—	—	—	—	—	—	—	—	—
12th Grade	—	—	—	—	—	—	—	—	—	9.2	—	—	—	—	—	—	—	—	—	—	—	—
College Students	—	—	—	—	—	—	—	—	—	—	—	—	—	—	—	—	—	—	—	—	—	—
Young Adults	—	—	—	—	—	—	—	—	—	—	—	—	—	—	—	—	—	—	—	—	—	—

TABLE 9.22

Trends in annual and 30-day prevalence of use of various drugs for eighth, tenth, and twelfth graders, college students, and young adults, 1991–2000 [CONTINUED]

	Annual											30-Day										
	1991	1992	1993	1994	1995	1996	1997	1998	1999	2000	'99–'00 change	1991	1992	1993	1994	1995	1996	1997	1998	1999	2000	'99–'00 change
Smokeless Tobacco[d,e]																						
8th Grade	—	—	—	—	—	—	—	—	—	—	—	6.9	7.0	6.6	7.7	7.1	7.1	5.5	4.8	4.5	4.2	-0.3
10th Grade	—	—	—	—	—	—	—	—	—	—	—	10.0	9.6	10.4	10.5	9.7	8.6	8.9	7.5	6.5	6.1	-0.5
12th Grade	—	—	—	—	—	—	—	—	—	—	—	—	11.4	10.7	11.1	12.2	9.8	9.7	8.8	8.4	7.6	-0.7
College Students	—	—	—	—	—	—	—	—	—	—	—	—	—	—	—	—	—	—	—	—	—	—
Young Adults	—	—	—	—	—	—	—	—	—	—	—	—	—	—	—	—	—	—	—	—	—	—
Steroids[k]																						
8th Grade	1.0	1.1	0.9	1.2	1.0	0.9	1.0	1.2	1.7	1.7	0.0	0.4	0.5	0.5	0.5	0.6	0.4	0.5	0.5	0.7	0.8	+0.1
10th Grade	1.1	1.1	1.0	1.1	1.2	1.2	1.2	1.2	1.7	2.2	+0.5s	0.6	0.6	0.5	0.6	0.6	0.5	0.7	0.6	0.9	1.0	0.0
12th Grade	1.4	1.1	1.2	1.3	1.5	1.4	1.4	1.7	1.8	1.7	-0.1	0.8	0.6	0.7	0.9	0.7	0.7	1.0	1.1	0.9	0.8	-0.1
College Students	—	—	—	—	—	—	—	—	—	—	—	—	—	—	—	—	—	—	—	—	—	—
Young Adults	0.5	0.4	0.3	0.4	0.5	0.3	0.5	0.4	0.6	0.4	-0.2	0.2	0.1	0.0	0.1	0.2	0.2	0.2	0.2	0.3	0.1	-0.2

NOTES: Level of significance of difference between the two most recent classes: s = .05, ss = .01, sss = .001.
'—' indicates data not available. '*' indicates less than .05 percent but greater than 0 percent.
Any apparent inconsistency between the change estimate and the prevalence of use estimates for the two most recent classes is due to rounding error.

Approximate Weighted Ns	1991	1992	1993	1994	1995	1996	1997	1998	1999	2000
8th Graders	17,500	18,600	18,300	17,300	17,500	17,800	18,600	18,100	16,700	16,700
10th Graders	14,800	14,800	15,300	15,800	17,000	15,600	15,500	15,000	13,600	14,300
12th Graders	15,000	15,800	16,300	15,400	15,400	14,300	15,400	15,200	13,600	12,800
College Students	1,410	1,490	1,490	1,410	1,450	1,450	1,480	1,440	1,440	1,350
Young Adults	6,600	6,800	6,700	6,500	6,400	6,300	6,400	6,200	6,000	5,700

[a] For 12th graders, college students, and young adults only: Use of "any illicit drug" includes any use of marijuana, LSD, other hallucinogens, crack, other cocaine, or heroin, or any use of other narcotics, amphetamines, barbiturates, or tranquilizers not under a doctor's orders. For 8th and 10th graders only: The use of other narcotics and barbiturates has been excluded, because these younger respondents appear to overreport use (perhaps because they include the use of nonprescription drugs in their answers).

[b] For 12th graders, college students, and young adults only: Data based on five of six forms in 1991–98; N is five-sixths of N indicated. Data based on three of six forms beginning in 1999; N is three-sixths of N indicated.

[c] Inhalants are unadjusted for underreporting of amyl and butyl nitrites; hallucinogens are unadjusted for underreporting of PCP.

[d] For 12th graders only: Data based on one of six forms; N is one-sixth of N indicated. For college students and young adults only: Data based on two of six forms; N is one-third of N indicated. Questions about nitrite use were dropped from the college student and young adult questionnaires in 1995. Questions about smokeless tobacco use were dropped from the college student and young adult analyses in 1989.

[e] For 8th and 10th graders only: MDMA data based on one of two forms in 1996; N is one-half of N indicated. Beginning in 1997, data based on one-third of N indicated due to changes in the questionnaire forms.. Smokeless tobacco data based on one of two forms for 1991–96 and on two of four forms beginning in 1997; N is one-half of N indicated.

[f] For 12th graders, college students, and young adults only: Data based on four of six forms; N is four-sixths of N indicated for each group.

[g] In 1995, the heroin question was changed in three of six forms for 12th graders and in one of two forms for 8th and 10th graders. Separate questions were asked for use with injection and without injection. In 1996, the heroin question was changed in all remaining 8th and 10th grade forms. Data presented here represent the combined data from all forms.

[h] For 8th and 10th graders only: Data based on one of two forms in 1995; N is one-half of N indicated. For 12th graders only: Data based on three of six forms; N is three-sixths of N indicated.

[i] Only drug use which was not under a doctor's orders is included here.

[j] For 8th and 10th graders only: Data based on one of four forms; N is one-third of N indicated.

[k] For 12th graders, college students, and young adults only: Data based on two of six forms; N is two-sixths of N indicated for each group.

[l] For 8th and 10th graders only: Data based on one of two forms in 1996–97; N is one-half of N indicated. Data based on three of four forms in 1998; N is two-thirds of N indicated. Data based on two of four forms beginning in 1999; N is one-third of N indicated.

[m] For 8th, 10th, and 12th graders only: In 1993, the question text was changed slightly in half of the forms to indicate that a "drink" meant "more than just a few sips." The data in the upper line for alcohol came from forms using the original wording, while the data in the lower line came from forms using the revised wording. In 1993, each line of data was based on one of two forms for the 8th and 10th graders and on three of six forms for the 12th graders. N is one-half of N indicated for these groups. Beginning in 1994, data were based on all forms for all grades. For college students and young adults, the revision of the question text resulted in rather little change in the reported prevalence of use. The data for all forms are used to provide the most reliable estimate of change.

SOURCE: Lloyd D. Johnson, Patrick M. O'Malley, and Jerald G. Bachman, "Table 2-2 Trends in Annual and 30-Day Prevalence of Use of Various Drugs for Eighth, Tenth, and Twelfth Graders, College Students, and Young Adults (Ages 19-28)," in *Monitoring the Future: National Survey Results on Drug Use 1975–2000, Volume II: College Students & Adults Ages 19-40*, NIH Publication No. 01-4925, National Institute on Drug Abuse, Bethesda, MD, August 2001

TABLE 9.23

Trends in 30-day prevalence of daily use of various drugs for eighth, tenth, and twelfth graders, college students, and young adults, 1991–2000

					Daily						
	1991	1992	1993	1994	1995	1996	1997	1998	1999	2000	'99–'00 change
Marijuana/Hashish, daily[e]											
8th Grade	0.2	0.2	0.4	0.7	0.8	1.5	1.1	1.1	1.4	1.3	0.0
10th Grade	0.8	0.8	1.0	2.2	2.8	3.5	3.7	3.6	3.8	3.8	0.0
12th Grade	2.0	1.9	2.4	3.6	4.6	4.9	5.8	5.6	6.0	6.0	0.0
College Students	1.8	1.6	1.9	1.8	3.7	2.8	3.7	4.0	4.0	4.6	+0.6
Young Adults	2.3	2.3	2.4	2.8	3.3	3.3	3.8	3.7	4.4	4.2	-0.2
Alcohol[d,e]											
Any daily use											
8th Grade	0.5	0.6	0.8	—	—	—	—	—	—	—	—
		1.0	1.0	0.7	1.0	0.8	0.9	1.0	0.8	-0.3s	
10th Grade	1.3	1.2	1.6	—	—	—	—	—	—	—	—
		1.8	1.7	1.7	1.6	1.7	1.9	1.9	1.8	-0.1	
12th Grade	3.6	3.4	2.5	—	—	—	—	—	—	—	—
		3.4	2.9	3.5	3.7	3.9	3.9	3.4	2.9	-0.4	
College Students	4.1	3.7	3.9	3.7	3.0	3.2	4.5	3.9	4.5	3.6	-0.8
Young Adults	4.9	4.5	4.5	3.9	3.9	4.0	4.6	4.0	4.8	4.1	-0.7
Been Drunk, daily[c,e]											
8th Grade	0.1	0.1	0.2	0.3	0.2	0.2	0.2	0.3	0.4	0.3	-0.1
10th Grade	0.2	0.3	0.4	0.4	0.6	0.4	0.6	0.6	0.7	0.5	-0.2
12th Grade	0.9	0.8	0.9	1.2	1.3	1.6	2.0	1.5	1.9	1.7	-0.2
College Students	—	—	—	—	—	—	—	—	—	—	—
Young Adults	—	—	—	—	—	—	—	—	—	—	—
5+ drinks in a row in last 2 weeks											
8th Grade	12.9	13.4	13.5	14.5	14.5	15.6	14.5	13.7	15.2	14.1	-1.1
10th Grade	22.9	21.1	23.0	23.6	24.0	24.8	25.1	24.3	25.6	26.2	+0.6
12th Grade	29.8	27.9	27.5	28.2	29.8	30.2	31.3	31.5	30.8	30.0	-0.8
College Students	42.8	41.4	40.2	40.2	38.6	38.3	40.7	38.9	40.0	39.3	-0.7
Young Adults	34.7	34.2	34.4	33.7	32.6	33.6	34.4	34.1	35.8	34.7	-1.1
Cigarettes											
Any daily use											
8th Grade	7.2	7.0	8.3	8.8	9.3	10.4	9.0	8.8	8.1	7.4	-0.7
10th Grade	12.6	12.3	14.2	14.6	16.3	18.3	18.0	15.8	15.9	14.0	-1.9s
12th Grade	18.5	17.2	19.0	19.4	21.6	22.2	24.6	22.4	23.1	20.6	-2.5s
College Students	13.8	14.1	15.2	13.2	15.8	15.9	15.2	18.0	19.3	17.8	-1.4
Young Adults	21.7	20.9	20.8	20.7	21.2	21.8	20.6	21.9	21.5	21.8	+0.3
1/2 pack+/day											
8th Grade	3.1	2.9	3.5	3.6	3.4	4.3	3.5	3.6	3.3	2.8	-0.5
10th Grade	6.5	6.0	7.0	7.6	8.3	9.4	8.6	7.9	7.6	6.2	-1.4ss
12th Grade	10.7	10.0	10.9	11.2	12.4	13.0	14.3	12.6	13.2	11.3	-1.9ss
College Students	8.0	8.9	8.9	8.0	10.2	8.4	9.1	11.3	11.0	10.1	-0.9
Young Adults	16.0	15.7	15.5	15.3	15.7	15.3	14.6	15.6	15.1	15.1	0.0
Smokeless Tobacco, daily[a,b]											
8th Grade	1.6	1.8	1.5	1.9	1.2	1.5	1.0	1.0	0.9	0.9	0.0
10th Grade	3.3	3.0	3.3	3.0	2.7	2.2	2.2	2.2	1.5	1.9	+0.3
12th Grade	—	4.3	3.3	3.9	3.6	3.3	4.4	3.2	2.9	3.2	+0.3
College Students	—	—	—	—	—	—	—	—	—	—	—
Young Adults	—	—	—	—	—	—	—	—	—	—	—

NOTES: Level of significance of difference between the two most recent classes: s = .05, ss = .01, sss = .001.
'—' indicates data not available. '*' indicates less than .05 percent but greater than 0 percent.
Any apparent inconsistency between the change estimate and the prevalence of use estimates for the two most recent classes is due to rounding error.

Approximate Weighted Ns	1991	1992	1993	1994	1995	1996	1997	1998	1999	2000
8th Graders	17,500	18,600	18,300	17,300	17,500	17,800	18,600	18,100	16,700	16,700
10th Graders	14,800	14,800	15,300	15,800	17,000	15,600	15,500	15,000	13,600	14,300
12th Graders	15,000	15,800	16,300	15,400	15,400	14,300	15,400	15,200	13,600	12,800
College Students	1,410	1,490	1,490	1,410	1,450	1,450	1,480	1,440	1,440	1,350
Young Adults	6,600	6,800	6,700	6,500	6,400	6,300	6,400	6,200	6,000	5,700

[a] For 12th graders only: Data based on one of six forms; N is one-sixth of N indicated. For college students and young adults only: Data based on two of six forms; N is one-third of N indicated. Questions about nitrite use were dropped from the college student and young adult questionnaires in 1995. Questions about smokeless tobacco use were dropped from the college student and young adult analyses in 1989.
[b] For 8th and 10th graders only: MDMA data based on one of two forms in 1996; N is one-half of N indicated. Beginning in 1997, data based on one-third of N indicated due to changes in the questionnaire forms.. Smokeless tobacco data based on one of two forms for 1991–96 and on two of four forms beginning in 1997; N is one-half of N indicated.
[c] For 12th graders, college students, and young adults only: Data based on two of six forms; N is two-sixths of N indicated for each group.
[d] For 8th and 10th graders only: Data based on one of two forms in 1996–97; N is one-half of N indicated. Data based on three of four forms in 1998; N is two-thirds of N indicated. Data based on two of four forms beginning in 1999; N is one-third of N indicated.
[e] For 8th, 10th, and 12th graders only: In 1993, the question text was changed slightly in half of the forms to indicate that a "drink" meant "more than just a few sips." The data in the upper line for alcohol came from forms using the original wording, while the data in the lower line came from forms using the revised wording. In 1993, each line of data was based on one of two forms for the 8th and 10th graders and on three of six forms for the 12th graders. N is one-half of N indicated for these groups. Beginning in 1994, data were based on all forms for all grades. For college students and young adults, the revision of the question text resulted in rather little change in the reported prevalence of use. The data for all forms are used to provide the most reliable estimate of change.

SOURCE: Lloyd D. Johnson, Patrick M. O'Malley, and Jerald G. Bachman, "Table 2-3 Trends in Daily Use of Various Drugs for Eighth, Tenth, and Twelfth Graders, College Students, and Young Adults (Ages 19-28)," in *Monitoring the Future: National Survey Results on Drug Use 1975–2000, Volume II: College Students & Adults Ages 19-40*, NIH Publication No. 01-4925, National Institute on Drug Abuse, Bethesda, MD, August 2001

CHAPTER 10

PUBLIC OPINIONS ABOUT EDUCATION

Every year, Phi Delta Kappa, the professional education fraternity, publishes a survey of the American public on education issues. This annual examination is considered one of the best measurements of current American attitudes towards education. Except where otherwise noted, the information in this chapter comes from "The 33rd Annual Phi Delta Kappa/Gallup Poll of the Public's Attitudes Toward the Public Schools" (Lowell C. Rose and Alec M. Gallup, *Phi Delta Kappan*, September 2001).

Keep in mind that these are surveys of peoples' opinions and feelings about public education. They may or may not coincide with facts about the nation's schools. Instead, the survey results illustrate trends in current American thought on educational subjects.

BIGGEST PROBLEMS FACING LOCAL PUBLIC SCHOOLS

Since Phi Delta Kappa began surveying the public's opinion of education in 1969, discipline has been at or near the top of the list of concerns. Between 1969 and 1985 (with the exception of 1971, when the top issue was finances), discipline was the most frequently mentioned problem. Drug abuse by students replaced discipline as the top concern from 1986 through 1991, and in 1992, drugs and lack of proper financial support tied, at 22 percent each. In 1993 lack of proper financial support was clearly the number-one concern, with 21 percent mentioning it as the biggest concern for public schools in their communities. In 1994 and 1995, lack of discipline was back on top. Drug abuse edged out discipline as the top concern of 1996. In 1998 and 1999 lack of discipline, violence in schools, and lack of financial support were the top three concerns.

In 2000 the public identified two problems as top concerns—lack of financial support and lack of discipline. The same two concerns topped the poll in 2001 as well (15 percent each). Fighting/violence/gangs and over-

crowded schools (10 percent each) tied for second place in 2001. (See Table 10.1.)

GRADING THE SCHOOLS

Every year, the Phi Delta Kappa survey asks respondents to grade the public schools on the same scale used to grade students. In general, the survey has found for many years that the respondents' ties to local schools influence the way they rank them. A school attended by a respondent's child, for example, is graded more highly than the schools in the community as a whole, and local community schools are generally given higher grades than are the nation's school system as a whole.

Overall the 2001 survey found that half (51 percent) of those surveyed felt the schools in their communities deserved an A or a B. Most (62 percent) public school

TABLE 10.1

Public school problems

What do you think are the biggest problems with which the public schools of your community must deal?

	National Totals		No Children In School		Public School Parents	
	'01 %	'00 %	'01 %	'00 %	'01 %	'00 %
Lack of financial support/ funding/money	15	18	15	17	17	19
Lack of discipline/more control	15	15	17	17	10	9
Fighting/violence/gangs	10	11	11	11	9	11
Overcrowded schools	10	12	7	10	15	14
Use of drugs/dope	9	9	9	10	10	9
Difficulty getting good teachers/quality teachers	6	4	6	4	6	4

SOURCE: Lowell C. Rose and Alec M. Gallup, "What do you think are the biggest problems with which the public schools of your community must deal?," in "The 33rd Annual Phi Delta Kappa/Gallup Poll of the Public's Attitude Toward the Public Schools," in *Phi Delta Kappan*, September 2001

TABLE 10.2

Grading of public schools by parents and non-parents

Students are often given the grades A, B, C, D, and FAIL to denote the quality of their work. Suppose the public schools themselves, in this community were graded in the same way. What grade would you give the public schools here—A, B, C, D, or FAIL?

	National Totals		No Children In School		Public School Parents	
	'01 %	'00 %	'01 %	'00 %	'01 %	'00 %
A & B	51	47	47	44	62	56
A	11	11	8	10	19	14
B	40	36	39	34	43	42
C	30	35	33	35	25	33
D	8	8	8	8	8	6
FAIL	5	3	4	3	4	3
Don't know	6	7	8	10	1	2

SOURCE: Lowell C. Rose and Alec M. Gallup, "Students are often given grades A, B, C, D, and FAIL to denote the quality of their work. Suppose the public schools themselves, in this community, were graded in the same way. What grade would you give the public schools here—A, B, C, D, or FAIL?," in "The 33rd Annual Phi Delta Kappa/Gallup Poll of the Public's Attitude Toward the Public Schools," in *Phi Delta Kappan*, September 2001

TABLE 10.3

National grading of public schools

How about the public schools in the nation as a whole? What grade would you give the public schools nationally—A, B, C, D, or FAIL?

	National Totals		No Children In School		Public School Parents	
	'01 %	'00 %	'01 %	'00 %	'01 %	'00 %
A & B	23	20	22	19	25	22
A	2	2	1	2	2	2
B	21	18	21	17	23	20
C	51	47	53	47	47	47
D	14	14	13	14	15	12
FAIL	5	5	5	6	4	4
Don't know	7	14	7	14	9	15

SOURCE: Lowell C. Rose and Alec M. Gallup, "How about the public schools in the nation as a whole? What grade would you give the public schools nationally—A, B, C, D, or FAIL?," in "The 33rd Annual Phi Delta Kappa/Gallup Poll of the Public's Attitude Toward the Public Schools," in *Phi Delta Kappan*, September 2001

parents awarded an A or B grade to their community schools. (See Table 10.2.) When asked to grade the school attended by their own oldest children, two-thirds (68 percent) of public school parents awarded an A or a B.

Respondents graded the American public school system as a whole much more harshly. Only 23 percent felt the nation's public schools, overall, deserved A or B grades, while 65 percent assigned grades of C or D. (See Table 10.3.)

According to the U.S. Department of Education, between 1993 and 1999 the proportion of children in grades three to twelve with parents who reported being very satisfied with their child's school decreased from 56 percent to 53 percent. In 1993 the proportion that reported being very satisfied increased as family income increased, but in 1999 this was not true. (See Figure 10.1.)

When asked what consequences a school that fails to meet state standards should face, about two-thirds of the public believed additional funds should be awarded rather than withholding funds. Half (51 percent) favored providing vouchers to parents, and half (49 percent) believed that the teachers' contracts should not be renewed. (See Figure 10.2).

IMPROVE AND STRENGTHEN THE EXISTING PUBLIC SCHOOLS?

The public was asked whether they preferred improving and strengthening the existing public schools or providing vouchers for parents to use in selecting and paying for private and/or church-related schools. In 2001, 71 percent said they favored improving and strengthening exist-

ing public schools, while 27 percent preferred providing vouchers to parents. (See Table 10.4.)

STANDARDS

Raising standards, accountability in meeting those standards, and requiring high school students to take a common core of courses are major issues in education reform. Participants in "The Sixth Phi Delta Kappa Poll of Teachers' Attitudes Toward the Public Schools" (Carol A. Langdon and Nick Vesper, *Phi Delta Kappan*, vol. 81, no. 8, April 2000) were asked about the student achievement standards in the public schools in their community. Most (57 percent) believed that standards were about right, although one-third felt standards were too low. More teachers (63 percent) than the general public believed standards were about right. (See Table 10.5).

In response to a specific question about social promotion—advancing children from grade to grade in order to keep them with others in their age group—nearly three-quarters (72 percent) of public school parents and more than three-quarters (76 percent) of teachers favored stricter standards even if it meant that significantly more students would be held back a grade. (See Table 10.6).

When asked if they would favor or oppose requiring high school students to take a standardized core curriculum, 78 percent of the public and 73 percent of teachers supported a standardized curriculum. (See Table 10.7).

In 2001 about half of the public (52 percent), and a majority (59 percent) of public school parents believed that all students have the ability to reach a high level of learning. These proportions were down slightly from 2000, when 55 percent of the public and 60 percent of public school parents believed all students have the ability to reach a high level of learning. (See Table 10.8.)

FIGURE 10.1

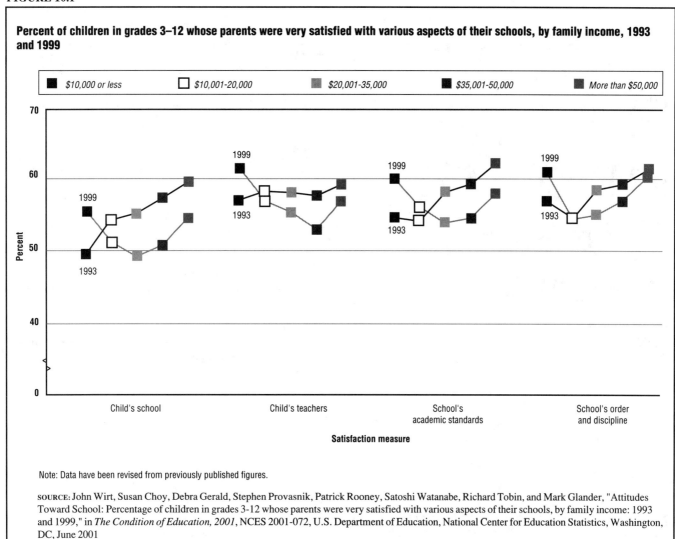

Percent of children in grades 3–12 whose parents were very satisfied with various aspects of their schools, by family income, 1993 and 1999

Note: Data have been revised from previously published figures.

SOURCE: John Wirt, Susan Choy, Debra Gerald, Stephen Provasnik, Patrick Rooney, Satoshi Watanabe, Richard Tobin, and Mark Glander, "Attitudes Toward School: Percentage of children in grades 3-12 whose parents were very satisfied with various aspects of their schools, by family income: 1993 and 1999," in *The Condition of Education, 2001*, NCES 2001-072, U.S. Department of Education, National Center for Education Statistics, Washington, DC, June 2001

DRUGS AND ALCOHOL AT SCHOOL

Teachers and the public's attitudes about the public schools are compared in the Sixth Phi Delta Kappa Poll. Although zero-tolerance policies toward alcohol and drug violations have been debated in the past two years, both the public and teachers strongly supported the automatic suspension of any student in possession of any illegal drug or alcohol. In 2000, 90 percent of respondents supported a zero-tolerance drug and alcohol policy. (See Table 10.9.)

TO TEACH OR NOT TO TEACH VALUES

The Phi Delta Kappa polls have been asking questions about the role of values or ethics/morals in public education since 1975, when 79 percent of the public favored public school instruction about morals and moral behavior. The following year, respondents rated "high moral standards" among the top four qualities that should be developed in children. A 1984 poll listed "develop

standards of right and wrong" as second only to "develop the ability to speak and write correctly" among the most important goals of public schools.

The Sixth Phi Delta Kappa Poll of Teachers' Attitudes Toward the Public Schools presented a list of 11 values and asked respondents to indicate whether or not each one should be taught in public school. In 2000 about 90 percent of the public and teachers favored teaching acceptance of people of different races and ethnic backgrounds, honesty, democracy, patriotism, caring for friends and family members, moral courage, and "the Golden Rule." Most respondents also wanted schools to teach acceptance of people who hold unpopular or controversial viewpoints. Support was mixed for teaching sexual abstinence outside of marriage (45 percent of the public, and 68 percent of teachers), and acceptance of people with different sexual orientations (35 percent of the public, and 55 percent of teachers). The public did not approve of teaching acceptance of the right of a woman to choose an

FIGURE 10.2

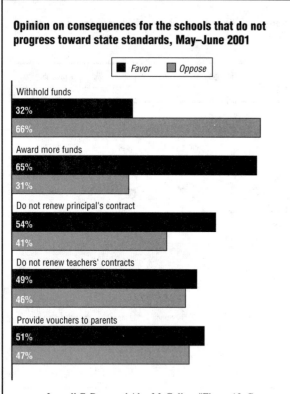

Opinion on consequences for the schools that do not progress toward state standards, May–June 2001

■ *Favor* ▇ *Oppose*

Withhold funds
32%
66%

Award more funds
65%
31%

Do not renew principal's contract
54%
41%

Do not renew teachers' contracts
49%
46%

Provide vouchers to parents
51%
47%

SOURCE: Lowell C. Rose and Alec M. Gallup, "Figure 13. Consequences for Schools That Do Not Progress Toward State Standards," in "The 33rd Annual Phi Delta Kappa/Gallup Poll of the Public's Attitude Toward the Public Schools," *Phi Delta Kappan*, September 2001

TABLE 10.5

Opinion on student achievement standards in public schools, 1999

In your opinion, are student achievement standards in the public schools in your community too high, about right, or too low?

	Teachers %	Public %
Too high	8	6
About right	63	57
Too low	29	33
Don't know	*	4

*This option was not presented to teachers.

SOURCE: Carol A. Langdon and Nick Vesper, "In your opinion, are student achievement standards in the public schools in your community too high, about right, or too low?," in "The Sixth Phi Delta Kappa Poll of Teachers' Attitudes Toward the Public Schools," *Phi Delta Kappan*, vol. 81, no. 8, April 2000

TABLE 10.4

Opinion on school improvement, May–June 2001

Which one of these two plans would you prefer — improving and strengthening the existing public schools or providing vouchers for parents to use in selecting and paying for private and/or church-related schools?

	National Totals %	No Children In School %	Public School Parents %
Improving and strengthening existing public schools	71	71	73
Providing vouchers	27	26	25
Neither (volunteered)	—	—	2
Don't know	2	3	—

SOURCE: Lowell C. Rose and Alec M. Gallup, "Which one of these two plans would you prefer - improving and strengthening the existing public schools or providing vouchers for parents to use in selecting and paying for private and/or church-related schools?" in "The 33rd Annual Phi Delta Kappa/Gallup Poll of the Public's Attitude Toward the Public Schools," *Phi Delta Kappan*, September 2001

TABLE 10.6

Opinion on standard for social promotion, 1999

Social promotion means moving children from grade to grade in order to keep them with others in their own age group. Would you favor stricter standards for social promotion in school even if it meant that significantly more students would be held back?

	Teachers %	Public %
Favor	76	72
Oppose	15	26
Don't know	9	2

SOURCE: Carol A. Langdon and Nick Vesper, "Social promotion means moving children from grade to grade in order to keep them with others in their own age group. Would you favor stricter standards for social promotion in school even if it meant that significantly more students would be held back?" in "The Sixth Phi Delta Kappa Poll of Teachers' Attitudes Toward the Public Schools," *Phi Delta Kappan*, vol. 81, no. 8, April 2000

abortion (16 percent), although almost half (48 percent) of teachers did. (See Table 10.10.)

NO CHILD LEFT BEHIND

On January 8, 2002, President Bush signed H.R. 1, the *No Child Left Behind Act*, into law. The new autho-rization was a major reform to the Elementary and Sec-ondary Education Act (ESEA) of 1965. H.R. 1 authorized $26.5 billion for the 2002 budget year for K-12 education, a nearly $8 billion increase over 2001 funding. The fol-lowing are some of the major provisions of the *No Child Left Behind Act*.

Accountability for Results

H.R. 1 created standards in each state for what a child should know and learn in reading and mathematics in grades three through eight. Student progress and achieve-ment are measured according to tests based upon those state standards and given to every child, every year. The results are available in annual report cards on school per-formance and on statewide progress. Statewide reports include performance data disaggregated according to race, ethnicity, gender, and other criteria to demonstrate student achievement overall, and to chart progress in clos-

TABLE 10.7

Opinion on core curriculum standardization, 1999

As you know, many high school students are allowed to choose many of their academic courses. Would you favor or oppose requiring high school students to take a standardized core curriculum of certain courses?

	Teachers %	Public %
Favor	73	78
Oppose	17	21
Don't know	10	1

SOURCE: Carol A. Langdon and Nick Vesper, "As you know, many high school students are allowed to choose many of their academic courses. Would you favor or oppose requiring high school students to take a standardized core curriculum of certain courses?," in "The Sixth Phi Delta Kappa Poll of Teachers' Attitudes Toward the Public Schools," *Phi Delta Kappan,* vol. 81, no. 8, April 2000

TABLE 10.9

Opinion on drugs and alcohol zero tolerance policy, 1999

Some public schools have a so-called zero tolerance drug and alcohol policy, which means that possession of any illegal drugs or alcohol by students will result in automatic suspension. Would you favor or oppose such a policy in the public schools in your community?

	Teachers %	Public %
Favor	93	90
Oppose	5	10
Don't know	2	*

*Less than one-half of 1%.

SOURCE: Carol A. Langdon and Nick Vesper, "Some public schools have a so-called zero tolerance drug and alcohol policy, which means that possession of any illegal drugs or alcohol by students will result in automatic suspension. Would you favor or oppose such a policy in the public schools in your community?" in "The Sixth Phi Delta Kappa Poll of Teachers' Attitudes Toward the Public Schools," *Phi Delta Kappan,* vol. 81, no. 8, April 2000

TABLE 10.8

Opinion on ability to reach high level of learning, May–June 2001

In your opinion, do all students have the ability to reach a high level of learning, or do only some have the ability to reach a high level of learning?

	National Totals		No Children In School		Public School Parents	
	'01 %	'00 %	'01 %	'00 %	'01 %	'00 %
All have the ability to reach a high level of learning	52	55	48	53	59	60
Only some have the ability	46	43	50	45	40	38
Don't know	2	2	2	2	1	2

SOURCE: Lowell C. Rose and Alec M. Gallup, "In your opinion, do all students have the ability to reach a high level of learning, or do only some have the ability to reach a high level of learning?," in "The 33rd Annual Phi Delta Kappa/Gallup Poll of the Public's Attitude Toward the Public Schools," *Phi Delta Kappan,* September 2001

TABLE 10.10

Opinion on values taught in public schools, 1999

Here is a list of different values that might be taught in the public schools. For each one, please indicate whether you think it should or should not be taught to all students in the public schools of your community.

Should be Taught	Teachers %	Public %
Acceptance of people of different races and ethnic backgrounds	98	93
Honesty	98	97
Democracy	93	93
Patriotism/love of country	90	90
Caring for friends and family members	88	90
Moral courage	87	90
The Golden Rule	86	86
Acceptance of people who hold unpopular or controversial political or social views	64	71
Sexual abstinence outside of marriage	45	68
Acceptance of people with different sexual orientations, that is, homosexuals or bisexuals	35	55
Acceptance of the right of a woman to choose abortion	16	48

SOURCE: Carol A. Langdon and Nick Vesper, "Here is a list of different values that might be taught in the public schools. For each one, please indicate whether you think it should be taught to all students in the public schools of your community," in "The Sixth Phi Delta Kappa Poll of Teachers' Attitudes Toward the Public Schools," *Phi Delta Kappan,* vol. 81, no. 8, April 2000

ing the achievement gap between disadvantaged students and other groups of students. A sample of students in each state participate in the fourth- and eighth-grade National Assessment of Educational Progress (NAEP) in reading and mathematics every other year.

Reading First

Federal funding for reading was increased from $300 million in fiscal year (FY) 2001 to more than $900 million in FY 2002, and will be about $1 billion in FY 2003. The Reading First initiative's goal is for every child to be able to read by the end of grade three. Awards are made to states, which then make competitive sub-grants to local communities to identify students at risk and to provide training to elementary school teachers on reading instruction. The Early Reading First program awards grants to Local Education Agencies (LEAs) to support language,

literacy and pre-reading development in preschool age children.

LEAs must use instructional strategies drawn from research, such as *Put Reading First* (Bonnie B. Armbruster and Jean Osborn, Center for Improvement of Early Reading Achievement and National Institute for Literacy, Washington, DC, September 2001) and the report of the National Reading Panel, *Teaching Children to Read: An Evidence-Based Assessment of the Scientific Research on Reading and Its Implications for Reading Instruction*

FIGURE 10.3

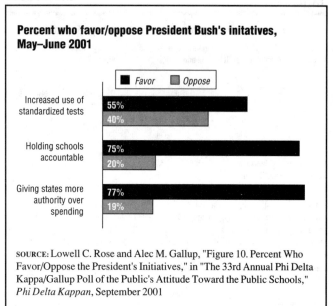

Percent who favor/oppose President Bush's initatives, May–June 2001

■ Favor   ▨ Oppose

Increased use of standardized tests	55% Favor / 40% Oppose
Holding schools accountable	75% Favor / 20% Oppose
Giving states more authority over spending	77% Favor / 19% Oppose

SOURCE: Lowell C. Rose and Alec M. Gallup, "Figure 10. Percent Who Favor/Oppose the President's Initiatives," in "The 33rd Annual Phi Delta Kappa/Gallup Poll of the Public's Attitude Toward the Public Schools," *Phi Delta Kappan*, September 2001

(National Institute of Child Health and Human Development, Bethesda, MD, 2000). "Reach Out and Read" and "Ready to Read" are two specific programs recommended by First Lady Laura Bush in her educational initiatives report, *Ready to Read, Ready to Learn* (2001).

These studies focus on the importance of instruction in phonics, reading comprehension, and literature appreciation; daily exposure to both fiction and nonfiction; and providing incentives to read. Instruction in vocabulary, reading comprehension (that includes summarizing, clarifying, questioning, and visualizing), and frequent opportunities to write are also stressed.

Flexibility at the State and Local Level

H.R. 1 reduced the overall number of ESEA programs at the U.S. Department of Education from 55 to 45. Up to 50 percent of the federal dollars school districts receive can be transferred among several education programs without separate approval. All 50 states can transfer up to 50 percent of the federal non-Title I state activity funds among ESEA programs without advance approval. Local school officials serving rural schools were also given more flexibility in how federal funds are used in their districts.

School Choice and Charter Schools

H.R. 1 created options for public school choice. Parents with children in failing schools are allowed to transfer their child to a better-performing public or charter school immediately after a school is identified as failing. Federal Title I funds (approximately $500 to $1,000 per child) can be used to provide supplemental educational services—including tutoring, after school services, and summer school programs—for children in failing schools. H.R. 1 expands federal support for charter schools by giving parents, educators and interested community leaders opportunities to create new charter schools.

Teacher Quality Program

H.R. 1 asked states to put qualified teachers in every public school classroom by 2005. The Eisenhower Professional Development and Class Size Reduction programs were combined to create the new Improving Teacher Quality State Grants program. States and local districts are permitted to use this funding for staff development for their public school teachers, principals, and administrators. States and districts are required to ensure that federal funds promote the use of scientific, research-based, and effective practice in the classroom. In addition to funding professional development, states and school districts are allowed to use their grants for reforming teacher certification or licensure requirements; alternative certification; tenure reform; merit-based teacher performance systems; bonus pay for teachers in high-need subject areas and in high-poverty schools and districts; and mentoring programs. Local school districts were given more flexibility and now can transfer non-Title I funds for use towards any authorized ESEA purpose, including hiring new teachers, increasing teacher pay, and improving teacher training and development.

English Proficiency

H.R. 1 consolidated the U.S. Department of Education's bilingual and immigrant education programs. The new federal program focuses on helping limited English proficient (LEP) students learn English. States and school districts are held accountable for making annual increases in English proficiency from the previous year. States set performance objectives to ensure LEP children achieve English fluency after they have attended school in the United States for three consecutive years. States that do not meet their performance objectives for LEP students could lose up to ten percent of the administrative portion of their funding for all ESEA state administered formula grant programs.

Public Opinion About *No Child Left Behind*

In 2001 *No Child Left Behind* had the support of those surveyed for the 33rd Annual Phi Delta Kappa/Gallup Poll. When asked whether they favored or opposed the President's education initiatives, more than three-quarters (77 percent) of the public approved of giving states more authority over education spending, three-quarters supported the idea of holding schools accountable, and more than half (55 percent) favored the increased use of standardized tests. (See Figure 10.3.)

IMPORTANT NAMES AND ADDRESSES

American Association for Employment in Education, Inc.
3040 Riverside Dr.
Suite 125
Columbus, OH 43221-2550
(614) 485-1111
FAX (614) 485-9609
E-mail: aaee@osu.edu
URL: http://www.aaee.org

American College Testing (ACT)
2201 N. Dodge St.
P.O. Box 1008
Iowa City, IA 52243-1008
(319) 337-1000
FAX (319) 339-3021
URL: http://www.act.org

American Federation of Teachers
AFL-CIO
555 New Jersey Ave. NW
Washington, DC 20001
(202) 879-4400
E-mail: online@aft.org
URL: http://www.aft.org

Centers for Disease Control and Prevention (CDC)
1600 Clifton Rd.
Atlanta, GA 30333
(404) 639-3311
(800) 311-3435
URL: http://www.cdc.gov

Child Trends
4301 Connecticut Ave. NW
Suite 100
Washington, DC 20008
(202) 362-5580
FAX (202) 362-5533
E-mail: jrobinson@childtrends.org
URL: http://www.childtrends.org

Children's Defense Fund
25 E St. NW

Washington, DC 20001
(202) 628-8787
E-mail: cdfinfo@childrensdefense.org
URL: http://www.childrensdefense.org

The College Board (SAT)
45 Columbus Ave.
New York, NY 10023-6992
(212) 713-8000
URL: http://www.collegeboard.org

Council of the Great City Schools
1301 Pennsylvania Ave. NW
Suite 702
Washington, DC 20004
(202) 393-2427
FAX (202) 393-2400
URL: http://www.cgcs.org

Educational Testing Service
Corporate Headquarters
Rosedale Rd.
Princeton, NJ 08541
(609) 921-9000
FAX (609) 734-5410
E-mail: etsinfo@ets.org
URL: http://www.ets.org

Higher Education Research Institute
UCLA Graduate School of Education
and Information Studies
3005 Moore Hall
Box 951521
Los Angeles, CA 90095-1521
(310) 825-1925
FAX (310) 206-2228
E-mail: heri@ucla.edu
URL: http://www.gseis.ucla.edu/heri/heri.html

Home School Legal Defense Association
P.O. Box 3000
Purcellville, VA 20134-9000
(540) 338-5600
FAX (540) 338-2733
E-mail: mailroom@hslda.org
URL: http://www.hslda.org

Institute of International Education
809 United Nations Plaza
New York, NY 10017-3580
(212) 984-5400
FAX (212) 984-5358
URL: http://www.iie.org

National Catholic Educational Association
1077 30th St. NW
Suite 100
Washington, DC 20007-3852
(202) 337-6232
FAX (202) 333-6706
E-mail: nceaadmin@ncea.org
URL: http://www.catholic.org/ncea

National Center for Children in Poverty
Mailman School of Public Health,
Columbia University
154 Haven Ave.
New York, NY 10032
(212) 304-7100
FAX (212) 544-4200
URL: http://cpmcnet.columbia.edu/dept/nccp

National Education Association
1201 16th St. NW
Washington, DC 20036
(202) 833-4000
URL: http://www.nea.org

National Law Center on Homelessness
and Poverty
1411 K St. NW
Suite 1400
Washington, DC 20005
(202) 638-2535
FAX (202) 628-2737
E-mail: info@nlchp.org
URL: http://www.nlchp.org

Phi Delta Kappa International
408 N. Union St.
P.O. Box 789
Bloomington, IN 47402-0789

(812) 339-1156
FAX (812) 339-0018
800-766-1156
URL: http://www.pdkintl.org

U.S. Census Bureau
Washington, DC 20233
(301) 457-2135
FAX (301) 457-3761
E-mail: webmaster@census.gov
URL: http://www.census.gov

U.S. Department of Education
National Center for Education Statistics
1990 K St. NW
Washington, DC 20006
(202) 502-7300
URL: http://nces.ed.gov

U.S. Department of Education
Office of Educational Research and
Improvement (OERI)
555 New Jersey Ave. NW
Washington, DC 20208-5500
URL: http://www.ed.gov/offices/OERI

U.S. Department of the Interior
Bureau of Indian Affairs
Indian Education Programs
1849 C St. NW
Washington, DC 20240
(202) 208-6123
FAX (202) 208-3312
URL: http://www.oiep.bia.edu

RESOURCES

The National Center for Education Statistics (NCES) of the U.S. Department of Education (Washington, DC) is a valuable source of information about the state of education in America. Its two annual publications, *Digest of Education Statistics* and *The Condition of Education*, provide a detailed compilation of education statistics from prekindergarten through graduate school. Many other NCES publications were of major assistance in the preparation of this book: *Distance Education at Postsecondary Education Institutions: 1997–98*; *Dropout Rates in the United States: 2000*; *Features of Occupational Programs at the Secondary and Postsecondary Levels* (2001); *Homeschooling in the United States: 1999*; *Mini-Digest of Education Statistics, 2000*; *NAEP 1998 Writing Report Card for the Nation and the States*; *National Education Longitudinal Study of 1988*; *Private School Universe Survey: 1999–2000*; *Projections of Education Statistics to 2011*; *Statistics in Brief: Changes in High School Vocational Coursetaking in a Larger Perspective* (2000); *Statistics in Brief: Revenues and Expenditures for Public Elementary and Secondary Education: School Year 1998–99*; *Teacher Quality: A Report on the Preparation and Qualifications of Public School Teachers* (1999); *Teachers' Tools for the 21st Century: A Report on Teachers' Use of Technology* (2000); *The Nation's Report Card: Fourth Grade Mathematics 2000*; *The Nation's Report Card: Fourth Grade Reading 2000*; *The Nation's Report Card: Science Highlights 2000*.

Other offices in the Department of Education, including the Planning and Evaluation Service and the Office of Educational Research and Improvement (OERI), routinely issue reports on specific areas of education. Publications consulted for this report were *Assessment of School-Based Management* (1996); *Challenge and Opportunity: The Impact of Charter Schools on School Districts* (2001); *Education for Homeless Children and Youth Program Report to Congress* (1997); *High Standards for All Stu-dents: A Report from the National Assessment of Title I on Progress and Challenges Since the 1994 Reauthorization* (2001); *National Excellence: A Case for Developing America's Talent* (1993); *Report on State Implementation of the Gun-Free Schools Act 1998–99*; *State ESEA Title I Participation Information for 1998–99: Final Summary Report*; *The State of Charter Schools 2000*; *21st Century Community Learning Centers: Providing Quality After-school Learning Opportunities for America's Families* (2000); and *22nd Annual Report to Congress on the Implementation of the Individuals with Disabilities Act* (2000).

The National Education Goals Panel (Washington, DC) published *The National Educational Goals Report: Building a Nation of Learners* (1999); *Promising Practices: Progress Toward the Goals 2000* (2000); and *Raising Achievement and Reducing Gaps: Reporting Progress Toward Goals for Academic Achievement* (2001).

The U.S. General Accounting Office (GAO: Washington, DC) has published numerous studies on American education. Reports that were consulted include *Bilingual Education: Four Overlapping Programs Could Be Consolidated* (2001); *Migrant Children: Education and HHS Need to Improve the Exchange of Participant Information* (1999); *School Facilities: Construction Expenditures Have Grown Significantly in Recent Years* (2000); and *School Finance: State Efforts to Equalize Funding Between Wealthy and Poor School Districts* (1998).

The Congressional Research Service (CRS) is a government research agency that works exclusively for members and committees of the U.S. Congress. *The Federal Migrant Education Program: An Overview* (1998) was referenced for this book.

The U.S. Department of Justice (Washington, DC) monitors the problem of crime and violence among the school-age population. *Criminal Victimization 2000: Changes 1999–2000 with Trends 1993–2000* was consulted for this book, and two publications produced by the Department of Justice in collaboration with the U.S. Department of Education also were used: *Working for Families and Children: Safe and Smart Afterschool Programs* (2000), and *Indicators of School Crime and Safety* (2001). The American Youth Policy Forum (Washington, DC) published *Less Hype, More Help: Reducing Juvenile Crime, What Works—and What Doesn't* (2000).

Two U.S. Census Bureau (Washington, DC) publications were consulted: *Poverty in the United States: 2000*, and *Dynamics of Economic Well-Being: Program Participation, 1993 to 1995, Who Gets Assistance?* (2001).

The Centers for Disease Control and Prevention (CDC; Atlanta, Georgia) published *STD Surveillance* (2000); "Youth Risk Behavior Surveillance—United States, 1999," in *CDC Surveillance Summaries* (2000); and *HIV/AIDS Surveillance Report* (2000). Dr. Lloyd Johnston of the University of Michigan's Institute for Social Research, with support from the National Institute on Drug Abuse (NIDA) annually performs the *Monitoring the Future* study, an in-depth survey of drug use among high school and college students. Also, *Journal of the American Medical Association* (Michael D. Resnick et al., "Protecting Adolescents from Harm," 1997) was utilized for this report. The U.S. Department of Health and Human Services, Administration for Children and Families produced the *Head Start Fact Sheet* (2000).

The Council of Great City Schools in Washington, DC, provided the National Urban Education Goals and compiled demographic details in *Beating the Odds* (2001). The Urban Teacher Collaborative (Belmont, MA) published *The Urban Teacher Challenge: Teacher Demand and Supply in the Great City Schools* (2000).

Key State Education Policies on K-12 Education (Council of Chief State School Officers, Washington, DC, 2000), and the 1998–99 *State of the States Gifted and Talented Education Report* (Council of State Directors of Programs for the Gifted, Austin, TX) were also valuable sources of information for this book.

The Advisory Committee on Student Financial Assistance (Washington, DC), *Access Denied: Restoring the Nation's Commitment to Equal Educational Opportunity* (2001) was referenced in this report.

America's Children: Key National Indicators of Well-Being (2001), a report in an annual series prepared by the Interagency Forum on Child and Family Statistics, provided statistics on early childhood education and "detached youth." Child Trends (Washington DC), in its 2001 *Facts at a Glance*, published data on teen pregnancy and births.

The Carnegie Council on Adolescent Development published *Turning Points* (Report of the Task Force on Education and Youth Adolescents, New York, 1989), and *Great*

Transitions: Preparing Adolescents for a New Century (1995). *A Nation Prepared: Teachers for the 21st Century* (Carnegie Forum on Education and the Economy, Washington, DC), and *Turning Points 2000* (Teacher's College Press, New York, 2000), were also referenced for this book.

Richard M. Ingersoll, in *Teacher Turnover, Teacher Shortages, and the Organization of Schools* (1999) and *Teaching Quality Policy Briefs: A Different Approach to Solving the Teaching Shortage Problem* (2001) (Center for the Study of Teaching and Policy, University of Washington, Seattle, WA), reported on his study of teacher attrition and migration.

The Consortium for Policy Research in Education published *Assessment and Accountability Systems in the United States: 1999–2000* (University of Pennsylvania, Graduate School of Education). Another publication that was useful in preparing this report was *2001 State Special Education Outcomes: A Report on State Activities at the Beginning of a New Decade*, (National Center on Educational Outcomes, University of Minnesota, Minneapolis).

The State of E-Learning in the States (National Governor's Association Center for Best Practices, Washington, DC, 2000) and *Distance Learning: Academic and Political Challenges for Higher Education Accreditation* (Council for Higher Education Accreditation, Washington, DC, 2001) were invaluable in providing information on current distance learning activities.

Phi Delta Kappa, a national teachers' fraternity, publishes numerous reports on the condition of education in the United States, including "The 33rd Annual Phi Delta Kappa/Gallup Poll on the Public Attitudes Toward the Public Schools" (*Phi Delta Kappan*, 2001), as well as "The Sixth Phi Delta Kappa Poll of Teachers' Attitudes Toward the Public Schools" (*Phi Delta Kappan*, 2000). Also, *Gallup Poll Topics A-Z*, an online source, was consulted for some topics.

The American Association for Employment in Education (AAEE) report, *Educator Supply and Demand in the United States* (AAEE, Columbus, OH, 2001) provided valuable information on teacher salaries, as did *Solving the Dilemmas of Teacher Supply, Demand, and Standards: How We Can Ensure a Competent, Caring, and Qualified Teacher for Every Child* (National Commission on Teaching and America's Future, New York, 2000); and *The Metropolitan Life Survey of The American Teacher, 1998* (Louis Harris and Associates, Inc., New York, 1998). The American Association of University Professors *Annual Report on the Economic Status of the Profession* (*Academe*, March/April 2001) supplied information on college faculty salaries.

The College Board (New York) published *2001 College Bound Seniors are the Largest, Most Diverse Group in History* and *Trends in College Pricing* (2000), which were consulted for this book, as were materials from the American College Testing Program's *2001 ACT National and State Scores*.

The American Federation of Teachers (AFT) was a valuable source of information on teacher salaries (Washington, DC, *Survey and Analysis of Teacher Salary Trends 1998*, *Survey and Analysis of Teacher Salary Trends 2000*) and distance learning (*A Virtual Revolution: Trends in the Expansion of Distance Education* (2001)). The Institute of International Education (New York) provided *Opendoors on the web* (2001).

Fourth Annual Report on School Performance (Edison schools, New York, 2001); *A Guide to Recent Studies of School Effectiveness by the Edison Project and the American Federation of Teachers* (Harvard University, Cambridge, MA, May 1998); and *An Evaluation of Student Achievement at Edison Schools Opened in 1995 and 1996* (Western Michigan University, Kalamazoo, MI, 2000) were used to summarize information on for-profit schools.

Centre for Educational Research and Innovation, Organisation for Economic Co-operation and Development, *Education at a Glance: OECD Indicators*, (Paris, France, 2001) provided charts and data about international comparisons of education.

Finally, a newspaper article, "Florida Clicks Into The Future, Offers An Online High School" (*The Miami Herald*, April 15, 2001) was referenced for this report.

INDEX

Page references in italics refer to photographs. References with the letter t following them indicate the presence of a table. The letter f indicates a figure. If more than one table or figure appears on a particular page, the exact item number for the table or figure being referenced is provided.

A

Ability to reach high level of learning, 181t
Access Denied: Restoring the Nation's Commitment to Equal Educational Opportunity, 164
Accountability
   charter schools, 118t, 119f
   No Child Left Behind Act, 180-181
   standards for schools, 178
Achievement
   level definitions, 54f, 66t
   National Education Goals for, 80-81, 84t
   reading levels for grade 4, 56f
   See also Testing
Acquired immunodeficiency syndrome (AIDS), 112, 113t
ACT (American College Test), 63, 66-67, 77-78t
Add Health study, 98-99
Adolescent Health Program, 98
Adult literacy, 82, 90-91t
Advanced Placement tests, 81, 85t
African-Americans, 5
   AIDS cases, 113t
   American College Test (ACT) scores, 78t
   college entrance exams, 69-70
   detached youth, 102t
   disabled children, 33
   enrollment in college, 149
   enrollment in public elementary/secondary schools by state, 15t
   faculty at colleges and universities, 158, 164t
   Head Start participants, 42
   high school dropout rates, 38t, 96

   historically black colleges and universities, 152-153
   mathematics proficiency scores, 58, 64-65t
   percentage of population enrolled in school, 4-5t
   poverty levels, 10, 96f
   reading proficiency scores, 57, 59f
   science proficiency scores, 58, 68f
   teen pregnancies, 112
   unemployment among dropouts, 99t
   writing proficiency scores, 60, 70t
   years of school completed, 2-3t
AFT (American Federation of Teachers), 120, 137
After-school programs, 17, 28f
Age
   AIDS cases, 113t
   enrollment in college, 147-149
   General Educational Development (GED) diplomas, 30t
   mathematics proficiency levels by, 64-65t
   percentage of population enrolled in school, 4-5t
   poverty levels by, 16t
   public assistance, 101t
   reading materials in home, 71f
   reading proficiency, 55t
   science scores by, 68t, 69t
   unemployment among dropouts, 99t
   violence in school, 114, 115t
   writing performance levels by, 70t
Agostini v. Felton (1997), 124-125
Aguilar v. Felton (1985), 124
AIDS (Acquired immunodeficiency syndrome), 112, 113t
Alabama, 9
Alaska
   computers in classrooms, 81
   parental participation with children's education, 83
Alaskan natives, 9
   See also Native Americans
Albanese, Strout v. (1999), 122
Alcohol use, 83, 92t
   attitudes towards, 101

   prevalence of among college students, 169-170, 173t, 175t
   prevalence of among high school students, 108t, 173t, 175t
   public opinion on, 179, 181t
Alliance for Equity in Higher Education, 154-155
Alt, Martha Naomi, 96
American Association for Employment in Education (AAEE), 133, 137
American College Test (ACT), 63, 66-67, 77-78t
American Federation of Teachers (AFT), 120, 137
American Indian Higher Education Consortium, 154
American Indians, 9
   See also Native Americans
Applegate, Brooks, 121
Argentina, 149
Arizona
   charter schools, 118, 119
   children's health, 80
   Kotterman v. Killian (1999), 122
Arkansas, 9
Armbruster, Bonnie B., 181
Asian-Americans
   American College Test (ACT) scores, 78t
   college entrance exams, 69, 70
   disabled children, 33
   enrollment in college, 149
   faculty at colleges and universities, 158, 164t
   Head Start participants, 42
   poverty levels, 96f
   reading proficiency scores, 59f
   science scores, 68f
   writing proficiency scores, 60, 70t
Assessment of education, 53-54, 53f
Assessment of School-Based Management (Wohlstetter and Mohrman), 127
Associate degrees, 155, 161t, 162t
At-risk students, 95-115
   alcohol use, 108
   charter schools for, 119
   detached youth, 98